NEW DIRECTIONS IN PSYCHO-ANALYSIS

Douglas Glass

MELANIE KLEIN—1954

NEW DIRECTIONS IN PSYCHO-ANALYSIS

The Significance of Infant Conflict in the Pattern of Adult Behaviour

Edited by

MELANIE KLEIN

PAULA HEIMANN

R. E. MONEY-KYRLE

With a Preface by
Ernest Jones

MARESFIELD LIBRARY
LONDON

First published in 1955 by
Tavistock Publications Limited
This edition printed in 1977
and reprinted in 1985
with permission of the Melanie Klein Trust
by H. Karnac (Books) Limited
58 Gloucester Road,
London S.W.7
England

ISBN 0 946439 13 3

The photograph of Melanie Klein
on the front cover is by
Dr Hans A. Thorner

Printed in Great Britain by
BPC Wheatons Ltd, Exeter

PREFACE

MRS. KLEIN's work of the past thirty years has been attacked and
defended with almost equal vehemence, but in the long run
its value can be satisfactorily estimated only by those who
themselves make comparable investigations. As is well known, I
have from the beginning viewed Mrs. Klein's work with the
greatest sympathy, especially as many of the conclusions coincided
with those I reached myself; and I have all along been struck by the
observation that many of the criticisms have been close echoes of
those with which I had been made familiar in the earliest days of
psycho-analysis. A good many of her findings and conclusions had
been adumbrated in quite early days by Freud, Rank and others,
but what is so distinctive and admirable in her work is the courage
and unshakable integrity with which she has quite unsparingly
worked out the implications and consequences of those earlier hints,
thereby making important fresh discoveries in her course.

It is a matter for wide satisfaction as well as for personal congratu-
lation that Mrs. Klein has lived to see her work firmly established.
So long as it was simply deposited in what she herself had published
there was always the hope, but by no means the certainty, that it
would be taken up by future students. The situation has now
moved beyond that stage; her work is firmly established. As a
result of her personal instruction, combined with the insight of
those who decided to accept it, she has a considerable number of
colleagues and pupils who follow her lead in exploring the deepest
depths. To the papers that many of them have contributed to *New
Directions in Psycho-Analysis* I have the pleasure of adding this *envoi*.

ERNEST JONES.

CONTENTS

Contents

INTRODUCTION

A SPECIAL issue of *The International Journal of Psycho-Analysis* was published in March, 1952, and dedicated to Melanie Klein on the occasion of her seventieth birthday. It consisted of a number of original essays by some of those who have been either associated with her work from the beginning or numbered among her pupils. The present book is a revised reproduction of eleven of these essays enlarged by the addition of ten more, including two by Melanie Klein herself.[1]

To those in the psycho-analytic field, it will need no further introduction. But, for the benefit of a wider audience, some preliminary remarks about the development of psycho-analytic theory and technique and Melanie Klein's part in this development would seem to be desirable.

*   *   *

Although we now know that there is no precise boundary between the states ordinarily described as mental health and mental illness, we have always tended to make one.[2] Indeed, until comparatively recent times mental illness seemed so unnatural a phenomenon that it was placed in the realm of the supernatural. The ill person was felt to be possessed by powerful spirits. As such, he was always feared; but whether he was honoured with gifts and appeals for help, or became the victim of relentless persecution, depended on the superstitions of his culture.

The first step from this to the more modern attitude was made by the early hypnotists who became prominent, especially in France, at the end of the eighteenth century and developed their technique throughout the nineteenth.[3] It was to two of their famous schools,

---

[1] The new papers are those numbered 1, 3, 6, 7, 9, 12, 13, 17, 20, and 21.
[2] Mental health can be precisely defined as a limiting concept. But the class so defined however useful it may be in psycho-analytic theory, is found to have no actual members.
[3] See Flugel, J. C., *A Hundred Years of Psychology*, 1933.

Introduction

Charcot's at the Salpêtrière and Bernhcim's at Nancy, that Sigmund Freud, at that time a brilliant young neurologist from Vienna, turned in 1885 and 1889, for help in the treatment of his patients.[1] But his initial satisfaction in using suggestion, as demonstrated by the French psychiatrists, was soon ended by the new discovery that the easy and seemingly miraculous cures he effected by its means were not lasting and had to be frequently repeated.

Meanwhile, he had become interested in the work of an older colleague in Vienna, Josef Breuer, who in treating the hysterical symptoms of a young woman had used hypnotism in a different manner, not to suggest away the symptoms, but to question her about them, and had noticed that they could be relieved "if she could be induced to express in words the affective phantasy by which she was at the moment dominated."[2] So now, in his dissatisfaction with a purely suggestive use of hypnotism, he repeated Breuer's experiment with a similar patient and, by its means, achieved a most encouraging measure of success.

For a time, Breuer and Freud collaborated in what had become the initial steps in the exploration of the unconscious, until Breuer, becoming anxious about the strength and nature of the forces that could be released from its depths, abandoned the research he had so brilliantly begun. Then Freud carried on for some years alone and in an atmosphere increasingly hostile to this work. It is not easy for those who now enjoy the more friendly attitude of their contemporaries—which is a direct result of his discoveries—to understand the enormous opposition he had to overcome, or the integrity required to maintain against it a balanced attitude, at once critical and confident, towards his own developing hypotheses. Yet, in this period of about ten years, when he seemed to have raised the entire academic world against him, he succeeded in laying the foundation on which analytic practice has been built.

His first advance beyond the point already reached by Breuer was a change, and a vast improvement, in technique. He abandoned hypnotism altogether and in its place developed the "free association" method which remains the only satisfactory way at once of exploring the unconscious and making it conscious to patients, and so relieving them of its irrational effects. With this new implement of research

---

[1] These brief notes are taken from Freud's *Autobiographical Study*. But for a full account the reader is referred to Ernest Jones' detailed biography: *Sigmund Freud—Life and Work*, Vol. I (London, 1953).

[2] Freud, S.: *An Autobiographical Study*, 1925. Authorized translation by James Strachey, 1935, p. 34.

at his disposal he made rapid progress in mapping out its hitherto uncharted depths.

It will perhaps be sufficient if the principal stages of Freud's exploration into the unconscious are very briefly listed. After the discovery of the Œdipus complex and of the existence of early sexuality, his next step was to follow, at first only in broad outline, the course of its development from its early oral and anal to its final genital form. Then came his discovery of the super-ego. That man was a moral being whose freedom was restricted by a conscience, a kind of mentor within but distinct from himself, had of course been recognized from very early times. What was new was Freud's discovery that this super-ego is a far more formidable and archaic being than the "conscious conscience", which is only a small part of it; new also was his theory of its origin. Since one of its most universal functions is to repress the incestuous and parricidal impulses of the Œdipus complex, he linked its origin with the conscious disappearance of this complex. When, from about the age of three to five, these impulses are at their height, their overt expression is certainly impeded by a more or less conscious fear of the parent of the same sex, whom the child wishes to displace; and Freud believed that this fear of a real external figure—not necessarily as it was but as the child imagined it to be—must be, at that age, the only ontogenetic force opposed to them. So when, at a somewhat later age, they are found to be wholly repressed and inhibited by an unconscious fear of the super-ego, he concluded that the super-ego must be the image of the same feared parent which had now been "introjected". Exactly how this process of "psychological incorporation" came about remained obscure. But from the beginning Freud regarded it as at least analogous to an oral process of physical incorporation.[1]

The last of his most important discoveries was that of the basic role played by aggression in the unconscious. This "Death Instinct", as he called it, is felt first as an indefinite threat to the self from within the self; but it is quickly "projected" outwards and felt as an external threat. There it can be dealt with more easily. The ego can seek to escape it, or to destroy it—in which case it becomes, as it were, its own object. But it was Melanie Klein who first made use of this discovery to explain the archaic severity of the super-ego, which is so much more ruthless than even the most brutal of real parents. When,

---

[1] Moreover, and this seems much more questionable, he believed that it was based on a phylogenetic memory of cannibalistic attacks on primal fathers—a theory which is perhaps itself a projection into the racial past of what was later recognized as an oral-cannibalistic phase of early infancy.

Introduction

at the height of his Œdipus complex, the child turns against the
parent he wishes to displace, he projects his own aggression upon this
parent, who in his imagination becomes a veritable ogre and is, as
such, introjected to form his super-ego.

By this time the period of Freud's isolation had long been over, and
he was surrounded by a large school of co-workers, with branches in
almost every country. One of the most brilliant of these co-workers
was Karl Abraham who, as a result of his own work with the severest
types of mental illness, and under the influence of Freud's new discoveries about the importance of aggression, was able to go a stage
further in the reconstruction of the earliest stages of development.
But unfortunately his own death, when he had barely reached the
most productive period of his life, prevented him from completing
his work.

Melanie Klein was his pupil, and during his life he encouraged
and supported her work in the direct application of analysis for the
treatment of children. Her first task was to develop a special
technique for the purpose. It would have been futile to ask children
who can hardly talk to give verbal "free associations". So she
provided them with toys, and encouraged them to "play freely"
instead. She then "interpreted" their play, that is, she described to
them the feelings and phantasies which seemed to be expressed by it.

With this new technique at her disposal she was at once able to
achieve therapeutic results that surpassed those usually obtained with
adults. She was also in a position, as it were, for the first time to
observe the early stages of development at close quarters, and so to
map it out in much greater detail than had ever been possible before.
Abraham was not slow to recognize the significance of this new
development. In 1924, at the first Congress of German psycho-
analysts, in summing up the paper on the Erna case (*The Psycho-
Analysis of Children*, Chap. 3) he said: "The future of psycho-analysis
lies in play-technique." In the thirty years that have elapsed since
then, his prediction has come true. Play technique has profoundly
influenced analysis.

The analytic picture of mental development as enlarged, and in
some points modified, by Melanie Klein's work, is not easy to summarize without distortion. But a brief mention of its two principal
stages need not be misleading provided we remember that earlier
stages co-exist or alternate with later ones—owing to "fixation" and
"regression". To emphasize this fact Melanie Klein herself speaks of
the successive "positions", rather than stages, of development.

The first of these results from the infant's unintegrated, and violently conflicting, attitudes to the vital objects of his world, particularly his mother's breasts. Both because her breasts are sometimes gratifying and sometimes frustrating and because the child's own impulses are projected into, or felt to come from, these objects, they are themselves felt to be sometimes good and loving, sometimes bad and dangerous. And since he also "introjects" or incorporates them in phantasy, he feels himself to be possessed, as well as surrounded, by alternatively protective and persecutory objects. The persecutory anxiety, which always arises in this period, retards, and often temporarily disrupts the gradual integration of his ego. In short, the early stage is characterized by what Melanie Klein has appropriately named the paranoid-schizoid position.

The next stage results inevitably from the increasing integration of the infant's impulses, so that he begins to realize, at first only intermittently, that the gratifying objects he needs and loves are but other aspects of the frustrating ones he hates and in phantasy destroys. With this discovery he begins to feel concern for these objects and to experience depression. This "depressive position" is so painful that to escape it he tends to deny either that his destroyed good objects are good or that they have been injured. In other words, he tends either to regress to the older persecutory position or to adopt a "manic defence" in which concern and guilt are strenuously denied. But so far as he can tolerate depressive feelings, they give rise to reparative impulses and to a capacity for unselfish concern and protective love. The extent to which he achieves or fails to achieve this normal outcome determines the stability of his health, or his liability to illness.

It should be mentioned at this point that, in her view, those two great discoveries of Freud, the Œdipus complex and the super-ego, have their roots in these periods of development and so begin much earlier than he thought.

The insight now gained into these positions and defences of early development enables us to recognize them as recurring in every analytic transference—that is, in a patient's changing attitudes to his analyst—where they can be pointed out and modified by being brought to light. The deeper understanding we owe to Melanie Klein has therefore substantially increased the power and range of both applied and clinical analysis. Moreover, by passing through some of the analytic limits accepted as impassable a few decades ago, her work encourages us to hope that others still impassable may in time be passed.   R. E. MONEY-KYRLE.

PART ONE

PAPERS IN CLINICAL PSYCHO-ANALYSIS

1

THE PSYCHO-ANALYTIC PLAY TECHNIQUE: ITS HISTORY AND SIGNIFICANCE [1]

MELANIE KLEIN

IN offering a paper mainly concerned with play technique as an introduction to this book, I have been prompted by the consideration that my work both with children and adults, and my contributions to psycho-analytic theory as a whole derive ultimately from the play technique evolved with young children. I do not mean by this that my later work was a direct application of the play technique; but the insight I gained into early development, into unconscious processes, and into the nature of the interpretations by which the unconscious can be approached, has been of far-reaching influence on the work I have done with older children and adults.

I shall, therefore, briefly outline the steps by which my work developed out of the psycho-analytic play technique, but I shall not attempt to give a complete summary of my findings. In 1919, when I started my first case, some psycho-analytic work with children had already been done, particularly by Dr. Hug-Hellmuth.[2] However, she did not undertake the psycho-analysis of children under six and, although she used drawings and occasionally play as material, she did not develop this into a specific technique.

At the time I began to work it was an established principle that interpretations should be given very sparingly. With few exceptions psycho-analysts had not explored the deeper layers of the unconscious—in children such exploration being considered potentially dangerous. This cautious outlook was reflected in the fact that then, and for years to come, psycho-analysis was held to be suitable only for children from the latency period onwards.[3]

[1] Based on a paper read to the Royal Medico-Psychological Association on 12th February, 1953.
[2] "On the Technique of Child Analysis", *Int. J. Psycho-Anal.*, Vol. II (1921).
[3] A description of this early approach is given in Anna Freud's book *Einführung in die Technik der Kinderanalyse,* 1927 (*Introduction to the Technique of Child Analysis*, Nervous and Mental Disease Monograph Series, No. 48, 1929).

Melanie Klein

My first patient was a five-year-old boy. I referred to him under the name "Fritz" in my earliest published paper.[1] To begin with I thought it would be sufficient to influence the mother's attitude. I suggested that she should encourage the child to discuss freely with her the many unspoken questions which were obviously at the back of his mind and were impeding his intellectual development. This had a good effect, but his neurotic difficulties were not sufficiently alleviated and it was soon decided that I should psycho-analyse him. In doing so, I deviated from some of the rules so far established, for I interpreted what I thought to be most urgent in the material the child presented to me and found my interest focusing on his anxieties and the defences against them. This new approach soon confronted me with serious problems. The anxieties I encountered when analysing this first case were very acute, and although I was strengthened in the belief that I was working on the right lines by observing the alleviation of anxiety again and again produced by my interpretations, I was at times perturbed by the intensity of the fresh anxieties which were being brought into the open. On one such occasion I sought advice from Dr. Karl Abraham. He replied that since my interpretations up to then had often produced relief and the analysis was obviously progressing, he saw no ground for changing the method of approach. I felt encouraged by his support and, as it happened, in the next few days the child's anxiety, which had come to a head, greatly diminished, leading to further improvement. The conviction gained in this analysis strongly influenced the whole course of my analytic work.

The treatment was carried out in the child's home with his own toys. This analysis was the beginning of the psycho-analytic play technique, because from the start the child expressed his phantasies and anxieties mainly in play, and I consistently interpreted its meaning to him, with the result that additional material came up in his play. That is to say, I already used with this patient, in essence, the method of interpretation which became characteristic of my technique. This approach corresponds to a fundamental principle of psycho-analysis—free association. In interpreting not only the child's words but also his activities with his toys, I applied this basic principle to the mind of the child, whose play and varied activities—in fact his whole behaviour—are means of expressing what the adult

[1] "The Development of a Child", *Int. J. Psycho-Anal.*, Vol. IV (1923); "The Role of the School in the Libidinal Development of the Child", *Int. J. Psycho-Anal.*, Vol. V (1924); and "Infant Analysis", *Int. J. Psycho-Anal.*, Vol. VIII (1926). These papers are also contained in *Contributions to Psycho-Analysis, 1921–45* (London, 1948).

expresses predominantly by words. I was also guided throughout by two other tenets of psycho-analysis established by Freud, which I have from the beginning regarded as fundamental: that the exploration of the unconscious is the main task of psycho-analytic procedure, and that the analysis of the transference is the means of achieving this aim.

Between 1920 and 1923 I gained further experience with other child cases, but a definite step in the development of play technique was the treatment of a child of two years and nine months whom I psycho-analysed in 1923. I have given some details of this child's case under the name "Rita" in my book, *The Psycho-Analysis of Children*.[1] Rita suffered from night terrors and animal phobias, was very ambivalent towards her mother, at the same time clinging to her to such an extent that she could hardly be left alone. She had a marked obsessional neurosis and was at times very depressed. Her play was inhibited and her inability to tolerate frustrations made her upbringing increasingly difficult. I was very doubtful about how to tackle this case since the analysis of so young a child was an entirely new experiment. The first session seemed to confirm my misgivings. Rita, when left alone with me in her nursery, at once showed signs of what I took to be a negative transference: she was anxious and silent and very soon asked to go out into the garden. I agreed and went with her—I may add, under the watchful eyes of her mother and aunt, who took this as a sign of failure. They were very surprised to see that Rita was quite friendly towards me when we returned to the nursery some ten to fifteen minutes later. The explanation of this change was that while we were outside I had been interpreting her negative transference (this again being against the usual practice). From a few things she said, and the fact that she was less frightened when we were in the open, I concluded that she was particularly afraid of something which I might do to her when she was alone with me in the room. I interpreted this and, referring to her night terrors, I linked her suspicion of me as a hostile stranger with her fear that a bad woman would attack her when she was by herself at night. When, a few minutes after this interpretation, I suggested that we should return to the nursery, she readily agreed. As I mentioned, Rita's inhibition in playing was marked, and to begin with she did hardly anything but obsessionally dress and undress her doll.

[1] (London, 1932). See also *On the Bringing up of Children* (London, 1936), and "The Œdipus Complex in the Light of Early Anxieties", *Int. J. Psycho-Anal.*, Vol. **XXVI** (1945), also in *Contributions to Psycho-Analysis*.

But soon I came to understand the anxieties underlying her obsessions, and interpreted them. This case strengthened my growing conviction that a precondition for the psycho-analysis of a child is to understand and to interpret the phantasies, feelings, anxieties, and experiences expressed by play or, if play activities are inhibited, the causes of the inhibition.

As with Fritz, I undertook this analysis in the child's home and with her own toys; but during this treatment, which lasted only a few months, I came to the conclusion that psycho-analysis should not be carried out in the child's home. For I found that, although she was in great need of help and her parents had decided that I should try psycho-analysis, her mother's attitude towards me was very ambivalent and the atmosphere was on the whole hostile to the treatment. More important still, I found that the transference situation—the backbone of the psycho-analytic procedure—can only be established and maintained if the patient is able to feel that the consulting-room or the play-room, indeed the whole analysis, is something separate from his ordinary home life. For only under such conditions can he overcome his resistances against experiencing and expressing thoughts, feelings, and desires, which are incompatible with convention, and in the case of children felt to be in contrast to much of what they have been taught.

I made further significant observations in the psycho-analysis of a girl of seven, also in 1923. Her neurotic difficulties were apparently not serious, but her parents had for some time been concerned about her intellectual development. Although quite intelligent she did not keep up with her age group, she disliked school, and sometimes played truant. Her relation to her mother, which had been affectionate and trusting, had changed since she had started school: she had become reserved and silent. I spent a few sessions with her without achieving much contact. It had become clear that she disliked school, and from what she diffidently said about it, as well as from other remarks, I had been able to make a few interpretations which produced some material. But my impression was that I should not get much further in that way. In a session in which I again found the child unresponsive and withdrawn I left her, saying that I would return in a moment. I went into my own children's nursery, collected a few toys, cars, little figures, a few bricks, and a train, put them into a box and returned to the patient. The child, who had not taken to drawing or other activities, was interested in the small toys and at once began to play. From this play I gathered that two of the toy figures represented herself and a little boy, a school-mate about whom I had heard before. It appeared that there was something secret about the behaviour of these two figures and that other toy people were resented as interfering or watching and were put aside. The activities of the two toys led to catastrophes, such as their falling down or colliding with cars. This was repeated with signs of mounting anxiety. At this point I interpreted, with reference to the details of her play, that some sexual activity seemed to have occurred between herself and her friend, and that this had made her very frightened of being found out and therefore distrustful of other people. I pointed out that while playing she had become anxious and seemed on the point of stopping her play. I reminded her that she disliked school, and that this might be connected with the fear that the teacher would find out about her relation with her school-mate and punish her. Above all she was frightened and therefore distrustful of her mother, and now she might feel the same way about me. The effect of this interpretation on the child was striking: her anxiety and distrust first increased, but very soon gave way to obvious relief. Her facial expression changed, and although she neither admitted nor denied what I had interpreted, she subsequently showed her agreement by producing new material and by becoming much freer in her play and speech; also her attitude towards me became much more friendly and less suspicious. Of course the negative transference, alternating with the positive one, came up again and again; but, from this session onwards, the analysis progressed well. Concurrently there were favourable changes, as I was informed, in her relation to her family—in particular to her mother. Her dislike of school diminished and she became more interested in her lessons, but her inhibition in learning, which was rooted in deep anxieties, was only gradually resolved in the course of her treatment.

II

I have described how the use of the toys I kept especially for the child patient in the box in which I first brought them proved essential for her analysis. This experience, as well as others, helped me to decide which toys are most suitable for the psycho-analytic play technique.[1] I found it essential to have *small* toys because their

[1] They are mainly: little wooden men and women, usually in two sizes, cars, wheelbarrows, swings, trains, aeroplanes, animals, trees, bricks, houses, fences, paper, scissors, a knife, pencils, chalks or paints, glue, balls and marbles, plasticine and string.

7

number and variety enable the child to express a wide range of phantasies and experiences. It is important for this purpose that these toys should be non-mechanical and that the human figures, varying only in colour and size, should not indicate any particular occupation. Their very simplicity enables the child to use them in many different situations, according to the material coming up in his play. The fact that he can thus present simultaneously a variety of experiences and phantasied or actual situations also makes it possible for us to arrive at a more coherent picture of the workings of his mind.

In keeping with the simplicity of the toys, the equipment of the play-room is also simple. It does not contain anything except what is needed for the psycho-analysis.[1] Each child's playthings are kept locked in one particular drawer, and he therefore knows that his toys and his play with them, which is the equivalent of the adult's associations, are only known to the analyst and to himself. The box in which I first introduced the toys to the little girl mentioned above turned out to be the prototype of the individual drawer, which is part of the private and intimate relation between analyst and patient, characteristic of the psycho-analytic transference situation.

I do not suggest that the psycho-analytic play technique depends entirely on my particular selection of play-material. In any case, children often spontaneously bring their own things and the play with them enters as a matter of course into the analytic work. But I believe that the toys provided by the analyst should on the whole be of the type I have described, that is to say, simple, small, and non-mechanical.

Toys, however, are not the only requisites for a play analysis. Many of the child's activities are at times carried out round the wash-hand basin, which is equipped with one or two small bowls, tumblers, and spoons. Often he draws, writes, paints, cuts out, repairs toys, and so on. At times he plays games in which he allots roles to the analyst and himself such as playing shop, doctor and patient, school, mother and child. In such games the child frequently takes the part of the adult, thereby not only expressing his wish to reverse the roles, but also demonstrating how he feels that his parents or other people in authority behave towards him—or *should* behave. Sometimes he gives vent to his aggressiveness and resentment by being, in the role of parent, sadistic towards the child, represented by the analyst. The principle of interpretation remains the same whether the

[1] It has a washable floor, running water, a table, a few chairs, a little sofa, some cushions and a chest of drawers.

8

phantasies are presented by toys or by dramatization. For, whatever material is used, it is essential that the analytic principles underlying the technique should be applied.[1]

Aggressiveness is expressed in various ways in the child's play, either directly or indirectly. Often a toy is broken or, when the child is more aggressive, attacks are made with knife or scissors on the table or on pieces of wood; water or paint is splashed about and the room generally becomes a battlefield. It is essential to enable the child to bring out his aggressiveness; but what counts most is to understand why at this particular moment in the transference situation destructive impulses come up and to observe their consequences in the child's mind. Feelings of guilt may very soon follow after the child has broken, for instance, a little figure. Such guilt refers not only to the actual damage done but to what the toy stands for in the child's unconscious, e.g. a little brother or sister, or a parent; the interpretation has therefore to deal with these deeper levels as well. Sometimes we can gather from the child's behaviour towards the analyst that not only guilt but also persecutory anxiety has been the sequel to his destructive impulses and that he is afraid of retaliation.

I have usually been able to convey to the child that I would not tolerate physical attacks on myself. This attitude not only protects the psycho-analyst but is of importance for the analysis as well. For such assaults, if not kept within bounds, are apt to stir up excessive guilt and persecutory anxiety in the child and therefore add to the difficulties of the treatment. I have sometimes been asked by what method I prevented physical attacks, and I think the answer is that I was very careful not to inhibit the child's aggressive *phantasies;* in fact he was given opportunity to act them out in other ways, including verbal attacks on myself. The more I was able to interpret in time the motives of the child's aggressiveness the more the situation could be kept under control. But with some psychotic children it has occasionally been difficult to protect myself against their aggressiveness.

III

I have found that the child's attitude towards a toy he has damaged is very revealing. He often puts aside such a toy, representing for

[1] Instances both of play with toys and of the games described above can be found in *The Psycho-Analysis of Children* (particularly in Chapters II, III and IV). See also "Personification in the Play of Children", *Int. J. Psycho-Anal.*, Vol. X (1929) also in *Contributions to Psycho-Analysis*.

Melanie Klein

instance a sibling or a parent, and ignores it for a time. This indicates dislike of the damaged object, due to the persecutory fear that the attacked person (represented by the toy) has become retaliatory and dangerous. The sense of persecution may be so strong that it covers up feelings of guilt and depression which are also aroused by the damage done. Or guilt and depression may be so strong that they lead to a reinforcing of persecutory feelings. However, one day the child may search in his drawer for the damaged toy. This suggests that by then we have been able to analyse some important defences, thus diminishing persecutory feelings and making it possible for the sense of guilt and the urge to make reparation to be experienced. When this happens we can also notice that a change in the child's relation to the particular sibling for whom the toy stood, or in his relations in general, has occurred. This change confirms our impression that persecutory anxiety has diminished and that, together with the sense of guilt and the wish to make reparation, feelings of love which had been impaired by excessive anxiety have come to the fore. With another child, or with the same child at a later stage of the analysis, guilt and the wish to repair may follow very soon after the act of aggression, and tenderness towards the brother or sister who may have been damaged in phantasy becomes apparent. The importance of such changes for character formation and object relations, as well as for mental stability, cannot be overrated.

It is an essential part of the interpretative work that it should keep in step with fluctuations between love and hatred; between happiness and satisfaction on the one hand and persecutory anxiety and depression on the other. This implies that the analyst should not show disapproval of the child having broken a toy; he should not, however, encourage the child to express his aggressiveness, or suggest to him that the toy could be mended. In other words, he should enable the child to experience his emotions and phantasies as they come up. It was always part of my technique not to use educative or moral influence, but to keep to the psycho-analytic procedure only, which, to put it in a nutshell, consists in understanding the patient's mind and in conveying to him what goes on in it.

The variety of emotional situations which can be expressed by play activities is unlimited: for instance, feelings of frustration and of being rejected; jealousy of both father and mother, or of brothers and sisters; aggressiveness accompanying such jealousy; pleasure in having a playmate and ally against the parents; feelings of love and hatred towards a newborn baby or one who is expected, as well as the ensuing anxiety, guilt, and urge to make reparation. We also find in the child's play the repetition of actual experiences and details of everyday life, often interwoven with his phantasies. It is revealing that sometimes very important actual events in his life fail to enter either into his play or into his associations, and that the whole emphasis at times lies on apparently minor happenings. But these minor happenings are of great importance to him because they have stirred up his emotions and phantasies.

IV

There are many children who are inhibited in play. Such inhibition does not always completely prevent them from playing, but may soon interrupt their activities. For instance, a little boy was brought to me for one interview only (there was a prospect of an analysis in the future; but at the time the parents were going abroad with him). I had some toys on the table and he sat down and began to play, which soon led to accidents, collisions, and toy people falling down whom he tried to stand up again. In all this he showed a good deal of anxiety, but since no treatment was yet intended, I refrained from interpreting. After a few minutes he quietly slipped out of his chair and saying "Enough of playing", went out. I believe from my experience that if this had been the beginning of a treatment and I had interpreted the anxiety shown in his actions with the toys and the corresponding negative transference towards me, I should have been able to resolve his anxiety sufficiently for him to continue playing.

The next instance may help me to show some of the causes of a play inhibition. The boy, aged three years nine months, whom I described under the name "Peter" in *The Psycho-Analysis of Children*, was very neurotic.[1] To mention some of his difficulties: he was unable to play, could not tolerate any frustration, was timid, plaintive, and unboyish, yet at times aggressive and overbearing, very ambivalent towards his family, and strongly fixated on his mother. She told me that Peter had greatly changed for the worse after a summer holiday during which at the age of eighteen months he shared his parents' bedroom and had opportunity of observing their sexual intercourse. On that holiday he became very difficult to manage,

---

[1] This child, whose analysis was begun in 1924, was another of the cases that helped to develop my play technique.

II

slept badly, and relapsed into soiling his bed at night, which he had not done for some months. He had been playing freely until then, but from that summer onwards he stopped playing and became very destructive towards his toys; he would do nothing with them but break them. Shortly afterwards his brother was born, and this increased all his difficulties.

In the first session Peter started to play; he soon made two horses bump into each other, and repeated the same action with different toys. He also mentioned that he had a little brother. I interpreted to him that the horses and the other things which had been bumping together represented people, an interpretation which he first rejected and then accepted. He again bumped the horses together, saying that they were going to sleep, covered them up with bricks, and added: "Now they're quite dead; I've buried them." He put the motor-cars front to rear in a row which, as became clear later in the analysis, symbolized his father's penis, and made them run along, then suddenly lost his temper and threw them about the room, saying: "We always smash our Christmas presents straight away; we don't want any." Smashing his toys thus stood in his un-conscious for smashing his father's genital. During this first hour he did in fact break several toys.

In the second session Peter repeated some of the material of the first hour, in particular the bumping together of cars, horses, etc., and speaking again of his little brother, whereupon I interpreted that he was showing me how his Mummy and Daddy bumped their genitals (of course using his own word for genitals) and that he thought that their doing so caused his brother to be born. This interpretation produced more material, throwing light on his very ambivalent relation towards his little brother and towards his father. He laid a toy man on a brick which he called a "bed", threw him down and said he was "dead and done for". He next re-enacted the same thing with two toy men, choosing figures he had already damaged. I interpreted that the first toy man stood for his father whom he wanted to throw out of his mother's bed and kill, and that one of the two toy men was again the father and the other represented himself to whom his father would do the same. The reason why he had chosen two damaged figures was that he felt that both his father and himself would be damaged if he attacked his father.

This material illustrates a number of points, of which I shall only mention one or two. Because Peter's experience of witnessing the sexual intercourse of his parents had made a great impact on his mind, and had aroused strong emotions such as jealousy, aggressiveness and anxiety, this was the first thing which he expressed in his play. There is no doubt that he had no longer any conscious knowledge of this experience, that it was repressed, and that only the symbolical expression of it was possible for him. I have reason to believe that if I had not interpreted that the toys bumping together were people, he might not have produced the material which came up in the second hour. Furthermore, had I not, in the second hour, been able to show him some of the reasons for his inhibition in play, by interpreting the damage done to the toys, he would very likely—as he did in ordinary life—have stopped playing after breaking the toys.

There are children who at the beginning of treatment may not even play in the same way as Peter, or the little boy who came for one interview only. But it is very rare for a child completely to ignore the toys laid out on the table. Even if he turns away from them, he often gives the analyst some insight into his motives for not wishing to play. In other ways, too, the child analyst can gather material for interpretation. Any activity, such as using paper to scribble on or to cut out. and every detail of behaviour, such as changes in posture or in facial expression, can give a clue to what is going on in the child's mind possibly in connection with what the analyst has heard from the parents about his difficulties.

I have said much about the importance of interpretation for play technique and have given some instances to illustrate their content. This brings me to a question which I have often been asked: "Are young children intellectually able to understand such interpretations?" My own experience and that of my colleagues has been that if the interpretations relate to the salient points in the material, they are fully understood. Of course the child analyst must give his interpretations as succinctly and as clearly as possible, and should also use the child's expressions in doing so. But if he translates into simple words the essential points of the material presented to him, he gets into touch with those emotions and anxieties which are most operative at the moment; the child's conscious and intellectual understanding is often a subsequent process. One of the many interesting and surprising experiences of the beginner in child analysis is to find in even very young children a capacity for insight which is often far greater than that of adults. To some extent this is explained by the fact that the connections between conscious and unconscious are closer in young children than in adults, and that infantile repressions are less powerful. I also believe that the infant's

13

intellectual capacities are often underrated and that in fact he understands more than he is credited with.

I shall now illustrate what I have said by a young child's response to interpretations. Peter, of whose analysis I have given a few details, had strongly objected to my interpretation that the toy man he had thrown down from the "bed" and who was "dead and done for" represented his father. (The interpretation of death-wishes against a loved person usually arouses great resistance in children as well as in adults.) In the third hour Peter again brought similar material, but now accepted my interpretation and said thoughtfully: "And if I were a Daddy and someone wanted to throw me down behind the bed and make me dead and done for, what would I think of it?" This shows that he had not only worked through, understood and accepted my interpretation, but that he had also recognized a good deal more. He understood that his own aggressive feelings towards his father contributed to his fear of him, and also that he had projected his own impulses on to his father.

One of the important points in play technique has always been the analysis of the transference. As we know, in the transference on the analyst the patient repeats earlier emotions and conflicts. It is my experience that we are able to help the patient fundamentally by taking his phantasies and anxieties back in our transference interpretations to where they originated—namely, in infancy and in relation to his first objects. For by re-experiencing early emotions and phantasies and understanding them in relation to his primal objects, he can, as it were, revise these relations at their root, and thus effectively diminish his anxieties.

v

In looking back over the first few years of my work, I would single out a few facts. I mentioned at the beginning of this paper that in analysing my earliest child case I found my interest focusing on his anxieties and defences against them. My emphasis on anxiety led me deeper and deeper into the unconscious and into the phantasy life of the child. This particular emphasis ran counter to the psycho-analytical point of view that interpretations should not go very deep and should not be given frequently. I persisted in my approach, in spite of the fact that it involved a radical change in technique. This approach took me into new territory, for it opened up the understanding of the early infantile phantasies, anxieties and defences, which were at that time still largely unexplored. This became clear to me when I began the theoretical formulation of my clinical findings.

One of the various phenomena which struck me in the analysis of Rita was the harshness of her super-ego. I have described in *The Psycho-Analysis of Children* how Rita used to play the role of a severe and punishing mother who treated the child (represented by the doll or by myself) very cruelly. Furthermore, her ambivalence towards her mother, her extreme need to be punished, her feelings of guilt and her night terrors led me to recognize that in this child aged two years and nine months—and quite clearly going back to a much earlier age—a harsh and relentless super-ego operated. I found this discovery confirmed in the analyses of other young children and came to the conclusion that the super-ego arises at a much earlier stage than Freud assumed. In other words, it became clear to me that the super-ego, as conceived by him, is the end-product of a development which extends over years. As a result of further observations, I recognized that the super-ego is something which is felt by the child to operate internally in a concrete way; that it consists of a variety of figures built up from his experiences and phantasies and that it is derived from the stages in which he had internalized (introjected) his parents.

These observations in turn led, in the analyses of little girls, to the discovery of the leading female anxiety situation: the mother is felt to be the primal persecutor who, as an external and internalized object, attacks the child's body and takes from it her imaginary children. These anxieties arise from the girl's phantasied attacks on the mother's body, which aim at robbing her of its contents, i.e. of fæces, of the father's penis, and of children, and result in the fear of retaliation by similar attacks. Such persecutory anxieties I found combined or alternating with deep feelings of depression and guilt, and these observations then led to my discovery of the vital part which the tendency to *make reparation* plays in mental life. Reparation in this sense is a wider concept than Freud's concepts of "undoing in the obsessional neurosis" and of "reaction-formation". For it includes the variety of processes by which the ego feels it undoes harm done in phantasy, restores, preserves, and revives objects. The importance of this tendency, bound up as it is with feelings of guilt, also lies in the major contribution it makes to all sublimations, and in this way to mental health.

Melanie Klein

In studying the phantasied attacks on the mother's body, I soon
came upon anal- and urethral-sadistic impulses. I have mentioned
above that I recognized the harshness of the super-ego in Rita
(1923) and that her analysis greatly helped me to understand the way
in which destructive impulses towards the mother become the
cause of feelings of guilt and persecution. One of the cases through
which the anal- and urethral-sadistic nature of these destructive
impulses became clear to me was that of "Trude", aged three years
and three months, whom I analysed in 1924.[1] When she came to
me for treatment, she suffered from various symptoms, such as
night terrors and incontinence of urine and fæces. Early on in her
analysis she asked me to pretend that I was in bed and asleep. She
would then say that she was going to attack me and look into my
buttocks for fæces (which I found also represented children) and that
she was going to take them out. Such attacks were followed by
her crouching in a corner, playing that she was in bed, covering
herself with cushions (which were to protect her body and which
also stood for children); at the same time she actually wetted herself and showed clearly that she was very much afraid of being
attacked by me. Her anxieties about the dangerous internalized
mother confirmed the conclusions I first formed in Rita's analysis.
Both these analyses had been of short duration, partly because
the parents thought that enough improvement had been achieved.[2]

Soon afterwards I became convinced that such destructive impulses and phantasies could always be traced back to oral-sadistic
ones. In fact Rita had already shown this quite clearly. On one
occasion she blackened a piece of paper, tore it up, threw the scraps
into a glass of water which she put to her mouth as if to drink from
it, and said under her breath "dead woman".[3] This tearing up and
soiling of paper I had at the time understood to express phantasies
of attacking and killing her mother which gave rise to fears of
retaliation. I have already mentioned that it was with Trude that I
became aware of the specific anal- and urethral-sadistic nature of
such attacks. But in other analyses, carried out in 1924 and 1925
(Ruth and Peter, both described in *The Psycho-Analysis of Children*),
I also became aware of the fundamental part which oral-sadistic
impulses play in destructive phantasies and corresponding anxieties,
thus finding in the analysis of young children full confirmation of

[1] Cf. The *Psycho-Analysis of Children*.
[2] Rita had eighty-three sessions, Trude eighty-two sessions.
[3] See "The Œdipus Complex in the Light of Early Anxieties", *Int. J. Psycho-Anal.*, Vol.
XXVI (1945), also *Contributions to Psycho-Analysis*, pp. 374-5.

Abraham's discoveries.[1] These analyses, which gave me further scope for observation, since they lasted longer than Rita's and Trude's,[2] led me towards a fuller insight into the fundamental role of oral desires and anxieties in mental development, normal and abnormal.[3]

As I have mentioned, I had already recognized in Rita and Trude the internalization of an attacked and therefore frightening mother —the harsh super-ego. Between 1924 and 1926 I analysed a child who was very ill indeed.[4] Through her analysis I learned a good deal about the specific details of such internalization and about the phantasies and impulses underlying paranoid and manic-depressive anxieties. For I came to understand the oral and anal nature of her introjection processes and the situations of internal persecution they engendered. I also became more aware of the ways in which internal persecutions influence, by means of projection, the relation to external objects. The intensity of her envy and hatred unmistakably showed its derivation from the oral-sadistic relation to her mother's breast, and was interwoven with the beginnings of her Œdipus complex. Erna's case much helped to prepare the ground for a number of conclusions which I presented to the Tenth International Psycho-Analytical Congress in 1927,[5] in particular the view that the early super-ego, built up when oral-sadistic impulses and phantasies are at their height, underlies psychosis —a view which two years later I developed by stressing the importance of oral-sadism for schizophrenia.[6]

Concurrently with the analyses so far described I was able to make some interesting observations regarding anxiety situations in boys. The analyses of boys and men fully confirmed Freud's view that castration fear is the leading anxiety of the male, but I recognized that owing to the early identification with the mother (the feminine position which ushers in the early stages of the Œdipus complex) the anxiety about attacks on the inside of the body is of great

[1] Cf. "A Short History of the Development of the Libido, Viewed in the Light of Mental Disorders", 1924. Reprinted in *Selected Papers* (London, 1927).

[2] Ruth had 190 sessions, Peter 278 sessions.

[3] This growing conviction about the fundamental importance of Abraham's discoveries was also the result of my analysis with him, which began in 1924 and was cut short fourteen months later through his illness and death.

[4] Described under the name "Erna" in *The Psycho-Analysis of Children*, Chapter III.

[5] Cf. "Early Stages of the Œdipus Conflict", *Int. J. Psycho-Anal.*, Vol. IX (1928); also reprinted in *Contributions to Psycho-Analysis*.

[6] Cf. "The Importance of Symbol-Formation in the Development of the Ego", read before the Eleventh International Psycho-Analytical Congress, Oxford, 1929. Published in *Int. J. Psycho-An·l.*, Vol. XI (1930); also reprinted in *Contributions to Psycho-Analysis*.

importance in men as well as women, and in various ways influences and moulds their castration fears.

The anxieties derived from phantasied attacks on the mother's body and on the father she is supposed to contain, proved in both sexes to underlie claustrophobia (which includes the fear of being imprisoned or entombed in the mother's body). The connection of these anxieties with castration fear can be seen for instance in the phantasy of losing the penis or having it destroyed inside the mother—phantasies which may result in impotence.

I came to see that the fears connected with attacks on the mother's body and of being attacked by external and internal objects had a particular quality and intensity which suggested their psychotic nature. In exploring the child's relation to internalized objects, various situations of internal persecution and their psychotic contents became clear. Furthermore, the recognition that fear of retaliation derives from the individual's own aggressiveness led me to suggest that the initial defences of the ego are directed against the anxiety aroused by destructive impulses and phantasies. Again and again, when these psychotic anxieties were traced to their origin, they were found to stem from oral-sadism. I recognized also that the oral-sadistic relation to the mother and the internalization of a devoured, and therefore devouring, breast create the prototype of all internal persecutors; and furthermore that the internalization of an injured and therefore dreaded breast on the one hand, and of a satisfying and helpful breast on the other, is the core of the super-ego. Another conclusion was that, although oral anxieties come first, sadistic phantasies and desires from all sources are operative at a very early stage of development and overlap the oral anxieties.[1]

The importance of the infantile anxieties I have described above was also shown in the analysis of very ill adults, some of whom were border-line psychotic cases.[2]

---

[1] These and other conclusions are contained in the two papers I have already mentioned, "Early Stages of the Œdipus Conflict" (*Int. J. Psycho-Anal.*, Vol. IX); and "The Importance of Symbol-Formation in the Development of the Ego" (*Int. J. Psycho-Anal.*, Vol. XI). See also "Personification in the Play of Children" (*Int. J. Psycho-Anal.*, Vol. X (1929)). All these papers are reprinted in *Contributions to Psycho-Analysis*.

[2] It is possible that the understanding of the contents of psychotic anxieties and of the urgency to interpret them was brought home to me in the analysis of a paranoic schizophrenic man who came to me for one month only. In 1922 a colleague who was going on holiday asked me to take over for a month a schizophrenic patient of his. I found from the first hour onwards that I must not allow the patient to remain silent for any length of time. I felt that his silence implied danger, and in every such instance I interpreted his suspicions of me, e.g. that I was plotting with his uncle and would have him certified again (he had recently been de-certified)—material which on other occasions he verbally expressed. Once when

There were other experiences which helped me to reach yet a further conclusion. The comparison between the undoubtedly paranoic Erna and the phantasies and anxieties that I had found in less ill children, who could only be called neurotic, convinced me that psychotic (paranoid and depressive) anxieties underlie infantile neurosis. I also made similar observations in the analyses of adult neurotics. All these different lines of exploration resulted in the hypothesis that anxieties of a psychotic nature are in some measure part of normal infantile development and are expressed and worked through in the course of the infantile neurosis.[1] To uncover these infantile anxieties the analysis has, however, to be carried into deep layers of the unconscious, and this applies both to adults and to children.[2]

It has already been pointed out in the introduction to this paper that my attention from the beginning focused on the child's anxieties and that it was by means of interpreting their contents that I found myself able to diminish anxiety. In order to do this, full use had to be made of the symbolic language of play which I recognized to be an essential part of the child's mode of expression. As we have seen, the brick, the little figure, the car, not only represent things which interest the child in themselves, but in his play with them they always have a variety of symbolical meanings as well which are bound up with his phantasies, wishes, and experiences. This archaic mode of expression is also the language with which we are familiar in dreams, and it was by approaching the play of

I had interpreted his silence in this way, connecting it with former material, the patient, sitting up, asked me in a threatening tone: "Are you going to send me back to the asylum?" But he soon became quieter and began to speak more freely. That showed me that I had been on the right lines and should continue to interpret his suspicions and feelings of persecution. To some extent a positive as well as a negative transference to me came about; but at one point, when his fear of women came up very strongly, he demanded from me the name of a male analyst to whom he could turn. I gave him a name, but he never approached this colleague. During that month I saw the patient every day. The analyst who had asked me to take over found some progress on his return and wished me to continue the analysis. I refused, having become fully aware of the danger of treating a paranoic without any protection or other suitable management. During the time when I analysed him, he often stood for hours opposite my house, looking up at my window, though it was only on a few occasions that he rang the bell and asked to see me. I may mention that after a short time he was again certified. Although I did not at the time draw any theoretical conclusions from this experience, I believe that this fragment of an analysis may have contributed to my later insight into the psychotic nature of infantile anxieties and to the development of my technique.

[1] As we know, Freud found that there is no structural difference between the normal and the neurotic, and this discovery has been of the greatest importance in the understanding of mental processes in general. My hypothesis that anxieties of a psychotic nature are ubiquitous in infancy, and underlie the infantile neurosis, is an extension of Freud's discovery.

[2] The conclusions I have presented in the last paragraph can be found fully dealt with in *The Psycho-Analysis of Children*.

the child in a way similar to Freud's interpretation of dreams that I found I could get access to the child's unconscious. But we have to consider each child's use of symbols in connection with his particular emotions and anxieties and in relation to the whole situation which is presented in the analysis; mere generalized translations of symbols are meaningless.

The importance I attributed to symbolism led me—as time went on—to theoretical conclusions about the process of symbol formation. Play analysis had shown that symbolism enabled the child to transfer not only interests, but also phantasies, anxieties, and guilt to objects other than people.[1] Thus a great deal of relief is experienced in play and this is one of the factors which make it so essential for the child. For instance, Peter to whom I have referred earlier, pointed out to me, when I interpreted his damaging a toy figure as representing attacks on his brother, that he would not do this to his *real* brother, he would only do it to the *toy* brother. My interpretation of course made it clear to him that it was really his brother whom he wished to attack; but the instance shows that only by symbolic means was he able to express his destructive tendencies in the analysis.

I have also arrived at the view that, in children, a severe inhibition of the capacity to form and use symbols, and so to develop phantasy life, is a sign of serious disturbance.[2] I suggested that such inhibitions, and the resulting disturbance in the relation to the external world and to reality, are characteristic of schizophrenia.[3]

In passing I may say that I found it of great value from the clinical and theoretical point of view that I was analysing both adults and children. I was thereby able to observe the infant's phantasies and anxieties still operative in the adult and to assess in the young child what his future development might be. It was by comparing the severely ill, the neurotic, and the normal child, and by recognizing infantile anxieties of a psychotic nature as the cause of illness in adult neurotics, that I had arrived at the conclusions I have described above.[4]

---

[1] In this connection, cf. Dr. Ernest Jones' important paper "The Theory of Symbolism", *Brit. J. Psychol.* Vol. IX (1916).

[2] "The Importance of Symbol-Formation in the Development of the Ego", *Int. J. Psycho-Anal.*, Vol. XI (1930). Also in *Contributions to Psycho-Analysis*.

[3] This conclusion has since influenced the understanding of the schizophrenic mode of communication and has found its place in the treatment of schizophrenia.

[4] I cannot deal here with the fundamental difference which, besides common features, exist between the normal, the neurotic and the psychotic.

VI

In tracing, in the analyses of adults and children, the development of impulses, phantasies, and anxieties back to their origin, i.e. to the feelings towards the mother's breast (even with children who have not been breast-fed), I found that object relations start almost at birth and arise with the first feeding experience; furthermore, that all aspects of mental life are bound up with object relations. It also emerged that the child's experience of the external world, which very soon includes his ambivalent relation to his father and to other members of his family, is constantly influenced by—and in turn influences—the internal world he is building up, and that external and internal situations are always interdependent, since introjection and projection operate side by side from the beginning of life.

The observations that in the infant's mind the mother primarily appears as good and bad breast split off from each other, and that within a few months, with growing ego integration the contrasting aspects are beginning to be synthesized, helped me to understand the importance of the processes of splitting and keeping apart good and bad figures,[1] as well as the effect of such processes on ego development. The conclusion to be drawn from the experience that depressive anxiety arises as a result of the ego synthesizing the good and bad (loved and hated) aspects of the object led me in turn to the concept of the depressive position which reaches its climax towards the middle of the first year. It is preceded by the paranoid position, which extends over the first three or four months of life and is characterized by persecutory anxiety and splitting processes.[2] Later on, in 1946, [3] when I reformulated my views on the first three or four months of life, I called this stage (making use of a suggestion of Fairbairn's)[4] the paranoid-schizoid position and, in working out its significance, sought to co-ordinate my findings about splitting, projection, persecution and idealization.

---

[1] "Personification in the Play of Children", *Int. J. Psycho-Anal.*, Vol. X (1929); also in *Contributions to Psycho-Analysis*.

[2] "A Contribution to the Psychogenesis of Manic-Depressive States", *Int. J. Psycho-Anal.*, Vol. XVI (1935); also in *Contributions to Psycho-Analysis*.

[3] "Notes on Some Schizoid Mechanisms", *Int. J. Psycho-Anal.*, Vol. XXVII (1946); also in *Developments in Psycho-Analysis* (London, 1952).

[4] Fairbairn, W. R. D., "A Revised Psychopathology of the Psychoses and Neuroses", *Int. J. Psycho-Anal.*, Vol. XXII (1941); also in *Psycho-Analytic Studies of the Personality* (London, 1952).

Melanie Klein

My work with children and the theoretical conclusions I drew from it increasingly influenced my technique with adults. It has always been a tenet of psycho-analysis that the unconscious, which originates in the infantile mind, has to be explored in the adult. My experience with children had taken me much deeper in that direction than was formerly the case, and this led to a technique which made access to those layers possible. In particular, my play technique had helped me to see which material was most in need of interpretation at the moment and the way in which it would be most easily conveyed to the patient; and some of this knowledge I could apply to the analysis of adults.[1] As has been pointed out earlier, this does not mean that the technique used with children is identical with the approach to adults. Though we find our way back to the earliest stages, it is of great importance in analysing adults to take account of the adult ego, just as with children we keep in mind the infantile ego according to the stage of its development.

The fuller understanding of the earliest stages of development, of the role of phantasies, anxieties, and defences in the emotional life of the infant has also thrown light on the fixation points of adult psychosis. As a result there has opened up a new way of treating psychotic patients by psycho-analysis. This field, in particular the psycho-analysis of schizophrenic patients, needs much further exploration; but the work done in this direction by some psycho-analysts, who are represented in this book, seems to justify hopes for the future.

---

[1] The play technique has also influenced work with children in other fields, as for example in child guidance work and in education. The development of educational methods in England has been given fresh impetus by Susan Isaacs' research at the Malting House School. Her books about that work have been widely read and have had a lasting effect on educational techniques in this country, especially where young children are concerned. Her approach was strongly influenced by her great appreciation of child analysis, in particular of play technique; and it is largely due to her that in England the psycho-analytic understanding of children has contributed to developments in education.

2

A CONTRIBUTION TO THE RE-EVALUATION OF THE ŒDIPUS COMPLEX—THE EARLY STAGES[1]

PAULA HEIMANN

Introductory Remarks

FOR the purpose of this paper I have decided to concentrate on the early stages of the Œdipus complex which Melanie Klein has discovered in her analyses of young children. Her contributions also influence the assessment of the later stages, but I think that the most useful way of approaching divergences of opinion lies in discussing the field in which they originate.

Although my presentation seems to emphasize the controversial points in our views on the Œdipus complex, this does not mean that we underrate the amount or the significance of the ground we share.

Before dealing with my subject matter I wish to define our position with regard to some basic concepts and to outline briefly the period preceding the Œdipus complex.

The Theory of the Instincts

All understanding of psychological phenomena rests on Freud's discovery of the dynamic Unconscious. The two primary instincts of life and death, the borderland entities between soma and psyche, from which all instinctual impulses are derived, are the source of mental energy; all mental processes start from an unconscious stage.

Freud's concept of an inherent antithesis in the deepest and the most dynamic levels of the mind is fully born out by Melanie Klein's work. More than this, her work has produced many observations which substantiate his theory, but precisely on this account major divergences between her views and classical theory have arisen.

I am referring to the position that the mental facet of the instinctual urges, which we call "unconscious phantasy", occupies in Melanie Klein's work.

[1] Read before the Seventeenth International Psycho-Analytic Congress at Amsterdam in August, 1951, as part of the Symposium on the Re-evaluation of the Œdipus complex.

Paula Heimann

Unconscious Phantasies

By the term unconscious phantasies we mean the most primitive psychic formations, inherent in the operation of the instinctual urges; and because these are inborn, we attribute unconscious phantasies to the infant from the beginning of his life. Unconscious phantasies occur not only in the infant, they are part of the unconscious mind at any time, and form the matrix from which the pre-conscious and conscious processes develop. In the earliest stages they are almost the whole of psychical processes, and, of course they are pre-verbal, or rather non-verbal. The words which we use when we wish to convey their contents and meaning are a foreign element, but we cannot do without it—unless we are artists.

Unconscious phantasies are associated with the infant's experience of pleasure or pain, happiness or anxiety; they involve his relation with his objects. They are dynamic processes, because they are charged with the energy of the instinctual impulses, and they influence the development of ego mechanisms. For example, introjection develops from the infant's unconscious phantasy of incorporating the mother's breast, which accompanies the desire for the breast and the actual sensation of sucking and swallowing when in contact with it.

Conversely, the mechanism of projection develops from the phantasy of expelling an object.

In order to understand the infant's psychic development and many of his physical processes, we must appreciate his unconscious phantasies.

Earliest Object Relations

The first childhood period is characterized by the infant's maximal dependence on his mother and by the maximal immaturity of his ego. The instinctual urges and the phantasies which they imply reign supreme. Perception of the reality of the self and of objects is poor, and phantasy flourishes the more. To obtain satisfaction, the infant needs his object. He wills it when he experiences his needs. He omnipotently possesses it when he is satisfied. When he is caressed and gratified, he has the ideally good breast. He loves this breast, he could eat it. He incorporates the gratifying breast and is one with it. He goes to sleep with his loved object. If things go well, he will do the same thing in adult life.

In states of hunger or pain, he does not believe that the pain is part of himself; it is the malicious breast which is responsible, and he hates it. His attempts at introjecting and keeping the good breast, and projecting his pain and the bad breast, have been without avail. He feels persecuted by the bad breast within his own self.

Throughout, in Melanie Klein's work, the focus has been on anxiety as the most dynamic element in frustration and conflict, By consistently analysing the phantasies associated with anxiety, and the defences determined by these phantasies, she discovered that the most primitive type of fear is the fear of persecutory objects (at first the bad breast), and that splitting mechanisms are amongst the earliest ego defences.

She has termed these early processes the paranoid-schizoid position, thus pinpointing the character of the anxiety and of the defences against it, which prevail during the first few months of life, and which underlie later schizophrenic illnesses.

Lack of cohesion in the early ego and the use of splitting mechanisms lead to the infant's living with a good and a bad double of his object, which correspond with his feelings of gratification or frustration.

Love, hate, and fear, the fundamental units of psychological experience, develop in the wake of instinctual urges and physical sensations.

The Whole Object Stage

At this stage, which begins roughly in the second quarter of the first year, the infant's ego is stronger and more coherent. Perception leads to more integrated objects. The infant sees more at the time, and remembers more of the past. He recognizes his parents as whole objects, that is, as persons. He has lost some of his omnipotence and gained more sense of reality. This holds not only for the external world of objects, but also for internal psychic reality.

The conflict of ambivalence begins to play its part in the infant's emotional life. Melanie Klein regards it as the nucleus of the infantile depressive position.

The infant begins to realize that when he loves and hates his mother, it is one and the same person whom he desires and attacks. He feels unhappy and guilty, he suffers from the pain which his destructive impulses inflict on her, and he fears that he will lose her and her love. These feelings concern also his internal mother.

Hatred against the loved object matters so much, because at this stage the belief in the omnipotence of evil outweighs the belief in the power of love. It is *depressive* anxiety that the infant now experiences.

The "infantile depressive position" represents the fixation point for later manic-depressive illness.

Normally the infant's depressive moods pass off quickly. Amongst the defences we distinguish a regressive type, the "manic defence", which revolves upon denial and flight, and a progressive one, which consists of the drive for reparation and attempts at inhibiting destructive impulses, in particular, greed, in order to spare the mother.

Moreover, other factors implied in the many advances at this stage of development help the child.

This leads to my main theme. When the infant begins to realize that his parents are persons, he also feels that they are not only objects for his needs and wishes, but that they have a life of their own, and with one another. With the widening of his emotional and intellectual orbit, the infant enters upon the triangular stage of his relation with his parents. He does not merely add the whole object to his part objects, it is also the relationship between his mother and his father which becomes a highly significant factor in his life. This first establishment of an emotional triangle with his parents is the beginning of the Œdipus complex. Increasingly the infant's emotions, impulses, and phantasies, centre upon the parental couple.

This new focus of interest in his life, which stimulates and exercises his mental energies, operates as another means of defence against the depressive position.

The Early Stages of the Œdipus Complex

The beginning of the Œdipus complex coincides with the polymorphously perverse condition of the child's instinctual impulses. Excitations from all parts of his body are active, and because the erotogenic zones are also the seat of the destructive impulses, the child fluctuates not only between one erotic desire and another, but also between libididinal and destructive aims. Such movements and fluctuations are characteristic for this phase.

The phantasies that accompany these excitations have specific contents. The child wishes to experience the gratification of each of his manifold urges by specific oral, anal, and genital contacts with his parents.

Under the dominance of the libido the child's phantasies are pleasurable. He imagines the fulfilment of his polymorphous desires. But this holds only up to a point, and polymorphous wishes recur as polymorphous fears, not only because his parents do in fact frustrate many of his desires, but because the destructive components of his wishes, his cruel cravings, are in phantasy experienced as actions, and lead to destroyed and destructive objects in his inner and outer world. At the beginning, the oral impulses lead in this orchestra of polymorphous urges, and, together with the urethral and anal zones, overshadow the genital for a time, so that genital excitations are in part linked with pre-genital phantasies. In the second half of the first year, however, genital stirrings gain in strength, and the wish for genital gratification includes the wish to receive and give a child. In our observation a child of eleven months is not only capable of feeling rival hatred and jealousy of a baby brother or sister, as Freud described, but the child *himself* desires the baby and envies his mother. His jealousy is double edged.

It is to this phase that we attribute the origin of the unconscious equation of breast, penis, fæces, child, etc., and the infantile sexual theories, which Freud discovered and related to the child aged three to five years. In our view these equations and theories express the infant's phantasies at the polymorphous stage of instinctual development, when the excitations from all bodily zones and libidinal and destructive aims rival one another.

Thus the theory of parental intercourse as a feeding or excretory act, of babies being conceived through the mouth and born through the anus, show the overlapping of oral, excretory, and procreative urges and phantasies. The notions of the "primal scene", or of the castrating phallic mother, betray the fusion of libidinal and cruel impulses characteristic of early infantile genitality.

A three-year-old child is capable of verbalizing some of these phantasies, but the time at which he expresses them does not coincide with the date of their origin. The three-year-old child who has achieved a considerable degree of organization has largely overcome the polymorphous condition of his instinctual impulses.

Our clinical observations in the analysis of children and adults have shown us that the most crucial contents of the Œdipus complex, and the most severe conflicts and anxieties, relate to the primitive impulses and phantasies which form the early stages of the Œdipus complex.

In passing I would mention that, apart from dreams, we can see the phantasies of this early stage clearly in certain states both of normal and of pathological regression. Adolescence normally shows the re-emergence of early infantile sexuality. When the adolescent in horror turns away from his impulses, it is not only because he discovers his incestuous object choice, the wish to sleep with his mother, but because he becomes aware that he is attracted and excited by perverse and cruel phantasies.

The regressed schizophrenic often expresses polymorphously perverse phantasies without any disguise and attributes his bizarre bodily sensations to his internalized parents and their intercourse.

After these general observations let us consider some features of the early Œdipus complex in more detail.

Melanie Klein holds that both the boy and the girl begin the Œdipus complex in the direct and in the inverted form.

The Early Œdipus Complex in the Boy

The boy's "feminine position" is due to several factors. The conflicts of the depressive position concern predominantly the mother, and act as an incentive for seeking another love object. In addition, he is in many ways frustrated by her, and particularly during weaning.

The loss of the external breast intensifies the identification with the mother which has been going on all along. In the triangular relationship with his parents this identification strengthens the homosexual component of the boy's bisexuality.

Predominant in his many desires for his father are the impulses for the father's *penis*, which at first is largely equated with the breast. The boy wants to suck, swallow, and incorporate it orally, as well as through his anus and penis, which he treats as receptive organs. There are also active versions of such phantasies; the boy wants to enter with his own penis the father's body, mouth, anus, and genital. In the latter part of the first year the desire to receive a child from the father plays an important part.

These wishes represent the roots of male homosexuality. In his feminine position the boy is his mother's enemy and rival.

The man's envy of the woman, of her ability to bear and feed children, has been underrated in classical theory. Yet the analyses of fathers give ample evidence of such envy. Whilst the occurrence of the "couvade" has been acknowledged, the conclusion has not been drawn that this manifestation of the man's desire to be a woman has its origin in the infant's early inverted Œdipus complex.

Envy and hatred of the mother, which accompany the first homo-sexual impulses in the boy, form an important source of the man's fear of the woman. The familiar notions of the *vagina dentata* and the so-called cloaca theory bear witness to the infant's jealous attacks on the mother's genital, and specifically to those phantasies in which the attacks are carried out by teeth and excrements.

Phantasies of attacking the mother's genital may lead to inhibition of heterosexuality in both the boy and the girl. For the boy, the woman's genital assumes qualities which threaten his penis; the girl, who identifies her own genital with that of her mother, comes to regard it as a dangerous organ, which she must not use with the man she loves.

The boy's feminine wishes for his father are in sharp conflict with his masculine desires for his mother.

In our view the infant assumes the existence of the vagina from his own genital sensations. His urge to penetrate is connected with phantasies about a corresponding genital opening in the mother's body. His primary libidinal desires for her are secondarily intensified by reparative tendencies. The drive to make amends to her by giving her genital pleasure and children contributes in the course of development a great deal to the establishment of the boy's heterosexual genitality.

These masculine impulses are associated with rival hatred against the father and with the corresponding fears of the father's retaliation.

In both his feminine and masculine position, the boy's desires are frustrated; and frustration is maximal when the infant witnesses or imagines that his parents are united in intercourse. The "combined parental figure" is the object of many phantasies in which libidinal and destructive aims are combined and opposed. Almost simultaneously, the infant aims at destroying both parents, and also at destroying only his rival while desiring the other parent. These phantasies lead to severe anxiety, the fear being that he destroys the desired object, be this mother or father, in the same attack which is aimed at the other parent, and his anxieties are multiplied because, owing to his incorporation phantasies, he feels that this hated "primal scene" takes place inside himself as well.

Anxieties of this kind play an important part in the boy's phallic manifestations. Pride in his penis is not only derived from his unconscious knowledge of its creative and reparative function. Such knowledge, we find, is a strong incentive for libidinal phantasies of intercourse with his mother. The narcissistic pleasure he derives from masturbation, urinary games, or exhibitionism is partly used as a defence against his fears of the mother's body which, as a result of his attacks, has become a battle ground, full of dangerous objects. And by his contempt for the female genital and denial of the vagina, he tries to escape from all notions about the inside of the body, his own as well as the mother's, because of the fears connected with

29

internal persecutors. The sight of his penis and its functions gives him again and again the reassurance that all is well with him, and that he need not be afraid of persecutory objects in his own body.

In this connection I would refer to Ernest Jones's lucid exposition of the factors which result in the "secondary nature of narcissistic phallicism".

Castration Complex

I have already described many of the anxieties that the boy experiences in connection with his early Œdipal impulses; when these anxieties are taken into consideration, Jones's suggestion that it is *aphanisis* which is dreaded, and not merely the loss of the penis, gains in significance. As far as the specific fears for the penis are concerned, in the early stages the boy is afraid of both parents.

In response to his own oral and anal attacks he fears that his penis will be bitten off, soiled, and poisoned.

After the establishment of the genital organization, his leading anxiety is castration by his father. This anxiety too has depressive as well as persecutory qualities; it is not only the fear of being deprived of the organ and power for sexual pleasure, but also the fear of losing the means for expressing love, reparative, and creative impulses. This depressive component is evidenced in the well-known equation between being castrated and being completely worthless.

The Early Œdipus Complex in the Girl

To turn now to the girl: her position in the early stages of the Œdipus complex is in many respects similar to that of the boy. She, too, oscillates between heterosexual and homosexual positions, and between libidinal and destructive aims, and experiences corresponding anxiety situations. She has the same motives for turning away from her mother, and in her case indentification with the mother intensifies the heterosexual impulses.

Here we consider merely the genital aspects of her early Œdipus phantasies.

Our observations are that vaginal sensations occur at this stage, not only sensations in the clitoris. Moreover, the clitoris has a conductor function and its excitations stimulate the vagina. Oral, urethral, and anal impulses also lead to vaginal sensations and phantasies.

The phantasies associated with vaginal urges have a specific

30

feminine character. The little girl wishes to receive and incorporate the father's penis, and to acquire it as an *internal* possession, and from here she soon arrives at the wish to receive a child from him. These wishes, partly because they meet with frustration, alternate with the desire to possess an external penis.

The masculine component of the sensations and phantasies connected with the clitoris can only be fully assessed if the girl's conflicts and anxieties which follow from her feminine position are taken into account.

When jealousy stimulates phantasies of attacking her mother's body, these attacks recoil upon herself, and she feels that her own genital will be mutilated, soiled, poisoned, annihilated, etc., and her own internal penis and children stolen from her by her internalized mother. These fears are the graver because she feels that she lacks the organ (i.e. the external penis), which could adequately placate or restore the avenging mother, and because she has no evidence that in reality her genital organs are unharmed. We consider that there is here a psychological consequence of the anatomical difference between the sexes which is of the greatest significance for the development of the girl.

We distinguish several sources for masculine drives in the little girl. Frustration of her feminine desires gives rise to hatred and fear of the father and drives her back to the mother. Anxieties related to her external and internal mother lead her to concentrate on phallic activities and phantasies. Her primary homosexual trends are thus most strongly increased by failure in her feminine position. She then comes to find that her male organ is inferior, that it is not a proper penis, that it cannot rival the father's penis. Because her phallicism is largely a secondary and defensive phenomenon, she comes to develop penis envy at the expense of femininity. She disowns her vagina, attributes genital qualities exclusively to the penis, hopes for her clitoris to grow into one and meets with disappointment. Devaluation of femininity underlies the overvaluation of the penis.

The familiar grievances of the girl against her mother for withholding the penis from her and sending her into the world as an incomplete creature are based on her need to deny her attacks on the mother's body and her rivalry with both parents. With her laments that she has come too short she protests that she never was greedy, never usurped the mother's position with her father, never stole the father's love, penis, and children from her.

31

To say this does not mean that we underrate the girl's intense admiration for the penis, or her greed, which makes her want to have whatever she regards as desirable. Nor do we doubt that penis envy plays an important part in female psychology. My point is that penis envy is a complex fabric of which only certain threads have been generally acknowledged.

The analysis of penis envy in a woman with pronounced rivalry with men shows us so clearly that it is built on the failure to master persecutory and depressive anxieties arising from her early femininity, and that these early anxieties lend the compulsive character to her demand that she must have a penis.

The conclusions from our work which I have here presented differ from Freud's view that there is a long period of pre-Œdipal mother fixation in the girl. The phenomena that Freud described under this heading in our view represents the inverted form of the girl's Œdipus complex, which alternates with the direct Œdipus complex.

The girl who shows an exclusive attachment to her mother, and hostility against her father, has failed to cope with the frustration of her first feminine wishes.

Our observations also lead us to disagree with the view that the woman's wish for a child takes second place to that for possessing a penis.

The Role of Introjection

I have endeavoured to show that throughout his development the child internalizes his parents, and that his internal objects have both a good and a bad aspect for him. In relation to the good internal object, he experiences a state of well-being, and in the earliest period, the good internal object fuses with the self; whereas states of anxiety of a persecutory or depressive kind are connected with the bad or destroyed internal objects.

This relation between the child and his parents prevails throughout the early stages of the Œdipus complex, and therefore the development of the Œdipus complex is throughout influenced by his feelings about his internal parents, by fears of being persecuted by them, and by guilt for harming them.

According to Freud, the super-ego is the result of the child internalizing his parents at the *decline* of the Œdipus complex; the tension between the ego and the super-ego is experienced as guilt and fear of retaliation.

Melanie Klein holds that all processes of internalization enter into the formation of the super-ego and that it begins with the first internalized object, the mother's breast. In her view there is throughout an interaction between the development of the ego, the Œdipus complex, and the super-ego.

Conclusion

In the light of Melanie Klein's work the Œdipus complex which Freud discovered appears as the *final* stage of a process which begins in early infancy. Its roots are set in a crucial phase of development. The child makes the first steps towards recognizing the reality of other persons, the first steps towards establishing full emotional relationships; he meets the full impact of the conflict of ambivalence; in his first experience of the triangular relationship with his parents his instinctual impulses are polymorphously perverse, and he oscillates between a heterosexual and a homosexual object choice.

In the early stages of the Œdipus complex the scales are weighted for the first time. Much of the way in which the child will enter and leave the final stage depends on the interplay of forces at this early period.

The understanding of the child's problems in the early infantile Œdipus complex makes us realize all the more the truth of Freud's discovery that the Œdipus complex is the *nuclear* complex in the individual's life.

POSTSCRIPT ON THE POLYMORPHOUS STAGE OF INSTINCTUAL DEVELOPMENT[1]

When preparing the above contribution to the Symposium on the Re-evaluation of the Œdipus Complex, I was compelled to think again, very thoroughly, about familiar matters. That is always a salutary experience because it counteracts the tendency to use terms glibly instead of thinking afresh about the conditions and processes to which these terms refer. I then found that certain topics came up in my thoughts, and one of these I wish to bring forward here.

It concerns the problem of the instinctual stages. Melanie Klein's discoveries which have necessitated a re-evaluation of the Œdipus complex lead also to a re-examination of our views on the course of instinctual development.

[1] Read before the British Psycho-Analytical Society, 16th January, 1952, as an Appendix to the Congress Paper.

33

Paula Heimann

In his *Three Essays on the Theory of Sexuality* (1905), which are the foundation of psycho-analytic theories of infantile sexuality, Freud speaks of the polymorphously perverse disposition of infantile sexuality. I shall quote only one passage. In his summary[1] he says: "Experience further showed that the external influences of seduction are capable of provoking interruptions of the latency period or even its cessation, and that in this connection *the sexual instinct of children proves in fact to be polymorphously perverse; . . .*" (My italics.)

Abraham in his *Development of the Libido* (1924) carried our knowledge of infantile sexuality further, mainly in three ways: (1) by showing the subdivisions of the oral and the anal stages; (2) by correlating the different sexual stages with the development of object-love; and (3) by stressing the development of the destructive strivings As to the third point, I regard it as noteworthy that, although his book appeared four years after *Beyond the Pleasure Principle*, Abraham does not refer to the death instinct. It seems to me possible to conclude that Abraham did not accept, or perhaps had not yet accepted, the theory of the death instinct, and this to my mind would explain why he maintained the idea that the first oral stage, the sucking stage, is free from destructive impulses, "pre-ambivalent", although in other connections he described the vampire type, i.e. the tendency to kill the object by sucking it to death. In passing I would repeat, what has often been pointed out before, that Melanie Klein's work does not endorse the view of a pre-ambivalent stage as Abraham describes it, but that her findings of the early splitting mechanisms which create an ideal and a persecutory breast represent an important modification of Abraham's concept of the pre-ambivalent stage. But this is only in passing, because my main interest in these short notes concerns the fact that in Abraham's scheme the notion of the polymorphously perverse disposition is not included.

As I endeavoured to show above, in Melanie Klein's work this notion is of considerable importance. She has often pointed out that the trends from the diverse zones overlap, and that this overlapping characterizes the instinctual climate of the early stages of the Œdipus complex.

We can to-day define the notion of a "polymorphously perverse" disposition in more detail. The infant tends to experience in an uncoordinated manner excitations from all parts of his body and to crave for their simultaneous gratification; further, equally he

[1] *Three Essays on the Theory of Sexuality* (London, 1949), p. 111.

34

simultaneously experiences and seeks to satisfy libidinal and destructive impulses.

The polymorphously perverse disposition arises thus from the fact that the infant from the beginning of life is under the influence of the two primary instincts of life and death. Their derivatives in the form of self-preservative and libidinal impulses on the one hand and of destructive and cruel cravings on the other are active from the beginning of life.

Both primary instincts operate in the infant's contacts with his first object, and thus begin in the manner which in respect of the libido Freud called "anaclitic". Freud attributed erotogenic qualities to all parts of the body. Melanie Klein's observations in the analyses of young children showed that there were also immensely cruel phantasies related to all parts of the body. It therefore follows from her work that Freud's statement about the way the libido operates has to be expanded to include the operation of the destructive impulses—a point which follows theoretically from the concept of the primary death instinct.

In addition, she has shown that the anxieties roused by the combination and opposition of the libido and the destructive impulses lead from the beginning to the development of ego-mechanisms, defence mechanisms.

The conclusion I wish to put forward here is that the transition from the oral to the anal stage is not direct, but that there is interpolated a period in which the infant's polymorphously perverse disposition becomes actually manifest and dominant.

This polymorphous period, or stage, occupying roughly the second half of the first year, could be regarded as one of the intermediate stations—in Abraham's analogy—which his time-table of the express trains does not mention.

I find it easy to bring the notion of this polymorphous period in line with Abraham's first anal stage, the stage in which the aim is to eject completely and annihilate the object. This tendency would appear as a kind of reaction formation against the turmoil which results from the simultaneous operation of so many inherently conflicting, inherently frustrating impulses with their corresponding anxiety situations. The developmental process which consecutively brings the different zones into a leading position implies a growing mastery by the ego of the instinctual urges and thus serves in part as a defensive function. The aim of the first anal stage of "relieving" the self by the complete evacuation of the internalized parents, equated as persecutors with the infant's own fæces, can be appreciated as a reaction to the overwhelming impact of the first Œdipal strivings (during the polymorphous stage). The experience of eliminating and getting rid of a bodily substance would come to occupy a central position, because in addition to the organ pleasure—libidinal pleasure—there is an *emotional* experience of relief. Many clinical observations suggest strongly that anal interests and gratifications are secondarily heightened for defensive purposes.

As a result of further development in the various spheres of the ego this massive defence by ejection is modified, and Abraham's second anal stage is established in which the predominant aim is to retain the object on the condition that it be dominated and controlled. The stronger the ego, the more can it deal with its sources of conflict intra-psychically and the less does it use the most primitive defence of expelling them.

Whilst I could connect the polymorphous stage easily with the next, the anal stage, I was confronted by difficulties when I tried to see its relation to the oral stage. What troubled me was the notion that if I thought of the polymorphously perverse condition of instinctual life, in which the Œdipus complex starts, as a *stage* extending for a certain time, if I thought that the oral stage did not proceed directly to the anal stage, I could not account for the powerful operation of the anal trends and mechanisms during the first three to four months of life, namely during the paranoid/schizoid position.

Ejecting—splitting—projecting: these are aims and mechanisms which are to be correlated with the anal function. Their nature is anal, even though there are oral and nasal forms of ejecting, such a spitting or breathing out. This accords with our clinical experience which shows that the phantasies underlying splitting and projecting are predominantly anal: the persecuting object is equated with fæces, the fæces are treated as internal persecuting objects. As long as I thought in terms of a direct transition from the oral to the anal organization I did not see a problem in accounting for the occurrence of anal elements in the stage of oral primacy. The two stages being neighbours, so to say, explained their making loans one from the other. But I then realized that the problem which baffled me was due to a mistake, an omission, on my part. I had failed to distinguish between the operation of *trends*, in this case anal trends, and that of an *organization*, in this case the oral organization. This distinction, however, is decisive. And if it is appreciated the question of nearness or distance between organizations becomes irrelevant.

During the first, the oral organization, the oral impulses reign supreme, but, of course, they are not the only ones in existence. Because they are of supreme power, they subordinate the other instinctual trends to their own purpose.

The oral impulses are essentially connected with an *inward* direction, they are receptive. The oral aim is to acquire and incorporate the object on whom the infant depends: the good, feeding, gratifying breast. Ejection and annihilation are derived from the anal organ and function. Under the predominance of the oral organization these anal trends are used as a complementary technique to achieve the oral aim of maintaining the blissful relation with the good breast with which the self fuses. The *cæsura* of birth, is, as Freud pointed out, less sharp than superficial impression might suggest. The infant strives to continue or regain his pre-natal oneness with his mother with all the means at his disposal. The oral impulses with their inward direction are eminently suitable to achieve it: the good breast is incorporated, loved, and treated as self. But the breast is not always good, the infant experiences a frustrating and persecuting breast and pain from the self, and against this painful experience the anal trends of ejection and annihilation are marshalled and put into operation. What is bad is split off, projected, eliminated; the predominantly oral aim of oneness with the good mother is preserved.

In an odd way, one might say, this aim of the oral organization (viz. to be one with the mother and to regain the pre-natal condition) is even pursued in the realm of splitting and projecting, because these mechanisms, amongst other consequences, result in identification, though of a certain kind—projective identification. The mother into whom the infant projects what he does not want to keep within himself, by this very process again comes to carry him in her body. By means of using the anal trends and mechanisms in a complementary way the infant pursues the policy of a double insurance against loss and separation.

The fact that he does achieve this aim only to a limited degree, and the complex *sequelæ* of his oral pursuits, are beyond the frame of my present considerations.

The notion, then, that there is a "polymorphously perverse" stage interpolated between the oral and the anal organization, is not in conflict with the theory of the oral organization of the instinctual impulses. If anything, the acknowledgment of this stage throws into relief how much it takes to undermine oral primacy.

Paula Heimann

Before concluding, I wish to refer very briefly to certain observations which can be better evaluated by the assumption that there exists a stage in which the polymorphously perverse disposition is manifest and dominant. These observations concern patients whose mothers became pregnant during this stage of their development, whose siblings were thus younger only by fifteen to eighteen months or so. While in many respects these patients differed in their personalities, they seemed to have in common certain inhibitions in their object-relations. They had the capacity for empathy and sensitivity, the readiness to help and understand the object, and well developed intellectual sublimations, etc., that is, genital character trends. But at the same time there was a very deep underlying resentment and an unforgivingness, an aggrieved attitude of "I do not expect to be loved and cared for. I know I must consider mother and her baby. Not for me the good things in life—but I understand, that is how it has to be"; that is, they also had character traits derived from the oral and anal stages. Much of this attitude could be traced to the Œdipal conflicts of the polymorphous stage heightened by the mother's pregnancy.

I believe that in the older literature such phenomena were described as a discrepancy between the development of the libido and that of the ego. I find it helpful to think in terms of a too early accentuation of the genital trends during the polymorphous stage when the oral and anal impulses are not yet sufficiently mastered and therefore give rise to particularly strong depressive and persecutory anxieties.

I do not, of course, wish to suggest that a child whose mother is pregnant when he passes through the polymorphous stage of instinctual development must unfailingly develop disturbances in object relationship. I am mentioning my observations because they illustrate the significance of this phase for the formation of character traits and social capacities.

That this stage deserves to be closely studied is also suggested by observations concerning the perversions. But it is not my aim to embark on this vast topic in the frame of these short notes. It is interesting, though, to remember that Freud developed his conclusions about infantile sexuality from the analysis of the sexual aberrations of adults.

3

A PSYCHO-ANALYTIC CONCEPT OF THE ORIGIN OF DEPRESSION[1]

W. CLIFFORD M. SCOTT

GENERAL interest in the psycho-analytic psychopathology of depression may have been kept in the background for a long time, owing to the rapid development of interest in the psychopathological understanding of the less complex symptoms common in neurosis, such as anxieties, phobias, obsessions, etc. The psychopathology of schizophrenic symptoms where the mechanisms sometimes seemed obvious and apparent, but where psycho-analytic treatment was not then helpful, interested more analysts in the early days than did the psychopathology of manic-depressive symptoms. Nevertheless since 1911, when Abraham first discussed depression, the psycho-analytic psychology of normal sorrow, depression, mourning, and grief, and the psychopathology of abnormal depressions have gradually developed until now concepts have been worked out which are to a considerable degree new and can be stated simply. Such new concepts have been found to be of essential value in psycho-analytic attempts at investigation and therapy of depressed states regardless of the degree of severity, regardless of the sex, and more or less regardless of the age—children as young as two and one-quarter and adults in the sixth decade having been treated.

The earlier work of analytic writers (Abraham, Sigmund Freud, Jones, Rado, etc.) was invaluable. The background of theoretical construction already developed was necessary to make the recent development possible. With the recent work courage was needed to make the new observations. The work done in this country in the past fifteen or twenty years, chiefly by and under the stimulation of

[1] This paper was read on 10th September, 1947, at a Symposium on "The Psychopathology of Depression" at the International Conference of Physicians (London). Published in the *British Medical Journal*, 20th March, 1948, Vol. I, p. 538.

Melanie Klein, has brought much clarification to the problem of abnormal depressed states, and incidentally points the way to further work with schizophrenia. Mrs. Klein published her first conclusions on this subject in 1935. She has added much to our knowledge of technique of investigation and attempts at therapy and has added to our theoretical constructions.

Most of the views I am putting forward are based on evidence personally obtained during the psycho-analytic treatment of neuroses with depression and with manic-depressive states in different sexes, of different ages from late infancy to late life.

To introduce the subject a brief outline needs to be given as to how the infant develops to a stage which allows depression to appear for the first time. What follows after this stage of development has been reached is the history of the different forms depression assumes at different periods of life. Just as the early stages of love and hate are significant in understanding their later development, so also may the varieties of adult depression come to be understood to a greater degree if we can become clearer about the genesis of depression in human life.

Regardless of different views about the source or nature of instinct, it can be said that from an early age the infant breathes air, sucks milk, passes water and stool, moves about and sleeps. These activities are normally pleasant. If any of these activities is frustrated, the infant becomes angry. Regardless of how intense or diffuse his anger may become, regardless of how many organs he uses to vent his anger, he will first show his anger in the situation where the frustration is; for instance, if breathing is frustrated he will breathe angrily, if sucking is frustrated he will suck angrily.

From the earliest period of life one aspect of each of these pleasant or angry activities is its direction, namely the direction of movement or interchange between what can be called the outer and the inner worlds, or the direction of interchange between this inner world and the outer world, for instance, breathing in, breathing out, swallowing in, vomiting out, etc.

Only slowly in the developing scheme of things are "people", as the adult knows them, included. Earlier the world consists of what adults would call "parts"—breasts, faces, hands, etc. Only slowly in the scheme of things does a "self" as a "whole person" or do "other people" as "whole people" develop. Only slowly do distinctions between what are later called perceptions, memories, images, etc., arise. Along this line of development, crucial points can be discovered, and it appears that at one of these crucial points depression becomes possible for the first time. Previously only simpler affects, such as anger, pleasure, pain, fear, are possible. It is in relationship to the manner in which these early depressive feelings arise and are dealt with that we can see the hope of understanding the symptoms of later depressions and understand how they can be dealt with. It is here that we see the beginnings of the development of normal tolerance of depression, of normal ways of dealing with depression, and also the beginnings of pathological depressed states.

Let us follow some of these early sequences in greater detail. Hunger *may* lead to sucking a breast or breast substitute, and to pleasure. Through the feelings of breathing, sucking, smelling, touching, swallowing, etc., the feeling of a "good something" going into or entering the inner world occurs. Technically this something is customarily referred to as an "object". During or following such an experience the child may pass water or stool or sleep with pleasure without as yet clearly appreciating that there is "a something" or "an object" associated with the experience of evacuation with the same clarity as later it will. Nevertheless he is already beginning to realize that an interchange between the outer world and the inner world, and between the inner and outer, is occurring. The general feeling of an infant feeding and later evacuating and sleeping is that both the inner and the outer world are "good" and that a "good" interchange in each direction has occurred. On the other hand, hunger *may not* be followed by such a satisfying experience. Instead it may be followed by frustration and bellowing and gnashing of toothless gums, by angry movements, by passing water and stool in his rage, and so forth. This leads to the feeling that the inner and outer worlds are "bad" and that any object differentiation in the inner or outer world is into many "bad" objects, and that any interchanges between the inner and outer world, which may have occurred in either direction, have been bad. Such a bout of anger may, of course, be followed later by satisfaction, but this type of satisfaction will be different from what it would have been had the bout of anger not preceded it. Similar experiences are repeated and repeated. The series of pleasures, frustrations, and annoyances build up on the one hand memories of attitudes to the inner and outer world in which the omnipotent, infantile loving imagination has had free play and, on the other hand, memories of persecutory attitudes to the outer and inner worlds in which

41

omnipotent, infantile hateful imaginations have had free play. Here much may be learned concerning the developing attitude to the external world, to the body and to the inner world of phantasy, memory, constructive thought, and so forth, and further work in this field should lead to our understanding of much of which we are ignorant in the psychopathology of schizophrenia.

But it is to the next step in development that I wish to refer specifically. Sooner or later sufficient integration occurs for the infant to realize that the memories of the loving, satisfying breast and the hated, frustrating breast are of one and the same breast, and that memories of the happy, sucking mouth and of the angry, frustrated, hungry mouth are of the same mouth. The significance of this integration for the genesis of depression is very great. I wrote above, sooner or later—the time will depend at least on the degree of maturity at birth, the constitutional intellectual endowment, and the quality of the previous emotional development. In other words, an integration seems to occur in which the belief in a continuing self, or what would later be called a part of the self, emerges, and continuing people in the environment, or what would later be called parts of these people, emerge. Coincident with this integration, a new affective state emerges. The realization that maximal love and maximal hate can both be expressed by the same bodily organs, that both maximal love and maximal hate can be felt towards the same object, and that this object can be both satisfying and frustrating, or can appear to be both loving and hating, is crucial. Another way of saying the same thing is that the earliest form of depression is the feeling which emerges: first, out of the realization that it is the same self that can both love and hate, and secondly, out of the realization that the ego can both hate and love the same object, and thirdly, out of the realization that the same object or person can be both gratifying or frustrating, or can appear to be loving or hating. Whether or not this new feeling is tolerated—whether or not it is accepted as a fact of developing human experience—is certainly important. Tolerance is related at least to whether love is believed to be greater than hate or hate is believed to be greater than love. When the store of love is greater than hate, love can be quickly used to overcome, to annul, to repair the effects of hate. Love can be used following separation from, or death of, a loved person, to keep the memory alive and to keep alive the belief in a capacity to love and be loved, and consequently to believe that people worth one's loving and people who may love oneself still exist in the outer world. The more normal methods of dealing with depression thus arise.

There are nevertheless many ways in which a partial and incomplete tolerance of a depressive situation arise, and these lead to the many forms and symptoms of the abnormal depressive states of all degrees of severity. The many ways in which the intolerance of the depressive situation is shown are at least related to whether the angry impulses, acts, and imaginations are greater than the loving ones. If the anger is greater than the love—if the memories (or their symbolic substitutes) of the many aggressive acts, impulses, and imaginations are greater in strength than the memories of love— then hopelessness and depressive anxieties connected with the belief that one can only do bad things and that only bad can be expected of oneself, arise. This may lead to a situation in which the self has to be destroyed to protect from one's badness the people and objects which go to make up one's inner and outer world. The self will be destroyed actually in suicide, or symbolically in a temper tantrum or a fit.

The situation I have tried to describe is the earliest example or one which will be repeated over and over again during later life. The changing methods by which the repetitions are dealt with have much to do with personality development and character; but an essential relationship to the realization that the person can both hate and love, and that the same objects can be both loved and hated, and believed to be lovable and hateful, remains and is crucial. Subsequent development, concerning the realization of oneself as a "whole person", and of other people as "whole people"; of oneself as of a certain sex, and of other people as each belonging to a certain sex, brings in many complexities, but the importance of the original situation remains. From the onset many—in fact most—of the developments mentioned have occurred unconsciously. Most of the normal ways of dealing with depression have developed unconsciously, as also have the various defences against depression.

The beginnings of depressive feelings related to the integrations already mentioned are concerned with the concepts of a continuing self and of other continuing persons. These beginnings are more in relation to what in adulthood we would call parts of a self or parts of another person. Nevertheless soon the emphasis shifts as further development occurs to the conception of whole people—to the whole self and the whole people in the environment. Throughout life, the conception of what a whole person is, the conception of what a human individual is, or is worth, what a lifetime is, or is worth, is continually changing and developing, and it is difficult to say what is the best or most useful formulation of a "whole person". At the present stage of human evolution, and being a part of our complicated, discontented civilization, one would hesitate to generalize concerning "wholeness". But at least one can be tolerably sure that a study of what constitutes a "good whole person" is intimately connected with the study of healthy and unhealthy ways of dealing with the depressive situation.

Connected with the integration that results in the belief in a whole self and in whole people (which often lasts more or less a life-time with relatively little alteration) the conscience begins to develop in an elaborate form. One might have thought that the complicated nature of the good and bad conscience in depressive states would have forced psychiatrists long ago to realize the need for using methods of investigation which would bring to consciousness further details regarding their development. Psycho-analytic methods bring to consciousness details of what has come to be called the super-ego. The super-ego is both a great hindrance and a great help. Gradually more concerning its development has been elucidated. The super-ego is a much more elaborate, inhibiting, and stimulating unconscious construct than all that is connoted by a good and bad conscience. With adults, of course, the manifold implications of conscience and the super-ego have their importance in the symptomatology of depressive states. Nevertheless, depressive states and depressive anxieties (guilt, remorse, regret, etc.) can arise in connection with simultaneous love and hate of part objects which are realized to have a continuing existence. In the analysis of depressed children and manic-depressive adults, the content of analysis may deal mostly with memories (or their symbolic substitutes) of repetitions of coincident love and hate of part objects, but part objects which are realized to have a continuing existence. It is this situation which appears to contain the most significant ego and object relationship for the understanding of the genesis of depression.

The content of behaviour and speech of the depressed person deals with his attempt to discover a satisfactory way of dealing with the realization that his hate for some person is greater than his simultaneous love for the same person, without at the same time denying that it is he who feels both love and hate, and without denying that it is to the same person that he feels both love and hate. The manifold symptom picture has to take account of the nature of the loving and hating impulses, acts, and imaginations at the early stage of development, when the integration already mentioned began. At this period, the impulses, acts, and imaginations are predominantly oral. Nevertheless, all organ activities that can reach consciousness may play some minor role at this time. Indeed I think it is difficult to substantiate the view that there is an early period when some organs—for instance the genital—play no role whatsoever. There is disagreement about the age at which depression can first occur, but I believe there is much evidence that it frequently occurs early in the first six months of life. It must also be remembered that the tests of reality which can be made at such a period are of an infantile type. The intensity and explosiveness of the infantile satisfactions and rages interfere with perception of reality, both inner and outer. The way each satisfaction and each rage is shown colours the outer world and the inner world by rapidly acting and complicated types of introjection and projection. The effects of these mechanisms lead to many of the later complexities of depressive states. Regardless of how old the person is, if he has not dealt successfully with the infantile depressive situation he will be left throughout life with an infantile attitude to the dangers of realizing that he is a being who can both love and hate simultaneously and can feel simultaneously both feelings for the same person. If treated, he may be brought face to face with the intensity of the complicated feelings appropriate to his present-day situation and may for a time suffer more severely while he is learning to deal healthily for the first time with depression.

In such a brief presentation little other than conclusions can be put forward and nothing can be said about the earlier analytic views. The conclusions I have put forward do not contradict the earlier views. These conclusions do little else than elaborate earlier views in the developmental sense.

Nevertheless, a few brief sketches can be given of the sort of patient whose study has led to these conclusions.

1. A boy of two years and one month became severly uninterested in everything and everybody, following a seemingly successful weaning at nine months. He became constipated. He was slow, quiet, and showed no interest in learning to speak. During seven months' treatment he became able to deal more normally with the depressive anxieties and situation already described. The subsequent mood changes were such that in retrospect it was easy to recognize his earlier state as a severe anergic depression. In analysis he showed by play florid content of depressive type. He did not speak a word

45

during analysis, but began to learn to speak at home. By play he could show much more complicated content than he could expect to speak of for years. He did nevertheless make tests of oral projective activity by yelling in rage once and by making a few sounds easily recognizable as signs of considerable pleasure.

2. A woman aged twenty, who had for at least ten years gradually become more uninterested and depressed and later suicidal showed during more than four years' treatment how homosexuality and severe masochistic and sadistic imaginations were the unhealthy attempts to cope with her forgotten wish to deal with the effects she believed her early aggression had had on her mother. Following much noisy dissatisfaction during the first month of her life during which she had been breast-fed, she was seemingly satisfactorily weaned. She showed no open oral aggression from the first month of life till many months after the beginning of her treatment. Only after learning to deal with almost simultaneous, or at least very rapidly alternating, hateful and loving impulses and acts of extreme intensity during treatment—which occurred in a hospital environment—was she able to begin to use her adult capacities to deal with the implications of her previously persistent infantile depression. During the crucial stages of her treatment her emotions were nearly, if not indeed quite, epileptic in intensity. During treatment stuporous states were interrupted by attacks of rage, which, I think, were related to epileptic furore. Such rages were followed by disturbances of consciousness. Later, intensely energetic loving outbursts occurred. These gradually lessened. The alternating love and hate gradually lessened in intensity as the depression connected with the realization that both were, had been, and would be, felt towards the same people, became more tolerable.

3. A man aged fifty-nine developed an agitated depression. During treatment he showed how a deep attachment to a grandfather in infancy might have led to the development of adult homosexuality had the grandfather not died at sixty when the patient was four. The patient did not grieve openly then, but his super-ego became to a large extent modelled on this grandfather. During treatment, when he realized the degree of his identification with his grandfather, and when he realized that he had unconsciously feared his own death at sixty, he began to be able after the lapse of fifty-five years to mourn the death of his grandfather openly. He then became able to plan a life on a scheme based more on the memory of the ambivalent love and hate for his own mother, whom he had ceased to feel

46

for in his infancy when he gave his love to his grandfather. Had he coped more healthily with depression in infancy, he might not have become so pathologically attached to his grandfather. Thus he might have avoided a severe depression at fifty-nine when his age was nearing that at which his grandfather died. Such a history demonstrates how difficult it would have been to predict, for instance, when he was forty, that he was seriously predisposed to an illness at fifty-nine.

One could also sketch many failures, but unfortunately the chief point with regard to the psychopathology of psycho-analytic failures is that the data on which one might base inferences as to why they failed cease to be collected. Here I would make a plea to those who have under observation depressed patients who have had psychoanalytic treatment and are still unable to deal healthily with depression to report the later developments. I am confident that the patient's previous analysts would co-operate.

In conclusion I do not think I can do better than suggest that the implications of the simple formula already outlined regarding the onset of depressed states be investigated fully. I restate the formula: out of the realization that at one and the same time it is possible for a person to love and to hate, and out of the realization that such love and hate can be felt for one and the same person, emerges the human capacity for depression both normal and abnormal. The vicissitudes of the imbalance between the loving and hating impulses determine the subsequent normal or abnormal development in respect of the capacity to deal healthily with depression.

REFERENCES

ABRAHAM, K. (1911) "Notes on the Psycho-analytical Investigation and Treatment of Manic-Depressive Insanity and Allied Conditions", in *Selected Papers*. London, Hogarth Press, 1927.
—— (1916) "The First Pregenital Stage of the Libido", in *Selected Papers*. London, Hogarth Press, 1927.
—— (1924) "A Short Study of the Development of the Libido", in *Selected Papers*. London, Hogarth Press, 1927.
FREUD, S. (1917) "Mourning and Melancholia". *Collected Papers*, Vol. IV. London, Hogarth Press, 1924.
JONES, E. (1929) "Fear, Guilt and Hate". *Int. J. Psycho-Anal.*, Vol. X (1929).
KLEIN, MELANIE (1935) "A Contribution to the Psychogenesis of Manic-Depressive States". *Int. J. Psycho-Anal.*, Vol. XVI (1935).
—— (1940) "Mourning and its relation to Manic-Depressive States". *Int. J. Psycho-Anal.*, Vol. XXI (1940).
RADO, S. (1927) "The Problem of Melancholia". *Int. J. Psycho-Anal.*, Vol. IX (1928).
SCOTT, W. C. M. (1946) "A Note on the Psychopathology of Convulsive Phenomena in Manic-Depressive States". *Int. J. Psycho-Anal.*, Vol. XXVII (1946).

4

EARLY ANXIETY SITUATIONS IN THE ANALYSIS OF A BOY IN THE LATENCY PERIOD

M. GWEN EVANS

THE material in this paper, selected to illustrate certain typical anxiety situations arising in early childhood, has been taken from the analysis of a boy, which spread over a number of years. For a number of reasons no case history is given and the relation of the chosen examples to many other important aspects of the analysis cannot be indicated. Environmental factors contributing to the illness are also not dealt with here but entered into the material continually and were analysed.

My main purpose is to demonstrate how such early anxiety situations and the respective defences erected against them are uncovered and dealt with according to the findings and analytic technique of Melanie Klein. The examples were selected from a mass of material and the interpretations based on more evidence than could be included, the aim being to introduce just enough of the child's associations to make clear which particular type of anxiety was being dealt with at any one point. Such anxieties occur regularly in the analyses of children between eight to ten years of age and are familiar to many of my colleagues.

When the analysis started, school inhibitions were the main external sign of the boy's hidden difficulties, and he knew that his parents had sent him to the analyst for a resolution of his inability to take a normal part in the work and play of the school. For some time he avoided all references to his past and present life at school, but when he gradually and indirectly began to talk about it the emphasis was at first placed on the difficulty he experienced in making friends with other children. It was soon evident to me that there was massive projection at work in relation to them.

He spoke more easily of his sibling, a sister younger than himself by a few years, and he was conscious of a very ambivalent relation

48

with her, stretching back as far as his memory could go. This type of relationship was in strong contrast to his conscious attitude to his mother, for whom his love was never in doubt. It was only when we reached very early patterns of relationship with her, through the acting out of infantile memories in the transference, that we came upon severe disturbances in oral and anal types of behaviour towards her. He had dealt with these difficulties to a certain extent by shifting them on to father and sister, and also used a number of symbolic substitutes for the mother to keep her own person free from conflicts, the school being one of the main substitutes.

The boy's approach to his father was full of difficulty and bound up with early environmental disturbances created by the father's unavoidable absence overseas for several years, during which time the small boy had to face many of the war situations alone with mother and baby sister, both of whom he felt it his duty to care for as though deputizing for the father. All conscious memory of the latter had faded before his return.

The general picture presented by the patient at the outset of analysis was one of imperturbable cheerfulness and friendly politeness, but he could not hide the look of terror in his eyes. He showed a constant desire to please and yet it was soon evident that, quite apart from the usual unconscious resistances, he was consciously planning to prevent the analyst discovering some of his well-guarded secrets. Alongside a superficial submissiveness was a strong negativistic attitude, coupled with ceaseless secret watchfulness against all kinds of possible control issuing from the analyst. Later on it emerged that he resorted to a number of magic controls over me, which often came into play as he approached the house and operated from a distance.

In so far as he could experience me as a friendly helper, he wished for and expected all kinds of extra-analytic contacts, such as visits to his home and school on the occasions when there were parties or functions, birthday and Christmas presents, the loan of money, instruction or helpful interference on his behalf in external events. Within the analysis itself he either looked for some pronouncement by me of magic formulæ which would suddenly put everything right, or expected methods of treatment similar to those experienced by him in physical medicine.

His attitude to the play-material was at first a very free one and he gave useful verbal associations, but as soon as he realized that the analyst could understand a number of things which he had no conscious intention of revealing, he became less willing to co-operate in this way, and the same massive resistances appeared that characterized his behaviour at school. Something of the underlying acute anxiety came through when he asked me if I possessed "second sight". It was customary for him to cover up, whenever possible, every sign of the disturbances created in him by my interpretations, and yet an underlying co-operation was maintained, so that after the nature of some specific resistances had become clear he could bring new material, which often came through like an outburst of something long dammed up.

His necessity to placate the analyst and the parents who sent him to analysis caused him at first to play somewhat compulsively with the material provided and to make an effort to talk, so that when he became less afraid of our immediate intentions towards him he could show more of his dissatisfaction and defiance. In many sessions he never spoke at all and yet found ways of conveying when he was ready for more interpretation. Some of the silent phases represented a reproduction of important early pre-verbal relationships with the mother.

In the initial stages of establishing the analysis, persecutory anxieties hidden behind his placid exterior were frequently pointed out to him, and I made it clear to him that I was aware of his terror of me and of analysis. We dealt with the element of secrecy and camouflage that entered into his superficial façade of good humour, placidity, and politeness, and his use of projecting outside himself and into other people everything unpleasant and frightening. Fear was explained to him as the dominant factor in his need to express hostility indirectly and to maintain a secret control over us all.

As soon as he became less afraid of me through the interpretation of the deeper persecutory terrors, he was able to become more openly aggressive and disobedient both at home, at school, and in the analysis. Unlike most patients who can accept the analyst's "no" regarding certain activities which are impractical in the analyst's home, he continued defiantly to attack some of my private possessions.

Although dominated by persecutory anxieties the early material showed depressive elements and reparative drives and a sad expression would occasionally pass across his face, but it was only after the analysis was well established that the depression emerged. Again it came out at last as though long dammed up and consciously withheld. He admitted to me and to his parents a deep and lonely despair, the misery of which had gone together with self-accusations and suicide impulses. The latter he demonstrated in analysis as consciously thought out in a number of detailed ways. From this point onwards the analysis dealt continually with a mixture of depressive and persecutory feelings which tended to alternate. When the persecutory anxiety increased the work became temporarily more difficult, but the link between the two kinds of relationship with me was often found and resolved through the analysis of the projection on to me of an internal persecuting mother or father. The threat from this very primitive, cruel and implacable figure attacking his body and mind from within was so great that it could only be ignored or defied, in line with his behaviour of defiance towards me in the analysis. Although much of this type of material came in connection with bad male figures, whom he was delighted to see overthrown in pictures, jokes, and tales, particularly if they were ridiculed and made to look silly, I found the very primitive nature of his super-ego to be an indication that his disturbances in ego-development had had their origin in early oral and anal difficulties in relation to the mother. This was confirmed as the analysis went on.

The uncovering of this mixture of depression, projection, and internal persecution led us on to the analysis of his states of confusion and to his conscious awareness of the abnormality of some of his mental processes. Very cautiously he began to test out the effect it would have on me if he demonstrated his inability at times to do quite simple arithmetic. We played games together in which he kept our scores and he made lists from catalogues of the things he wanted to buy and then could not add up a small column of figures. The conflict between wanting me to see his difficulty and the need to try and hide the fact that he was hopelessly confused usually ended in his giving up all attempt to carry on. But sometimes he voluntarily admitted that he could not go on talking because he had forgotten what he wanted to say, and he described an inability to remember what he learnt at school, etc. In speech with me he would mix up affirmatives and negatives, "I" and "you", "he" and "she", etc., sometimes noticing it and then trying to hide his mistake. To him confusion and such inabilities as these were closely linked with madness. He was consciously afraid of being mad but preferred to think that parents, teachers, and analyst too would regard him as lazy and ungrateful rather than let them know of the frightful muddle in his head. In this connection he represented himself one day as a "monster-calf" born with two heads and photographed in the magazine he showed me. He asked if it were true that such objects were called "freaks". At another time he conveyed to me that he was reading avidly, but secretly, accounts in daily papers of a murderer who was described as a split personality, and then began to tell me of outbursts of uncontrollable rage which came over him at times, particularly in connection with other children.

In many places in her writings Melanie Klein has emphasized the central place among early anxiety situations occupied by the phantasied attacks on the internal contents of the mother's body, explaining how guilt and anxiety derived from these phantasies contribute to inhibitions in learning. She stated, in 1930: "The child expects to find within the mother (*a*) the father's penis, (*b*) excrement, (*c*) children, and these things it equates with food." And: "The object of sadism at its zenith and of the epistemophilic impulse arising simultaneously with sadism, is the mother's body with its phantasied contents."[1]

She described in the same paper how an analysis was started with "Dick", a very inhibited and backward child, by her interpretation of his attempts to go into or towards places that stood for the mother's body and the associated fear of the aggressiveness in his penis.

In a paper[2] published the next year she described how "John's" fear of the inside of his mother's body, with which his own body was equated, made him unwilling to consider the nature of his own inside. His phantasied attacks on the young brother, while still inside mother, were bound up with his intellectual difficulties, and the resolution of his particular trouble with the word *fish* was through an understanding of its connection with the things inside mother's body as well as with his own and father's penis. My patient had many anxieties and phantasies in common with "Dick" and "John".

I

The first example to be given in detail from my patient's material belongs to his relation with his mother and sister, and includes those early sadistic phantasies against the inside of the mother's body. His mother's babies were symbolized as tortoises and there was an interesting equation between the dental plate inside his own mouth

[1] "The Importance of Symbol-Formation in the Development of the Ego", (1930), in *Contributions to Psycho-Analysis, 1921-48* (London, 1948).
[2] "A Contribution to the Theory of Intellectual Inhibition", 1931. Op. cit.

and the tortoise as the baby in mother's womb. The material came after several sessions during which he didn't speak at all. He had been suffering some pain with the dental plate he had to wear, and which was introduced for the first time by the dentist after his analysis had been in existence for some months. Interpretations had frequently been made to the effect that he regarded me as the instigator of this torture. On the day in question he again sat silent, reading to himself, and I reminded him that the appearance of this pattern of completely silent sessions had set in at the time when the dentist arranged for his first plate. I suggested that at that moment he was experiencing the plate as a part of myself, pushed into him to act both as a punishment and as a lever to make him speak to me. This resulted in his telling me in great detail about an incident that had taken place a few days before and which had made a great impression on him.

A kind woman had been cheated by some bad men. She had bought a tortoise as a present for her little boy because she knew that he wanted a playmate but, when she got it home and when they had examined it together, they found that it had only one eye and was lame in one foot. He inquired if I knew how awful the conditions could be inside *some* of the boats which brought these tortoises from foreign countries. In this case the conditions had been so terrible that most of them died and of those that survived (including this very tortoise) most were ill or damaged. Nevertheless, he continued, the woman and her little boy would of course not send the poor tortoise away because at the very first sight of it they became fond of it. The woman, however, would undoubtedly take the matter up with the men who had cheated her, forcing them to repay her at least some of the money they had charged her.

Although I did not begin my interpretations at this point, it will help in the understanding of the material if we consider its meaning here. There is a reference to the birth of his sister, whom he regarded as castrated when he first saw her (he and his mother examine the tortoise together and find she has only one eye and is lame in one foot). He blames the bad men, standing for father, projecting his own aggressive attitudes. He believes all his mother's unborn children were killed inside her because of the terrible conditions there (inside the ship). His sister is one of the survivors, whom he and his mother became fond of at first sight, partly because they pity her. But since he feels responsible, guilty, and frightened, he has to hide from mother and from father (the bad men) what he has done, because he is sure mother will demand an awful penalty. What he has done has to be hidden from the sister too. He had often shown me how intolerant his anxiety and guilt could make him when his sister is ill, naughty, or in some way a failure, and he always begins to defend himself from the imputation of responsibility for it.

Having told the story, he suddenly asked me if I would like to see what it was that interested him, while previously reading in silence and picking continually at his dental plate. As he turned to find the right page, he said that the picture he had been looking at had reminded him of the woman and the tortoise. When he showed me the page, which turned out to be a series of small pictures, he announced that he would need my help in understanding what it meant, for he had the feeling when he looked at it, that he might have missed the point. (Unconscious self-punishment like a mental castration, in identity with the castrated sister whose "point" is missing.)

In all the pictures there were little gnomes engaged in various sadistic activities, and each one had a long nose and peaked cap on his head. He pointed to one in which a gnome was standing threateningly behind another one, who with knife and fork in hand was bending over a tortoise on the ground before him. It seemed quite clear that the tortoise was going to be cut up and eaten by the gnome in front and that the "super-ego"-gnome behind his back showed the punishment coming to the one in front, when he had eaten the tortoise.

The patient asked me to tell him what I thought the first gnome was going to do, but I encouraged him to try and associate, and he made great efforts to do so, returning to the picture several times, but unconscious resistances were too great. I asked him about the second gnome and he at once ventured a guess that "the second gnome is going to hit the backside of the first". He was quite despairing about understanding the real meaning of the scene, but was equally sure that I understood it very well and wished that I would tell him. This I did not do because the co-operation and trust coming from him seemed sufficient to cope with the frustration. Later it will be seen from the subsequent material that his difficulty was due to an inability to see the knife and fork, but I did not know this at the time.

He could give me no more associations, so I started to interpret along the lines indicated above, and added that the long nose and peaked cap of the gnome stood for the father's penis which he has acquired, but which he feels is too big for him. Both gnomes were shown to be aspects of himself (his "split" self), and the punishing half has been at work causing him to "miss the point" of the picture; that this punishing part is fused with the internal father, whom he feels threatens him with the stick; that in the same way he feels the dental plate hurts him like the internal mother punishing him together with father for aggression towards both breast and baby (the tortoise).

We left the problem picture still unsolved and he turned to another one. In the one he selected there were again two gnomes with the super-ego behind as before, and he showed me how this one had "thrown a lasso towards the other". The loop was in fact already around the neck of the poor gnome who looked extremely frightened. A smoker's pipe was falling from his hand and he had lost control of a basket of apples which he had been carrying. On his head there sat a duck, and it was significant that the patient asserted that the lasso was aimed at the duck only, denying the fact that the loop was lying around the gnome's neck. A recurrent fear, expressed again and again in analysis, of being beheaded or hung as a murderer, lay behind his misobserving the position of the loop. This was interpreted as belonging to his castration fears and linked with phantasied attacks on both mother and father, who have been robbed of so many things. The pipe (father's penis), and the basket of apples (mother's breasts and the contents of her body) are dropped in a desperate attempt to escape from the hidden figure attacking suddenly from behind. This super-ego figure was described to him as standing for the threatening internal parents, as his own conscience. The live duck seemed to symbolize the ultimate source of all the stolen things, i.e. the unique omnipotent breast and penis, the possession of which would give him the power to get anything he wanted. I interpreted his wish to believe that if he gives back the duck, he can still escape castration and death by hanging.

There was an important link too with his previous reports of outbursts of rage being connected with attacks coming suddenly from behind, even when playfully done by another child. I showed him that one factor in this was the splitting of himself into the two gnomes, with projection of the attacking gnome into another child. A further interpretation connected with splitting at last made it possible for him to return to the problem picture and deal with it successfully. It was of the split into two parts, one that can see and understand, and another that is stupid and blind, with the projection of the sensible, effective part into me. This was the deeper reason of his conviction that it was I who saw the meaning in the picture, while he could do nothing about it. Only if I (as one part) would make a communication to him (the other part), was there any hope of an understanding. When he looked again and saw the knife and fork held over the tortoise, he was amazed and told me that he had only at that moment noticed them. He now realized that since the gnome represented himself he had not been able to bear the sight of himself about to cut up and eat the tortoise, that he had been forced through unconscious guilt and terror to interfere with his perceptive powers and to land himself in a number of difficulties, and that in this interference with his own mental capacities he had also actually punished himself by a kind of castration, since he could not "see the point" without using "his point" (equation between penis and head). He also understood with more conviction why he experienced my mouth and speech so often like a cannibalistic attack on his body.

After this phase in the analysis, during which other material of the same kind was worked through, his relations with his sister and with other children at school underwent a change. He began to see that he really believed intensely in the existence of the unborn babies (tortoises on the voyage in the mother-ship) who had either died inside mother, or had escaped in a damaged condition, and that he was always looking for these missing babies among the children he met at school, expecting them, of course, to be violently hostile to him.

II

My second example illustrates still further the connection between his intellectual difficulties and phantasies of this kind. The session was on the first day of a new term at school. On coming into the room he began at once to hunt for spiders, and having found two he put them temporarily into a match box, while he set about constructing an elaborate structure of several match boxes fitted together in such a way that only one very small opening was left as exit. He made sure that I had noticed this hole and ordered me to keep watch over it, saying "I am going to put the two spiders into the pen and you must tell me at once if they discover any other way out, which I may have overlooked. Only if they are *very clever* will they be able to find the little hole."

He named the spiders Alfred and Billy, "A" being the initial letter of his own name, and he talked to them as an adult might talk to children, telling Alfred that he was the adventurous one and accusing him of many bad things. Signs of confusion soon appeared, particularly in his uncertainty about the identities of the spiders. The pair of spiders signified at one and the same time: himself and his sister (changed into a boy), the parents (changed into children), and the two contrary parts of himself (adventurous and naughty or alternatively quiet and stupid). His rivalry with his sister and the denial of his feeling of inferiority regarding her came into the play by the assertion that Alfred (standing for himself) was the adventurous one who dared to be naughty, whereas in reality the reverse is the truth. I could remind him that in a recent session he had described himself as a dull, unenterprising spider, sticking in a corner all day by himself, reading books in a way that annoyed and disappointed his parents. Only by turning his sister into a younger brother can he believe in there being a chance for him to keep ahead of her, so relatively powerful does he think the female sex to be.

The roles I had to play in the transference were, first, that of mother in a conspiracy with him, the father, and secondly, that of sister, also in a conspiracy to shut up the parents after turning them into spiders (children), punishing them by a revengeful pattern of reversal. I explained to him the fear that lay behind this play, that seemed on the surface to be so enjoyable and amusing, telling him that I knew how frightened he was in the treatment room and that when he often sat and read by himself, he was secretly planning how to escape from the room and from analysis, that he was looking for the one small hole through which he could get away, and concentrated all his intellectual powers at times on this problem (the spiders must be *very clever* to find the hole). On the whole he is more conscious of such fears at school or with me, because he tries to keep his home and parents less frightening by the use of displacement.

But I reminded him that he had sometimes shown me that he had ideas about running away from home, and that when very depressed he had talked openly of suicide, which was also to him like escaping through a small hole out of a world which he sometimes regarded as too dangerous a place for him to live in. Symbolically the pen stood for the mother's body, into which the cruel parents put the two children, whom they had first hunted and captured, in accordance with a primitive birth-phantasy. But the outside world (from which the children had been taken and to which they tried to return through the small hole at birth), was also equated with the inside of the mother's body, and the terrors he experienced of people and events in this world were partly in terms of a feeling that he was living inside a big mother, meeting the babies and innumerable versions of the father, who he believed lived inside mother. From both babies and father-figures he expected hostility and attacks, as retaliation for his various aggressive attitudes to the pregnant mother and her contents.

III

In the third example taken from the session of the following day this kind of play was elaborated still further. He stated that he was going to make a different type of "pen", which would be a copy of one that his father had recently made for their pet mice. It became my role, as son, to help the patient in the role of father just as he in reality had actually assisted his father. In the homosexual phantasy, father and son prepare a home for mother and her babies and thus express the patient's reparation impulses. But he voiced one of the inherent difficulties in such an attempt by remarking, "It is a pity that we can't have mice for our pen here, because they are really the right sort of thing. Never mind, we'll use ants instead." Mice were standing at this point for real children and the ants for excrements, which are all that he can produce when he takes up the female role with his father, and tries to produce children. His "never mind" attitude showed a typical attempt at denying pain and frustration (manic defence).

He went on to tell me that the spiders he used yesterday were not as good as ants, the former being no good because they sit about in corners, hiding and doing nothing, whereas the ants are clever and industrious, running about very fast. This contrast referred mainly to the difference between girls and boys. After looking for a while in the corners and cracks of the room, which stood for his own inside, he gave up the search there and went out into my garden, where he had been very destructive on many occasions to my plants. This time he merely looked for ants, representing my excrements, the garden being the inside of my body, as mother. He found a few ants but his mood changed suddenly and he was unable to continue the play. Looking miserable and disturbed, which was very unusual for him, he sat down at the table and began to look in silence at the pictures in a magazine he had brought down to the treatment room from my waiting room. This was one of the first occasions on which his underlying depression began to break through the surface picture of indifference and good humour.

58

While interpreting the break-down of his reparative attempt to make good, with father's help, the harm done to the two females, mother and sister, I reminded him that when he was a small boy he felt deserted by his father, who, he thought, had left him to carry on the task of looking after mother and sister alone and unaided. By leaving me alone when he went out into the garden, he reversed the roles and now he ignored me, making no communication at all, just as he felt the father became absorbed in his new interests and did not bother about the family. But since he looked unhappy and disturbed, he was showing that he now believes that father was unhappy as well as mother and children. I also pointed out that his reparative play had broken down mainly for two reasons: he and father as two males can't make real babies (the mice), and no substitutes (ants and spiders representing fæces) are of any use; secondly, in order to get the babies or material to make the babies (ants, as fæces), he has to force his way into the mother's body (my garden) and steal the necessary things. On previous occasions I had checked him in his activities in my garden, telling him that it belonged to that part of my property which was not available for purposes of the analytic work. He envies his sister's potential capacity to produce real babies which she can offer to the parents as reparation.

His silence continued and after a while I interpreted my magazine as an alternative place in which to find my babies, less dangerous than my garden, because the people and things he took out of the magazine (my body) with his eyes (substituted for mouth and penis) were not real and could not therefore be hurt like the plants. At this point he pushed the book towards me, asking me to look at an animal with a big wound on the side of its neck, made by the spade that some men had used to dig it out of its burrow. His unusually worried and unhappy expression remained. I linked this picture with others that he had shown me in which it was always adult men who had done the damage, and I told him that it is because his own guilt and fear is so unbearable that he continually puts all the responsibility on to father-figures. Although the depression was more manifest in this session, the persecutory element was also very strong, and so I interpreted his identification with the hurt animal in reference to my analytic attempts to dig him out of his hole, when he was silent and unco-operative. The early training in cleanliness seems to have been rather strict and premature, so he felt also that I was digging his thoughts and words out of him, like a mother putting a dangerous spade into him to get out his excrements (his babies=

animals). He showed that both he and the contents of his body have been hurt in consequence, and believed that analysis might really do him harm.

IV

The fourth example shows the relation between this kind of material, which in fact had to be worked through again and again, and his stealing tendencies. On many occasions after periods of great resistance, when he did not talk at all, he would suddenly stand up in order to clear out of his pockets an enormous collection of things, which he placed on the table before me. One day he showed me a gold chain which he said he had stolen from his sister. He would give no associations beyond this bare statement and seemed to be testing out what I would do about it. I said nothing and he proceeded to demonstrate what he wanted the chain for. He selected two round bottles from his drawer and fastened them together with an elastic band, into which he fixed the gold chain and then made the bottles dance up and down in front of me. To summarize what came out of this play, we could see how he envied his sister's power to make the parents dance to her tune, through the use of her feminine charms and attributes, represented by a gold chain. Several times he pushed his finger through a small loop in the chain and thus dangled the bottles, showing that a sexual relationship with the sister gives him indirect control over the parents. This relationship with the sister is also felt to be stolen and gives rise to much guilt and fear.

At a deeper level, associated with an earlier time in his life, he is still jealous of the baby sister's possession of the mother's breasts (the two bottles). The close connection between penis and eye (penis= forefinger in this play), which had appeared very often in his analysis, was interpreted here as a link with his penetrating eye, trying to see through holes how the mother was feeding the baby. The mother's habit had been to keep such a sight away from him as far as possible, and this contributed to his feeling that what he saw as the "Peeping Tom" either in fact or in phantasy was stolen knowledge. But another component of his guilt came from the use he made of knowledge gained in this way to appropriate (in phantasy) the breasts of both mother and sister. Later on in the analysis we reached masturbatory phantasies connected with his own nipples. Also he often used his mother, in reality as well as in imagination, to exert her influence with father to get things for him.

V

My fifth example which is also concerned with stealing is taken from a much later phase of the analysis. Just before the incident he had deliberately and openly stolen money from me and had attempted to deny it. He now showed how confused he was about what he had or had not done. It was his custom to borrow magazines from the waiting room to look at during the session and he always returned them to the waiting room before going away. He had been looking at some pictures in *Punch* with me and wanted to continue talking when I closed the session at the usual time. Instead of bringing the magazine out of the room he absentmindedly locked it up in his drawer—and then for three weeks never went near the drawer again. On no occasion did I draw his attention to what he had done. When he at last opened the drawer again he looked genuinely surprised and horrified to see the magazine there. Only once before had I seen him blush, and this time a crimson colour spread over face and neck, but he quickly recovered himself and brought the *Punch* to me, asking me to look at it with him. It was interesting to note that he selected, without realizing it, the very picture we had come to previously at the end of the session when he had no time to give his associations to it. His anger with me at the frustration and his subsequent method of retaliation had been completely covered up but now came out into the open, and was again linked with the old feeding pattern. A strong reparation drive was shown in his wish to bring the magazine to me at once and to continue where we left off. The unconscious decision to open the drawer again after three weeks could be interpreted to him as a sign that he had forgiven me for hurting him, when I stopped the session at the usual time. During the interval his behaviour and expression had been quiet and carefree, but underneath had been a conflicting turmoil of anger, guilt, fear and unhappiness.

The picture we now looked at was of an old lady in a museum looking at a model of a bee, and he said that he had been in that same museum and had also looked at the bee which "was a beautiful bit of work and very realistic". He laughed heartily at the old woman desperately covering the artificial flowers on her hat as she gazes with horror at the bee. I remembered that a few days before he had brought a tooth to show me, which the dentist had extracted because, in the words of the patient, "it was an extra one coming on top of the other as though two teeth were trying to come through in the place of one". He had used exactly the same phrase to describe this tooth, saying "it was a beautiful bit of work". I now reminded him of this and showed him the equation between tooth and bee. I pointed out that, although it was obvious that the old lady stood for myself and his mother, he had spoken of being in the same place as the old lady also looking at the bee and that, just before showing me the picture, he had looked at the *Punch* magazine in his drawer with this same expression of frightened astonishment on his face. *Punch* therefore was also equated with the bee and the tooth, because he felt that the extra tooth was just as much stolen by him and put in his body as the magazine was stolen and put in his drawer.

It was possible to show him the projection on to us of his fears of the bee as a persecutor, and to draw his attention to the fact that he pictures us as stupidly afraid of his penis (and that of the father), when attacking us from outside but that his bee-persecutor is also the second tooth attacking him in his mouth, and that he regards this tooth as the father's penis punishing him because he has stolen it in imagination. His fears of being silly, which are always closely linked with madness, were also projected on to the old woman, because he cannot bear the realization that he is not sure what he has done in reality and what only in phantasy, what he has done consciously and what he has done in the same way as he took the magazine. The acute anxiety and guilt associated with his homosexual attitudes, which derived from this stealing of bodily parts, interfered with the normal establishment of a good love relation with his father. Moreover, the use of his heterosexual powers in the mother-and-sister relationships for purposes of indirectly attaining love-gifts from father interfered with the normal development of his masculinity.

VI

In the sixth example we return to the earlier sessions which dealt with his sister's stolen chain. He began a session one day by telling me of a recent incident at school. A boy had taken and put in his pocket something which did not belong to him, and the cord attached to the object protruded from the pocket. A master ordered the boy to hand it up but the boy refused, and when the master thereupon pulled at the cord, the boy whipped out a pocket knife and quickly cut through the cord in defiance. I told him that he often experienced me as this kind of figure; although he had that day turned out his pockets voluntarily to show me stolen property, on many occasions he had done something similar to what the boy did at school, when he cut off all connection with me and retreated into himself; that he was afraid of school, the dentist's surgery, and the analytic room, as dangerous places to which the parents send him in the hope that teachers, dentists, and analysts will be cleverer than they in discovering and removing the stolen property. Such ideas made it difficult for him to co-operate with us. He then announced in a lighthearted way that the headmaster could not possibly expel the boy from school because the father was rich and the school needed his money. It was easy to see that he was dealing with his fears of being sent away from school and analysis by resorting to the mechanisms of denial and reassurance, and this was pointed out to him. His fears concerned both the waste of time and money he caused us all, and his secret activities which he judged to be so bad that expulsion or worse would follow their discovery.

The next day he emptied his pockets again and drew my attention to a match box. Having opened it, without speaking, so that I could see some insects and bits of grass within, he left the box open on the table in front of me and proceeded to unbolt the doors leading into my garden. Outside, he gathered some grass, and returned to moisten it under the tap before putting it in the box with the other grass. Still silent, he shut the box, where it lay before me, and then placed it in his drawer till the next day.

Although no interpretation of the play was given at this point, I could understand some of its symbolic meaning and its relation to the previous day's material. The drawer stood for the mother's body, containing among other things the match box as the womb. Through his vivid identification with his mother the match box was his imaginary womb, and the robbery associated with his homosexual and heterosexual attitudes was expressed by the unbolting of the doors and forced entry into my garden to get the grass. The grass together with the water from the tap was the contribution of the father to the making of the baby, and in leaving the match box and its contents in the drawer undisturbed and without any comment, he identified himself with the parents, who observed a similar silence about their creative activities when the mother became pregnant.

He next took string from the drawer and began silently to twist it to make rope, which he knew how to do very efficiently, and for a long time was leaning up against me so that our bodies were in close contact. In this way he demonstrated his knowledge of the umbilicae cord and of the close bodily connection between the baby (himself) and mother (the analyst). Later on in the session, when the work of interpretation began, we discovered that the rope (umbilical cord) represented also every type of affectionate bond possible between two human beings, including the expression of love through physical contact, but some of his difficulties arose from the fact that he considered only the most intense physical connection as sure proof of love, namely being as close as a baby is by means of the navel cord, etc. When he began to talk, it took the form of teaching me how rope was made. He then went on to describe the difference in structure and function between two contrasting types of rope. His voice and manner were gentle, and everything was explained very clearly as though he were a kind and patient teacher instructing a small child. I was standing for his sister, and he once again showed me what an advantage he feels she had over him by being the younger, because he had no elder brother to explain things to him in lieu of the parents, who observed a strict silence. His sister need not steal the information or feel driven to be a Peeping Tom.

He told me that one rope was made for strength and durability, and gave window cord as an example, saying that it was the type in general use, but quite unsuitable for certain situations in which it might even be a real menace. A second kind of rope was necessary which should have reasonable strength and yet could be cut through easily and quickly with a sharp knife. If ships were caught in a terrific storm when tied up to a wharf or fastened together, they must be cut free to stop them banging about and being bashed in by bumping together. "A good sailor would," he said, "always have a knife on him and hasten to cut the ship free."

When interpreting, I pointed out that he had been obliged to show his knowledge of the father's role in the making of a baby, by silent demonstration, partly because he wanted to indicate the way knowledge had come to him, partly because the fact of a woman's pregnancy is not usually referred to in general conversation, and also because his guilt and fear prevented him talking freely to me about these things. A few weeks later after more work had been done along the lines of these two sessions, he called to me from the garden one day and asked me spontaneously and excitedly to come and look at two insects coupled together in the act of intercourse.

The lesson he gave me about ropes was evidence of his growing awareness of the fact that such things as weaning are necessary and beneficial, and that his clinging to the more primitive bonds with the parents, as well as his demands for impossible forms of physical gratification, are damaging and dangerous to himself and others. The knife which all good sailors have and keep sharp represented his penis, which if cherished and developed could be used to free himself from an overstrong desire for the mother's breast and father's penis, in real acts of incorporation.

Referring to the previous session with the quarrel between the schoolmaster and the boy who cut the cord, I showed him that his attempts to grow up and free himself and his parents from relationships of too great intimacy and overdependence were interfered with by his feelings of guilt and need to make reparation on account of his stealing tendencies: that at least from the mother's pregnancy onwards he had never felt that he could come really near to the parents emotionally, and that the insecurity of the relationship had increased his need to keep on trying to put right even the earliest forms of contact suitable to a very small child and its parents, but not suitable at a later age: that he was anxious to develop a loving and yet breakable type of bond between himself and his family (represented by the second type of rope): that the only people in the family between whom he felt the other unbreakable bond should and could safely exist now, were the parents (first type of rope): that the difference between affectionate relationships on the one hand and sexual ones on the other (suckling and genital intercourse) were shown in the play with the rope.

In his behaviour to me he had always shown an oscillation between almost complete withdrawal to an affectionate and confiding communicativeness, and in this latter mood he always ended up by making demands for further intimacy, which had to be refused, e.g. borrowing money (sometimes acceded to), invitations to birthday parties and to school functions, requests to have my cat or dog in the room, questions regarding my private life, and finally the need to touch me in a way that gave direct sexual gratification. The same thing was also shown symbolically in a number of ways, for instance, in the request that he might open the lid of the anthracite stove (symbolizing my genital) in order to suspend inside it a very hard ball of plasticine (his penis), which he wanted to warm and soften before it was in a condition to be used creatively. He stated that to hold it outside the stove, even close up against it, was not sufficient since the ball was so very hard.

VII

The seventh illustration brings his relation with his sister in the rivalry situation, where he struggled for a dominant place in the father's affections, and was brought to me in the analysis as some proof of an improvement in his way of dealing with envy and jealousy.

Their father's birthday was just ahead, and he told me that this year he and his sister together would give him a joint present. It was to be a heater for the car to be placed close to the engine and left there all night to prevent it freezing up on cold winter nights. He explained that his father often had difficulty in the mornings to get the car started for his journey to work. There was also a reference to the mother's present to the father which, he said, was of course a much bigger one. Interpretation dealt with his growing realization of his father's need for the love of his children, as well as for that of his wife, to help him through the day's work by means of which he supported the family. In recent sessions there had been more manifest guilt regarding his lack of appreciation of the many gifts given to him at the cost of his father's hard work. I pointed out how the jealousy of both mother and sister, who he felt could give father so much more than he, had interfered with his impulses to show affection to his father. I reminded him too of the ways in which he had previously described an alliance with the sister against the parents. The heater was also explained to him as representing mother's genital, which he wished to restore to father, whom he believed to have been deprived of it during nights of coldness, on account of his attempts to interfere with the parents' intercourse.

While I was speaking he settled down to read a serial story in a magazine which he had brought with him that day. It was a story he had read in previous instalments in other sessions but without giving any associations. On this occasion his whole bearing and posture as he sat at the table reading was rather unusual for him. Instead of the more typical childish behaviour, with thumb-sucking, rhythmical rocking, picking of the nose, and body scratch-ings, etc., he sat upright and like an adult with one arm flung across the table and the other hand placed quietly on the open page. The impression he gave was of a child trying to copy a grown-up's position, probably his father's.

After a while he stopped reading and volunteered a résumé of the whole story up to date, emphasizing the things which interested him most. It was about the daughter of a Red Indian chief and how she was discovered in an act of disobedience so bad that the father arranged for a public ceremony of expulsion. She was banished from the chief's territory and the special badge worn as the chief's daughter was taken from her. With the loss of the badge went the special protection which had formerly been given to her as well as the deference paid to her by her subordinates. Memories of the sister's arrival and of the father's pride and pleasure in her had been stirred up by the preparations for the father's birthday, and the underlying death-wishes against the sister came out in this story in their earliest forms, namely, she was to be sent away never to return; she was to be starved and neglected. The tortoise story had expressed the opposite attitude of love and pity towards the new-born baby, and during this session he showed an attempt to deal with the underlying hostility shown in the story by an acceptance of the sister and a satisfactory association with her in the shared giving of a present.

Without going into any detail I will add that the actual misdeed of the girl in the story was one of which he had in fact been guilty himself, and this having been discussed in the analysis previously, it made it possible to show him the connection and to point out the projection of this aspect of himself into the sister. This projection had added to his need to get rid of the sister and increased his fear of her, while the depression connected with his feelings about being a very unsatisfactory and disappointing son added to his conviction that his father preferred his daughter.

The giving of presents on a birthday had stimulated his expectation of gifts to himself and his sister from the father, and he showed how the badge stood for a promise of the ultimate bestowal of the father's penis on one or other of the children, who would then rule in his place. In spite of demonstrating in many sessions his rejection of his masculinity and his grievance against the parents for assigning the male role to him and not to his sister, he shows here how much he wants to be able to identify with his father and keep the badge (his penis) using it in a predominantly friendly way.

The compulsive nose-picking, etc., which usually tormented him, related to the need also to internalize the father in order to bring about the desired identification, but showed that he had not succeeded in establishing a good and helpful father within.

Castration anxiety came to the fore more strongly at this time, partly owing to his greater effort to maintain the masculine position.

While talking to me about the story, he was continually pulling at the handle of the drawer in the table at his end. He kept on unscrewing it and then screwing it in again, and seemed unaware of what he was doing; so I interpreted his unconscious fear that his father would take his penis away from him in just that way, by catching hold of it and unscrewing it, linking this fear not only with his aggressive use of his penis, but also with the retention in his mind of infantile ideas about the male genital as a movable object, like a badge or a handle, which could be taken away, exchanged, or replaced. I reminded him of the many different kinds of badges which he had made from varying materials during other sessions, and of the way he used to come at times with a large number of badges in the lapels of his coat. He had told me too that he sold some of these badges to other children at school. I indicated the reassurance value of these primitive phantasies and his retention of them therefore in order to allay a number of fears.

VIII

In the eighth example, we can see some of his fears about the aggressive nature of his penis and the association in his mind between his father's genital and his own. The symbols used were a ruler, a pendulum, an engine, a puppy, and paint brushes. The plasticine ball of which the pendulum weight was made has been mentioned in a previous example, but I will now add that at one stage in the analysis he had often swung the ball backwards and forwards, while holding it suspended with his hand in front of his genital, so that I could point out the equation he was making between his penis and a pendulum.

On this occasion he spent a long time at the beginning of the session making fruitless efforts to set up and demonstrate to me the nature and functions of a pendulum as taught recently at school. The objective reason for his failure to make it swing satisfactorily in the session was that he hung it from the curtain rod, which lay between two projecting parts of the wall around the window, and the ball banged against them. It became obvious that he gradually realized the need for a horizontal support projecting at right angles to the window to bring the pendulum into a different vertical plane. Nevertheless he said that he was sure that, if he went on trying, he could make it work without introducing this support. Finally he gave up such an unrealistic way of approach to the problem (the pendulum also stood for his head, which he no longer banged against reality represented by the wall) and fetched from his drawer a much damaged ruler, which he had attacked with his penknife in an earlier session when expressing anger against school teachers and all other figures of authority. At that time we had talked of the ruler as representing the internal figures also, whom he experienced as an unpleasant conscience ruling him arbitrarily from within.

When in this session he could bring himself to give up his attempts to force the pendulum to work through his omnipotent control of it, he chose this very ruler for the necessary support, although other equally suitable pieces of material were available. Without detaching the string from the curtain rod he now passed the string along the ruler, inserting the latter between the window and the vertical part of the string pulled downwards by the plasticine weight, and he found that the pendulum swung freely in the new plane in which there was no obstruction. The analyst then got her lesson on the nature and use of pendulums, and this was followed by the work of interpretation, the main points of which will be summarized.

The ruler in the drawer was representing the father's penis within him, felt to be within his body (the drawer) and in a damaged condition through his own attacks upon it. His reluctance to use the internal father to help him with his intellectual problems, and his rejection of the father's penis as an object to be placed within his own (along the string to support it), to give it the power of erection, was due mainly to his fears: (1) of the father and the penis being too damaged to function properly; (2) of their being hostile to him because he had hurt them; (3) of their being such implacable and dominating rulers that to come under their direction would involve the loss of all freedom of action. Fears derived from the opposite position which he had at first taken up were also pointed out to him, because he had shown that when trying to manage things alone he both "banged his head against a wall" and also continually came into conflict with people and things, banging and being banged by them.

He was soon talking about an old toy engine of his which he said "has been very much knocked about by me, but it was given to me when I was much too small to know how to take care of it. I was only a kid so how could I help knocking it about! Sometimes I think of taking it to the toyshop to get it repaired but I never do, because I would be too ashamed to show it to the man there." He

69

had decided to ask the parents to give him a completely new and different type of engine and railway set instead.

While talking about the engine he had got out his painting book and went on with the painting of a puppy commenced but left unfinished some weeks before. It had been copied from a photograph of a puppy in one of my magazines and a careful drawing was made before any painting was attempted. Within a few minutes of going on again with the painting, he asked me if I thought I could provide him with two more brushes for his drawer, because "with the two I already have I can't help making a mess of my painting. One is too small and the other too large." He showed manifest anxiety about not being able to keep entirely within the lines of his drawing, and when the paint came very slightly over the edge, he said again: "You see! I can't help spoiling the picture with these brushes." I agreed to the need for intermediate size brushes and promised to provide them, but then took up the work of interpretation.

I pointed out that he was dealing with engine, puppy, and paint brushes as part of the same theme shown in the pendulum-ruler play. The engine and puppy came in as damaged objects that he had not succeeded in protecting from his aggression through disturbances in his relation with the helpful parent figures within, represented by the ruler and the paint brushes. I reminded him of an earlier account he had given of a puppy he had once owned, when a small boy, but could not keep because he didn't treat it properly. He at once repeated the remark he had made about his damaged engine, "I was too small then to know how to behave." To this I replied that he was not only describing his own failures but criticizing the parents (the paint brushes) and asking me to give him two new and different parents. Any conscious and direct criticism of his parents played a very small part in his analysis, and the unconscious criticisms that had appeared before were mostly in terms of sadistic triumph over them.

Although the request for new paint brushes might seem to indicate rejection of both parents and relate to the real external ones, I think that the main emphasis throughout the session was on the difficult relationship with the internal father and his penis. The drawer into which I was to put the new brushes had been standing for himself, and, in my experience, any objects held in the hand during creative work stand predominantly for the internalized objects, with whom an intense emotional relationship is being experienced unconsciously while the work goes on. That the father and his penis appeared in duplicate (the two paint brushes) referred to substitute father figures who had played important roles in the boy's life, when his own father was not available. After interpretations had been made along these lines, I added that he was now more able to try to sort out his own responsibility for these failures from the role played by the parents in creating difficulties for him. His criticism of them took the form of a complaint that they gave him gifts and forced him into situations when he was still too young and inexperienced to handle them satisfactorily.

I also suggested to him that through the equation between himself (and his penis) and his damaged objects he showed me that he felt too ashamed to show me his damaged head and penis, as he had been too ashamed to show his engine to the man in the toyshop.

The reparative element in drawing and painting is well known, and one can see here his imaginative recreation of the real lost puppy, as well as the repairing and bringing to life of the phantasy objects. He believed the puppy to have been destroyed on his account, when it was sent away after attacking a neighbour's chickens. Several weeks before this session we had been talking about the use he made of various objects for purposes of projecting his aggression, and the puppy had come into that discussion, so that the engine and the ruler could now be understood in relation to the puppy. Guilt towards the puppy, and towards all the objects symbolized in this session, was combined with acute anxiety lest a similar fate awaited himself or his genital, and this guilt and anxiety lay behind his inability to use his mental and physical powers. The fear of uncontrolled aggression had an inhibiting effect continually. I took it that by copying a puppy in one of my magazines he was not only asking me to help him find his puppy again but also to help in his efforts to recreate the puppy by explaining to him the structure of a dog's body, an exchange lesson for the many lessons he had given me in his sessions, e.g. the one on the pendulum. One of the tragic aspects of a child's attempt to repair and recreate damaged objects is his lack of knowledge, and this applies both to real and phantasy attempts to put things right. And when a child has had to separate himself from internal or external helping figures, his despair becomes very great. In this patient the hopelessness was shown in his inactivity which alternated with a manic assertiveness such as the statement that he could *make* the pendulum work even against his common sense.

Another useful connection could be made in this session between

71

the tortoise material, already described, and these other damaged objects, engine, ruler and puppy. He was wearing his dental plate but found it very troublesome and took it out several times. Once he said: "I have to try to keep it in, but I am not forced to if it hurts too much." I reminded him that the plate had been equated with the damaged tortoise, which had stood for an internal persecutor, and that he now shows how strongly he feels that the lost puppy is within him, hitting back and biting him as it once bit the chickens. His assertion, displaced on to his remark about the plate, that he does not have to keep an internalized object within him, is a pitiful denial of the existence of the internal persecutor, and I interpreted both this denial and the use he makes of an accompanying psychic act of projection, whenever he removes the plate from his mouth.

He came to the next session as I had never seen him before. I found him sitting motionless in the waiting-room in a dejected attitude, bent forward with his head in his hands. Even when I spoke to him, he did not move for a while, and then looked up with a start to say: "I did not know that you were there." Downstairs in the treatment room he took up the same position and told me that he had slept badly, and one could see that he had not brushed his hair. He wanted to go to sleep with his head on the table, but kept struggling against sleep, and I interpreted his fear of me as someone trying to put him to sleep as he believed "the vet put the puppy to sleep". I pointed out also the confirmation he was giving me of my remarks about the dying and dead objects within him and of his struggle against a need to identify with them.

IX

One of the psychic tasks all children are faced with, for the satisfactory attainment of a unified personality, is the bringing together in a stable union of the two internalized parents. Such a union is a step towards the assimilation of the parents, together with their good qualities, in successive identifications. A number of symptoms as well as inhibitions have their basis in the child's relation with this internal combined figure. My patient showed me in many different kinds of material that this combined figure was for him a strange and frightening one, disturbing his comfortable feelings about his own body and contributing to his hypochondriacal fears.

His conception of parental intercourse was that of a sadistic act in which he more often portrayed mother as the more powerful partner, being successful in gaining all the good things which money symbolized. His mother's money bag was to him the womb in which she unfairly stored up an undue share of everything that could be desired. The strong identification with mother and sister was often expressed in the remark that the one and only thing he wanted to be was a millionaire. He announced that a millionaire could control anybody or anything and thereby get all he wanted, but went straight on to complain of the unfairness of the usual arrangement in marriage where the man was forced to have a job and earn money to support the woman. He brought money from his collection of coins to demonstrate his grievance against his mother, as Britannia. There were coins from all the reigns back to Victoria, and he sorted out those that had on them the heads of kings, but turning them over said to me: "You see! It doesn't matter whether the coin belongs to a queen or a king, Britannia sits on them all!"

When interpreting this material in connection with his unconscious picture of the dominant female in a sadistic parental intercourse and his choice of the female for his predominant identification, I also spoke of the concreteness of his unconscious phantasies, according to which the king-and-queen-parents, as well as their excrements and genitals, were felt to be inside his body in the same way as the coins lay in his pocket. It was possible also in this session to explain to him some of the unconscious connections with his stealing tendencies which he had demonstrated by taking money from his mother's bag and from me. In the realm of phantasy he stole from mother and sister to fit himself out with the bodily parts needed to play a female role in relation to father, and much of his guilt and anxiety derived from these unrealistic imaginary activities. Through his identification with the bad Victoria-Britannia mother, he was also feeling himself to be dominating and sadistic in his homosexual attitudes.

His hatred and fear of the powerful robbing female caused him to employ his father, in his imagination, to carry out violent attacks upon her. Indirectly he brought conscious and unconscious memories of bombing during the war through a play in one session with marbles. He placed some on the floor and then from a considerable height tried to drop other marbles exactly on his targets. It became clear only a few days later that there had been a specific attack upon the females in this play. He drew my attention to some pictures of men filling up a number of planes with jelly-bombs, explaining to me that such bombs were used in warfare to drop with precision-bombing on the tops of certain buildings. He insisted that the poor pilots were *made* to go up with these bombs and drop them as directed by these bad men who were filling up the planes.   So I interpreted in the first place his persecutory feelings about the bad father making him attack mother and sister, and his experience of bombing as though the absent father had sent the enemy bombers to search them out and kill them. But subsequently I pointed out the element of projection that always turned up in his material, when he draws my attention to what the bad men are doing, while the children (here represented by the pilots) are quite innocent.

The same theme of father and son attacking the mother and sister was shown in a more genital form a few days later when he asked me if I knew about the two famous ships the *M——— I*, and the *M———II*, the latter built to replace the former which he said "had lived out her full span of life". His mood was a very anxious one with more manifest anxiety than usual, and he showed a loving concern for the *M——— II* (obviously standing for his sister) when he told me that unlike the one whose place she took, she had been unable to weather a frightful storm during her maiden voyage and was smashed to pieces on the rocks. When I interpreted his great anxiety and concern for his sister, whom he feared would never become adult like her mother, he became very uneasy but was able to co-operate by turning to another picture, this time of ships in a canal. "It is very dangerous," he said, "for a wooden ship like that to go into a canal, because in such places they are likely to get riddled with worms, which penetrate right into them so that in the end they become quite hollow and then the slightest bang and—down it goes!" My first interpretation was of the worms as the bad penises which he, and the father whom he controls, put into the sister like the bad men filling up the bombing planes to attack the buildings below; that the storm and rocks which wrecked the *M——II* are also the weapons of the bad males—mother has been able to withstand their attacks, but the sister will not have enough strength to resist. There was also a reference to previous material which had shown his concern lest his sister had been damaged in sexual play with him. But I also pointed out his anxiety concerning his own state as a female in the homosexual situation, for he has in imagination pushed the sister out and taken her place, only to find that he is full of anxiety about becoming more and more hollow,

74

through his persistent incorporation of a number of penises in the passive homosexual experiences.

So great were his difficulties that he could only maintain his masculine identification with father for short periods and even then with accompanying partial inhibition. The aggressive nature of the penis, his father's, was one important reason for his failure, and the impoverishment of his personality and lack of energy were exemplified by the hollow ship ready to collapse at the slightest bang on its sides. The identification with either mother or father, or both, as internal sexual figures meant being involved in a sadistic dangerous act. One of his main defences was regression to an identification with an earlier undifferentiated parent figure in which mother and father, male and female entities were confused and mixed up with each other. This confusion in the internal figure added to the strangeness of his feelings about himself and also made him fear and try to avoid an identification with it. This regression was also to oral contact with the object and involved important displacement from the genital-urethral-anal parts of the body up to the head. Nose, mouth, eyes and ears became burdened with the functions derived from these other organs, and this affected his concept of the bodies of the internal parents, turning them as well as himself into distorted monstrosities.

Denial of his anxieties was a very strong and well established defence, and he sought to prove to me that this loss of function in some of his organs and doubling of function in another part of the body was a very great advantage, and in fact quite an achievement. With great enthusiasm he described a man whom he had known intimately during early childhood. It was a long story and I am only using one point in it here. The man had been involved in a bad accident that was nearly fatal, and on recovery it was found that, through damage to his nose, the sense of smell was permanently and hopelessly lost. It was when my patient was describing the wonderful way in which this man dealt with his loss that the maximum amount of affect appeared in voice and facial expression. The man made no trouble at all but rather rejoiced in the acquisition of a strange new power, for he developed the capacity to smell with his eyes and this power never failed him.

I explained to him his internalization of this man and identification with him in the displacement from damaged nose (the penis) to the eyes (standing for the vagina) which also involved for him displacement from the genital up to the head, and in the use of cheerful good humour for purposes of denial. That he spends so much time at home and in his sessions reading was explained as a retreat from masculine to feminine activity, and that the kind of reading he fears is of this type, because he feels that he becomes full of the wriggling worms, which make his head hollow and empty of knowledge which can't be acquired by using his head and eyes in a penetrating masculine activity. I showed him how strong this attitude of denial and indifference was and how he maintains super-ficially a superior feeling about himself and other males, who deal with their illness and impotence by asserting that a homosexual male is an improvement on a normal male. But I also reminded him that he does occasionally reveal how unhappy and frightened he is about his condition and about the strangeness and abnormality of the internal parents with whom he is identified.

One day he asked me to look at some of the illustrations to a serial story that he had read at home and now read again during his session. The pictures he selected all contained a centaur and the title of the story was "I Don't Wanna be a Hoss". As usual his laugh covered up underlying anxiety. He undertook to give me a summary up to the incidents illustrated in these pictures. The sheriff of a town in America had passed harsh judgment on an Indian for ill-treatment of his horse, to which the Indian responded by vindictively offering the sheriff something to eat which turned him into a centaur. My patient was delighted with this and clearly identified himself with the Indian, showing me that the sheriff stood for the father who blames and punishes him for ill-treating his mother and sister, who are turned thereby into mere beasts of burden. The horse appears very frequently in children's symbolic representations as the mother, but it is usually a very special aspect of the mother that is empha-sized by the use of a four-footed animal. It appeared in this case, for the mother is thought of as containing the father and making therefore one of the early forms of the combined parent figure. The identification with this kind of mother eliminates the sexual father in the sense that the combined figure is not of the two parents in the act of intercourse (fused with each other from the outside of their bodies); the father and his penis have been completely incorporated by mother. My patient felt a superior homosexual identification with what to him was a more powerful and frightening figure. The identification is really expressed by the centaur, and it became clear as we went on with the work that the sheriff stood un-consciously for my patient, who experienced his homosexual condition as a punishment and as a shame which he sought to hide.

In the story, the centaur-sheriff was terrified lest his ridiculous condition should be discovered, and he was driven to a number of humiliating expedients to hide the lower part of his body from the public, so that he might continue his functions as sheriff. He was helped in his adventures by a young nephew upon whose goodwill he became utterly dependent. From one point of view this nephew stood for his sister with whom he wanted to change places and imagined there had been an exchange of genitals, and in many accounts of their joint reality activities he emphasized unconsciously his great dependence on her initiative, though superficially speaking of her condescendingly. From another point of view the nephew was linked with different boys with whom he had been friendly. He showed me a picture of a blindfolded blacksmith shoeing the centaur, while the nephew stood on guard covering the blacksmith with a loaded gun. His explanation of this picture was that the nephew had concocted a wonderful trick to help the uncle. He had led the blacksmith on to boast that he could shoe any horse blind-folded. My patient looked straight at me at that moment and said how awful it would be if the bandage happened to fall from the blacksmith's eyes. I told him that he felt as though he were the centaur sitting in the analyst's room as a blacksmith shop and that in imagination he had a friend of his (the nephew) in the room covering me with a gun. If I should understand what lay behind his being the centaur, I was in danger of being killed by the nephew, and he felt that I did not know what danger I ran through under-taking and going on with his analysis. On another occasion he had told me that he had a real friend slightly older than himself, who possessed a gun and a licence to shoot. He himself had come to different sessions armed with weapons, sword, gun, arrow, and knife, once jumping out at me from behind the waiting-room door saying: "Your money or your life."

One of the reasons why I was in such danger was because he thought of me as one who would kill him or the nephew (one of his friends), if I discovered their secrets. He was also afraid that he might betray those represented by the nephew, who might then shoot him. After one session when he took no notice of me through-out the whole time, he spoke at last on the doorstep when outside the house, saying: "I am going straight from you to the dentist, to be murdered, you know."

77

It was part of the work of the analysis to help him in sorting out the anxieties and guilt that had their connections with real external happenings and those that were primarily derived from phantastic situations. The analysis of real happenings uncovered realistic elements of danger to himself and others which were at times exaggerated and confused with irrational fears, and at other times were denied and under-estimated also. The analysis of the centaur material was very much fuller than can be given in this paper. The centaur was dealt with as a representation of the real parents too, and some of the links worked out between his contribution to their appearing in his inner world in this unsatisfactory and humiliating union and the factors that he felt derived from the limitations and difficulties of the real parents.

x

To conclude, I will draw attention to the fact that when the more persecutory aspect of his anxiety situations diminished as a result of analytic work, he could show for a while a mood of true depression, with more acceptance of responsibility and more trust in me. His birthday came soon after the sessions with the centaur, and he celebrated it by bringing me an analytic present. He arrived with his stamp collection and asked for help with the large number of stamps waiting to be fastened into his stamp album. He said he had been too lazy to deal with it before, a favourite defensive explanation of states of inhibition due to unmanageable acute anxieties. He estimated that he had a very large collection for a boy of his age, but said that it was in a disgraceful state because he took no trouble to fasten the stamps into the book.

He was chiefly interested during this session in the difference between countries that were monarchies and those that were republics and got confused between the two. He passed a stamp over to me asking me to identify the country to which it belonged, that we might then classify it in these terms. "Republique Française" was very clearly written on the stamp, so I passed it back and said it must be standing for something else he wanted me to examine inside him, since he could obviously read it for himself. He smiled and read out the French words with correct pronunciation and then said the stamp had become so dirty that he was not sure about seeing it correctly. A minute later he handed me another stamp and with a very anxious look on his face said, "That republic is the one that has just been wiped out, isn't it?" Before I started to interpret he had added that he now had the chance to have his father's stamp collection, but was not going to accept the offer yet, because he was still unable to take care of things. While fastening some stamps which he said were very good ones into his book he made a sudden sound of disgust and pulled off one of the attachment slips saying: "That's a disgusting one and no good."

My interpretations were along the lines of the book being himself, the stamps (like the coins he had brought previously) being the internal mothers and fathers, internalized at different ages in his life (the different reigns). Different people (the countries) have different internal organizations, some choosing republics and others monarchy (the earliest type of internal world for the child). The stamps he doesn't look after sufficiently well are the parents, and their children, inside him. Some of them have become so dirty through his attitudes to them that he can't bear to look at them and can't even recognize them. If his method of producing a republic inside is by the destruction of the king and queen he feels that he, as the republic, will be wiped out in revenge. His internalization processes have been held up (sorting out and placing stamps in the album) not so much because of laziness, which is his frequent substitute explanation, but more because he fears that his inside is a place in which they cannot be kept alive. His fear of externalizing his aggression drove him to turn it inwards and added to the devastation within. The adhesive label for the stamp was his own penis and that of the father (hand, head, etc.) which must be used to join the king and queen together and to join them to himself. Pulling it off and throwing it away, as too disgusting, expressed his dissatisfaction with the penis, which still caused him at this stage in the analysis to retreat again and again from the genital position.

SUMMARY

The main purpose of the foregoing is to demonstrate in the case of a boy-patient how certain early anxiety situations are uncovered and dealt with according to the analytic technique of Melanie Klein. The reason for which he came to analysis was the parents' concern about severe inhibitions at school in work and play. At the outset of analysis this attitude of non-co-operation was not shown in the transference situation but appeared as soon as the patient's need to placate the analyst had diminished.

Depression and persecutory fears, open aggression and defiance, as well as passive negative attitudes of great strength began to emerge both at home and in the analysis. The patient was able later on to reveal conscious concern about such symptoms as mental confusion and hypochondriacal fears which he had been trying to hide.

The following examples were taken from his analysis which lasted for several years. The first three dealt with anxieties relating to phantasies of attacks made upon the inside of the mother's body.

Example 1. The mother's babies were symbolized as tortoises and as the dental plate in his mouth, which he experienced as a persecutory object. His companions at school were equated with the mother's unborn children.

Example 2. The connection between such anxieties and intellectual inhibition was shown and their effect upon his relation with his sister.

Example 3. Spiders and ants were captured in the treatment room to be placed in pens constructed during the session. The picture of a damaged animal in a magazine was used together with the spiders and ants to represent the objects as he imagined them to be inside the mother.

Example 4. Stealing tendencies were shown in connection with his envy of the female functions. He demonstrated the material by means of dancing bottles suspended from a gold chain stolen from his sister.

Example 5. Dealt with stealing in relation to the analyst, and led to the discovery of important links between conscious and unconscious thefts. Confusion arising from uncertainties about the separation of real and imaginary theft was also discussed.

Example 6. Describes the bringing to analysis of some of the stolen property. Fears of schoolteachers, the dentist and the analyst were connected with the idea that we were searching for the things stolen in phantasy as well as for those objects which he had really pilfered. Stolen knowledge about the parents' sexual functions, and about the facts of birth, were shown to contribute to his difficulties in learning.

Example 7. Described something of his rivalry with the sister for a dominant place in the father's affections, and was brought to analysis at the time of the father's birthday when the children decided to give a joint present. Some of the material was given in the form of a summary which he made for me of a serial story he had read during several sessions. The story was of a chief's daughter who lost her badge and was banished by her father for disobedience.

Example 8. Showed some of his fears about the aggressive nature of his penis and the association in his mind between his father's genital and his own. He set up a pendulum and explained to me how it worked, introducing a broken school ruler as part of the arrangement. Other symbols of the penis used in the session were a toy engine, a puppy, and paint brushes.

Example 9. Illustrated the importance of the internal figure of the combined parents, which the patient showed as a strange and frightening figure disturbing his good relation with his body. One form of it was shown as a centaur in another serial story read during the sessions.

Example 10. Described his reactions to his own birthday and showed how a mood of depression could appear and be worked through after some severe persecutory anxieties had been partially analysed. The parents appeared as kings and queens on coins and stamps.

5

THE ROLE OF ILLUSION IN SYMBOL FORMATION[1]

MARION MILNER

PSYCHO-ANALYTIC CONCEPTS OF THE TWO FUNCTIONS OF
THE SYMBOL

MUCH has been written by psycho-analysts on the process by which the infant's interest is transferred from an original primary object to a secondary one. The process is described as depending upon the identification of the primary object with another that is in reality different from it but emotionally is felt to be the same. Ernest Jones and Melanie Klein in particular, following up Freud's formulations, write about this transference of interest as being due to conflict with forces forbidding the interest in the original object, as well as to the actual loss of the original object. Jones, in his paper "The Theory of Symbolism" (1916), emphasizes the aspects of this prohibition which are to do with the forces that keep society together as a whole. Melanie Klein, in various papers, describes also the aspect of it which keeps the individual together as a whole; she maintains that it is the fear of our own aggression towards our original objects which makes us so dread their retaliation that we transfer our interest to less attacked and so less frightening substitutes. Jones also describes how the transfer of interest is due, not only to social prohibition and frustration and the wish to escape from the immanent frustrated mouth, penis, vagina, and their retaliating counterparts, but also to the need to endow the external world with something of the self and so make it familiar and understandable.

The identification of one object with another is described as the forerunner of symbolism, and Melanie Klein, both in her paper "Infant Analysis" (1923) and in the "The Importance of Symbol

[1] This paper originally appeared in a slightly longer form, under the title "Aspects of Symbolism in comprehension of the Not-Self". A postscript has been added to this version.

Formation in the Development of the Ego" (1930), says that symbolism is the basis of all talents. Jones describes this identification as a process of symbolic equivalence through which progress to sublimation is achieved, but adds that symbolism itself, in the sense in which he uses the word, is a bar to progress. Leaving aside for a moment this difference over the use of the word symbol, there is one point about wording which, I feel, requires comment. Jones describes the process of identification that underlies symbol formation as being not only the result of the forbidding forces, but also a result of the need to establish a relation to reality. He says that this process arises from the desire to deal with reality in the easiest possible way, from "the desire for ease and pleasure struggling with the demand of necessity". It seems to me that this way of putting it is liable to lead to misunderstanding. The phrase "desire for ease and pleasure" set against the "demand of necessity" gives the impression that this desire is something that we could, if we were sufficiently strong-minded, do without. The phrase reflects perhaps a certain puritanism which is liable to appear in psycho-analytic writing. Do we really mean that it is only the desire for ease and pleasure, and not necessity, that drives us to identify one thing with another which is in fact not the same? Are we not rather driven by the internal necessity for inner organization, pattern, coherence, the basic need to discover identity in difference without which experience becomes chaos? Actually I think Jones himself implies such an idea when he says that this confounding of one thing with another, this not discriminating, is also the basis of generalization; and he indicates the positive aspect of this failure to discriminate, in relation to discovery of the real world, when he says:

"... there opens up the possibility ... of a theory of scientific discovery, inventions, etc., for psychologically this consists in an overcoming of the resistances that normally prevent regression towards the infantile unconscious tendency to note identity in differences."

This was written in 1916. In 1951 Herbert Read writes:

"The first perceptions of what is novel in any science tend to assume the form of metaphors—the first stages of science are poetic."

Jones quotes Rank and Sachs when they make a distinction between the primary process of identification which underlies symbolism and symbolism itself. He quotes their description of how the original function (demonstrable in the history of civilization) of the identification underlying symbolism was a means of adaptation to reality, but that it "... becomes superfluous and sinks to the mere significance of a symbol as soon as this task of adaptation has been accomplished". He quotes their description of a symbol as the "unconscious precipitate of primitive means of adaptation to reality that have become superfluous and useless, a sort of lumber room of civilization to which the adult readily flees in states of reduced or deficient capacity for adaptation to reality, in order to regain his old long-forgotten playthings of childhood". But they add the significant remark that what later generations know and regard only as a symbol had in earlier stages of mental life full and real meaning and value.

Jones goes on to quote Rank's and Sachs' statement that symbol formation is a regressive phenomenon, and that it is most plainly seen in civilized man, in conditions where conscious adaptation to reality is either restricted, as in religious or artistic ecstasy, or completely abrogated, as in dreams and mental disorders. Here it seems to me that a valuable link has been made between symbolism and ecstasy, but the context in which these two ideas have been brought together leaves out, in respect of the arts, what Jones has described in respect of scientific invention: that is, that it may be a regression in order to take a step forward. Thus Rank's and Sachs' statement does not draw attention to the possibility that some form of artistic ecstasy may be an essential phase in adaptation to reality, since it may mark the creative moment in which new and vital identifications are established. In fact Rank and Sachs do not here allow for the possibility that truth underlies the much quoted aphorism that Art creates Nature; and so also they miss the chance of indicating an underlying relation between art and science.[1]

I think some of the difficulty arises here from lack of a sufficiently clear distinction between the two uses of the process which has been given the name of symbolization. Fenichel (1946) has made this distinction more clear. He says:

> "In adults a conscious idea may be used as a symbol for the purpose of hiding an objectionable unconscious idea; the idea of a penis may be represented by a snake, an ape, a hat, an airplane, if the idea of penis is objectionable. The distinct idea of a penis had been grasped but rejected."

[1] Rank, in his later work, does in fact take a much wider view of the function of art.

But he then goes on to say that symbolic thinking is also a part of the primal prelogical thinking and adds:

"... archaic symbolism as a part of prelogical thinking and distortion by means of representing a repressed idea through a conscious symbol are not the same. Whereas in distortion the idea of penis is avoided through disguising it by the idea of snake, in prelogical thinking penis and snake are *one and the same;* that is, they are perceived by a common conception: the sight of the snake provokes penis emotions; and this fact is later utilized when the conscious idea of snake replaces the unconscious one of penis." (The italics are mine.)

A distinction between two uses of the word symbol has also been described by a non-analyst. Herbert Read (1950) says:

"But there is a very general distinction to be made between those uses of the word which on the one hand retain the sense of a throwing together of tangible, visible objects, with each other or with some immaterial or abstract notion, and those uses which on the other hand imply no such initial separation, but rather treat the symbol as an integral or original form of expression. A word itself may be a symbol in this sense, and language a system of symbols."

The similarity between this second use of the word symbol and Fenichel's second use of it, is clear; although Read says earlier that he feels that it is a pity that he and analysts have to use the same word to describe different things.

ILLUSION AND FUSION

It is the use of symbolism as part of what Fenichel calls prelogical thinking that I wish to discuss here. In particular I wish to consider what are the conditions under which the primary and the secondary object are fused and felt as one and the same. I want to study both the emotional state of the person experiencing this fusion and what conditions in the environment might facilitate or interfere with it; in fact, to study something of the internal and external conditions that make it possible to find the familiar in the unfamiliar—which, incidentally, Wordsworth (1798) said is the whole of the poet's business.

85

Marion Milner

When considering what concepts are available as tools for thinking about this process of fusion or identification, the concept of phantasy is obviously essential, since it is only in phantasy that two dissimilar objects are fused into one. But this concept is not quite specific enough to cover the phenomenon; the word illusion is also needed because this word does imply that there is a relation to an external object of feeling, even though a phantastic one, since the person producing the fusion believes that the secondary object *is* the primary one. In order to come to understand more about the meaning of the word illusion I found it was useful to consider its role in a work of art. I had already, when trying to study some of the psychological factors which facilitate or impede the painting of pictures,[1] become interested in the part played by the frame. The frame marks off the different kind of reality that is within it from that which is outside it; but a temporal spatial frame also marks off the special kind of reality of a psycho-analytic session. And in psycho-analysis it is the existence of this frame that makes possible the full development of that creative illusion that analysts call the transference. Also the central idea underlying psycho-analytic technique is that it is by means of this illusion that a better adaptation to the world outside is ultimately developed. It seemed to me that the full implications of this idea for analytic theory had still to be worked out, especially in connection with the role of symbolism in the analytic relationship.

In considering the dynamics of the process the concept of anxiety is clearly needed. Melanie Klein has laid great stress on the fact that it is dread of the original object itself, as well as the loss of it, that leads to the search for a substitute. But there is also a word needed for the emotional experience of finding the substitute, and it is here that the word ecstasy may be useful.

There is also another ordinary English word, not often used in psycho-analytic literature, except to talk about perversion, or lack of it, in neurotic states, and that is the word concentration. I wish to bring it in here because, in analysing children, I have found myself continually noticing the varying moods or quality of concentration shown by the children, and have tried to understand the relation of these variations to the kind of material produced. These observations have not been confined to the analytic situation; I have often noticed, when in contact with children playing, that there occurs now and then a particular type of absorption in what they are doing, which gives the impression that something of great

[1] This study was published under the pseudonym "Joanna Field" (1950).

86

importance is going on. Before becoming an analyst I used to
wonder what a child, if he had sufficient power of expression, would
say about these moods, how he would describe them from inside.
When I became an analyst I began to guess that the children were in
fact trying to tell me, in their own way, what it does feel like. And
I thought I recognized the nature of these communications the more
easily because I had already tried for myself, introspectively, to find
ways of describing such states, most particularly in connection with
the kinds of concentration that produce a good or a bad drawing.

Before going on to present and discuss some clinical material,
there is one other concept which I think needs clarifying; and that is,
the meaning of the term "primary object". Earlier psycho-analytic
discussions of symbol formation most often emphasized the child's
attempts to find substitutes for those original objects of interest
that are the parents' organs. But some also emphasized the aspect
of the child's attempts to find his own organs and their functioning
in every object. In more recent work these two views tend to be
combined and the idea develops that the primary "object" that
the infant seeks to find again is a fusion of self and object, it is mouth
and breast felt as fused into one. Thus the concept of fusion is
present, both in the primary situation, between self and object, and
in the secondary one, between the new situation and the old one.

CASE MATERIAL: A GAME OF WAR BETWEEN TWO VILLAGES

Moments when the original "poet" in each of us created the outside world for us, by finding the familiar in the unfamiliar, are perhaps forgotten by most people; or else they are guarded in some
secret place of memory because they were too much like visitations
of the gods to be mixed with everyday thinking. But in auto-
biographies some do dare to tell, and often in poetry. Perhaps, in
ordinary life, it is good teachers who are most aware of these
moments, from outside, since it is their job to provide the conditions
under which they can occur, so to stage-manage the situation that
imagination catches fire and a whole subject or skill lights up with
significance. But it is in the analytic situation that this process can
be studied from inside and outside at the same time. So now I
will present some material from child analysis which seems to me
to be offering data about the nature of the process.

The patient is a boy of eleven who was suffering from a loss of talent for school work. During his first school years, from four to six, he had been remarkably interested and successful and always top of his form; but he had gradually come to find himself very near the bottom, and at times had been totally unable to get himself to school at all.

The particular play that I wish to discuss had been preceded by a long period in which all the toys had been set out in the form of a village, full of people and animals; the boy would then bomb the village by dropping balls of burning paper upon it, my role being to play the part of the villagers, and try to save all the toys from actual destruction. The rules of the game were such that this was often very difficult, so that gradually more and more of the toys were burnt, and from time to time I had replaced them by new ones. (This boy had, in fact, lived through part of the blitz on London, and had started this play some time after my own house had been damaged by blast; and he had shown delayed interest in the extent of the damage when he came to my house for his analysis.)

In the session which I have chosen to describe, he begins by saying that we are to have two villages and a war between them, but that the war is not to begin at once. My village is to be made up of all the people and animals and houses; his of toy trucks, cars, etc., and "lots of junk and oddments to exchange", though I am to have some oddments as well. He begins by sending along a truck from his village with half a gun in it, and takes various things in exchange. He then brings a test-tube and exchanges it for a number of objects, including a little bowl, bits of metal, a ladder, etc. When I comment on the amount taken in exchange he says: "Yes, the test-tube is equal to a lot," but on the return journey to his own village he adds: "I think those people were a bit odd, I don't think I like those people much, I think I will give them just a little time-bomb." So he takes back his test-tube, sticks some matches in it, and drops it over my village. He then drops a whole box of matches on my village, and says the villagers have to find it and put it out before it explodes. But then I have to come and bomb his village, and when I drop a flare, instead of putting it out he adds fuel to it. Then he says: "You have got to bring all your people over to my village, the war is over." I have to bring the animals and people over in trucks, but at once he says they must go back because they all have to watch the burning of the whole stack of match boxes (which he has bought with his own money). He makes me stand back from the blaze, and shows great pleasure.

He now decides that his "people" (empty trucks) are to call on mine; his are explorers and mine are to think his are gods. The trucks arrive, my people have to be frightened. He tells me to make them say something; so I make the policeman ask what they want; but he replies: "You've forgotten, they think it's gods." He now borrows the "Mrs. Noah" figure from my village and stands her in one of his trucks. Then, in a god-like voice, he commands that the villagers go into their houses and prepare food.[1] It is now the end of the session and while I am beginning to tidy up he plays with some melting wax, humming to himself the hymn-tune "Praise, my soul, the King of Heaven". He smears some wax on both my thumbs and says he is double-jointed, and asks if I am too.

At first I saw this material in terms of his bisexual conflict and I tried to interpret it in that way. I told him that I thought the war between the two villages was expressing his feeling that I, as the mother, the woman, have all the human values, while he has only the mechanical ones. This interpretation linked with earlier material in which he had spent weeks making Meccano models with sets that he brought to the session, and had continually shown me the models illustrated in the handbook, assuring me that "You can make *anything* with Meccano"; but this play had stopped suddenly after he had tried to make a mechanical man, as specified in the book, and it had failed to work, i.e. move. And I had told him then how disappointed he was that he could not make a live baby out of his Meccano. So, in this village play, I pointed out how he had now attempted some rearrangement and exchange in which I was to be given some of the maleness (gun and test-tube), and he was to have something of the femaleness (ending up with getting the "Mrs. Noah" figure). I explained also how this compromise had not entirely worked, since jealousy had broken through, as was shown in his attempt to justify his impending envious attacks by saying "I don't like these people"; that is to say "I am not guilty because they are bad anyway, so it doesn't matter hurting them." Also I told him that by burning his own village he was not only punishing himself, but at the same time expressing (externalizing) the state of anxiety in which he felt full of explosive fæces which might at any

[1] I have had to omit some of the play in the middle of the session for reasons of space. It was connected with the theme of the previous months, in which there had been only one village, which he had continually bombed and burnt. I had interpreted it as partly an attempt to gain reassurance about his attacks on his mother's body, by acting them out in this comparatively harmless way and with my approval; I had also linked it with the aggression he had actually shown when his mother was pregnant.

moment blow up his own body; and added that he had returned
to the attempt to avoid the cause of jealousy by trying to mitigate the
absoluteness of his split between "mechanized" male and "human"
female. I suggested that he was trying to tell me how he could not
stand the empty, depersonalized gods (trucks), so effected a compromise by borrowing the good mother figure to fill the empty truck.
I pointed out how, after this, he could tell me that he was double-
jointed; that is, he combined both positions, and he hoped I could too.

In the next session immediately following this one, he spent the
whole hour mending his satchel, a job that he said ordinarily his
mother would do for him. Here I interpreted that the two villages
were also mother and father, and that he felt he had succeeded in
bringing them together inside him.

Certainly he did seem to be working out his conflicts about the
relation between father and mother, both internally and externally,
and trying to find ways of dealing with his jealousy and envy of his
mother in what Melanie Klein (1928) has called the "femininity
phase". Considered in this light, his mechanized village then also
stood for his feeling about his school. For at this time he was constantly complaining how utterly uninteresting and boring his school
work was, and he frequently brought material to do with waste
lands and desert places: this being in marked contrast with the early
school years during which he had been interested and successful.
Thus one way of trying to describe the situation was in terms of the
idea that the school, the place in which he must seek knowledge, had
become too much identified with the destroyed mother's body, so
that it had indeed become a desert; for the game of attacking and
burning the village had been played throughout the period of his
most acute school difficulties. But at the same time it was also too
much identified with the desired mother's body, for such material
certainly also pointed to intense conflict in the direct Œdipus situation, as well as in the "femininity phase"; and for a long time it had
seemed to me that the school difficulty was being presented largely
in these terms. Thus the entry into the world of knowledge and
school work seemed to be identified with the entry into the mother's
body, an undertaking at once demanded by the schoolmaster-father
figure but forbidden under threat of castration by the sexual rival
father. In fact one could describe the situation here in terms of the
use of symbolism as a defence, and say that because the school had
become the symbol of the forbidden mother's body this was then a
bar to progress.

The defence against the anxiety aroused by this symbolic identification took the form of a reversal of roles in his play with me; he himself became the sadistic punishing schoolmaster and I had to be the bad pupil. For days, and sometimes weeks, I had to play the role of the persecuted schoolboy: I was set long monotonous tasks, my efforts were treated with scorn, I was forbidden to talk and made to write out "lines" if I did; and if I did not comply with these demands, then he wanted to cane me. (When asked if he were really treated as badly as this at school he always said "no"; he certainly was never caned, and the school, though of the conventional pattern, did try most generously to adapt to his difficulties.) Clearly then there was a great amount of resentment and fear to be worked through in the Œdipus situation, but I did not feel this was the only reason for the persistence of this type of play. It was other aspects of the material which finally led me to see the problem as also something to do with difficulties in establishing the relation to external reality as such.

One of these was the fact that he frequently adopted a particularly bullying tone when talking to me, even when he was not playing the schoolmaster game, but he always dropped this tone as soon as he began imaginative play with the toys. This observation suggested that perhaps this boy could drop the hectoring tone, during this kind of play, because it was a situation in which he could have a different kind of relation to external reality, by means of the toys; he could do what he liked with them, and yet they were outside him. He nearly always began the session with the bullying tone and insistence that I was not ready for him at the right time, whatever the actual time of starting; but as soon as he had settled down to using the toys as a pliable medium, external to himself, but not insisting on their own separate objective existence, then apparently he could treat me with friendliness and consideration, and even accept real frustration from me.

THE RECEPTIVE ROLE OF THE TOYS

This observation set me wondering about the exact function of this relation to the toys, and in what terms it could be discussed. I noticed how, on days when he did play with the toys, there seemed to develop a relationship between him and them which reminded me of the process I had myself tried to observe introspectively when doing "free" drawings (1950). I thought that there was perhaps something useful to be said about the actual process of playing with the toys as compared with, on the one hand, pure day-dreaming, and on the other, direct expedient muscular activity directed towards a living object. In the play with the toys there was something half-way between day-dreaming and purposeful instinctive or expedient action. As soon as he moved a toy in response to some wish or phantasy then the play-village was different, and the new sight set off a new set of possibilities; just as in free imaginative drawing, the sight of a mark made on the paper provokes new associations, the line as it were answers back and functions as a very primitive type of external object.

About two months after the war-of-the-villages play something occurred which seemed to offer a further clue as to what was happening when he played with the toys; for the bullying tone suddenly vanished for four days, beginning with a day when he told me about something that had happened at school which clearly gave him great pleasure. For many weeks before he had been intensely preoccupied with a photography club that he and his particular friends had organized in their out-of-school hours; now he reported that their form master had given him permission to hold their meetings in school, during a time set aside for special activities, and had even given them a little room in which to work.

This sudden disappearance of his dictatorship attitude gave me the idea that the fact of his spontaneously created activity being incorporated in the framework of the school routine was a fulfilling, in external life, of the solution foreshadowed in the war between the villages play. What he had felt to be the mechanized, soulless world of school had now seemed to him to have become humanized, by the taking into its empty trucks of a bit of himself, something that he had created. But what was particularly interesting was the fact that he had only been able to respond to the school's gesture at this particular moment; for there had been many efforts on their part to help him before this, such as special coaching after his continual absences. One could of course say that it was because of the strength of his own aggression and his anxiety about it, that he had not been able to make more use of the help offered; but it seemed to me that these earlier efforts on the part of the school had not had more apparent effect also because they had not taken the particular form of the incorporation of, acceptance of, a bit of his own spontaneous creation. Now the school, by being receptive, by being in-giving as well as out-giving, had shown itself capable of good mothering; it was a male world which had become more like his mother, who had in fact

92

been a very good mother. Much earlier he had foreshadowed this same need by one of his rare dreams, in which his mother had been present at school in his Latin class, Latin being the bugbear of his school subjects.

This view of the meaning of the villages play as partly to do with problems of this boy's whole relation to what was, for him, the un-mitigated not-me-ness of his school life, threw light on one of the elements in the original situation when his difficulties first became apparent. Not only had his father been called away to the war just at the time when his baby brother had been born and when London was being bombed, but he had also lost his most valued toy, a woolly rabbit. As the analysis advanced I had come to realize how significant this loss had been, for it became more clear that one of my main roles in the transference was to be the lost rabbit. He so often treated me as totally his own to do what he liked with, as though I were dirt, his dirt, or as a tool, an extension of his own hand. (He had never been a thumb sucker.) If I was not free the moment he arrived, even though he was often thirty minutes early, I was re-primanded or threatened with punishment for being late. In fact it certainly did seem that for a very long time he did need to have the illusion that I was part of himself.

PLAY AND THE BOUNDARY BETWEEN INNER AND OUTER

Here I tried to review the various psycho-analytic concepts of mechanisms that can be forerunners of or defences against object relations, and see which might be useful to explain what was hap-pening. Certainly he split himself and put the bad bit of himself into me when he punished me as the pupil. Certainly he used threatening words which were intended to enter into me and cow me into doing what he wanted and being his slave. Certainly he tried to make me play the role of the all-gratifying idealized phantasy object; he once told me that he did feel himself quite special and that the frustrating things that happened to other people would not happen to him. I thought that this did mean that he felt at times that he had this mar-vellous object inside him which would protect and gratify him. And this linked with the fact that he would sometimes hum hymn tunes, such as "Praise, my soul, the King of Heaven", although he explicitly expressed great scorn for religion. Certainly also he found it very difficult to maintain the idea of my separate identity; in his demands

93

he continually denied the existence of my other patients or any family ties. The way he behaved could also be described by saying that he kept me inside him, since he continually used to insist that I knew what he had been doing or was going to do, when I had in fact no possible means of knowing. Yet I did not feel that these ways of talking about what happened were entirely adequate; for all of them take for granted the idea of a clear boundary, if I am felt to be inside him then he has a boundary, and the same if a bit of him is felt to be projected into me.

But there was much material in this analysis to do with burning, boiling down, and melting, which seemed to me to express the idea of the obliteration of boundaries. And I had a growing amount of evidence, both from clinical material and introspective study of problems in painting, that the variations in the feeling of the existence or non-existence of the body boundary are themselves very important. In this connection Scott (1949) restates Winnicott's view (1945, 1948) about how a good mother allows the child to fuse its predisposition to hallucinate a good situation with the earliest sensations of a good situation. Scott then describes this as an "oscillation between the illusion of union and the fact of contact, which is another way of describing the discovery of an interface, a boundary, or a place of contact, and perhaps at the same time is another way of describing the discovery of 'the me' and 'the you' ". He goes on to say "But I think only a partial picture of union and contact is given by discussing the good situation. Equally important is the evil union and the evil contact and the discovery of the evil me and the evil you."[1] He also talks of the extremes of the states in which all discriminations and interfaces are destroyed as in what he calls "cosmic

[1]Winnicott, in a private communication, states that he does not entirely agree with Scott's restatement of his view, as quoted above. He adds the following modification:

"I agree with Scott's comment only if he is looking back at early infancy, starting from the adult (or child). Regression is a painful and precarious business partly because the individual regressing goes back with experiences of forward emotional development and with more or less knowledge in his pocket. For the person regressed there must be a denial of 'evil union' and of 'evil me' and 'evil you' when an 'ideal union' between 'good self' and 'good mother' is being lived (in the highly specialized therapeutic environment provided, or in the insane state).

"This begs the whole question, however, of the earliest stages of an individual's emotional development studied there and then. For an infant, at the start, there is no good or bad, only a not yet de-fused object. One could think of separation as the cause of the first *idea* of union; before this there's union but no *idea* of union, and here the terms good and bad have no function. For union of this kind, so important for the founding of the mental health of the individual, the mother's active adaptation is an absolute necessity, an active adaptation to the infant's needs which can only come about through the mother's devotion to the infant.

"Less than good enough adaptation on the part of a mother to her infant's needs at this very early stage leads (it seems to me) to the premature ego-development, the precocious abandonment of illusion of which M. Milner writes in this paper."

94

bliss" and "catastrophic chaos". And these extremes relate, I think, to behaviourist observations that can be made, both in and out of analysis, of the variations of facial expression between extreme beauty and extreme ugliness. I had, for instance, a child patient of six who would at times show an extremely seraphic face, and it occurred in connection with great concentration on the use or lack of use of outline in painting. I also observed a schizophrenic patient (adult) who would at times have moments of startling physical beauty counterbalanced by moments of something startlingly repellent.

One could certainly think of this phenomenon in terms of complete union with a marvellous or atrocious inner object, with the obliteration of inner boundaries between the ego and the incorporated object. But there was also the question of where the actual body boundary was felt to be. Did it mean that the skin was felt to include the whole world and therefore in a sense was denied altogether? Certainly the introspective quality of what have been called oceanic states seems to include this feeling, as does also the catastrophic chaos that Scott refers to. For the schizophrenic patient described above constantly complained that she could not get the world outside her and that this, rather than being a source of bliss, was agony to her. Certainly there is very much here that I do not understand. Also the whole question of beauty appearing in analysis, perceived by the analyst either as a varying physical quality of the patient or as a quality of the material, has not been much discussed in the literature, though Sharpe (1937) does mention dreams that the patient describes as beautiful. When perceived by the analyst it can clearly be described in terms of the counter-transference, and used, just as any other aspect of the counter-transference can be used (Paula Heimann, 1950), as part of the analytic data. Thus in trying to understand all that this boy was trying to show me I had to take into account the fact that at times there was a quality in his play which I can only describe as beautiful—occasions when it was he who did the stage managing and it was my imagination which caught fire. It was in fact play with light and fire. He would close the shutters of the room and insist that it be lit only by candle light, sometimes a dozen candles arranged in patterns, or all grouped together in a solid block. And then he would make what he called furnaces, with a very careful choice of what ingredients should make the fire, including dried leaves from special plants in my garden; and sometimes all the ingredients had to be put in a metal cup on the electric fire and stirred continuously, all this carried out in the half darkness of candle light. And often there had to be a sacrifice, a lead soldier had to be added to the fire, and this figure was spoken of either as the victim or the sacrifice. In fact, all this type of play had a dramatic ritual quality comparable to the fertility rites described by Frazer in primitive societies. And this effect was the more striking because this boy's conscious interests were entirely conventional for his age; he was absorbed in Meccano and model railways.

ÆSTHETIC EXPERIENCE AND THE MERGING OF THE BOUNDARY

The fact that in this type of material the boy's play nearly became "a play", in that there was a sense of pattern and dramatic form in what he produced, leads to many questions about the relation of a work of art to analytic work, which are not relevant here. But the particular point I wish to select for further consideration is that he seemed to me to be trying to express the idea of integration, in a variety of different ways. Thus the fire seemed to be here not only a destructive fire but also the fire of Eros; and not only the figurative expression of his own passionate body feelings, not only the phantasy representative of the wish for passionate union with the external object, but also a way of representing the inner fire of concentration. The process in which interest is withdrawn temporarily from the external world so that the inner work of integration can be carried out was, I think, shown by the boiling or melting down of the various ingredients in what he called "the fire cup", to make a new whole. And the sacrifice of the toy soldier by melting it down both expressed the wish to get rid of a bad internal object, particularly the cramping and cruel aspect of his super-ego, and also his sense of the need to absorb his inner objects into his ego and so modify them. But in addition to this I think it represented his feeling of the need to be able, at times, to transcend the common-sense ego; for common sense was very strong in him, his conscious attitude was one of feet firmly planted on the ground. For instance, when he did tell a dream, which was rarely, he usually apologized if it was at all nonsensical. And formerly also this boy had told me that he was "no good at art" and he was extremely tentative in any attempts at drawing. But later this changed. For he told me one day, with pride, that he was good at both science and art, which he felt was not very usual amongst his schoolfellows; though he was still inclined to be apologetic about his æsthetic experiences. When he told me of the delight he took in the colours of the various crystals he had studied in his chemistry he added, "It's childish to like them so much."

Although an important factor in this development of his capacity to feel himself "good at art" was his growing belief in his power to restore his injured objects, this is not the aspect of the material that I wish to discuss here; for I am concentrating on the earlier problem of establishing object relationships at all, rather than on the restoration of the injured object once it is established. Granted that these two are mutually interdependent and that anxiety in the one phase can cause regression to the earlier one, there is still much to be said about the earlier phase as such. Thus a central idea began to emerge about what this boy was trying to tell me; it was the idea that the basic identifications which make it possible to find new objects, to find the familiar in the unfamiliar, require an ability to tolerate a temporary loss of sense of self, a temporary giving up of the discriminating ego which stands apart and tries to see things objectively and rationally and without emotional colouring. It perhaps requires a state of mind which has been described by Berenson (1950) as "the æsthetic moment".

"In visual art the æsthetic moment is that fleeting instant, so brief as to be almost timeless, when the spectator is at one with the work of art he is looking at, or with actuality of any kind that the spectator himself sees in terms of art, as form and colour. He ceases to be his ordinary self, and the picture or building, statue, landscape, or æsthetic actuality is no longer outside himself. The two become one entity; time and space are abolished and the spectator is possessed by one awareness. When he recovers workaday consciousness it is as if he had been initiated into illuminating, formative mysteries."

Now I think it is possible to add something to my attempts to describe what happened in this boy during the play when his whole behaviour to me changed, and to link this with what an artist or a poet does. For observations in analysis suggest that experiences of the kind described by Berenson are not confined to the contemplation of works of art, but that art provides a method, in adult life, for reproducing states that are part of everyday experience in healthy infancy. Sometimes poets have explicitly related such states to their early experience: for instance, Traherne, and also Wordsworth, in his note on "Intimations of Immortality from Recollections of Early

Marion Milner

Childhood". Thus Wordsworth says that as a child he was unable to think of external things as having external existence, he communed with all he saw as something not apart from but inherent in his own immaterial nature; when going to school he would often grasp at a wall to recall himself from the abyss of idealism. I suggest that it is useful, in child analysis, to look out for the ways in which the child may be trying to express such experiences, when he has not yet sufficient command of words to tell what he feels, directly, but can only use words or whatever other media the play-room offers him, figuratively: for instance, as this child used candle light and fire and the activities of melting and burning, as well as the actual toys. And I think it may be useful also to bear in mind that if, when talking about this state, one uses only those concepts, such as introjection and projection, which presuppose the existence of the organism within its boundaries in a world of other organisms within boundaries, one may perhaps distort one's perception of the phenomenon. Thus it is important not to forget the obvious fact that we know the boundaries exist but the child does not; in the primal state, it is only gradually and intermittently that he discovers them; and on the way to this he uses play. Later, he keeps his perception of the world from becoming fixed, and no longer capable of growth, by using art, either as artist or as audience; and he may also use psychoanalysis. For, as Rank (1932) says, art and play both link the world of "subjective unreality" and "objective reality", harmoniously fusing the edges but not confusing them. So the developing human being becomes able deliberately to allow illusions about what he is seeing to occur; he allows himself to experience, within the enclosed space-time of the drama or the picture or the story or the analytic hour, a transcending of that common-sense perception which would see a picture as only an attempt at photography, or the analyst as only a present-day person.

THE NEED FOR A MEDIUM BETWEEN THE SELF-CREATED AND
EXTERNAL REALITIES

What I want to suggest here is that these states are a necessary phase in the development of object relationships and that the understanding of their function gives a meaning to the phrase "Art creates Nature". In this connection a later phase in the transference phenomena shown by this boy is relevant. It was after he had become deeply interested in chemistry that there occurred in analysis, for several weeks, a repeated catechism. He would say "What is your name?" and I would have to say "What is my name?" Then he would answer with the name of some chemical, and I would say "What is there about that?" And he would answer "It's lovely stuff, I've made it!"; and sometimes he would give me the name of the chemical which is used as a water-softener.

Here then is the link with the artist's use of his medium, what the *Concise Oxford Dictionary* defines as an "intervening substance through which impressions are conveyed to the senses"; and this pliable stuff that can be made to take the shape of one's phantasies, can include the "stuff" of sound and breath which becomes our speech. (This boy would sometimes tell me that I was a gas, or that he was going to dissolve me down or evaporate me till I became one.) So it seemed that he had become able to use both me and the play-room equipment as this intervening pliable substance; he had become able to do with these what Caudwell (1937) says the poet does with words, when he uses them to give the organism an appetitive interest in external reality, when he makes the earth become charged with affective colouring and glow with a strange emotional fire.

As regards the use of the medium of speech,[1] there was a stage, after the war of the villages play, when it was very difficult to get this boy to talk. He would play, but silently, and when he did talk, it was always to try and teach me something; sometimes it was the language of chemistry, which he knew and I did not. And this I think expressed the need of the artist in him (and also the scientist, for he soon became determined to make science his career) to have a bit of his own experience incorporated in the social world, just as he had been able to have his own club incorporated in the world of school. For, as Caudwell points out, the artist is acutely aware of the discrepancy between, on the one hand, all the ways of expressing feeling that are provided by the current development of speech and art, in our

---

[1] Unfortunately I was not able, before writing this paper, to read S. Langer's (1942) detailed discussion of the nature and function of symbolism, as it was not yet published in England and I could not obtain a copy. Had I been able to obtain the book in time I would have made specific reference to some of Langer's statements about speech and symbolism. Particularly relevant to my problem is her emphasis on the advantages of small sounds made with part of one's own body as a medium for symbol formation. One of these advantages is the intrinsic unimportance, in their own right, of these sounds. This relates to my point about the effectiveness of the toys as a medium for thought and communication being due to their pliability; that is, that their real qualities are unimportant for practical expedient living, so they can be given arbitrary or conventional meanings and thus be used as a language. I would also like to have elaborated on the relation of Langer's conception of the function of symbols to Jung's (1933) and to have considered the bearing of both on the material presented here.

particular culture and epoch; and, on the other hand, our changing experiences that are continually outstripping the available means of expression. Thus the artist wishes to cast his private experiences in such form that they will be incorporated in the social world of art and so lessen the discrepancy. Caudwell points out that it is not only the artist who feels this discrepancy and not only the discrepancy between feeling and current forms of expression of it; it is also the scientist, in respect not of feeling, but of perception and currently accepted ways of formulating it, currently accepted views of "reality", who wishes to contribute something of his own to the changing symbols of science. Perhaps even he must do this if the already discovered symbols are to become fully significant for him.

EFFECTS OF PREMATURE LOSS OF BELIEF IN THE SELF–CREATED
REALITY

The phenomenon of treating the world as one's own creation is mentioned by Fenichel. He says:

"There always remain certain traces of the original objectless condition, or at least a longing for it ('oceanic feeling'). Introjection is an attempt to make parts of the external world flow into the ego. Projection, by putting unpleasant sensations into the external world, also attempts to reverse the separation of ego from non-ego."

And he goes on to refer to the child who "when playing hide-and-seek closes his eyes and believes he now cannot be seen". Fenichel then says, "The archaic animistic conception of the world which is based on a confusion of ego and non-ego is thus illustrated."

Although there are differences of opinion about what he calls here "the original objectless condition", about whether or not there is some primitive object relation from the very beginning, which alternates with the "objectless" or fused condition, I think Fenichel's description is valuable. The example of the child playing hide-and-seek vividly shows the belief in a self-created reality; just as analytical material shows related phenomena such as the child's belief that when he opens his eyes and sees the world, he thereby creates it, he feels it is the lovely (or horrible) stuff that he has made.

The idea that these states of illusion of oneness are perhaps a recurrently necessary phase in the continued growth of the sense of twoness leads to a further question: What happens when they are prevented from occurring with sufficient frequency or at the right moments?

This boy had had in general a very good home and been much loved. But he had suffered very early environmental thwartings in the feeding situation. In the early weeks of his life his mother had had too little milk and the nurse had been in the habit of not getting the supplementary feed ready in time, so that he had had to wait to finish his meal and had shown great distress: an experience that was re-lived in the transference, when whatever time I was ready for him, he always said I was too late.

Although it is obvious that a child must suffer frustration, there is still something to be said about the way in which it should occur and the timing of it. I suggest that, if, through the pressure of un-satisfied need, the child has to become aware of his separate identity too soon or too continually, then either the illusion of union can be what Scott calls catastrophic chaos rather than cosmic bliss, or the illusion is given up and premature ego-development may occur; then separateness and the demands of necessity may be apparently accepted, but necessity becomes a cage rather than something to be co-operated with for the freeing of further powers. With this boy it was clear how the imposed necessities, regulations, non-self-chosen tasks, of a conventional school, had provided a setting for a repetition of his first difficulties in relation to the environment. In fact he often told me what his ideal school would be like, and it amounted to being taught by a method very like what modern educationists call the project method.

If one asks the question, what factors play an essential part in the process of coming to recognize a world that is outside oneself, not one's own creation, there is one that I think has not been much stressed in the literature. Thus, in addition to the physical facts of the repeated bodily experiences of being separated from the loved object, and being together with it, and the repeated physical experiences of interchange with the not-self world, breathing, feeding, eliminating: in addition to the gradually growing capacity to tolerate the difference between the feeling of oneness, of being united with everything, and the feeling of twoness, of self and object, there is the factor of a capacity in the environment. It is the capacity of the environment to foster this growth, by providing conditions in which a recurrent partial return to the feeling of being one is possible; and I suggest that the environment does this by the recurrent providing of a framed space and time and a pliable medium, so that, on occasions, it will not be necessary for self-preservation's sake to distinguish clearly between inner and outer, self and not-self. I wish to suggest that it was his need for this capacity in the environment that my patient was telling me about in his village play, when he said there was to be a war, "but not yet". It was as if he were saying that the true battle with the environment, the creative struggle of interacting opposites, could not begin, or be effectively continued, until there had also been established his right to a recurrent merging of the opposites. And until this was established necessity was indeed a mechanized god, whose service was not freedom but a colourless slavery.

Looked at in this way the boy's remark, "I don't like those people", was not only due to a denial of an uprush of feared uncontrollable jealousy and envy, it represented also the re-enactment of a memory or memories of a near breakdown of relationship to the outside world. It was the memory, I suggest, of actual experience of a too sudden breaking in on the illusion of oneness, an intrusion which had had the effect of preventing the emergence from primary narcissism occurring gradually in the child's own time. But it represented also a later situation; for the premature ego-development, referred to by Melanie Klein as inhibiting the development of symbolization (or, in Jones's terms, of symbolic equivalents) was also brought about by the impingement of the war. For the sake of self-preservation, it had been necessary for him continually and clearly to distinguish between external and internal reality, to attend to the real qualities of the symbol too soon. Thus it was reported to me that this boy had shown remarkable fortitude when, with his father away in the Navy, he and his baby brother and mother had lived through the blitz on London. And also, later on, his reports indicated that he was very self-controlled in school, in that situation where self-preservation demands a fairly continual hold upon objectivity, since day-dreaming and treating the external world as part of one's dream are not easily tolerated by schoolmasters. But the fact that this amount of objectivity was only achieved at a fairly high cost in anxiety was shown in his analysis, for at one time he was continually punishing me for imagined lapses into forgetfulness, inattention, unpunctuality. It was only later that he was able to tell me about what he now called his absentmindedness, in a tolerant way and without anxiety.

IMPLICATIONS FOR TECHNIQUE

The considerations I have tried to formulate here are not only matters for theory, they have direct bearings upon technique. With this boy there was always the question of whether to emphasize, in interpreting, the projection mechanisms and persecutory defences and to interpret the aggression as such; but when I did this the aggression did not seem to lessen and I was sometimes in despair at its quite implacable quality. At times he treated me as if I were like the man in the Bible from whom a devil was driven out, but into whom seven more came, so that he went on attacking me with almost the fervour of a holy war. But when I began to think along the lines described above, even though I knew that I was not succeeding in putting these ideas clearly into words in my interpretations, the aggression did begin to lessen and the continual battle over the time of the beginning of each session disappeared. Of course I may be mistaken in thinking that the change in the boy's behaviour which accompanied the change in my idea of the problem was a matter of cause and effect, since the issue is very complicated and brings in many debatable questions of theory. But I think that it was significant that, near the end of his analysis, this boy told me that when he was grown up and earning his own living he would give me a papier-mâché chemical clock, which would keep perfect time and would be his own invention. He said it would be of papier-mâché because I had an ornament, a little Indian dog, made of this, and also I remembered how he himself had tried, during his play with me, to make papier-mâché bowls, but unsuccessfully. Granted that the idea of the giving of the clock stood for many things, including returning to me the restored breast and restored penis, and also represented his gratitude for the recovery of his own potency, I thought he was telling me something else as well. I thought that the malleability of the papier-mâché provided him with a way of expressing how he felt about part of the curative factor in his analysis. It was his way of saying how, in the setting of the analytic play-room, he had been able to find a bit of the external world that was malleable; he had found that it was safe to treat it as a bit of himself, and so had let it serve as a bridge between inner and outer. And it was through this, I suggest, as well as through the interpretations I had given about the content of his wishes towards outer and inner objects, that he had become able to accept the real qualities of externality, objective time standing as the chief representative of these. And in those phases when he could not make this bridge, because the fact that I had to work to a time-table forced on him an objective reality that he was not yet ready for, then I became merely the gap into which he projected all his "bad" wishes, or internal objects representing these. When he could not feel that he had "made" me, that I was his lovely stuff, then I was the opposite, not only bad but also alien, and bad because alien; so I became the receptacle for all that he felt was alien to his ego in himself, all the "devil" parts of himself that he was frightened of and so had to repudiate. It seemed as if it was only by being able, again and again, to experience the illusion that I was part of himself, fused with the goodness that he could conceive of internally, that he became able to tolerate a goodness that was not his own creation and to allow me goodness independently. Exactly how an infant does come to tolerate a goodness that is recognized to exist independently of himself seems to me to have not yet been entirely satisfactorily explained; though the factor of the relief obtained from giving up the illusion of omnipotence is mentioned in the literature and was clearly apparent in this boy. The repeated discovery that I went on being friendly, and remained unhurt by him, in spite of the continual attacks on me, certainly played a very important part. For instance, there was another ritual catechism which would begin with "Why are you a fool?" and I had to say, "Why am I a fool?" Then he would answer, "Because I say so". Clearly if he had to feel that all the foolishness of adults was his doing, as well as their goodness, then he was going to bear a heavy burden. But I think he could not proceed to the stage of experiencing the relief of disillusion until he had also had sufficient time both to experience and to become conscious of the previous stage; he had to become aware that he was experiencing the stage of fusion before he could reach the relief of de-fusion. And it was only when he could become conscious of the relief of de-fusion that we were then able to reach his depression about injuries that he had felt he was responsible for, both internally and externally, in his family situation and in relation to me.

On looking back it seems to me that the greatest progress in his analysis came when I, on the basis of the above considerations, was able to deal with the negative counter-transference. At first, without really being aware of it, I had taken for granted the view of infantile omnipotence which is described by Fenichel:

"Yet even after speech, logic, and the reality principle have been established we find that pre-logical thinking is still in operation and even beyond the role it plays in states of ego regression or as a form of purposeful distortion. It no longer fulfils, it is true, the function of preparing for future actions but becomes, rather, a *substitute* for unpleasant reality."

I had accepted this view but grown rather tired of being continually treated by this boy as his gas, his breath, his fæces, and had wondered how long the working through of this phase would take. But when I began to suspect that Fenichel was wrong here, and that this pre-logical fusion of subject and object does continue to have a function of preparing for future action, when I began to see and to interpret, as far as I could, that this use of me might be not only a defensive regression, but an essential recurrent phase in the development of a creative relation to the world, then the whole character of the analysis changed; the boy then gradually became able to allow the external object, represented by me, to exist in its own right.

Caudwell says that the artist and the scientist

"are men who acquire a special experience of life—affective with the artist, perceptual with the scientist—which negates the common ego or the common social world, and therefore requires refashioning of these worlds to include the new experience."

This boy had, I think, indicated the nature of this process by his reaction to the school's refashioning of a tiny bit of itself and its routines. For this had happened in response to the vividness of his belief in the validity of his own experience; a vividness which also had contributed to a refashioning in me of some of my analytic ideas.

Conclusion

On the basis of the study of such material as I have described here, and also from my own experiments in painting, I came to see the pertinence of Melanie Klein's statement that symbolization is the basis of all talents; that is, that it is the basis of those skills by which we relate ourselves to the world around us. To try to restrict the meaning of the word symbolization, as some writers tend to do, to the use of the symbol for purposes of distortion, may have the advantage of simplification, but it has other disadvantages. One of these is that it causes unnecessary confusion when one tries to communicate with workers in related disciplines, such as epistemology, æsthetics, and the philosophy of science; it interferes with what might be a valuable collaboration in the work of clarifying some of the obscure issues about the nature of thought. This isolation of psycho-analysis, by its terminology, from related fields, may not have been a disadvantage in the early days of the struggle to establish analytic concepts in their own right, but now such isolation, can, I think, lead to an impoverishment of our own thinking.

Another advantage of not limiting the meaning of the word symbol to a defensive function would be a clarification of theory by bringing it more in line with our practice. The analytic rule that the patient shall try to put all that he is aware of into words does seem to me to imply a belief in the importance of symbolization for maturity as well as for infancy; it implies the recognition that words are in fact symbols by means of which the world is comprehended. Thus in the daily battle with our patients over the transference we are asking them to accept a symbolic relation to the analyst instead of a literal one, to accept the symbolism of speech and talking about their wants rather than taking action to satisfy them directly. And, as all analytic experience shows, it is when the patient becomes able to talk about all that he is aware of, when he *can* follow the analytic rule, then in fact he becomes able to relate himself more adequately to the world outside. As he becomes able to tolerate more fully the difference between the symbolic reality of the analytic relationship and the literal reality of libidinal satisfaction outside the frame of the session, then he becomes better.

POSTSCRIPT

After completing this paper I began the analysis of another child, also aged eleven, who presented a somewhat similar problem of persistence in what looked like aggressive attacks. This child, a girl, fervently and defiantly scribbled over every surface she could find. Although it looked as if it were done in anger, interpretation in terms of aggression only led to increase in the defiance. In fact, the apparent defiance did not change until I began to guess that the trouble was less to do with fæces given in anger and meant to express anger, than with fæces given in love and meant to express love. In this sense it was a battle over how she was to communicate her love, a battle over what kind of medium she was going to use for the language of love. So intense were her feelings about this that, after the first two days of analysis, she did not speak to me again, except when outside the play-room, for six months, although she would often write down what she wanted to say. Gradually I had come to look at the scribbling in the following way: by refusing to discriminate and claiming the right to scribble over everything, she was trying to deny the discrepancy between the feeling and the expression of it; by denying completely my right to protect any of my property from defacement she was even trying to win me over to her original belief that when she gave her messes lovingly they were literally as lovely as the feelings she had in the giving of them. In terms of the theory of symbolism, she was struggling with the problem of the identity of the symbol and the thing symbolized, in the particular case of bodily excretions as symbols for psychic and psychosomatic experiences. She was also struggling with the very early problem of coming to discriminate not only between the lovely feelings in giving the mess and the mess itself, but also between the product and the organ which made it.

When I began to consider what she was doing in these terms I also became able to see the boy's battle of the villages in a wider perspective. Both the children were struggling with the problem of how to communicate the ecstasies of loving, as well as the agonies; and the boy's "lovely stuff" was certainly both the lovely stuff of his lovely dreams *and* his lovely sensations which, at one level, he could only think of in terms of "lovely" fæces. The phrase "denial by idealization" is familiar, but the denial here is, I suggest, in the nature of the mess, not in the nature of the psychic experience of which it is the symbol. For this is the maximum experience of joy, ecstasy, which is a psychic fact, a capacity for heavenly or god-like experience possessed by everyone. The psychic agony came, and the anger, when this boy had to face the fact that there was discrepancy between the objective qualities of his messes, that is, how they looked to other people, and his subjective evaluation of them as actually being the same as the god-like experiences. Thus both children were struggling with the agony of disillusion in giving up their belief that everyone must see in their dirt what they see in it: "my people" are to see his empty trucks and "think it's gods". In fact, he is saying what the poet Yeats said: "Tread softly, because you tread on my dreams."

But was this struggle to make me see as they saw in essence any different from the artist's struggle to communicate his private vision? I have suggested that both the artist and the scientist are more acutely aware than the "average" man of the inadequacies of what Caudwell calls "the common ego", the commonly accepted body of know-ledge and ways of thinking about and expressing experience, more sensitive to the gap between what can be talked about and the actuality of experience. If this is true, then it is also true to say that what is in the beginning only a subjective private vision can become to future generations, objectivity. Thus the battle between the villages seemed to me to be not only a symbolic dramatization of the battle of love and hate, the struggle with ambivalency towards the object, but also a genuine work of dramatic art, in which the actual process by which the world is created, for all of us, is poetically represented.

The battle over communicating the private vision, when the battleground is the evaluation of the body products, has a peculiar poignancy. In challenging the accepted objective view and claiming the right to make others share their vision, there is a danger which is perhaps the sticking point in the development of many who would otherwise be creative people. For to win this battle, when fought on this field, would mean to seduce the world to madness, to denial of the difference between cleanliness and dirt, organization and chaos. Thus in one sense the battle is a very practical one; it is over what is a suitable and convenient stuff for symbols to be made of; but at the same time it is also a battle over the painful recognition that, if the lovely stuff is to convey the lovely feelings, there must be work done on the material.

REFERENCES

BERENSON, B., *Æsthetics and History*. London, Constable, 1950.
CAUDWELL, C., *Illusion and Reality*. London, Lawrence and Wishart, 1937.
FENICHEL, O., *The Psycho-Analytic Theory of Neurosis*. London, Kegan Paul, 1946.
HEIMANN, PAULA, "On Counter Transference", *Int. J. Psycho-Anal.*, Vol. XXXI, 1950.
JONES, E., *Papers on Psycho-Analysis*. London, Baillière, Tindall and Cox, 1948.
JUNG, C., *Psychological Types*. London, Kegan Paul, 1933.
KLEIN, MELANIE, *Contributions to Psycho-Analysis, 1921–45*. London, Hogarth Press, 1948.
LANGER, SUSAN, *Philosophy in a New Key*. Cambridge, Harvard University Press, 1942.
MILNER, MARION, (JOANNA FIELD), *On Not Being Able to Paint*. London, Heinemann, 1950.
RANK, O., *Art and Artists*. New York, Knopf, 1932.
READ, H., "Psycho-Analysis and the Problem of Æsthetic Value", *Int. J. Psycho-Anal.*, Vol. XXXII, 1951.
—— *Art and the Evolution of Man*. London, Freedom Press, 1951.
SCOTT, W. C. M., "The Body Scheme in Psychotherapy", *Brit. J. of Med. Psych.*, Vol. XXII, 1949.
SHARPE, ELLA F., *Dream Analysis*. London, Hogarth Press, 1937.
WINNICOTT, D. W., "Primitive Emotional Development", *Int. J. Psycho-Anal.*, Vol. XXVI, 1945.
—— "Pediatrics and Psychiatry", *Brit. J. of Med. Psych.*, Vol. XXII, 1948.
WORDSWORTH, WILLIAM, Preface to *Lyrical Ballads*, 1798.

6

STEPS IN EGO-INTEGRATION OBSERVED IN A PLAY-ANALYSIS

LOIS MUNRO

I T is the purpose of this paper to demonstrate the connection between the severe disturbance of emotion and the lack of ego-integration in a boy of three years of age.

By giving a brief account of his history and general behaviour it is intended to show that up to the age of three years, when his analysis began, there was evidence of a profoundly disorganized ego. Material has been selected from the first, third, and eighth months of the analysis to illustrate the contention that the strength and character of his destructive impulses, with their attendant anxieties and defences, had led to a particular state of disorganization. This was responsible for the child's unawareness of having a self.

By the eighth month of analysis the child had developed considerably both in the sphere of object relationships and of sublimations. I shall describe the steps by which these changes were brought about and seek to demonstrate the mechanism of the underlying process of ego-integration.

HISTORY

Colin's parents did not recognize their child's illness until he was nearly three years of age. His baby sister Katy was born when he was two years and eight months old, and it was by comparison with her that they realized how seriously disturbed he was, and always had been. I shall refer later to the part his mother's own emotional difficulties played in the long denial of her son's illness. However, once she could acknowledge this she sought advice and proved very co-operative. She gave me at the beginning of the analysis the following full and detailed history.

Colin's birth was protracted. There were signs of fœtal distress which alarmed the midwife, who in turn frightened his mother. This midwife, who was engaged to stay for a month as nurse, was not only exceedingly over-anxious but clumsy and incompetent in her handling of the new baby. The parents, too, found her disturbing, and only managed after a battle to get rid of her a fortnight after the baby was born. During the first four months the baby hardly slept; he cried continuously, and was constipated. There was breast milk for him so long as his mother rested in bed. For at least an hour after each feed in the first two weeks the midwife "banged his back to bring up the wind". Even when she left, feeding was an endless struggle. He was fed on demand with breast and bottle, but was so slow in taking his food that there seemed to be no time of the day when he was not being fed. At ten months he began to "eat like a horse", but his appetite started to decline at his first birthday coincidentally with his mother becoming pregnant. When Colin was fourteen months old she miscarried, and by fifteen months his eating was severely inhibited, and remained so. At three years of age, when he started analysis, meals were long-drawn-out conflicts; he would never feed himself, demanded that food should be prepared in a "special" way, turned away from it, and then had a temper-tantrum because he was not being fed. He did not give up his night bottle until he was nearly three years old.

Save for an attack of gastro-enteritis at four months, he was generally constipated, passing hard motions. By means of diet and mild medication his motions were kept soft, but he always passed them incontinently. He never used his pot until he first saw his baby sister do so; he was two years and nine months old at the time. From then onwards, he used it to produce daily, after lunch, an exceptionally large motion, which he showed with great pride to each member of the household, demanding that they should admire it. However, at other times he continued to let his fæces drop from him all over the house, apparently unaware of what he was doing. He wore nappies until he was nearly three years old, and was unhappy at parting with them. He was never dry by night or by day.

Colin's development was slow; he was still lying when he was nine months old, not because he could not sit up, but because he wanted someone to pull him up. Sleep was always broken and, as he grew older, he developed an obsessional ritual. He would call for his mother to come to his room, in order to pick up a fallen toy, or to give him a drink of water. Half an hour after this he would come into her bed, lie there without movement and forbid her to touch him. He then returned to his room, only to repeat the ritual an hour or so later.

At eighteen months old he had a severe traumatic experience, when flying to America with his parents. He became acutely terrified, screamed the whole time and had what appeared to be a fit. Unfortunately, his four cellular blankets, called "Nammies", which he had sucked and eaten since he was seven months old, had been washed. This distressed him considerably and, though he accepted them, he never sucked or ate them again. On landing he clutched both parents with his hands, refusing to be parted from them even when they went to the lavatory. This necessitated all three of them going everywhere together. After this journey he seemed to be unable to make contact with people other than his parents, and when any of his American cousins played with him he lay on the ground and whimpered.

A nanny was employed when he was two years and four months old, that is, four months before his sister's birth. For three of these months he would not let her do anything for him; he then became very fond of her and treated her as his property. Though he was told of the baby's coming, he was very frightened and upset when he first saw her. Later he climbed into his mother's bed with tears running down his cheeks, looking like "a broken-hearted old man". He paid little attention to his sister, save to remark that he hated her crying.

He was always sensitive to correction, and became acutely distressed when anything was broken. He pleaded with his parents to tell him it was not damaged, or begged his father to mend it. He taught himself letters and colours, but did not play by himself: he would say: "You do it", while he watched. He had a few words, but did not use them to converse with people or to answer their questions.

He was extremely fond of his father, especially admiring him for his skill in mending and constructing. His relationship with his mother was chiefly concerned with getting her to comply with his obsessional demands and rituals. He showed little need to receive affection from her or to give any himself, but if he was parted from her for any time in the day, he appeared white and strained when next they met. His mother summed up the situation in the following words: "We have two children and two different lives for each. Colin's is organized independently from his sister's because he has to have it so, and it is easier for us all this way." Thus, it was his parents' policy to fall in with his obsessional demands, since to refuse led to such a state of anxiety in the child.

He masturbated openly to the accompaniment of violent rocking, and with yells and shrieks. This stopped abruptly after he had seen his sister bathed for the first time. But his parents noticed that he used to rock and roll whenever he was put into a room by himself, the only form of punishment they employed.

TECHNIQUE

In the consultation interview with Colin's mother before starting the analysis, I asked her for the names he had for the members of his family. These were: Mummy, Daddy, Katy, and Nanny. I learned that he had never had a name for himself, but on his sister's birth, when he was two years and eight months old, he called himself Katy. He only began to call himself Col, short for Colin, three months later, just before his third birthday. I also asked what he called the different parts of his body and their products, and was told that the breast was "feeder"; the penis "penis"; urine was "po-po"; and fæces "grunts".

The technique I used in Colin's analysis is that described by Melanie Klein in her *Psycho-Analysis of Children* (1932). Colin came with his nurse to the waiting-room of the clinic, and was supposed to stay there until I fetched him. The play-room was across the passage. It was furnished with a couch, an armchair for me, a small metal chair for Colin, a second small wooden chair, and a table. There was a sink with running water from a tap accessible to him. Underneath it was a basin, a soap dish, and a floor-cloth. A chest of drawers contained an unlocked cupboard in which there were two ashtrays, one black and one red, and seven locked drawers, six of which belonged to other children, and the seventh to Colin. In his drawer were the small toys described by Melanie Klein: small coloured human and animal figures, trains, carts, ships, aeroplanes, houses, and trees. There were marbles in a bag, a ball, plasticine, blocks of wood, paper, pencil, chalks, and a mug.

At the beginning of the session I unlocked the drawer before I fetched the child from the waiting-room, and aimed at maintaining this routine. However, as the analysis continued, Colin often leaned out of the waiting-room window, if it was open, and saw me coming. At times he ran to meet me, at other times he commanded me to wait for him, or to go to the play-room without him. I generally acceded to these modifications, but treated them as part of the analytical situation and interpreted them.

In my interpretations I made use of the child's own words and phrasing, trying to be as simple and succinct as possible. After each session it was my practice to make full notes, which included recording as exactly as I could the wording of my interpretations. In this paper I shall give some of these interpretations practically verbatim, but for the most part I shall repeat the gist of them or summarize interpretations of one or several sessions. In assessing which part of the material needs to be interpreted at any particular point in the analysis, account must be taken of those aspects of the child's emotional conflicts that are most important at that moment. The appropriate interpretation then includes appreciation of the transference and counter-transference (Paula Heimann, 1950), and aims at bringing about a mutative interpretation (James Strachey, 1934).

THE FINDING GAME

Colin started his analysis a month after his third birthday. He was undersized for his age and gave an impression of frailty. However, he was easy and natural in his movements and showed considerable dexterity. Though he had a friendly smile and came readily into the play-room, he was at first inhibited in his play, preferring me to do everything. However, interpretation of the anxieties and defences preventing freedom of play soon enabled him to become more active.

The first important game the child played with me was a form of Hide and Seek, which I am calling here the Finding Game. He began and ended each session with it from the first until the tenth week, and significantly returned to it from time to time later in the analysis. I learned from his mother that he had played it at home from an early age, and that his parents called it "Where's Colin?"

This is how he played it. When I went into the waiting-room, found him sitting on his nurse's knee, often holding a paper in front of him. I had, at his request, to ask: "Where's Colin?" to which he replied: "He's not here," or "It's Nanny." I had then to speculate aloud as to whether he might be under the table or behind the door and only when I said: "On Nanny's knee" would he appear smiling from behind the paper, and come with me into the play-room. At

113

the end of the session, he hid under the rug on the floor, and I had to fetch his nurse. He became very excited, and on several occasions he shouted: "Dainty Dish". This comes from the nursery rhyme in which, it will be remembered, the four and twenty blackbirds were baked in a pie to be a dainty dish to set before the king.[1] Nurse had to look for Colin as I had done. Later, as he became more articulate, he asked from under the rug: "Are Col's arms here? Are his legs here?" and several times he stood up with his eyes closed, asking: "Are Col's eyes here?" It was not until these questions had been answered affirmatively that he opened his eyes, took his nurse's hand, and walked out of the room.

THE HUMPTY-DUMPTY-CHRISTMAS-TREE GAME

Throughout the first week of analysis he began each session with the same play. Following the Finding Game he came into the play-room, took the ball out of the drawer and threw it into the corner by the window, saying: "Where is it? It's not here." I understood that the ball represented himself, partly because he used the same words for the ball as he used in the Finding Game for himself, and partly because in earlier sessions he had made it clear that the ball stood for himself. The meaning, then, of the play action with the ball was that he felt lost because he did with his ego what he did with the ball. I felt the child showed me an intra-psychic process in a dramatic way. It was as if a state of depersonalization with a loss of the sense of self followed when he split off and projected a part of his own self into the outer world.

The fourth session of the first week of the analysis opened with this routine, which I briefly interpreted as his showing me that he felt afraid and lost. He then took out every toy from the drawer, examined it for any sign of damage, and placed it upright on the table. He selected a conical tree, which he called the Humpty-Dump-ty-Christmas-Tree, and held it in front of his body. He was lying on the couch at the time, and at this point started to rock and roll. He told me I was to do the same thing with another tree. I took a tree, but only held it in my hand.

The appearance of the masturbatory equivalent showed that he

[1] *Sing a song of sixpence, a pocket full of rye,*
Four and twenty blackbirds baked in a pie.
When the pie was opened the birds began to sing.
Oh what a dainty dish to set before a king.

was employing auto-erotic gratification as a defence against the anxieties inherent in the feeling of being lost. It will be recalled that masturbation had stopped, though the rocking persisted, when he had first seen his baby sister bathed. Following this session I began to realize that there was an important relationship between the feeling of being lost and the birth of his sister.

He again began the fifth session by throwing the ball into the corner by the window, where he left it for the greater part of the hour. He then took out the bag of marbles, emptied them carefully on to the table, and asked me to pick up any that fell on to the floor. He returned to the drawer to take out the toys, examined them and stood each one upright on the table. This time, however, he asked me to select a "special one", and pointed to a wooden sheep. Lying on the couch by the table, he put two toy figures, a man and a red woman, into a lorry and said: "Are all the toys out? Is the drawer empty? Go and see." He then took the Christmas tree and put it beside him, asking: "What was Munro yesterday?" I pointed to the lorry, which he had called Munro's car. He asked: "Who are the Man and the Red Lady?" and taking out the red woman figure, threw her into the corner where the ball was lying. "You want to have a Special-Munro, like the sheep, here," I said, "and a Red-Lady-Munro to be there in the corner where you have thrown the Ball-Col."

Before I could say more, he interrupted me and, looking up in surprise, said: "Col isn't here. Are there two Cols?" He picked out a pig and, putting it into my hand, said: "This is Little Col. What does he do?" I addressed the pig, saying: "What is Little Col doing in Munro?" thus interpreting the meaning of his putting the pig into my hand as his wish to do something inside my body. Colin confirmed the correctness of the interpretation by replying: "He wants to eat up all the 'tatoes" (potatoes), and taking a second pig, said: "These are the 'tatoes." He added two sheep, one of which was the "special" one, and said: "These are knives and forks." He swept all the toys off the table into my lap, including the lorry and the toy man, saying, "These are all 'tatoes. Col is cutting up roast beef for Daddy and Mummy."

Pointing to the pile of toys, I said, "Little Col wants to be inside Mummy-Munro to cut and eat up her 'tatoes. He feels the Daddy-Man in the Munro-car is inside her, and wants to eat him too."

At this point he asked: "Where is Munro?", fetched the Red Lady from the corner and added her to the pile of toys on my lap.

"Where is the other bit of Munro? Find her," he demanded, looking towards the Christmas tree. I picked it up, and he took it and added it to the rest of the toys. He then ran in great excitement for the ball, and threw it about the room, giving the impression that he was chasing it and did not dare to hold it. When the ball fell, apparently by chance, into the empty drawer, he climbed on to the table and stretched across the gap to retrieve it, only to throw it away from him again. His behaviour with the ball is difficult to describe because the acute anxiety and manic excitement combined to produce a chaotic and distraught effect. Finally he told me to get the ball. I had first to put all the toys from my lap on to the couch, but some marbles fell. As I stooped to pick them up, he shouted: "No, Col wants to. Give him the ones you picked." He then collected all the marbles, and put them in their bag, which he held against his stomach.

The interpretations which I gave to him during this complex phase of play were that Little Col, the pig, was the greedy part of himself, which wanted to get inside me, standing for his parents, to eat us and our contents. He then felt we were inside him threatening to devour him. This made him very frightened so that he had, by putting part of himself into the ball, to keep himself safe by running away. At the same time he felt that the parents he had eaten were in bits and should be put together. This he tried to do in three ways; by feeding them with roast beef, by putting the two "bits of Munro"—the Red Lady and the Christmas tree—on to my lap, and by sweeping all the toys off the table on to my lap. He also felt he was in bits and wanted to put himself together inside himself. This he showed when he insisted on picking up the marbles, putting them in their bag and holding it against his stomach.

The implications of the analytical material of this last session are considerable. Munro's car containing the Red Lady and the toy man stood for his parents. By taking out and throwing the Red Lady into the same corner as the ball he was expressing his direct Œdipal wishes to separate his parents and to have his mother to himself. At the same time, by retaining the Christmas tree, representing his father, beside him on the couch he demonstrated his homosexual desires. But he could only fulfil these wishes at the cost of dividing himself between his parents, and this was one reason which made him feel he had no self.

The play on my lap, which followed my indication of his desire to enter his mother's body, expressed his phantasies about her contents—the 'tatoes. The first pig stood, as he said, for Little Col, and the second pig for his sister. The "special" sheep which I had to select at the outset meant, as he explained to me later, good food that "melted and did not have to have the badness taken out of it first by cooking". This sheep further represented the good breast, which was sucked and gave good milk. He equated melting with vanishing, so emphasizing his feeling that good things never lasted. The sheep, which he had called knives and forks, represented the cutting and biting aspects of eating and led to the phantasy of a cut and bitten-up breast. He felt, moreover, that when this breast was inside him it would cut and bite him. He had shown me in his play two fundamental phantasies surrounding his early feeding experiences. They had been revived when seeing his baby sister fed. He felt he had never had enough of the good breast and milk, and so had no conviction of there being an enduring good breast. This deprivation had intensified his sadistic impulses, and had led to the feeling that the breast was both dangerous and destroyed.

In his play he was describing a nightmare inner world in which he and his objects were devouring each other. His defence against anxieties associated with a relationship of mutual devouring was to split himself into two Colins. One, represented by the ball in the corner, was to be kept apart from himself, his family, the analyst, and the events around him; it was to be preserved by remaining passive and by not participating. The second, represented by the pig, Little Col, stood for his greedy impulses directed towards his mother and the contents of her body. When he projected his impulses into her, she came to take on the character of a devouring mother. This is projective identification described by Melanie Klein (1946). He dramatized this phantasy by sweeping all the toys into my lap saying: "These are all 'tatoes." Colin also employed his defence of splitting to preserve his objects. The Red Lady was that part of his mother which he was separating in order to keep her safe in the same corner where he had thrown his Ball-Self; the Christmas tree was representing a similar part of his father to be kept beside him on the couch.

Under the pressure of sexual excitement and greed his anxiety mounted. By adding the Red Lady and the Christmas tree—"both bits of Munro"—to the pile of toys, he showed he could no longer preserve his parents. His defence of splitting and projecting failed and he came to feel that he had devoured his parents, that they were inside him and that he was identified with them. His manic and distraught pursuit of the ball expressed the phantasy of being about to be caught and eaten. He felt, to recall his words in the Finding Game, that he was to be put into a pie, baked, and eaten.

At the same time it can be seen that Colin had quite strong reparative drives, which extended beyond the wish to preserve his parents by keeping them safe from his greedy impulses. His words: "He wants to eat up all the 'tatoes" were followed by: "Col is cutting up roast beef for Daddy and Mummy", and implied a wish to feed them. Then his addition of all the toys and both "bits of Munro" meant not only reuniting his parents but restoring them by returning all the bitten-up pieces. It meant giving to his mother his father's penis, her breasts, and her two children. These reparative drives failed, as the play with the ball showed, because his devouring impulses led to the feeling in the child that to feed his parents meant giving them flesh to eat, both their own and his. I was left with the chaotic pile of toys on my lap, and he with the marbles in their bag held against his stomach, that is, the many small balls represented the disintegrated parts of the big ball, and, hence, a self in pieces. He was showing how attempts at introjection were fraught with danger. It meant taking into himself by eating both the destructive parts of himself and the damaged object, and in these circumstances he could not maintain either himself or the object intact. In consequence he came to feel that he could not put himself together; at best his ego was like the marbles in the bag, at worst a chaos of mutually devouring objects.

This session throws light on the Humpty-Dumpty-Christmas-Tree game of the preceding day. The phantasy accompanying this masturbatory equivalent is shown in his play. The tree stood for his father with a present-giving penis, and Humpty Dumpty, the egg of the nursery rhyme, stood for his mother. He was representing them in a pleasurable and productive intercourse. But the end of the nursery rhyme is that Humpty Dumpty has a great fall and cannot be put together again.[1] Colin showed himself clearly familiar with the rhyme, thus indicating his fear that the intercourse would end disastrously. Though this catastrophe was not enacted in this session, the dread of its happening was expressed in his attitude to the toys in the drawer at the beginning of the next session (the fifth). It will be recalled that, having thrown the ball

---

[1] *Humpty Dumpty sat on a wall,*
Humpty Dumpty had a great fall.
All the King's horses and all the King's men
Couldn't put Humpty together again.

into the corner and taken out the bag of marbles, he returned to the drawer and, taking out each toy, examined it and stood it upright on the table. That is, having first made sure of his own safety and that aspect of his mother which he wanted to preserve, he sought for more information about his mother's state. The drawer symbolized her body and the toys her contents, in particular the marbles the bits of himself inside her (as he had shown by the end of the session). His examination of them expressed his fear that they might be damaged. By standing each toy upright he was reassuring himself that they were alive, whole, and uncastrated. In later sessions, not here described, he used to end a sequence of play by emptying the drawer and saying: "When the wind blows, down will come cradle, baby and all."[1] This gave one of the reasons why Colin wanted his parents' intercourse to fail: he knew it would be followed by the birth of a baby, and this he regarded as a disaster for everyone. His mother's account of his profound distress when he first saw the new baby will here be recalled. His request, then, that I should play the Humpty-Dumpty-Christmas-Tree game, meant that I should be the restored mother of his phantasy, who would give him both his mother's good breast and his father's good penis, for him to combine inside himself. Thus his masturbation was an omnipotent attempt both at reuniting his parents, and, in addition to his libidinal wishes, at denying his destructive wishes towards them.

It will be recalled that he had given up masturbating after he had seen his baby sister bathed. It is well known, and was true of Colin, that the sight of a sister's genitals stimulates the boy's castration fears, and acts as a repressing agency in his struggles against masturbation. It seems to me, however, that the appearance of the rocking in the analysis has additional meaning. For, in dramatizing the accompanying phantasies, in the fifth session, he showed how the phantasies of his parents' relationship were dominated by his oral-sadistic impulses, and how he dreaded the outcome of their union—a baby sister, or worse. According to his history, when he first saw the baby, he was frightened, and later profoundly depressed; but there had been an earlier traumatic experience. At ten months of age, after severe difficulties in feeding, he began to "eat like a horse". At twelve months, coincidentally with his mother becoming pregnant, his appetite declined, and was inhabited by fourteen months when

---

[1] *Hush-a-by Baby on the tree top,*
When the wind blows the cradle will rock.
When the bough breaks the cradle will fall,
Down will come cradle, Baby and all.

she miscarried. This would suggest that by ten months he might to some extent have overcome his oral anxieties and made a sufficiently good relationship to internalize a more satisfactory mother. In view of the many indications of this child's perceptiveness I am inclined to believe that at twelve months he had become aware of her pregnancy. This would reactivate with increased intensity his anxieties concerning his greed and the phantasies of her inside, foster his aggressive attacks with their concomitant fear of persecutory retaliation, and cause him to turn away from her as a good feeding mother. Thus, the non-appearance of the baby, i.e. the miscarriage, confirmed his belief in his own destructive powers, and in the dangers inherent in the union either between his parents, or between himself and them. His phantasy, shown in the chaos of toys on my lap and his chanting :"Down will come cradle, baby and all", was that his mother's inside was a confusion of dead and damaged objects. Though his masturbation was genital in form, it was strongly influenced by his early oral anxieties. Because his impulses were of a devouring character, the expected reprisal would take the form of his penis being bitten off. He saw in his sister's genital what was to him evidence that a part of her body had been bitten off, and showed in his play with the ball and in the Finding Game that his fears were not limited to castration, but extended to the whole, and every part, of his body. The miscarriage was for him proof of total loss. The rocking was a desperate attempt to keep himself alive; that is, the cradle still rocked, the bough had not broken causing the cradle to fall, and he was not in pieces. At the same time he saw the baby as an integral part of his mother which, having been cut from her inside, left her mutilated.

The Finding Game, then, was a presentation of his problem. In the waiting-room he was showing that he felt himself to be lost inside his mother, represented by his nurse. ("Where's Colin? He's not here," or, "It's Nanny".) By looking for him, naming him, and finding him, "on Nanny's knee", I was to be the helpful aspect of his mother, who by extricating him from her inside would give him independent existence. At the end of the session, when he hid under the rug, called out excitedly "Dainty Dish", and asked whether his arms, legs, and eyes were there, he showed that he felt himself to be in pieces inside a devouring mother, the analyst. He needed his nurse to be the mother who would not only extricate him but, by naming the different parts of his body, would put him together and enable him to function. He was showing that his ego was split and projected to such a degree and in such a scattered way that he had no awareness of a self. He needed the analysis to find and put together the scattered parts of his ego.

The effect of this state of his ego was seen in his object relations. Though he smiled indiscriminately at everyone, and rarely protested at being handed over to strangers, his mother's report of his being white and strained when next they met indicates the great anxiety which he felt in her absence and tried to deny. Every contact meant for Colin that he was eaten up by each object in turn and had to exist inside them. His passivity expressed his feeling that as he was inside his objects they had to function for him. At the same time by tyrannical demands and obsessional rituals he tried to maintain control of his objects and his environment, and hence of the scattered parts of himself. The absence of an integrated ego explains why he could do so little for himself, i.e. feed, dress, and play. It accounts too for his incontinence of urine and fæces. The birth of his sister, then, was of great significance, for he saw in her a representation of himself as a baby, who could exist and function separately from his mother. He identified himself with her, not only by calling himself Katy, but also by learning to function as she did, notably to produce the large motion in the pot after he had first seen her do so.

THE NAUGHTY BOILERS

Since the fourth week of the analysis there had been a background of anxiety at home. Colin's father had fallen ill with a renal calculus, which the child called the Kidney Stone. He was constantly in his father's room, and persistently demanded large drinks of water. During the third month his father went to hospital for an operation and returned three weeks later. Colin kept asking that there should be plenty of food in the house, and that the door should be kept open "for when Daddy comes back". Meanwhile, in the play-room, the table and wooden chair were being damaged by another child who used the play-room prior to Colin. He noticed and remarked upon every new item of damage. He also noticed any small piece of fluff, or paper, which might have been left by the other child. Sometimes he just commented upon what he saw, at other times he disgustedly picked up the piece of debris and put it into my hand. On one occasion he said: "Col doesn't like to pick the Nasty Baby." His comments further made it clear that the two pieces of furniture represented his parents, the chair standing for his father and the table for his mother. He showed that he connected the damage to his parents with the presence of the Nasty Baby.

In the analysis the Finding Game had ended. He began to talk about the Naughty Boilers, and in his play dramatized their activities by throwing the marbles under the couch. They were naughty boys, the bad aspects of himself and his parents. They did damage with boiling, bubbling water which was, in his phantasy, a mixture of fæces, urine, and cooking food—food broken up and inherently poisonous. The Naughty Boilers were the representatives of Colin's sadistic attacks directed towards the inside of his mother's body, and symbolized internal persecutors as described by Melanie Klein (1932). The tap had come to play an increasingly important part in the analysis, and Colin insisted that it should be turned on and the water left running throughout the session. He called it at this time the "straight, white water" and it had feeding, cleansing, and healing properties. It represented Colin's good object. It is likely that his belief in the goodness and efficacy of the "straight, white water" was supported by seeing his father drink large quantities for relief of his renal condition. However, both at this time and later, he frequently maintained it would make him "big like Daddy". This suggests that the "straight, white water" was not only a panacea against illness but represented the contents of his father's penis. At this stage of the analysis it was felt as good urine because of Colin's reparative impulses to feed and heal, and it was unconsciously equated with milk which flowed abundantly. Thus, in the Naughty Boilers and the "straight, white water", he showed the division of his objects into bad and good.

During this period there was a pattern in his play, which appeared in whatever material he used. It consisted in filling his mug, red lorry, or large wheel-barrow—which he brought to the analysis—with water, marbles, or toys, and then emptying the contents. Initially this was on to the floor, when he would ask me to pick them up. If it was water that he emptied he would move away to a dry part of the floor and start the game again. Later the contents were emptied into another receptacle and this in turn into a third, and eventually on to the floor. Frequently there was defiance in this last act, but despair soon appeared, when he would say: "All mixed up." It could be seen that he was struggling with his phantasies about the Naughty Boilers who, he felt, were everywhere, and contaminated everything. He felt that the only way to deal with their destructiveness was to turn them out and to start again at the beginning. Even when he found an object which could contain them safely, their destructive power prevailed. He was showing that nothing could be kept inside himself because it was so bad, and must be turned out. He then searched for an object to relieve him of his bad contents, but as it too became contaminated, he never could evade the ultimate confusion and chaos. All was "mixed up" and he despaired of ever being able to put things right.

Once in the tenth week he put a piece of fluff into my hand, and said: "Frogs, blood, muck, and sick; that's for you." He then went across the room to sit behind the table. He became increasingly more anxious during this and subsequent sessions. He told me to sit at the far end of the room and, if I had occasion to approach him, would call out warningly: "Zebra Crossing." (This, as is well known, is the name given to safety zones in the road which cars are forbidden to cross when being used by a pedestrian.) If I began to interpret, he would say: "Don't speak, don't say." It was clear that he pictured me as a car filled with frogs, blood, muck, and sick— the horrible alive excrements of which the Nasty Baby was made. He wished to attribute the excrements to the Naughty Boilers, to deny that they could belong to himself and to project them into me. He feared that contact with me would result in my pouring them back into him, and so controlled me by keeping me at a distance and forbidding me to open my mouth. However, in contrast to the repetitive emptying, he was now trying to separate the good from the bad in himself—"Frogs, blood, muck, and sick; that's for you"—and to separate himself from me—"Zebra Crossing". These controls he imposed upon me were evidence of a greater capacity to bring into focus his diffused persecutory feelings, and to cope with psychotic anxiety by obsessional means. (This behaviour in the analysis recalls his obsessional ritual at night, when he would climb into his mother's bed and lie there forbidding her to touch him.)

I shall now describe two sessions in the eleventh week. He started, as usual, asking me to turn on the tap. He then told me to sit on the far side of the room by the door. He busied himself with the basin, mug, and running water in the sink. After a time, he came over to me—this was the first time he had come near me for several sessions —and he gave me a full mug of water, saying: "Drink it, because you are ill." I accepted the mug, and pretended to drink. He ran to the couch, lay down with his eyes closed for a moment, and then ran to the sink, saying "It mustn't get all over." Here he sat watching the bubbles made by the running water, and rocking himself. After a time he asked to be taken to the lavatory to urinate. I said: "You felt I was ill because of the frogs, blood, muck, and sick which you wanted to put into me. I am standing for Daddy who is ill with the Kidney Stone, and Mummy with the Nasty Baby inside her. You felt you made them ill with your Naughty Boilers, the bad po-po and grunts. The straight white water is from the good Daddy's penis and the good Mummy's feeder which you want to give to make ill-Daddy-Mummy-and-Munro well. You want your po-po to be good so you can make well with it, and you want me to help you put the bad po-po and grunts in the lavatory where they will not be dangerous." I linked these wishes with his fears at night—shown by his lying on the couch, and by his excitement and rocking when watching the tap-water running. He phantasied his parents having a dangerous intercourse because of his own hostile impulses to attack them with his urine and fæces. He then felt the parents of his phantasies—his internal parents—would retaliate, so to save himself he threw out these parents by wetting his bed and by dropping his fæces all over the house. I interpreted his rocking when watching the tap as expressing his masturbation phantasy of sucking in the contents of the good penis and breast in a magical way so that he would only have good parents inside. They could then make a good baby between them. This was represented by the large motion which he passed in the daytime.

In this session he had begun by splitting off the bad things and projecting them into me, and splitting off the good things and projecting them into the tap. When he brought me water to drink, "because you are ill", he was attempting to bring the good and bad aspects of his object together in me. But because in this feeding situation sexual excitement and greed were aroused, he could not sustain his restitutive and reparative drives. His flight to the couch, where he lay with his eyes closed, was the expression of his anxiety. He dared not look at me and see the consequences of his act. For he feared that he had aroused my greed, which would be followed by my incontinence—a flood of "frogs, blood, muck, and sick" which he wanted to wash out of me, and also a flood of lost goodness which he wanted me to keep. He split off this latter wish, projected it, and expressed his anxiety that the sink would overflow. Then by his rocking he employed magical means to control, and so keep, the desired goodness inside himself and me. By urination he was able to rid himself of the consequences of greed. The intensity of the anxiety caused him to break contact with me as an external figure, and to take flight into phantasy in which he magically controlled his objects.

When I arrived for the next session, Colin was looking out of the waiting-room window. He asked me what I was hiding (it was the floor-cloth which I was carrying), told me to go into the play-room, and said that he would follow. He noticed that the broken table was propped up by the broken chair. "What will it do?" he asked. He went to the sink, and this time he himself turned on the tap to fill and empty his mug, while watching the bubbles in an absorbed way. He brought the mug over to me and said: "Because you are ill with frogs, sick, po-po, and grunts." He returned to the sink—not to the couch as he had done on the previous day—and watched the tap, making mouth movements suggestive of drinking. He looked round at me and said: "I have a wee sore in my mouth." This was a startlingly unusual form of communication—he had never before used the pronoun "I". It indicated that he now had an inside, and hence contents. I said: "To-day you feel you have a sore Daddy and Mummy inside you. They make your mouth sore. You want to make them and yourself well with the straight, white water, the good penis and feeder." He came over to me with his full mug, and standing beside me—not in front as he had done on previous occasions—drank with increasing pleasure and enjoyment. I said: "Because you wanted to make me well yesterday and to-day you feel you can take and keep my good water and good talk inside you to make Daddy, Mummy, and yourself better." He looked at me with some concern, and noticing some water spilt on my sleeve said: "You are wet all over. What will you do?" He took the mug to the sink, saying as he poured out the water: "Lavatory hole." I said: "You are afraid that I have turned into a greedy Munro, and have swallowed all the water from the tap-penis and the tap-feeder so that I shall be flooded inside and wet all over. Then you tell me that I can let out the water from my lavatory hole, and be safe." I went on to remind him that he had said "What will it do?", when he had seen the table propped up by the chair. They stood for his damaged but good parents supporting and feeding each other in intercourse. They had aroused his greedy desires to bite off the breast and penis, and to swallow the milk and semen. But, though he had wanted to make them well by feeding back into them the bitten-off penis and feeder, he was afraid the milk and semen might turn into urine and flood them. I linked this material

125

with his feeding experiences as a baby. Then he had felt as if the breast, which he had wanted to bite off, had bitten him inside, and that all the milk he had wanted to drink had flooded him. He had come to feel that the breast could not be kept good inside him.

He then took the floor-cloth, which he had never been able to touch before, and placed it under the table. He poured water from his mug on to the top of the table and watched with pleasure the stream of water being absorbed by the cloth below. I said: "Now you are wanting to make the table Mummy well by giving her the good milk and the good po-po from Daddy's penis. You are looking inside her to see whether she has a po-po hole to let out the water so that she will not be flooded. You want her to be able to keep the good things." At the end of the hour he returned to the Finding Game; he hid under the rug, but took the floor-cloth with him. I said: "The floor-cloth is a good bit of Munro, whom you want to help you with your grunts and po-po. It is like the nappies you used to wear when you were a baby."

His mother reported a few days later that he now defæcated regularly in his pot in the mornings, as well as at noon. This he continued to do with only very occasional lapses.

The session just described had begun with considerably less persecutory anxiety and some belief in his reparative impulses. It was possible for him to make a closer contact with me both to find out what I contained (the floor-cloth) and, as the modification of his words showed—frogs, blood, muck, and sick into frogs, sick, po-po, and grunts—to acknowledge that the damage in me had resulted from his excretory attacks. He turned on the tap himself because he was now able to approach his good object directly. He then showed it was possible to introject in a less magical way, for he appeared to be sucking and had dispensed with rocking. The growing awareness of his own inside found direct expression in his communication "I have a wee sore in my mouth". He had taken back the hurt into himself and so came to realize the damage in his own ego. Because he had restored me, both by relieving me of his attacks and by restoring to me the good breast and penis, he could now expect me to help him and accept my help. When he stood beside me and drank the water, as he had asked me to do on the previous day, he was showing me that he could now internalize and identify with a helpful figure. Moreover, since I did not overflow, it meant that I could hold the goodness and he could do likewise. At the same time he felt he was doing this in his own right, and that he was a separate person. He could moreover sustain his contact with me as an external and more real person.

The prevailing emotion throughout the session was one of delight and pleasure. It first showed in his sucking movements when looking at the running water, declared itself openly when he drank the water from his mug, and appeared at the end of the hour when he took the floor-cloth with him underneath the rug in the Finding Game. His mother had told me that he had recently been sucking his fingers and dribbling; he had never done so as a baby. Several times previously he had tentatively explored his mouth with his fingers, but he had never in the analytic sessions swallowed anything. In other words, his mouth and his inside had been so great a source of anxiety to him, and had led to such a degree of oral-erotic inhibition, that he had failed to develop those consolatory activities that help a child to overcome frustration and play an important part in sustaining his inner security. The way by which he had come in the analysis to find this pleasure was based on his having restored his mother, both by withdrawing his excretory attacks from her and by returning to her the good feeding properties of the breast and penis. He could then bring into focus his phantasies concerning her anus. He could differentiate it from her mouth, and see in it a means whereby dangerous things might be voided, thus enabling her to retain the goodness uncontaminated. Finally he could internalize such a mother, identify with her, and find within himself similar possibilities. When in the Finding Game he took the floor-cloth with him under the rug, he was demonstrating his own achievement in finding a lost part of himself.

There is a phrase in popular use, "the bottom has fallen out of the world", which might be used to describe Colin's state. The floor-cloth symbolized the finding of the bottom or floor of himself. The meaning of the cloth nearest consciousness was that it represented his nappies to which he had been deeply attached. He had regretted parting with them, and openly expressed his longing to be like his baby sister and to wear them again. He also found his earlier relationship with his "Nammies", which he had ceased to suck and eat after he had found they had been washed, as if an essential ingredient was missing. This was on the terrifying trip to America. I learned that his first word for food was "Nam". D. W. Winnicott (1952) has introduced the term Transitional Object for such a possession as the Nammie. He described transitional phenomena occurring in an intermediate area between the

127

subjective and that which is objectively perceived—boundary phenomena of Schilder. As I see it, the appearance of the Nammie in the Finding Game had more meaning than the recovery of a Transitional Object. It means that Colin recovered his early experience of contact with his mother's body, ultimately his memories of feeding at her breast. His Transitional Object, the Nammie, was the symbol of his experience of himself with his first object, the breast, and, as such, was an integral part of his ego.

Colin's first use of the pronoun "I" showed that he had come to recognize that he had a self. It was as if by discovering his mouth and distinguishing it from his anus he found that he had a body cavity in between, wherein it was possible to hold something. This was, in essence, his good object, and his good self identified with it. This is in line with Freud's statement (1923) that the ego is first and foremost a body-ego.

The illness of Colin's father stirred his anxieties most profoundly. It threatened the shaky security of his whole world, based, as it was, on the existence of a strong, loving, external father with capacities for repair and control. The illness increased his fears of his destructive impulses, and forced him to become aware of his own ineffectual reparative abilities. The Kidney Stone inside his father was comparable to the Nasty Baby inside his mother, and threatened the return of the disaster which had overtaken his mother at the time of her miscarriage, and later at the birth of his sister. It will be remembered that in Colin's phantasies he felt his mother had been dreadfully mutilated by giving birth. When, as the result of the analysis, Colin felt himself able to restore his parents, he felt that the lost good breast and penis were now available, and that they could combine to make good babies. He has showed he felt he was doing this for himself when he produced the large motion in his pot for everyone to admire at noon. Now he felt he could do this at all times. It was to him evidence of constructiveness, and not, like the scattered fragments of his fæces, hopeless destruction.

There was a change in his object relations, most noticeable in his attitude to his father on his return from hospital a few days after this period of analysis. He did not repeat the compulsive demands he had made before, and showed more real solicitude and consideration.

I mentioned at the beginning of this paper that denial of Colin's disturbed state was a symptom of his mother's emotional difficulties.

I had the opportunity several times during the analysis of seeing his mother, her conscious reason for visiting me being that she wanted to give me information about her son. But her own problems broke through, and I was confronted with severe psychotic anxieties. I wish to make it clear, as I did to Colin's mother, that I did not intend analysing her, and confined myself to interpreting her anxiety in terms of her transference to me, her son's analyst. She told me that she had had a previous pregnancy before Colin, but had miscarried at the sixth month. The foetus was dead and macerated. She had denied the reality of this, maintaining that she had lost a beautiful child. When first she saw Colin she turned away from him saying: "He's not my Johnnie." (This was the name she had proposed giving to the child of her first pregnancy.) During the few interviews with me—nine in as many months—there was an outpouring of repressed guilt for her rejection of Colin, and her wish that he should die. In consequence, she had not trusted herself to make close contact with him lest she should give vent to her destructive feelings. This accounted for her difficulties in feeding him, her readiness to submit to his exacting demands, and her feeling that his father and nurse were better for him than she was. Further, she had to deny that Colin was in any way disturbed until it was forced upon her by comparison with her next child, Katy. The unconscious phantasy seemed to be that, having lost her first baby, she expected him to be restored to her in her second pregnancy, but in an idealized form. At this point the depression for the loss of her first baby appeared and centred upon Colin. It was clear that she was driven to seek a compulsive solution, both in her need to become pregnant, when he was a year old, and again when her daughter was born, one and a half years later. This seemed to expiate her guilt for producing dead or ill babies, and she was able to face the fact of Colin's illness and to seek help for him. When I come to review the factors which contributed to Colin's seriously disturbed development, account must be taken of his mother's illness. Undoubtedly he suffered from her unconscious aggression. He did not receive from her the loving support he needed against his own persecutory fears. His homosexual desires for his father were encouraged by his mother, who, being unable to feel herself to be a good mother, overvalued the role of her husband as father. However, her wish to make amends led her to choose a kind, tolerant nurse for him, to seek psychological help and to co-operate loyally throughout the analysis at considerable sacrifice to herself.

FURTHER STEPS IN EGO-INTEGRATION

The period from which I shall select the next material covers the eighth month of analysis, which followed the summer holiday. The analytical material was dominated by the anxieties stimulated by my having gone away, and included the fear that when I returned I should be pregnant. The week-end breaks during this period enhanced these fears. In addition, Colin started going to school. His behaviour in this connection was interesting; for he met his mother without the strained and anxious expression with which she had been familiar in the past; further he was unusually communicative, telling her everything that the children and the teachers did, and volunteered proudly that he did nothing when he was there. This was confirmed by his teacher, who said that he sat quite passively doing nothing and speaking no word to anyone. This attitude he maintained for several weeks.

At the beginning of one Monday session, i.e. after the week-end break, he killed a ladybird which he found in the play-room and insisted on sweeping it not only out of the room but out of the building into the yard. On the following Monday he put a white house on the rubber doorstop inside the play-room, and poured water over it, saying: "Under the water. Down will come baby, cradle and all." These two play activities expressed his murderous wishes towards a baby he phantasied I had. He also found how he could manipulate the tap so that the water squirted across the room.

I should at this point describe his method of urinating, as it developed in the analysis. At first he used to take my hand and, saying: "Col feels a po-po coming", pull me to the play-room door. I had to open it and take him to the lavatory. Here he stood quite passively telling me in a remote and rather abstracted way what I had to do. I complied with these instructions in so far as they referred to his clothes and position. He had to be lifted on to the seat and then he allowed his urine to run from him. As the analysis proceeded he started to urinate standing up, but did not handle his penis or watch the flow. This gradually changed and he began to take an increasing interest and participate more actively in the experience. In the sixth month he handled his penis and directed the stream, and a month later he opened the door and went to the lavatory by himself. I do not propose giving in this paper all the child's associations by play and word together with my interpretations which led to these changes, and to the understanding of the phantasies involved. I can only mention that by the eighth month the squirting tap stood for urinating in a masculine way and pouring water meant urinating in a feminine way.

On the third Monday session of this post-holiday period, he commented on the evidence of another child having wet the floor. He then picked a small, white woman figure from the drawer, put it on the arm of my chair and knocked it into the corner by the door. He threw out all the contents of his drawer, something he had not done for weeks. He turned on the tap and threw mugfuls of water, first over the white woman and then over the doorstep. He poured it around my chair and with increasing vehemence over the room. As he did so, he said: "I am going to water like Munro's girl, and more." This referred to a little girl who came to the clinic and who had appeared in the analytical material in direct sequence to the piece of fluff—the Nasty Baby—quoted earlier in this paper. He often found the play-room wet, and had recently attributed this to "Munro's girl". He was very jealous of her and felt her to be his rival. He felt she received from me unlimited supplies of love and gratification and complete liberty to wet or soil. He intended to have all these supplies and privileges himself. Thus, throwing the mugfuls of water meant claiming all the abundance, and urinating as he phantasied his sister and mother did meant being feminine. In contrast, squirting the tap, though it represented having a penis and being masculine, meant, at this moment, deprivation and restriction. He was also expressing by this act not only his rivalry with Munro's girl, his sister and his mother, but also his wish to drown and kill them. He became more excited and aggressive in his play with the water, but guilt supervened, so when running across the room, which he had flooded with water, he slipped and fell flat. His mood changed suddenly; he lay quite passive, then he began to cry desolately, but quietly. This was unusual—he generally screamed and demanded that the hurt should be "blown away", when I used to blow gently on the hurt part. On this occasion, as I picked him up, I said: "You felt Munro's girl had been sitting on my chair and had got from my feeder tap all my good milk. You wanted it yourself and to get more than she did. Because you were angry with me for giving it to her, and angry with her for getting it, you turned it into po-po to kill and drown us both. You feel the same way about Katy when she stays at home with Mummy and you go to school, and you felt like that when she was a baby inside

131

Mummy. You wanted the cradle with baby Katy to fall down, so she would be killed. Now you feel that Munro and Munro's girl join with Mummy and Katy to throw you down into the water and to kill you." He then went over to the corner by the door where the white woman lay, and stood silently in the pool of water there; after a minute he moved to the doorstop and stood there in the same way. Then he walked slowly to the couch, lay down and said repeatedly in a monotonous voice: "It's a removal van; take it to the sink." I moved the couch as he directed, and he took a black ashtray, put in some marbles and asked me to squeeze the dirty water from the floor-cloth into it. He looked at it mournfully and tipped the contents into the plug hole of the sink. I said: "The ashtray with the dirty water stands for your bad self filled with bad po-po and grunts. The marbles are your Mummy's good feeders, Daddy's good penis, and their good babies, all turned bad inside you by what you feel you have done to them. You feel so bad for this that you feel you should be taken away by the removal van, and thrown away down the lavatory hole. You feel you are like the Nasty Baby, whom no one would like to pick (up), and the ladybird, who should be killed and swept out of the building."

In response to my interpretations Colin took his mug and put in the marbles. He held it under the tap and squirted water into it. He then used the filled mug standing under the running water as a basis on which to build what he called a Fountain. This Fountain had often appeared before in his play, and it stood for his actual family restored and brought to life, his mother's inside restored, and himself rehabilitated. In this session the restoration was affected by the tap—the live-giving penis—and the helpful analysis. He asked at the end of the session that the Fountain should be left like this. I heard him go into the yard with his nanny and inspect the outside drain, down which the water was running. He returned to the play-room to look at the Fountain, and then went out into the yard and home.

This session showed clearly the feared outcome of the murderous attacks he felt he had made and was making on his mother's body. The play-room, my chair, the drawer, and myself stood for his mother's body. The little girl who preceded him stood for my child and for his sister—his rival. The white woman represented the baby whom his mother fed and attended to, and the doorstop represented the baby inside his mother. His jealousy of his sister who stayed at home with his mother when he was sent to school

132

reactivated his jealousy during his mother's pregnancy and, in turn, the earlier envy of her body and its contents. This he demonstrated by throwing away the white woman and emptying the drawer, saying: "Down will come cradle, baby and all." His fear of retaliatory persecution by the external mother and sister led him to redouble his attacks with the aim not only of outdoing his rivals but also of killing them by drowning. But the more he attacked the representatives of his mother and baby sister, the more persecuting he felt they became, and though he tried to maintain this as an external situation, the defence by projection failed. His external figures were internalized as persecutors and now attacked him from inside. He became overwhelmed from within, feeling himself now to be the victim of murderous attacks, and, in identification with the attacked little girl, fell down on to the wet floor. This symbolized death; both his fear of dying and his suicidal impulses.

At this point his hatred turned upon himself, for he found, under the stress of rivalry and jealousy, that in attacking his sister he was also attacking his mother's child—which was himself. He was showing, by standing in the corner where the white woman lay in a pool of water, and where the doorstop was, that he was identified with the child he was wanting to drown. The dead child was felt to be fæces only fit to be thrown away, for he had called the sink in earlier sessions the "lavatory hole".

His passivity represented more particularly a state of being dead. I would in this context recall the significance of the corner of the room by the window, into which he threw his Ball-Self; it was the place where he tried to preserve the alive and good part of himself and his mother from his current play-room activities which were then concerned with his devouring impulses. In this last interview he was showing that there was a place in which there was a dead part of himself, one that he could not own and which none of his family could love. The events of this hour demonstrated that the undoing of the split resulted momentarily in the feeling that the whole of himself was flooded, drowned, turned into worthless fæces, and abandoned; that is, he was dead. This phantasy affords an explanation of his passivity at school. He felt he had been sent there as rubbish by his family, and that while they and the teacher and children at school were alive, he was dead. Herbert Rosenfeld (1950) described an acute confusional state occuring when splitting processes lessen and the libidinal and aggressive impulses become temporarily more active with the latter predominating. Colin, under the stress of his greed and jealousy, abandoned his splitting devices and, his destructive impulses being the stronger, a momentary acute confusion appeared. To use his words from an earlier interview, he was "all mixed up", both in respect of his impulses and his objects; and for Colin, "all mixed up" meant being dead. However, his confusion was resolved by my interpretation of his guilt for his aggressive impulses. This strengthened his libidinal impulses, differentiation became possible, and brought his reparative tendencies to the fore. He could now find the tap which stood for his father's penis, and squirt the water to represent the love he desired. So that his action with the tap expressed his wish that his father should inject life into him. The structure called the Fountain stood, as we have seen, for the family rebuilt and brought alive within himself, and also for the mother's body restored by the life-giving father. The restoration included her having a baby—not only Katy but himself. By identification with this mother, he felt himself to be restored. To inspect the drain from outside and then to return to the play-room to look at the Fountain was a means of reassuring himself against a number of anxieties, many of which were worked out in greater detail later. But the important meaning which I wish to single out here was that he was again playing the Finding Game. This time, however, it was he who was the finder, and he who was putting himself together. He was correlating the state of the inside with that of the outside, both of his mother and of himself. He was linking the experience of himself in the analysis with me in the play-room, with himself who was going home with his nurse. He was thus reassuring himself that both of us could survive a separation and remain alive and undamaged. It might be said that in seeking, finding, and linking these experiences himself he was finding evidence of the continuity of life and refuting his fear of death.

Now it was apparent that the means he used on this occasion to initiate the integrating process was the life-giving penis—the tap, which squirted water into the mug containing the marbles, representing himself with the broken-up breast inside. Colin was identified with his destroyed mother and received the penis in the feminine position. Thus his own coming to life was dependent upon the restoration of his internal mother and her child. It could be seen that his homosexuality was less due to the strength of his libidinal impulses for his father than to his need for protection from a persecuting and damaged mother. He also needed his father to mend the destroyed mother. As mentioned before, his parents had noticed his admiration for his father's ability to repair and construct. For integration to take place, father and mother must come together within himself, but this very act, while promising restoration, meant bringing about a very dangerous situation. It meant the making of a baby, which was compounded of the "Nasty Baby", who became his rival sister, and the miscarriage, an unborn, and so dead, baby. These babies played such an important role in his phantasies because, by projecting on to them his own sadistic and jealous wishes towards his mother, they came to be the representatives of a hated and dead part of himself.

Before I consider the implication of these two split-off parts of himself for the integration of his ego, I shall describe another form of the Finding Game. I shall only enumerate the details and summarize my interpretations. This play took place at the beginning of the ninth month; that is, following the week containing the last described session. He took my bunch of keys and hid with it under the table, which he covered by a rug. The bunch of keys from the beginning had represented my family, home, and possessions. He told me to look for it in different parts of the room according to his direction. As he named each place, I interpreted that he was asking me to find and put together the various events of the analysis, in which I had represented different aspects of his parents and family. Thus, under the sink was Mummy-Munro, whom he had felt to be full of po-po and grunts and wanted to throw down the "lavatory hole", and I recalled the interpretations given at that time. The cupboard in the chest of drawers was Munro-Daddy who had got broken by the Kidney Stone, and Munro-Mummy who was broken by the Nasty Baby. Finally, when I was allowed to look under the table, I was Mummy-and-Daddy-Munro, whom he had hidden in himself. I said that he was wanting me not only to put Mummy and Daddy together, but also to find and put together the various parts of himself that had got lost in his parents. He wanted me to give them to him, like the bunch of keys, so that he could be put together inside himself. Next day he returned to the drawer and pointed out the meaning of each toy as it had been used by him in the analysis. He said, for example: "The Mummy-house, which I broke with po-po when I was cross: the Christmas tree which I lost: the white lady who was baby Katy and whom Col hated." Thus the Finding Game had changed into finding out. He then asked for materials suitable for making good, and several interviews were employed in gumming and painting the toys. He also spent part of the interviews writing and reading. He began to tell me of events at home and at school, and to give me details of some of his earlier experiences, notably of what he had felt when Daddy was ill and what he remembered being told of his aeroplane journey. His vocabulary increased, his use of sentences developed, and he was able to give verbal expression to phantasies which previously he had only demonstrated in his play. His enuresis improved, and he had several runs of consecutive dry nights. He found out the name of Munro's girl, and now referred to Mary, and attempted the more correct pronunciation of his sister's name. I was given information about children at school by name. Because he was less persecuted and less split, people ceased to be merely figures but became real personalities. In particular he began playing with his sister and at times could be protective towards her. Further, because he was freer of anxiety, his capacity to love was liberated, and reparative and sublimatory activities appeared. After this his direct Œdipal rivalry also came to the fore in his analytic play.

Since then analysis has continued and the early improvement has been maintained. Among other things, he has made much progress at school, giving evidence of considerable intelligence. I had a chance meeting with a colleague, who knew the child. He had been impressed by the changes that had taken place, and remarked that it was like seeing a dead child come to life.

In the analysis we had come to see that Colin's defence against chaotic confusion—"All mixed up"—was to split himself into the Ball-Self and the Nasty Baby—little Col, the pig, of the first session described. These parts he projected into his objects. He came to feel that such existence as he had was in them but not in himself—"Col isn't here." His Ball-Self was his good self and the relationship with his mother's good breast. It was bound up with his feeding experiences and gave rise to the feelings that the breast's goodness was transitory; it readily vanished and could not be sustained with security for any length of time. Further, he felt that his own devouring impulses endangered the good breast. In consequence, his good impulses, together with the good breast, could only exist apart from himself, i.e. in the corner of the room by the window. His bad self, the Nasty Baby, contained his destructive impulses towards his mother's breast and included the inside of her body and its contents. This was shown in the nightmare world of the parents and himself cutting and eating up each other, and in the "frogs, blood, muck, and sick", the products of the Naughty Boilers. In these phantasies, any meeting between his objects was destructive, and any product of their meeting a "Nasty Baby". This was so bad an object that it was regarded as dead, and worthy only of being taken away by the removal van and thrown down the lavatory hole. The interview in which he expressed his murderous attacks on the rival child gave evidence of the feelings aroused by his mother's pregnancy with his sister, and of the earlier pregnancy which miscarried. His distress, described by his mother when first seeing his baby sister, could be understood as expressing his horror and despair at his mother's production. As if he, at this point, derived no reassurance at the sight of a living baby, but only saw the Nasty Baby of his phantasies. The inhibition of his appetite at the time of the miscarriage suggests that the absence of a baby meant a dead baby, already carried away and disposed of, and a mutilated mother. Though he tried to maintain that it was the Nasty Baby and not himself—using projection and splitting mechanisms—it could be seen that he felt there was a part of himself which was quite unlovable and unloving. It was a dead part and was associated with a destroyed mother. It contained those experiences bound up with his earliest contact with his mother —perhaps his distraught first months of ceaseless crying and frustrated feeding, possibly even his difficult birth. Certainly his mother's own conflicts and their reflection in her attitude towards him at that time were included. The American trip at eighteen months reactivated these terrors. Because so much of himself was involved in his phantasies of his mother, he was unable to feel he existed apart from her, and only if she was restored could he exist in his own right. This implies an innate and very strong capacity for love. He showed this in his belief in the efficacy of the "straight white water", standing for the good milk, which he split off and attributed to his father. His father's illness deprived him of the reassurance which he found in this phantasy of a potent, repairing father, and showed how closely he felt his mother's phantasied destroyed condition coincided with his own. Both of them were suffering from the loss of a good breast. In the analysis, particularly that part described under the heading of the Naughty Boilers, he showed, by taking the floor-cloth with him under the rug, how highly he valued my interpretation. For in consequence of my becoming, in the transference, a restored mother by having the good penis and breast given to me, he became able not only to internalize a helpful figure, but also to differentiate himself from me. More importantly he came to find in himself an ego which was damaged.

From this moment the recovery of the lost experience of pleasurable feeding in the finding of the "Nammie" became possible. Being able to recognize the "Nasty Baby" as part of himself was followed by his asking me to put myself together—by recalling all the roles I had played in the analysis. This led to his identification with me as an integrating mother who was capable of making a whole, living child. In doing the same for his part of the analysis he came to be able to form within himself a child who was himself—his ego. He showed that for integration of his ego he needed to be able to internalize an object which was integrated and so was capable of integration. For the strength and violence of his impulses repeatedly endangered his deeply loved object, and nullified his own capacity for reparation. The need to find and use this aspect of himself was essential if he was to be able to put together the scattered parts of himself. The Finding Game which he made me play at the outset was indeed a plain statement of his unconscious appreciation of what he needed analysis to do for him.

Before Colin came to me he was seen in consultation by a child-psychiatrist/analyst, who diagnosed psychotic symptoms. He considered that the analysis would be a long one in view of the need to heal the injury arising in the very early relationships. In spite of the delay in development he thought the child's intelligence was normal. My experience in the anlaysis supports these views.

It might be suggested that the difficult birth played a particularly traumatic part, leading to specific cerebral damage, and thus accounting for the child's delayed development and psychotic behaviour. I do not think this was so. In my opinion it was rather that the birth intensified the primary persecutory anxiety, which derives from the working of the death instinct at that time (Melanie Klein, 1952). This state of anxiety received further reinforcement from his early relationship with his mother, whose own problems interfered with the establishment of satisfactory feeding. There can be no doubt that there were extreme degrees of splitting within the ego, which gave rise to a form of depersonalization. However, he showed from the first a strong innate capacity for love which, though from time to time inaccessible to him, could always be seen and felt to be present. His reaction following the terrifying experience in the aeroplane, when he refused to be parted from his parents, implied a considerable tenacity of belief in the goodness of his parents as a means of preserving himself. Thus, I am inclined in view of this and other evidence of the strength of the life instinct and in spite of the degree of the psychotic disorder present, to maintain that this child was not schizophrenic.

Freud (1924) refers to the need to know in what circumstances and by what means the ego succeeds in surviving the strains which beset it. He suggests that the relative strength of the forces should be assessed together with the possibility of the ego submitting itself to deformity and mutilation to avoid rupture. Without analysis I think Colin would have developed into a rigid personality with the likelihood of a psychotic breakdown at puberty, or, possibly, into an eccentric and withdrawn individual. The value of analysis in early childhood lies in the greater chance of reaching and resolving those anxieties and defences which are responsible for perpetuating the split state of the ego. When the rigid and chaotic behaviour of the early sessions and life at home is compared with the richness of play and rapid development just described, the losses which his ego suffered as a result of splitting can be appreciated. In my view the disorganized parts of the ego not only interfere with maturation, but contain at worst the seeds of future maldevelopment and illness and at best the restriction of personality with limitation of sublimation and impoverishment of object relationships.

REFERENCES

Freud, S., *The Ego and the Id*. London, Hogarth Press, 1927.
——"The Economic Problem in Masochism." *Collected Papers*, Vol. II. London, Hogarth Press, 1924.
——"Neurosis and Psychosis." *Collected Papers*, Vol. II. London, Hogarth Press, 1924.
Heimann, Paula, "On Counter-Transference." *Int. J. Psycho-Anal.*, Vol. XXXI, Parts 1 and 2 (1950).
——"A Contribution to the Re-Evaluation of the Œdipus Complex—The Early Stages." *Int. J. Psycho-Anal.*, Vol. XXXIII, Part 2 (1952).
Klein, Melanie, *The Psycho-Analysis of Children*. London, Hogarth Press, 1932.
——"Mourning and its Relation to Manic-Depressive States." *Int. J. Psycho-Anal.*, Vol. XXI, Parts 1 and 2 (1940); and *Contributions to Psycho-Analysis, 1921–45*. London, Hogarth Press, 1948.
——"Some Notes on Schizoid Mechanisms." *Int. J. Psycho-Anal.*, Vol. XXVII, Parts 3 and 4 (1946); and *Contributions to Psycho-Analysis, 1921–45*. London, Hogarth Press, 1948.
——"Some theoretical conclusions regarding the emotional life of the Infant." *Developments in Psycho-Analysis*. London, Hogarth Press, 1952.
Rosenfeld, H., "Note on the Psychopathology of Confusional States in Chronic Schizophrenias." *Int. J. Psycho-Anal.*, Vol. XXXI, Parts 1 and 2 (1950).
Strachey, J., "Nature of the Therapeutic Action of Psycho-Analysis." *Int. J. Psycho-Anal.*, Vol. XV, Parts 2 and 3 (1934).
Winnicott, D. W., "Transitional Objects and Transitional Phenomena." *Int. J. Psycho-Anal.*, Vol. XXXIV, Part 2 (1952).

7

THE ANALYSIS OF A THREE-YEAR-OLD
MUTE SCHIZOPHRENIC

EMILIO RODRIGUÉ

THE present paper is based on the clinical material of a psychotic boy who began treatment when he was just over three years of age. His pronounced withdrawal and the negativistic features of his condition raised special problems, which I should like to outline first, particularly those encountered at the beginning of treatment; I should also like to point out what sources I drew on for assistance in understanding the child's psychotic behaviour.

The immediate problem was one of communication. The child did not speak, having lost the few words he had once mastered more than a year before treatment began. He did not utter any articulated sound, only an occasional guttural scream. There was, further, an absence of manual or facial expressive behaviour. He remained quite silent and did not try to communicate either by means of sounds or of gestures. Nor did any emotional significance emerge from his way of carrying out such bodily skills as he commanded; walking, unbuttoning his jacket, taking off his cap, for example, were all performed mechanically.

Faced with this mute and seemingly meaningless behaviour my first aim was obviously to understand him, and to make it possible for him to understand me. This paper, covering the first seven months of analysis, particularly the first five months, attempts to describe how contact was established and a means of mutual communication evolved, and how, in the course of the analytical work, the child's means of expression developed and his contact with me progressed to a fuller relationship. I have chosen to describe the first seven months of analysis because it was near the end of that period, in the fifth month, that the child began to speak.

It is not my main purpose to give a detailed account of the technique of the analysis. I would emphasize, however, that I did not depart from the essential technical requirements of child-analysis devised by Melanie Klein.[1] By this I mean that, as far as possible, I consistently interpreted both the child's positive and negative transference manifestations and did not rely on other measures, such as reassurance, coaxing, or gifts, for bringing about therapeutic results. What is more, realizing that this child was very sensitive to routine alterations and bitterly resented even minor changes in my attitude to what he was permitted to do, I soon learned to be more consistent with him than with the average neurotic child. With regard to the arrangement of the play-room and the toys that were used in treatment I also followed Melanie Klein's suggestions, and I shall comment upon this later.

Needless to say, my interpretations in the early weeks of treatment were highly tentative, for I found only slight and scattered indications in the child's behaviour on which to build interpretations. Besides, as he gave no sign that he heard what I said, the usual criterion for assessing an interpretation—observation of a direct emotional response—was lacking.[2]

Another difficulty arose regarding the wording of my interpretations, and quite often I had to struggle with the limitation inherent in having to use a very simple and reduced vocabulary to describe complicated emotional processes.

One important reason for the difficulty in finding the right words came from the fact that some, if not most, of these processes could be said to belong to a pre-verbal stage of development. In addition it must be emphasized that the evidence for interpretation often lay in imponderables in the child's behaviour which are impossible to reproduce—being by their very nature outside the realm of discursive thought—but which made an impression on my mind and led me to interpret in a given way. I believe such an experience to be familiar to all analysts and to occur to some extent in every analysis, so that they are to be the more expected when drawing inferences from the behaviour of an autistic child. For that reason the use of counter-transference feelings, in the way described by Paula Heimann,[3] as an instrument for furthering

[1] See *The Psycho-Analysis of Children* (London, 1932). Ch. II, "The Technique of Early Analysis" in particular.
[2] These difficulties were greater during the first six weeks of analysis, but even then the fact that the child did not openly react to my interpretations—as a less disturbed child would do—does not mean to say, as we shall see, that he was wholly unresponsive.
[3] "On Counter-Transference", *Int. J. Psycho-Anal.*, Vol. XXXI (1950).

Emilio Rodrigué

insight had here a wider application, I believe, than in most cases.

A knowledge of Melanie Klein's work on early mental processes was essential for understanding the "autistic" behaviour of the child; I think that this paper illustrates that point throughout. Besides her general theoretical and technical formulations, I found the specific orientation needed in the paper[1] in which she described the analysis of a psychotic child (Dick, four years old). The technique used in that analysis and the conclusions drawn from it were extremely illuminating, and specially so because Dick's symptomatology was strikingly similar to that of my child patient.

HISTORY

Raul was three years and three months old when treatment began. His principal symptoms were marked withdrawal, mutism, negativism, automatic obedience and general intellectual backwardness.

Although a deterioration of his condition had set in only about the middle of his second year, the basic problem, that of emotional dissociation, could be traced back to his first months of life. A first child, he was born in an asphyxiated state after prolonged labour, and his first responses seemed to be typical of the "inert suckling" described by Merell Middlemore,[2] for he was unable to grasp the breast, and showed considerable torpor. The sucking reflex started only on the fourth day. As an infant he was always sleepy; when roughly handled he stiffened, but only half came out of his lethargic state. Difficulties with feeding existed from the beginning; his constant lack of appetite troubled his parents. The change-over to bottle-feeding in the fourth month, when his mother returned to work, took place with surprisingly little resistance: but though he accepted the bottle he showed no enthusiasm for it. To sum up, therefore, he was a quiet baby, neither crying nor laughing much, and it was only his persistent lack of appetite that worried his parents.[3]

Raul's physical and intellectual development did not grossly

[1] See "The Importance of Symbol Formation in the Development of the Ego" (1930), in *Contributions to Psycho-Analysis 1921–45* (London, 1948).
[2] See *The Nursing Couple* (London, 1941), p. 77.
[3] A neurological examination did not reveal any evidence of a brain lesion.

deviate from the parents' notion of normality until after he was sixteen months old. He sat up and walked within the normal time. His first word was heard at the end of his first year and was preceded by a rather feeble lalling stage. When sixteen months old he had a vocabulary of six words. At that time too, although toilet training had not been achieved, he showed occasional discomfort and disgust on seeing his soiled nappies.

A deep and sudden regression took place after his sixteenth month, when his mother became pregnant again,[1] and his condition further worsened when, a few days after his second birthday, she gave birth to a second boy, Raul's only sibling. In a few months he lost most of his social achievements; his scanty vocabulary disappeared, and this was followed by the loss of articulated sounds. His face lost expressiveness; he neither wept nor laughed, though occasionally he smiled to himself; his hands, too, became unexpressive. Play became unimaginative and solitary; he would continue monotonously, for hours on end, spinning the lid of a pan or bouncing a ball, and at such times he seemed to be deeply engrossed in a private world of his own. He had no favourite toy. In the social sphere, he showed complete emotional detachment from his environment, to the extent of rarely recognizing his parents. He forcibly repelled all attempts at getting in touch with him, for he did not allow any caresses or contact apart from the routine handling involved in such things as bathing and changing.

He soiled and wetted himself, and did not seem to mind even if he remained unchanged for hours. He showed insensibility to pain also and in particular to cold.

He seemed to have a craving for routine. He wanted things always to be done in the same way. This was specially noticeable at meals. Difficulties over food had been present from birth onwards, but became more marked when solids were introduced at the end of the first year. He flatly refused them at first, and only gradually came to accept mashed vegetables and a limited number of other pap-like mixtures. He resented the slightest variation in his diet, which thus became very monotonous. He had, moreover, a peculiar way of approaching a "suspect" food: he would very slowly approach the spoon, having first examined it from all angles before "sampling" a tiny bit from the tip. He could not bite any

---

[1] His parents were certain that these adverse changes coincided with the beginning of his mother's second pregnancy, probably not because he noticed it in its early stage, but because he reacted to her changed emotional relationship to him.

solid food, meat, toast, or candy, and had the habit of spitting out food he did not like.[1]

PARENTS

When Raul was four months old his mother went to work and left him almost exclusively in the care of nurses who came and left often enough to prevent the child from becoming attached to any one of them. She saw more of him after having her second child (a normal baby) whom she much preferred. Her personality and her relation with her elder son constitute a topic which is difficult to deal with briefly without distorting it. In many ways she was a "bad" mother. She was unstable in her emotions, rather inclined to brood over her ill fate, and would sometimes regard her son as a hopeless case, and, sometimes as just a "nervy" child. She lacked the ability to keep herself at a proper emotional *distance* from him, for she was either too detached and indifferent or she stubbornly insisted on trying to shake his aloofness away. I shall give two examples of this latter feature. She was over-anxious to make him eat, and often lost her temper over it, so that when he spat his food out she forced it angrily back into his mouth. The other example has to do with a habit Raul developed some time before treatment started, which consisted in closing his ears by folding them forward. His mother looked upon this as a "naughty" device to enable him not to hear, and had the unfortunate idea of swaddling him. In both instances she displayed the same exasperated drive to force her way into the child's private world.

It must be said, however, that these examples show her at her worst. I would add, therefore, that she began to co-operate in her son's treatment when she saw signs of improvement in him and, later on, she changed quite a lot and proved to be, on the whole, helpful beyond expectations. Raul's father made a good impression; he treated his son kindly and was genuinely distressed but not discouraged by his illness.

[1] With what I have already said of Raul a parallel can be drawn from Dick's symptomatology (cf. reference to Melanie Klein's paper on Symbol Formation). This four-year-old boy suffered from an intense emotional and intellectual inhibition to the extent that his whole mental life had come to a standstill. His detachment from his environment was almost complete and he did not show any interest in play or in any other expressive activity. His speech had echolalic features and it was of an "autistic" type. An oscillation between automatic obedience and negativistic behaviour completed his more overt symptoms. Dick also had a history of feeding difficulties starting from birth, which included the same struggle over solids. Significantly enough, he was also inhibited in biting hard food. Melanie Klein's description of Dick's first interview could, in its essentials, apply to Raul's behaviour on the same occasion.

The analysis of a three-year-old mute schizophrenic

INITIAL INTERVIEW AND EARLY COURSE OF THE ANALYSIS[1]

At the first interview, the extreme nature of the child's lack of contact with his environment was the most apparent feature. He behaved as if the playroom were an empty space and, although he must have been aware of obstacles, since he circumvented them, he acted, so to say, as if the boundary formed by the walls of the room was not really there. He looked beyond them and did not react to the fact of being in a strange room. The unknown setting aroused neither fear, apprehension, curiosity, nor excitement—nothing but indifference. He seemed not to hear and not to see anything, but just ran round and round, during the whole hour, in what seemed to be a purposeless zig-zag. I had placed some toys[2] on the table and on the floor, which were plainly visible; Raul did not even look at them. When his parents tried to make him play by picking up a toy and dangling it in front of him, he screamed in anger and made desperate efforts to free his body if they held him to fix his attention.

What most impressed me in that first session was the realization that this child, who behaved as if he were deaf[3] and dumb, yet had a remarkably intelligent face. He struck me as a child with an interesting personality and was far from conveying that impression of sheer dullness so often given by defective children. Moreover, he was an unusually attractive child—of the kind people turn round to look at—well proportioned, stronger perhaps than the average, and he moved gracefully and on the tips of his toes.

Raul's second session was a repetition of the initial interview—

---

[1] Raul had four analytic sessions a week.

[2] I had selected the following toys for Raul to play with: bricks of two sizes, small figures of people and animals, and miniature fences, tables, trees, which made up a toy farm; little plastic cars and aircraft, and somewhat larger wooden boats and trucks with sufficient space to put the smaller toys in; a couple of balls and marbles; string, wooden and tin boxes of various sizes, pencils, crayons, plasticine, paper, and a pair of blunt scissors. During the first weeks of analysis some of these toys were openly displayed on the floor and on the table before the child entered the room. Later on, he was shown the place where his toys were kept. Apart from these toys, which were for him alone to play with, there were a number of rectangular pieces of plywood in one corner of the room, and this playing material, together with a blackboard, and a set of cups and containers for water-playing, were objects that all child-patients shared. With regard to the play-room furniture, it consisted of a table, five chairs and a couch. The bathroom adjoined this room and contained a basin and a chest of drawers where the toys were kept.

[3] The possibility of deafness had been previously considered, but the otologist established that his hearing was not impaired. This is significant because Kanner, in his description of "Early Infantile Autism", mentions that most children in that group were admitted for suspected deafness or mental deficiency (see pp. 173-9).

Emilio Rodrigué

the same cold, absent indifference could be observed. I had questioned his parents, who had witnessed part of the first interview,[1] for I wanted to know if the behaviour shown on that occasion was typical, and I was told that he was not, as a rule, so completely withdrawn at home, but that it was his usual behaviour when taken to an unfamiliar place. It was upon this fact, in addition to what I knew of the child's history, that I started interpreting. I told him that he was afraid of me, because he did not know me and did not know my room either. I was like bad food (or like new food); he was afraid of taking it in, and the same applied to the toys round him. I added that, because he was afraid, he did not want to hear or look at me for fear that I might get inside him and hurt him.[2]

In the child's history the birth of his baby brother, when he was just two, stood out as a very traumatic experience; from that occurrence dated the onset of his sudden deterioration. It seemed to me that all new-comers in his life might become a new version of the intruding baby. Accordingly, in that second session, I also interpreted that he saw me as his younger brother taking the "good mummy" away from him. Whilst interpreting I watched him closely, especially when naming his brother, but his face remained expressionless.

His lack of response was interpreted as an active rejection. Several times during the session he closed his left ear by folding it forward, and this action led me to insist on his fear that my words might get inside him.

Although the third session started on a similar autistic pattern,

[1] On that occasion, the child did not seem to realize that his parents had left the room and no change was observed in his attitude when they were absent.

[2] The interpretations I made will not be given here literally, for the words that were actually said lose much of their meaning when taken out of their context and put on paper. For instance, the verbatim transcription of a fragment of the interpretation given above would run as follows: "Raul . . . Raul afraid, fear . . . yes, Raul fear . . . Raul not know me, not know me. I a-m n-e-w (several times repeated; then kneeling down and pointing at the toys and making a little noise with some of them) t-o-y-s new. Room new, house new . . . why? Why? Raul don't know and afraid. I (kneeling in front of him and pointing at my chest) am bad food in spoon (I made the appropriate gesture and made a sign of fear at an imaginary spoon). All *here* bad food, *burns*, etc., etc." Needless to say these words, disjointed and "queer" in print, were made clear in speech with the help of tone, gesture, pause and emphasis. I would like to add, however, that from the second month onwards I employed a larger vocabulary, realizing that the child followed me better when my sentences ran more freely; but even then, I believe literal transcriptions would be rather hard to follow. Nevertheless, some sample interpretations will be given.

It should be mentioned here that the analysis was conducted in Spanish and that the original sound of the words used allowed for "phonetic links", which are, of course, incapable of translation. For instance, "*chiche*" in Spanish baby-talk means toy which sounds almost the same as "*cheche*", the nursery word for milk. Accordingly, the connection between his fear of food and his fear of toys was easier to establish than may be apparent from the above translation.

146

slight changes were observed towards the middle of the hour; for the child whilst pacing round the toys occasionally glanced at them in a way that betrayed curiosity. His general attitude was one of such indifference that I might easily have been misled into thinking that he did not care at all for the toys. But while he disregarded what was more prominently displayed, for example, those toys placed on the table or in the middle of the room, he went nearer those standing in less obvious places. The first toy he actually handled was a small brick he found lying apart under the couch, at the end of the third session.

His initial approach to toys reminded me of his parents' description of his feeding habits. Toys were like "suspect" food that he had to reconnoitre from all aspects and check before "sampling" them.

My interpretations in that hour focused on this similarity between food and toys. Besides, his behaviour showed distrust and concealment, and I tried to relate these features to what seemed to me to be the underlying persecutory anxiety—his fear of being eaten up by me.

It seemed that Raul had a basic tendency not to betray his desires, as if it were dangerous to wish something or to let people know that he had a wish. I tried to put this notion into simple words, adding that all things given to him were felt to be bad (he had only the "bad mummy" who stuck food into his mouth) whilst the "good mummy" went to his younger brother.

In the subsequent sessions the child gradually began to handle a larger number of toys. His interest at the start was in bricks and pencils; next, in a truck and some little toy cars. He just picked them up or moved them along. Once his mind was made up he did not hesitate to handle a toy and did not seem to be afraid of it. Although he tended to play more freely towards the end of sessions, this was not always the case. He often started moving toys around as soon as he came into the play-room, but did not seem particularly interested in what he was doing and his "play" was absent-minded.

At the end of the second week Raul began to play in a way that became characteristic. He took a small number of bricks and little toy figures, sometimes marbles or pencils, and scattered them on the floor in front of him. Then he began very carefully to place each toy in a certain spot, an operation which took him a long time. Often he changed his mind and displaced a toy a couple of inches

147

to the left or right, only to replace it in its original position. Frequently he would spend the whole hour making these minute alterations in the pattern of the toys. The patterns were asymmetrical and the toys looked like chessmen scattered on a chessboard. Moreover, the child behaved somehow like a chess-player, for he arranged and moved the toys one at a time, as if each move had meaning and purpose; and yet, no meaning emerged. The toys did not seem to be related to one another and the whole affair lacked that interplay of basic regularities and significant variations that allow an onlooker to detect the "rules of the game". But his *attitude* when playing was significant because he played for himself alone and behaved towards the arrangement of toys as if they were a part of him, pushing me away if I came too near the area of his play-activities. He did this although he shrank away from bodily contact, and even if he himself was not near the pattern of toys at the time, he would come back to push me away.

I have mentioned chess. The comparison helps to formulate the assumptions I drew at the time. His play impressed me as a one-man game. He was the "player" who made the rules and moved the figures according to a plan; but no other participant existed; his moves were not the response to somebody else's move. Hence, I felt the child could only experience those facets of reality that came near the rigid scheme of his controlling phantasies. People's ways were too unpredictable, they did not fit into his patterned world, their existence, as persons, had therefore to be denied. Only in phantasy could they be accepted, for there he felt that he controlled people as tightly as toys were controlled in his games—a control which must have stood for his attempt to arrange, and gain mastery over, his internal objects. Thus, I tried to interpret the toy patterns that emerged in his play, as showing the way he wished to control me. If the "real" me came too near the toy-pattern, I had to be rejected for fear of losing his phantasied control over me.

These notions were difficult to convey to the child. I interpreted his omnipotent control of his internal and external objects in terms of his having eaten up everything (that is to say his mother's breast and body and his father's penis) and of himself now being a "big mummy" who had everything. During several sessions I kept interpreting along similar lines and I believe only half succeeded in my efforts. Although signs of immediate response to these interpretations were absent, subsequent events suggested that somehow they had an effect on him. Raul's persecutory anxieties had so far appeared indirectly and were mainly inferred from his distrust, negativism, and autistic withdrawal. I suggest that the fact that his persecutory fears came more into the open in the following weeks can be regarded as an indication that the early interpretations were operative.

The child played placidly and on the whole apathetically during the second, third and fourth weeks of treatment. His chief occupation was still making patterns of toys, and as a rule he seemed mildly happy and obediently followed me in and out of the play-room at the beginning and end of each session. Signs of restlessness appeared, however, at the end of the third week and subsequently became much more evident. He became demanding, and screamed with rage when frustrated, and also showed great curiosity for certain objects that were outside his reach, either in drawers or behind closed doors. He was especially attracted by the chest of drawers. Some of the drawers were open; others, containing other children's toys, were locked, and towards these Raul began to behave in a particular way. When faced with a drawer that roused his interest, he would make a feeble attempt to open it, but if he failed to do so, he usually ceased trying altogether and went into a screaming fit of rage. It was extremely rare to see him trying to open a drawer again after failing once, even when it was an unlocked drawer that he had previously been able to open. If, on the other hand, Raul (or I, for that matter) opened the drawer, his attitude invariably underwent a striking change; for all his burning curiosity vanished as soon as the contents of the drawer were exposed. He did not even glance at them. Very soon, however (fourth session of the fourth week), an interesting feature was added: the child, after failing in his task, quite often took my hand—or my arm—and pushed it towards the desired goal. If I did not comply with his wish he kept insistently pushing my hand, screaming wildly and showing great despair.

Raul's total incapacity to act aggressively was fully revealed at this stage. When frustrated he looked very angry and yet his grip on my hand was light; the gentle grip contrasting oddly with his violent screaming. He made not the slightest attempt to hit or kick me, nor was he violent towards material objects.[1] Accordingly, I considered his feeble attempts at opening the drawers as instances

---

[1] Raul began to be violent towards toys and material objects in the third month of treatment, this coinciding, as we shall see, with a marked improvement in his condition.

of a profound inhibition of his aggressive impulses. Thus, I understood that the act of opening was equated in his mind with tearing, bursting, and other violent deeds; in other words, this act meant destroying the object he was actively seeking. The drawer and its contents were interpreted as standing for his mother and those possessions (penises, babies, food) he imagined her body to contain. I felt that the child's despair was grounded in his utter incapacity to get any good from the external object. He was doomed to fail, for the desired object turned bad *in the act of getting it*. I got that impression of doom, I think, from witnessing the sudden way his high expectations vanished as soon as the drawer lay open. It was, so to say, the reversal of the alchemist's dream, for everything he touched turned bad. I interpreted that to open a drawer, or to touch, or take a toy, was like greedily eating me up and destroying me.[1]

But this interpretation does not cover the whole field. The accent fell on persecution. Everything coming from outside, that is, from me, was bad because I (standing for his mother and the world at large) was felt to be hostile. Accordingly he could not *receive* (incorporate) the good I was withholding from him, but had to get inside me *to control and take possession* of me. Only by projecting himself inside the object could he get something from it. That could be seen in the way the child "took possession" of my hand. When he pushed my hand towards a goal he dealt only with my hand and not with me as a whole person. He did not look at my face, but just looked at my hand and pushed it as if it were a tool, an appendage of *his* hand. Probably because my hand was felt to be both better and more able to take the consequences, it had to perform the aggressive act "his hand" could not do. I told him he had put his own hurting, tearing "bad hand" into mine and also said that he took possession of other people by putting parts of himself into them. Moreover, this was a way of "sampling" the different bits of my body, following the pattern of his feeding technique.[2] I considered his attitude to be an active way of splitting

[1] Greed certainly played a part here; in this respect a sharp swing had taken place in his behaviour; instead of the former inhibition of his oral desires, excessive greediness appeared in his curiosity.

[2] Later on there were many instances of his treating me as a "part-object"; if he wanted me to walk I was pushed by my knee, or he made me stand by lifting me up by my lapel. On one occasion (sixth month of analysis) he played a game in which three chairs and I took part. The game, similar to that of the asymmetrical patterns of toys described above, consisted in pushing me in the same way as he pushed the chairs. Raul laughed mischievously when asked if I was a chair and, by way of reply, he put a rug on my lap while I had to take a crouching position.

my body (rather than a mere incapacity to perceive whole objects) aimed at denying that I was a whole person, independent of him, and with a will of my own. One element in his behaviour, omitted so far for the sake of clarity, fully endorsed that view. It often happened at that time that when I actively withdrew my hand from his grasp his anxiety seemed to become overwhelming, for he would suddenly fall limply as if all strength had, in a flash deserted him. Because of a generalized lack of muscular tone, his limbs took on puppet-like postures when he collapsed on the floor. It was clear that the cause of Raul's fall was my hand's rebellious act. That is to say, when the object was felt to be outside his control, it turned into the persecutor that might attack and destroy him. I interpreted that he was afraid that my "bad hand" might force itself inside him and break him up. The puppet-like way in which he fell suggested that the complete loss of body control was the visible result of an inner experience of disintegration.[1] The fear of the forceful re-entry of the persecutory object was no doubt increased by the fact that his mother to some extent acted in that way in reality (cf. her way of feeding him p. 144).

Herbert Rosenfeld has described how in the analysis of schizo-phrenics the patient at times could not differentiate himself from others, and found that this confusion of identity originated in the patient's feeling that a large part of his own self had been lost inside the external object, owing to an excessive use of the mechanism of *projective identification*.[2] States of loss of identity were a fairly frequent occurrence in Raul throughout the seven-month period covered by this paper, especially at the stage here being described. To give an instance: at the end of a stormy hour (fourth week), I sat down on the floor without the child at first noticing me. When he saw me, he looked as if he had seen a ghost. The next moment he fell down limply in the way he did when frustrated but for a longer period. Finally, he crawled towards me, making frantic efforts to lift me up, by my knees, shoes, lapel; thus, it could be said that if "I fell", he fell, no distinction being made between what happened to him or to me.

[1] See Melanie Klein, "Notes on Some Schizoid Mechanisms" (1946) in *Developments in Psycho-Analysis*, London, 1952, 292, and H. Rosenfeld, "Analysis of a Schizophrenic State with Depersonalization" (1947), *Int. J. Psycho-Anal.*, Vol. XXVIII, 130, and "Notes on the Psycho-Analysis of the Super-ego Conflict of an Acute Schizophrenic Patient", in this book.
[2] See "Notes on the Psycho-Analysis of the Super-ego Conflict of an Acute Schizophrenic Patient", in this book. For the description of the mechanism of Projective Identification, see Melanie Klein's paper: "Notes on Some Schizoid Mechanisms", in *Developments in Psycho-Analysis*, London (1952).

Emilio Rodrigué

THE NOTION OF AN IDEAL OBJECT

I intend to deal here with several features in the child's personality which were baffling in that they did not at all fit into the overall autistic and negativistic background. Here is an example. In the fourth week of analysis, although he had hardly looked at my face, he made gestures mimicking someone who has taken off his glasses, and only later did I realize that this was because I had on a new pair. (They were, by the way, so much like the old pair that of all my patients he was the only one to notice it.) Also, this child, who up to then had hardly dared to do more than push a toy about, suddenly one day (at the close of the first month of treatment) unexpectedly began building a high tower of bricks, using far greater skill than is generally found in his more normal contemporaries. But these feats of skill or ingenuity were flashes in the darkness—they vanished just as they had appeared, being once more replaced by the autistic behaviour. After witnessing these brief changes I gradually came to feel that there was much more going on in the deeper layers of his mind than I had been prepared to believe.

I would like to deal here with those elements in Raul's behaviour or general appearance that did not fit into the autistic pattern. I have already mentioned, in connection with the initial interview, the child's intelligent expression and gracefulness. The above example illustrates his uncommonly good manual dexterity and sense of equilibrium. He also had an intuitive mechanical knowledge,[1] but, at this stage of his analysis, he was not particularly fond of mechanical things. Besides, his sense of orientation was superior to what might have been expected of him. He seemed also to have a good memory and knew after a few days where to find an object he had seen only once or twice. To this I would add that in his history a precocious musical disposition had been observed by his parents (as early as the sixth month). His father, who had an ear for music, noticed that the child's early lalling utterances quite soon became song-like. Certain types of music had an instantaneously soothing effect and he would stop crying in the middle of a fit to listen attentively to a given piece of music even before he was one year old.[2]

---

[1] His father, when questioned with regard to this skill, told me that not long before (he believed it was after analysis had started) Raul had taken the mincing-machine to pieces, a rather difficult operation involving the unscrewing and disconnecting of several pieces of machinery. A few months later he was also able to put the pieces together again. I should add that *tours de force* such as these had taken place *before* analysis started.

[2] Raul always fell into blissful concentration when listening to Bing Crosby's voice and, oddly enough, other American crooners left him unmoved.

Now comes a piece of material (second session, fourth week) that gave me further insight into what might be called the "gifted" side of the child's personality. In the hour preceding that here described, Raul had been making patterns with toys (in the way described on pages 147-8, but he soon gave up playing and flew into a rage, the cause of which eluded me. At the next session he played along the same lines, but the game this time had far greater meaning. At the beginning of the hour he placed a thin rectangular piece of three-ply wood (5 in. × 7 in.), one of a set, flat on the floor and surrounded it with toy fences, leaving no gap. In the enclosure thus formed he placed bricks and other small toys (figures of people, animals, marbles, etc.) at first carefully, and then just piled them up. If a fence fell down when the pile was in the making, he immediately stood it up again. Once the confined space was filled to the top with toys he proceeded to lay other rectangular pieces of wood, first round the fenced piece, then leading away from it as if he were setting out dominoes. All these pieces, roughly twelve, were left *unfenced*. On them the child placed some *extra* toys, distributing them in such a way that only a few stood *near* the fenced-in part, or enclosure, and none at all were placed on the pieces farthest away.

I believe Raul's main conflict—his isolation from the external world—was vividly depicted in the way these toys were distributed. For the pile of toys was confined in an enclosed space (and Raul's main concern had been that it should be enclosed) lacking all communication with the pieces outside. The arrangement looked like a diagram of his autism, illustrating the way he had withdrawn from external reality into his autistic shell.

I began interpreting whilst the game was going on and, here again, I understood the material mainly in oral terms. I spoke of his having eaten up all that was good (the good breast, the good penis, etc.)[1] and that nothing, or nothing but badness, existed in the external world. The notion of loneliness was brought into my interpretations when I asked myself what motive the child had had for bringing this game into the analytical situation; I told him that he felt cold and lonely with no "mummy" and no "daddy" outside him, and that he was asking me for help.

[1] I also referred here to Raul having eaten up the "good Raul", for I wanted to convey the impression his autistic behaviour gave me, that the good part of his self was, as it were, within his ego-boundaries. To convey the notion of something external to him I pointed at the "enclosure" and said "Raul", and then to the other boards and said "Not Raul, outside Raul". Needless to say, here as elsewhere I made full use of the arrangements of toys to convey my interpretations.

Emilio Rodrigue

I felt that he was listening to my interpretations. There was a certain alertness in his face which was new to me.

Later, when he had finished laying out his toys, I began to understand the game (and partly, to interpret it) as also representing an inner situation where the "enclosed" part stood for a source of goodness or of bounty that was split off and inaccessible to the remaining part of his self. In other words, I thought that something similar to the autistic barrier, which kept him shut away from the outside world, existed between parts of his inner world as well.

When I go back over my notes I find I have no record of the point when I became fully aware of the importance of an ideal "unassimilated" object which accounted for severel features in the child's condition, such as the "gifted" split-off part of his personality; what I do know is that I became aware of it, as an assumption, at the time of the "enclosure game", and that it grew in significance two weeks later when the child started to hallucinate. I assumed (and most of this was interpreted in the following sessions) that he kept his ideal object cut off from the remaining part of his self out of fear of his internal and external persecutory objects and the destructive parts of his ego. Furthermore, owing to the intensity of his persecutory anxiety and the excessive splitting of his ego, all the forces that the weakened ego could summon up had to be used for clustering, so to speak, round the object and protecting it from a constant danger. The intensity of this dread would account for the child's not being able to benefit from the inner source of bounty. In other words, the ideal object could not be *assimilated*. Such a process has been described by Melanie Klein and by Paula Heimann.[1] The incapacity to assimilate the "enclosed" arises, as Melanie Klein has shown, both from excessive idealization which is needed to counteract the intensity of the persecutory anxiety and from a basic doubt regarding the goodness of the ideal object itself. The way Raul *hastily* piled up toys in the enclosure suggested distrust of the ultimate nature of the ideal object—he did not dare to look too closely at it.

[1] Cf. Paula Heimann's paper "A Contribution to the Problem of Sublimation and its Relation to the Processes of Internalization" (1942), *Int. J. Psycho-Anal.*, Vol. XXIII, Part I, where the concept of "assimilation" is introduced in relation to successful sublimation, the unassimilated object (either persecutory or idealized) being that which makes continuous demands on the subject, whose work (sublimation) is done out of slavery towards an inner master. Melanie Klein, "Notes on Some Schizoid Mechanisms" (1946) in *Developments in Psycho-Analysis* (1952), applied this concept when dealing with early disturbances in ego-development brought about by what she called "the flight to the internal idealized object" (p. 302) owing to the intensity of persecutory anxiety.

HALLUCINATORY EXPERIENCES

By the end of the first month of analysis the child played, on the whole, in a livelier way. Generally speaking, several attitudes alternated throughout the sessions. Autistic withdrawal still predominated, but bouts of restless and demanding behaviour often upset his apathy. The child now used to look at me (just passing glances) in almost every session, and on several occasions he smiled brightly, but I could not trace the smile back to anything in particular. Several ways of playing were also present simultaneously. He went on with the monotonous, chess-like patterns of small toys; but quite often he used toys in what might be described as a curiously *functional* way; that is to say, each object was given its correct use: a hammer for nailing, a car to roll along, a fence, for fencing, and so on. Imagination seemed to be excluded and toys were not used as symbols for something else. Some features of this unimaginative playing soon predominated, however, adding interest to his games. His play had more and more to do with opening and closing things, with making one object slide over another, or with putting objects into a container and taking them out again. The common factor in these activities lay in his more sustained interest in what he was doing, and in the objects themselves.

The following game occurred at this time. As Raul had been interested in things that opened and shut I included a small lead-gate among his toys. He did not play with it during the first two sessions. At the third, however, he first opened and closed the play-room door and then examined the toy gate closely. Then he made a toy animal go through it several times, opening and closing the gate on each occasion. Finally, he tried to make a crumpled piece of paper go through the gate and screamed anxiously when the paper ball stuck and would not pass through. The game was discontinued after this incident, and it may be added that months passed before he came back to the little gate. Several interpretations were attempted here. I spoke of my ("the Friend's")[1] words and my body getting inside him like a big lump of fæces that hurt; also like the food his mother stuck in his mouth. I also said that he felt suspicious of me for bringing the new toy (he did not play for two sessions) and that he felt I wanted to open him up (I used the

---

[1] Raul's parents at the time spoke of "the Friend" at home when mentioning me to the child.

gate as a demonstration) to take away his "good" things and put my bad food, dirt, fæces in him. I felt that the child was attempting to make a clearer distinction between what was outside and what was inside him. I said (putting the toy gate near him) that "Raul has a mouth, a mouth between Raul and Friend, and Raul does not know if this is Friend's good food (I showed him the toy animal which had had no trouble with the gate) or Friend's bad food (I showed the paper ball) which hurts and bursts". It was significant that the child, although he had interrupted the game in anxiety, did not start doing anything else and looked at the objects I made use of in support of my interpretations.

This material becomes more important when we remember that it immediately preceded the child's hallucinations. Indeed it might be said that it ushered in the following phenomena, which were observed a few sessions afterwards, about the sixth week of analysis. The child had probably been hallucinating, though I did not realize it, for a couple of sessions. Then I observed that the sessions assumed a definite pattern maintained for a few days in which his behaviour alternated between states of concentration (in the sense defined by Marion Milner in her paper)[1] and states of withdrawal or restlessness, the change-over being abrupt. His new attitude showed expectation and eagerness. At times, but not often, he seemed to be in a blissful state. His eager concentration was reminiscent of a person stopping suddenly in the midst of a trivial action when a significant sound is heard; it carried that note of suspense, of arrested movement. Indeed, I realized that he was listening to something that came from the direction of the ceiling; the way he looked upward and became closely attentive was unmistakable. He seemed to be *seeing* things projected on the ceiling as well, for he followed the invisible orbit of an object with his eyes. It struck me as most significant that these blissful and eager hallucinations took place, as a rule, whilst I was interpreting and that the duration of these phenomena was approximately that of my speech. My voice then appeared to be instrumental in conditioning the hallucinatory response.[2]

The immediate outcome of this phenomenon was to lessen the gap between us. I had the feeling that the "visions" were a bridge that allowed greater ease of communication. It showed me that

[1] See "Aspects of Symbolism in Comprehension of the Not Self" in this book.
[2] The child first hallucinated during sessions and only several days later was this observed at home. He had never hallucinated before and it was a very alarmed mother who told me the child had been having "visions". (I had not informed her about the occurrence of this phenomenon.)

he had listened to me attentively. To judge from his expression when hallucinating I had become a very important object for him. His hallucinations then could be regarded as a sign of considerable improvement, allowing him, as they did, greater means of contact with an external object; the "visions" were thus instrumental in bringing about an increase in introjection and projection.

Raul's "visions" may be compared to the wish-fulfilling hallucinations of infants. Melanie Klein[1] has shown that in that state the child fully possesses an idealized inexhaustible breast—a psychic experience of bliss which is based on the omnipotent conjuring up of an idealized breast and on the omnipotent denial (annihilation) of a persecutory one. I suggest that this was also true in Raul's case, the "vision" representing the projection of the idealized internal object. I believe that his *ability* to hallucinate was a result of the analytic work so far done, for this state implied that a lessening of persecutory anxiety allowed the child to have greater contact with the idealized object which had so far been kept "enclosed" in his ego (cf. the enclosure game 147–8). As he was less afraid, he could now reveal the possession of that ideal object to me. In this respect the game of a few days before with the paper ball that got stuck in the toy gate might be related to the projection of this ideal object, illustrating the child's anxiety as to whether he had to keep it within himself or could externalize it. But, as I said before, the "vision" helped me to establish a closer relationship with the child, and this suggests that he was conjuring up not only an ideal breast but also *a part of his own self.* This part was hallucinated outside him and met the external object half-way. It seemed that what he projected (an object and a part of his ego) was felt to be good; the hallucination being ultimately a compromise between a drive towards libidinizing the world and his fear of it. Hence, that which he externalized was suspended mid-way, as it were, between himself and the external object. When interpreting I emphasized these two aspects: his wish to put the good breast and the good Raul into me, and his fear that I should take those good things away from him and do harm to them.

These eager and blissful "visions" were for a very short time the only type of hallucinations present. Frightening hallucinations appeared a few sessions afterwards and both phenomena alternated

[1] Cf. "Some Theoretical Conclusions Regarding The Emotional Life of the Infant", and "Notes on Some Schizoid Mechanisms" (1946), in *Developments in Psycho-Analysis* (London, 1952)

for more than a month—the blissful ones becoming less and less frequent till they almost disappeared. The appearance of frightening hallucinations confirmed Melanie Klein's findings that wish-fulfilling hallucinations cannot be maintained for long, built as they are on the omnipotent denial of the split-off persecutory object and of persecutory anxiety. Raul's frightening hallucinations at their worst were pathetic to watch, for through them the acute character of his persecutory anxieties and the intensity of his suffering became evident. His frightening hallucinations mainly followed one pattern, the differences being chiefly in intensity and frequency. They would start with Raul flying into a rage, with or without a discernible cause. Next he would stare at the ceiling, his eyes showing fear. The room soon appeared to be crowded with persecutors, to judge from the way he would suddenly jerk round to stare at the corners (sometimes he would literally spin round like a top, screaming). He seemed to be ringed about by foes. A state of panic would follow and Raul would dash across the room in such a way that one almost "saw" the ring of pursuers closing in on him. When his panic was at its height he gave a stifled scream and fell on the floor. It was the same puppet-like collapse already described in the episode of "my hand" (p. 151). When the child collapsed, here again, one could "see" that this was due to his vivid phantasy that the pursuers were bursting their way into him.[1]

I referred above to these experiences as being pathetic, and I think they impressed me as such mainly because of the utter helplessness of this child. Although Raul trembled with fear, he did not attempt to defend himself, not even by raising his arm to shield his eyes. In fact, he seemed completely at the mercy of his hallucinatory pursuers. A scene such as I have described lasted a few minutes only and he sometimes had up to five or more collapses of the kind in a session. Occasionally, he banged his head against the wall before falling down.

Although this new symptom might appear as anything but reassuring, I in fact felt it to be the sign of a considerable improvement. For the hallucinations showed that he was now able to *experience* acute persecution and provided the medium for it; and I felt that his terror of persecutory objects, hitherto strongly denied, was able to come into the open because of a lessening of anxiety and a greater

---

[1] As in the case quoted by Dr. Lois Munro elsewhere in this book, it is probable that this total collapse represented the child's "death" both at the hands of his persecutors and as an escape from them.

ego integration. In other words, it was now possible for him to become aware of his own terrifying psychic reality because he was less disintegrated.

I believe that the child did not hallucinate before because his ego lacked sufficient coherence for such an experience. Formerly, owing to excessive splitting, his ego made little differentiation between internal and external events and his impulses were too diffused to enable him to conjure up the hallucinations clearly and to hold them for some time. It might also be said that he could only then be *observed* hallucinating because he had ceased to hallucinate all the time. I mean by this that the complete denial of external reality shown in his autism might well be considered a continuous *negative hallucination*.

With regard to the *content* of the frightening hallucinations, I think that again they represented both an object and a part of his ego; in this case, the persecutory breast or mother and the aggressive part of his self. The relation between these "visions" and myself could be clearly perceived on those occasions when Raul hallucinated as a result of frustrations inflicted by me; for it was then obvious that he hallucinated a persecutor in order not to see me as one. Hence, I often interpreted the "vision" as my split-off double which the child "made up" for me to remain good—good but ineffective. He did not appeal to me or ask for my assistance when hemmed in by persecutors; I was just a witness to the drama. My inefficiency reminded me of the ideal but barren "enclosed" object, already described (p. 154). This is significant, because the hallucinations became less terrifying when he turned to me for protection.

The protection consisted in his using my body as a sort of shield or parapet to hide him from his pursuers. It was very typical of this phase that he would start seeing persecutors everywhere and feel panicky, just as described above (cf. p. 158), but then, at the critical moment, instead of falling down, he would rush towards me and nestle up against my body. There he seemed to feel safe. Now and then he peeped out in the direction of the danger.[1]

[1] The first time the child used my body for protection had an interest of its own. He had been calmer than usual that session, when he suddenly grasped my wrist-watch. I gave it to him and he inspected it closely and then, surprisingly enough, placed the dial against his eye, like a monocle, as if he wanted to hear the tick-tock with his eye. He kept the watch there for quite a time before holding it to his ear. I did not know what to make of this "mistake", which is, by the way, a good example of how unpredictable an autistic child can be. The child obviously knew that he saw and did not hear with his eyes, and I am inclined therefore to consider this incident as a variant of his sampling technique: he had to taste me with his eyes to see if I (represented by one of my possessions) was dangerous or could be trusted. There were, incidentally, further indications that Raul considered his eyes more protected than his ears, owing perhaps to the fact that the former can be closed whilst the latter are always exposed to outer stimuli (cf. the way he stopped his ear by folding it forward).

I also observed that the "visions" tended to become more and more *localized*—usually in one upper corner of the room, and this appeared to be the outcome of his capacity to use me as a shield. But when anxiety was too great he no longer sought my protection and his hallucinations again became diffused and terrifying.

That he used me as a protector indicated that I had become a safer object, or a stronger one. His way of using me—crouching as if against a shield—suggested that he looked for safety *inside* my body. I would also refer here to the reversal of roles that had taken place with regard to the "enclosure game" (p. 153): there I assumed that the child protected the ideal object with a shield or barrier (the fences round the pile of toys); here I—the object—was protecting him by a similar device. This was an improvement, for the whole evidence suggests that it was far easier, for this child, to protect than to be protected. More than a month passed before his hallucinations became less frightening.

WATER-PLAY

Raul began to play with water a couple of sessions after he had first used my body as a screen. His attitude, cautious at first, soon became free and easy; nevertheless seven sessions exclusively devoted to water-playing elapsed before he dared to taste water. During those sessions he enjoyed filling the basin up to the top and then dipping both arms in up to the arm-pits, stirring the water with such turbulence that he usually got extremely wet. At other times he would very gently lower his naked arms into the basin, and seemed to relish contact with the cold water. On such occasions I heard him laughing aloud for the first time.[1] The child showed no sign of anxiety when he soaked himself or flooded the room.

Here I shall describe only two sessions, one in which he drank and the following one when depressive anxiety became the main feature.

The first was one in which his enjoyment of the water was keener than ever. He repeatedly filled a tumbler and kept pouring water all over the bathroom: under the basin, over the taps and, especially, into tin boxes and other containers. He went on doing this for a time and then took a drink from the tumbler. This surprised me, for he

---

[1] This was also the first occasion on which he showed a bodily sensation. Once, when he had soaked his clothes, he made a gesture for me to take off the overall he was wearing. There were other indications at the time that made me "feel" that he felt his body.

had not led up to it in any way. A few moments afterwards he took another sip, but before the end of the hour he found a far more exciting way of drinking, which consisted in sucking and licking all round the rim of the basin while letting the water overflow. In doing this his eyes shone and his body quivered with pleasure.

When the session was over, his mother came into the play-room to change his wet clothes. The child greeted her with a sunny smile and while he was being rubbed down with a towel and powdered, he seemed completely happy. Her attitude was a surprise to me, for on this occasion she showed a tender and sensitive understanding of her son's needs. This happy mother-child relationship seemed to be the consummation of the important and well rounded experience Raul had had that day; it reminded me of Dr. Winnicott's observation of the importance a *total experience* has in the emotional development of the child.[1]

I shall deal here with only one aspect of this over-determined material: that which concerned the child's blissful relationship with the breast. He had been able to be fed by it and to enjoy the feeding fully. The way he played at the basin, his gently dipping his arms into the water, seemed indicative of a fusion, a feeling of oneness with the ideal breast, this experience being the opposite of the one he had previously had with the "enclosed", ungiving ideal object.

In the transference, I think I played two roles: I was the bountiful breast or the mother who gave such a breast, on the one hand; and, on the other, Raul's baby brother or his father with whom he could now share the breast. With regard to the former role it was significant that the child should first feel me as a protector, or a shield, and that he was only later able to feel that I could feed him—by means of the basin that obviously stood for the breast. That I was predominantly felt as a sheltering and giving object indicated that a clearer distinction existed in his inner world between the good and bad object, and that the former was not in such constant danger of being overwhelmed by the latter (cf. the "enclosure game", p. 153).

But I think I also stood for Raul's brother, because to play at the basin was like showing the breast to me, and I consider, sharing it as well. I might add here that I approached the basin a couple of times to mimic what he was doing (when interpreting) and that he *did not mind* my intrusion. The fact that the wash-basin was an overflowing breast must have been significant, for it thus became inexhaustible and he could feel that he was neither emptying it with his

[1] *The Ordinary Devoted Mother and her Baby*, Nine Broadcast Talks, 1949.

Emilio Rodrigué

greed nor in danger of being deprived of it if he shared it with his brother. Melanie Klein[1] has repeatedly emphasized that idealization is used by the child both to defend himself against persecutory anxiety and to deny the harm done to the object. The outcome of this material as we shall now see confirms her views.

Raul continued to play with water in the following session. He played as on the preceding day, and even sucked from the rim of the basin, but *the mood* of the game was quite different: he was worried and tense and far from enjoying himself freely. He had taken a lampshade[2] from a nearby cupboard, at the beginning of the hour, and placed it carefully on the bathroom table before starting to play with water. He was obviously concerned for the lampshade's safety, often glancing at it whilst playing, and finally interrupting his game when he realized that the lampshade had been sprinkled with water. He reacted to this with anxiety and began immediately to hallucinate. This time the hallucination was focused on the electric light bulb hanging over the basin. Although badly frightened by the light, the child did not escape at once but went across the room and "rescued" the lampshade before running away. For the rest of that session he kept the lampshade beside him and did not return to the bathroom.

The important development shown in the session was Raul's concern for an object. He did love and care and worry for the lampshade. Guilt and distress were experienced when the lampshade got wet. These traits indicated a move towards depression, never shown before. The fact that he took a risk to save the lampshade was especially significant; it indicated a new capacity to defend what he loved. It should be noted, too, that Raul's attitudes and actions had a clearer meaning in this session. The thread of his emotions ran uninterruptedly from a mood in which he cared for and worried about the object to one in which guilt and anxiety were combined with his decision to defend it. His actions built up a coherent plot, and the reason for this is to be found, I think, in his greater capacity to bear guilt and experience depressive feelings.

When the lampshade got wet, the child could not cope with the anxiety of having harmed the loved object without splitting it. The

[1] See "Some Theoretical Conclusions Regarding the Emotional Life of the Infant", in *Developments in Psycho-Analysis* (London, 1952).
[2] This cupboard, containing bits of lumber, stood facing the play-room door and the child had opened it on other occasions. I gave him the lampshade and other objects in that cupboard because, at the time, he preferred to play with household objects rather than with toys.

electric bulb thus became the frightening (i.e. destroyed) object. But an electric bulb and a lampshade go naturally together; so the fact that he chose them to embody the good and the bad object suggests a lessening of his splitting mechanisms.

Finally, the lampshade was the first clear symbol to appear; the first of a series to come. It was the first object with which the child formed a stable emotional tie. It was clearly a symbol of the breast and I interpreted it as the outcome of that *total experience* he had had on the preceding day—the sucking from the rim of the basin in particular. Both the wash-basin and the lampshade stood for the breast, but the former was *too near* the breast to function as a symbol.[1]

AGGRESSIVE DISPLAY AND GREATER CONTACT WITH REALITY

Up to then (third month) Raul obediently stopped playing and left the room at the end of sessions. He never looked at me when I said goodbye to him. He did not want to take a toy home either. He had a different attitude, however, at the end of the session just described, for he wanted to take the lampshade home. Thus, he desired to possess the loved object. I told him that he wanted to take me with him and to keep me inside him. I also said that his body was felt to be safe, and that he wished to keep his loved object for himself alone.

His present attitude contrasted with the complete detachment he had previously shown at the end of sessions. To take the lampshade with him amounted to keeping me inside instead of drastically denying both my existence and his love for me when we parted. Later, thinking this over, I realized that to show possessiveness also meant a lessening of omnipotence: one must feel there are things not possessed that one needs in order to form a wish for possession.

I decided not to allow Raul to take the lampshade home and a fit of anger followed this frustration. Raising my voice so that he might hear me I tried to deal with his rage and the frustration that caused it. The good breast was taken away from him. But the lampshade did not stand for the ideal breast only; it was the symbol of the recent happy experiences at the basin; so I think that it also stood for a part of himself. I was, therefore, taking away from him

---

[1] The lampshade was not, *in itself*, a substitute for the breast; it had that essential quality of a symbol whereby "the connotation remains with the symbol when the object of its denotation is neither present nor looked for . . ." Susanne K. Langer, *Philosophy in a New Key* (Cambridge, 1942, and London, 1951), p. 52.

that experience of blissful union with the breast. This was not interpreted. The uproar was then too great for him to listen and for me to have a clear mind. I repeatedly came to it, however, on the following days.

When Raul's anxiety-state showed signs of subsiding I took him along and showed him the place where the lampshade would be kept. This reassured him but he was still restless when his mother took him home. I think I made the right decision. I felt sorry for the child in his despair and had doubts about my attitude. But I acted upon my previous experience with Raul which had taught me to be as consistent as I could be with regard to what he could or could not do.[1] What followed in Raul's analysis seemed to endorse my views: overt aggressiveness came to the fore.

Next day he was withdrawn. He did go for the lampshade but soon left it in one corner. He then became restless and had a fit of anger that went on for most of the hour. This session was the first of a stormy period that went on for a couple of weeks. Raul had many terrifying hallucinations at the time and, for several days, my body was not felt to be a safe shield. It looked as if a setback had taken place, but for one fact: the child became more openly aggressive. When rage was at its height he violently threw or kicked objects around. The aggressive act usually occurred at that stage of the hallucinatory persecution when he had previously fallen down; indeed, it seemed to be the substitute for bodily collapse. If that was so, Raul could now externalize, and thus act out, the destructive anxiety-situation which previously took place inside him. Besides, in general he showed a greater capacity for making a stand against his persecutors. He now threatened or even "exorcized" them, for he clenched his teeth, knit his brow and pulled all sorts of "fearful" faces at the ghostly apparitions. On one occasion he opened the window, made a commanding gesture with his arms ordering the persecutors to leave the room, and then closed the window, very pleased with himself. He was not disturbed again in that hour.

The child's restlessness was perhaps greater during the first five

---

[1] I believe M. Mahler has an opposite view in these matters. Discussing "Autistic Infantile Psychosis" in her paper "On Child Psychosis and Schizophrenia" (*The Psycho-analytic Study of the Child* (Vol. VII (1952), p. 286) she presents a case-history (Lotta, three years and four months) and explicitly says: "During therapy, by using *every conceivable device*, she was slowly brought to sensory perception of the outer world . . ." p. 290 (italics mine). Later on she qualifies this statement. With regard to the autistic child in general she writes: "Hence he must be lured out of his autistic shell with all kinds of devices such as music, rhythmic activities, and pleasurable stimulation of his sense organs," p. 302. But I believe that interpretations of the unconscious processes underlying the autism render these other devices unnecessary. In Melanie Klein's view they are disturbing to analysis and make interpretations difficult.

sessions following the lampshade incident. Near the end of the fifth session an interesting and sudden change in his mood appeared. He had upset all the chairs in the play-room at the beginning of the hour, and was particularly angry and noisy. Then, suddenly, he stood motionless and silent. It was an amazing transition from din to silence. The former enhanced the latter. Raul remained still for a while; he then took a chair and delicately placed it on top of another so that it balanced. He observed the chairs for a time as if wanting to make sure that the swaying upper chair would not lose its balance and fall. Next he took a fairly large metallic ruler (from the cupboard in which he found the lampshade) and holding it with both hands, like a balancing pole, he again remained motionless in the middle of the room. I was struck by the inquisitive, almost astonished, way he gazed round the room. He looked intensely and yet peacefully happy. This experience had a strong æsthetic import. I *knew* that something momentous was taking place in the child's mind or was about to take place. I could not but feel carried away by the mystery and suspense that the scene conveyed.[1] The impression I had was that he was discovering something in the surrounding space, as if recreating the world, and that everything he had, in phantasy, destroyed was coming back to life again. I tried to put these notions into words; for that purpose my interpretations focused on the important role reparation seemed to play here.

I referred to the violent way he had thrown the chairs around and how that had been like breaking up my (the Friend's) body, stressing his present urge to put the pieces of my body together again. Here, as in the preceding sessions, I came back to the incident of the lampshade that appeared to be the starting-point of his greater aggressiveness, and said that I had been the "bad mummy" who had taken the breast away from him and had made him feel like breaking her up. But the point needing special emphasis seemed to me to be that of his reparative phantasies and, in particular, that of reparation carried through by means of his penis. For in that session, the metallic ruler appeared clearly as a penis-symbol. I interpreted that he was able to throw things around because he was less afraid of his

[1] Marion Milner, in her paper "Aspects of Symbolism in Comprehension of the Not-Self" (in this book), describes a situation in the analysis of a boy of eleven that seems to me to be very similar in its æsthetical significance to that which I here describe. The assumptions she made in order to explain the material have been very illuminating for my understanding of Raul's æsthetic experiences; specially those views she puts forward in the section of her paper under the heading "Æsthetic Experience and the Merging of the Boundary".

aggression and of the aggressive qualities of his penis in particular, and thus could believe in its "good" reparative functions also. The child's response to this interpretation was remarkable: he listened attentively and seemed fully to understand my words; he then took my hand and pressed it tenderly against his cheek. His body was lightly poised over mine so that we seemed to be doubling the arrangement of the two balanced chairs that stood in front of us. I told him how he was less afraid of my penis too and that this made it possible for him to take in (to understand) my words, for they were felt to be the good penis or to come from it. Finally, I said that he felt he was a "mummy" and I was a "daddy" and that we were having a "good baby"—"we were making a new Raul".

Here I would like to give a brief summary of the main events in the fifteen weeks of analysis so far covered. Raul had begun to hallucinate in the sixth week and it took another six weeks for this phenomenon to diminish in intensity. By then water-play had begun and this game reached its climax in less than two weeks (seven sessions) when he drank. The lampshade came in on the following day. A week and a session more passed by, characterized by his aggressive outbursts, until the session above described was reached. This sequence of events shows that the pace of the child's improvement quickened once his persecutory hallucinations subsided, for after that several changes took place within a period of three weeks. In the period I shall now describe, up to the time when he spoke his first word and covering almost a month, a number of changes took place simultaneously, so I cannot do more than give the main trend of these developments with only some of the salient material.

Raul continued to be aggressive during this period. But he also developed a new way of dealing with spatial elements, for, apart from showing greater interest in a wider range of objects, he started to have definite ideas about how to use and where to put them. For instance, several sessions were devoted to "re-designing" the playroom. He worked very energetically at his new schemes, moving all the furniture round, sometimes carrying separate pieces out of the room altogether and bringing them back again and showing great ingenuity in varying his arrangements. Toys were more freely handled and Raul began to have definite likes and dislikes with regard to them. Those toys he liked were treated with the utmost care and delicacy, but he was careless and often violent with the group he rejected. He had a delicate way of approaching certain objects that he loved best, of lightly touching them with his fingertips and of raising his hands again as pianists sometimes do.

Raul also used his hands creatively in a game he often repeated, which involved kneeling by my side on the couch, taking off my glasses, and skilfully putting them on again several times, and then patting my face and pressing it gently as if he were modelling or shaping it. This game, amounting to a ritual, showed a desire for an intimate contact with me and the child chuckled with glee and uttered a soft gurgling sound while playing it.[1]

I believe he was beginning to make a far greater use of symbols. It could clearly be seen that he was dealing with external reality in a new way: he was *libidinizing* external objects, modelling them into symbols. Toys were increasingly used in a symbolic way: a piece of chalk, for instance, ceased to be exclusively employed as an object for drawing and now also stood for a nail in a game of make-believe, where a brick was a hammer, or was stuck in a bottle *as if* it were a candle, etc.

The greater use which he made of symbols coincided with his uttering his first articulated sounds, and here again, just as in the case of his hallucinations, they first appeared in a session and, subsequently, at home. His first significant sound was uttered six sessions after the one in which the two balanced chairs and the metallic ruler were interpreted as indications of his reparative phantasies (see p. 165). This happened after he had given me a particularly warm reception, for he smiled when entering the play-room and pressed my hand against his cheek. He then moved a chair up and leaned the ruler against it; then, standing on it, he began switching the electric light on and off and, with every flicker, he uttered a command-like "uuah-uuah". He was certainly delighted by this game in which the light "obeyed" him and he kept it up for ten minutes or so. This game suggested to me several lines of interpretation. I told him that Raul was like "Daddy" and had "Daddy's" ("the Friend's") big penis that made "uuah-uuah". With this "uuah-uuah", I went on, Raul was big and strong and could make the light come and go. As the child had become rather afraid of light (since the day he had wetted the lamp-shade and had been afraid of the electric light in the bathroom), I interpreted the "uuah-uuah" as coming from the good penis which was so strong that it turned the "bad light-penis" into a weak baby

---

[1] A variety of rituals appeared at the time, and I think that the first clear ritualistic attitude in the child occurred in that session where he held the metallic ruler in his hands whilst he was "re-creating the world".

which had to do what it was told: when Raul said "uuah-uuah", the "bad" penis went away.[1] I also spoke of his magic control over things, such as making day and night with his sound or controlling the parental intercourse. Finally, and whilst the light still went on and off, I spoke of his need for a good internal penis for the purpose of controlling his urine.

The child listened to my interpretations but it could not be said that he evinced much interest in them. After playing with the light, he went to the blackboard and chalked a series of vertical lines on it. I asked him if that was Raul and he stopped drawing to look at me and smile. He then proceeded to draw a circular scribble and responded in the same way when asked if it stood for a "mummy".

The twice-repeated sequence of meaningful responses such as these to a question of mine had never before occurred; never before had he come so near a direct answer. This was followed immediately by his climbing on to the table, lying on his back and opening his legs. It seemed that for him acknowledging my question was the same as the act of receiving the male organ; hence, I interpreted that my words were like a penis that got inside him and gave him "baby-words" like the sound "uuah-uuah".[2] Thus it might be said that, for Raul, to understand was literally to *conceive*.

On the following days other sounds appeared in rapid succession, "buuh", "ghuih", "baah", and in settings not unlike that described in connection with this first one; for he often made gestures that were feminine; moreover, his whole attitude was of a receptive feminine kind. I also noticed that vocalizations were frequently made when he happened to be handling objects that had a clear sexual symbolism.[3]

This receptive attitude was of significance. I believe it to be the counterpart of his other accomplishment: his greater use of symbols which represented a libidinizing of the outer world by pouring good parts of himself into it. The greater interplay of the child's inner and outer world resulted in a much less autoplastic type of behaviour. He was now able, to some extent, to modify the external world by

[1] I should explain that not one of these articulated sounds is a word in Spanish.

[2] This is an almost literal interpretation. The fact that he placed the metallic ruler by the chair before starting to play, lends support, I think, to my assumption that his articulated sound was related to the possession of a "good" penis.

[3] Once he vocalized when struggling to go up a narrow stairway holding the metallic ruler in one hand and the lampshade (resuscitated for the occasion) in the other. He also vocalized in a session in which the ruler and an electric radiator played important roles. With regard to his feminine gestures, his mother then reported that he was particularly attracted by her clothes and was often found wearing her hat and gloves, and carrying a bag.

acting upon it instead of magically denying or changing it. I believe that this was due to a diminution of his persecutory anxiety which allowed him to feel less distrustful of his external and internal objects and thus enabled him to give out more of the good "enclosed" in his inner world. The fact that he was more overtly aggressive was very important in this connection, for it showed that his destructive impulses were less denied and that those parts of his self felt to be aggressive were no longer so completely split off as before, in particular his penis, of which he was now less afraid and which could thus be felt as reparative and not solely destructive.

HIS FIRST WORD AND ITS SETTING

As an introduction to the session in which he first spoke, I would like to say that at the close of the period described above the child became interested in the problem of perspective and spent considerable time contemplating an object from different angles. To give an example: there was a skylight in the building visible from the waiting-room. The outward aspect of the skylight (a rectangular turret) had interested him whenever he went up on to the roof. Once, after he had inspected it closely, an idea seemed to strike him and he hurried downstairs, going straight into the waiting-room to fix his eyes on the square patch of light on the ceiling. The child had obviously understood that the outward and inward aspects of the skylight were two different facets of the same object. A similar interest in the different perspectives of objects was apparent on other occasions and, in particular, in the session when he first spoke. This occurred on the first day on which I saw him after treatment had been interrupted for a week for the Easter holiday.

At the beginning of the hour he looked for a long time down the lift shaft through the space between the door of the lift and the landing. He then went up and down the stairs and behaved in the following way: when he was on the top landing he looked at the lower landing and vice versa. In other words, he was looking from the place at which he had arrived towards the place from which he had come. This activity was interpreted as depicting the feelings of separation that the child had felt during the interruption, and how he had then felt the distance separating us.

I soon realized that Raul had changed. His mother told me that after a couple of "naughty days" he had been gay and affectionate for the rest of the week. On his return he recognized me at once and seemed delighted to see me again. I was, above all, impressed by his greater independence. Instead of holding my hand, as he had always done when leaving the room, he now went in and out of the room and up and down stairs by himself. I first interpreted this attitude as a sign of resentment, as if he were trying to tell me "I can get on all right without you". But upon considering the general impression the child gave, I came to stress his feeling of having been able to keep me inside himself (to remember me) during the seven days' break. I told him that he had felt angry and empty when I did not appear and that he had searched for me (I interpreted his staring at the lift-shaft as looking inside himself) and felt he had destroyed me—during the "naughty period"—but had afterwards restored me to life again.

His independence was interpreted as the result of having kept me safely as an internal, helpful object he could *depend on.*

But other relevant features appeared in this session: not only was he more independent of me, he also openly asked for help, in a way that had no precedent. Thus, when he came back from the stairs, he leaned out of the window and made a gesture indicating that I should hold him even more tightly so that he could lean farther out. This implied a realistic notion of danger, my assistance being asked for at the right moment.

The child asked to be helped again soon afterwards. He became angry without apparent reason and gave vent to his anger by knocking a chair away. No sooner had he done this than he showed great fear of the chair and ran towards me. This time, he did not shield himself against my body as usual, but *urged me to pick him up.* Once I had done so, he calmed down and immediately afterwards went to the bathroom, and there, without looking at me, he twice said quite clearly "Mummy".

The setting of this session proved to have features in common with the following sessions in which he introduced other words; the conclusions given here, therefore, though made specifically in relation to this particular session, apply broadly to the general trend of the period.[1]

[1] As with the wordless articulations, once the first word was spoken, others followed, and in less than a month he had used more than half a dozen words. His speech was "autistic" at first: the child seemed to speak to himself and his utterances occurred at random moments although he often applied his vocabulary correctly. After a month this achievement was lost again as a result of the removal of the play-room to another building. There he began slowly to speak again and now, in the seventh month of treatment, Raul has already uttered two-word sentences (the first being "water-mummy"). Speech tends to become communicative but improvement is slow. Of particular significance is the fact that he has not yet learned to say "yes" or "no".

What was interesting in that session was the child's new way of dealing with aggression. The chair he had knocked about became the object to be dreaded; what he injured became the persecutor. Such a clear causal link between his aggression and persecution had never appeared before. The "injured" chair was interpreted as standing for the analyst, who had frustrated him, and whom Raul had in phantasy destroyed. But there were other facts that made me add to this interpretation. He had been able to recognize his own aggression and he had shown a realistic notion of danger at the window. Of what danger had he become aware? I think that, ultimately, it was the danger of his own aggressive impulses, which were now felt to come from within himself, and that his acceptance of them had enabled him to become aware of external dangers too. Accordingly, I also interpreted the chair as standing for his own aggressive self which he felt to be so frightening that he could not cope with it without my help.

The following features were present in the session: recognition of me after separation, independence, realistic awareness of danger, and greater realization of his own aggressive impulses. These features indicated that his ego was more integrated, that a greater synthesis between his libidinal and aggressive impulses had taken place and that his perception of external and internal reality had improved. It seems clear then that this new psychic perspective had given rise to his first word.

A full discussion of the reasons that led the child to speak, and of the meaning words had for him, would be outside the scope of this paper. The onset of verbal symbolism would have to be considered in relation to other symbolic modes of expression, such as rituals, gestures, and imaginative play. That task I cannot undertake here. Therefore, I would like to draw attention only to the fact that Raul's first word appeared at that moment of his analysis when depressive features seemed to be coming nearer to the surface.

Melanie Klein has shown the importance of the depressive position in mental development.[1] At that stage, basic changes take place in a child's way of experiencing the world. The boundaries of knowledge—perceptions, reactions, feelings, ideas—are widened. And this ensues from the ego's capacity to experience guilt, and to care for its objects; also from the ego's realization that its love and hate

[1] "A Contribution to the Psychogenesis of Manic-Depressive States" (1935), in *Contributions to Psycho-Analysis, 1921–45* (1948). There is also a useful short description of the depressive position in Hanna Segal's paper, "A Psycho-Analytic Approach to Æsthetics", in this book.

relate to one and the same object and that this object is not a part of the self but has a life of its own.

Raul's analysis seems to show that an intimate connection exists between the depressive position and symbol-formation. Every move he made towards that position brought in a constellation of symbols, which were ever richer in meaning and embraced an ever wider range of objects and interests. I think the connection clearly existed in his case; but of course further work will be needed before it can be established as a general rule.[1]

DEVELOPMENT IN THE COURSE OF ANALYSIS

In the first seven months of analysis much progress was observed, but there is still a lot to be done if the psychotic condition is to be successfully overcome. In this paper I have concentrated on the series of changes that appeared in the child's behaviour. These changes tell a story of quick improvement, and this might give a one-sided picture if attention were not drawn to the fact that the background of the child's behaviour is still predominantly autistic. Most of the symptoms described at the beginning are still present at the close of the seventh-month period, but their frequency and intensity have considerably diminished. States of emotional detachment and withdrawal often occur, but they seldom last for a whole session, while fits of rage, with or without hallucinations, are still very common.

Raul's behaviour at home has considerably improved. He is much more affectionate to his parents—his father in particular. Towards his brother he is able to show jealousy and, lately, affection as well. He loves to play with children he knows well and he prefers those games that demand a lot of running. Although his aggression is still very inhibited, he has been seen hitting other children once or twice.

A dramatic change has taken place over food. Raul has acquired a voracious appetite, so much so that his mother complains how difficult it is to keep him quiet while food is being cooked. He now likes meat and his diet includes a variety of new dishes.

Progress in speech is slow. As I said elsewhere he is still unable to say "yes" or "no". He understands much better now and often does what he is told. At the time of writing this paper he has achieved

[1] Some further evidence of this connection is to be found in Bion's paper, in this volume.

sphincter control. This habit was acquired quite suddenly and in less than a fortnight he was clean both night and day.

Finally, I noticed that his hallucinations seem slowly to be changing into phobias. His visual hallucinations tend to become a fear of bright light. The way he screws up his eyes or turns his face away from the light suggests photophobia. He also shows phobic reactions towards unfamiliar objects—the vacuum cleaner, for instance. There are many signs indicating that his original insensibility has turned into a generalized hypersensibility.[1] For example, he screams if a tiny piece of food falls on him or his napkin; he cannot tolerate the feel of certain rough materials and is very particular about the clothes he wears.

EARLY INFANTILE AUTISM

Under the heading of "Early Infantile Autism" Kanner has presented a group of children with a symptomatology very similar to Raul's. What follows is a brief account of Kanner's findings.[2]

These children are usually withdrawn and unemotional from early infancy. They are, as a rule, quiet and well-behaved, and may be left by themselves for long periods without crying. As their symptoms are of the silent kind and do not disturb grown-ups, their parents usually do not detect any abnormality until the second or even the third year. The parents then complain chiefly of the aloofness of their child. The autistic child makes no distinction between people he knows and complete strangers; all are treated alike. Even his mother is treated in a detached, unemotional way. These children seem to want from people only to be left alone; when alone they play placidly for long hours, and their games, like Raul's, are as a rule unimaginative and meaningless. They respond with anger and anxiety if their activities happen to be interfered with, either by people or by unforeseen events. It seems, indeed, that what they dread most in their lives is the unforeseen; they show what Kanner describes as an "obsessive desire for the maintenance of sameness",[3] and they can be driven to despair by any change in their daily routines. They get on better with inanimate

---

[1] P. Bergmann, and S. K. Escalona, have reported on several children, whose clinical picture they relate to that of Kanner's "Early Infantile Autism", presenting hypersensibilities not unlike that of Raul. See "Unusual Sensitivities in Very Young Children", in *The Psycho-Analytic Study of the Child*, Vol. III–IV, 1949, p. 333.

[2] For a more detailed account see Kanner's description of Early Infantile Autism in his book *Child Psychiatry* (Springfield, Ill., 1935), p. 716.

[3] Ibid., p. 718.

than with animate objects; indeed, to some extent, they treat people as inanimate objects, for they consider only that part of a person's body with which they happen to be in immediate contact.

Nearly two-thirds of the thirty or more children seen by Kanner (up to 1948) learned to speak. Their speech has the following features: naming and pronunciation present no difficulty, on the contrary they usually learn by rote and remember with astonishing accuracy long lists of words, but their vocabulary is not used for communication. Words do not express meaning to others. *Echolalia* and *"pronominal inversal"* (they cannot distinguish "I" from "you") are general occurrences, and Kanner considers the latter almost to be the pathognomic sign of that condition.

These children have a very low general intellectual performance, but their faces are usually intelligent and they nearly always excel in some one intellectual or artistic field. Such giftedness has led to many of them being considered child prodigies, but it soon appears that their talent, however great, is one-sided, and strangely out of keeping with the rest of the personality. Lastly, they often come from cold, ultra-intellectual families.

Raul's condition undoubtedly comes under Kanner's heading of Early Infantile Autism.[1] His symptoms, one by one, are included in Kanner's scheme and the reader is referred to his history for the purpose of correlation. I found this author's excellent description of "Early Infantile Autism" very illuminating; for, besides its inherent diagnostic value, it enabled me to set the experience I had gained from a single case against the background of a well-defined nosological entity. Moreover, I feel that Kanner's phenomenological description adds a wealth of confirmatory data to some of Melanie Klein's statements regarding the earliest stage of mental

[1] Dr. and Mrs. E. Pichon Riviere had opportunities for studying ten cases of Early Infantile Autism, seven of which are now under analysis by P. Riviere and his co-workers. Their findings, using Melanie Klein's play technique, are in the main similar to mine and I am deeply grateful to them for putting their case material and their valuable experience at my disposal. On the basis of their material it seems that practically all such children have feeding difficulties from birth onwards and are nearly always extremely unaggressive. Kanner does not explicitly refer to these features, but they seem to be implicit in his description.

No definite reference that I know of has been made by Kanner or others to hallucinations in these children. This surprises me, for I have come across another autistic child who hallucinates. He is a boy of twelve, whom I have just started to analyse, and whose symptomatology is surprisingly like Raul's, except that he speaks. At the first interview I could see that he hallucinated, and, when asked about what he saw, he said that a man was playing football on the ceiling. Two sessions afterwards he saw the devil behind me and showed acute anxiety.

This child, by the way, shows a real gift for music; I am told that he can tell who is conducting a given symphony on the radio even when he has not heard the conductor before in that particular piece of music, for he knows the style of every well-known conductor.

development—the paranoid-schizoid position. It is signikcant that Kanner himself has done no more than give a phenomenological description of the group he has defined and has not gone into its underlying psychopathology.[1] This may be because he does not conceive the multiplicity of autistic symptoms as active attempts to master anxiety. It appears that he regards them merely as an expression of an abnormally undeveloped mind resulting from an innate autistic disposition coupled with an unfavourable environment. Thus, for instance, in his view the child deals with persons as "part-objects" only because he cannot apprehend whole objects.

Melanie Klein's formulations account for and bring together the various features of autistic behaviour in a way that, as far as I know, no other theory has done. Based on her views I shall sketch some conclusions that I believe apply generally to the autistic group of children.

These children's moods alternate between two extremes. They either look placid, even blissful, or they look frightened and in despair. They usually swing sharply from one state into the other, without intermediate states. They look placid when left alone among their things; anxiety suddenly appears when an external object intrudes in a way that cannot be ignored.

They seem to hate and fear the external world. Their lack of interest in it, when placid, results from denying its existence. This denial appears to be extreme in infantile autism. I suggest that in some severe cases, like Raul's, it amounts to a *negative hallucination* of the environment. Hence, they live in an empty space; our voice is not heard nor is our body seen. It is significant here that many autistic children were thought to be deaf.[2]

---

[1] Kanner, *op. cit.*, discusses Melanie Klein's views on techniques of child-analysis at length and disagrees with them. His criticism shows that he was acquainted with her work. In the chapter on Infantile Schizophrenias he mentions that "Klein, Rapoport, and Cottington could report improvement as a reward for psycho-therapy". Unfortunately, however, Melanie Klein's name is omitted from the bibliography, so that the reader cannot trace the "rewarding" results to any case in particular (that obtained in Dick's analysis for instance). Rapoport's paper, on the other hand, was not omitted; significantly it concludes: "To summarize, I have quoted at length from Melanie Klein's paper ('The Importance of Symbol-Formation in Ego-Development') because, first, it is an important contribution to the problems of childhood sch zophrenia, and second, because in certain instances her observations on psychodynamics parallel the clinical picture described in our patient. Therapeutic contact was established and an insight into the child's problem gained when, after using a play technique similar to Melanie Klein's, the meaning of the patient's obscure symbolism became intelligible." Rapoport's patient, a boy of eleven, showed "striking similarities" with Dick: refusal to eat, inhibition of biting, withdrawal ("he would ignore people for days"), echolalia, dissociation of pain, etc. See J. Rapoport's paper: "Therapeutic Process in a Case of Childhood Schizophrenia", *The Nervous Child* (1942), p. 188.

[2] See Kanner, *op. cit.*, p. 717.

Emilio Rodrigué

These children deny the external world's existence because they have projected into it all (objects, feelings, situations) that is hateful and painful and frightening. The quantitative factor is extremely important and accounts for their extreme withdrawal: they seem to project and deny *en bloc* the whole of their aggressive selves. This massive disowning would explain, first, why their external object can suddenly turn into a fearful persecutor and secondly, why they are unaggressive to the point of even lacking self-preservative drives. In the twelve-year-old boy I am treating, his lack of aggression went so far that he could not shield his face with his arms when he fell (he had a dent in his forehead). Raul's case is a clear illustration both of the intensity of his persecutory anxiety (cf. his frightening hallucinations) and of his unaggressive helplessness. When the projecting and disowning of impulses is done on such a vast scale a large part of the ego is also split off, so that it is considerably weakened. The weak ego needs to defend itself. The autistic child defends himself by magic means.

The autistic child is an omnipotent creature. In many ways he is the despotic ruler of a static world peopled by those who have the blind obedience of inanimate objects. His behaviour suggests that he only participates in those external situations in which the "sameness" of the environment provides a suitable background for his controlling phantasies. Melanie Klein's theories regarding the mechanism of projective identification are essential for an understanding of the way in which the autistic child comes to feel that he omnipotently controls the world.[1] By projecting parts of his self into the object he feels that he controls it, for he identifies the object with the projected part of the self. I consider that it is because of the extreme use the autistic child makes of projective identification that he comes to think of the external world as a part of his self, which can be completely denied and/or completely controlled. He has the omnipotent belief that people are puppets whose disjointed parts, like my hand in Raul's case, are tools and appendages to be used to fit his own purposes.

But this phantasy can be, and often is, shattered. This usually happens when the external object (or event) behaves *suddenly*, so to speak, in such an unpuppet-like way that the child's omnipotent belief breaks down. When his defensive mechanism fails, he feels confronted by, and at the mercy of, a persecutory object that can

---

[1] For a description of projective identification see "Notes on Some Schizoid Mechanisms" (1946), in *Developments in Psycho-Analysis*, 1952.

be said to embody all the content of his destructive impulses. When this takes place he fears his own annihilation, for I think the intensity of the autistic child's anxiety is similar to that to which imminent death gives rise. The experience of annihilation comes about when he feels that the persecutory object is bursting its way into his body and destroying it (cf. Raul's puppet-like collapses, p. 151, 158). This forceful re-entry of the persecutors seems to be the main anxiety-situation in infantile autism.

There is a counterpart to the alternation of moods in these children that has to do with their body-schemes.[1] It is difficult to describe autistic behaviour without the use of such terms as "shell", "barrier", "being wrapped up", etc., to account for our impressions. By these terms we convey our impression that a sharply defined boundary lies between ourselves and the withdrawn child. But neither can we dispense with concepts such as "disintegration", and "chaos", for example, when describing the frightening experiences of ego-annihilation also experienced by these children. We feel then that their shell-like boundary no longer exists. This suggests that the autistic child clings to a boundary dividing that which is felt to be good and to be his self, from that which is felt as bad and alien. He has made a shell of a boundary out of fear of a persecutory world—a shell which is a defence against confusion and loss of differentiation between an inner "good" and an outer "bad" world. The state of confusion occurs, as Herbert Rosenfeld has shown in his work with schizophrenics, from the inordinate use of projective identification,[2] and it can be clearly observed in an autistic child who has acquired speech. The peculiar grammatical construction, called "Pronominal Inversal", in which he "... comes to speak of himself always as 'you' and of the persons addressed as 'I' "[3] is obviously related to the underlying confusion between "me" and "not-me". Echolalia in an autistic child analysed by Mrs. G. Racker could also be seen to represent this confusion and the defence against it: by repeating the word, he was the other person (confusion), but by being the other person's echo, he was reflecting the word outside without assimilating it.[4]

[1] I am using the concept of "body scheme" in the sense defined by W. C. M. Scott, and hope I am not misapplying his ideas. Cf. his paper "A Problem of Ego Structure", *Psycho-Anal. Quart.* (1948), 71, in which he develops Paul Schilder's concept of the "body-image" (*The Image and Appearance of the Human Body*, Psyche Monographs No. 4, 1935).

[2] See "Notes on the Psychopathology of Confusional States in Chronic Schizophrenias", 1950, *Int. J. Psycho-Anal.*, Vol. XXXI, 132; see also "Notes on the Psycho-Analysis of the Super-ego Conflict of an Acute Schizophrenic Patient" in this book.

[3] Cf. Kanner, *op. cit.*, p. 718.

[4] Personal communication.

The autistic child is highly narcissistic. He relates himself to an external object only in so far as he comes to feel that it is a part of his self (projective identification). The work of Melanie Klein has shown that in narcissistic states the relation to an internal object is retained. The relation to an ideal internal object came out clearly in Raul's analysis, and I believe it accounts for several phenomena in infantile autism. It would account, for instance, for those blissful moments such children often have. Besides, the fact that even self-preservation can be hampered in them cannot be solely explained by the massive denial of aggression. It suggests a disregard for the body, because there is something else—the ideal internal object—which the child is trying to protect and really cares for. His body would then be, in Melanie Klein's words, "only a shell for it (the ideal object)".[1] This attitude might have something to do with the frequent insensibility of these children to bodily pain.

Finally, the notion of an ideal internal object offers an explanation for one most interesting problem raised by infantile autism: that of the beauty, the talent for music, and the graceful movements of such children. Kanner mentioned, in a private communication,[2] that only one out of the thirty or so cases he studied did not have a gift for music. Besides, they are often remarkably beautiful and graceful. Kanner does not explicitly mention their beauty and gracefulness, but he refers to these qualities (beauty, in particular) in several case histories—qualities which were also present in the children studied by Pichon Riviere and his co-workers, and in the children I have seen.

The autistic child, like Narcissus, is beautiful.[3] In this connection there is a highly significant passage in Freud's paper "On Narcissism"[4] where he remarks on the "fascination" of narcissistic women: "Such women have the greatest fascination for men, not only for æsthetic reasons, since as a rule they are the most beautiful, but also for certain interesting psychological constellations". Freud proceeds to relate their fascination to narcissism and adds: ". . . the charm of a

---

[1] Cf., "Notes on Some Schizoid Mechanisms" in *Developments in Psycho-Analysis*, p. 302. Referring to excessive idealization as a defence mechanism, Melanie Klein mentions that the ego can be so entirely dependent on his ideal object that he becomes "only a shell for it". I believe that her statement specifically applies to the autistic child.

[2] Reported by P. Bergmann and S. K. Escalona's paper: "Unusual Sensitivities in Very Young Children" in *The Psycho-analytic Study of the Child*, Vol. III–IV, 1949, p. 333.

[3] I feel that the fate of these children embodies, in condensed form, the Greek myth of Narcissus. They are both Narcissus and Echo (the nymph whose love Narcissus rejected). Like Narcissus they cannot distinguish between themselves and others and, like Echo, they do not distinguish whether words belong to them or to others (echolalia).

[4] Cf. "On Narcissism: an Introduction", 1914, *Collected Papers*. IV, p. 30.

child lies to a great extent in his narcissism, his self-sufficiency and inaccessibility, just as does the charm of certain animals, which seem not to concern themselves about us, such as cats and large beasts of prey".

I was surprised to find that Freud's terms in this passage are those one specifically uses when speaking of autistic children: "beauty", "self-sufficiency", "inaccessibility". Even his reference to cats reminded me of the tip-toe quality of Raul's walk, and of the light springy gait so frequently possessed by these children in general. Moreover, they are certainly attractive. Freud suggests that the spell cast by narcissistic creatures might be due to the fact that "we envy them their power of retaining a blissful mind". I believe Freud's remark becomes even more significant if, following Melanie Klein's contributions to the study of narcissism, we think of the blissful state of mind as the result of an ideal relationship with an ideal object. Wrapped up in his phantasies the autistic child lives in an inner world of love and harmony, where nothing but the ideal object is felt to exist. The ultimate content of this inner world would be an ideal relationship with a bountiful, everlasting, ever-present breast.

I suggest that the beauty and other æsthetic gifts and qualities of the autistic child may be the result of that ideal relationship. Perhaps in the blissful emotional tie with the ideal object, feelings are phrased in a pattern akin to music. In other words, music may be the medium of expression, the language of love with an ideal object. Does the ideal object also create the autistic child's beauty?

But we must not forget that this is only one side of the picture. The very perfection of his inner paradise is a measure of his horror of the outer world into which he has projected all his devils.[1]

---

[1] There were times when this same child could become extremely ugly. His screams too were peculiarly unpleasant.

8

NOTES ON THE PSYCHO-ANALYSIS OF THE SUPER-EGO CONFLICT IN AN ACUTE SCHIZOPHRENIC PATIENT

HERBERT ROSENFELD

IN analysing a number of acute and chronic schizophrenic patients during the last ten years, I have become increasingly aware of the importance of the super-ego in schizophrenia. In this paper I shall present details of the psycho-analysis of one acute catatonic patient in order to throw some light on the structure of the schizophrenic super-ego and its relation to schizophrenic ego-disturbances. I also wish to discuss the controversy about methods of approach to acute schizophrenic patients.

THE CONTROVERSY CONCERNING THE APPROACH TO SCHIZOPHRENIC PATIENTS BY PSYCHO-ANALYSIS

In discussing the value of the psycho-analytic approach to schizophrenia, we have to remember that psychotherapists with widely different theories and equally different techniques claim success in helping the schizophrenic in the acute states of the disease. The attempt to concentrate on producing a quick therapeutic result in the acute schizophrenic state, irrespective of the method of approach, may be temporarily valuable to the individual patient and gratifying to the therapist; but these "cures" are generally not lasting and the therapists often neglect the importance of continuing the treatment during the chronic mute phase of the disease which follows the acute state.[1] The psycho-analytic method can be used for both the acute and the chronic phase of the disease. I have found

[1] Eissler (1951) suggested the terms: "acute or (first) and mute or (second) phase of schizophrenia". He pointed out that the acute phase may last many years and the illness may take its course entirely either in the first or in the second phase. Eissler's contention is that the whole question of the psycho-analysis of schizophrenia can be decided only in the second phase.

that when used in the acute phase it can be carried on in the chronic phase without any fundamental change in technique; in fact, the use of the analytic technique in the acute phase prepares and assists the psycho-analytic treatment of the mute phase. The ultimate success of the treatment seems to depend on the handling of the mute phase. But, if a non-analytic method of forcible suggestion or of reassurance is used in the acute phase, psycho-analysis has been found to be exceedingly difficult in the chronic phase and its ultimate success may be prejudiced. Therefore if analysis is to be used at all in the treatment of schizophrenia, it is advisable to start with it in the acute phase.

There are many who would disagree with this view that the psycho-analytic technique can be used in the treatment of acute schizophrenia. Most American psycho-analytic workers on schizophrenia, for example, Harry Stack Sullivan, Fromm-Reichmann, Federn, Knight, Wexler, Eissler, and Rosen, have changed their method of approach so considerably that it can no longer be called psycho-analysis. They all seem agreed that it is futile to regard psycho-analytic method as useful for acute psychosis. They all find re-education and reassurance absolutely necessary; some workers like Federn have gone so far as to say that the positive transference must be fostered and the negative one avoided altogether. He has also warned us against interpreting unconscious material. Rosen seems to interpret unconscious material in the positive and negative transference, but he also uses a great deal of reassurance, a problem which I shall discuss later on in greater detail. But a number of English[1] psycho-analysts, stimulated by Melanie Klein's research on the early stages of infantile development, claim to have been successful in treating acute and chronic schizophrenics by a method which retains the essential features of psycho-analysis. Psycho-analysis in this sense can be defined as a method which comprises interpretation of the positive and negative transference without the use of reassurance or educative measures, and the recognition and interpretation of the unconscious material produced by the patient. The experience of child analysts may help us here to define in more detail the psycho-analytic approach to acute schizophrenics, because the technical problems arising in the analysis of acute psychotics are similar to those encountered in the analysis of small

[1] There may be a number of workers in the U.S.A. and South America such as Kaufmann and Pichon Riviere who have treated schizophrenic patients by psycho-analysis. They have, however, not described their clinical approach. (Pichon Riviere's papers on schizophrenia are only theoretical.)

children. In discussing the analysis of children from the age of two years and nine months onwards, Melanie Klein has pointed out that by interpreting the positive and negative transference from the beginning of the analysis, the transference neurosis develops. She regards any attempts to produce a positive transference by non-analytic means, such as advice or presents or reassurance of various kinds, not only as unnecessary but as positively detrimental to the analysis. She found certain modifications of the adult analysis necessary in analysing children. Children are not expected to lie on the couch, and not only their words but their play is used as analytical material. Co-operation between the child's parents and the analyst is desirable, as the child has to be brought to his sessions and the parents supply the infantile history and keep the analyst informed about real events. In the analysis of children as described by Melanie Klein, however, the fundamental principles of psycho-analysis are fully retained.

All the experience thus gained has been used as guiding principles in the analysis of psychotics, particularly acute schizophrenic patients. If we avoid attempts to produce a positive transference by direct reassurance or expressions of love, and simply interpret the positive and negative transference, the psychotic manifestations attach themselves to the transference, and, in the same way as a transference neurosis develops in the neurotic, so, in the analysis of psychotics, there develops what may be called a "transference psychosis". The success of the analysis depends on our understanding of the psychotic manifestations in the transference situation.

There are some technical points which should be mentioned here. I never ask an acute schizophrenic patient to lie down on the analytic couch. After the acute schizophrenic condition has passed, one has to consider very carefully when the lying position should be introduced. This decision is by no means an easy one, as I have found that there are many chronic schizophrenic patients who are better treated in the sitting-up position. Schizophrenic patients frequently change their position in the consulting-room during any one session and also from one session to another, and this behaviour is significant as an expression of the patient's unconscious phantasies. I use as analytic material the whole of the patient's behaviour, his gestures and actions of various sorts, to a far greater extent than with neurotic patients. Close co-operation by parents and nurses is essential, particularly if the patient has to be seen in a mental hospital or nursing home or has to be brought to the analyst by a nurse or relative. Another important question is how often and how long at a time the patient should be seen. I have found that acute schizophrenic patients have to be seen at least six times a week, and often the usual fifty minutes' session has seemed to be insufficient. In my own experience it is better not to vary the length of time of any one session, but to give the patient, if necessary, longer sessions (ninety minutes) while the acute phase persists. It is also unwise to interrupt the treatment for more than a few days while the patient is still in the acute state, since it may cause a prolonged setback in his clinical condition and in the analysis.

The analysis of schizophrenic patients has many pitfalls, since the nature of the schizophrenic process makes the analytic task exceedingly difficult. The analyst has to cope with disturbing counter-transference reactions in himself and is often tempted to change or abandon his analytic technique. This may be one of the reasons for the controversy about the possibility of an analytic approach. The solution of the controversy can only be found in practice: namely, by showing that a transference analysis of acute schizophrenic patients is possible; and by examining the nature of the schizophrenic transference and other central schizophrenic problems and anxieties.

I have the impression that the need to use controlling and reassuring methods is related to the difficulty of dealing with the schizophrenic super-ego by psycho-analysis. Milton Wexler (1951) has contributed to the understanding of this point in his paper "The Structural Problem in Schizophrenia". In criticizing the view of Alexander, who denies the existence of a super-ego in schizophrenics, Wexler says: "To explain the schizophrenic's conflicts (hallucinations and illusions) wholly as expressions of disorganized instinctual demands that have lost their inter-connection, is a travesty of the clinical picture of schizophrenia, which often reflects some of the most brutal morality I have ever encountered. Certainly we are not dealing with a super-ego intact in all its functions, but a primitive, archaic structure in which the primal identification (incorporated figure of the mother) holds forth only the promise of condemnation, abandonment and consequent death. Though this structure may only be the forerunner of the super-ego which emerges with complete resolution of the Œdipus situation, its outline and dynamic force may be felt both in young children and schizophrenic patients, and if we do not see it (the super-ego), I suspect it is because we have not yet learned to recognize the most archaic aspects of its development."

183

While fully recognizing the importance of the archaic super-ego, Wexler has, however, deviated considerably from psycho-analysis in his clinical approach. Apparently he did not attempt to analyse the transference situation. He tried to identify himself deliberately with the super-ego of his patient by agreeing with the patient's most cruel, moral self-accusations. In this way he established contact with his patient which he had failed to do before. The treatment continued while the therapist was taking over the role of a controlling and forbidding person (for example, he forbade the patient any sexual or aggressive provocations which threatened to disturb the therapeutic relationship). Wexler made it quite clear that he also acted in a very friendly, reassuring manner towards his patient. The theoretical background of his approach is his attempt as a therapist to identify himself with the super-ego of the patient. As soon as he has made contact with the patient in this way he feels that he has succeeded in his first task, and he (the therapist) then begins to act as a controlling but friendly super-ego. He claims that in this manner a satisfactory super-ego and ego-control is gradually established which brings the acute phase of schizophrenia to an end. The patient who had been distinctly helped by Wexler's method was a schizophrenic woman who had been in a mental hospital for five years.

Rosen (1946) described a technique in approaching acute, excited, catatonic patients who felt pursued by frightening figures. He established contact by "deliberately assuming the identity, or the identities, of the figures which appeared to be threatening the patient and reassured the latter that, far from threatening him, they would love and protect him". In another case, Rosen (1950) directly assumed the role of a controlling person by telling his woman patient to drop a cigarette which she had grabbed. He also controlled her physically and told her to lie still on the couch and not to move. But towards the end of the session described, he changed his attitude by saying, "I am your mother now and I will permit you to do whatever you want." In Wexler's and Rosen's case it is clear that the particular approach aims at a modification of the schizophrenic super-ego by direct control and reassurance. Wexler suggests that Knight's and Hayward's success in the treatment of their schizophrenic patients must have been also due to their taking over super-ego control. It seems likely that all these methods which use friendly reassurance have a similar aim, i.e. the modification of the super-ego.

Indeed, from this critical survey, it would seem that all these psychotherapeutic methods are aimed at a direct modification of the super-ego. But I should add that none of the workers I have quoted have so far made clear whether they tried to approach the acute schizophrenic patient by a psycho-analytic technique and, if so, why they failed.

SOME PSYCHO-ANALYTIC VIEWS ABOUT THE SUPER-EGO IN SCHIZOPHRENIA

Freud (1924) said: "A transference neurosis corresponds to a conflict between ego and id, a narcissistic neurosis to that between ego and super-ego, and a psychosis to that between ego and outer world." Freud did not explicitly discuss schizophrenia in this paper; however, this formula seems to suggest that he did not think the super-ego could play any significant role in schizophrenia (dementia præcox). But earlier, in 1914, he pointed to a parallel between delusions of observation such as the hearing of voices in paranoid disorders, and the manifestations of conscience. He suggested that "the delusion of being watched presents the conscience in a regressive form, thereby revealing the genesis of this function". He then proceeded to link the ego-ideal with homosexuality and the influence of parental criticism. Later on in the same paper he said that in paranoid disorders the origin or "evolution of the conscience is regressively reproduced". These statements of Freud (1914) imply that he did appreciate the importance of the super-ego in schizophrenia. He seems also to hint that the analysis of regressed schizophrenics suffering from auditory hallucinations might help to explain the origin of the super-ego.

E. Pichon Riviere (1947) stressed the importance of the super-ego in schizophrenia. He suggested that the psychoses (including schizophrenia) as well as the neuroses are the outcome of a conflict between the id on the one hand and the ego at the service of the super-ego on the other. He says: "In the process of regression there arises a dissociation of the instincts, and that of aggression is channelled both by the ego and the super-ego, thus determining the masochistic attitude of the former and the sadistic attitude of the latter. Tension between the two instincts originates anxiety, guilt feelings and the need for punishment. . . ."

Pious (1949) stated that he "became convinced that the fundamental structural pathology in schizophrenia most probably lies in the formation of the super-ego". He believes in the early development of the super-ego, but only stresses its positive aspects. He says:

Herbert Rosenfeld

"The super-ego develops from several loci, the earliest of which is the introjection of the loving and protecting mother-image. I believe that the development is jeopardized by prolonged privation and by hostility in the mother." In his opinion the schizophrenic has a defective super-ego, but the structure of this defective super-ego is not explained.

Nunberg expressed his views on the super-ego in schizophrenia in 1920. His patient, who suffered from an extremely severe feeling of guilt, claimed that he had destroyed the world; and it became clear that he believed he had done so by eating it. Nunberg says: "In his cannibalistic phantasies the patient identified the beloved person with the food and with himself. To the infant the mother's breast is the only loved object, and this love, at that stage, bears a predominantly oral and cannibalistic character. There cannot yet exist a feeling of guilt." Nunberg, however, suggests that certain feelings and sensations of the oral and anal zone, which cannot yet find expression in speech, "form the emotional basis for the development of that ideational complex known as guilt-feeling". Reading Nunberg's description of his patient, we are surprised at his statement that "there cannot yet exist a feeling of guilt" at the oral stage. For his case suggests that guilt-feelings and a super-ego exist at a preverbal period and seems to show that the sensations of the oral tract to which he refers are related to phantasies of consuming objects.

Melanie Klein[1] has contributed most to our understanding of the early origins of the super-ego. She has found that, by projecting his libidinal and aggressive impulses on to an external object which at first is his mother's breast, the infant creates images of a good and a bad breast. These two aspects of the breast are introjected and contribute both to the ego and the super-ego. She has also described two early developmental stages corresponding to two predominant early anxieties of the infant; "the paranoid-schizoid position", which extends over the first three to four months of life, and "the depressive position", which follows and extends over most of the remaining months of the first year. If, during the paranoid-schizoid phase, aggression and therefore paranoid anxieties become increased through internal and external causes, phantasies of persecutory objects predominate and disturb the ability to maintain good objects inside on which normal ego and super-ego development depend.

[1] I do not attempt to present here a detailed description of Melanie Klein's views; I only try to concentrate on those points which are relevant to the theme of my paper.

She has emphasized that "if persecutory fear and, correspondingly, schizoid mechanisms are too strong, the ego is not capable of working through the depressive position. This in turn forces the ego to regress to the paranoid-schizoid position and reinforces the earlier persecutory fears and schizoid phenomena."[1]   In such cases the internal objects, including the super-ego, will be only slightly modified by the later development, and so will retain many of the characteristics of the early paranoid-schizoid position, i.e. objects are split into good and bad ones.   There is an inter-relationship between these good and bad objects in that, if the bad objects are extremely bad and persecutory, the good objects as a reaction-formation will become extremely good and highly idealized.   Both the ideal objects and the persecutory objects contribute to the early super-ego and in patients who have regressed to the paranoid position we can observe that some idealized and also some persecutory objects have super-ego functions.   In the analysis of many acute schizophrenic patients we have difficulty in detecting the ideal objects functioning as the super-ego and we are impressed only by the persecutory quality of the super-ego.   This may be due partly to the extreme demands of idealized objects, which make it so difficult to differentiate them from the demands of the persecutory objects.

Generally speaking, in schizophrenic patients the capacity to introject and maintain good objects inside is severely disturbed. However, even in acute schizophrenic patients we can occasionally observe attempts, which coincide clinically with the appearance of depressive anxieties, to introject good objects.   As the infant during his normal development moves towards the depressive position, the persecutory anxiety and the splitting of objects diminishes, and the anxiety begins to centre round the fear of losing the good object outside and inside.   After the first three or four months of life, the emphasis shifts from the fear that the self will be destroyed by a persecuting object, to the fear that the good object will be destroyed. Concurrently there is a greater wish to preserve it inside.   The anxiety and guilt about the inability to restore this object inside, and secondly outside, then come more to the fore and constitute the super-ego conflict of the depressive position.   The normal outcome of the depressive position is the strengthening of the capacity to love and repair the good object inside and outside.

In schizophrenic patients there has been a failure of normal

---

[1] Melanie Klein: "Notes on Some Schizoid Mechanisms", in *Developments in Psycho-Analysis*, p. 308.

Herbert Rosenfeld

working-through of the depressive position, and regression to the paranoid phase has taken place. The process does not become stationary at this point and frequent fluctuations involving progression and regression take place.[1]

This may explain why in an acutely regressed schizophrenic patient one often observes a super-ego which shows a mixture of persecutory and depressive features. Clinically the patient may be observed to be in a "struggle" with objects inside, which attack him by criticizing and punishing him, and which seem to represent a persecutory super-ego. But often quite suddenly the nature of the internal objects seems to change and they assume a more complaining character and make insistent demands for reparation, features which are more characteristic of what might be called a "depressive" super-ego.[2] The conflict can rarely be maintained on the depressive level for any length of time and persecution increases again.

In the following description of the struggle of a patient with his internal objects I have purposely concentrated on those internal objects which go to form the super-ego. The contribution of internalized objects to the ego and their relation to the id are also of vital importance, but I have not discussed them in detail in this paper.

The investigation of the psychopathology of schizophrenia has also shown the importance of certain mechanisms such as splitting of both the ego and its objects, which were named by Melanie Klein "schizoid mechanisms". For example, she described, among others, the splitting of the ego caused by aggression turning against the self and by the projection of the whole or parts of the self into external and internal objects—a process which she has called "projective identification".[3]

In previous papers I have drawn attention to the importance of projective identification in schizophrenia. In the transference analysis of acute schizophrenic patients it is often possible to trace the mechanism of projective identification to its origin. I have observed that whenever the acute schizophrenic patient approaches an object in love or hate he seems to become confused with this object. This confusion seems to be due not only to phantasies of oral incorpora-

---

[1] Melanie Klein: "Notes on some Schizoid Mechanisms".

[2] In Melanie Klein's view, the super-ego of the depressive position, among other features, accuses, complains, suffers and makes demands for reparation, but, while still persecutory, s less harsh than the super-ego of the paranoid position.

[3] For the more detailed study of these mechanisms I refer to Melanie Klein (1946) and H. Rosenfeld (1947).

tion leading to *introjective* identification, but at the same time to impulses and phantasies in the patient of entering inside the object with the whole or parts of his self, leading to "*projective* identification". This situation may be regarded as the most primitive object relationship, starting from birth. In my opinion the schizophrenic has never completely outgrown the earliest phase of development to which this object relationship belongs and in the acute schizophrenic state he regresses to this early level. While projective identification is based primarily on an object relationship, it can also be used as a mechanism of defence: for example, to split off and project good and bad parts of the ego into external objects, which then become identified with the projected parts of the self. The chronic schizophrenic patient makes ample use of this type of projective identification as a defence. If, however, projection as a defence becomes too extensive, the ego, instead of being strengthened, loses its own capacity to function and an acute schizophrenic state of disintegration may result. In neurotic patients the severe super-ego often causes the projection of impulses unbearable to it into the outside world, or in mania the super-ego is projected into the outside world to rid the ego of its internal tormentor. In acute schizophrenia I found that not only internal objects, including the super-ego, are often projected into external objects, but the projection of the super-ego was accompanied by massive projection of parts of the self into external objects, which caused severe splitting and disintegration of the ego.

I cannot discuss in this paper all the mechanisms of ego-splitting, but shall draw attention to ways in which the super-ego is responsible for *ego-splitting*. I also wish to show that a primitive super-ego exists in the acute schizophrenic patient, that the origin of this super-ego goes back to the first year of life, and that this early super-ego is of a particularly severe character, owing to the predominance of persecutory features.

DISCUSSION OF CERTAIN ASPECTS FROM THE PSYCHO-ANALYSIS OF AN
ACUTE SCHIZOPHRENIC PATIENT

Diagnosis

When I saw the patient for the first time he had been suffering from acute schizophrenia for about three years. He had always responded for a short time to electric shock or insulin comas, of which he had had at least ninety. There was a query whether he was hebephrenic, because of his frequent silly giggling, but, in spite of some hebephrenic features, practically all the psychiatrists who saw him diagnosed a catatonic type of schizophrenia of bad prognosis. Leucotomy had been suggested to diminish his violence and to help the nursing problem, but at the last minute his father decided to try psycho-analysis.

History of Patient

The patient, who was twenty-one, was born abroad, after a difficult forceps delivery. He was the eldest child (a brother was born four years later). He did not do well at the breast and after four weeks was changed over to the bottle. He cried for hours as a baby because his parents were advised not to pick him up. Difficulties over taking food were present throughout childhood and the latency period. A change occurred several years before the beginning of his illness, when he suddenly developed an enormous appetite. He had frequent attacks of nervous vomiting from childhood onwards. Other symptoms were disturbing sensations like deadness and stiffness in his arms and legs, and a feeling in his tongue that it got twisted. He could never stand being hurt, and when he had pain he often tried to pinch his mother as if he were angry with her about it. He was popular at school and had a number of friends. There was a period of exhibitionism between nine and eleven years of age. When he was about sixteen an incident occurred which frightened the parents and made them aware that there was something seriously wrong with the patient. He and his brother occupied a bedroom next door to that of their parents during holidays. His mother saw the patient on the parapet of the balcony, which was on the fourth floor, and thought he was about to commit suicide by throwing himself to the ground below. She managed to stop him and he "broke down" and accused his father of not telling him the facts of life. Apparently the patient had had a period of intense masturbation before this episode. At seventeen he fell in love with a ballet dancer. She jilted him and soon afterwards he had his first schizophrenic breakdown.

Parents of the Patient

His mother had not felt well during her pregnancy, and, after her confinement, developed asthma and could not look after the baby, who was handed over to a nurse. It is very difficult to assess clearly her relationship to him, but it seems that she preferred the younger boy.[1] When the patient grew up he frequently quarrelled with her, and got on much better with his father. When he fell ill, she would not have him at home and later on she was strongly opposed to his having psycho-analytic treatment. His father was an emotional man, very fond of his eldest boy, but undecided and unreliable.

The Treatment

At the time when I first saw the patient he was socially withdrawn, suffered from hallucinations and was almost mute, and sometimes he was impulsive. The first fortnight he was brought by car from the mental nursing home where he was looked after. Later I saw him there and he had two private male nurses. For the first four to five weeks of the treatment he was at times dangerously violent. From then on the violence lessened a good deal and he became much easier to handle. This changed again at a time when the nurses and I began to realize that his parents, particularly his mother, intended to stop the treatment. I had the strong impression that, although the patient had not been directly informed about this, he must have sensed it through his surroundings. I was driven to this assumption because from that moment he became progressively more violent, though even then he never attempted to attack me. Till then he had co-operated with me in negative and positive states.

Technique

I saw him regularly for about one hour and twenty minutes every day, with the exception of Sundays. When he spoke he rarely used whole sentences. He nearly always said only a few words, expecting me to understand. He frequently acknowledged interpretations which he felt were correct, and he could show clearly how pleased he was to understand. When he felt resistance against interpretations, or when they aroused anxiety, he very often said "No", and "Yes" afterwards, expressing both rejection and acceptance. Sometimes he

[1] In some papers on schizophrenia particularly by American writers like Pious and Fromm Reichmann the mother's hostile and "schizophrenogenic" attitude has been stressed. The mother in this case seems to have been unconsciously hostile to the patient and the patient's illness increased her guilty feelings. But we ought not to forget that in all mental disturbances there is a close inter-relationship between external factors acting as trauma and internal ones which are determined mostly by heredity. In our analytic approach we know that it is futile and even harmful to the progress of an analysis to accept uncritically the patient's attempts to blame the external environment for his illness. We generally find that there exists a great deal of distortion of external factors through projection and we have to help the patient to understand his phantasies and reactions to external situations until he becomes able to differentiate between his phantasies and external reality.

showed his understanding by the clarity and coherence of the material he produced after an interpretation. At times he had great difficulty in formulating words and he showed what he meant by gestures. At other times, in connection with certain anxieties, he altogether lost his capacity to speak (for example, when he felt that everything had turned into fæces inside him), but this capacity improved in response to relevant interpretations. Later on in the course of treatment he began to play in a dramatic way, illustrating in this manner his phantasies, particularly about his internal world.

THE PROBLEM OF CASE PRESENTATION

In presenting certain aspects of an analysis like this, it is impossible to reproduce all the material given by the patient and all the interpretations. It has also to be remembered that, with such a severely ill patient, the analyst cannot understand everything the patient says or tries to say.

However, I hope that I shall be able to show that this deeply regressed patient, who had great difficulty in verbalizing his experiences, conveyed his problems to me not only clearly enough to make a continuous relationship possible, but also in a manner which gave a fairly detailed picture of his guilt conflict in the transference situation, and the ways and means by which he was trying to *deal with it.*

Since some analysts, such as Eissler, deny the importance of interpretations in acute schizophrenia, it is necessary to discuss the significance of verbal interpretations. Eissler stressed the schizophrenic's awareness of the primary processes in the analyst's mind, and it is these primary processes on which, in his opinion, the result of treatment depends and not on the interpretations. I understand this to mean that the schizophrenic is extremely intuitive and seems to be able to get help from a therapist who *unconsciously* is in tune with his patient. Eissler seems to regard it as unimportant and leading to self-deception to consider whether or not the psychotherapist consciously understands the schizophrenic patient. He writes: "I did not get the impression that in instances in which interpretations were used during the acute phase there was a specific relationship between interpretation and clinical recovery. It may be assumed that another set of interpretations might have achieved a similar result."

In my opinion the unconscious intuitive understanding by the psycho-analyst of what a patient is conveying to him is an essential factor in *all* analyses, and depends on the analyst's capacity to use his counter-transference[1] as a kind of sensitive "receiving set". In treating schizophrenics who have such great verbal difficulties, the unconscious intuitive understanding of the analyst through the counter-transference is even more important, for it helps him to determine what it is that really matters at the moment.

But the analyst should also be able to formulate consciously what he has unconsciously recognized, and to convey it to the patient in a form that he can understand. This after all is the essence of all psycho-analysis, but it is especially important in the treatment of schizophrenics, who have lost a great deal of their capacity for conscious functioning, so that, without help, they cannot consciously understand their unconscious experiences which are at times so vivid. In presenting the following material, I would therefore ask the reader to remember that I had continuously to watch for the patient's reactions to my interpretations, and often to feel my way until I could be sure of giving them in a form that he could use. For example, I was surprised to find that he could follow without much difficulty the interpretation of complicated mechanisms if I used simple words.

Even so, it was at times obvious that he was unable to understand verbal communication, or at least that he misunderstood what was said. We know from the treatment of neurotics that the analyst's words may become symbols of particular situations, for example, a feeding or a homosexual relationship; and this has to be understood and interpreted. But with the schizophrenic, the difficulty seems to go much further. Sometimes he takes everything the analyst says quite concretely. Hanna Segal (1950) has shown that if we interpret a castration phantasy to the schizophrenic he takes the interpretation itself as a castration. She suggested that he has a difficulty either in forming symbols or in using them, since they become equivalents instead of symbols. In my experience I found that most schizophrenics are only temporarily unable to use symbols, and the analysis of the patient under discussion contributed to my understanding of the deeper causes of this problem. This patient had certainly formed symbols, for instance his symbolic description of internalized objects was striking. But whenever *verbal* contact was

---

[1] Cf. Paula Heimann (1950): "On Counter-transference".—"My thesis is that the analyst's emotional response to his patient within the analytic situation represents one of the most important tools for his work. The analyst's counter-transference is an instrument of research into the patient's unconscious."

Herbert Rosenfeld

disturbed, through the patient's difficulty in understanding words as symbols, I observed that his phantasies of going into me and being inside me had become intensified, and had led to his inability to differentiate between himself and me (projective identification). This confusion between self and object, which also led to confusion of reality and phantasy, was accompanied by a difficulty in differentiating between the real object and its symbolic representation. Projections of self and internalized objects were always found to some extent, but did not necessarily disturb verbal communication. For it is the *quantity* of the self involved in the process of projective identification that determines whether the real object and its symbolic representation can be differentiated. Analysis of the impulses underlying projective identification may also explain why the schizophrenic so often treats phantasies as concrete real situations and real situations as if they were phantasies. Whenever I saw that projective identification had increased, I then interpreted his impulses of entering inside myself in the transference, whereupon his capacity to understand symbols, and therefore words and interpretations, improved.

THE PROGRESS OF TREATMENT

Before describing certain stages of the treatment which gave me some detailed and inter-related material about my patient's superego problem, I will sketch briefly the first four weeks of treatment, during which time he co-operated particularly well. In the first few sessions he showed clear signs of both positive and negative transference. His predominant anxieties were his fear of losing himself and me, and his difficulty in differentiating between himself and me, between reality and phantasy, and also between inside and outside. He talked about his fear of losing and having lost his penis: "Somebody has taken the fork away"; "Silly woman." He was preoccupied with being a woman, and he had a wish to be re-born a girl:[1] "*Prince* Ann." By analysing material like "The Virgin Mary was killed", or "One half was eaten",[2] and "Bib (penis) was killed",

[1] Compare Rosen who described the frequent re-birth phantasies of schizophrenic women wanting to be re-born as boys.

[2] During the analysis it became clear that the patient felt he had split off or killed those parts of himself which were felt by him to be bad and dangerous to his good objects. In attributing the dangerous aggressive impulses to his penis, he felt that his penis was to be killed, to be eaten or destroyed, and consequently lost, which greatly increased his castration anxiety.

194

we began to realize that he attributed his dangerous, murderous feelings against his mother, and against women in general, to his male half and his penis. We also understood that his phantasies of being a woman were greatly reinforced by his desire to get rid of his aggression. When he began to understand this method of dealing with his aggression, his wish to be a woman lessened and he became more aggressive.

Sometimes his aggression turned outward and he attacked the nurses, but frequently it turned against himself. He then spoke of "Soul being killed", or "Soul committing suicide", or "Soul being dead": "Soul" being clearly a good part of himself. Once when we discussed these feelings of deadness, he illustrated this turning of his aggression against himself by saying "I want to go on—I don't want to go on—vacuum—Soul is dead", and later astonished me by stating clearly "The problem is—how to prevent disintegration." (The turning of the aggression against the self has been described as part of the splitting process causing disintegration in schizophrenia by Melanie Klein 1946, and H. Rosenfield, 1947).

A predominant anxiety in the analytic situation, which the patient on rare occasions was able to formulate, related to his need for me. My not being with him on Sundays seemed at times unbearable, and once on a Saturday he said, "What shall I do in the meantime, I'd better find someone in the hospital." On another occasion he said, "I don't know what to do without you." He gave me repeatedly to understand that all his problems were related to "Time", and when he felt he wanted something from me, it had to be given "instantly".

Whenever he attacked somebody physically, he reacted with depression, guilt, and anxiety; and it gradually became clear that when his aggression did not turn against himself, but against external or internal objects, a guilt and anxiety problem arose which in fact occupied most of the time in the analysis.

I will now give some detailed material which followed an attack on Sister X four weeks after the beginning of his treatment. A few days before the attack, he seemed preoccupied with phantasies of attacking and biting breasts and with fear of women ("witchcraft"). He was inarticulate and difficult to understand. He talked about "three buns", which probably meant three breasts, but it was not clear at the time why there were three. He attacked Sister X suddenly, while he was having tea with her and his father, hitting her hard on the temple. She was affectionately putting her arms round his shoulders at the time. The attack occurred on a Saturday, and I found him silent and defensive on Monday and Tuesday. On Wednesday he talked a little more. He said that he had destroyed the whole world and later on he said, "Afraid." He added, "Eli" (God) several times. When he spoke he looked very dejected and his head drooped on his chest. I interpreted that when he attacked Sister X he felt he had destroyed the whole world and he felt only Eli could put right what he had done. He remained silent. After continuing my interpretations by saying that he felt not only guilty but afraid of being attacked inside and outside, he became a little more communicative. He said, "I can't stand it any more." Then he stared at the table and said, "It is all broadened out, what are all the men going to feel?"[1] I said that he could no longer stand the guilt and anxiety inside himself and had put his depression, anxiety, and feelings, and also himself, into the outer world. As a result of this he felt broadened out, split up into many men, and he wondered what all the different parts of himself were going to feel. He then looked at a finger of his which is bent and said, "I can't do any more, I can't do it all." After that he pointed to one of my fingers which is also slightly bent and said, "I am afraid of this finger." His own bent finger had often stood for his illness, and had become the representative of his own damaged self, but he also indicated that it represented the destroyed world inside him, about which he felt he could do no more. In saying that he can't do it all, he implied a search for an object outside. But what kind of object relations do we find in the transference situation? I immediately seemed to become like him and was frightening. I interpreted to him that he put himself and the problems he could not deal with inside me, and feared that he had changed me into himself, and also that he was now afraid of what I would give back to him. He replied with a remark which showed his anxiety that I might stop treatment and he added explicitly that he wished that I should continue seeing him.

I shall now examine this material from the theoretical point of view. After his attack on the sister, the patient felt depressed and anxious. His behaviour, gestures, and the few sentences and words he uttered, showed that he felt he had destroyed the whole world outside, and he also felt the destroyed world inside himself. He makes this clearer later on in the analysis; but it is very important to realize at this stage that he felt he had taken the destroyed world into himself and then felt he had to restore it. To this task he was driven

[1] "It is all broadened out" refers also to the world which is destroyed; but his ego is included in the destroyed world and this seemed to be the relevant factor to recognize.

by an overpowering super-ego, and his omnipotence failed him. He also felt persecuted by the destroyed world and was afraid. Under the pressure of both overwhelming guilt and persecution anxiety, which were caused by the super-ego, his ego began to go to pieces: he could not stand it any more and he projected the inner destroyed world, and himself, outside. After this everything seemed broadened out and his self was split up into many men who all felt his guilt and anxiety. The pressure of the super-ego is here too great for the ego to bear: the ego tries to deal with the unbearable anxiety by projection, but in this way ego-splitting, and in this case ego-disintegration, takes place.[1] This is, of course, a very serious process, but if we are able to analyse these mechanisms in the transference situation, it is possible to cope analytically with the disastrous results of the splitting process.

The patient himself gave the clue to the transference situation, and showed that he had projected his damaged self containing the destroyed world, not only into all the other patients, but into me, and had changed me in this way. But instead of becoming relieved by this projection he became more anxious, because he was afraid of what I was then putting back into him, whereupon his introjective processes became severely disturbed. One would therefore expect a severe deterioration in his condition, and in fact his clinical state during the next ten days became very precarious. He began to get more and more suspicious about food, and finally refused to eat and drink anything. He became violent, and appeared to have visual hallucinations and also hallucinations of taste. In the transference he was suspicious of me, but not violent, and in spite of the fact that he was practically mute we never lost contact entirely. He sometimes said "Yes" or "No" to interpretations. In these I made ample use of previous material and related it to his present gestures and behaviour. It seemed to me that the relevant point had been his inability to deal with his guilt and anxiety. After projecting his bad, damaged self into me, he continuously saw himself everywhere outside. At the same time, everything he took inside seemed to him bad, damaged, and poisonous (like fæces), so there was no point in eating anything. We know that projection leads again to re-introjection, so that he also felt as if he had inside himself all the destroyed and bad objects which he had projected into the outer world: and he indicated by coughing, retching, and movements of his mouth and fingers that

[1] See the more detailed discussion of the relation of ego-splitting and ego-disintegration which follows.

197

he was preoccupied with this problem. The first obvious improvement occurred after ten days when the male nurse had left some orange juice on the table which he (the patient) viewed with great suspicion. I went over previous material and showed him that the present difficult situation had arisen through his attempt to rid himself of guilt and anxiety inside by putting it outside himself. I told him that he was not only afraid of getting something bad inside him, but that he was also afraid of taking good things, the good orange juice and good interpretations inside, since he was afraid that these would make him feel guilty again. When I said this, a kind of shock went right through his body; he gave a groan of understanding, and his facial expression changed. By the end of the hour he had emptied the glass of orange juice, the first food or drink he had taken for two days. There was a distinct general improvement in his taking food from that time, and I felt it was significant that a patient, in this very hallucinated state, was able to benefit by an interpretation which showed him the relationship of the acute hallucinated state to his guilt problem.

The analytic material and the mechanisms I have described here are not an isolated observation. They seem to be typical of the way an acute schizophrenic state develops. I have stressed that it is the inability of the schizophrenic patient to stand the anxiety and guilt caused by his introjected object or objects, including the super-ego, which causes the projection of the self, or parts of the self containing the internalized object, into external objects. This results in ego-splitting, loss of the self and loss of feelings.[1] At the same time a new danger and anxiety situation develops which leads to a vicious circle and further disintegration. Through the projection of the bad self and all it contains into an object, this object is perceived by the patient to have changed and become bad and persecuting, as the clinical material above indicated. The persecution expected after this form of projection is a forceful aggressive re-entry[2] of the object into the ego. During this phase therefore introjection may become inhibited in an attempt to prevent the persecuting object from entering.

Thus a most important defence against the re-entry of the objects into which projection has taken place is negativism, which may show itself as a refusal to have anything to do with the world outside including the refusal of food. Such a defence is, however, rarely

[1] In my paper "Analysis of a Schizophrenic State with Depersonalization" I have dealt in greater detail with the problem of ego-splitting, loss of self and loss of feelings.
[2] This process has been described by Melanie Klein, "Notes on some Schizoid Mechanisms".

successful, since almost simultaneously with the projection of the self into an external object, the external object containing the self is also introjected. This implies that the object exists in phantasy externally and internally at the same time. In the process the ego is in danger of being completely overwhelmed, almost squeezed out of existence. In addition, we have to remember that the whole process is not stationary, because as soon as the object containing parts of the self is re-introjected, there is again the tendency to project which leads to further introjection of a most disturbing and disintegrating nature. This means that we are dealing not just with one act of splitting, projection and introjection, but with a process where multiple projections and introjections can take place in a very short time.

Clinically and theoretically it is important to consider the process from at least two angles: first the projection takes place to safeguard the ego from destruction, and may therefore be considered a defensive process which is unsuccessful and even dangerous because ego-splitting, and therefore ego–disintegration, takes place; secondly, there is also an object relation of an extremely primitive nature connected with the projection, because the introjected objects and parts of the self are projected *into an object*. This is important to understand because the strength of the persecutory fears about the re-entry of the object depends on the strength of the aggressive impulses pertaining to this primitive object relationship. In a previous paper (1951) I described this object relationship in greater detail, so I only want to repeat here that there is evidence that, in addition to the relation to the breast, the infant from birth onwards has libidinal and aggressive impulses and phantasies of entering into the mother's body with parts of himself.[1] When there are phantasies of the self entering the mother's body aggressively, to overwhelm and to take complete possession, we have to expect anxiety, not only about the mother and the entering self being destroyed, but also about the mother turning into a persecutor who is expected to force herself back into the ego to take possession in a revengeful way. When this persecutory mother figure is introjected, the most primitive super-ego figure arises which represents a terrible overwhelming danger to the ego from within. It is most likely that the inability of the schizophrenic ego to deal with introjected figures arises from the nature of this early object relationship.

[1] These impulses and mechanisms have been described by Melanie Klein, "Notes on some Schizoid Mechanisms".

In the clinical material described above I have not explained why the patient attacked Sister X. I wish to add here that at a later date I had more material about the incident and I understood that at the moment when Sister X put her arms round him he became afraid that she was going to force herself into him in order to take possession of him. As I interpreted this, he shuddered and raised his arm as if to ward off an assault.

A fortnight later

I shall now report material which was obtained about a fortnight later. On a Monday, before I saw the patient I learnt from the male nurse that on the previous Sunday he seemed tense and had been about to make an attack on him. The attack did not materialize, but the patient turned very pale and said "Hiroshima".

When I approached him on the Monday, he received me by saying "You are too late." His limbs were trembling and he jumped in fright when the nurse sneezed in the room next door. He later said "I cannot look," and he repeated several times, "I can't do anything." He mentioned death several times and then became silent. He opened his mouth as if to speak but no words came out. I said that he could not speak because he was afraid of what he felt inside and what would come out of him. He replied "Blood". In my interpretations I told him that he had missed me over the week-end and had felt very impatient. He felt that he had killed me inside himself, and thought that as an external person I was too late now to do anything to help him and to help myself inside him. He was afraid to look at the destruction inside, and his difficulty in speaking, and his fear that blood might come out of him, showed how real this murderous inner attack had felt to him.

On the Tuesday, he said, "We have to stop, I can't do it any more." He again showed his bent finger, mentioned death and blood, and shrugged his shoulders. After I had again stressed how real and concrete his inner, killing attack on me had been, and that he could do nothing to make me alive, he pointed to a certain part of the hospital and said, "I want to have shock treatment." When I asked him what shock treatment meant to him, he replied without the slightest hesitation, "Death." I said that having killed me, he now felt that he ought to be killed as a punishment, to which he agreed.

What is significant in these two interviews is that he was more aware of having made an attack on me as an internal object. By greeting me on my arrival with the words: "You are too late," he was recognizing me as an external object and had to some degree differentiated this external me from the internal murdered me (blood). He was struggling to repair the damage he had done, but felt quite unable to do so. He felt less persecuted and more guilty, and his desire to have shock treatment expressed his need for punishment to relieve his guilt. However, the process did not stop here. As before, under the pressure of guilt, the splitting process temporarily increased. When I saw him on Wednesday, he looked very confused. He asked, "Can I help you?" He looked round all over the floor as if he were searching for something he had lost, and he picked up imaginary bits and pieces. I interpreted that he felt himself to be confused with me as a helpful person, that he had put himself inside me for help because he could not deal with his inner problems any more, but that he now felt split and all over the place, and was therefore trying to collect himself. He made a movement with his shoulders as if he wanted to say, "Of course, what else can I do?" After this he made eating movements and I interpreted that he felt he was eating me up to get something good inside himself, and also to swallow back the self he had put into me. He immediately stopped and said, "One can't go on eating. What can I do?"

The patient's response to my interpretation gives the impression that he took my interpretation that he was eating me up as a reproach. In schizophrenic patients the misunderstanding of interpretations is generally due to their attribution of concreteness to their thought-content and thought-processes, i.e. whatever they think of exists in actual concrete form. On this occasion the patient reacts to what the analyst said with the thought that he is in fact actually eating the analyst up, therefore he must not do it. From the technical point of view one may attempt to interpret to the patient that he has taken the interpretation simply as a reproach and that he felt attacked by this interpretation. This may be sometimes helpful but a more effective approach is to understand the deeper causes for the misunderstanding. When I discussed the temporary inability of the schizophrenic to use symbols (on p. 193), I suggested that when projective identification is reinforced the patient loses some of his capacity to understand symbols and therefore words, and he takes interpretations very concretely. I felt that the projection of the internal object (the super-ego) into me, leading to projective identification, was in this instance the essential factor, on which I concentrated in my interpretations. So I again explained to the patient that he had put himself into me as an external object because he could not deal with his guilt about having killed me inside himself. As a result of this interpretation, he said, "Blood and death", which seemed to indicate that he had reversed the process of projection and reintrojected the damaged object, and then he talked about Eli in an attempt to find an omnipotent solution of the conflict which we had previously discussed. Then he looked more relaxed and said, "My son, my son", in a friendly, loving way, and added, "Memory." I showed him that he had been able to revive the memory of a good relationship with his father and so with me, and that he had begun to realize that the good feelings and memories about his father and myself were helping him to deal with his hatred and guilt. During this interview the patient had repeated a method of dealing with his guilt by projecting himself into an external object—a process which I have already described in discussing earlier sessions (after the attack on Sister X.) The projective identification was on both occasions accompanied by confusion and splitting, but this time, after the interpretation, he was able to reverse the process and attempted other means of dealing with his guilt.

I will attempt to explain some of the differences between these two guilt situations, which both ended in projecting the guilt and parts of the self into an external object. In the first instance the patient did attack an external object, Sister X, and he felt he had destroyed the whole world. It appeared that he felt the destruction outside and inside. After the projection of the guilt situation into me he felt that I had been changed and had become persecuting. In the second instance (when the patient said "Hiroshima") he must have felt violently aggressive and his description afterwards of what he experienced inside himself emphasized that he felt he had killed an object inside (blood, death), but at the time of the violent anger he managed to control himself and did not attack a real person. Later, when he projected his guilt and his self into me, he did not think that he had changed me into his bad self, but he felt that he had changed into me and so had become the helpful person whom, on this occasion, he felt me to be.

A Few Days Later

The following interview showed another variation of the patient's attempts to deal with his super-ego. At the beginning of the interview he touched my hand several times, looking at me anxiously. I interpreted that he wanted to see if I was all right. He then asked me directly, "Are you all right?" I pointed out that he was afraid of having hurt me, and that he was now more able to admit his concern about me as an external person. He then said "chicken"—'heat'—"diarrhœa". I replied that he liked chicken and that he felt he had eaten me like a chicken and his diarrhœa made him feel that he had destroyed me as an inner object in the process of eating me up. This increased his fear that he had also destroyed or injured me as an external object. He now became more concerned about his inside. At first he said "movement" and "breath" which I interpreted as a hope that I was alive inside him. But afterwards he kept his leg rigidly stiff for several minutes, and on being asked what this implied, he said "Dead". This I interpreted as a feeling that I was dead inside him. He then said, "Impossible"—"God"—"Direct", which I interpreted as meaning that he felt I should be all-powerful like God and do something directly to make this impossible inner situation better. He then said, several times, "frightened", and he looked very frightened indeed. Suddenly he said "No war". He got up and shook hands with me in the most amiable manner, but while he was doing so he said "Bluff". I said that he felt at war with me inside after having had the phantasy of eating me up and killing me, and that he was now afraid of my revenge from inside and outside. He wanted to be at peace with me outside and inside, but he felt no real peace was possible, that it was only "bluff". I related this to his past life, to his feeling that his good relationship with people outside had been built on bluff, but also that he had felt that his coming to terms with his guilt and anxiety had often been based on bluff and deception.

In considering this session I suggest that my patient tried to make it clear that his guilt and fear were related to an introjected object which he believed he had killed by devouring. He showed that his relationship to this internalized object was a mixture of concern and persecution; when the fear of the persecution by the dead internal object increased, the only solution, apart from an omnipotent one, seemed to be to appease the persecutors, which also represented his super-ego. This he felt to be bluff.

In the following session the patient discovered a different method of helping me to understand his inner relationship to me, and so his super-ego conflict. When I approached him he was sitting very quietly on a chair, looking intently at his hand, at first examining it from the outside. Afterwards he stared fixedly at the inside: it looked as if he imagined that he was holding something there. I asked him what he saw, and he replied "Crater". I then asked whether there was anything inside the crater. He replied, as if to put me off, "Nothing—empty". I now interpreted that he was afraid that I was in the crater, and that I was dead. Later he closed his hand and squeezed it tightly. I interpreted that he felt that he imprisoned me inside his hand and that he was crushing me. He continued squeezing his hand for some time, looking withdrawn. Suddenly he got up, looked round in a frightened way, and escaped from the treatment room, which was not locked. The nurses brought him back, and he sat down again without any struggle. I pointed out to him that, while he was phantasying holding and squeezing me inside himself, the room had suddenly turned, for him, into a dangerous prison from which he tried to escape. I interpreted also that he had identified himself with me, because he felt guilty about what he was doing to me inside him. While I was interpreting the fear of the room, his anxiety seemed to lessen, and he returned to squeezing his hand.

The next day the nurses reported that the patient had become very frightened during a walk. He had suddenly stopped, staring at the ground. He would not go any further. On questioning him the nurses found that he heard voices threatening to punish him with death. He stopped walking because he saw an abyss in front of him. After some time he calmed down. Later on he had what seemed to be two cataleptic attacks in which he suddenly fell forward as if dead. The nurses were sure that he was not unconscious during this attack. I used this information next day with the patient, although he made no reference to it himself, and I explained this frightening experience as a continuation of what we had been discussing during the previous session. I related the abyss to the crater and interpreted that not only did he feel that he had killed and destroyed me in the crater, but also that he felt he had changed me into a retaliating object which was threatening him with punishment and death. The cataleptic fits represented both his own and my death. The striking feature about this experience is the distinct connection between the threatening super-ego voices and his own aggressive phantasies against me. The super-ego is here again persecuting and threatening him according to the talion principle.

So far we have seen that the patient was mainly preoccupied with me as an internal object, which he had killed with his oral sadistic impulses. In surveying these sessions it seems that he felt guilty and persecuted by this internal object which, particularly in its persecutory form, had a super-ego function.

He showed various methods of dealing with this frightening super-ego. He attempted to expel it by projecting it into an external object. But this did not lead to a clinical improvement, because in projecting the super-ego he also projected parts of his self. In the first instance (after the attack on Sister X), where he projected his bad self into an external object in an aggressive manner, not only the splitting but also the persecution from without increased. In the second instance of projection (Can I help you?), the super-ego was also projected, but here the emphasis was on projecting the good side of the self and the object which needed to be restored into an external object, the analyst. This did not create a feeling of external persecution. But the projection of goodness produced a splitting of the ego which is felt as a depletion of goodness in the self. In this case it led to an increased oral greed in an attempt to recapture the good self and a good object by eating it up in phantasy.

These two instances illustrate the relation of the super-ego to ego splitting, and I suggest that, as methods of dealing with the super-ego, they commonly occur in acute schizophrenic states with confusion.

The other methods shown by the patient in this material are the desire for punishment and the appeasement of persecutors: the two cataleptic fits[1] seem to imply a complete masochistic[2] submission to the killing super-ego, and the same explanation applies to the need for punishment in asking for electric shock (death) treatment. In the latter case the masochistic submission, however, was not to the internal super-ego, but to an external object. This, incidentally, throws some light on the psychological importance of electric shock treatment[3] which subjects a patient to the experience of death without actually killing him. The appeasement of the persecutory super-ego by bluff, as illustrated by my patient, is a very common mechanism, particularly in chronic schizophrenics. It also plays a considerable part as a defence against an acute schizophrenic state. Moreover, the strengthening of the appeasement mechanisms may bring about a remission of an acute attack; but recovery by this means is unsatisfactory, because it completely stifles any development of personality.

[1] These attacks resembled a catatonic stupor. The psycho-pathology suggested here may also contribute to our understanding of the catatonic stupor.

[2] Cf. A. Garma's (1932) and P. Riviere's (1946) theory of the masochistic ego and the sadistic super-ego in schizophrenia.

[3] If the patient had been submitted to electric shock treatment at the time when he asked for it, his guilt conflict would have been temporarily alleviated, and very likely he might have had a remission of the acute state which still persisted, but this would have meant abandoning further psycho-analytic understanding of his conflict.

Herbert Rosenfeld

The *"Helpful"* Super-ego

In the following session, which I shall refer to as (a), we came to understand more of the positive relationship of the patient to his super-ego. In the beginning of the session he was looking for something in his pocket. He could not find it and it turned out that it was his handkerchief he wanted. I interpreted that he was not only looking for his handkerchief but also for the part of himself which helped him to control himself, but which he could not find. I pointed out to him that he had frequently lost himself and his inner control because he felt he could not stand anxiety and guilt.[1] He then looked me straight in the face and said, "The problem is how to feel the fear." I interpreted that he wanted to feel the fear which meant anxiety and guilt inside because he realized his need of control. He then looked out of the window where a man was trimming the hedges.[2] He was watching him in a fascinated way, without apparent fear. I pointed out that this man was trimming the hedges, and was in this way keeping them in shape, and in control, without damaging them. That was the relationship he wanted to feel with me inside himself; a helpful control without feeling damaged. The patient's remark "The problem is how to feel the fear" is significant because it implies his realization that he had avoided the experience of guilt and anxiety and so was without an inner means of control. The nurses reported that after this session he was rational for the first time since he had been in hospital. He was able to converse with doctors and nurses. This state lasted for several hours, and recurred almost every day for about three weeks. The improvement coincided with a greater capacity to acknowledge the need for an internal object as a helpful, controlling figure, and a lessening of his persecutory anxiety. During the next session (b) he became more able to verbalize his super-ego conflict. I found him sitting in a rigid position. It took more than twenty minutes before the rigidity lessened. He then said, "No energy"—"Struggle", and later on "I am wrong". He sighed and continued, "Worn out". "Hercules". Later during the session he said "I can only do my best, I cannot do any more." (He was looking very tired.) He also said "Religion", but was not able to discuss in

---

[1] From the patient's whole attitude I felt that this interpretation was needed at that moment, but I do not want to give the impression that looking for a handkerchief in an acute schizophrenic patient always has this particular meaning. One has always to consider a multitude of factors to understand the meaning of schizophrenic actions.

[2] One might of course think that the man with the shears aroused his castration anxiety. But I think this aspect was not in the foreground at that moment.

detail what he meant. I interpreted that he was trying to face his sense of guilt which was a struggle, that the demands of his conscience were so enormous that he felt quite worn out, and that he thought he would have to be a Hercules to do all that he felt he ought to do. At the end of the session he opened a black box which stood in a corner of the room where I was treating him. This box contained human bones, used for teaching students and nurses.[1] Almost every time from now on he opened the box once or twice during or at the end of a session, until, at a later date, he gave a full illustration of what this skeleton in the box (his super-ego) seemed to be like.

I suggest that we may view this analytical material from two angles: (a) The patient was in this hour willing to face and accept his destroyed internal world. This experience was accompanied by greater depression. It seemed to me that his opening of the box symbolized his looking inside himself. The contents of the box were actually bones of a skeleton, and from his previous remarks it can be assumed that the object he felt he had inside was a destroyed one. (b) This destroyed object had previously threatened him with destruction, but during this session it seemed that there were internal demands for its reparation, which were felt by him to be overwhelming and made him feel worn out. It would appear that either this internal destroyed object itself had a super-ego function or that another object having this function made demands for the reparation of this destroyed object.

Primary Envy

During the next session (c) the patient was preoccupied with envy and how to get rid of it. In the session after that (d) he sat silently on a chair, looking anxiously at the outside and inside of his hand. I asked, "What are you afraid of?" He replied, "I am afraid of everything." I then said he was afraid of the world outside and inside, and of himself. He replied "Let's go back," which I took to mean that he wanted to understand the early infantile situation in the transference. He stretched out his hands towards me on the table, and I pointed out that he was trying to direct his feelings towards me.

---

[1] The hospital unfortunately had no proper consulting rooms. I had several times to change the room where I treated the patient, and in the end the superintendent thought that I would be least disturbed in the lecture room. One day the patient discovered the black box with the bones. I had no knowledge of its presence beforehand. I decided not to have the box removed but to analyse the patient's interest in it. But I want to stress that I was in this room only by force of external circumstances, not by my own choice.

He then touched the table tentatively, withdrew his hands and put them into his pockets, and leaned back in his chair. I said that he was afraid of his contact with me, who represented the external world, and that, out of fear, he withdrew from the outer world. He listened carefully to what I said and again took his hands out of his pockets. He then said, "The world is round", and continued clearly and deliberately, "I hate it because it makes me feel burnt up inside". And later he added, as if to explain this further, "Yellow"— "envy". I interpreted to him that the round world represented me felt as a good breast, and that he hated the external me for arousing his envy, because his envy made him feel he wanted to kill and burn me inside himself. So he could not keep me good and alive himself, and felt he had a bad and burning inside. This increased his envy and his wish to be inside me, because he felt I had a good inside. At the end of the session (d) he touched the burning hot radiators in the treatment room and the wooden shelf over them.

This session (d) is particularly significant because it throws some light on the patient's fundamental conflict with the world, and his deep-seated envy of the good mother and breast.

In the analysis of neurotic and pre-psychotic patients this early envy has frequently been described. It is, however, interesting that this inarticulate, regressed patient should so stress his envy and jealousy in his earliest infantile object relationship with his mother. Sometimes he referred it to the beginning of life, repeatedly stressing birth and envy, and it was clear that the jealousy of his brother, which was also frequently discussed, was not the problem he had most in his mind. It seems that some of the earliest aggression, starting from the separation of the infant from his mother at birth, is experienced as envy, because everything that makes the infant feel comfortable seems to belong to the outer world—the mother.

This conflict became manifest in the transference situation when I was equated with the good mother and the good breast. Historically the patient had had a short, unsatisfactory time at the breast, and his mother was unable to look after him because of her asthma. Previously he had shown that he hated me when I was absent, but in this session (d) it is his envy of me which makes it difficult for him to take good things from me.

The envy of the good mother and her good inside also increases the greedy impulses to force the self inside the mother, because, if the mother has all the goodness, the child wants to be inside her. But the envy and jealousy with which in phantasy the child enters the mother's body create images of a destroyed mother. At the end of the hour, the patient touched the hot radiators which burned his hand, and afterwards he touched the wooden shelf, which may have meant that he feared that by entering me he changed me, so that my inside was as burning as his own.

Another interesting feature is the way the patient, through the gestures of his hands, showed whether his cathexes were directed to external or internal objects. If he turned his instinctual impulses towards an external object, he took his hands out of his pockets, and indicated by the movement of his fingers that he was trying to make contact with the external world. When he withdrew the cathexis from the outer world, and directed it towards what was going on inside him, he put both his hands back into his pockets. When his feelings were directed outside and inside simultaneously, he kept one hand in his pocket and laid the other one on the table.[1]

During the following session (e) he looked inside the box with the bones and again touched the radiators. Then he took some crumpled-up paper out of his pocket and tried to straighten it out, but soon he looked frightened again. He walked past me and looked out of the window. At the next session (f) he emphatically said, "My own birth." He kept looking inside his hand and repeated several times, "Birth, Time and Jealousy."

I suggest that he was trying to indicate the connection of birth and envy. It is the birth situation which starts the envy of the mother and her good inside. The patient's looking out of the window was probably an expression of his feeling that he was inside me.[2] I pointed out before that when an object is introjected, which through projective identification has been identified with parts of the ego, a particularly complicated situation arises: here the patient was trying to deal with an internal object, but he also felt himself to be inside this object.

During this period he again seemed to misunderstand my interpretations. For example: When I interpreted to him during session (g) that he felt envious of me, he suddenly got up and moved away from me. He then went to the box and took a bone from it, showed it to me and put it back again. After this he seemed to get more frightened of me, and tried to get out of the room. Then he sat on the radiator, at a distance, and laughed at me in an aggressive and

---

[1] I do not want the reader to think that I would always interpret the play with hands in this way, but at this point I was convinced that this was its meaning.

[2] In my experience with other schizophrenic patients looking out of the window frequently meant that the patient felt he was inside the analyst.

challenging manner. Afterwards he walked about the room, ignoring me, and looking contemptuous; he made movements with his legs as if he were dancing. His attitude to me had changed after my interpretation of his jealousy. It seemed that he felt that by my interpretation I had made an attack on him, blaming him for his impulse. His taking a bone from the box here emphasized the concreteness of his experiences: namely, that he identified me with whatever the bone meant to him, probably a threatening super-ego. His dancing suggested that he had killed me and that he felt triumph and contempt. He was treating me like dirt. This concreteness of the patient's experiences continued after the session. The nurses reported that after I had left he had a large bowel motion, and used at least five times as much toilet paper as usual to cover it up.

When I arrived the next time (session h), he sat in his usual chair. In front of him on the table were two little heaps: one little heap of half-burnt cigarette tobacco and cigarette paper was on one side, next to it there was a little heap of grey ashes. The tobacco and the paper looked like a miniature fæcal mess and paper. The patient kept his eyes fixed on the heaps for some time. He came very close to it with his mouth, then he moved away again. He repeated this several times. He did not show that he noticed my presence. I interpreted that the heap which looked like a bowel motion represented me. I added that he felt he had changed me into a motion last time. The little heap of ashes seemed to represent those parts of himself mixed up with me, which he also felt were burnt up and destroyed. He continued staring at the heaps, making eating movements. I interpreted that he had both burnt up and destroyed me and himself, and that he wanted to take me and himself back again by eating. He was now picking up different bits and pieces and trying to sort them out, but they all dropped again into the mess. After the looking and mouthing, the touching and playing with the heap became much more intense. His playing with the mess seemed to be an unsuccessful attempt both to differentiate himself from me and to restore us. After the play he looked first at his hands, which were dirty, and then for a little time at a whitish spot on the table. I pointed out that he seemed to get mixed up between playing with his fæces and playing with his penis, because the glistening spot on the table seemed to be connected with masturbation (emission). When his confused look lessened I gave him a more detailed interpretation, showing him in detail how the present situation had arisen. I also linked it with the past, particularly with the earliest relations to his mother.

From the material presented, it may be difficult to see why I referred here to my patient's masturbation phantasies, but as I explained before, it is not always possible in an analysis such as this to show all the reasons for giving an interpretation. My patient had never during his breakdown really played with fæces, or eaten fæces, but he masturbated a great deal. He seemed to me confused, and he probably felt that he himself actually was the concrete mess that he had shown me in his play. So the interpretations had to be given in a way that helped him to recognize that his impulses differed from one another, and also to differentiate between himself and the objects with which he felt confused.

These last two sessions (g and h) are related to the earlier sessions (after the attack on Sister X and "Can I help you?") in which the patient had projected his self and his super-ego into me as the representative of the external world. In the earlier instance he had refused food, and he probably at that time had phantasies that he was forced to eat fæces—poison—representing his own bad self and persecuting objects. In the later one he had tried to recapture himself and me as a lost good object through eating. In the present instance (g and h) he illustrated his experience in play, and made it clear that the fæces represented me as the accusing super-ego which he tried to expel and destroy. When the persecutory anxiety relating to objects inside, including the super-ego, increased, he expelled the super-ego, but his phantasy of eating the heap of fæces and his playing with and sorting out the heap seemed to me to point to phantasies of regaining and restoring a good object, which would imply that he was attempting here to deal with his conflict on the depressive level.

I would like to refer to Abraham's (1924) observation on coprophagic phantasies in melancholia. Abraham suggested that the coprophagic phantasies of his patient turned out to be the expression of a desire to take back into his body the love object which he had expelled from it in the form of excrement. Abraham thought that "the tendency to coprophagia seems to contain a symbolism which is typical for melancholia". He described impulses of expelling (in an anal sense) and of destroying (murdering): "The product of such a murder—the dead body—became identified with the product of expulsion—with excrement."

My experience with this schizophrenic patient would seem to confirm the view that the coprophagic phantasy can represent a depressive mechanism of re-incorporating a lost object identified with fæces. But then the question has still to be answered: Why is coprophagia and playing with fæces in the adult typical for schizophrenia? I would like to suggest a tentative answer: The schizophrenic is trying to take back not only the object he has lost but also the parts of his ego which are mixed up with the object. Moreover, the actual eating of fæces is a sign not only of regression but also of having lost the capacity for symbolic representation. It depends on the degree to which his (mental) experiences actually have a concrete character for him, whether the schizophrenic can differentiate between phantasies of fæces as a destroyed object and fæces themselves.

In his experience during this session the patient came dangerously near to losing his ability to differentiate between symbol and actual object, because of the intensification of the projective identification process, which I had not sufficiently interpreted in session (g) (in which his envy was again so strong). In session (h) where he played with the heap, I took care to help him to differentiate again.

During the same session (h) the patient had difficulty in talking, but the nurses reported that afterwards he talked rationally and did not seem confused. But it must be remembered that these rational periods never lasted more than a few hours.

In the next session (i) he began looking away from me and remaining silent; but he looked eager and less confused, so I decided to go over the last sessions with him, showing him in detail in what way he was repeating experiences and phantasies of his early relationship with his mother and her breasts. I connected his silence with his anger and with his jealousy of the breast. I spoke of the roundness which at first represented the world to him, and of his difficulties in feeding from the breast because of his anger and his feelings of being burnt up inside. I reminded him of his feelings that the breast inside him had turned into fæces, and was threatening him; that, as we had seen last time, he wanted to free himself from this inner persecution, but that he could not bear to lose this internal breast even if it had turned into fæces, and that he was preoccupied with taking it back as he wanted an object he could love. I said he refused to have anything to do with me because of his fear of attacking me as an external object representing the breast, and that he was so angry and jealous because I was separate from him and not his own possession, his own self. After this interpretation he held his head in his hands. I interpreted to him that he wanted to hold me and have a good relationship with me outside and inside himself. He agreed, but very soon withdrew his hands into his pockets, which seemed here to indicate a withdrawal of libidinal cathexis from the outside.

I interpreted that the aggressive feelings had become stirred up in him against me as an external object representing the breast, and that he was afraid of his aggressive biting mouth. That was the reason why he had turned away from me. He at first said, "I can't do anything." Then he got up and went slowly to the black box and looked into it intently. He then took out a lower jaw bone (mandible). I asked him whether he knew what kind of bone this was. He did not answer but turned to me and held the bone in the position of his lower jaw to show me that he knew. He then put the bone back into the box and repeated the behaviour of session (g), only this time he showed more clearly that he was frightened of me, and he walked quickly away from me. I interpreted that he was afraid that I would attack and bite him, because he thought that I had changed into an attacking mouth. Then he came towards me and gave me a very slight punch (which obviously was not meant to hurt but was part of the dramatization of the situation). After this he walked up and down the very large room in a most peculiar manner, with hunched-up shoulders, and a fierce expression. He moved his legs as if he had hallucinations that bodies were lying on the floor and that he had to step over them. He looked so much like a wolf, who was running up and down in a cage, that I called out to him, "You behave like a wolf in a cage." He agreed with loud laughter, and went on running up and down and twice he tried to get out of the room.

During the next session (k) he was much more rational. He asked me how all this related to the past, to fears at night, and to me, which we discussed in detail. Then he said again, "I am wrong", which suggested to me that he felt that all we had been working over together during the last sessions (g to k) was related to his guilt feelings. He said, "Lupus", "Brown cow", "Yellow cow". After this he took a match out of his pocket which he broke into three pieces. He asked, "How are there three parts?" I said that he showed me that at present he felt his conscience was divided into three pieces: "Lupus", "Brown cow", and "Yellow cow". And I explained to him that he had shown this to me during the last few days. He had dramatized "Lupus", the wolf, last time, after taking the lower jaw bone from the black box. The jaw bone represented the internalized breast which he had attacked like an aggressive, hungry wolf, and which in his phantasies had turned into an aggressive, biting mouth. The brown cow seemed to be the breast he felt he had destroyed and changed into fæces; while the yellow cow seemed to be a breast which he had changed through envious and urinary attacks, and which had also become bad and threatening. The three pieces of the match seemed here to correspond to three aspects of his super-ego. The number three had previously appeared when he talked about three buns, which seemed to represent three breasts. But he also sometimes talked about the third penis and at a later date he referred to the third man. It is quite likely that further analysis would have revealed that the third man and the third penis did not only refer to his real brother or father but also to three male aspects of his super-ego.

It is, of course, impossible to clarify all these details, but I thought it was clear enough that the patient used the box containing the bones to illustrate in a concrete way phantasies and sensations of internal objects also representing his super-ego. In particular, these were dramatically represented by "brown cow", the destroyed breast which had turned into fæces, and "lupus" representing the persecuting, internalized, attacking mouth (the biting conscience). "Yellow cow" referred to the times when he talked about envy, birth and yellow, which I had linked with phantasies of entering the mother. But these phantasies were probably more difficult to represent in a dramatic way.

During the next few weeks the patient was more depressed, and seemed less manic and persecuted. He was eager during the session, showed in words and actions that he was trying to bring things together inside, and felt he wanted to give the good things up to God and the analyst. There was sometimes a distinct desire to be guided by me, but there was also a fear of giving everything back to me lest he should have nothing left himself. To guard against this he played a game in which he kept something hidden from me. For example, he held something in one hand while he allowed me to see only the other one. During this period he once said to the nurse that he had a great deal to worry about, but he felt it would be all right in the end. At times he again projected his depression with parts of himself into me; and at such times he was more preoccupied with losing his self and being inside an object than with objects inside himself. When he smoked a cigarette, he seemed to identify the ashes with a projected part of his own self. This seemed to me the explanation of the fact that he got anxious and disturbed when he dropped the ashes to the ground. His looking for the ashes seemed to symbolize that he was attempting to recapture this lost self. Once he said: "How can I get out of the tomb?" I felt here that he implied that in projecting his self, his depression, into me, he felt enclosed by me and so I became a tomb from which he wanted my help to be released. At other times, when in his depressed state, he seemed entirely preoccupied with attempts to restore a good, idealized object inside. He sat quietly and thoughtfully, and when I asked him what he was doing, he replied that he was rebuilding heaven. During this period the depressions lasted longer and the periods of excitement were shorter.

About the time of the arrival in England of the patient's mother, he ceased to co-operate as well as he had done hitherto, and it was obvious that there were considerable difficulties to overcome. It is very hard to assess how far the expected arrival of the mother was related to the worsening in the patient's co-operation, which might be considered a temporary difficulty. But it is quite clear that when she did arrive, and showed her disapproval of psycho-analysis, asked for further opinions, and considered leucotomy, he became rapidly violent and uncontrollable. We have to remember that, in treating acute psychotic patients, we are in the same position as the child analyst treating a young child. There is no way of preventing parents from interfering with or stopping the treatment, should they so wish.

However, before this problem arose, he had co-operated with me so well, in spite of the severity of his condition, that I regard the progress made in the analysis, and the understanding derived from it, as deserving of consideration in its own right.

After the three months of treatment preceding the arrival of the patient's mother, the nurses, the hospital doctors, and myself were agreed that there had been a distinct improvement in the patient's condition which had gradually come about since the beginning of the analysis when he had been acutely excited and had refused food altogether. After such a short treatment improvement could not of course in any case be considered stable. It seemed, however, that the analysis had at times distinctly diminished the patient's persecutory fears and had also affected to some extent the process of splitting the ego. As a result of this work the depression was coming more clearly to the surface, which coincided with a lessening of the persecutory character of the super-ego.

I wish to stress here that in treating severe schizophrenics by psycho-analysis one has to keep in mind that the tendency to fluctuations in their clinical state is to be expected to a far greater extent than in neurotic patients, even when the analysis is making good progress. But nevertheless the points just now discussed can be considered as criteria by which the progress in the psycho-analysis of a schizophrenic patient may be judged over *prolonged* periods: stable improvement depends on a gradual lessening of persecutory anxiety and ego splitting, and greater capacity to deal with conflicts on the depressive level, which would imply a greater capacity to maintain good objects outside and inside. These changes also affect the super-ego so that positive features of the super-ego become more noticeable.

CONCLUSION

In this paper I have approached the problem of the super-ego in schizophrenia by illustrations from the analysis of an acute schizophrenic patient. My findings in this case are not an isolated observation, as in other schizophrenics I also encountered a particularly severe super-ego of a persecutory nature.

In neurotic cases it takes a long and deep analysis to follow the development of a super-ego of this kind to its source into early infancy. In treating an acute regressed schizophrenic patient, however, we get an insight into early infantile processes near the beginning of the analysis, which may give us a certain amount of confirmation of the theories and concepts which have gradually been built up from the deep analysis of neurotic and psychotic adults and children. I found Melanie Klein's concept of the early infantile development, including her view of the early origin of the super-ego, most valuable because it enabled me to understand the varying and difficult problems which one meets in such cases, and my experience fully confirmed her views.

Analysts who are anxious to treat schizophrenics must remember that they will be faced with a great number of difficulties which may at first appear insurmountable, but which yield to deeper psycho-analytic understanding. If we abandon the psycho-analytic approach because of these difficulties, we give up the hope of further psycho-analytic insight. In watching the development of the super-ego conflict during an analysis such as I have described, one may often be tempted to change one's approach. Some American workers may argue: Why not cut right across the super-ego death-theme by saying to the patient, "I am not dead, I am not going to kill you, I love and protect and control you." Rosen has shown that such an approach often works, though it is not sufficiently clear how it works. Nevertheless, I should like to refer to the session where my patient said "No war" and where he most amicably shook hands with me, saying "Bluff". Was his previous adjustment based on successful bluff? If so, a forceful reassurance may again build up a more stable bluff situation. I have had the opportunity of analysing a chronic schizophrenic who had an acute schizophrenia many years ago. During the acute state and afterwards for about twelve years, he was treated by a great deal of reassurance and friendliness by a therapist who was very interested in him. The patient had made a better adjustment, but had developed other very disturbing symptoms. When we analysed the superstructure of his illness, it became clear that his improvement and co-operation were due to a terror of the outer world, and that he was continually appeasing phantasied persecutors. The friendly doctor was a persecuting figure to him, and the previous treatment and the first part of the treatment with me were dominated by continuous appeasement and bluffing. It took several years of analytic work to modify this attitude which had been reinforced by reassurance.

I do not think there is a central bluff situation in all schizophrenics, but I think it is very common. In judging the success of reassurance methods one has also to remember that every schizophrenic patient keeps on projecting his self and his internal objects, including his super-ego, into the therapist. The fact that the therapist does not alter, and remains friendly, is important both for the psycho-analytic and the psycho-therapeutic situation. The psycho-therapist who uses reassurance relieves the patient's anxiety temporarily about his dangerous super-ego and his dangerous self. When the therapist says: "I love you and will look after you", he implies: "You are not bad and I will not retaliate", and also: "You can put all your badness into me; I will deal with it for you." This may help, but it is the therapist's unconscious understanding and acceptance of the feelings of his patient which causes the reassurance to be effective, and it is doubtful whether such a patient can ever become independent of the therapist, and whether he can ever develop his personality. In the psycho-analysis of schizophrenia, we are also confronted with and accept the schizophrenic's projection of his internalized objects, including his super-ego and himself, continuously into the analyst; but the analyst interprets this situation and the problems connected with it, until the patient is gradually able to acknowledge and retain both his love and hate and his super-ego as belonging to himself. Only then can we consider that the analysis of a schizophrenic has been successful.

Herbert Rosenfeld

I have recorded a fragment of the analysis of this severely ill patient in order to contribute to the research into the psycho-pathology of schizophrenia. The problem of the super-ego and its development and origins is not only important for schizophrenia, but for all the neuroses and psychoses. Melanie Klein's research on the early origins of the super-ego, and the earliest anxieties, has been accepted by many but by no means all analysts. Some of the doubts they have about her view that these origins are to be found in earliest infancy arise from their difficulties in assessing the developmental period to which certain material belongs. It has frequently been suggested that the analysis of very young children, and of severely regressed schizophrenics, will help to throw further light on this problem.

My aim here has been to show that a transference analysis of a deeply regressed schizophrenic is possible, and that it can throw light on the earliest introjected objects and on their super-ego functions.

REFERENCES

ABRAHAM, K. (1924). "A Short Study of the Development of the Libido viewed in the light of Mental Disorders", *Selected Papers*. London, Hogarth Press, 1942.

ALEXANDER, F. "Schizophrenic Psychoses. Critical Considerations of the Psycho-Analytic Treatment", *Arch. Neurol. Psychiat.*, Vol. 26 (1951).

EISSLER, K. R. "Remarks on the Psycho-analysis of Schizophrenia", *Int. J. Psycho-Anal.*, Vol. XXXII, 139 (1951).

FEDERN, P. "Psycho-Analysis of Psychoses", *Psychiatric Quart.*, Vol. 17, 3–19, 246–257, 470–487 (1943).

FREUD, S. (1914) "On Narcissism: an Introduction", *Collected Papers IV*. London, Hogarth Press, 1925.

FROMM REICHMANN, FRIEDA, "Psycho-Analytic Psychotherapy with Psychotics", *Psychiatry*, Vol. 6, 277–279 (1943).

GARMA, A. (1932) "Die Realität und Das Es in der Schizophrenie", *Int. Zeitschrift f. Psycho-Anal.*, Vol. 18, 183.

HAYWARD, M. L., "Direct Interpretation in the Treatment of a Case of Schizophrenia", *Psychiatric Quart.*, Vol. 23, No. 4 (1949).

HEIMANN, PAULA, "On Counter-transference", *Int. J. Psycho-Anal.*, Vol. XXXI, 78 (1950).

KATAN, M., "A Contribution to the Understanding of Schizophrenic Speech", *Int. J. Psycho-Anal.*, Vol. XX, 353 (1939).

KAUFMANN, M. R., "Some Clinical Data on Ideas of Reference", *Psycho-Anal. Quart.*, Vol. 1 (1932).

—— "Religious Delusions in Schizophrenia", *Int. J. Psycho-Anal.*, Vol. XX, 363 (1939).

KLEIN, MELANIE, "A Contribution to the Psychogenesis of Manic Depressive States", *Int. J. Psycho-Anal.*, Vol. XVI (1935) and in *Contributions to Psycho-Analysis*. London, Hogarth Press, 1948.

—— (1946) "Notes on Some Schizoid Mechanisms", *Int. J. Psycho-Anal.*, Vol. XXVII, 99 and in *Developments in Psycho-Analysis*. London, Hogarth Press, 1952.

—— (1948) "A Contribution to the Theory of Anxiety and Guilt", *Int. J. Psycho-Anal.* Vol. XXIX, 114 and in *Developments in Psycho-analysis*. London, Hogarth Press, 1952.

KNIGHT, R., "Psychotherapy of an Adolescent Catatonic Schizophrenic with Mutism" *Psychiatry*, Vol. IX, No. 4 (1946).

NUNBERG, H., *Practice and Theory of Psycho-Analysis*. New York. Nervous and Mental Disease Monographs No. 74 (transl. 1948).

—— *On the Catatonic Attack* (1920).

—— *The Course of the Libidinal Conflict in a Case of Schizophrenia* (1921).

Psycho-Analysis of the Super-Ego Conflict in an acute schizophrenic

Pious, W. L., "The Pathogenic Process in Schizophrenia", *Bul. Menninger Clinic*, Vol. 13 (1949).

Riviere, E. Pichon, "Psicoanalisis de la Esquizofrenia", *Revista de Psicoanalisis*, Vol. 5, 293 (1947).

Rosen, J., "A Method of Resolving Acute Catatonic Excitement", *Psychiat. Quart.*, Vol. 20, 2, 183 (1946).

—— "The Treatment of Schizophrenic Psychoses by Direct Analytic Therapy", *Psychiat. Quart.*, Vol. 21, 3 (1947).

—— "The Survival Function of Schizophrenia", *Bul. Menninger Clinic*, Vol. 14, 3, 81 (1950).

Rosenfeld, H., "Analysis of a Schizophrenic State with Depersonalization", *Int. J. Psycho-Anal.*, Vol. XXVIII, 130 (1947).

—— "Note on the Psychopathology of Confusional States in Chronic Schizophrenias", *Int. J. Psycho-Anal.*, Vol. XXXI (1950).

—— "Transference Phenomena and Transference Analysis in an Acute Schizophrenic Patient", *Int. J. Psycho-Anal.*, Vol. XXXIII, 4 (1952).

Segal, Hanna, "Some Aspects of the Analysis of a Schizophrenic", *Int. J. Psycho-Anal.*, Vol. 31, 268 (1950).

Sullivan, H. Stack, "The Modified Psycho-analytic Treatment of Schizophrenia", *Amer. J. Psychiat.*, Vol. 2 (1931).

Wexler, M., "The Structural Problem in Schizophrenia: Therapeutic Implications", *Int. J. Psycho-Anal.*, Vol. XXXII, 157 (1951).

9

LANGUAGE AND THE SCHIZOPHRENIC[1]

W. R. BION

INTRODUCTION

IN this paper I shall discuss the schizophrenic patient's use of language and the bearing of this on the theory and practice of his analysis. I must make it clear, for the better understanding of what I say, that even where I do not make specific acknowledgment of the fact, Melanie Klein's work occupies a central position in my view of the psycho-analytic theory of schizophrenia. I assume that the explanation of terms such as "projective identification" and the "paranoid" and "depressive positions" is known through her work.

Freud made numerous references to the bearing of psycho-analysis on psychosis, but for the purpose of introducing my paper I shall refer only to one or two of these. In his 1924 paper on "Neurosis and Psychosis" he gives a simple formula for expressing perhaps the most important genetic difference between neurosis and psychosis, as follows: "Neurosis is the result of a conflict between the ego and its id, whereas psychosis is the analogous outcome of a similar disturbance in the relation between the ego and its environment (outer world)."[2] As it stands this statement would appear to equate an endo-psychic conflict with a conflict between the personality and the environment and to open the way to confusion. I do not think it unjust to his views to assume they are more correctly represented by passages in which the dynamics of neurosis and psychosis are uncompromisingly based on the concept of endo-psychic conflict. Yet Freud's formula does, by pointing to the psychotic patient's hostility to reality, and conflict with it, help us to grasp one element that

---

[1] The theme of this paper was stated in a much compressed form in a contribution to the International Congress of Psycho-Analysis in 1953.
[2] *Collected Papers*, Vol. II (London, 1924).

determines the nature of the endo-psychic conflict, and I remind you of it for that reason.

I would now turn to some passages from his paper, written in 1911, entitled, "Formulations regarding the Two Principles in Mental Functioning".[1] I shall consider that succession of adaptations, which the new demands of the reality principle make necessary, in the mental apparatus which, Freud says, "on account of insufficient or uncertain knowledge, we can only detail very cursorily", for I believe that certain experiences that have come my way enable me to make some suggestions about them.

He says, "The increased significance of external reality heightened the significance also of the sense organs directed towards that outer world, and of the consciousness attached to them; the latter now learned to comprehend the qualities of sense in addition to the qualities of pleasure and 'pain' which hitherto had alone been of interest to it." It will be one of my contentions that the conflict with reality, of which Freud speaks in my first quotation, leads the psychotic patient to developments which make it doubtful whether he has ever learned to "comprehend the qualities of sense in addition to the qualities of pleasure and 'pain'." Further I shall suggest there is evidence which may indicate that destructive attacks have been directed by the patient, or the patient's id, against the newly significant sense organs and "the consciousness attached to them". In my view, what Freud describes as the institution of the reality principle is an event that has never been satisfactorily achieved by the psychotic, and the main failure takes place at the point which Melanie Klein describes as the development of the depressive position. The reality principle, if it were allowed to operate, would make the psychotic infant aware of his relationship with whole objects, and thereby of the feelings of depression and guilt associated with the depressive position. It is at this point however that the patient makes destructive attacks on all those aspects of his personality, his ego, that are concerned with establishing external contact and internal contact. What are these special aspects of the ego? Freud cites (i) "attention"; (ii) "notation", which he says is a part of that which we call memory; (iii) "an impartial passing of judgment"; (iv) a new function entrusted to motor discharge, which is now concerned with action, and (v) restraint of action "by means of the process of thought, which was developed from ideation". Freud says, "thought was endowed with qualities which made it possible for the mental

[1] *Collected Papers*, Vol. IV (London, 1925).

apparatus to support increased tension during a delay in the process of discharge. It is essentially an experimental way of acting, accompanied by displacement of smaller quantities of cathexis together with less expenditure (discharge) of them."

I shall explain why I think that all these special adaptations, except (iv) (about which I shall have something to say in another context), are really aspects of the establishment of verbal thought; further, that this development is one aspect of the synthesizing and integrating forces which Melanie Klein has described as characteristic of the depressive position. I hope also to show that I regard disturbances in the development of verbal thought as an important aspect of psychosis, particularly, but not exclusively, of schizophrenia, even though I do not wish it to be supposed that I ignore the peculiarity of the schizophrenic's object relations, of which verbal thought, for all its importance, is but a subordinate function. I may best do this by a quotation from a paper to which I shall have occasion to refer later—Freud's paper, in 1911, on the Unconscious.[1] In discussing one of the cases I quote, he says, "Analysis shows that he is working out his castration complex upon his own skin." I shall suggest, relating my experiences to Freud's formula that in psychosis the conflict is between the ego and the environment, that this view of his patient would be even more fruitful if we suppose that the psychotic's castrations are worked out on his mental skin—i.e. on the ego; more precisely still, castration of the ego is identical with destructive attacks on (i) the consciousness attached to the sense organs; (ii) attention—the function which Freud says is instituted to search the outer world; (iii) the system of notation which he describes as a part of memory; (iv) the passing of judgment which was developed to take the place of repression; and finally, (v) thought as a way of supporting the increased tension produced by restraint on motor discharge. With regard to this last point I would add that in my view verbal thought is the essential feature of all five functions of the ego and that the destructive attacks on verbal thought or its rudiments is inevitably an attack on all.

To pass now to the nature of these attacks: I shall suggest that they are all true examples of the mechanisms described by Melanie Klein in her discussion of the paranoid and depressive positions, and particularly of projective identification. In her paper on "The Importance of Symbol-formation in the Development of the Ego" (1930),[2] she

[1] *Ibid.*

[2] *Int. J. Psycho-Anal.*, Vol. II (1930); also in *Contributions to Psycho-Analysis* (London, 1948).

describes the child's phantasies about the contents of the mother's body and the sadism with which the child makes attacks upon these supposed contents. It is my belief that the same oral, urethral, anal, and muscular sadism that she describes as typical of the attack on the mother's body and on the sexual parents, is in action against the ego. The "castration" of the ego, then, is manifested in extremely sadistic attacks on (i) the consciousness attached to the sense organs; (ii) attention; (iii) the system of notation; (iv) the passing of judgment; (v) the capacity to support frustration of motor discharge and therefore upon the whole development of verbal thought of which all these, and not merely the last, as Freud says, are particular aspects. Prominent amongst the methods by which the sadistic attacks on verbal thought are given effect is the splitting which Freud and others have so frequently described. But the point is that the splitting of verbal thought is carried out cruelly, and the attempts at synthesis which are typical, in psychotics as in others, of the depressive position, are frustrated because the splits are brought together cruelly.

I shall also hope to show that the splitting mechanism is brought into action to minister to the patient's greed and is therefore not simply an unfortunate catastrophe of the kind that occurs when the patient's ego is split in pieces as an accompaniment of his determination to split his objects; it is the outcome of a determination which can be expressed verbally as an intention to be as many people as possible, so as to be in as many places as possible, so as to get as much as possible, for as long as possible—in fact timelessly.

The material is derived from the analysis of six patients; two were drug addicts, one an obsessional anxiety state with schizoid features, and the remaining three schizophrenics, all of whom suffered from hallucinations which were well in evidence over a period of between four to five years of analysis. Of these three, two showed marked paranoid features, and one, depression.

With one exception I made no conscious departure from the psycho-analytic procedure I usually employ with neurotics, being careful always to take up both positive and negative aspects of the transference. For a short period I had to visit one patient in hospital but otherwise all visited me, sometimes with a male nurse in attendance. The exception I shall make clear by approaching the main theme of my paper. This, as I have indicated, is the Theory of Schizophrenia as it appears when it is approached through analysis of the difficulties that attend communication between the schizoid patient and the analyst. For the most part the discussion centres on the rudimentary stages of what, for want of a better term, I have called verbal thought. But, before that stage is reached in analysis, much work has to be done, and it is in the course of this work that I make interpretations that most analysts will criticize as exceptions to sound analytic procedure, and therefore matter for scrutiny.

The analyst who essays, in our present state of ignorance, the treatment of such patients, must be prepared to discover that for a considerable proportion of analytic time the only evidence on which an interpretation can be based is that which is afforded by the counter-transference. What this means in practice I shall attempt to indicate by a description of part of one such session; this is how it went. The patient had been lying on the couch, silent, for some twenty minutes. During this time I had become aware of a growing sense of anxiety and tension which I associated with facts about the patient which were already known to me from work done with him in the six months he had already been with me. As the silence continued I became aware of a fear that the patient was meditating a physical attack upon me, though I could see no outward change in his posture. As the tension grew I felt increasingly sure that this was so. Then, and only then, I said to him, "You have been pushing into my insides your fear that you will murder me." There was no change in the patient's position but I noticed that he clenched his fists till the skin over the knuckles became white. The silence was unbroken. At the same time I felt that the tension in the room, presumably in the relationship between him and me, had decreased. I said to him, "When I spoke to you, you took your fear that you would murder me back into yourself; you are now feeling afraid you will make a murderous attack upon me." I followed the same method throughout the session, waiting for impressions to pile up until I felt I was in a position to make my interpretation. It will be noted that my interpretation depends on the use of Melanie Klein's theory of projective identification, first to illuminate my counter-transference, and then to frame the interpretation which I give the patient.

This mode of procedure is open to grave theoretical objections and I think they should be faced. I need not mention the debate which still centres on Melanie Klein's theories, but I would discuss further the use which I make of counter-transference.

The objection that I project my conflicts and phantasies on to the patient cannot and should not be easily dismissed. The defence must lie in the hard facts of the analytic situation, namely that in the present state of psycho-analytic knowledge the analyst cannot rely on a body of well-authenticated knowledge. Further, he must assume that his own analysis has gone far enough to make disastrous misinterpretation unlikely. Finally, I think there are signs that as experience accumulates it may be possible to detect and present facts which exist, but at present elude clinical acumen; they become observable, at second hand, through the pressure they exert to produce what I am aware of as counter-transference. I would not have it thought that I advocate this use of counter-transference as a final solution; rather it is an expedient to which we must resort until something better presents itself.

To some extent, for reasons I give later, it has to be accepted that the psychotic patient "acts out", but I have no doubt whatever that the analyst should always insist, by the way in which he conducts the case, that he is addressing himself to a sane person and is entitled to expect some sane reception. This point is of importance for, as I shall show later, patients will use the mechanism of projective identification to rid themselves of their "sanity". If the analyst appears by his conduct to condone the feasibility of this, the way is open to massive regression, and in my experience, if the patient is once allowed to do this, a great deal of work has to be done to retrieve the position. In this respect I am absolutely in agreement with Maurits Katan in his views on the importance of the non-psychotic part of the personality in schizophrenia.[1]

I may mention two reasons for hoping that the procedure I have outlined may be sound. The first is that a safeguard exists in the psychotic patient's readiness to indicate when he thinks he is the victim of the analyst's projections. His view is not proof that projection is taking place, but it does deserve attention. My second point is that the procedure works.

SCHIZOPHRENIC LANGUAGE

Language is employed by the schizophrenic in three ways; as a mode of action, as a method of communication, and as a mode of thought. He will show a preference for action on occasions when other patients would realize that what was required was thought; thus, he will want to go over to a piano to take out the

[1] M. Katan, "The Importance of the Non-Psychotic Part of the Personality in Schizophrenia", *Int. J. Psycho-Anal.*, Vol. XXXV, 2 (1953).

movement to understand why someone is playing the piano. Reciprocally, if he has a problem, the solution of which depends on action, as when, being in one place, he should be in another, he will resort to thought—omnipotent thought—as his mode of transportation.

At the moment I want to consider only his use of it as a mode of action in the service either of projective identification or of splitting the object. It will be noted that this is but one aspect of schizophrenic object relations in which he is either splitting or getting in and out of his objects.

The first of these uses is in the service of projective identification. In this the patient uses words as things, or as split-off parts of himself, which he pushes forcibly into the analyst. Typical of this is the belief of a patient who felt he got inside me at the beginning of each session and had to be extricated at the end of it.

Language is employed also as a mode of action for the splitting of his object. This obtrudes when the analyst becomes identified with internal persecutors, but it is employed at other times too. Here are two examples of this use of language: The patient comes into the room, shakes me warmly by the hand, and looking piercingly into my eyes says, "I think the sessions are not for a long while but stop me ever going out." I know from previous experience that this patient has a grievance that the sessions are too few and that they interfere with his free time. He intended to split me by making me give two opposite interpretations at once, and this was shown by his next association when he said, "How does the lift know what to do when I press two buttons at once?"

My second example has wide implications, which I cannot take up here, because of its bearing on insomnia. The technique depends on the combination of two incompatible elements thus: the patient speaks in a drowsy manner calculated to put the analyst to sleep; at the same time he stimulates the analyst's curiosity. The intention is again to split the analyst who is not allowed to go to sleep and is not allowed to keep awake.

You will note a third example of splitting later on when I describe a patient splitting the analyst's speech itself.

Before I consider the schizophrenic's difficulties with language as a mode of thought, I want to turn for a moment to a discussion of semantics. I think that our difficulties as analysts are made to appear greater than they are by an inadequate theory of semantics, and in particular the use of the Augustinian theory as if it were valid for the whole field. Wittgenstein[1] has deprecated this view and seems to me to put forward a theory which is both more comprehensive and more realistic. In ordinary speech the meaning of any given word, and still more the meaning of the sum total of what a man says, depends upon the synthesis of a complex variety of elements; sounds have to be combined to form words, and words, sentences. Culture and personality of the person to whom the remark is addressed is also rapidly assessed and integrated with other elements in the speaker's mind. The appropriate intonation and pronunciation must be employed, and so on. As I shall show later, reasonably correct colloquial speech can be so treated by the listener that its meaning is destroyed. Reciprocally the speaker can be so incapable of synthesis or show such aberration in his modes of integration that a deal of work has to be done merely to appreciate what has happened to the verbal communication, let alone to grasp the meaning. I shall hope to make these points clearer by actual clinical examples which I shall cite in the development of my theme.

To turn now to the schizophrenic's difficulties with language as a mode of thought. Here is a sequence of associations all in one session, but separated from each other by intervals of four or five minutes.

"I have a problem I am trying to work out."

"As a child I never had phantasies."

"I knew they weren't facts so I stopped them."

"I don't dream nowadays."

Then after a pause the patient went on in a bewildered voice, "I don't know what to do now." I said, "About a year ago you told me you were no good at thinking. Just now you said you were working out a problem—obviously something you were thinking about."

Patient: "Yes."

Analyst: "But you went on with the thought that you had no phantasies in childhood; and then that you had no dreams; you then said that you did not know what to do. It must mean that without phantasies and without dreams you have not the means with which to think out your problem." The patient agreed and began to talk with marked freedom and coherence. The reference to the inhibition of phantasy as a severe disability hindering development supports Melanie Klein's observations in her paper, "The Theory of Intellectual Inhibition".

[1] L. Wittgenstein, *Philosophical Investigations* (Oxford, 1953).

The severe splitting in the schizophrenic makes it difficult for him to achieve the use of symbols and subsequently of substantives and verbs. It is necessary to demonstrate these difficulties to him as they arise; of this I shall shortly give an example. The capacity to form symbols is dependent on:
(i) the ability to grasp whole objects,
(ii) the abandonment of the paranoid-schizoid position with its attendant splitting, and
(iii) the bringing together of splits and the ushering in of the depressive position.

Since verbal thought depends on the ability to integrate, it is not surprising to find that its emergence is intimately associated with the depressive position which, as Melanie Klein has pointed out, is a phase of active synthesis and integration. Verbal thought sharpens awareness of psychic reality and therefore of the depression which is linked with destruction and loss of good objects. The presence of internal persecutors, as another aspect of psychic reality, is similarly unconsciously more recognized. The patient feels that the association between the depressive position and verbal thought is one of cause and effect—itself a belief based on his capacity to integrate—and this adds one more to the many causes of his hatred, already well in evidence, of analysis, which is after all a treatment which employs verbal thought in the solution of mental problems.

The patient at this stage becomes frightened of the analyst, even though he may concede that he feels better, but, and this is where the kernel of our problem lies, he shows every sign of being anxious to have nothing whatever to do with his embryonic capacity for verbal thought. That is felt to be better left to the analyst; or, as I think it more correct to say, the analyst is felt to be better able than he to harbour it within himself without disaster. The patient seems, despite all the work done, to have reverted to the use of language that I have described as characteristic of the schizophrenic before analysis. He has greater verbal capacity, but prefers to employ it as he did when it was slight.

DEVELOPMENT OF CAPACITY FOR VERBAL THOUGHT

To explain why the patient is so chary of using his increased capacity I must tell you of an experience which seems to have peculiar significance for him. A patient said to me. "I am a prisoner of psycho-analysis." Later in the session he added, "I can't escape." Some months later he said, "I can't get out of my state of mind." A mass of material, to which quotation cannot do justice, had accumulated over a period of three years to give the impression that the patient felt unable to escape from the prison which seemed sometimes to be me, sometimes psycho-analysis and sometimes his state of mind, which is a constant struggle with his own internal objects.

The problem to which I am addressing myself can best be understood if it is seen to appertain to the moment when the patient feels he has effected his escape. The escape appears to contribute to the patient's feeling, which he occasionally reports, that he is better; but it has cost him dear. This same patient said, "I have lost my words", and meant by this, as further analysis disclosed, that the instrument with which he had effected his escape had been lost in the process. Words, the capacity for verbal thought, the one essential for further progress, have gone. On expansion it appears that he thinks he has reached this pass as a penalty for forging this instrument of verbal thought and using it to escape from his former state of mind; hence the unwillingness I described to use his greater verbal capacity except as a mode of action.

Here now is the example I promised when I was speaking of the difficulty that schizophrenic splitting caused in the formation of symbols and the development of verbal thought. The patient was a schizophrenic who had been in analysis five years; I describe some essentials of two sessions. I must warn you that compression has compelled me to leave out many repetitive formulations which in fact would mitigate the baldness of the interpretations as I report them here. I think interpretation should be in language that is simple, exact, and mature.

Patient: "I picked a tiny piece of skin from my face and feel quite empty."

Analyst: "The tiny piece of skin is your penis, which you have torn out, and all your insides have come with it."

Patient: "I do not understand . . . penis . . . only syllables."

Analyst: "You have split my word 'penis' into syllables and it now has no meaning."

Patient: "I don't know what it means, but I want to say, 'If I can't spell I can't think.'"

Analyst: "The syllables have now been split into letters; you cannot spell—that is to say you cannot put the letters together again to make words, so now you cannot think."

The patient started the next day's session with disjointed associations and complained that he could not think. I reminded him of the session I have just described, whereupon he resumed correct speech thus:

Patient: "I cannot find any interesting food."

Analyst: "You feel it has all been eaten up."

Patient: "I do not feel able to buy any new clothes and my socks are a mass of holes."

Analyst: "By picking out the tiny piece of skin yesterday you injured yourself so badly you cannot even buy clothes; you are empty and have nothing to buy them with."

Patient: "Although they are full of holes they constrict my foot."

Analyst: "Not only did you tear out your own penis but also mine. So to-day there is no interesting food—only a hole, a sock. But even this sock is made of a mass of holes, all of which you made and which have joined together to constrict, or swallow and injure, your foot."

This and subsequent sessions confirmed that he felt he had eaten the penis and that therefore there was no interesting food left, only a hole. But this hole was now so persecutory that he had to split it up. As a result of the splitting, the hole became a mass of holes which all came together in a persecutory way to constrict his foot. This patient's picking habits had been worked over for some three years. At first he had been occupied only with blackheads, and I shall quote from Freud's description of three cases, one observed by himself, one by Dr. Tausk, and one by R. Reitler, which have a resemblance to my patient. They are taken from his paper on "The Unconscious" of 1915.[1]

Of his patient Freud said, he "has let himself withdraw from all the interests of life on account of the unhealthy condition of the skin of his face. He declares that he has blackheads and that there are deep holes in his face which everyone notices." Freud says he was working out his castration complex on his skin and that he began to think there was a deep cavity wherever he had got rid of a blackhead. He continues: "The cavity which then appears in consequence of his guilty act is the female genital, i.e. stands for the fulfilment of the threat of castration (or the phantasy representing it) called forth by onanism." Freud compares such substitute formations with those of the hysteric, saying "A tiny little hole such as a pore of the skin will hardly be used by an hysteric as a symbol for the vagina, which otherwise he will compare with every imaginable object capable of

[1] *Collected Papers*, Vol. IV (London, 1925).

enclosing a space. Besides we should think that the multiplicity of these little cavities would prevent him from using them as a substitute for the female genital."

Of Tausk's case he says, "in pulling on his stockings he was disturbed by the idea that he must draw apart the knitted stitches, i.e. the holes, and every hole was for him a symbol of the female genital aperture."

Quoting Reitler's case he says the patient "found the explanation that his foot symbolized the penis, putting on the stocking stood for an onanistic act. . . ."

I shall now return to my patient at a session ten days later. A tear welled from his eye and he said with a mixture of despair and reproach, "Tears come from my ears now."

This kind of association had by now become familiar to me, so I was aware that I had been set a problem in interpretation. But by this time the patient, who had been in analysis some six years, was capable of a fair degree of identification with the analyst and I had his help. I shall not attempt a description of the stages by which the conclusions I put before you were reached. The steps were laborious and slow even though we had the evidence of six years of analysis on which to draw.

It appeared that he was deploring a blunder that seemed to bear out his suspicion that his capacity for verbal communication was impaired. It seemed that his sentence was but another instance of an inability to put words together properly.

After this had been discussed it was seen that tears were very bad things, that he felt much the same about tears which came from his ears as he did about sweat that came from the holes in his skin when he had, as he supposed, removed blackheads or other such objects from the skin. His feeling about tears from his ears was seen to be similar to his feeling about the urine that came from the hole that was left in a person when his penis had been torn out; the bad urine still came.

When he told me that he couldn't listen very well I took advantage of his remark to remind him that in any case we needed to know why his mind was full of such thoughts at the present juncture, and I suggested that probably his hearing was felt to be defective because my words were being drowned by the tears that poured from his ears.

When it emerged that he couldn't talk very well either I suggested that it was because he felt his tongue had been torn out and he had been left only with an ear.

231

This was followed by what seemed to be a completely chaotic series of words and noises. I interpreted that now he felt he had a tongue but it was really just as bad as his ear—it just poured out a flow of destroyed language. In short it appeared that despite his wishes and mine, we could not, or he felt we could not, communicate. I suggested that he felt he had a very bad and hostile object inside him which was treating our verbal intercourse to much the same kind of destructive attack which he had once felt he had launched against parental intercourse, whether sexual or verbal.

At first he seemed to feel most keenly the defects in his capacity for communication or thought, and there was a great deal of play with the pronunciation of tears (*teers* or *tares*), the emphasis being mostly on the inability to bring together the objects, words, or word plus pronunciation, except cruelly. But at one point he seemed to become aware that his association had been the starting point for much discussion. Then he murmured, "Lots of people." On working this out it appeared that he had swung away from the idea that his verbal capacity was being irretrievably destroyed by the attacks to which our conversation was being subjected, to the idea that his verbal communication was extremely greedy. This greed was ministered to by his splitting himself into so many people that he could be in many different places at once to hear the many different interpretations that I, also split into "lots of people", was now able to give simultaneously instead of one by one. His greed, and the attacks on verbal communication by the internal persecutors, were, therefore, related to each other.

This patient's belief that splitting had destroyed his ability to think was the more serious for him because he no longer felt that action provided a solution for the kind of problem with which he was struggling. This state was equated by the patient with "insanity".

The patient believes he has lost his capacity for verbal thought because he has left it behind inside his former state of mind, or inside the analyst, or inside psycho-analysis. He also believes that his capacity for verbal thought has been removed from him by the analyst, who is now a frightening person. Both beliefs give rise to characteristic anxieties. The belief that he has left it behind has, as we have seen, helped to make the patient feel he is insane. He thinks that he will never be able to progress unless he goes back, as it were, into his former state of mind in order to fetch it. This he dare not do because he dreads his former state of mind and fears that he would once more be imprisoned in it. The belief that the analyst has removed his capacity for verbal thought, makes the patient afraid of employing his new found capacity for verbal thought, lest it should arouse the hatred of the analyst and cause him to repeat the attack. He thus shows the same attitude to verbal thought as he has to his potency and his equipment for work and love. From the patient's point of view the achievement of verbal thought has been a most unhappy event. Verbal thought is so interwoven with catastrophe and the emotion of depression that the patient, resorting to projective identification, splits it off and pushes it into the analyst. The results are again unhappy for the patient; lack of this capacity is now felt by the patient to be the same thing as being insane. On the other hand, reassumption of this capacity seems to him to be inseparable from depression and awareness, on a reality level this time, that he is "insane". This fact tends to give reality to the patient's phantasies of the catastrophic results that would accrue were he to risk reintrojection of his capacity for verbal thought.

It must not be supposed that the patient leaves his problems untouched during this phase. He will occasionally give the analyst concrete and precise information about them. The analyst's problem is the patient's dread, now quite manifest, of attempting a psychoanalytic understanding of what they mean for him, partly because the patient now understands that psycho-analysis demands from him that very verbal thought which he dreads.

So far I have dealt with the problem of communication between analyst and schizophrenic patient. I shall now consider the experience that the patient has when he lives through the process of achieving sufficient mastery of language to emerge from the "prison of psycho-analysis", or state of mind in which he previously felt himself to be hopelessly enclosed. The patient is apparently unaware of any existence outside the consulting room; there is no report of any external activity. There is merely an existence away from the analyst of which nothing is known except that he is "all right", or "better", and a relationship with the analyst which the patient says is bad. The intervals between sessions are admitted and feared. He complains that he is insane, expresses his fear of hallucination and delusion, and is extremely cautious in his behaviour lest he should become insane.

The living through of the emotions belonging to this phase leads to a shift towards higher valuation of the external object at the expense of the hallucinated internal object. This depends on the analysis of the patient's hallucinations and his insistence on allotting to real objects a subordinate role. If this has been done, the analyst sees before him the ego and more normal object relations in process of development. I am assuming that there has been an adequate working through of the processes of splitting and the underlying persecutory anxiety as well as of reintegration. Herbert Rosenfeld has described some of the dangers of this phase.[1] My experiences confirm his findings. I have observed the progress from multiple splits to four, and from four to two, and the great anxiety as integration proceeds with the tendency to revert to violent disintegration. This is due to intolerance of the depressive position, internal persecutors, and verbal thought. If splitting has been adequately worked through, the tendency to split the object and ego at the same time is kept within bounds. Each session is then a step in ego development.

REALIZATION OF INSANITY

The penalty for attempting a clarification of the complexity of the schizophrenic patient's relationship with his objects is that if the attempt is successful it is delusively misleading. I would redress the balance by approaching the facts I have described from a different angle. I shall take up the story at the point where splits are brought together, the patient escapes from the prison of his state of mind and the depressive position is ushered in. I wish particularly to draw attention to this concatenation of events when it is suffused by the illumination achieved through the development of a capacity for verbal thought. I have made it clear that this is a most important point in the whole analysis and I may therefore have given the impression that thereafter the analysis enters calm waters. What takes place, if the analyst has been successful, is a controlled schizophrenic breakdown, and with it the patient directs powerful feelings of hatred against the analyst. If care has been taken throughout the analysis to deal with the transference, negative as well as positive, I am inclined to think the patient will not actually make a murderous attack on the analyst—though it is probably as well not to count on this—but will be content to say with intense conviction and hatred that the analyst has not merely led him to realize he is hallucinated and deluded but is responsible for having brought him to this pass.

[1] "Analysis of a Schizophrenic State with Depersonalization". *Int. J. Psycho-Anal.*, Vol. XXVIII, 1947.

Until we know more about the treatment of such cases it is quite likely that the patient, if he is not already in hospital, will have to go there now. The analyst must expect that concern for the patient's welfare will cause the family to intervene. He should oppose any proposal for surgical or shock treatment and concentrate on not allowing the patient to retreat from his realization that he is insane or from his hatred of the analyst who has succeeded, after so many years, in bringing him to an emotional realization of the facts which he has spent his life trying to evade. This may be the more difficult because, when the first panic begins to subside, the patient himself will suggest that he is better. Due weight must be given to this, but care must be taken to prevent its being used to delay investigation, in detail, of the ramifications in the analytic situation of the changes brought about in the patient's object relationships, by the realization by himself of his insanity.

SOME SUBSEQUENT DEVELOPMENTS

I wish now to give some idea of a session when this phase is well established and the patient has accepted both his insanity and the necessity for the analytic work demanded of him. The examples I give are typical of the sessions which I have described as "steps in ego development". The first is of a patient whose psychological problem may be summarized as a lifelong rebellion against the depression to which he was compelled to cling, with the utmost tenacity, through fear of the "catatonic schizophrenia" (his words) which would take its place were he to abandon it. The session took place some fifteen months after what his doctor had described as a schizophrenic breakdown: he had been called in to see him when he was in a "depressive stupor". At the time of this session he had become able to discuss, without much fear, whether various experiences that arose from day to day were what he severally called "visual images", or "delusions", or "hallucinations", or "nightmares", or "dreams", or "real". He accepted that it was necessary to make the distinction and showed, implicitly and explicitly, that it was more important to know whether something was true than whether it was pleasant. He was also prepared to accept the fact, which I was able to demonstrate, that he was frequently passing from "depression" to "schizophrenia" and vice versa; in short, that the dreaded breakdown was not a thing of the past, over and done with, but a recurrent phenomenon. He still tended to deny it by drawing my attention to the fact that he was now regularly attending lectures and courses in engineering. I always acknowledged that, but pointed out that this fact did not necessarily refute my interpretations.

In the session I am describing, I had been giving an interpretation to the effect that his inability to make a judgment, of which he had just complained, had followed associations in which he was once more experiencing difficulty in the use of words.

Patient: "I can't properly remember all you have just said."

Analyst: "Since you feel you lack words you also feel you lack the means to store ideas in your mind. This feeling is so strong that it makes you think you have forgotten, whether you have or not."

Patient: "Oh yes; I remember now." (Then, becoming depressed.) "I am afraid I am a great trouble to you."

Analyst: "As soon as you feel able to think, and so to remember, you feel you have done me an injury, been a trouble to me, and the depression comes on."

Patient: "My muscles are becoming stiff. (Stretching out his arms, each in turn, rather stiffly but with much of the character of the movement accompanying a yawn, or the gesture of an athlete limbering up.) Is this schizophrenia?"

Analyst: "We know how you dread depression; but now you need not be depressed because you have this very bad 'schizophrenia' inside controlling your arms."

Patient: (Depressed). "I don't know how I shall get through the day."

Analyst: "Now you are depressed again—either you feel you have this bad 'schizophrenia' or bad 'depression'; nothing but one or the other."

Patient: (Puzzled.) "Funny. Because I go to lectures now and enjoy them."

Analyst: "You cannot understand how you can be working or happy when you feel, as you have felt all your life, that you can only be depressed or what you call 'schizophrenic'."

I have chosen this example because it gives a good idea of the way a patient will compress into a few associations the whole of a "breakdown" which it has taken years to accomplish in the first instance; the experience against which he has mobilized so much of his resistance is now lived through with comparative ease. It shows how the depressive position can be used as an escape from the paranoid-schizoid position and vice versa; and it shows the part that is played in these changes by the integration and disintegration of verbal thought.

My next example I include as one showing the kind of difficulty that a schizophrenic patient encounters in his attempt to employ words. This patient had been working through the "breakdown" for some nine months at the time of this episode. The session had been marked by a good deal of rather abstract speculation over some difficulty he had had at work, and in the course of it he used the word "selexual". He reacted to this by a gesture of angry impatience. "What was that?" I asked him. "Oh, nothing; two words got on top of each other and became sexual." I replied, "You are feeling that your words will not help you when you want them to, but instead become sexual with each other. They seem to be behaving rather like the parents inside you who, you remember, seem always to persecute you by having sexual intercourse." He remembered the reference as we had done a great deal of work about the primal scene in its many aspects and he was familiar with manifestations of it as an internal object. The striking thing about this association was that it showed a synthesis in which his objects were coming together, or were being allowed to come together, in a far more creative manner than had been the case before the "breakdown". Then they had never been able to come to life even when brought together, and more often than not had been brought together cruelly—i.e. incongruously and frustratingly. Further, the patient was angry but not persecuted. Finally, there was an emotional quality about the episode which I find difficult to convey, but which I must attempt because I have no doubt of its importance. It was the first time in his whole analysis that I had felt amused and able to believe that, had he been aware of my amusement, he would have forgiven it. Before this time there had been occasions, such as that on which he reported a dream of animals composed of two incompatible halves joined together, where I seemed to be invited to share in what I can only describe as an "unfunny" joke; there had been a number of occasions when he had felt, with dangerously mounting anger, that he was being laughed at. But there had been no occasion, such as this, where asperity seemed to be softened by an element of tenderness. For the first time it seemed possible that a day might come when the patient would show a sense of humour. I pointed out to him immediately, while

237

the intonation he had employed was presumably fresh in his mind, that he had spoken of the sexual behaviour of these two objects with exasperation but also with love; and I reminded him, for contrast, of the unrelieved hatred with which he had previously spoken of the sexual parents.

My last example from this phase is a reply which a schizophrenic patient made when I pointed out to him that he, as I supposed, was doubting the accuracy of an interpretation I had given him. "I was concentrating on whether it was pleasant or unpleasant," he replied, "so I didn't know anything about its being true or not." I suggested that this might explain his complaint, a few days previously, of the anxiety he suffered through not being sure whether an experience was an hallucination or not. "If you feel you only want to know if something is pleasant or unpleasant you would naturally suppose that you had not learned how to tell the difference between real and unreal."

The developments that sprang from my patient's flash of insight persuaded me that a feeble deployment of the depressive position was very closely associated with the continued dominance of the pleasure principle and the destructive attacks on the ego which I have discussed in this paper. I am disposed also to attach importance to the fact that in this patient and one other, hatred of pain was apparently a stronger motive than love of pleasure. (I would further suggest, as a theory for testing, that in the paranoid-schizoid position pain becomes identified with the early super-ego.) That is to say, attacks on the ego were stimulated by the patient's determination to avoid pain at any cost, even the cost of sacrificing and chance of experiencing pleasure. But the attacks on the ego are, I believe, the source of the fears, extremely acute fears, of disintegration, annihilation, death. In so far as the destructive attacks are felt to have been a success, the patient seems to feel that an inner disaster has taken place, that the absence of painful stimuli achieved is evidence that death has supervened; that he has gone back to where he was; gone back to the state of mind in which he was before he was born.

RESULTS

I am not yet prepared to offer any opinion about the prospects of treatment except to say that two of the three schizophrenics of whom I am speaking are now earning their living. I consider that if the course I have indicated above is followed, there is reason to anticipate that the schizophrenic may achieve his own form of adjustment to reality which may be no less worthy of the title of "cure" because it is not of the same kind as that which is achieved by less disordered patients. I repeat that I do not think that any cure, however limited, will be achieved if, at the point I have tried to describe to you, the analyst attempts to reassure the patient and so undoes all the good work that has led to the patient's being able to realize the severity of his condition. At this point an opportunity which must not be lost has been created for exploring with the patient what it means to do analytic or any other kind of work when insane.

The experiences I have described compel me to conclude that at the onset of the infantile depressive position, elements of verbal thought increase in intensity and depth. In consequence, the pains of psychic reality are exacerbated by it and the patient who regresses to the paranoid-schizoid position will, as he does so, turn destructively on his embryonic capacity for verbal thought as one of the elements which have led to his pain.

10

A COMBINATION OF DEFENCE MECHANISMS IN PARANOID STATES

PAULA HEIMANN

I. INTRODUCTION

PSYCHOPATHOLOGY of everyday life abounds in examples of paranoid delusions. We are all apt to feel at times that it always rains when we have planned to spend a day out of doors, that the bus going in the opposite direction to ours always comes first, that some unfortunate experience we have had was directly due to somebody's ill-will or at least to fate's. Usually, however, this type of paranoid delusion is easily corrected. On second thoughts we remember many occasions when the weather was kind, when our bus came immediately, or even when we were particularly lucky; and we know that our unpleasant experiences are not caused by enemies, personal or impersonal, but result from other factors, including our own errors of judgment and other imperfections.

Following this line of thought we come to discern a rising scale of severity in delusional attitudes. There is the momentary reaction—"Damn that fool!" Ascending the scale, there is the mood which may persist for some hours—"I knew everything would go wrong with me to-day, and it has!" Neither of these leads as yet to harmful consequences; both are entirely compatible with sound mental health. Next in severity might be a paranoid state lasting for days or weeks, or more. Finally, there is the psychosis in which the person's life is totally determined by his belief in a persecution, the delusion having become permanent, and the focus of a rigid system. I am not, however, suggesting that the duration of the paranoid delusion is the only criterion to be considered in assessing the significance of the different types of paranoid delusional states. Another, for example, is its intensity; the degree to which the subject's feelings and thoughts are absorbed by it or the drive for action it engenders against the supposed persecutor.

To say that transient paranoid delusions are found in every analysis is only repeating the observation that they form part of the psychopathology of everyday life.

We have learnt from Freud not to draw a sharp line between normal and abnormal psychological processes. The Œdipus conflict is ubiquitous; it forms the nucleus of every neurosis, and every child passes through the infantile neurosis. We do not regard this infantile neurosis as an illness, although unfortunate inheritance and environment may cause it at the time to change so that it becomes an illness. Normally the child grows out of it successfully; if he is not sufficiently successful, he will take too many traces of it into adult life and at some time develop an overt neurosis.

Melanie Klein's work has shown us that early infantile development embraces two phases in which, characteristically, anxieties of a psychotic nature occur: namely, both persecutory and depressive delusional feelings and phantasies. Normally these anxiety states are transient and interspersed in healthy and happy moods; but here, too, adverse inherited and environmental factors may actually turn them into conditions of illness. In the second of these phases, the "infantile depressive position", Melanie Klein has found the roots of the Œdipus complex.[1] The infantile neurosis, the neurotic manifestations after the first year, represents partly the working over of the earlier psychotic anxieties just mentioned, and partly the response to the current and actual Œdipal conflicts. Failure in each developmental phase establishes the fixation-points for later mental illness; those for psychosis lying, as Abraham was the first to show, in earliest infancy.[2]

This brief sketch of mental development, with its danger points for the achievement of mental health, gives us the theoretical explanation of the psychopathology of everyday life. Observation in analyses shows that the absolutely "normal" person is a creature of fiction, not of reality.

The patients on whose analyses the present paper is based showed marked paranoid states, either at the beginning of the analysis or at a later stage. The conscious reasons for which they came to seek analysis varied, and so did their presenting symptoms; they included

[1] Cf. Ch. 2 in this book.
[2] "A Short Study of the Development of the Libido, Viewed in the Light of Mental Disorders" (1924). *Selected Papers* (London, 1942.)

difficulties in work or in social and sexual relationships, as well as severe anxiety states connected with a dread of impending break-down into psychosis. Whether or not in adverse circumstances and without analysis the paranoid condition in some of my patients would have deteriorated into psychosis I wish to leave an open question. The incident in analysis which I quote as an illustration is from one of the more seriously affected patients, but it should not be regarded as an isolated or atypical occurrence. I am using the terms "paranoid state" and "paranoid patient" merely descriptively and without implying a psychiatric diagnosis. Psycho-analytic observations are not easily brought into line with psychiatric schemes of classification. Psychiatry began and developed long before Freud's pioneer discoveries of the unconscious parts of the mind, and thus it is rooted in a mode of thought that is fundamentally different from the psycho-analytic approach. Some psycho-analytic concepts have been accepted by many psychiatrists, and psycho-analysts have carried their work into the psychiatric wards. The gap between psychiatry and psycho-analysis has narrowed, but it is still true, as Ernest Jones pointed out in 1929,[1] that the psychiatrist uses a macro-scopic investigation, whereas the psycho-analyst employs a micro-scopic technique. When they discuss their findings, they have to make adjustments.

II. CHARACTERISTIC FEATURES OF THE ANALYSIS OF PARANOID PATIENTS

The analysis of paranoid patients has characteristic features. The patient's associations focus on his persecutory experiences and on the person (or persons) whom he holds responsible. He describes in much detail how, as a result of this person's hostile actions, he is thrown into a condition of anguish, pain, and mental and physical incapacity. He asserts over and over again that he is a helpless and innocent victim. Usually he feels that his present enemy follows in the footsteps of an important figure in his past, for example one of his parents, and he concludes with bitterness that history repeats it-self and that he is doomed to suffer.

The analytic sessions are filled by the patient's reporting ever new incidents in which he has been attacked, humiliated, and harmed in one way or another. His state of panic and agony is intolerable;

[1] "Psycho-Analysis and Psychiatry", Ch. XIX in *Papers on Psycho-Analysis* (Fifth Edition). (London, 1948.)

he cannot find peace anywhere. Attempts at activity give him no relief but, on the contrary, add infinitely to his suffering; often he cannot accomplish what he has started, either his mind goes blank, or a turmoil of ideas overwhelms him. Then he cannot read or talk with people because he cannot follow a train of thought, and a new terror sweeps over him. People will pounce on him and he will be scorned and ridiculed. And so one misery follows another; persecution and anticipation of persecution follow each other continuously.

When his persecutory fears are transferred to the analyst, the analytic sessions become devoted to the enumeration of the analyst's wrongdoings. At such a point in an analysis I have been accused of having no human sympathy with the sufferer—indeed I make my living out of him; I have no interest in helping him since that would end my sinecure; I am conceited, dictatorial, and intent on putting over my stupid theories, to the patient's detriment; my interpretations are taken from the textbooks, which I have learnt by heart, and which have no bearing on the patient's individual and specfiic condition; analysts think they are God Almighty, but in fact nobody has ever been helped by analysis. The patient is convinced that his condition has deteriorated through the analysis; he never was so ill as now. In fact he was quite well before the analysis. He feels that the analyst sides with his enemies—is his enemy.

This situation differs greatly from the usual pattern of analytic sessions in which the patient associates more or less freely and although at times in a state of resistance expects his analyst to interpret his material and show him its unconscious meanings. Paranoid patients lack this co-operative attitude, they are full of suspicion, fear, and hostility, intent on rejecting the analyst and proving him wrong. This does not make it easy for the analyst to maintain his analytic attitude; in particular, difficulties in his counter-transference may arise, and he may be tempted to modify his technique. Instead of using the specific tool of analysis, interpretation, he may attempt to change the atmosphere of the analytic session by deliberately using reassurance techniques, such as comforting the patient or commiserating with him, appealing to his intellect and common sense, or placating him in one way or another.[1] For this reason I will digress here to sketch in outline some main lines of the necessary technique in such cases.

[1] I would refer here to my remarks on Counter-transference in "On Counter-Transference" *Int. J. Psycho-Anal.*, Vol. XXXI, Parts I and II, and in "Problems of the Training Analysis", *Int. J. Psycho-Anal.*, Vol. XXXV, Part II, 1954.

Analytic sessions with such patients often follow this pattern. They begin the hour by complaining about their condition and reporting in great detail on their sufferings, each of which is felt to be due to analysis in general and to the analyst in particular. Whilst they themselves are quite unaware of it, it is obvious that by thus reporting their painful experiences to me they find ample opportunity for criticizing, mocking, and attacking me. Consciously they are merely distressed and alarmed; unconsciously they give themselves the pleasure of satisfying their sadistic impulses. In such cases I adopt the method of listening to their complaints for some time in silence. When they feel that they have expressed themselves sufficiently, and their fury is to some extent spent, I take up the accusations in detail, and make explicit what has been merely implied or hinted at. One can often recognize that an interpretation that has been accepted at the time has later been distorted into an attack and invested with some malicious and dangerous meaning. I put into words as completely and specifically as possible whatever has been hinted at or left as an innuendo or a vague allusion.

I do not attempt to reassure or comfort such patients or to argue and appeal to intellectual reasoning. I do not try to convince them of my goodwill or protest against the distortion of my interpretations or behaviour. My conviction is that only by fully verbalizing their conscious and preconscious ideas of persecution can I establish contact. It is very important to restore the links between expressed feelings of persecution and the particular incidents, such as change of times, an imagined quality in my voice, words, or movements, or interpretations in recent or earlier analytic sessions that have fostered paranoid delusions.

In my experience this technique is necessary in general for patients in an acute paranoid state. It bears out Freud's rule that the analyst must start with the material which is on the surface of the patient's mind. When a patient is actually under the sway of a paranoid delusion, it is this delusion which is on the surface. It cannot be bypassed, but must be thoroughly dealt with. No attempt can be made to argue intellectually against it or to dissuade the patient from it by the deliberate assumption of the attitude of a kindly friend. The patient's feelings of persecution and their origins in certain situations need to be fully verbalized and brought clearly into his consciousness.

When I have traced the patient's explicit references or dark allusions to interpretations and incidents in earlier sessions, it becomes to some extent obvious to him that he had tendentiously distorted my remarks or behaviour, and his paranoid fears will lessen. Thus, even in this part of the analytic session, during which we focus on his actual complaints—which at first he treated as founded on fact— the patient gains some insight into his own hidden motives, impulses, and phantasies. The realization that his sense of being insulted and wronged by me was based on his own tendency to give malicious significance to my interpretations then emerges, so to say, effortlessly as a by-product.[1] Gradually this feature (i.e. ordinary interpretative work), becomes dominant, while paranoid preoccupations recede, and the patient corroborates by associating with relevant experiences of his present life, dreams or memories. These then bring his unsolved conflicts with his original objects more clearly into the open and show the historical factors of external and internal reality that determine his actual condition.

In this way, by an exclusively analytic procedure, the patient's initial state of persecutory anxiety is reduced, and he will often say spontaneously that he feels better and that his alarm and restlessness have gone. Such patients, however, hardly ever give one any thanks for the relief which on their own statement they are actually experiencing. One patient often made this very relief a cause for complaint, i.e. that by my "nice voice and pleasant personality" I seduced him and lulled him into a false sense of security which, he declared, was not founded on any "real" improvement. Indeed, whenever in his introductory report on his condition he did mention an improvement, he almost unfailingly attributed it to some person having been nice to him and explicitly denied that the analytic work could have helped him.

III. PROBLEMS OF DEFENCES IN PARANOID STATES

The defence mechanisms which enable an ill ego to keep functioning deserve the analyst's attention no less than the pathogenic processes themselves. Listening to the patient's descriptions of their wretched condition, of their intense fears and helplessness, we wonder how it is that they have not long ago broken down and become totally incapacitated. In view of the intense misery and suffering

[1] Cf. James Strachey: "Symposium on the Theory of the Therapeutic Results of Psycho-Analysis", *Int. J. Psycho-Anal.*, Vol. XVIII, Parts II and III (1937). Strachey shows that it is important to enable the patient to make ". . . a comparison between his archaic and imaginary objects and his actual and real ones" (p. 142).

experienced in the paranoid state, in the sense of being hated and
persecuted, of being rendered helpless and incapable, the problem
of the resources that the ego possesses for its own support requires
close consideration. There must be some way in which patients,
although not feeling this consciously, are enabled to find some support, some measures of defence which, even in the state of persecution, the ego can yet marshal as a protection from crumbling under
the pressure of fear and helplessness.

As already mentioned, the analyst is impressed by the fact that
paranoid patients actually derive a good deal of sadistic gratification
when they dwell on their misery and enumerate in detail what they
are suffering. They attack the analyst when they lament that the
analyst persecutes them. One special meaning soon emerges. The
habit, which these patients display, of opening the analytic session
with a detailed report on their pains and sufferings can be seen to
represent the emotional equivalent of an anal evacuation (into the
analyst) which gives them relief and sadistic pleasure.

When I interpreted this meaning of her complaints to one patient, she agreed immediately. It was true that after such a morning
evacuation of anger, fear, scorn, etc. (equated with excrements) into
me, the analyst, she felt relieved and more at ease and could face her
family with greater tolerance, even friendliness. In the course of the
day she felt maltreated and persecuted by them, and accumulated
hatred and anger which she promptly discharged in the next analytic session. When occasionally she felt sorry for me, she comforted
herself with the thought that, after all, that was what I was paid for;
usually she changed course, denied her pleasure in attacking me, and
asserted my guilt and my partisanship of the persons who persecuted her.

Thus I could see that paranoid patients experience sadistic pleasure
in situations which, consciously, they register only as persecutory
and most painful; and I came to regard this unconscious gratification of sadistic impulses as providing some defence and support for
the ego. However, the processes involved in this defensive function
of sadistic pleasure need to be defined more clearly.

From the case-history of one patient, there follows some material
leading up to an incident in his analysis which, in my view, illustrates some of the defence mechanisms used by the ego in a paranoid
state.

This patient habitually used in the analysis the method I have
described as a preliminary anal evacuation into the analyst.

246

Superficially his anal-sadistic behaviour in the analysis was a repetition of experiences he had had with a mistress to whom he was alternately cruel and kind, exploiting and generous. In sexual situations with her he particularly enjoyed breaking wind while with her, and it was important for him that she disliked this but quietly tolerated it. He used to go to prostitutes as well, for beating and masturbation; he did not have sexual intercourse with them. These experiences also were re-enacted in the transference. By his complaints—the phrase "letting off steam" is an apt description—he repeated the anal activities (breaking wind) in the presence of his sexual object, and when he moaned that he suffered at my hands and that my treatment was the cause of his pain and misery, he reproduced in the transference his beating experiences with the prostitutes. (Behind this transference of more recent experiences infantile material emerged which, however, need not be related in the present context.)

Of the many phantasies which determined his wish to be beaten, only the few that are relevant to my main theme will be mentioned here. The wish to be beaten was by no means altogether a wish to suffer pain. The obvious passive-masochistic aspect of his beating experiences is misleading, and loses much in significance when the total situation is taken into account. Since the woman who beat him was employed and controlled by him, he could determine and regulate the amount of pain he wanted to experience. Besides this consciously accepted fact, the dominating unconscious phantasies revealed in the analysis considerably reduced the masochistic quality of the beating episodes. He was strongly identified with the prostitute and in phantasy was taking her role. Such identification with the manifestly sadistic partner in masochistic relations has long been recognized by psycho-analysis. In his case it meant that, whilst the beating woman represented himself, he who was beaten represented his father. On many occasions the patient traced all his misery to his upbringing by his father, whom he described as a ruthless and cruel dictator. He asserted that his father had the power of thrusting himself into his victims, depriving them not only of their freedom, but of their individuality.[1] He felt that he carried this loathsome and

---

[1] Another patient, with severe paranoid delusions centring on her father, described her father's personality and effect on his family in almost identical terms. She too stressed his power of thrusting himself into the people he wished to dominate. Individual psychology provides the prototype of facts quite familiar to us in other circumstances. After all in war an army of occupation not only controls and dominates the victim country, but also enforces a change of its laws and customs.

cruel father within himself, and this feeling was so strong that he attributed all the features of his appearance and the character-traits that he disliked to this internal father. Whenever he admitted anything bad in himself, it was not really part of himself, but belonged to his internal father. It transpired that the blows in the beating practices were not directed at himself, but at the father whom he carried in his body.

In addition to this phantasy that made the father experience the pain and indignity of being beaten on the buttocks, beating represented an exorcizing ceremony. When the patient was beaten, it meant to him that the persecuting and hated father was beaten out of his system and that he got rid of him. Here again the anal pattern of relief through evacuation was in evidence.

A condition of his pleasure was the prostitute's frustration. She had to be subservient to his will—his instrument, not his partner. While she had to carry out the beating at his bidding and to give him pleasurable sensations by the accompanying genital orgasm, she was not to have any pleasure herself. This was one of the determinants for his avoiding sexual intercourse. In this way he enacted the primal scene as in his Œdipal phantasies he wished it to be; his mother should never have loved his father, she should have married him only for his money, and she should loathe and punish the father's sexual advances. The father should feel the humiliation of being rejected and of being impotent to give pleasure to his partner.[1] The son's gratification was based on depriving his parents of pleasure and making them hate each other.

Another type of action in my patient's history is significant for an understanding of his behaviour in the incident next described. He often spoke with great love and admiration of his mother and illustrated her kindness and forbearance by various incidents. He remembered, for example, how he once took her into his car and drove off with her, and how, when they had gone a good distance from home, he unburdened himself by accusing her of the many wrongs he felt she had done him. She had listened patiently and with her characteristic kindness.

In one particular session Mr. X began as usual with a report on his wretched life, his anxieties and inabilities, and the torments caused

---

[1] The homosexual aspects of the beating practices which include hatred against the rival-mother are omitted because I am not concerned with presenting a comprehensive case-history. For the same reason also I do not mention the way in which shame and horror affected the patient and how in certain situations he attempted to make reparation to the women he maltreated.

by his fears and his futile attempts to ward them off. Scornful and mocking references to the analyst were there in plenty. He felt at the end of his tether. His situation was aggravated that day because he had to make a change in his business. He knew what he wanted to do, yet felt unable to make the decision. He felt maximally persecuted, and his problems appeared to him to be of a vital order. He demanded that analysis, which in his view had utterly failed to improve his condition, should now be put aside, that I should give him advice about the "real" problem which was so pressing, and intervene directly in his external situation. I did not comply with his demand, but proceeded in the ordinary way; and he became less anxious and less persecuted and also gained more understanding about the problems with which he was confronted. His attacks on the analysis and on me, and his pleasure in insulting and accusing me, seemed rather stronger, perhaps, than usual; and on leaving, though much relieved and with more insight about his actual problem, he stated that I had not helped him at all and that he would be as much tormented after the hour as he had been before it.

The way, however, in which he made this statement did not accord with an anticipation of misery. It was with relish that he flung this parting shot at me. The effect accompanying his remark was triumphant and menacing. Manifestly his words contained two statements, one about my failure to help him and the other about the condition of torment he foresaw for himself. The hostile triumph in his attitude clearly related to the first statement—my failure as an analyst—and was in line with the many scornful remarks he had so often made; but in connection with the second part of his remark another meaning emerges. There was also an unmistakable threat in his attitude, which, if put into words, would run like this: "I shall torment *you* after the hour exactly as I have done here. You cannot escape from me!"

The unconscious meaning of the patient's parting words was that *I* was going to suffer. What he said about himself unconsciously related to his object, which he could triumphantly control and torment because he had *introjected* it.

It takes much longer to describe than to perceive a process which takes place in a moment. It seemed to me that I could actually witness in operation the process of the patient's introjection of myself; indeed, the fact that such an introjection occurred when he was about to leave me brings to mind Freud's suggestion that introjection may be the sole condition on which the ego can give up an object.[1] Throughout the hour the patient had attacked and scorned me and tried to force me to take part in his life outside the analysis. At the point of leaving me he introjected me in order to continue his attacks, and it could be seen that the power wielded by the ego over its introjected object(s) forms part of its defensive techniques. When my patient tried to make me leave the sphere of analysis and follow him into his life outside, he re-enacted in the transference situation his relation with his mother. In the past he took the original object of his sadistic love, his mother, into his car and removed her physically from her home in order to attack her. It is not difficult to see that the car was a symbol of himself and that in unconscious phantasy the patient took his mother into himself, introjecting her once more, as often on earlier occasions. In the transference relationship he introjected the substitute object, the analyst. As in those incidents with his mother, he felt only wronged and victimized, and his tyrannizing and cruel impulses were being completely denied.

IV.   INTRA-PSYCHIC OBJECT RELATIONS

The observation that a patient in the course of his analysis introjects his analyst is so familiar that it would seem not to merit any special description. In fact we have come to regard such introjection as an important part of the therapeutic process of analysis, in particular since Strachey, connecting his conclusions with many of Melanie Klein's theories, defined it as the means by which the patient's archaic super-ego is modified and assumes a more realistic and a kinder character.[2]

Two conditions, however, must be fulfilled in order to bring about this beneficial result. The patient must regard the analyst at the moment of such introjection as a good and helpful parental figure, and the introjected object must be absorbed into the super-ego system.

In the clinical instance just described the analyst was in the role of a persecutor and, as will be shown, the introjected object was predominantly maintained as such, an object, something foreign to the self and not fusing with it.

[1] Freud, S. (1923). *The Ego* and *the Id* (London, 1927). Cf. also Freud's (1921) discussion of introjection of an object that is renounced in male homosexuality, in *Group Psychology and the Analysis of the Ego* (London, 1923), p. 67.

[2] The Nature of the Therapeutic Action of Psycho-Analysis", *Int. J. Psycho-Anal.*, Vol. XV, Parts II and III (1934).

A combination of Defence Mechanisms in Paranoid States

When Freud, in his analysis of group behaviour, introduced the concept of a "grade" in the ego,[1] he clearly envisaged the intra-psychic situation following introjection as an internal object-relationship. The relevant passage may be quoted: "Let us reflect that the ego now appears in the relation of an object to the ego-ideal which has been developed out of it, and *that all the interplay between an outer object and the ego as a whole*, with which our study of the neuroses has made us acquainted, may possibly be repeated upon this new scene of action inside the ego." (My italics.) In his subsequent writings this wide notion of an intra-psychic emotional relationship has not been worked out. It has been overshadowed by the concept of the mental structure composed of the id, the ego, and the super-ego; the latter, according to Freud, being established at the decline of the Œdipus complex by the child's introjecting his parents. Later introjections then affect only the ego and shape its character by identification with the introjected objects. It appears that Freud thought that introjection strengthened either the super-ego or the ego, e.g. when he described how identification with the love object was specific for women and that consequently their super-ego was less severe than that of men.

This development of psycho-analytic theory which replaced the ego-ideal by the super-ego has tended to narrow intra-psychic objection-relationship to the relation between the ego and the super-ego.

In another connection I have tried to show[2] that introjection can affect simultaneously both the ego and the super-ego, although sometimes the emphasis may lie more on the one than the other, according to the emotions prevailing in any given instance of introjection.

In the present context I wish to stress the significance of Freud's first notion of an intra-psychic emotional object-relation, comparable to inter-personal relationships, resulting from introjection. Melanie Klein's research concerning emotional life in early infancy[3] has given new meaning to Freud's description "that all the interplay between an outer object and the ego as a whole" may take place intra-psychically. Introjection occurs from the beginning of life, and

---

[1] *Group Psychology and the Analysis of the Ego*, London, 1923.
[2] See Ch. IV, *Developments in Psycho-Analysis* by Melanie Klein, Paula Heimann, Susan Isaacs, Joan Riviere. (London, 1952.)
[3] For a fuller presentation of these processes the reader is referred to Melanie Klein's original work, *The Psycho-Analysis of Children*, London, 1932, and in *Contributions to Psycho-Analysis*, London, 1948.

the first introjected objects are the two aspects, gratifying and frustrating, in which the infant experiences and conceives of his mother's breast (or its substitute). As the infant's awareness widens, more part-objects, relating to both his parents, are introjected, and his ego and super-ego develop gradually and in an inter-acting fashion.

Both systems are built upon the introjected objects, but while they are in the process of being formed, the condition is fluid and the introjected objects persist, as such, and are not yet assimilated or fused with the psychic organization.[1]

Therefore the topographical results of introjection can be summed up as being threefold: the introjected object may be taken into the super-ego system and increase or decrease its severity; it may be absorbed into the ego and alter its character (identification); or it may remain as part of an inner world of objects with which the ego maintains emotional relations similar to external, inter-personal relationships. The introjected object which acts as the judge of the ego, i.e. the super-ego, thus represents only one part of the relation between the ego and its introjected objects. In fact the range of the child's emotions towards his parents is far wider than simply a super-ego relation, which means fear or relief from fear, subjection to their orders on rebellion. All his feelings of love and hate, which in the long period of his life with his parents are continually developing and becoming richer in quantity and quality, come into play, inter-acting with the rich and complex feelings on the part of his parents. And it is the whole of this multi-faceted and multi-coloured relation-ship that is internalized; thus the super-ego does not exhaust all the emotional experiences that the ego derives as the result of intro-jecting the parents (and their substitutes).

Melanie Klein's theories of mental development just referred to can be brought into line with Freud's explanation of the primitive behaviour of members of a group with a leader. The condition in the adult ego which Freud describes as a "new scene of action inside the ego", an emotional relationship between the ego and its introjected object, has its prototype in an early stage of development before the systems of the ego and the super-ego have been formed and before the psychic capacity for integration has become predominant. The degree to which the primitive mode and results of introjection prevail

---

[1] It should be noted that even in mature persons the feeling of having an internal object may occur, and by no means necessarily as part of a momentary regression. Artists frequently attribute their creative productions not to themselves (their ego), but to something, some agency, within themselves.

in an individual may be taken as indicative of his maturity; indeed, the tendency in joining a group to manifest primitive group behaviour, such as blind obedience to the leader, uncritical acceptance of his views, cessation of self-interest and of moral principles otherwise maintained, for example, will not be found in mature and stable individuals.

Freud's statement that the ego-ideal has been developed out of the ego raises a question which he himself did not pursue, namely, that concerning the method by which this grade in the ego is established. Melanie Klein's work has provided the answer; it is the mechanism of splitting.[1] The ego splits itself and severs one part from the rest. This split-off part of the ego contains the introjected object, and on account of the separation between it and the remaining ego the introjection of the object does not lead to identification; but instead an *intra-psychic object-relationship* ensues, similar to interpersonal relationships, as has been shown in the quoted instance.

V. A COMBINATION OF DEFENCE MECHANISMS IN PARANOID STATES

The paranoid type of introjection internalizes a hated and dreaded object, and the intra-psychic situation which results from this introjection repeats and continues the relation between the individual and his external persecutor. The same sadism which the subject, the "ego as a whole", directs to the outer object is turned by the ego (as a systematized part of the total personality) against its introjected object.

A part of the ego, that part which harbours the introjected object, the "persecutor", is sacrificed; it is split off from the rest and put apart from the ego organization, thus losing the "me"-quality. If one is inclined to phylogenetic considerations, one may compare splitting with the technique of those lizards which when caught by the tail sever it from the body, and, albeit mutilated, escape. At the cost of sacrificing a part, the ego is protected from being identified with the object which it attacks and torments. By adding splitting to introjection a "new scene of action inside the ego" is arranged on which the ego continues its sadistic relationships.

In its attacks on the internal object, the ego discharges intrapsychically the destructive impulses which issue from the id, and

[1] "Notes on Some Schizoid Mechanisms" (Ch. IX), *Developments in Psycho-Analysis*.

Paula Heimann

which otherwise would endanger the ego itself, e.g. drive it towards self-injurious behaviour.[1] It binds these destructive forces in some measure by cathecting the internal object with which as a result of splitting it is not identified. At the same time it disowns its cruel impulses and makes them over to the internal object; and therefore guilt does not arise. Ultimately this process of intra-psychic projection amounts to an *intra-psychic deflection* of the death instinct—hence its great defensive value.

It is possible that such intra-psychic projection of cruel impulses on the internal persecutor to some extent spares the external original object and facilitates the libidinal cathexis of other objects in the external world. This might account for the fact that these paranoid patients continue the analysis in spite of their conscious conviction that the analyst harms them, and also for their capacity to enjoy some measure of social life.

The process of internal projection readily suggested itself to me when I observed incidents similar to the one described above; but it was not clear how such intra-psychic projection took place, until the part played by the mechanism of splitting could be understood. In the light of Melanie Klein's concept of the paranoid-schizoid position and through her presentation of the defensive processes of splitting in early infantile life, it could be seen that intra-psychic as well as external projection is preceded by a split in the ego.

Freud suggested that projection does not merely mean that an internal perception is replaced by an external one, but that it amounts to the annihilation of an internal process. It seems that the view that projection is secondary to a split in the ego, and to the loss of a certain part of the ego, lends support to the notion that in projection something is "abolished internally".[2] Certain parts of the ego, certain impulses and ideas, are no longer appreciated and perceived as part of the self.

This combination of introjection, splitting, and intra-psychic (as well as external) projection seems to represent defences characteristic of paranoid states, and of very great significance in preventing the patient from breaking down under the stress of his hatred and paranoid fears. To put it in an over-simplified manner: the paranoid patient is endangered only to the extent to which he is identified with the internal object which he persecutes. By means of splitting

[1] It is more correct to say: towards *even more* self-injurious behaviour. Cf. Section VII.
[2] "Psycho-Analytic Notes upon an Autobiographical Account of a Case of Paranoia (Dementia Paranoides)", also referred to as the "Schreber case", *Collected Papers*, Vol. III, p. 458. (London, 1925.)

and projection this identification is controlled and limited.[1] It seems, moreover, that whereas usually these protective inner processes of splitting and internal projection remain completely unconscious, occasionally their successful effect breaks through into consciousness. Several of my patients who suffered from paranoid states have told me that sometimes, without any accountable reason, the whole torment, panic, whirlpool of incoherent ideas, etc., would disappear in a flash, and they would feel free, capable, and even happy.

VI. ABSENCE OF GUILT IN PARANOID STATES

Since Freud's essay on "Mourning and Melancholia",[2] we have become familiar with the connection between introjection and depression, and regard the use of introjection in the sphere of psychopathology as specific for depressive states. It is in striking contrast to these well-established observations that this same mechanism of introjection in paranoid states does not lead to guilt and depression.

Incidentally, I do not intend to imply that the total condition of the paranoid patient lacks depressive elements or, conversely, that paranoid feelings are entirely absent in the state of depression. In the frame of the present paper, however, I am concerned with the specific defences used by the ego in paranoid states, and I have therefore singled out and followed only these.

The paranoid patient introjects the objects which he unconsciously attacks and consciously regards as his persecutors, in order to dominate and torment them, to rejoice in his power over them and enforce his gratification from them. He does not identify himself with the maltreated object, but remains aloof from it; he denies his cruel impulses, projects them on to the object, and consciously considers himself the victim of persecution by this object.

This condition in the first place derives from the split in the ego which in his case follows upon introjection.

Such a split does not occur in the depressive mode of introjection. Here the ego retains its coherence and, as Freud has shown,[3] is identified with the introjected object and therefore shares its injured condi-

[1] The beating incidents reflect these intra-psychic events. Since the patient employed the prostitute, he could control and limit the amount of pain which she inflicted on him.
[2] *Collected Papers*, Vol. IV (London, 1925).
[3] "Mourning and Melancholia", *op. cit.*

Paula Heimann

tion. Moreover, the introjected object, which is felt to be suffering, hurt, in bits, and so on, through the subject's sadism, is in contact with the super-ego and issues complaints and demands, which the ego feels unable to fulfil and to which it responds with the sense of guilt and unworthiness. In the paranoid introjection identification with the injured object and feelings of depression, of guilt and unworthiness, are circumvented by the mechanism of splitting, which maintains the introjected object as such, i.e. prevents its being taken into the ego or the super-ego.

The defensive and ego-supporting aspect of sadistic gratifications, which can be directly observed in the paranoid patient's behaviour, depends on this splitting, this division in the ego, which comes into play after introjection.

I have just suggested that as a result of splitting the introjected object is also kept apart from the super-ego, and that this accounts for the absence of guilt and for the sense of self-righteousness so pronounced in the paranoid delusion. It may be argued that the introjected object is in fact taken into the super-ego, without, however, altering the balance of power between it and the ego, because the ego so fully overrules the super-ego that an addition to the latter does not effectively increase its strength. To my mind this would mean stretching the concept of the super-ego beyond good sense. It seems more convincing to conclude that in the paranoid state the ego's tendency to split is an aspect of a general lowering of the intrapsychic integrative forces. The super-ego too is affected by it and is incapable of taking in and absorbing the introjected object. In the last resort this would mean a relative weakness of the life instinct, of the forces which bind, seek connections and unity, and counteract disruption.

With regard to the absence of feelings of guilt in the paranoid patient there is a remark of Freud's, an aside, as it were, in the context that he was studying, which is most revealing; it has been neglected in the bulk of analytic literature. Freud said: "The person who is now hated and feared as the persecutor was at one time loved and honoured. *The main purpose of the persecution constructed by the patient's delusion is to serve as a justification for the change in his emotional attitude.*"[1] (My italics.) By means of the delusion of being persecuted the patient can deny his love feelings and hate the object of his delusion without feeling guilty.

[1] "Psycho-Analytic Notes upon an Autobiographical Account of a Case of Paranoia (Dementia Paranoides)", *Collected Papers*, Vol. III (London, 1925).

Clinical observation shows abundantly that when the patient admits his violent hatred against his persecutor, he does indeed say in so many words that his hatred is justified and that he need not feel guilty. He declares that his hatred is merely a reaction, not spontaneous. In fact he goes further than that. He treats his own cruel impulses not as his own, but his persecutor's. One of my patients, immediately after revelling in most sadistic revenge phantasies, said calmly that she was altogether innocent of hating, it was alien to her nature; the hatred against her father which she had just expressed came from the father within herself.[1]

Freud's remark about the purpose of the delusion of persecution is, as mentioned, only incidental to his main interest, which is devoted to the analysis of the patient's homosexual phantasies and conflicts, upon which this autobiographical report essentially revolves. It has the character of an intuition rather than of a carefully elaborated conclusion and Freud himself did not carry it further, but concentrated on the role which the defence against homosexual impulses plays in the causation of paranoia.

This paper of Freud's, his analysis of what a man remembered and put on paper of his illness and recovery, which was confirmed by certain biographical data obtained later from other sources, has fundamentally influenced psycho-analytic thought and theory of paranoia. It has led to an almost monopolistic position of homosexuality in the pathogenesis of paranoia, and this has happened in spite of Freud's earlier findings in his analytic treatment of a woman suffering from chronic paranoia.[2] In this case, which unfortunately seems to have fallen into oblivion, Freud traced the illness to the patient's conflicts about incestuous relations with her brother when both were children, i.e. to heterosexual conflicts.

In my view, this development of psycho-analytic theory of paranoia involves the loss of these two important observations of Freud's which both concern the effect which the defence against guilt has on the formation of paranoid delusions. The one occurs in the last-mentioned paper, i.e. guilt for heterosexual (incestuous) impulses, and the second occurs in the Schreber case, written fifteen years

---

[1] I would here record my observation that the impulse to avenge oneself (for real or imagined wrongs) is connected with the unconscious phantasy that if the wrongdoer is made to suffer, the subject will be relieved of suffering. The conscious formula so often encountered in ordinary life: "That'll teach him" is unconsciously continued into: "I myself shall no longer be afflicted by the wrong which he has done to me. I have returned it to him, where it belongs."

[2] "Further Remarks on the Defence Neuro-Psychoses", *Collected Papers*, Vol. I (London, 1924).

later, and concerns the guilt for hating the formerly loved object. I would suggest that these two ætiological factors can be reinstated on the basis of Melanie Klein's work.

As mentioned briefly at the beginning of this paper, Melanie Klein holds that the roots of the Œdipus complex, which Freud discovered in its more advanced form in the child aged three to five years, lie in early infancy. In its initial stages the Œdipus complex is characterized by a confusion of instinctual urges in regard both to their sources (zones) and their object-choices. Pre-genital and genital impulses, heterosexual and homosexual aims co-exist, and furthermore libidinal wishes are fused and confused with cruel urges of an archaic and most savage nature. This "polymorphous" stage of instinctual development[1] which is interpolated between the oral and the anal organizations represents the fixation-points for later perversions. It accounts for the anxieties associated with the Œdipus complex, for the frightening phantasies about parental intercourse, the "primal scene", which reflect the infant's own instinctual condition, polymorphous and mixed, libidinal and destructive, in relation to his love objects. In my view it is this admixture of cruel aims in his love impulses characteristic of the early infantile Œdipus complex which leads to guilt and horror for the incestuous wishes, be they of a heterosexual or of a homosexual kind. This polymorphous state of the instinctual urges constitutes a serious difficulty for the early infantile ego, underlying as it does the fluid condition of the ego, its need to achieve integration and unification, and the alternation that occurs between coherence and incoherence. As Melanie Klein has shown, advance in integration at this stage leads to the poignant conflict of ambivalence with guilt and despair for the hatred experienced against the loved objects, and for directing cruel impulses towards them, the "infantile depressive position". In response to this conflict of ambivalence there are forward, constructive movements representing the drive to make reparation, as well as regressive techniques, such as denying the conflict by taking flight from unity, splitting the emotions and doubling the objects, so that two separate relations arise: love is then felt to be directed towards a good object and hatred towards its bad double. Conflict is by-passed, because there is happiness in the love relation and persecution in the hate relation. Instead of feeling guilt for hating the loved object the infantile ego oscillates between the delusion of bliss from the one and the delusion of persecution from the other

[1] Cf. Postcript to Ch. 2 in this Book.

object; and that in fact it is one and the same object which is loved and hated, desired and dreaded as a persecutor is denied. In these regressive techniques the earlier type of object relation is reinstated, the "schizoid-paranoid position".

Guilt for incestuous, heterosexual and homosexual wishes, guilt for cruelty towards the sexual object, and guilt for the change from love to hatred—all occur as elements of the same early infantile phase. If we take this psychic condition pertaining in the early stages of the Œdipus complex into account, we can incorporate the defence against heterosexual wishes as well as that against homosexual impulses and the need to deny the change from love and honour to hatred and contempt in our theories of the pathogenesis of paranoid delusions.

VII.   IMPAIRMENT OF EGO FUNCTIONS BY PARANOID DEFENCES

The combined action of introjection, splitting, and intra-psychic (as well as outward) projection which the ego sets in motion in order to protect itself against the persecutor is in various respects damaging to the ego. Such a self-contradictory result of a defensive process is characteristic of defences which involve denial or distortion of reality and subsequent failure in meeting its demands, because the ego's essential function for the organism lies in its capacity to perceive external and internal reality and to act in conformity with it. "In the ego perception plays the part which in the id devolves upon instinct. The ego represents what we call reason and sanity . . ."[1]

This basic function of perception, however, presupposes coherence within the ego and a free passage between its various elements. An ego which too readily has recourse to the mechanism of splitting has only a low degree of coherence, and again the frequent occurrence of splits in its structure in turn weakens its coherence and imposes barriers and limitations to the various processes which take place in the ego.

It follows that a (relatively) beneficial outcome of splitting after introjection will depend largely on quantitative factors. It must be very important that the loss which the ego incurs should be kept minimal, so that a much larger proportion of it remains relatively intact and functioning. It would further appear necessary that that

[1] Freud, S.. *The Ego and the Id* (London, 1927), p. 30.

part of the ego which through the introjection of the persecuting/persecuted object has ceased to operate within the ego, ceased to possess the "me"-quality, should be kept widely apart from the remaining ego. To use a spatial analogy it must be very important that the line of severance should detach only a small portion of the ego and not interfere with the rest which is maintained as ego ("me").

This would ensure that a sufficient amount of ego-function remains relatively unimpaired and available for the subject's needs. An assumption of this kind is in keeping with the fact that all the patients under my observation who suffered from paranoid states were capable of living in an ordinary milieu and of carrying out social and professional activities without conspicuous incompetence.

It is justifiable to conclude that only small losses in the ego take place in those mild delusions of everyday life mentioned at the beginning of this paper. There is an impairment of ego-functions: memory is deficient, perception is wrongly interpreted, ideas of reference falsify judgment. But the delusion is soon over, the split in the ego is swiftly repaired, and the individual once more assumes a reasonable and sane attitude.

In the paranoid states I am considering here the delusion of persecution is maintained for a long time and actuated repeatedly. Repeatedly and frequently the persecutor is introjected; introjection is followed by splitting and projecting. Thus the associative and integrative functions of the ego are interfered with and so is its capacity for establishing object-relations of a realistic and gratifying kind.

I may here briefly compare the damage to the ego from splitting with that from repression. In repression too certain parts of the ego—impulses, affects, ideas—are removed from consciousness, and the ego is thus reduced in its breadth and moreover loses a certain amount of energy by maintaining repression and erecting counter-cathexes. Within these limitations, however, the ego functions well, the person is fully coherent and largely free from anxiety. These differences follow from the condition of the ego when these mechanisms are originally in operation. Splitting is characteristic for the rudimentary ego, whereas repression is characteristic for the much more advanced ego (the phase which Freud called "phallic"). The frequent use of splitting is evidence of a deeper regression than is that of repression. Clinically the atmosphere of the analytic situation is different when the work is concerned with the one or the other mechanism. To put this in a simple formula: when repression has been lifted, the patient, as Freud described, says: "Actually, I have always known this." When a split in the ego is repaired, the patient says: "Oh, I see *now*."

It is obvious that in the paranoid state the ego fails in its task of mastering anxiety by realistic measures, i.e. by behaviour and actions based on correct thinking. Apart from brief respites, para-noid patients are in a state of anxiety, and their thinking is over-whelmed by the theme of their persecution. Subjective and objective reality are assessed incorrectly. Paranoid patients are reputed to be sharp observers and highly intelligent, but in my experience there are serious flaws in both these capacities. Observation is extremely one-sided; the patients approach the external world with the blind spots of their paranoid bias, and their attention is focused on what-ever fits in with it and feeds their suspicions. They easily detect unconscious hostility, but they overlook unconscious and manifest kindness. Moreover, conclusions from observation are distorted by ideas of reference.

In dealing with a problem they are unable to give due weight to its complexity. They cannot embrace its manifold aspects, but isolate and exaggerate that one particular line which fits in with their emotional preoccupation. They reiterate, lack intellectual resilience and are unimaginative. They cannot approach the situa-tion from a new angle and reject it if it is suggested by another per-son. They are shallow in their thinking, spread over a wide surface, making the same point over and over again, but avoid the depth. (This suggests that the splitting lines run between surface and depth of the ego, horizontally as it were.)

One of my patients accused me of seeing things only in black and white and of trying to enforce this on her, and she prided her-self on her capacity to discern subtle differences in tone, but in fact she was hair-splitting and the heart of the matter escaped her. It seems that the impression that paranoid patients are highly intelli-gent is based on their capacity for arguing. They are often gifted speakers, find words easily, and have a rich and varied vocabulary. They argue expertly, but they argue too much and think too little and with specious facility. Verbiage covers poverty of concepts. They prove their own foregone conclusion which is that they are right, good, and superior, and the other person is wrong, bad, and inferior; they almost entirely lack humour.

The restriction of their intellectual activities is due to their fears.

Paula Heimann

When the ego is predominantly engaged in defensive manœuvres, it lacks the internal freedom which is necessary for sublimation and creative work.[1] It is indeed often quite striking to see the extent to which a person, otherwise intelligent, sensitive, and imaginative, can become dull, rigid, and monotonous, in fact, stupid, when actually swayed by paranoid fears and hatred.

The paranoid type of introjection with its sequelae is the pathological version of the pattern of introjection in normal development. The child's ego grows by introjecting his parents whom he loves and admires, and by assimilating its good objects the child's ego is encouraged to test and develop its own potential capacities and expand in various respects, social, practical, intellectual, and artistic. When introjection, however, is determined by hatred and fear, the introjected object is not assimilated. The ego gains nothing, but suffers losses in the manœuvres of defence against this object.

VIII. COMMON ELEMENTS IN PARANOID AND MANIC STATES

The triumph which the paranoid person shows when convicting his persecutor of incompetence, stupidity, cruelty, and so on, links the paranoid with the manic state. Exaltation of the self occurs in the manic and the paranoid patient alike. Freud and Abraham have shown that the delusion of persecution implies ideas of grandeur. The paranoid split in the ego leads to a condition similar to mania where the ego, as Freud described, has "mastered the complex, or thrust it aside, or surmounted the object itself".[2] The question arises whether the ego's triumph over the super-ego in the manic state may not also be based on some kind of splitting and disintegration of the super-ego which for the time being renders it helpless.

Consciously the manic patient feels cheerful, loved and loving, elated, and capable of achieving whatever he likes, whilst the paranoid patient feels persecuted, bitter, wretched, and interfered with in his activities. Behind this impressive difference, however, there are great similarities. If the manic person meets contradiction, his amiable, hearty expansiveness gives way to violent aggression. Other similarities lie in the impaired thought-processes, such as shallowness, flight of ideas, change of issues, inability to accept a

[1] Heimann, Paula, "A Contribution to the Problem of Sublimation", etc., *Int. J. Psycho-Anal.*, XXIII, Part I, 1942.
[2] "Mourning and Melancholia", *op. cit.*

different view,[1] failure to comprehend external and internal reality.

The common denominator of both the manic and the paranoid conditions is the infant's inability to bear the conflict of ambivalence towards the loved object with the attendant guilt, anxiety on behalf of the object, and distress about his failure to love in a constructive way. This conflict of ambivalence originates in the infantile depressive position, which in normal development is mastered by means of a predominance of the love feelings. We should perhaps assume that the manic or paranoid adult failed in that early phase on account of unfavourable factors which at the time accentuated the normal conflict of ambivalence, such as lack of understanding and love on the part of the parents, or illnesses, or traumatic events which affected his parents as well as himself, or an inherent weakness—congenital— of the child's capacity for love and trust in goodness, ultimately an unfavourable balance between the life and the death instincts. By various factors then the infant's belief in the omnipotence of his own hostile feelings and of his inability to counter them and restore his injured love-objects may have been aggravated and the normal feelings of depression increased to overwhelming despair as well as extended in time. Then every single element in the state of despair had to be warded off by means of denial rather than dealt with by restorative phantasies and actions. In the group of feelings which Melanie Klein termed the "manic defence", hatred is either denied or welcomed. Love is denied or treated as exceedingly beneficial for the object; or the significance of the object is denied because there are plenty of objects and it does not matter if some are destroyed and lost because new ones can always be found; or the infant feels omnipotent and can do without any objects or can control everybody. In the regressive flight from the depressive to the paranoid-schizoid position, the infant escapes from the conflict of ambivalence and returns to the characteristic doubling of his relationships

---

[1] Intolerance of an opinion different from his own which occurs in both the paranoid and the manic patient shows that both have regressed to an early infantile phase in which the gratifying mother fuses with the self, whilst the frustrating mother is felt as different from the self and its enemy. The patient from whose analysis I have quoted found it exceedingly frustrating if his sexual partner showed any initiative, and often in the analysis he longed for me to be completely passive, absolutely silent, and not to express any opinion of my own different from his. I found that all my paranoid patients resented interpretations because they "had not thought of this" themselves. This resentment was not only an expression of a general attitude that whatever comes from an enemy must be dangerous and is better rejected. It had the specific quality that a thing is dangerous if it is different from the person himself.

The manic patient's attitude is illustrated by the German saying: "*Und willst Du nicht mein Bruder sein, so schlag ich Dir den Schädel ein*". ("If my brother you won't be, I shall just slay thee.") The paranoid patient makes the same statement in a less humorous manner.

alternating between abject helplessness in relation to the persecuting object, whom he hates freely, and complete happiness with the ideal object, who is his own possession. Both the manic and the paranoid states deny that there is any cause for sadness, guilt and depression.

The paranoid state in adult life would then represent regression to the original relationship with the persecuting object, whilst the relation to the ideal object is replaced by a narcissistic attitude expressed in the ideas of grandeur and self-righteousness. In the primitive behaviour of groups which Freud traced to the fact that the group leader becomes a substitute for the ego-ideal, we see the reproduction of infantile idealized object-relationships, with the characteristic deflection of implacable hatred on to the persecuting object, represented by everybody who is opposed to the group leader.

IX. BREAKDOWN OF THE PARANOID DEFENCES

I can only briefly point to the consequences of the breakdown of these paranoid defences. When the division(s) in his ego cannot be maintained and the different parts of his ego fuse, the paranoid patient realizes that his state of persecution was built on delusion, not on fact. He becomes identified with the attacked internal and external object and acknowledges his guilt towards it, and a state of depression ensues; the degree of this state depends on the degree of the patient's sadism, on the strength of his former delusions of persecution, on the length of time these delusions lasted, involving the disintegration of his ego and the corresponding rigidity of his divided condition, that is to say, on the damage the ego has suffered in the process of building up and maintaining the delusions. The notion of an "atrophy" of the ego is perhaps not out of place. How much of its integrative functions, of its capacity for contact with objects, ultimately of the capacity for love has been maintained beneath the screen of paranoid delusions, and how much of it can be resuscitated by analysis and favourable circumstances decides the issue.

By way of speculation, not based on experience, I would suggest that the breakdown of the defences can also lead to the absolute converse of depression, namely to a full-scale attack on the object of the paranoid delusion. I have in mind those incidents of sudden violent crimes committed by hitherto unobtrusive citizens. It happens not infrequently that the daily Press reports a murder in circumstances which to the psychiatrist immediately suggest that the criminal must have been a paranoiac. In the court proceedings then this fact is established. The victim of the crime was held to be the murderer's deadly enemy and had to be annihilated in self-defence.

To return to analytic experiences: in the dissolution of paranoid delusions usually a swing from persecution to either depression or mania is observed, and as analysis progresses such swings occur with diminishing intensity. In a successful analysis the patient works through his conflicts with his original objects, achieves some tolerance towards the bad parts of his past, and recovers its good parts. At the same time his internal objects assume friendlier and more realistic characters. By re-living in the analytic relationship the beneficial parts of his earlier development, too, the patient comes to introject helpful objects which are assimilated both by the ego and the super-ego. Such introjections involve the re-introjection of good aspects of the ego earlier projected on to the object, and this factor may be thought to facilitate the process of assimilation in the ego. The ego gains in strength and cohesion, the standards (demands) of the super-ego become more acceptable and realistic, and experiences with the external world assume a more beneficial give-and-take character. Having come to know himself better, the patient recognizes the danger of launching out into a delusion of persecution before it is strong. His strengthened and more coherent ego then begins to work through the persecutory anxieties so that a state of paranoid fear is weakened or aborted, and the subsequent swings into a manic or depressive mood take milder and more transient forms as well.

11

AN OBSESSIONAL MAN'S NEED TO BE "KEPT"

BERYL SANDFORD

THE patient about whom I am writing, and whom I will call Mr. A, seemed at the beginning of his analysis four years ago to suffer from practically every known neurotic symptom. And, since he produced analytic material as lavishly as he produced symptoms, I have had some ado to condense this paper to a reasonable length and, at the same time, make it comprehensible.

He is a typical obsessional with marked paranoid and agoraphobic features, and with a neurosis of such long standing that it gives the impression of having become part of his total personality. In this paper I am going to discuss one particular aspect of his case, and that is his need to be "kept". This does not mean that he cannot work; it means that he cannot work for money.

Mr. A, who is a Clinic patient, comes from a superior working class family, and is now aged forty-one. Before the war he had had three years' psychotherapy, but this had to be stopped because of the outbreak of war. Mr. A was exempted from all forms of National Service because of his mental illness.

He is a fine figure of a man, about six feet tall and broad in proportion. His hair is black and brilliantined. He has a magnificent speaking voice, and used to lie on the couch declaiming flamboyantly as though acting in Victorian melodrama.

Everything about him, both mental and physical, seemed to give the impression of being a little larger than life. He talked in rounded periods. He alluded to anyone who was hard up as being "financially embarrassed"; if he owed someone eighteen-pence he talked of a "pecuniary obligation"; and anyone of average intelligence was always said to have a "brilliant intellect".

His mother, who is still alive, was a children's nurse before she married. She appears to share many of her son's contamination fears. His father, who was a builder, died of pulmonary tuberculosis at

266

the beginning of the war. Mr. A is the youngest of three children—
his sister and brother being twins, two years older than he is. Both,
according to Mr. A, have "brilliant intellects". The brother, who is
married but childless, is a chartered surveyor earning good money;
the sister is married to a factory inspector and has four children.

The twins went to a secondary school, but Mr. A himself had only
attended an elementary school, where he was considered lazy and was,
he said, always a year or two older than the average of his class.
His comments on school work were significant: he could not bear
history because it was "all about kings losing their heads"; he could
not bear geography because it was "a great bore going into ins and
outs of countries".

When he started analysis Mr. A had been married for ten years.
He is childless. He lives on a housing estate in an outer London
suburb. His wife, who is now forty-four, is a pretty woman and
appears bright and intelligent. Nowadays she has a job as secretary,
but during the first two years of Mr. A's analysis she was suffering
from varicose ulcers and could not work. They were both receiving
sickness benefit, he 13s. and his wife 8s. a week. Their combined
fares to the Clinic five times a week came to more than this, and
they were living on money borrowed from Mr. A's brother.
Under these circumstances, it seemed to me to be unreasonable to
expect Mr. A to pay more than the very heavy fare to the Clinic, and
I therefore agreed that he should pay nothing for treatment until
times were better. It soon became apparent, however, that his need
to be dependent was so great that unconsciously he was using
Machiavellian methods to make sure that times did *not* get
better.

Superficially Mr. A appeared to be collaborating in every way,
but his prompt attendance, his flow of pre-arranged associations, his
protests of always telling the truth and his apparent insight were all
part of a magnificent façade. Hidden behind this obsessional facade
were psychotic features.

Mr. A's obsessional symptoms go right back into early childhood,
when he used to go through various rituals and touching cere-
monials at bedtime, such as going in and out of the door so many
times, carrying a glass of water in a special way, and knocking on the
floor after he went to bed to make sure his parents were alive.

He alleges that his mother continually thwarted any sort of
activity on his part. First, she would refuse to allow him to do whatever it was he wanted to do, and then she would say, "Very well,

please yourself—but you'll be sorry." She appears to have been extremely over-anxious about cleanliness and forbade the children to use any lavatory except the one at home. According to Mr. A she hated people visiting her house on the grounds that it was not good enough. One of her methods of punishment was to refuse to eat until "he was good again".

When he started his analysis with me in November, 1946, he was quite unable to go out of the house alone. His wife brought him to the Clinic each day and waited to take him home again. His anxiety was so great after each session that he could not go out into the street for perhaps an hour or longer, and he and his wife would wait together in the Clinic waiting-room until he felt equal to leaving. The three-quarter-hour journey took them about three hours each way, sometimes longer. Mr. A could never satisfy himself that he had not damaged the passers-by—for example, knocked them down area stairs—and it was necessary to stand, sometimes for half an hour or longer, and watch people safely out of sight. He was quite incapable of coping with such a busy station as Baker Street, and so they came to Regent's Park. It took them nearly an hour and a half to come from Regent's Park to Gloucester Place. I once left the Clinic and saw him and his wife standing at the corner of York Street; when I returned nearly three-quarters of an hour later they were still there; and this was on one of those dreadful days in the winter of 1947 when it was snowing hard and the ice was inches thick on the roads. How his wife bore it I cannot imagine, as she was at that time suffering from severe varicose ulcers. One can only conclude that it satisfied some masochistic tendencies in herself, and I am sure that unconsciously she still encourages his dependence.

Most of his contamination fears are typical. The majority of these fears still exist but they have diminished considerably in intensity. He felt his house to be contaminated and no one, and in particular his mother, was allowed inside it. The house was full of what he called "pockets of resistance", that is to say, large heaps of "contaminated objects" which he had not had time to clean, and which must not be touched by anyone. No dustbin could be emptied until he had sifted the contents; no envelope or piece of paper thrown away until thoroughly examined again and again and yet again, probably ending up in a "pocket of resistance" as being too dangerous to throw away. After having intercourse with his wife, the sheets had to be changed; they both had to wash from top to toe and everything they had touched or might have touched had to be washed. When he first came to analysis he was washing almost continuously all day; if he took his hands out of the basin clean they would be contaminated by the towel, and the whole business started all over again. He was also afraid of swallowing dirt while he was asleep and had, he said, trained himself not to swallow all night. Conversely, he felt that whatever came out of him was dangerous and he was extremely constipated, and had bad pains in his stomach. He very rarely had dreams.

He derived enormous satisfaction from writing letters, particularly to well-known politicians; for example, he once showed me a very long and very rude letter which he had written in a very neat hand to Mr. Attlee. He did not post these letters; he put them in a cupboard until it was "overflowing with them", and when there were too many he burnt them. It transpired later that when he was a boy he used to masturbate into a handkerchief and then, terrified of contaminating someone with the handkerchiefs, he used to put them all into a suitcase, where they remained for years until he burnt them.

He got his first job, that of office boy, at the age of sixteen, and lost his first week's wages on the way home. Later he had various clerical jobs, but was forced to give up work as book-keeper and agent in an insurance company fourteen years ago, soon after he got engaged, owing to the increasing severity of his obsessional symptoms. Mr. A says that the contamination symptoms became insupportable from the moment he touched his future wife's genitals.

Since that time he has been unable to do any paid work, with the exception of one job which he held down for eighteen months during the war. This was at a corn-merchant's, selling animal foodstuffs. Gradually, however, he became more and more anxious about the stuff they were selling; he was convinced that the grain being sold was damaged and full of broken glass, and that it would be his fault if hundreds of animals died. He finally had to give up the job, and for the next eighteen months, until he started analysis with me, he shut himself up in one room in his house. His fear that hundreds of animals had died through his fault was now extended to human beings. It became delusional in character, and he soon really believed that he was the cause of all the starving people in Europe. He dared not listen to the wireless for fear of hearing about starving people, and when he first started coming to analysis he had to sit in the train with his eyes shut, to prevent himself reading anyone's newspaper and learning that the whole world was in a state of chaos and destruction, caused by him.

During the early months of analysis he lay rigidly on the couch crying or bullying me. He told me exactly how I was to conduct the analysis. I was not, he said, to stick too closely to what he called "The Freud Handbook". He hated transference interpretations, and at the end of the first week he said firmly that those were the sort of interpretations he was not going to allow, adding kindly, "But all others are welcome."

He did his best to infuriate me, and I must admit that there were times when he almost succeeded. He bullied, hectored, cried, whined, and hurled insults at me. He always tried to force me into being the opposition; he wanted me to disagree with him so that he could argue and win the argument. This need for opposition was —and still is to a certain extent—of immense importance to him. He has to surround himself with people who will frustrate him. If they do not frustrate him, he soon sees to it that they do, crying out the whole time that he is persecuted beyond endurance, but that he will get the better of his persecutors.

The reason for this became clearer towards the end of the first year of analysis, during which time he produced a mass of material showing his terror of his unconscious oral and anal sadistic phantasy attacks on his parents. It is this terror which leads him to seek the satisfaction of knowing that the parents are able to control him and stop him destroying them. Also, he enjoys repeating the process of getting them to fight him in order to prove to himself that he can win the fight. This pattern of being controlled by the parents and then proving to himself that he can control them is being worked out in all his activities.

He always fought hard to keep the analysis on an intellectual level, but gradually more and more phantasies began to come to light. He unconsciously equated talking with defæcating and was, therefore, in constant terror that he had completely destroyed me with his outpourings, which were certainly copious. At the same time, he used talking as a method of defending himself; as long as he was continually pouring fæces into me he felt that he was preventing me pouring fæces into him.

He was terrified of masturbating and of having sexual intercourse. His ideas on these subjects were almost delusional. He insisted that he believed that semen contained millions of live babies and he feared that when he masturbated he would cause the death of these millions

of babies, since when spilt out they would die of starvation. He said
he was sure that these dead babies turned into fæces and produced
V.D. He felt intercourse to be "a filthy business like going to the
lavatory". When his wife became pregnant some years before the
analysis started, he was so frantic with anxiety that he alleges he made
her produce a miscarriage by getting her to take doses of castor oil.
He said to me: "Don't blame me—you know as well as I do that I
couldn't have filthy babies crawling all over the floor of my house."
Nor could he bear "sparrows coming into his house, messing and
pecking at everything with their beaks". Nor could be bear his
mother coming into his house. The analytic material produced at
this time showed clearly his unconscious terror that he himself would
be broken into, and attacked orally and anally by his mother who,
he feared, would do to him what he in phantasy had done to her.[1]
After many months working through the fear of retaliation by his
mother, he did allow his brother to come into his house. This was
the first time that anyone had been allowed in since he was married.
He can now allow friends to come into the house, but his mother is
still forbidden admission.

At the end of eighteen months or thereabouts, he began to talk
more freely about his childhood and youth. He said that he stopped
masturbating at the age of fifteen because the Vicar terrified him
by telling him that "self-abuse" would send him mad. He also
described playing what he called "dirty games" with his brother and
sister, when he was about six. This game consisted in sticking their
fingers up each others' anuses. The twins, however, finally decided
that they preferred to play this game alone. After this, he used to
shut himself up in the W.C. and push up his anus large rusty screws
which he found in his father's tool-box. He would then screw them
into the wall and fear that the wall was for ever contaminated. He
would also go out to the chicken run and amuse himself by sticking
his finger up the hens' anuses in an attempt to extricate the eggs.

He had many ideas about twins; he felt very much his lack of a
twin, and this has a bearing on his need for his wife to go everywhere
with him. He imagined that he once had a twin but that this twin
was left dead inside his mother. As a child at home he was always the
solitary one; mother had father, the girl twin had the boy twin, but
he had no one and felt surrounded by enemies in duplicate.

Towards the end of the second year of analysis there was some

---

[1] See Melanie Klein, *The Psycho-Analysis of Children* (1932) and *Contributions to Psycho-Analysis* (1948).

decrease in the severity of the obsessional and agoraphobic symptoms. He was much freer in his movements; he had cleared up many of the "pockets of resistance" in his house and made life more comfortable at home; he occasionally visited friends and could allow himself to read the newspapers and listen to the wireless. But with the reduction in the obsessional symptoms there was an increase in the paranoid features.

In July, 1948, his sickness benefit was raised to 26s. a week and soon afterwards his wife was well enough to start work as a shorthand-typist. From now on, for some months, analytic material was brought in the form of tirades against the Government, the Social Services and the Clinic. He wrote long and acrimonious letters— which were no longer relegated to the cupboard but were actually sent—in connection with his sickness benefit. If the money was a few days late he really believed that he was being specially selected for this type of treatment. Unconsciously he was afraid that he had drained the good breast dry and was being punished for his oral greed.

He was in constant terror that the Ministry of National Insurance would summon him to go before a Medical Board to judge whether his 26s. should be continued or not, and in the autumn of 1948 this dreaded thing happened. He had never been able to stand a medical examination because of his obsessions, and ordered me to write to the authorities and tell them that he was too ill to attend. For about a week he behaved like a terrified child in a tantrum. He felt that he was at the mercy of omnipotent parents who would strip him and force their way into him and find inside him the breast destroyed by his oral greed, and the penis stolen from father, his rival. After this interpretation his anxiety diminished somewhat and he decided to write to the Ministry himself and explain his difficulty. The letter began in a well-balanced manner but ended with a blatantly paranoid outburst. The result was that he was visited at his home by a doctor from the Ministry of Pensions who, according to Mr. A, told him not to worry but to continue with his analysis and rest assured that his 26s. would continue indefinitely.

Mr. A, however, continued his complaints against me and the Clinic for not intervening between him and the Medical Board. He threatened to report us to the Minister of Health who, he said, would not only "bring us down into the mud" but would "flood us with inspectors who would kick up a stink and blow us sky high". At the same time he proceeded to worry his mother, trying, much against her will, to install a gas stove in her house. He shouted: "I'll see to it that she has gas in her house." I linked this with his threats about the inspectors who were to blow us all sky high, and I interpreted his attempts to force his way into his mother and myself in order to control us omnipotently from within with fæces and flatus. After this he gave up the gas stove project and concentrated on getting a pension for his mother, who was living on an allowance paid to her by her elder son. Mr. A got into contact with the Ministry of Pensions and, by a long and complicated process which I need not go into here, he managed, not only to make his mother less well-off than she might have been, but he succeeded in stopping his brother paying her the allowance and thus did him out of some Income Tax rebate.

In stopping his brother from paying this allowance, Mr. A was expressing his jealousy of his mother's relationship to the brother, here identified with father; and also his jealousy of the twins' relationship to each other. He was putting a stop to the parents' intercourse and to the twins' "dirty games". The sum he finally obtained for his mother was 26s. a week, the same as he himself receives as sickness benefit.

By the spring of 1948 he was making the journey as far as Baker Street alone, but he still needed his wife's help from there to the Clinic. He had been to the theatre for the first time in twelve years; went shopping for his wife; visited friends and attended local whist drives. Again, as the obsessions and agoraphobic symptoms decreased, the paranoid anxieties increased and we entered on a new and very turbulent phase.[1]

A big cemetery was to be built near Mr. A's house. He was terrified at the idea and he made up his mind to attend a Protest Meeting of the Residents' Association and, if need be, to make a speech denouncing the plan. His fear of talking to strangers had very much diminished in the past year, but he had never before made a public speech. However, he went to the meeting which was attended by the local Mayor and Councillors and their legal adviser, and he got up and made a long speech. His speech was a great success. He admitted to me, however, that he had made a curious mistake in the speech and during the discussion afterwards. He had insisted that he would be able, from his bed, to see all that went on in the cemetery. When he got home he went up to his bedroom to verify this and

---

[1] For a discussion of the link between obsessional symptoms and paranoid anxieties see Melanie Klein, *The Psycho-Analysis of Children* (1932), Ch. IX.

found that he could hardly see anything at all, even by leaning out of the window. Nothing at all could be seen from his bed. However, he would be able to see the "big black hearses" going by, and the thought made him shudder. He was told at the meeting that the cemetery would be hidden by trees and bushes, but this was no comfort to him. He said, "Just think of the horror of going through the dark damp alley-ways, through the bushes, to arrive in the midst of all those dead and decaying bodies." This, he said, "would be a terrible psychological shock for any little children running up and down the dark alley-ways and penetrating the bushes". Children running up and down alley-ways were a source of great anxiety to him. He complained bitterly of the "dirty little brats" who, he said, rushed to and fro screaming and making an "unholy mess" in the path which joined his house to his neighbour's; he was also terrified of crossing the railway bridge at his local station, where children were always playing. Also, as I have said, he could not manage, without his wife's help, the short but crowded walk which joined Baker Street to Gloucester Place. It was clear that his fear of the dark damp alley-ways, leading to the cemetery full of dead and decaying bodies, reflected his phantasy of forcing his way into his mother and destroying everything inside her. At the same time the bridge and the walk from Baker Street and the alley-ways all represented the parents' genitals joined in intercourse, and he identified himself with the children making the "unholy mess", in other words, attacking the parents' genitals with fæces.

By insisting that he could see the cemetery from his bed, and publicly protesting against it, he was, on the one hand, proving how innocent he was of sexual curiosity about the parents and, on the other hand, expressing his terror of seeing father and mother having intercourse that was lethal as the result of his own projected sadistic wishes. He had slept in his parents' room until he was about five years of age and remembered once when about three years old hearing his father moaning in pain and his mother crying in the night. He had cried too and tried to get into their bed, but he was not allowed to, and he remembers thinking to himself, "That is because the bed is dirty".

His success at the meeting, which really appears to have been considerable, led to an invitation to become a member of the Committee of the Residents' Association, followed by an invitation to join the Committee of the Conservative Association. This delighted him as he was, in his own words, an "ardent Conservative", though I think he would always be "ardent opposition" no matter who was in power. He was made Chief Canvasser of a big district during the General Election, and was doing continuous full-time voluntary work, making public speeches and being honorary treasurer of one organization and honorary secretary of another. But he made no attempt to get any paid work.

His new-found gift for public speaking now shows every sign of becoming a good sublimation of his oral and anal sadism, but at the time of which I am writing, his manic reactions were very disquieting. At analysis he lay on the couch shouting over and over again that he was surrounded by enemies who whispered and plotted, but insisting that he knew he could vanquish them all. He cried triumphantly: "I'll pick them off one by one, like Hitler did." He felt he was at the mercy of the attacking, avenging, omnipotent parents, and all his energies were given to the work of proving that he also was omnipotent and could control them.

Whenever I could manage to make myself heard, I interpreted the transference implication of all this, that is to say, his terror of me and his need to control me. I was the breast which was being drained dry; I was the combined parents; I was the cemetery and the hearse; and I was the house full of contaminated objects soiled and torn to bits by himself, the pecking sparrow. He felt he could never put me together again, and he was in a state of despair and terror; despair that I was damaged beyond repair, and terror that I would force my way into him as he in phantasy had forced his way into me.

At the end of a few months, there was some reduction in the persecutory fears, but the pattern of his activities remained the same. He would manage somehow or other to get himself at cross purposes with the Chairman and Secretary of the Conservative Association. The Chairman was a man and the Secretary was a woman, and he invariably accused them of being "up to dirty tricks" behind people's backs. He would quarrel with them in Committee and then enjoy giving the impression that he was the one who was losing the fight. Then having fostered this situation carefully for a few weeks he would "drop his bombshell", as he called it, by bringing infallible proof that he was in the right, and the Chairman and Secretary in the wrong. In doing this, he was repeating an anal phantasy in which he retained the fæces as long as possible and then had the satisfaction of using them in one tremendous attack on the parents and the twins, in order to stop the parents' intercourse and the twins' "dirty games". This pleasure in retention was also expressed by his occasional promises to send a vast cheque to the Clinic in the distant future. Needless to say, I was identified with the Chairman and Secretary who got "up to tricks" behind people's backs.

More material in connection with his inability to work for money now began to come to light. He had, as I have already said, managed to get his mother a pension; he had collected considerable sums on behalf of the Conservative Association; he made a good sum of money for a charity fête; but money for himself or for his analysis was not forthcoming. He decided that I, like his mother and himself, was to be paid by the State. I was to become a National Health Analyst, and he was the one who was going to force Aneurin Bevan, whom he both hated and admired, to nationalize the Clinic. On the one hand, he was trying to relieve his guilt about not paying for his analysis; while on the other hand, by getting the Government to pay for his mother, for himself and for me, he would be safeguarding himself from a frightening castrating father, and this was a way of coping with his Œdipal fears. Not only did he preserve himself from being castrated by a bad dangerous father by ceasing to be a rival, he also became, by identification with his mother, the one who was loved and protected by the good father.

Last year, when he first started coming to my consulting room instead of the Clinic, he talked of the dangers of "opening up new channels" and wondered what he would find "in my private place". He feared that a dark, frightening man would open the door and that the house would be dark and full of hostile people. He wondered whether people would hear what he was saying; he was sure my telephone was tapped. "Coming into my private place" meant exploring into my inside and finding there an angry father and many pairs of hostile twins all plotting against him and waiting to attack him. He still cannot open his eyes in my room. This is in order that he shall not see the death and destruction which he imagines he has caused by his entry; it is also a method of shutting out persecutors. Another reason for shutting his eyes is that he feels that if he cannot see others, they cannot see him.

His need for his brother to be his protecting twin, and his efforts to force me into the roles of protecting twin and father, came to the fore when, about six months ago, he started trying to get paid work. He applied to the Rehabilitation Department of the Labour Exchange, but he announced that nothing would induce him to give up his 26s. a week. He was, therefore, only asking for £1 a week even if he did full-time work, since he was not entitled to earn more than £1 so long as he received sickness benefit. He said angrily that I should arrange for him to have occupational therapy for which he could be paid £1 a week. I asked him what he meant by occupational therapy and he said, "Oh, you know, weaving and so forth; after all I am quite incapable of doing real work." I pointed out that he was doing full-time unpaid real work and had been doing so for months; what he could not do was to work for money.

At the same time that he was demanding that I supply him with occupational therapy, he was also trying to get his brother to find him work, with the same stipulation that he earned only £1 a week. He said, however, that he knew that his brother would never help him to get a job. He said: "My brother's afraid that I'll get a bigger job than he's got. He has always kept me out of everything. All he will do is to lend me money." All the material brought at this point expressed his fear of getting the bigger job, the bigger penis, and thus being at the mercy of a castrated and envious brother, with whom I was identified. After some weeks of shilly-shallying he finally refused as unsuitable a job offered to him by his brother. He also refused two jobs offered to him by the Labour Exchange on the same grounds. It is true that the jobs offered were not suitable for someone with his obsessional symptoms, but I am sure that he managed to get himself offered the wrong type of job.

In the end he asked his brother to lend him some more money for his keep, which his brother did. In this way, by keeping his 26s. a week and achieving the loan, he satisfied his need to be kept by his father and brother, and, by paying nothing for his analysis, he was satisfying his need to be kept by me. Whenever I interpreted this "need to be kept" in terms of homosexual wishes towards his father and his brother, he became confused, developed eye-ache, got earache, went deaf and said he had not heard a word. On this occasion it was followed by an attack of hæmorrhoids, and a change in the pattern of his voluntary work. There was less of the "bombshell"; the accent was now on "kudos". He saw to it that *he* did all the work and that others finally got all the kudos. He was at this time made organizer of a big charity fête in aid of the Conservative Association. He wrote a forty-page report on how a fête should be run. He was complimented by the Chairman and Secretary of the Association, who said that it was a valuable piece of work. From that moment Mr. A began unconsciously to arrange things in such a way that, in the end, he would get no kudos at all for the success of the enterprise. He said, "I shall resign from the Association when the fête is successfully over. I shall just pack up and fade out." I told him that the long and successful report was the erect penis. He wanted to display it but he feared that he would be attacked by the parents if he did so. This was because he never really felt that the penis was his own to display; it was father's penis stolen from mother's inside and, in stealing it, he felt that he had deprived both parents. Therefore, he had to hand back the penis to the parents in the same way as he handed back the "kudos" to the Chairman and Secretary. I told him that although he blamed those around him for getting the kudos that should be his, in reality he was all the time deliberately divesting himself of it and forcing others to accept it.

He then told me about an incident in his childhood which, he said, he had vowed to himself never to divulge. When he was three years old, he and the twins were given cricket bats. The twins' bats were real ones, good and solid; his was made of matchwood and broke the first time he used it. Ten years later, his school was entered for a local sports competition. He made up his mind that he would win the first prize, which was a magnificent cricket bat and real leather ball. He said: "I was determined to bash my way to victory." What actually happened was most significant. He won every event outright until the finals of the high jump. He then did a five-foot jump which made him equal with the other competitor and, although he had often jumped higher than that without any strain, he collapsed on landing and lay there quite unable to move. He has no memory of feeling at all ill; he remembers thinking to himself that he must "fade out" for a bit. He was at once examined by the doctor who was attending the sports, and he was forbidden to jump again. And so this particular event was a tie. He had, however, won all the other events and the cricket bat and ball were his. Naturally his schoolfellows crowded round him cheering, ready to carry him in triumph on their shoulders. But he crept away to his mother, and to quote his own words, "I buried my head in her; I just blotted myself out and clung to her with my eyes shut all the way home." He felt that he must not even *see* the cheering crowd of schoolboys, and added: "You see I was about a couple of years older than they were." He never used the bat or ball; he packed them up carefully and put them in a cupboard and has not unpacked them to this day. He said: "The bat must be cracked and dry and quite useless by now, and the leather ball must be rotten."

This closely guarded reminiscence is, obviously, rich in meaning.

Firstly, by tying equal in the high jump, he is expressing his wish to identify himself with the twins. But the moment he becomes the twins, he feels himself to be in danger from those who are two years younger, since he has endowed these younger ones with his own hostile feelings towards the twins, who are two years older than he is. He replied to this interpretation by being surprised that he had said "two years". He admitted that he had made a mistake; the other competitors were actually only a few months younger. He also said that now he came to think of it, it was extraordinary how often he tied equal with other children, not only in sport but in lessons.

He told me that he "warned" the headmaster of his school that he was going to win that cricket bat and ball and the headmaster said: "Good, go ahead, but I doubt if you'll win the high jump." The high jump represents the erect penis and is followed immediately by the symbolic castration implicit in the collapse on landing. But, not only has the headmaster-father warned him that he will not achieve the erection, the doctor-father comes along and forbids him to try again. He identifies himself with his mother, "blotting himself out in her" while he tries to protect himself from the attacks of his rivals by shutting his eyes.

Secondly, this incident expresses his intention to "bash" his way into his mother and, omnipotently, to possess and control from within the breast and father's penis—the good leather ball and the magnificent cricket bat. But the cricket bat, once he possesses it, becomes cracked and dry, and the good leather ball goes rotten, both victims of his oral greed, and he must keep them hidden in the cupboard for ever, that is to say, inside himself where he feels them as destroyed and persecuting objects. After telling about the sports, the pains in his stomach did actually become very acute and he felt as though there were a hard lump and "something stretched out to breaking point" inside him.

There was some change in his behaviour at this time. He could now be surprised at the way he had reacted to a local newspaper report of the Sports. The report had said that the day was "marred" by the collapse of the young hero of the day, who had been over-whelmed by his efforts in winning the championship. Mr. A had translated this as meaning that he had completely destroyed every-one there, and had himself been destroyed. He could never use the word "marred" again because it filled him with such horror. He detested the newspaper-man who wrote the article and who, he felt, accused him of such wholesale murder, and it was only now, more than twenty-five years later, that he suddenly realized that the article was a sympathetic one.

Mr. A's fears, when out in the street, have changed somewhat; instead of being afraid that others will fall under buses and down area stairs, he now fears that he himself will do so. The material connected with the fear of falling to his death, which includes the fear of being hanged—referred to by him as "the biggest drop of all"—suggests that the collapse after the five-foot jump was not only a castration but a symbolic suicide. While relating the story of the high jump he showed, for the first time in analysis, real grief, and since then the feelings of persecution have begun to give place to feelings of depression. The pompous façade crumbled and I found myself face to face with a desperately unhappy little boy.

A change which suggests that he is feeling more integrated is that he no longer isolates one session from another. He can now remember material from one session and carry it on to the next. Also, he can admit that certain improvements in himself are due to the analysis; for years he completely denied that any changes could have been caused by the treatment. To admit that my interpretations had in any way helped would mean that I had succeeded in penetrating inside him, and he felt that that would be tantamount to disaster.

Melanie Klein in her "Notes on Some Schizoid Mechanisms" wrote: ". . . introjection may be felt as a forceful entry from the outside into the inside, in retribution for violent projection." The process of forcing the self into another object has also been discussed by Joan Riviere in her "Remarks on Paranoid Attitudes", and by Herbert Rosenfeld in his paper on Homosexuality. In my opinion, anxieties attached to phantasies of violent projection and introjection are at the root of Mr. A's inability to earn and to spend. To earn means to him that he is forcing his way inside an object to rob it with violence; to spend money or give a present of any kind means that he himself is being penetrated and robbed with violence.

In opening the cupboard door and letting me in to see the cricket bat and ball, Mr. A was showing that he felt introjection to be less dangerous than before. A few days after telling me this story, he was able, for the first time in fourteen years, to allow the window cleaner to come in through the back door to clean the windows, and to allow the dustman to come in through the back door to collect the dustbin. He had, at the same time, begun to earn a little money.

It is, I think, of interest that he is earning this money as an insurance agent persuading people to take out policies against burglary.

He has now started making plans for paying his debts. The idea of a vast cheque for the Clinic in the dim and distant future is giving place to more realistic plans for payment in the present. Naturally, his obsessional make-up, which causes the insight of to-day to become the obsession of to-morrow, makes progress difficult; but there are, I think, definite signs that he is gradually relinquishing his great need to be "kept".

BIBLIOGRAPHY

FREUD, S., *Collected Papers*, Vol. III. London, Hogarth Press. "Notes upon a Case of Obsessional Neurosis" (1909). "A Case of Paranoia" (1911).
—— *Inhibitions, Symptoms and Anxiety*. London, Hogarth Press, 1936.
KLEIN, MELANIE, *The Psycho-Analysis of Children*. London, Hogarth Press, 1932.
—— "Notes on Some Schizoid Mechanisms", *Int. J. Psycho-Anal.*, Vol. XXVII (1946).
—— *Contributions to Psycho-Analysis*. London, Hogarth Press, 1948.
RIVIERE, JOAN, "Remarks on Paranoid Attitudes seen in Analysis and Everyday Life." (Unpublished paper read before the British Psycho-Analytical Society, 1948.)
ROSENFELD, H., "Remarks on the Relation of Male Homosexuality to Paranoia, Paranoid Anxiety and Narcissism", *Int. J. Psycho-Anal.*, Vol. XXX (1949).

12

THREE DEFENCES AGAINST INNER PERSECUTION

Examination Anxiety, Depersonalization and Hypochondria

HANS A. THORNER

In the following paper I describe the reaction of certain patients to an unconscious sense of internal persecution, that is, to the phantasy of being in danger from bad internal objects, representing the patient's own aggressive urges. Consciously this may be experienced in many ways: as a feeling of inner badness or unworthiness, or, when projected outside, as threats of external danger.

The first part seeks to show that this anxiety reaction is very similar to examination anxiety which I found in a number of the patients. It is evident that the anxiety connected with academic examinations is well suited to represent a fear that one's evil tendencies (worthlessness), no matter how deeply hidden and denied, will be uncovered and exposed, with consequent ruin.

The second and third sections discuss patients in whom the defence by externalization of an internal danger is complicated by a splitting of the ego, leading to symptoms of depersonalization and feelings of unreality. Connections are made between these sensations and hypochondria.

I. EXAMINATION ANXIETY

Examination anxiety has mainly been investigated in patients who had had difficulties in examinations. These difficulties may consist of excessive anxiety, inability to study, or repeated failure in examinations. But the same patients also complain of similar anxiety in situations that are far removed from an examination proper. For example, in a classic case recorded by Sadger, the patient, in discussing a dream, gave the following description of his sexual difficulties: "Each attempt at sexual intercourse appears to me like an examination . . . in my imagination a fear of the next

282

examination remains: thus every fresh attempt at intercourse unconsciously means an examination and I am unable to solve this problem. Therefore I must try to deceive the woman by feigning passion which I do not feel. In the dream I do not succeed in the deception."[1]

The patients I quote had, as their analysis revealed, certain features in common: impotence, or frigidity, together with a marked readiness to react with anxiety resembling examination anxiety. They came to analysis with such complaints as impotence (Case A), hysteria (Case B), or depression (Case C), and were not at first specifically aware of "examination anxiety". But they were ready to acknowledge it after they had experienced it in the transference situation.

The analytic work on examination anxiety and castration fear has been summarized by Flugel, who, however, omitted Sadger's paper.[2] Flugel, following Rank and others, dealt with examination from the historical and anthropological point of view as an initiation rite. From this point of view, *which is mainly that of the examiner*, the examinee appears as someone who, willingly or unwillingly, has to submit to the procedure of examination. In contrast to this point of view, the present paper deals with *that of the examinee*, or more precisely with that of persons who feel as if they were being examined; the accent of interest lies on their reaction to this and, as I shall try to show, on their implicit demand for an examination.

So far as examinations are derived from puberty rites, and puberty rites from the ritual castration of the younger generation by the "fathers", the examinee's point of view should not be difficult to understand. It is that of someone threatened with castration. Broadly speaking, in the classical analytic literature, this is how such anxiety has always been explained.[3]

The later development of psycho-analytic theories traced this type of anxiety to pre-genital levels. Ernest Jones[4] considered the removal of fæces to be the precursor of castration anxiety, and

<hr/>

[1] Sadger, J. (1920). "Über Prüfungsangst und Prüfungsträume", *Int. Z. Psychoanal.* Vol. 6.
[2] Flugel, J. C. (1939). "The Examination as Initiation Rite and Anxiety Situation", *Int. J. Psycho-Anal.*, Vol. XX.
[3] Stengel, E. "Prüfungsangst und Prüfungsneurose", *Z. f. psychoanalytische Pädagogik*, Vol. 10 (1936).
Freud, S. *The Interpretation of Dreams*, pp. 273–6 (London, 1954).
Sadger, J., *loc. cit.*
Blum, E. "The Psychology of Study and Examination", *Int. J. Psycho-Anal.*, Vol. VII (1926).
[4] "Cold, Disease, Birth", *Papers on Psycho-Analysis*, 5th Ed., Ch. XV.

Hans A. Thorner

A. Starcke[1] showed that weaning from the nipple causes an anxiety analogous to castration anxiety.

At the same time another development proceeded. Ernest Jones[2] recognized that the threat of castration is only a "partial threat, however important a one, against sexual capacity and enjoyment as a whole. For the main blow of total extinction (of the capacity for sexual enjoyment) we might do well to use a separate term, such as the Greek word 'aphanisis'." Meanwhile, Melanie Klein[3] analysed small children and found that their phantasied attacks against the inside of the mother's body and the objects in it (particularly the father's penis) were experienced in their projected form as threats of attacks on the child's own inside. In other words, the precursor of (genital) castration anxiety is the fear of total extinction, not only of the sexual capacity, as in aphanisis, but of the person as a whole. Here Melanie Klein[4] does not follow Freud in regarding the fear of death as arising out of the fear of castration.

Case A

The patient was a man of early middle age who complained that he was impotent, and that all his love relationships came prematurely to an end. He was at times quite able to make preliminary contact with women, but as soon as he felt that they were interested in him he had to break off. His impotence in the sexual sphere could easily be linked with other situations in his life. For instance, he was very fond of music, in which he had reached a certain standard of accomplishment, but could not play in public, or before his friends. He noticed that through the anatomical connection of the extensor tendons to the third, fourth and fifth fingers, their movements were not as independent of each other as he would like them to be for his piano playing, and he conceived the idea that an operation might help to make them more independent. (It is interesting, not only that a patient should conceive the idea of improving his piano-playing by an operation, but also that he was able to find a surgeon willing to perform it. This has a particular significance at a time when surgeons venture into so

---

[1] "The Castration Complex", *Int. J. Psycho-Anal.*, Vol. II (1921).
[2] "Early Development of Female Sexuality", *Papers on Psycho-Analysis*, 5th Ed., Ch. XXV, p. 440.
[3] *The Psycho-Analysis of Children* (London, 1932).
[4] "A Contribution to the Theory of Anxiety and Guilt", *Int. J. Psycho-Anal.*, Vol. XXIX (1948), also in *Developments in Psycho-Analysis*, London, 1952.

problematic a field as "psycho-surgery".) There is no doubt that his handicap in piano-playing, in particular his inability to play in the presence of another person, was in fact psychological and closely related to his impotence. It was an inhibition similar to those more common inhibitions of writing, the symbolic meaning of which is well known.[1] But this patient was skilful with his fingers in other ways; he took an interest in machinery and enjoyed putting broken machinery together, mending cars, etc.

So far I have said nothing to suggest that his inhibition could not be explained solely in terms of a castration anxiety which disturbed both his piano-playing (as a symbolic masturbation) and actual intercourse. But behind this lay other fears and dangers, and these became clearer when he was faced with a situation which approximated to an examination. He applied for a new post and had to face an interview. This roused great anxiety, because he felt unable to face his interviewers and to answer their questions.

Shortly before the interview he spoke of an incident in which he had heard someone delivering a lecture. The speaker had an impediment in his speech, and listening to him was agony. He constantly put himself in the speaker's place. Another incident was associatively connected with this: the farewell speech of the Duke of Windsor had been broadcast in the interval of a public concert, when a man sitting next to him made an uncomplimentary remark about the Duke. In both these incidents the relationship between the speaker and audience was strained. In other words, the audience was hostile to the speaker because it was dissatisfied with what it was receiving from him. In this incident the material showed that the speaker represents the patient, as an impotent man. The second incident, in which he identified himself with the Duke of Windsor, shows a frankly hostile reaction in the audience. Both have to be taken as illustrations of his unconscious phantasies about the coming interview, where he would be the speaker, and the interviewers would be the audience undoubtedly felt to be hostile. He was particularly afraid of certain questions which would reveal what he considered to be his black record, although, from the reality point of view, there was very little black in his record.

A dream which he reported in one of these sessions now throws light upon the nature of this black record. Red spiders were crawling in and out of his anus. The doctor who examined him told the

---

[1] See Melanie Klein, "The Role of the School in the Libidinal Development of the Child" 1923), in *Contributions to Psycho-Analysis, 1921–1945*, p. 68.

patient that he was unable to see anything wrong with him, to which the patient replied: "Doctor, you may not see anything, but they are there all the same." Here the patient expresses his conviction that he harbours bad objects (red spiders) and even the doctor's opinion cannot shake this conviction. The associative link between "black record" and "red spiders" shows the anal significance of his "black record". He himself is afraid of these objects against which he, like the man in the dream, asks for help. This help must be based on a recognition of these objects and not on their denial; in other words he should be helped to control them. It is clear that we are here dealing with a feeling of persecution by bad internal objects. From this point of view many of his statements become more comprehensible. In the first place, the lecturer with the impediment of speech, with whom he identified himself, is his impotent and clumsy self, and the hostility of the audience, which he felt when listening to the lecture, was, among other things, his own reaction to his bad and impotent self. But knowing the patient's link between the "black record" and the "red spiders", we may add that the hesitant speaker was also experienced as full of bad objects. We are therefore led to assume that the patient connected the impediment of speech with the presence of bad internal objects, or applying this to himself, that he connected his impotence with his sense of internal persecution by bad (black) internal objects. That a sense of internal persecution may lead to an inhibition (stammer or impotence) can be understood; this symptom is an attempt at dealing with an internal danger by projecting it outside so that the disturbance seems to result from the anticipated hostile or critical attitude of external people.

His further complaint that he has to withdraw from women as soon as they show interest in him also becomes comprehensible in terms of his feeling that they might discover what is unconsciously apparent to him, namely, his own badness. In the lecturer with the impediment of speech he gave a representation of his anxieties about women. The audience also represents women who will become hostile when they recognize the speaker's, that is his own, badness. Therefore, so far as women are concerned, the patient prefers to withdraw before they become hostile, that is, as soon as they become observant of him. Further, his fear of women has also another root. They are experienced by him as devouring, greedy figures, reacting in this way to his greedy demands and to his meanness towards them; this was in accordance with an archaic image of his mother. Even in later years his relationship to his mother was a strained one; he accused her of being selfish and demanding.

The analysis of the patient's fear that he harbours bad objects in himself was accepted with great relief. As a result of it he could, for the first time, recognize that there might be something good in himself. Whatever his own feelings were, the interviewers might also recognize certain things in his favour. At this point he remembered that for some time he had not given me fresh infantile memories in his associations. These infantile memories stood for good and helpful objects because he felt his analysis could not progress unless he was able to remember incidents of his childhood. Apparently good objects could not be produced side by side with bad and dangerous ones, of which the "red spiders" were representatives. Since he had to control the bad objects, he had to suppress the good ones at the same time, and he was thus left with a feeling of emptiness.

Case B

The patient is a woman in the thirties, who has been in analysis for several years on account of severe hysteria. Paranoid traits were prominent in her clinical picture. She has improved very much, and is now again in full employment. But she developed an acute anxiety state, accompanied by over-activity and insomnia, when she received notification of the date of an examination which was due two weeks later. At first she felt that everything was well, but this manic reaction did not last long; a few days later she showed signs of exhaustion and depression. At the same time she voiced paranoid ideas, which seemed to her to be justified by the personality of her examiner whom she pictured as an enemy. She walked about my room touching almost every object as if she wanted to test the room in every detail, and while doing so explained that she would have to go through her work and read it with the eyes of the examiner to find the questions which the examiner might ask. She also mentioned certain imaginary answers which she proposed to give; all of them were exceedingly aggressive and based on the assumption that the examiner was a sadistic attacker. At the same time she felt that I also was attacking her; in fact, she experienced the whole situation of examination in the consulting room; and finally she hid in a corner of the room so that I could not see her.

Hans A. Thorner

Case C

This patient a woman of forty, showed an element regularly observed in examination anxiety, namely that the anxiety is most severe in anticipation. She also gave material that demonstrated the excretory character of the internal bad objects. This patient had a marked difficulty in speaking in analysis, which was more pronounced at the beginning of the session; it could be overcome and dissolved when I was able to understand the nature of the anxiety at the particular moment. Alone, and before any reassurance by reality, she was faced with the full force of her unconscious phantasy of an internal persecution she was unable to control.

But not all anxiety reactions can be mitigated by reality testing. Patients with phobias have other defences; they try to avoid situations that precipitate anxiety. The same patient also said that, were she able to speak freely, she might say things which she did not want to say. She had marked anxiety when she felt that she had to say things which she wanted to conceal. Her anxiety was based on similar processes to that described by patient A, who was afraid of his "black record". As the analysis of the frightening phantasies concerning bad objects of patient A showed that we were dealing with anal objects, it is not surprising to hear that this patient was not only afraid of the things she would have to say, but of the things she would have to "pass". She produced dreams in which she was afraid that she would not control her urge to pass water, and she confirmed that she was afraid of wetting my couch. In another dream she felt there was something coming out of her which was not real urine but a dangerous acid. When she looked at her clothes she saw that they had been burnt by this dangerous fluid. Like the first patient she felt herself to be full of bad and dangerous material which resulted in anxiety about what would happen in the analysis. In the transference situation I appeared sometimes as a dangerous persecutor and sometimes as the good object which is endangered by the bad things that may come out of her. It was often difficult to say whether she was more afraid of the positive or the negative transference situation.

Looking back on the material, the deepest distress of these patients is their conviction that they are unworthy or bad, in that they are unable to do the good that is expected of them. So far I have argued that this sense of incompetence, no less than the sense of badness, is the result of an unconscious feeling that there are bad and dangerous objects in them. The question now arises as to the origin and

288

meaning of these objects. This feeling of having bad objects is ultimately the result of the patient's own aggression. Case C felt unwanted all her life. Her younger sister, who was born so soon after her that her own breast-feeding was cut short, appeared to have had the affection of the family. On the other hand she felt that her mother grudged her anything she had achieved herself during her life. This was seen often, but became clear to the patient when she concealed some presents she received from her husband for fear that her mother would spoil them for her out of envy. My patient felt a similar envy towards her own daughter. One Christmas when her daughter had for the first time decorated the Christmas tree by herself, my patient felt that now she had lost this function— now she was quite useless. The feeling of her greed towards her mother was projected on to her daughter—what she once must have felt towards her mother, now she attributed to her daughter. Similarly she reacted to her daughter's first menstruation: her daughter's growing up led to a feeling that she was declining and to the fear that now she was going to lose her own procreative function.

This patient was particularly incapable of experiencing her own greed and aggression. She projected it outside and was thus faced by her greed in others—or she felt empty—or she felt there was something bad in her, something which I described previously as bad internal objects.

The bad internal objects were not felt as greed or aggression, but a link could be established with a hypochondriacal fear of cancer. Throughout her analysis she expressed fears of having cancer, or suffering from tuberculosis. Immediately after her daughter's first period these anxieties increased, and she was convinced that she had cancer of the breast. This was interpreted to her as the greedy daughter inside her who was eating her up. But the greedy daughter was ultimately the representative of her own feelings about her mother and her attacks on her mother's breast.

A patient of Blum—a woman who also developed examination anxiety—has much in common with the one I have just quoted. Both had difficulties in being loved. Blum's patient said: "It seems to me that it was not right that my parents were so nice to me yesterday."[1] This was related to her hostile attitude to her mother which she described at length and which, in a different form, was dealt with in a dream. In this dream her sister threatened her with

[1] *Op. cit.*, p. 461.

289

the removal of her liver, i.e. with an attack on her inside. The meaning of the attack on her inside becomes clear from a second dream, in which the patient was forced to eat an object that appeared as a woman's head or a small fœtus, which reminded her of the facial features of her own mother. In the words of the patient, "she had to eat it from hatred of her sister."[1] At the same time a characteristic of this patient was her persistent denial that she had, or was allowed to have, anything. "She was not allowed to do anything; she was not allowed to *know* anything."[2] Her own greed for everything the mother was and possessed appeared as being "forced" to eat what she wanted, so that she could deny her guilt for this greed. The incorporated mother is a stolen, damaged and hated possession which she dreaded having exposed in her by the examination. She denied that she had stolen, and accused her objects of robbing her of good things and forcing bad into her.

Blum's case appears of particular interest because he showed so clearly the pre-genital elements which caused the difficulties. This patient, like my own in whom dangerous objects (red spiders) seemed to be harboured, felt bad and worthless, and full of bad objects,[3] who represented the patients' own evil activities towards others, as well as those others whose goodness had been destroyed by his attacks.

Such patients continuously try to deal with their internal bad objects, which are felt to be not only dangerous to others but also to themselves (e.g. the acid fluid in the dream of one of my patients), either by projection outside (they are then faced with external persecution), or by denial, which has other disastrous results. These may be manifold: apart from anxiety and depression, denial may lead to an inhibition of initiative, resulting in impotence and frigidity, and to feelings of unworthiness, emptiness or depersonalization (discussed in the second part of this paper), as well as to a sense of persecution. But reparative elements are also always to be found, for example, in the preoccupation of one of my patients in repairing machinery, which represented his attempt to restore his damaged objects. If I have not done justice to them here, this is because I have abstracted one aspect only from these cases.

It can be seen that these patients will use any situation which

[1] *Op. cit.*, p. 464.
[2] *Op. cit.*, p. 463.
[3] Both patients have the wish to have the bad internal object removed. Blum's patient dreamt that her liver (bad object) was being removed, while my patient came to be analysed after leucotomy had been suggested.

contains elements of a test as a means of dealing with the dangers threatening from their internal world. The anxiety they feel is not only a reaction to the test. They also use the experience of the test to diminish their anxiety; for, in it, they can make an internal danger become external, and convert a universally bad internal object into something specific and so limited. An examination may lead to failure, but it is a failure in one situation, not in every situation. To fail in everything is, of course, the deepest fear. Here the sexual failure is of paramount importance. Failure in sexuality, as a result of a sense of internal persecution, is not a failure in one situation—it is experienced as a general failure. In that sense examinations, successful or not, are a means of dealing with the sense of impotence, and in particular are attempts at limiting or providing counter-evidence against it.

II. THE FEELING OF UNREALITY

An interesting outcome of the difficulty of maintaining good and bad internal objects side by side is a feeling of pretence or deception. For instance, Sadger's patient complained that he had to feign passion to deceive the woman. In a similar way one often hears patients say that although they gave the right answers in their examination, they really did not know the subject, so that success could not have any value for them in raising their self-esteem. In these cases the good internal object is partially denied and felt merely as a pretence and thus loses much of its reality.

Similar processes may lead to a feeling of unreality of which depersonalization is an example. In "derealization" the patient has a feeling that the world has changed, has become unreal; while in "depersonalization" he feels that he himself, that is his ego, has changed. Both feelings, derealization and depersonalization, can be experienced separately or mixed with each other in various proportions.

Such states of mind are found in many clinical conditions, and I shall now quote two cases, one of a schizoid personality with acute states of depersonalization, and one of hysteria with hypochondria. The hypochondria at times disappeared but could again be recognized in anxieties about a changed appearance of the world (derealization). Both conditions had many features in common: e.g. a sense of persecution by bad internal objects, which under certain conditions were projected outside; also strong oral greed and sadism. Both showed schizoid mechanisms, a split ego, but the nature of the split was different in the two cases. Both patients had difficulties in introjecting good objects.

1. *Case D: Schizoid Personality with acute states of depersonalization*

A young man aged twenty-three, who has been under my observation for eighteen months,[1] had had a number of episodes of depersonalization as a result of which he was invalided from the Services. He was at first treated with E.C.T. in a military hospital, and later had treatment in a civilian hospital on two occasions; but was still having periodic attacks of anxiety associated with depersonalization when he was admitted to hospital and treated by analysis under my supervision. The attacks recurred whenever his analysis was interrupted for external reasons, such as holidays. At all times he was aloof and distant. Apart from these attacks he did not consider that anything was wrong with him. At the same time he was co-operative and showed a positive attitude to his treatment; he attended regularly in spite of difficulties. During the treatment he improved, and eventually became engaged and married. His aloofness, which changed during treatment, led to some difficulties with his girl-friend who resented his indifference and threatened to break off the engagement. Although he admitted that he had doubts whether he could marry, he felt that he could not face a separation. In other words, in his relationship to his girl-friend he showed an attitude similar to that in his treatment. Although he came regularly and obviously wanted to be treated, he had great resistances which showed themselves in his difficulties in speaking freely during analysis.

As I have said, the precarious balance which he called his normal state was upset by any interruption of his treatment. A dramatic change then came over him and he showed all the characteristics of an acute state of depersonalization and derealization. He became anxious, had great difficulty in taking food, lost weight, refused to leave his room, and felt ghastly and changed. At the same time, the world around him took on a different complexion. He lost contact with his surroundings, that is, he heard and saw people, but they lost reality for him since he could not believe in what he saw and heard. People around him appeared automatic. But he also felt as if he had a mysterious influence on the external world,

---

[1] I saw this patient about once a week during his treatment at the hospital; but his actual analysis was carried out by Dr. N. A. Cohen, to whom I am indebted for the details of the case.

and that when the telephone rang he had willed it to do so and when people spoke they seemed to express his thoughts and not their own.

These were the words in which the patient described his state of mind during such a period. In the analysis, by correlating the change in himself with the change in his surroundings it was possible to show that he felt he had forced his way into objects and persons around him whom he now controlled from inside, and was correspondingly impoverished in his ego, for instance, by feeling that a part of himself was in the telephone which he had willed to ring. At the same time, other people thought his own thoughts while he had lost them. He also felt that he controlled time; during these periods he avoided wearing a watch, for he felt the watch was no use to him since it showed the time he made it show.

A similar reaction occurred in another situation which combined the loss of the analysis with another danger-situation. He was about to go on a motor-cycling holiday with his girl-friend. On the day he was to leave he broke down. In addition to the usual feelings of change in himself and his world, which, as I said, he seemed to control from within, he had two other anxieties: that his motor cycle, which had often appeared as an external representative of himself, was also damaged; and that he could not meet the demands of his girl-friend. It seemed not only that he could not meet her demands for love because something standing for his penis was damaged, but as if her demands had caused the damage because meeting them means being bitten up and swallowed by her. Here then there seems to be the link, which Melanie Klein first showed, between the phantasy of a forceful entry into a person and the fear of being swallowed up by them, in the quoted instance, by his girl-friend whom he felt he could not satisfy. In both cases he found himself in another person, but in one he felt he controlled the person (or object) and in the other he felt he was controlled by him (or by it).[1]

---

[1] In this connection it is of interest to recall Freud's description of the feeling of unreality which he gave in the Schreber case. "Psycho-Analytical Notes upon an Autobiographical Account of a Case of Paranoia (Dementia Paranoides)". *Collected Papers*, Vol. III (London, 1933), p. 456. Schreber's view of other people as being "cursory contraptions" is part of his phantasy of a world-catastrophe. Freud ascribes this phantasy to a "projection of the internal catastrophe; for his subjective world has come to an end since he has withdrawn his love from it." In a later passage Freud returns to the same point when he suggests that "Schreber's 'rays of God', which are made up of a condensation of the sun's rays, of nerve fibres, and of spermatozoa, are in reality nothing else than a concrete representation and external projection of libidinal cathexes." Schreber believed "that the world must come to an end because his ego was attracting all the rays to itself". We would interpret the idea of having attracted all the "rays of God" to itself as an expression of oral greed.

Except for the first few weeks after his admission it was possible to analyse him as an out-patient for most of the time. Only during his acute attacks was it necessary to re-admit him. In this way, continuity of treatment could be assured. During the attack before this holiday he was re-admitted. After a few days in hospital he had recovered sufficiently to go on holiday, but he did not enjoy it. While he was away he again developed his protective layer of aloofness and indifference.

During another phase of depersonalization further observations were made. The feeling of controlling the external object was linked with a fear of losing control over himself. When riding on his motor cycle he had the feeling that he might run over someone, that is, he could not trust his control over his motor-cycle (himself), while, at the same time, he felt that he could stop an oncoming motor-car by his will-power.

How can these reactions be understood? In the first place we came to see that as the result of strong oral wishes which were projected outside he felt that he was damaged and swallowed up by the object of his love. As a protection against this danger situation he kept a precarious balance by maintaining a distant relationship, which we recognized in the transference as aloofness, and his girl-friend complained of as indifference.

This balance he called his "normal" state of mind.[1] It was easily upset by any situation of frustration. At this point the usual defence of aloofness became insufficient, and fresh mechanisms were put into action. He became afraid that he would not be able to control himself (motor cycle) which meant he felt that he would not be able to control his aggression. Thus, in order to get rid of it, he projected his aggression outside into an object, with the result that the object appeared dead and powerless. He felt that he had forced his way

[1] "Aloofness" and indifference is a basic clinical phenomenon in schizoid personalities. In her paper on "The Importance of Symbol-formation in the Development of the Ego" (1930) (*Contributions to Psycho-Analysis, 1921 1945*), Melanie Klein describes a child showing this phenomenon. She says (p. 242): "His lack of interest in his environment and the difficulty of making contact with his mind were, as I could perceive from certain points in which his behaviour differed from that of other children, only the effect of his lack of a symbolic relation to things. The analysis, then, had to begin with this *fundamental* obstacle to establishing contact with him."

Among others who have investigated schizoid aloofness may be mentioned:

Fairbairn, "Schizoid aloofness is the fear of loving lest one's love should destroy" (see H. Guntrip, "Fairbairn's Theory of Schizoid Reactions". *Brit. J. Med. Psychol.* (1952), Vol. XXV, Part II and III, p. 90). H. Rosenfeld ("Transference Phenomena and Transference Analysis in an Acute Catatonic Schizophrenic Patient", *Int. J. Psycho-Anal.*, Vol. XXXIII, Part IV (1952), p. 458) relates these phenomena to negativism, which he considers a defence of the schizophrenic against his paranoic fear of being invaded by the external object (analyst), or of invading the external object.

into it and now controlled it from inside, though it was no more than an empty shell, as in the instances quoted.

Several additional features remain to be considered. At a time when he felt damaged he mentioned that his motor cycle was not working, and took the sparking plugs to his place of work in order to clean (restore) them. He felt there was something bad and dirty in him that was responsible for his not functioning, and he wanted to bring this into his analysis which was represented by his place of work. But then the idea that he had to put these objects into his analyst aroused anxiety. In the same session he said, with an expression of shame, that he practised fellatio, which in this context seemed to mean that analysis was, to him, something like fellatio. In my opinion his shame was linked with his fear of poisoning the analyst with "dirty" objects. This also suggests a reason why he found it so difficult to speak freely in analysis. At the same time, because he felt he had poisoned the outside world he had to guard himself against taking anything into himself, and this he showed by loss of appetite and unwillingness to eat. As a consequence he lost a good deal of weight during the attack.[1]

Herbert Rosenfeld[2] gives an account of a woman patient which might almost have been applied to ours: "The frustration had stirred up her greedy aggressive wishes. They had taken the form of phantasies in which she was forcing her way into him (the wanted external object) to compel him to do what she wanted and at the same time she felt she was emptying him of all that was good in him. The result of this greedy aggressive attack was that she felt herself to be inside him . . . the object she had forced herself into was dead, emptied through her oral demands. . . . She felt dead through the projective identification with the object. On the other hand, the feelings lost through this process seemed to correspond with that part of herself and her libido which through the projection had become split off from herself."

Four points seem to emerge from the survey of our own case. First, the patient felt that he had bad objects in himself which he might put into the analyst, as in his fellatio phantasy. This led to a

[1] At the same time his ego was felt to be impoverished of good objects because they could not be maintained alongside the bad ones. This feeling is a consequence of, or may lead to, a severe disturbance of introjection of good objects, as Melanie Klein has repeatedly described. ("Psychogenesis of Manic Depressive States". *Contributions to Psycho-Analysis*, p 292.) She has also pointed out that feeding difficulties in children are often connected with similar problems (*op. cit.*, p. 284).

[2] "Analysis of a Schizophrenic State with Depersonalization", *Int. J. Psycho-Anal.*, Vol. XXVIII (1947), p. 138.

difficulty in speaking (giving things) and also became apparent in his difficulties with his girl-friend and with other people in general. Second, he felt that he himself, as a whole, was entering objects. Third, he was unable to eat, since the food might have been poisoned —Rosenfeld described a similar trend in his case. Fourth, his personality was split up. This fourth element was not stressed in the previous account although it could already be seen in the material. His lack of emotion, which was a constant source of bewilderment and anxiety to him, had always been noticed by the people surrounding him and played a significant part in his analysis. Physically it showed itself in a vacant facial expression. I have already described this symptom as a defence against the dangers of being swallowed up by the object, but it is also an indication that he had split off emotional responses. A similar split occurred in his sensory perceptions which lost their feeling-component in periods of depersonalization and derealization, when he saw and heard people without being able to believe in their reality. He was partially conscious of these splitting processes when he said that he could not speak and think because his thoughts were in bits.

When the splitting processes in this patient are compared with those in the following patient it can be seen that splitting may occur in different "planes". This topographical expression is justified because patients experience splitting processes in different places. The following patient (Case E) felt certain sensations in her body which were recognized as split-off persecutors, i.e. internal objects that were being kept apart from her ego inside herself because they were felt to be dangerous. The split followed the body–mind border, while the former patient (Case D) felt the split between his emotional and intellectual self; the split went through the core of the ego.

This patient's symptoms can, I think, in accordance with my main argument, be shown to be the result of unsuccessful defences against a sense of persecution by bad internal objects. His attempts to rid himself of internal persecutors by projection failed. For the bad internal objects were felt to be so intimately rooted in his ego that his attempt to get rid of them ended only in the sense of having split and projected parts of his ego and so of having lost contact with himself. In other words, projection failed in its aim of dissolving the connection between the good and bad in him; instead, the inner persecutors were projected, together with parts of the ego. This is what occurred when he was frustrated—for instance, during an interruption of his analysis. He projected his internal persecutors, but at the same time also parts of his ego, and he then felt that *he* entered outside objects, which thus came under his control. But this invasion by his self of the outside world did not rid himself of internal persecutors. Therefore he did not succeed in turning an inner sense of persecution into an external sense of persecution.

One of the essential elements of an inner persecution situation of this kind is that it is felt to be inseparably connected with the person that is, it cannot be shaken off. A persecution so closely combined with the personality forms an intimate relation to the ego of the person. If the patient tries to externalize the danger (i.e. by projection of an inner persecuting object), but is unable to sever the intimate connection between the inner persecuting object and his ego, he does not lose the feeling of an inner persecution. After a "successful" projection the persecution is felt to come from outside as an external threat: the patient feels threatened, but does not feel internally changed. In contrast to this our patient felt that things outside were dangerous, but at the same time he himself felt deeply changed, or, as he put it, he felt ghastly. The projection of inner persecuting objects without their successful separation from the ego is a special case of the situation which Melanie Klein has described as projective identification.

Theoretically, we may agree that internal objects are always modified parts of the ego, like the super-ego, the best studied of all internal objects, which is a part of the ego modified by the introjection of parental figures. My thesis that projection of an internal object can be successful if it is accomplished without the projection of a noticeable part of the ego may appear to conflict with the view that internal objects are always parts of the ego. But, from our clinical experience, we know that some internal objects are felt to be more closely fused with the ego than others. Good internal objects are more easily accepted as ego-syntonic; bad objects are usually felt to be separate from the ego, but, in certain conditions, they are felt to be inseparable. The degree of intimacy is quantitatively different in every case, and it is this difference that allows me to make the statement that in some cases the internal object can be successfully projected, and in others that its projection is accompanied by the projection of a noticeable part of the ego with the consequences I have described.

This quantitative difference is described by Paula Heimann[1]

---

[1] "On some Defence Mechanisms in Paranoid States" (Ch. 10 in this volume).

when she points to the combination of introjection, splitting and intra-psychic projection as a characteristic defence in paranoid states. She shows that "together with the introjection of the object a splitting in the ego takes place". The part of the ego which becomes identified with the introjected object is split off from the rest. "The success of the defensive splitting appears to depend on how much of the ego remains free and separated from that part which through the introjection of the persecuted/persecuting object is lost and no longer operates within the organization of the ego."

2. *Projective Identification and Primitive Thinking*

I cannot leave this subject without mentioning the intimate connection between these mechanisms and primitive thinking. In infancy and in mythopoeic thinking, thoughts are experienced as "real", that is, the thought is identified with the object. This is the basis for magical thinking. If the Egyptians of the Middle Kingdom solemnly smashed pottery bowls which were inscribed with the names of hostile tribes or their rulers, they thought they had killed their enemies. "But if we call the ritual act of breaking the bowls symbolical, we miss the point. The Egyptians felt that real harm was done to the enemies by the destruction of their names."[1]

Since Melanie Klein's paper on the "Importance of Symbol-formation in the Development of the Ego",[2] symbolic representation in schizophrenic thought has increasingly received attention. The clinical observation that the schizophrenic may experience thoughts as a concrete substance and words as concrete objects is generally accepted. This fact led some observers to suppose that the concrete nature of schizophrenic thinking is due to the schizophrenic's incapacity to form or use symbols. The capacity for symbol-formation is in certain cases restricted, as we know from Melanie Klein's patient; but the attempt to couple concrete thinking with the restriction in symbol-formation ignores what Ernest Jones, in his paper on "The Theory of Symbolism",[3] has made abundantly clear, namely that the development of abstract thinking from concrete thinking is not the same as symbol-formation. He showed that a symbol— in the restricted sense as used in psycho-analysis—is a concrete object which represents another primary object. The use of symbols

[1] Frankfurt, H. & H. A., *Before Philosophy*, Penguin Edition, p. 21.
[2] *Contributions to Psycho-Analysis, 1921-1945.*
[3] *Papers on Psycho-Analysis*, 5th edition, p. 87-144.

in this sense is clearly involved in concrete thinking. Strictly speaking, therefore, the development from concrete to abstract thinking is not equivalent to the development of a capacity to use symbols, but rather to the development of a capacity to use them in a more abstract way, which is probably akin to their use in generalizations. In contrast to this view Hanna Segal says "The difficulty of forming or using symbols is, I think, one of the basic elements in schizophrenic thinking. This certainly is at the root of the concrete thinking described in schizophrenics".[1]

One of my patients who has not otherwise been quoted in this paper described his recovery from an acute schizophrenic breakdown, which was associated with feelings of homosexual persecution, by saying that he could not handle nails during the early phases of his illness because they were connected with crucifixion; after recovery he regained the feeling that "nails were nails". The capacity for forming symbols was never impaired during his illness, but the symbol (nails) was so closely identified with the repressed idea of a dangerous penis which would homosexually pierce the father that he could not touch them. Such examples are common. Segal gives similar examples, but she takes the view that if the repressed idea is so strongly represented by the substitute object that it creates "all the anxiety belonging to the original object" the substitute idea ceases to be a symbol; hence the suggestion referred to above.

Any explanation of the genesis and nature of concrete thinking has to take into account the fact that this is a quality which is not confined to schizophrenics, but is characteristic for primitive thinking, infantile or mythopoeic, which makes free use of symbols. It is agreed that the quality of concreteness is connected

---

[1] Hanna Segal, "Some Aspects of the Analysis of a Schizophrenic", *Int. J. Psycho-Anal.* Vol. XXXI (1950), para. 4, p. 270. In a later paper she developed this idea ("A Psychoanalytical Approach to Æsthetics", *Int. J. Psycho-Anal.*, Vol. XXXIII, Part II, p. 202, and in Ch. 16 of this book). I am not in a position to enter into a detailed discussion of problems of symbolism in psycho-analysis, for which a full study would be required and which is outside the scope of this paper. Since this paper was written Dr. Segal read an important paper on symbol-formation before the Medical Section of the British Psychological Society (27th April, 1955). Her distinction between symbolic equation—the concretely experienced indirect representation of a primary object—and symbol, and the genetic link of the former with the paranoid-schizoid position, and the latter with the depressive position represents a great advance. What I describe in this section as a symbol that becomes frighteningly concrete would be called by Segal a symbolic equation. She also recognizes that a symbol can revert to a symbolic equation by means of projective identification. This is the process I describe in this section of my paper which primarily deals with the experience of concreteness and not symbol-formation. A point for further consideration which so far as I know has not been dealt with by Dr. Segal is that abstraction and generalization have to be genetically distinguished from symbol-formation.

299

Hans A. Thorner

with the perceptive element in thinking which is an ego-activity. In the primitive ego, objects may not yet be fully differentiated from itself, as an "outside" and "not-me" is not fully differentiated from an "inside" and "me". In this state the "thought" of an object will scarcely be different from the "feel" of an object which is only gradually experienced as a separate entity from the ego. This primitive state can be reproduced by the more mature, but sick, ego through projective identification, and the presence of the sensual aspects of the ego lends the quality of concreteness to the thought (or word). Then a state of confusion between ego and object arises, which is described in this paper as a sense of unreality. Another consequence is that objects are felt to be animated. Mythopoeic thinking assumes the action of a will where the normal adult of our civilization thinks in terms of mechanical causality. In primitive, i.e. magical, thinking an outside object seems to be influenced by what is done to a thought or a word, because the thought or word appears to be identical with the object. This is the basis of the omnipotence of infantile thought, a fundamental concept of psychoanalytical theory. The word is also experienced as part of the ego, and therefore word and object have both the sensual quality which we call concrete. It is my hypothesis that the concreteness and the animation of the object or its symbol is the consequence of the endowment of the object or its symbol with ego-qualities. If these are inseparably mixed with those belonging to the aggressive instinct (death instinct) they become very frightening. In the example of the nails which my patient was unable to handle I maintained that the phobic reaction was due to the patient's projection of his own aggressive self into them; as a consequence they ceased to be "nails", but became alive with his own murderous feelings, in short became the concrete symbol of his own dangerous penis with which he would pierce the father. This patient's difficulty was not that he could not form or use symbols, but that his symbols, like other objects, were liable to become possessed with his own aggressive self, a process with which we have become familiar under the term "projective identification".

Depersonalization is here seen as a defence against internal persecution—a defence which involves a splitting of the ego, which becomes impoverished of good objects and is partly projected outside into external objects. Since the perception of these objects is thereby disturbed, the feeling of depersonalization is closely linked with that of derealization.

300

III. HYPOCHONDRIA

This leads me to another group of cases which also suffer from internal persecution, with this difference, that the persecutory objects are not felt to be within the core of the ego but within the body-ego, namely, to cases of hypochondria and conversion hysteria.[1] Internal persecution is linked with both hypochondria and hysterical conversion-symptoms. As Melanie Klein[2] writes: "The fundamental factor common to both (hypochondriasis and hysterical conversion-symptoms) is the fear relating to persecution within the body (attacks by internalized persecutory objects, or to the harm done to internal objects by the subject's sadism, such as attacks by his dangerous excrements) all of which is felt as physical damage inflicted on the ego. The elucidation of the processes underlying the transformation of these persecutory anxieties into physical symptoms might throw further light on the problems of hysteria."

Freud, who dealt with hypochondria in his paper "Narcissism: an Introduction", saw the key to an understanding of hypochondria in the withdrawal of interest from external reality, in the simultaneous preoccupation of the hypochondriac with his inner world and in the relationship of this condition to schizophrenia (paraphrenia). These observations, among others, prompted him to introduce the concept of narcissism. It is of particular interest that Freud visualized libido as capable of being attached to real (external) or to imaginary (internal) objects. He says: "Now it is in the first instance a matter of indifference for the internal process of 'working-over' (of excitation) if this is accomplished *on real or imaginary objects* (my italics). The difference does not appear until later, when the turning of the libido towards the unreal object (introversion) has led to a damming-up."[3] Freud considered the preoccupation with inner objects important enough to merit a special term, and he suggested restricting Jung's term of introversion to describe this relationship.[4]

In appraising Freud's theory of hypochondria it should be remembered that it was published as early as 1914, well in advance

---

[1] A differentation between the core of the ego and the body-ego is not a new one. It is widely accepted that the body is part of the "self", but not identical with it. This does not contradict Freud's formulation that genetically "the ego is first and foremost a body-ego".

[2] *Developments in Psycho-Analysis*, Ch. VI, p. 225.

[3] "On Narcissism: An Introduction". *Collected Papers*, Vol. IV, p. 43 (translation of first sentence slightly altered to render it more like the German original).

[4] *Op. cit.*, p. 31.

of his introduction of the concept of the aggressive instinct, which in our present understanding of hypochondria plays an important part. The absence of this concept at that time also accounts for his need of a special theory to explain how pain can arise from a damming-up of libido.

Case E

A case of hysteria. The patient was a single woman of thirty-three who appeared younger than her age. She used to suffer from a fear of blindness. She also complained of a number of hypochondriacal symptoms: sometimes she felt that one leg was heavier than the other so that she had difficulty in raising it from the ground, or it was weak and could not support her, and was felt to be hollow; or one side of her body was numb. During the night she sometimes felt that she could not see and had to switch on the light to test her sight. These feelings constitute a change in ego-feelings; to be precise, a change in the body-ego. When some of these feelings, particularly the fear of blindness, receded, a new experience came to the fore: she felt that not she, but the world, had changed; people appeared to have a changed expression, they looked dead. What used to be the fear of blindness turned into a state in which the external object had changed its quality and become what she called a "dead object". At such moments she felt a compulsion to touch objects in order to prove that they were alive.

At the age of twenty-one, when she was to accompany her father on a trip abroad, she had her first breakdown. Conflicts between her own unconscious sexual impulses towards her father and her loving and aggressive feelings for her mother led to an acute phobia which prevented her from leaving the house. These elements need not be considered in this context in which we are concerned only with the patient's attitude to her mother's jealousy. From early youth she remembered frequent quarrels between her parents when her mother accused her father of infidelity. Her mother's jealousy and her tormenting suspicions were a significant feature of her family background.

She complained bitterly of her mother's possessiveness; her mother always wanted her daughters around her and prevented them, in more ways than one, from starting a life of their own away from home. At the same time, she was aware that she was as jealous as her mother. She could not tolerate my other patients; she felt that they took me away from her. In an early phase of her analysis she said she could not visualize being married as she would be afraid that her husband would be taken away by another woman. It is clear not only that she felt she was as jealous as her own mother but that she also projected her own envy, jealousy, possessiveness and aggression into others—hence her fear that others would take her husband away if she should ever marry.

Her feeling of "badness" could be traced to aggressive feelings, which took the form of obsessional thoughts of an irresistible impulse from which she asked to be protected; for instance, at one time she was afraid of an impulse to kill her mother. Similarly she was afraid of an impulse to pierce her own eyes. This irresistible impulse was experienced as a special form of persecution by bad inner objects, in particular her quarrelling parents, who seemed to be compelling her to give way to it. For it appeared as something foreign in herself, which did not come from her, but from another person in her. This impulse, and with it her fear, changed from time to time in intensity. Often it was replaced by the hypochondriacal symptoms I have already mentioned, i.e. by a fear of blindness or a sense of heaviness in her limbs; what had been felt as an aggressive impulse was now experienced as a blind or heavy object in her body.

At the same time she complained of unworthiness or inferiority. She could not understand that anyone could see anything desirable in her. She felt that nothing was good in her. It was, indeed, one of her characteristics that she disowned her own possessions (good objects). She had the habit of giving things away, such as pieces of jewellery, books, etc. Money had no value for her and she was embarrassed when she had not spent what she earned. Her compulsion to disclaim possessions was not restricted to the material plane. She envied people who, like her family, could believe in God, but she felt unable to have any faith—she felt empty and alone, had no possessions and did not belong to anybody. With her severe persecution by internal bad objects went a severe disturbance of her relationship to the internal good object, which could not be maintained in her together with the introjected bad objects.

The instability of her inner good objects was also shown by her constant demands for treatment. She usually felt better after a session but often this wore off before the next session. Even if treatment could not cure her, a permanent supply of treatment became a necessity for her well-being. This was obviously a repetition of a feeding situation in which she destroyed or lost the good food almost as quickly as she took it in.[1] In my patient, as in those described by Melanie Klein, the difficulty of maintaining her good objects resulted from her aggression which threatened them.[2]

As she was unable to maintain a good object in herself, it was necessary for her to deposit it in me, as her analyst and as an outside good object, instead of an inner one. During periods of positive transference she would be more inclined to experience her inner persecution as hypochondriacal feelings, that is, the bad inner objects were felt to be in her body, while the good object was mainly outside, in her analyst. When her relation to me turned to anger, or even hatred, her feeling of inner persecution also changed. Her hypochondria turned into a feeling of derealization. She projected her internal persecution outside and the good objects were withdrawn from me, that is, from the external world; I then had nothing, or very little good, to give her. She became depressed and the world appeared to her blank and empty. In periods like these she had feelings as described above, namely, people looked dead, but the hypochondriacal fears were reduced even if they had not disappeared.[3] This relation between hypochondriacal fears and fears about outside objects has often been observed. One of my hypochondriacal patients seemed to be equally preoccupied with the condition of his "purse" and with the condition of his body: financial and hypochondriacal fears replaced each other from time to time.

Cases D and E have the same defence against internal persecution, and both show the same strong oral aggressive tendencies. They differ clinically in that one is a case of depersonalization with marked splitting processes, while the other is a case of hysteria in which the splitting of the ego is, as it were, on a different plane. While the first patient felt that he was in the object, so that the split between the core of his ego and body did not appear in the foreground of his psychopathology, the split in the hysterical case was on this very boundary. Here the persecutors were felt to be within

---

[1] The difficulty of building up a stable inner good object may be the basis of the famous play "Peep-bo", which children are never tired of repeating. For so long as the child has not yet built up a safe and secure inner object, he may feel its external equivalent to be lost when out of sight and so needs and takes pleasure in its repeated reappearance.

[2] *Developments in Psycho-Analysis*, pp. 258, 269.

[3] Another feature of this patient was her almost uncanny ability to guess other people's thoughts (telepathy). This ability appeared to be connected with her oral greed, or with her compulsion to take objects inside her. Such patients experience the outside person as if he is inside their own body and they can feel what the other person feels as if it was their own self. It is my impression that a capacity of this kind is often found in hysterical patients, and in particular in those with hypochondriacal or conversion mechanisms.

the body, for instance, when the patient felt her eyes could not see. She also felt that her aggression would be directed against her body, that is, that she would pierce her eyes; but after she had projected these persecutors outside, not she, but others were bad (or dead). In addition to hypochondria she was also subject to many frequent minor physical illnesses. This supports Melanie Klein's view that there is a strong link between hypochondriasis, hysterical conversion symptoms, and physical ailments.

CONCLUSION

In this investigation I have tried to trace a few reactions, or defences, against inner persecution. In the first group of patients the inner persecutors were projected outside and experienced as an external danger. For the description of this form of anxiety I took examination anxiety as a pattern, and we could see that the anxiety reaction also arose in situations that were far removed from a real examination. We came to the conclusion that the patients used the situation of a test to diminish their anxiety by externalizing an inner danger, and to limit a universal (genital) danger to a specific situation.

In the second group, the externalization was complicated by a split ego. In the attempt to project the internal persecutor, parts of the ego were also projected. As the patient was unable to separate the inner persecutor from his ego he did not succeed in externalizing an inner danger situation, but was faced with a situation of "inner persecution" outside himself. In other words, a situation arose which Melanie Klein has described as projective identification. At the same time, the patient's ego became impoverished. He could not take in good objects since he would be unable to protect them from his own aggressive attacks which were invested in the bad internal objects.

In the case of hypochondria, the ego-split followed the body-mind boundary[1] and the persecuting inner objects were expelled from the core of the ego into the body, that is, they were prevented from permeating the ego as a whole. Sometimes they were expelled from the body-ego too, and then a state of derealization arose; that is, the hypochondria was relieved, but the world appeared bad (or dead). The peculiar form of the inner persecution that led

[1] In this context I mean by "mind" all parts of the ego that are not "body".

305

Hans A. Thorner

to hypochondria (physical illness) remained noticeable in a sense of derealization.

Another outcome of hypochondria which I do not follow up here, but which often occurs, is that the whole ego becomes invaded by the internal persecuting objects. When they are no longer restricted to the body, they threaten the ego with disintegration: hypochondria turns into psychosis.

Summing up, it is possible to say that a feeling of unreality develops when two conditions are fulfilled: when (i) a strong sense of inner persecution by bad objects is combined with (ii) splitting processes within the ego. Inner persecution is part of every psychoneurosis or psychosis. The clinical form .of the neurosis depends less on the underlying anxiety-situation than on the defence-mechanisms of the ego. If the externalization of inner persecution is unsuccessful owing to a split ego, the persecutor remains attached to a greater part of the ego, causing a feeling of unreality.

PART TWO

PAPERS IN APPLIED PSYCHO-ANALYSIS

13

ON IDENTIFICATION

MELANIE KLEIN

INTRODUCTION

IN "Mourning and Melancholia"[1] Freud showed the intrinsic connection between identification and introjection. His later discovery of the super-ego,[2] which he ascribed to the introjection of the father and identification with him, has led to the recognition that identification as a sequel to introjection is part of normal development. Since this discovery, introjection and identification have played a central role in psycho-analytic thought and research.

Before starting on the actual topic of this paper, I think it would be helpful to recapitulate my main conclusions on this theme: super-ego development can be traced back to introjection in the earliest stages of infancy; the primal internalized objects form the basis of complex processes of identification; persecutory anxiety, arising from the experience of birth, is the first form of anxiety, very soon followed by depressive anxiety; introjection and projection operate from the beginning of post-natal life and constantly interact. This interaction both builds up the internal world and shapes the picture of external reality. The inner world consists of objects, first of all the mother, internalized in various aspects and emotional situations. The relationships between these internalized figures, and between them and the ego, tend to be experienced—when persecutory anxiety is dominant—as mainly hostile and dangerous; they are felt to be loving and good when the infant is gratified and happy feelings prevail. This inner world, which can be described in terms of internal relations and happenings, is the product of the

---

[1] *Collected Papers* (1917), Vol. IV (London, 1925). Abraham's work on melancholia, as early as 1911 ("Notes on the Psycho-Analytical Investigation and Treatment of Manic-Depressive Insanity and Allied Conditions") and 1924 ("A Short History of the Development of the Libido, viewed in the Light of Mental Disorders") was also of great importance in this connection. Cf. *Selected Papers on Psycho-Analysis*, Karl Abraham (London, 1927).

[2] *The Ego and the Id* (1923) (London), 1927.

infant's own impulses, emotions, and phantasies. It is of course profoundly influenced by his good and bad experiences from external sources.[1] But at the same time the inner world influences his perception of the external world in a way that is no less decisive for his development. The mother, first of all her breast, is the primal object for both the infant's introjective and projective processes. Love and hatred are from the beginning projected on to her, and concurrently she is internalized with both these contrasting primordial emotions, which underlie the infant's feeling that a good and a bad mother (breast) exist. The more the mother and her breast are cathected—and the extent of the cathexis depends on a combination of internal and external factors, among which the inherent capacity for love is of utmost importance—the more securely will the internalized good breast, the prototype of good internal objects, be established in the infant's mind. This in turn influences both the strength and the nature of projections; in particular it determines whether feelings of love or destructive impulses predominate in them.[2]

I have in various connections described the infant's sadistic phantasies directed against the mother. I found that aggressive impulses and phantasies arising in the earliest relation to the mother's breast, such as sucking the breast dry and scooping it out, soon lead to further phantasies of entering the mother and robbing her of the contents of her body. Concurrently, the infant experiences impulses and phantasies of attacking the mother by putting excrements into her. In such phantasies, products of the body and parts of the self are felt to have been split off, projected into the mother, and to be continuing their existence within her. These phantasies soon extend to the father and to other people. I also contended that the persecutory anxiety and the fear of retaliation, which result from oral-, urethral- and anal-sadistic impulses, underlie the development of paranoia and schizophrenia.

It is not only what are felt to be destructive and "bad" parts of the self which are split off and projected into another person, but also parts which are felt to be good and valuable. I have pointed out earlier that from the beginning of life the infant's first object, the mother's breast (and the mother), is invested with libido and

[1] Among them from the beginning of life the mother's attitude is of vital importance and remains a major factor in the development of the child. Cf., for instance, *Developments in Psycho-Analysis*, London, 1952.
[2] To put it in terms of the two instincts, it is a question whether in the struggle between the Life and Death instincts the Life instinct prevails.

that this vitally influences the way in which the mother is internalized. This in turn is of great importance for the relation with her as an external and internal object. The process by which the mother is invested with libido is bound up with the mechanism of projecting good feelings and good parts of the self into her.

In the course of further work, I also came to recognize the major importance for identification of certain projective mechanisms which are complementary to the introjective ones. The process which underlies the feeling of identification with other people, because one has attributed qualities or attitudes of one's own to them, was generally taken for granted even before the corresponding concept was incorporated in psycho-analytic theory. For instance, the projective mechanism underlying empathy is familiar in everyday life. Phenomena well known in psychiatry, e.g. a patient's feeling that he *actually is* Christ, God, a king, a famous person, are bound up with projection. The mechanisms underlying such phenomena, however, had not been investigated in much detail when, in my "Notes on Some Schizoid Mechanisms",[1] I suggested the term "projective identification"[2] for those processes that form part of the paranoid-schizoid position. The conclusions I arrived at in that paper were, however, based on some of my earlier findings,[3] in particular on that of the infantile oral-, urethral- and anal-sadistic phantasies and impulses to attack the mother's body in many ways, including the projection of excrements and parts of the self into her.

Projective identification is bound up with developmental processes arising during the first three or four months of life (the paranoid-schizoid position) when splitting is at its height and persecutory anxiety predominates. The ego is still largely unintegrated and is therefore liable to split itself, its emotions and its internal and external objects, but splitting is also one of the fundamental defences against persecutory anxiety. Other defences arising at this stage are idealization, denial, and omnipotent control of internal and external objects. Identification by projection implies a combination of splitting off parts of the self and projecting them on to (or rather into) another

[1] Read to the British Psycho-Analytical Society on 4th December, 1946, published in *Int. J. Psycho-Anal.*, Vol. XXVII (1946), and in *Developments in Psycho-Analysis* (London, 1952).
[2] In this connection I refer to the papers by Herbert Rosenfeld, "Analysis of a Schizophrenic State with Depersonalization", *Int. J. Psycho-Anal.*, Vol. XXVIII, 1947; "Remarks on the Relation of Male Homosexuality to Paranoia, Paranoid Anxiety, and Narcissism", *Int. J. Psycho-Anal.*, Vol. XXX (1949); and "A Note on the Psychopathology of Confusional States in Chronic Schizophrenias", *Int. J. Psycho-Anal.*, Vol. XXXI (1950), which are relevant to these problems.
[3] Cf. my *Psycho-Analysis of Children*; for instance, pp. 186 ff.

Melanie Klein

person. These processes have many ramifications and fundamentally influence object relations.

In normal development, in the second quarter of the first year, persecutory anxiety diminishes and depressive anxiety comes to the fore, as a result of the ego's greater capacity to integrate itself and to synthesize its objects. This entails sorrow and guilt about the harm done (in omnipotent phantasies) to an object which is now felt to be both loved and hated; these anxieties and the defences against them represent the depressive position. At this juncture a regression to the paranoid-schizoid position may occur in the attempt to escape from depression.

I also suggested that internalization is of great importance for projective processes, in particular that the good internalized breast acts as a focal point in the ego, from which good feelings can be projected on to external objects. It strengthens the ego, counteracts the processes of splitting and dispersal and enhances the capacity for integration and synthesis. The good internalized object is thus one of the preconditions for an integrated and stable ego and for good object relations. The tendency towards integration, which is concurrent with splitting, I assume to be, from earliest infancy, a dominant feature of mental life. One of the main factors underlying the need for integration is the individual's feeling that integration implies being alive, loving, and being loved by the internal and external good object; that is to say, there exists a close link between integration and object relations. Conversely, the feeling of chaos, of disintegration, of lacking emotions as a result of splitting, I take to be closely related to the fear of death. I have maintained (in "Schizoid Mechanisms") that the fear of annihilation by the destructive forces within is the deepest fear of all. Splitting as a primal defence against this fear is effective to the extent that it brings about a dispersal of anxiety and a cutting off of emotions. But it fails in another sense because it results in a feeling akin to death—that is what the accompanying disintegration and feeling of chaos amount to. The sufferings of the schizophrenic are, I think, not fully appreciated, because he appears to be devoid of emotions.

Here I wish to go somewhat beyond my paper on "Schizoid Mechanisms". I would suggest that a securely established good object, implying a securely established love for it, gives the ego a feeling of riches and abundance which allows for an outpouring of libido and projection of good parts of the self into the external world without a sense of depletion arising. The ego can then also feel that

312

it is able to re-introject the love it has given out, as well as take in goodness from other sources, and thus be enriched by the whole process. In other words, in such cases there is a balance between giving out and taking in, between projection and introjection.

Furthermore, whenever an unharmed breast is taken in, in states of gratification and love, this affects the ways in which the ego splits and projects. As I suggested, there are a variety of splitting processes (about which we have still a good deal to discover) and their nature is of great importance for the development of the ego. The feeling of containing an unharmed nipple and breast—although co-existing with phantasies of a breast devoured and therefore in bits—has the effect that splitting and projecting are not *predominantly* related to fragmented parts of the personality but to more coherent parts of the self. This implies that the ego is not exposed to a fatal weakening by dispersal and for this reason is more capable of repeatedly undoing splitting and achieving integration and synthesis in its relation to objects.

Conversely, the breast taken in with hatred, and therefore felt to be destructive, becomes the prototype of all bad internal objects, drives the ego to further splitting and becomes the representative of the death-instinct within.

I have already mentioned that concurrently with the internalization of the good breast, the external mother too is cathected with libido. In various connections Freud has described this process and some of its implications: for instance, referring to idealization in a love relation, he states[1] that "the object is being treated in the same way as our own ego, so that when we are in love, a considerable amount of narcissistic libido overflows on to the object. . . . We love it on account of the perfections which we have striven to reach for our own ego. . . ."[2]

In my view, the processes which Freud describes imply that this loved object is felt to contain the split-off, loved, and valued part of the self, which in this way continues its existence inside the object. It thereby becomes an extension of the self.[3]

[1] (1921) *Group Psychology and the Analysis of the Ego* (London, 1922), p. 74.
[2] Anna Freud has described another aspect of the projection on to a loved object and identification with it in her concept of "altruistic surrender". *The Ego and the Mechanisms of Defence*, London, 1937, Ch. X.
[3] On re-reading recently Freud's *Group Psychology and the Analysis of the Ego*, it appeared to me that he was aware of the process of identification by projection, although he did not differentiate it by means of a special term from the process of identification by intro-jection with which he was mainly concerned. Elliott Jaques, in his contribution to this book (Ch. 20), quotes some passages from *Group Psychology* as implicitly referring to identification by projection.

The above is a brief summary of my findings presented in "Notes on Some Schizoid Mechanisms".[1] I have not confined myself, however, to the points discussed there but have added a few further suggestions and amplified some which were implied but not explicitly stated in that paper. I now propose to exemplify some of these findings by an analysis of a story by the French novelist Julian Green.[2]

A NOVEL ILLUSTRATING PROJECTIVE IDENTIFICATION

The hero, a young clerk called Fabian Especel, is unhappy and dissatisfied with himself, in particular with his appearance, his lack of success with women, his poverty, and the inferior work to which he feels condemned. He finds his religious beliefs, which he attributes to his mother's demands, very burdensome yet cannot free himself from them. His father, who died when Fabian was still at school, had squandered all his money on gambling, had led a "gay" life with women, and died of heart failure, thought to be a result of his dissolute life. Fabian's pronounced grievance and rebellion against fate are bound up with his resentment against his father, whose irresponsibility had deprived him of his further education and prospects. These feelings, it appears, contribute to Fabian's insatiable desire for wealth and success, and to his intense envy and hatred of those who possess more.

The essence of the story is the magic power to change himself into other people which is conferred on Fabian by a compact with the Devil, who seduces him by false promises of happiness into accepting this sinister gift; he teaches Fabian a secret formula by which the change into another person can be effected. This formula includes his own name, Fabian, and it is of great importance that he should—whatever happens—remember the formula and his name.

Fabian's first choice is the waiter who brings him a cup of coffee which is all that he can afford for his breakfast. This attempt at projection comes to nothing because at this point he still considers the feelings of his prospective victims, and the waiter, on being asked by Fabian whether he would like to change places with him, refuses. Fabian's next choice is his employer Poujars. He greatly envies this man who is wealthy, can—as Fabian thinks—enjoy life

[1] Cf. also "Some Theoretical Conclusions Regarding the Emotional Life of the Infant" in *Developments in Psycho-Analysis* (London, 1952), pp. 202–3.

[2] *If I Were You* (Translated from the French by J. H. F. McEwen), (London, 1950).

314

to the full, and has power over other people, in particular over Fabian. The author describes Fabian's envy of Poujars in these words: "Ah! the sun. It often seemed to him that M. Poujars kept it hidden in his pocket." Fabian is also very resentful of his employer because he feels humiliated by him and imprisoned in his office.

Before he whispers the formula into Poujars' ear, Fabian speaks to Poujars in the same contemptuous and humiliating way as Poujars used to speak to him. The transformation has the effect of making his victim enter Fabian's body and collapse; Fabian (now in the body of Poujars) writes out a large cheque in Fabian's favour. He finds in Fabian's pocket his address which he carefully writes down. (This slip of paper with Fabian's name and address he carries with him into his next two transformations.) He also arranges that Fabian, into whose pocket he has put the cheque, should be taken home, where he would be looked after by his mother. The fate of Fabian's body is very much in Fabian-Poujars' mind, for he feels that he might one day wish to return to his old self; he therefore does not want to see Fabian recover consciousness because he dreads the frightened eyes of Poujars (with whom he has changed places) looking out of his own former face. He wonders, looking at Fabian who is still unconscious, whether anybody ever loved him, and is glad that he got rid of that unprepossessing appearance and those miserable clothes.

Fabian-Poujars very soon finds out some drawbacks to this transformation. He feels oppressed by his new corpulence; he has lost his appetite and becomes aware of the kidney trouble from which Poujars suffers. He discovers with dislike that he has not only taken on Poujars' looks but also his personality. He has already become estranged from his old self and remembers little about Fabian's life and circumstances. He decides that he is not going to stay a minute longer than necessary in Poujars' skin.

On leaving the office with Poujars' pocket-book in his possession he gradually realizes that he has put himself into an extremely serious situation. For not only does he dislike the personality, outlook, and unpleasant memories which he has acquired, but he is also very worried about the lack of will-power and initiative which are in keeping with Poujars' age. The thought that he might not be able to muster the energy to transform himself into somebody else fills him with horror. He decides that for his next object he must choose somebody who is young and healthy. When he sees in a café an athletic young man with an ugly face, looking arrogant and quarrelsome but whose whole bearing shows self-assurance, vigour, and health, Fabian-Poujars—feeling increasingly worried that he might never get rid of Poujars—decides to approach the young man although he is very afraid of him. He offers him a packet of banknotes which Fabian-Poujars wants to have after the transformation, and while thus distracting the man's attention he manages to whisper the formula into his ear and to put the slip with Fabian's name and address into his pocket. Within a few moments Poujars, whose person Fabian has just left, has collapsed and Fabian has turned into the young man, Paul Esménard. He is filled with the great joy of feeling young, healthy, and strong. He has much more than in the first transformation lost his original self and turned into the new personality; he is amazed to find a packet of banknotes in his hand and in his pocket a slip of paper, with Fabian's name and address. Soon he thinks of Berthe, the girl whose favour Paul Esménard has been trying to win, so far without success. Among other unpleasant things Berthe told him that he has the face of a murderer and that she is afraid of him. The money in his pocket gives him confidence and he goes straight to her house, determined to make her comply with his desires.

Although Fabian has become submerged in Paul Esménard, he feels increasingly bewildered about the name Fabian which he has read on the slip of paper. "That name remained in some way at the very core of his being." A feeling of being imprisoned in an unknown body and burdened with huge hands and a slow-working brain takes possession of him. He cannot puzzle it out, struggling unavailingly with his own stupidity; he wonders what he could mean by wishing to be free. All this goes through his mind as he goes to Berthe. He forces his way into her room although she tries to lock the door against him. Berthe screams, he silences her by clapping his hand over her mouth, and in the ensuing struggle strangles her. Only gradually does he realize what he has done; he is terrified and does not dare to leave Berthe's flat since he hears people moving about in the house. Suddenly he hears a knock at the door, opens it and finds the Devil whom he does not recognize. The Devil leads him away, teaches him again the formula which Fabian-Esménard has forgotten, and helps him to remember something about his original self. He also warns him that in future he must not enter a person too stupid to use the formula and therefore incapable of effecting further transformations.

The Devil takes him into a reading-room in search of a person into whom Fabian-Esménard could change himself and picks out Emmanuel Fruges; Fruges and the Devil recognize each other immediately, for Fruges has all the time been struggling against the Devil, who has "so often and so patiently hung about that unquiet soul". The Devil directs Fabian-Esménard to whisper the formula into Fruges' ear and the transformation is effected. As soon as Fabian has entered into Fruges' body and personality, he recovers his capacity to think. He wonders about the fate of his last victim and is somewhat concerned about Fruges (now in the body of Esménard) who will be condemned for Fabian-Esménard's crime. He feels partly responsible for the crime because, as the Devil points out to him, the hands which committed the murder belonged to him only a few minutes ago. Before parting from the Devil he also inquires after the original Fabian and after Poujars. While recovering some memories of his former selves, he notices that he is more and more turning into Fruges and acquiring his personality. At the same time he becomes aware that his experiences have increased his comprehension of other people, for he can now understand better what went on in the minds of Poujars, Paul Esménard, and Fruges. He also feels sympathy, an emotion he has never known before, and goes back once more to see what Fruges—in the body of Paul Esménard—is doing. Yet he relishes the thought not only of his own escape but also of what his victim will suffer in his place.

The author tells us that some elements of Fabian's original nature enter more into this transformation than into either of the previous ones. In particular the inquiring side of Fabian's character influences Fabian-Fruges to discover more and more about Fruges' personality. Among other things he finds that he is drawn to obscene postcards which he buys from an old woman in a little stationer's shop, where the cards are hidden behind other articles. Fabian is disgusted with this side of his new nature; he hates the noise made by the revolving stand on which the cards are arranged, and feels that this noise will haunt him for ever. He decides to get rid of Fruges whom he is now able to judge to some extent with the eyes of Fabian.

Soon a little boy of about six comes into the shop. George is the picture of "apple-cheeked innocence" and Fabian-Fruges is at once very much attracted to him. George reminds him of himself at that age and he feels very tender towards the child. Fabian-Fruges follows George out of the shop and observes him with great interest. Suddenly he is tempted to transform himself into the boy. He fights this temptation as he has never, he thinks, fought temptation before, for he knows that it would be criminal to steal this child's personality and life. Nevertheless he decides to turn himself into George, kneels down beside him and whispers the formula in his ear, in a state of great emotion and remorse. But nothing happens, and Fabian-Fruges realizes that the magic does not work with the child because the Devil has no power over him.

Fabian-Fruges is horrified at the thought that he might not be able to get away from Fruges whom he dislikes more and more. He feels he is the prisoner of Fruges and struggles to keep the Fabian aspect of himself alive, for he realizes that Fruges lacks the initiative which would help him to escape. He makes several attempts to approach people but fails and is soon in despair, being afraid that Fruges' body will be his tomb, that he will have to remain there until his death. "All the time he got the impression that he was being slowly but surely shut in; that a door which had stood open was now gradually closing on him." Eventually he succeeds in changing himself into a handsome and healthy young man of twenty, called Camille. At this point the author introduces us for the first time to a family circle, consisting of Camille's wife Stéphanie, her cousin Elise, Camille himself, his young brother, and the old uncle who had adopted them all when they were children.

When he enters the house Fabian-Camille seems to be searching for something. He goes upstairs looking into different rooms until he comes into Elise's room. When he sees there his reflection in a mirror he is overjoyed to find that he is handsome and strong but a moment later he discovers that he has actually turned himself into an unhappy, weak, and useless person and decides to get rid of Camille. At the same time he has become aware of Elise's passionate and unrequited love for Camille. Elise comes in, and he tells her that he loves her and should have married her instead of her cousin Stéphanie. Elise, amazed and frightened since Camille has never given her a sign of returning her love, runs away. Left alone in Elise's room Fabian-Camille thinks with sympathy of the girl's sufferings and that he could make her happy by loving her. Then he suddenly thinks that if this were so he could become happy by turning himself into Elise. However, he dismisses this possibility because he cannot be sure that Camille, if Fabian were to turn himself into Elise, would love her. He is not even sure whether he himself—Fabian—loves Elise. While he wonders about this, it occurs to him that what he loves in Elise are her eyes which are somehow familiar to him.

Before leaving the house, Fabian-Camille takes revenge on the uncle, who is a hypocritical and tyrannical man, for all the harm he has done to the family. He also particularly avenges Elise by punishing and humiliating her rival Stéphanie. Fabian-Camille, having insulted the old man, leaves him in a state of impotent rage and goes away knowing that he has made it impossible for himself ever to return to this house in the shape of Camille. But before leaving he insists that Elise, who is still frightened of him, should listen to him once more. He tells her that he does not really love her and that she must give up her unfortunate passion for Camille or she will always be unhappy.

As before, Fabian feels resentment against the person into whom he has turned himself, because he has found him to be worthless; he therefore pictures with glee how Camille, when Fabian has left him, will be received at home by his uncle and his wife. The one person he regrets leaving is Elise; and suddenly it occurs to him whom she resembles. Her eyes have "in them all the tragedy of a longing which can never be satisfied"; and all at once he knows that they are Fabian's eyes. When this name, which he has completely forgotten, comes back to him and he says it aloud, its sound reminds him dimly of "a far country" known only in the past from dreams. For his actual memory of Fabian has completely disappeared, and in his hurry to escape from Fruges and transform himself into Camille he has not taken with him either Fabian's name and address or the money. From this moment onwards the longing for Fabian gets hold of him and he struggles to recover his old memories. It is a child who helps him to recognize that he himself is Fabian, for when the child asks what his name is, he straightway answers "Fabian". Now Fabian-Camille physically and mentally moves more and more in the direction where Fabian can be found, for, as he puts it, "I want to be myself again". Walking through the streets he calls out this name, which embodies his greatest longing, and waits to get a reply. The formula which he has forgotten occurs to him and he hopes that he will also remember Fabian's surname. On his way home every building, stone and tree takes on a particular meaning; he feels that they are "charged with some message for him" and walks on, driven by an impulse.

This is how he comes to enter the old woman's shop which had been so familiar to Fruges. He feels that in looking round in this dark shop he is also "exploring a secret corner of his own memory, looking around his own mind, as it were" and he is filled with "abysmal depression". When he pushes the revolving stand with the postcards on it the squeaking noise affects him strangely. He leaves the shop hurriedly. The next landmark is the reading-room in which, with the Devil's help, Fabian-Esménard was turned into Fruges. He calls out "Fabian" but gets no answer. Next he passes the house where Fabian-Esménard killed Berthe and feels impelled to go in and find out what happened behind that window at which some people are pointing; he wonders whether this is perhaps the room in which Fabian lives, but he is filled with fear and slinks away when he hears the people talking about the murder which was committed three days before; the murderer has not yet been found. As he walks on, the houses and shops become even more familiar to him, and he is deeply moved when he reaches the place where the Devil first tried to win Fabian over. At last he comes to the house in which Fabian lives and the concierge lets Fabian-Camille in. When he begins to climb the stairs a sudden pain grips his heart.

During the three days when all these events took place Fabian had been lying unconscious in his bed, looked after by his mother. He begins to come to and grows restless when Fabian-Camille approaches the house and comes up the stairs. Fabian hears Fabian-Camille call out his name from behind the door, gets out of bed and goes to the door, but is unable to open it. Through the keyhole Fabian-Camille speaks the formula and then goes away. Fabian is found by his mother lying unconscious by the door, but he soon comes to and regains some strength. He desperately wants to find out what happened during the days when he was unconscious and in particular about the encounter with Fabian-Camille, but is told that nobody has come and that he has been lying in a coma for three days ever since he collapsed in the office. With his mother sitting by his bedside he is overcome by the longing to be loved by her and to be able to express his love to her. He wishes to touch her hand, to throw himself into her arms, but feels that she would not respond. In spite of this he realizes that if his love for her had been stronger she would have loved him more. The intense affection which he experiences towards her extends suddenly to the whole of humanity and he feels overflowing with an unaccountable happiness.

His mother suggests that he should pray, but he can only recall the words "Our Father". Then he is again overcome by this mysterious happiness, and dies.

INTERPRETATIONS

I

The author of this story has deep insight into the unconscious mind; this is seen both in the way he depicts the events and characters and—what is of particular interest here—in his choice of the people into whom Fabian projects himself. My interest in Fabian's personality and adventures, illustrating, as they do, some of the complex and still obscure problems of projective identification, led me to attempt an analysis of this rich material almost as if he were a patient.

Before discussing projective identification, which to me is the main theme of this book, I shall consider the interaction between introjective and projective processes which is, I think, also illustrated in the novel. For instance, the author describes the unhappy Fabian's urge to gaze at the stars. "Whenever he stared like this into the all-enveloping night he had a sensation of being lifted gently above the world. . . . It was almost as if by the very effort of gazing into space a sort of gulf in himself, corresponding to the giddy depths into which his imagination peered, was being opened." This, I think, means that Fabian is simultaneously looking into distance and into himself; taking in the sky and the stars as well as projecting into the sky and stars his loved internal objects and the good parts of himself. I would also interpret his intent gazing at the stars as an attempt to regain his good objects which he feels are lost or far away.

Other aspects of Fabian's introjective identifications throw light on his projective processes. On one occasion, when he is lonely in his room at night, he feels, as so often, that he longs "to hear some signs of life coming from the other inhabitants of the building around him". Fabian lays his father's gold watch on the table; he has a great affection for it and particularly likes it because of "its opulence and glossiness and the clearly marked figures on its face". In a vague way this watch also gives him a feeling of confidence. As it lies on the table among his papers he feels that the whole room acquires an air of greater order and seriousness, perhaps

owing to "the fussy and yet soothing sound of its ticking, comforting amid the pervading stillness". Looking at the watch and
listening to its ticking, he muses upon the hours of joy and misery
in his father's life which it has ticked away, and it seems to him
alive and independent of its dead former owner. In an earlier
passage the author says that ever since childhood Fabian "had been
haunted by a feeling of some inner presence which, in some way
which he could not have described, was ever beyond the reach of
his own consciousness. . . ." I would conclude that the watch has
some qualities of a fatherly nature, such as order and seriousness,
which it imparts to his room and in a deeper sense to Fabian himself;
in other words, the watch stands for the good internalized father
whom he wishes to feel ever present. This aspect of the super-ego,
which links with the highly moral and orderly attitude of his
mother, is in contrast to his father's passions and his "gay" life, of
which the ticking of the watch also reminds Fabian. He identifies
himself with this frivolous side too, as is shown in his setting so
much store on his conquests of women—although such successes
do not afford him much satisfaction.

Yet another aspect of the internalized father appears in the shape
of the Devil. For we read that when the Devil is on his way to him,
Fabian hears footsteps resounding on the stairs: "He began to feel
those thudding footsteps as a pulse beating in his own temples."
A little later, when face to face with the Devil, it seems to him that
"the figure in front of him would go on rising and rising until it
spread like a darkness through the whole room". This, I think,
expresses the internalization of the Devil (the bad father), the
darkness indicating also the terror he feels at having taken in such
a sinister object. At a later point, when Fabian is travelling in a
carriage with the Devil, he falls asleep and dreams "that his com-
panion edged along the seat towards him" and that his voice
"seemed to wrap itself about him, tying his arms, choking him with
its oily flow". I see in that Fabian's fear of the bad object intruding
into him. In my "Notes on Some Schizoid Mechanisms" I described
these fears as a consequence of the impulse to intrude into another
person, i.e. of projective identification. The external object intruding into the self and the bad object which has been introjected
have much in common; these two anxieties are closely linked and apt
to reinforce each other. This relation with the Devil repeats, I
think Fabian's early feelings about one aspect of his father—the
seductive father felt to be bad. On the other hand, the moral

322

component of his internalized objects can be seen in the Devil's ascetic contempt of the "lusts of the flesh".[1] This aspect was influenced by Fabian's identification with the moral and ascetic mother, the Devil thus representing simultaneously both parents.

I have indicated some aspects of his father which Fabian had internalized. Their incompatibility was a source of never-ending conflict in him, which was increased by the actual conflict between his parents and had been perpetuated by his internalizing the parents in their unhappy relation with each other. The various ways in which he identified himself with his mother were no less complex, as I hope to show. The persecution and depression arising from these inner relations contributed much to Fabian's loneliness, his restless moods and his urge to escape from his hated self.[2] The author quotes in his preface Milton's lines "Thou art become (O worst imprisonment) the Dungeon of thyself."

One evening, when Fabian has been wandering aimlessly through the streets, the idea of returning to his own lodgings fills him with horror. He knows that all he will find there is himself; nor can he escape into a new love affair, for he realizes that he would again, as usual, grow tired of it very quickly. He wonders why he should be so hard to please and remembers that somebody had told him that what he wanted was a "statue of ivory and gold"; he thinks that this over-fastidiousness might be an inheritance from his father (the Don Juan theme). He longs to escape from himself, if only for an hour, to get away from the "never ending arguments" which go on within him. It would appear that his internalized objects were making incompatible demands on him and that these were the "never ending arguments" by which he felt so persecuted.[3]

---

[1] The various and contradictory characteristics—both ideal and bad—with which the father, as well as the mother, are endowed are a familiar feature in the development of the child's object relations. Similarly such conflicting attitudes are also attributed to the internalized figures some of which form the super-ego.

[2] I have suggested ("Notes on Some Schizoid Mechanisms") that projective identification arises during the paranoid-schizoid position which is characterized by splitting processes. I have pointed out above that Fabian's depression and his feeling of worthlessness gave additional impetus to his need to escape from his self. The heightened greed and denial which characterize manic defences against depression are, together with envy, also an important factor in projective identifications.

[3] In *The Ego and the Id* (1923), Freud writes (p. 38): "If they [the object-identifications] obtain the upper hand and become too numerous, unduly intense and incompatible with one another, a pathological outcome will not be far off. It may come to a disruption of the ego in consequence of the individual identifications becoming cut off from one another by resistances; perhaps the secret of cases of so-called multiple personality is that the various identifications seize possession of consciousness in turn. Even when things do not go so far as this, there remains the question of conflicts between the different identifications into which the ego is split up, conflicts which cannot after all be described as purely pathological."

He not only hates his internal persecutors but also feels worthless because he contains such bad objects. This is a corollary of the sense of guilt; for he feels that his aggressive impulses and phantasies have changed the parents into retaliatory persecutors or have destroyed them. Thus self-hatred, although directed against the bad internalized objects, ultimately focuses on the individual's own impulses which are felt to have been and to be destructive and dangerous to the ego and its good objects.

Greed, envy and hatred, the prime movers of aggressive phantasies, are dominant features in Fabian's character, and the author shows us that these emotions urge Fabian to get hold of other people's possessions, both material and spiritual; they drive him irresistibly towards what I described as projective identifications. At one point, when Fabian has already made his pact with the Devil and is about to try out his new power, he cries out: "Humanity, the great cup from which I shall shortly drink!" This suggests the greedy wish to drink from an inexhaustible breast. We may assume that these emotions and the greedy identifications by introjection and projection were first experienced in Fabian's relations to his primal objects, mother and father. My analytic experience has shown me that processes of introjection and projection in later life repeat in some measure the pattern of the earliest introjections and projections; the external world is again and again taken in and put out—re-introjected and re-projected. Fabian's greed, as can be gathered from the story, is reinforced by his self-hatred and the urge to escape from his own personality.

II

My interpretation of the novel implies that the author has presented fundamental aspects of emotional life on two planes: the experiences of the infant and their influence on the life of the adult. In the last few pages I have touched on some of the infantile emotions, anxieties, introjections and projections which I take to underlie Fabian's adult character and experiences.

I shall substantiate these assumptions by discussing some further episodes which I have not mentioned in the account of the novel. In assembling the various incidents from this particular angle, I shall not follow the chronological order either of the book or of Fabian's development. I am rather considering them as the expression of certain aspects of infantile development, and we have to remember that especially in infancy emotional experiences are not only consecutive but to a large extent simultaneous.

There is an interlude in the novel which seems to me of fundamental importance for understanding Fabian's early development. Fabian–Fruges has gone to sleep very depressed about his poverty, his inadequacy, and full of fear that he might not be able to change himself into someone else. On waking he sees that it is a bright, sunny morning. He dresses more carefully than usual, goes out and, sitting in the sunshine, becomes elated. All faces around him appear to be beautiful. He also thinks that in this admiration of beauty there is not "any of that lustful covetousness which was so apt to poison even his moments of really serious contemplation; on the contrary, he simply admired and with a touch of almost religious respect". However, he soon feels hungry because he has had no breakfast, and to this he attributes a slight giddiness which he experiences together with hopefulness and elation. He realizes, though, that this state of happiness is also dangerous because he must spur himself on to action so as to turn himself into somebody else; but first of all he is driven by hunger to find some food.[1] He goes into a baker's shop to buy a roll. The very smell of flour and warm bread always reminds Fruges of childhood holidays in the country in a house full of children. I believe that the whole shop turns in his mind into the feeding mother. He is engrossed in looking at a large basket of fresh rolls and stretches his hand out towards them when he hears a woman's voice asking him what he wants. At this he jumps "like a sleepwalker who has been suddenly woken up". She too smells good—"like a wheat-field"—he longs to touch her and is surprised that he is afraid to do so. He is entranced by her beauty and feels that for her sake he could give up all his beliefs and hopes. In watching with delight all her movements when she hands him a roll, he focuses on her breasts, whose outlines he can see under her clothing. The whiteness of her skin intoxicates him and he is filled with an irresistible desire to put his hands round her waist. As soon as he has left the shop he is overwhelmed with misery. He suddenly has a strong impulse to throw the roll on the ground and trample on it with "his shiny black shoes . . . in order to insult the sacredness of bread itself". Then he remembers that the woman touched it and "in a passion of thwarted desire he bit

[1] This state of elation is, I think, comparable to the wish-fulfilling hallucination (Freud). which the infant under the stress of reality, in particular of hunger, cannot maintain for long.

furiously into the thickest part of the roll". He attacks even its remains by crushing them in his pocket and at the same time it seems to him as if a crumb were sticking like a stone in his throat. He is in agony. "Something was beating and fluttering like a second heart just above his stomach but something large and heavy." In thinking again of the woman, he concludes with bitterness that he has never been loved. All his affairs with girls had been sordid and he had never before encountered in a woman "that fullness of breast the very thought of which was now torturing him with its persistent image". He decides to return to the shop to have at least another look at her, for his desires seem to be "burning him up". He finds her even more desirable and feels that his looking at her almost amounts to touching her. Then he sees a man talking to her, with his hand laid affectionately on her "milk-white" arm. The woman smiles at the man and they discuss plans for the evening. Fabian-Fruges is sure that he will never forget this scene, "every detail being invested with tragic importance". The words which the man had spoken to her still ring in his ears. He cannot "stifle the sound of that voice which from somewhere within went on speaking yet". In despair he covers his eyes with his hands. He cannot remember any occasion when he has suffered so acutely from his desires.

I see in the details of this episode Fabian's powerfully revived desire for his mother's breast with the ensuing frustration and hatred; his wish to trample on the bread with his black shoes expresses his anal-sadistic attacks, and his furiously biting into the roll his cannibalism and his oral-sadistic impulses. The whole situation appears to be internalized and all his emotions, with the ensuing disappointment and attacks, apply also to the internalized mother. This is shown by Fabian-Fruges furiously crushing the remains of the roll in his pocket, by his feeling that a crumb had stuck like a stone in his throat and (immediately afterwards) that a second and bigger heart above his stomach was fluttering inside him. In the very same episode the frustration experienced at the breast and in the earliest relation to the mother appears to be closely linked with the rivalry with the father. This represents a very early situation when the infant, deprived of the mother's breast, feels that someone else, above all the father, has taken it away from him and is enjoying it—a situation of envy and jealousy which appears to me part of the earliest stages of the Œdipus complex. Fabian-Fruges' passionate jealousy of the man who he believes possesses the baker-woman at night refers also to an internal situation, for he feels that he can hear inside him the man's voice speaking to the woman. I would conclude that the incident he has watched with such strong emotions represents the primal scene which he has internalized in the past. When, in this emotional state, he covers his eyes with his hand he is, I think, reviving the young infant's wish never to have seen and taken in the primal scene.

The next part of this chapter deals with Fabian-Fruges' sense of guilt about his desires which he feels he must destroy "as rubbish is consumed by fire". He goes into a church only to find that there is no holy water in the stoup, which is "bone-dry", and is very indignant about such neglect of religious duties. He kneels down in a state of depression and thinks that it would need a miracle to relieve his guilt and sadness and solve his conflicts about religion which have reappeared at this moment. Soon his complaints and accusations turn against God. Why had He created him to be "as sick and bedraggled as a poisoned rat"? Then he remembers an old book about the many souls who might have come to life but had remained unborn. It was thus a question of God's choice, and this thought comforts him. He even becomes elated because he is alive and "he clasped his side with both hands as if to assure himself of the beating of his heart". Then he reflects that these are childish ideas, but concludes that "truth itself" is "the conception of a child". Immediately after that he places votive candles in all the vacant places in the stand. An internal voice tempts him again, saying how beautiful it would be to see the baker-woman in the light of all these little candles.

My conclusion is that his guilt and despair relate to the phantasied destruction of the external and internal mother and her breasts, and to the murderous rivalry with his father, that is to say to the feeling that his good internal and external objects had been destroyed by him. This depressive anxiety was linked with a persecutory one. For God, who stood for the father, was accused of having made him a bad and poisoned creature. He fluctuates between this accusation and a feeling of satisfaction that he had been created in preference to the unborn souls and is alive. I suggest that the souls which have never come to life stand for Fabian's unborn brothers and sisters. The fact that he was an only child was both a cause for guilt and— since he had been chosen to be born while they had not—for satisfaction and gratitude to the father. The religious idea that truth is "the conception of a child" thus takes on another significance. The greatest act of creation is to create a child, for this means perpetuating life. I think that when Fabian-Fruges puts candles in all the vacant places in the stand and lights them, this means making the mother pregnant and bringing to life the unborn babies. The wish to see the baker-woman in the light of the candles would thus express the desire to see her pregnant with all the children he would give her. Here we find the "sinful" incestuous desire for the mother as well as the tendency to repair by giving her all the babies he had destroyed. In this connection his indignation about the "bone-dry" stoup has not only a religious basis. I see in it the child's anxiety about the mother who is frustrated and neglected by the father, instead of being loved and made pregnant by him. This anxiety is particularly strong in youngest and only children because the reality that no other child has been born seems to confirm the guilty feeling that they have prevented the parents' sexual intercourse, the mother's pregnancy and the arrival of other babies by hatred and jealousy and by attacks on the mother's body.[1] Since I assume that Fabian-Fruges had expressed his destruction of the mother's breast in attacking the roll which the baker-woman gave him I conclude that the "bone-dry" stoup also stands for the breast sucked dry and destroyed by his infantile greed.

III

It is significant that Fabian's first meeting with the Devil happens when he is feeling acutely frustrated because his mother, who insisted that he should go to communion next day, had thereby prevented him from embarking that evening on a new love affair; and when Fabian rebels and actually goes to meet the girl, she does not appear. At that moment the Devil steps in; he represents in this context, I think, the dangerous impulses which are stirred up in the young infant when his mother frustrates him. In this sense the Devil is the personification of the infant's destructive impulses.

This touches, however, only upon one aspect of the complex relation to the mother, an aspect illustrated by Fabian trying to project himself into the waiter who brings him his meagre breakfast (in the novel, his first attempt to assume another man's personality). Projective processes dominated by greed are, as I have repeatedly

[1] I touch here on one of the essential causes for guilt and unhappiness in the infantile mind. The very young child feels that his sadistic impulses and phantasies are omnipotent and therefore have taken, are taking, and will take effect. He feels similarly about his reparative desires and phantasies, but it appears that frequently the belief in his destructive powers far outweighs his confidence in his constructive abilities.

remarked, part of the baby's relation to the mother, but they are particularly strong where frustration is frequent.[1] Frustration reinforces both the greedy wish for unlimited gratification and the desires to scoop out the breast and to enter the mother's body in order to obtain by force the gratification she withholds. We have seen in the relation to the baker-woman Fabian-Fruges' impetuous desires for the breast and the hatred which frustration aroused in him. Fabian's whole character and his strong feelings of resentment and deprivation support the assumption that he had felt very frustrated in the earliest feeding relation. Such feelings would be revived in relation to the waiter if he stands for one aspect of the mother—the mother who fed him but did not really satisfy him. Fabian's attempt to turn himself into the waiter would thus represent a revival of the desire to intrude into his mother in order to rob her and thus get more food and satisfaction. It is also significant that the waiter—the first object into whom Fabian intended to transform himself—is the only person whose permission he asks (a permission which the waiter refuses). This would imply that the guilt which is so clearly expressed in the relation to the baker-woman is even present in relation to the waiter.[2]

In the episode with the baker-woman, Fabian-Fruges experiences the whole gamut of emotions in relation to his mother, i.e. oral desires, frustration, anxieties, guilt, and the urge to make reparation; he also re-lives the development of his Œdipus complex. The combination of passionate physical desires, affection, and admiration indicates that there was a time when Fabian's mother represented to him both the mother towards whom he experiences oral and genital desires and the ideal mother, the woman who should be seen in the light of the votive candles, i.e. should be worshipped. It is true that he does not succeed in this worship in church, for he feels he cannot restrain his desires. Nevertheless, times at she represents the ideal mother who should have no sexual life.

In contrast to the mother who ought to be worshipped like the Madonna there is another aspect of her. I take the transformation into the murderer Esménard to be an expression of the infantile impulses to murder the mother, whose sexual relation with the

[1] As I have pointed out in various connections, the urge for projective identification derives not only from greed but from a variety of causes.

[2] In putting forward this interpretation I am aware that this is not the only line on which this episode could be explained. The waiter could also be seen as the father who did not satisfy his oral expectations; and the baker-woman episode would thus mean a step further back to the mother relation with all its desires and disappointments.

father is not only felt to be a betrayal of the infant's love for her, but is altogether felt to be bad and unworthy. This feeling under- lies the unconscious equation between the mother and a prostitute which is characteristic of adolescence. Berthe, who is obviously thought of as a promiscuous woman, approximates in Fabian- Esménard's mind to the prostitute type. Another instance of the mother as a bad sexual figure is the old woman in the dark shop, who sells obscene postcards which are hidden behind other articles. Fabian-Fruges experiences both disgust and pleasure in looking at obscene pictures, and also feels haunted by the noise of the rotating stand. I believe that this expresses the infant's desire to watch and listen to the primal scene as well as his revulsion against these de- sires. The guilt attached to such actual or phantasied observations, in which sounds overheard frequently play a part, derives from sadistic impulses against the parents in this situation and also relates to masturbation which frequently accompanies such sadistic phan- tasies.

Another figure representing the bad mother is the maid in Camille's house, who is a hypocritical old woman, plotting with the bad uncle against the young people. Fabian's own mother appears in a similar light when she insists on his going to con- fession. For Fabian is hostile towards the father-confessor and hates confessing his sins to him. His mother's demand is, therefore, bound to represent to him a conspiracy between the parents, allied against the child's aggressive and sexual desires. Fabian's relation to his mother, represented by these various figures, shows devaluation and hatred as well as idealization.

IV

There are only a few hints about Fabian's early relation to his father, but they are significant. In speaking of Fabian's introjective identifications I have suggested that his strong attachment to his father's watch, and the thoughts it aroused in him about his father's life and premature end, showed love and compassion for his father and sadness about his death. Referring to the author's remarks that Fabian had ever since childhood "been haunted by a feeling of some inner presence . . ." I concluded that this inner presence represented the internalized father.

I think that the urge to make up for his father's early death and in a sense to keep him alive contributed much to Fabian's impetuous and greedy desire to live life to the full. I would say he was also greedy on his father's behalf. On the other hand, in his restless search for women and disregard of health, Fabian also re-enacted the fate of his father who was assumed to have died prematurely as a result of his dissolute life. This identification was reinforced by Fabian's bad health, for he had the same heart disease from which his father had suffered, and he had often been warned not to exert himself.[1] It would thus appear that in Fabian a drive towards bringing about his death was in conflict with a greedy need to prolong his life, and thereby his internalized father's life, by entering other people and actually stealing their lives. This inner struggle between seeking and combating death was part of his unstable and restless state of mind.

Fabian's relation to his internalized father focused, as we have just seen, on the need to prolong his father's life or to revive him. I wish to mention another aspect of the dead internal father. The guilt relating to the father's death—owing to death wishes against him—tends to turn the dead internalized father into a persecutor. There is an episode in Green's novel which points to Fabian's relation to death and the dead. Before Fabian has entered into the pact the Devil takes him at night on a journey to a sinister house where a strange company is assembled. Fabian finds himself the centre of intense attention and envy. What they envy him for is indicated by their murmuring "It's for the gift . . ." The "gift", as we know, is the Devil's magic formula which will give Fabian the power to transform himself into other people and, as it appears to him, to prolong his life indefinitely. Fabian is welcomed by the Devil's "underling", a very seductive aspect of the Devil, succumbs to his charm and allows himself to be persuaded to accept the "gift". It seems that the assembled people are meant to represent the spirits of the dead who either did not receive the "gift" or failed to use it well. The Devil's "underling" speaks contemptuously of them, giving the impression that they have been incapable of living their lives to the full; perhaps he despises them because they sold themselves to the Devil, and in vain. A likely conclusion is that these dissatisfied and envious people also stand for Fabian's dead father, because Fabian would have attributed to his father—who in fact had wasted his life—such feelings of envy and greed. His corresponding anxiety lest the internalized father would wish to suck out Fabian's life both added to Fabian's need to escape from his self and to his greedy wish

[1] This is an instance of the mutual influence of physical (possibly inherited) and emotional factors.

(in identification with the father) to rob other people of their lives.

The loss of his father at an early age contributed much to his depression, but the roots of these anxieties can again be found in his infancy. For if we assume that Fabian's powerful emotion towards the baker-woman's lover are a repetition of his early Œdipus feelings, we would conclude that he experienced strong death-wishes against his father. As we know, death-wishes and hatred towards the father as a rival lead not only to persecutory anxiety but also—because they conflict with love and compassion—to severe feelings of guilt and depression in the young child. It is significant that Fabian, who possesses the power to transform himself into whomsoever he wishes, never even thinks of changing himself into the envied lover of the admired woman. It seems that were he to have effected such a transformation, he would have felt that he was usurping his father's place and giving free rein to his murderous hatred towards him. Both fear of the father and the conflict between love and hatred, i.e. both persecutory and depressive anxiety, would cause him to retreat from so undisguised an expression of his Œdipus wishes. I have already described his conflicting attitudes towards his mother—again a conflict between love and hatred—which contributed to his turning away from her as a love object and to repressing his Œdipus feelings.

Fabian's difficulties in relation to his father have to be considered in connection with his greed, his envy, and his jealousy. His transforming himself into Poujars is motivated by violent greed, envy, and hatred, such as the infant experiences towards his father who is adult and potent and who, in the child's phantasy, possesses everything because he possesses the mother. I have referred to the author's describing Fabian's envy of Poujars in the words: "Ah! the sun. It often seemed to him that M. Poujars kept it hidden in his pocket."[1]

Envy and jealousy, reinforced by frustrations, contribute to the infant's feelings of grievance and resentment towards his parents and stimulate the wish to reverse the roles and deprive *them*. From Fabian's attitude, when he has changed places with Poujars and looks with a mixture of contempt and pity at his former unprepossessing self, we gather how much he enjoys having reversed the

---

[1] One of the meanings of the sun in his pocket may be the good mother whom father has taken into himself. For the young infant, as I pointed out earlier, feels that when he is deprived of the mother's breast it is the father who receives it. The feeling that the father contains the good mother, thus robbing the infant of her, stirs up envy and greed and is also an important stimulus towards homosexuality.

roles. Another situation in which Fabian punishes a bad father-figure arises when he is Fabian-Camille: he insults and enrages Camille's old uncle before leaving the house.

In Fabian's relation to his father, as in the relation to his mother, we can detect the process of idealization and its corollary, the fear of persecutory objects. This becomes clear when Fabian has turned himself into Fruges, whose inner struggle between his love for God and his attraction to the Devil is very acute; God and the Devil clearly represent the ideal and the wholly bad father. The ambivalent attitude towards the father is also shown in Fabian-Fruges accusing God (father) of having created him as such a poor creature: yet he acknowledges gratitude for His having given life to him. From these indications I conclude that Fabian has always been searching for his ideal father and that this is a strong stimulus towards his projective identifications. But in his search for the ideal father he fails: he is bound to fail because he is driven by greed and envy. All the men into whom he transforms himself turn out to be contemptible and weak. Fabian hates them for disappointing him and he feels glee over the fate of his victims.

V

I have suggested that some of the emotional experiences which occurred during Fabian's transformations throw light on his earliest development. Of his adult sexual life we gain a picture from the period preceding his encounter with the Devil, that is to say when he is still the original Fabian. I have already mentioned that Fabian's sexual relations were short-lived and ended in disappointment. He did not seem capable of genuine love for a woman. I interpreted the interlude with the baker-woman as a revival of his early Œdipus feelings. His unsuccessful dealing with these feelings and anxieties underlies his later sexual development. Without becoming impotent he had developed the division into two trends, described by Freud as "heavenly and earthly (or animal) love."[1]

Even this splitting process failed to achieve its aims, for he never actually found a woman whom he could idealize; but that such a person existed in his mind is shown by his wondering whether the only woman who could fully satisfy him would be "a statue of ivory and gold". As we have seen, in the role of Fabian-Fruges, he

[1] "Contributions to the Psychology of Love: the most Prevalent Form of Degradation in Erotic Life" (1912). *Collected Papers*, Vol. IV (London, 1925), p. 207.

experienced a passionate admiration, amounting to idealization, for the baker-woman. He was, I should say, unconsciously searching all his life for the ideal mother whom he had lost.

The episodes in which Fabian turns himself into the rich Poujars or the physically powerful Esménard, or lastly into a married man (Camille who has a beautiful wife), suggest an identification with his father, based on his wish to be like him and to take his place as a man. In the novel there is no hint that Fabian was homosexual. An indication of homosexuality is to be found, however, in his strong physical attraction to the Devil's "underling"—a young and handsome man whose persuasion overcomes Fabian's doubts and anxieties about entering into the pact with the Devil. I have already referred to Fabian's fear of what he imagines to be the Devil's sexual advances towards him. But the homosexual desire to be his father's lover manifests itself more directly in relation to Elise. His being attracted to Elise—to her longing eyes—was, as the author indicates, due to an identification with her. For one moment he is tempted to turn himself into her, if only he could be sure that the handsome Camille would love her. But he realizes that this could not happen and decides not to become Elise.

In this context Elise's unrequited love seems to express Fabian's inverted Œdipus situation. To place himself in the role of a woman loved by the father would mean displacing or destroying the mother and would arouse intense guilt; in fact, in the story Elise has the unpleasant but beautiful wife of Camille as her hated rival—another mother figure, I think. It is of interest that not until near the end did Fabian experience the wish to become a woman. This might be connected with the emergence of repressed desires and urges, and thereby with a lessening of the strong defences against his early feminine and passive-homosexual impulses.

From this material some conclusions can be drawn about the serious disabilities from which Fabian suffers. His relation to his mother was fundamentally disturbed. She is, as we know, described as a dutiful mother, concerned above all with her son's physical and moral welfare, but not capable of affection and tenderness. It seems likely that she had the same attitude to him when he was an infant. I have already mentioned that Fabian's character, the nature of his greed, envy, and resentment, indicate that his oral grievances had been very great and were never overcome. We may assume that these feelings of frustration extended to his father; for, in the young infant's phantasies, the father is the second object from whom oral gratifications are expected. In other words, the positive side of Fabian's homosexuality was also disturbed at the root.

Failure to modify the fundamental oral desires and anxieties has many consequences. Ultimately it means that the paranoid-schizoid position has not been successfully worked through. I think this was true of Fabian, and therefore he had not dealt adequately with the depressive position either. For those reasons his capacity to make reparation had been impaired and he could not cope later on with his feelings of persecution and depression. In consequence his relations to his parents and to people in general were very unsatisfactory. All this implies, as my experience has shown me, that he was unable to establish securely the good breast, the good mother, in his inner world[1]—an initial failure which in turn prevented him from developing a strong identification with a good father. Fabian's excessive greed, to some extent derived from his insecurity about his good internal objects, influenced both his introjective and projective processes and—since we are also discussing the adult Fabian—the processes of re-introjection and re-projection. All these difficulties contributed to his incapacity to establish a love relation with a woman, that is to say, to the disturbance in his sexual development. In my view he fluctuated between a strongly repressed homosexuality and an unstable heterosexuality.

I have already mentioned a number of external factors which played an important role in Fabian's unhappy development, such as his father's early death, his mother's lack of affection, his poverty, the unsatisfactory nature of his work, his conflict with his mother about religion and—a very important point—his physical illness. From these facts we can draw some further conclusions. The marriage of Fabian's parents was obviously an unhappy one, as is indicated by his father finding his pleasures elsewhere. The mother was not only unable to show warmth of feeling but was also, as we may assume, an unhappy woman who sought consolation in religion. Fabian was an only child and no doubt lonely. His father died when Fabian was still at school and this deprived him of his further education and of prospects for a successful career; it also had the effect of stirring up his feelings of persecution and depression.

We know that all the events from his first transformation to his return home are supposed to happen within three days. During these

---

[1] The secure internalization of a good mother—a process of fundamental importance—varies in degree and is never so complete that it cannot be shaken by anxieties from internal or external sources.

three days, as we learn at the end when Fabian-Camille rejoins his former self, Fabian had been lying in bed unconscious, looked after by his mother. As she tells him, he had collapsed in his employer's office after having misbehaved there, was brought home and had remained unconscious ever since. She thinks, when he refers to Camille's visit, that he has been delirious. Perhaps the author intends us to take the whole story as representing Fabian's phantasies during the illness preceding his death? This would imply that all the characters were figures of his inner world and again illustrate that introjection and projection were operating in him in closest interaction.

VI

The processes underlying projective identification are depicted very concretely by the author. One part of Fabian literally leaves his self and enters into his victim, an event which in both parties is accompanied by strong physical sensations. We are told that the split-off part of Fabian submerges in varying degrees in his objects and loses the memories and characteristics appertaining to the original Fabian. We should conclude therefore, (in keeping with the author's very concrete conception of the projective process) that Fabian's memories and other aspects of his personality are left behind in the discarded Fabian who must have retained a good deal of his ego when the split occurred. This part of Fabian, lying dormant until the split-off aspects of his personality return, represents, in my view, that component of the ego which patients unconsciously feel they have retained while other parts are projected into the external world and lost.

The spatial and temporal terms in which the author describes these events are actually the ones in which our patients experience such processes. A patient's feeling that parts of his self are no longer available, are far away, or have altogether gone is of course a phantasy which underlies splitting processes. But such phantasies have far-reaching consequences and vitally influence the structure of the ego. They have the effect that those parts of his self from which he feels estranged, often including his emotions, are not at the time accessible either to the analyst or to the patient.[1] The feeling that he does not know where the parts of himself which he has dispersed

[1] There is another side to such experiences. As Paula Heimann describes in a paper in this book (p. 240), a patient's conscious feelings can also express his splitting processes.

into the external world have gone to, is a source of great anxiety and insecurity.[1]

I shall next consider Fabian's projective identifications from three angles: (i) the relation of the split off and projected parts of his personality to those he has left behind; (ii) the motives underlying the choice of objects into whom he projects himself; and (iii) how far in these processes the projected part of his self becomes submerged in the object or gains control over it.

(i) Fabian's anxiety that he is going to deplete his ego by splitting off parts of it and projecting them into other people is expressed, before he starts on his transformations, by the way he looks at his clothes heaped untidily on a chair: "He had a horrible sensation in looking at them that he was seeing himself, but a self assassinated or in some way destroyed. The empty sleeves of his coat had, as they drooped limply to the ground, a forlorn suggestion of tragedy."

We also learn that Fabian, when he turned himself into Poujars (that is to say, when the processes of splitting and projection have just occurred), is very concerned about his former person. He thinks he might wish to return to his original self, and being, therefore, anxious that Fabian should be taken home, writes out a cheque in his favour.

The importance attaching to Fabian's name also denotes that his identity was bound up with those parts of himself which were left behind and that they represented the core of his personality; the name was an essential part of the magic formula, and it is significant that the first thing which occurs to him when, under the influence of Elise, he experiences the urge to regain his former self, is the name "Fabian". I think that feelings of guilt about having neglected and deserted a precious component of his personality contributed to Fabian's longing to be himself again—a longing which irresistibly drove him home at the end of the novel.

(ii) The choice of his first intended victim, the waiter, becomes easily understandable if we assume, as I suggested above, that he

[1] I suggested in "Schizoid Mechanisms" that the fear of being imprisoned inside the mother as a consequence of projective identification underlies various anxiety situations and among them claustrophobia. I would now add that projective identification may result in the fear that the lost part of the self will never be recovered because it is buried in the object. In the story Fabian feels—both after his transformation into Poujars and into Fruges—that he is entombed and will never escape again. This implies that he will die inside his objects. There is another point I wish to mention here: besides the fear of being imprisoned inside the mother, I have found that another contributory factor to claustrophobia is the fear relating to the inside of one's own body and the dangers threatening there. To quote again Milton's lines, "Thou art become (O worst imprisonment) the Dungeon of thyself".

stood for Fabian's mother; for the mother is the first object for the infant's identification both by introjection and by projection.

Some of the motives which impelled Fabian to project himself into Poujars have already been discussed; I suggested that he wished to turn himself into the wealthy and powerful father, thereby robbing him of all his possessions and punishing him. In doing so he was also actuated by a motive which in this connection I wish to emphasize. I think that Fabian's sadistic impulses and phantasies (expressed in the desire to control and punish his father) were something he felt he had in common with Poujars. Poujars' cruelty, as Fabian thought of it, also represented Fabian's own cruelty and lust for power.

The contrast between Poujars (who turned out to be ailing and miserable) and the virile young Esménard was only a contributing factor in Fabian's choice of the latter as an object for identification. I believe that the main cause for Fabian's decision to turn himself into Esménard, in spite of his being unprepossessing and repellent, was that Esménard stood for one part of Fabian's self, and that the murderous hatred which impels Fabian-Esménard to kill Berthe is a revival of the emotions which Fabian experienced in infancy towards his mother when she frustrated him, as he felt, orally and genitally. Esménard's jealousy of any man whom Berthe favoured renews in an extreme form Fabian's Œdipus complex and intense rivalry with his father. This part of himself, which was potentially murderous was personified by Esménard. Fabian, by becoming Esménard, thus projected into another person and lived out some of his own destructive tendencies. Fabian's complicity in the murder is pointed out by the Devil who reminds him, after his transformation into Fruges, that the hands which strangled Berthe were only a few minutes ago his own.

Now we come to the choice of Fruges. Fabian has a good deal in common with Fruges, in whom, however, these characteristics are much more pronounced. Fabian is inclined to deny the hold religion (and that also means God—the father) has over him and attributes his conflicts about religion to his mother's influence. Fruges' conflicts about religion are acute, and, as the author describes, he is fully aware that the struggle between God and the Devil dominates his life. Fruges is constantly fighting against his desires for luxury and wealth; his conscience drives him to extreme austerity. In Fabian the wish to be as rich as the people he envies is also very pronounced, but he does not attempt to restrain it. The two also have in common their intellectual pursuits and a very marked intellectual curiosity.

These common characteristics would predispose Fabian to choose Fruges for projective identification. I think, however, that another motive enters into this choice. The Devil, playing here the role of a guiding super-ego, has helped Fabian to leave Esménard and warned him to beware of entering a person in whom he would submerge to such an extent that he could never escape again. Fabian is terrified of having turned himself into a murderer, which, I think, means having succumbed to the most dangerous part of himself— to his destructive impulses; he therefore escapes by changing roles with somebody completely different from his previous choice. My experience has shown me that the struggle against an overwhelming identification—be it by introjection or projection—often drives people to identifications with objects which show the opposite characteristics. (Another consequence of such a struggle is an indiscriminate flight into a multitude of further identifications and fluctuations between them. Such conflicts and anxieties are often perpetuated, and further weaken the ego.)

Fabian's next choice, Camille, has hardly anything in common with him. But through Camille, it appears, Fabian identifies himself with Elise, the girl who is unhappily in love with Camille. As we have seen, Elise stood for the feminine side of Fabian, and her feelings towards Camille for his unfulfilled homosexual love for his father. At the same time Elise also represented the good part of his self which was capable of longing and loving. In my view Fabian's infantile love for his father, bound up as it was with his homosexual desires and his feminine position, had been disturbed at the root. I also pointed out that he was unable to change himself into a woman because this would have represented a realization of the deeply repressed feminine desires in the inverted Œdipus relation to his father. (I am not dealing in this context with other factors which impede the feminine identification, above all castration fear.) With the awakening of the capacity to love, Fabian can identify himself with Elise's unhappy infatuation with Camille; in my view he also becomes able to experience his love and desires towards his father. I would conclude that Elise has come to represent a good part of his self.

I would furthermore suggest that Elise also stands for an imaginary sister. It is well known that children have imaginary companions. They represent, particularly in the phantasy life of only children,

339

older or younger brothers or sisters, or a twin, who have never been born. One may surmise that Fabian, who was an only child, would have gained much from the companionship of a sister. Such a relation would also have helped him to cope better with his Œdipus complex and to gain more independence from his mother. In Camille's family such a relationship actually exists between Elise and Camille's schoolboy brother.

We shall remember here that Fabian-Fruges' overwhelming feelings of guilt in church appeared to relate also to his having been chosen, whereas other souls never came to life. I interpreted his lighting votive candles and picturing the baker-woman surrounded by them both as an idealization of her (the mother as saint) and as an expression of his wish to make reparation by bringing to life the unborn brothers and sisters. Particularly youngest and only children often have a strong sense of guilt because they feel that their jealous and aggressive impulses have prevented their mother from giving birth to any more children. Such feelings are also bound up with fears of retaliation and persecution. I have repeatedly found that fear and suspicion of schoolmates or of other children were linked with phantasies that the unborn brothers and sisters had after all come to life and were represented by any children who appeared to be hostile. The longing for friendly brothers and sisters is strongly influenced by such anxieties.

So far I have not discussed why Fabian in the first place chose to identify himself with the Devil—a fact on which the plot is based. I pointed out earlier that the Devil stood for the seducing and dangerous father; he also represented parts of Fabian's mind, super-ego as well as id. In the novel the Devil is unconcerned about his victims; extremely greedy and ruthless, he appears as the prototype of hostile and evil projective identifications which in the novel are described as violent intrusions into people. I would say that he shows in an extreme form that component of infantile emotional life which is dominated by omnipotence, greed, and sadism, and that it is these characteristics which Fabian and the Devil have in common. Therefore Fabian identifies himself with the Devil and carries out all his behests.

It is significant—and I think expresses an important aspect of identification—that when changing himself into a new person Fabian to some extent retains his previous projective identifications. This is shown by the strong interest—an interest mixed with contempt—which Fabian-Fruges takes in the fate of his former victims, and also in his feeling that after all he is responsible for the murder he committed as Esménard. It shows most clearly at the end of the story, for his experiences in the characters into whom he had turned himself are all present in his mind before he dies and he is concerned about their fate. This would imply that he introjects his objects, as well as projects himself into them—a conclusion which is in keeping with my view restated in the introduction to this paper that projection and introjection interact from the beginning of life.

In singling out an important motive for the choice of objects for identification I have, for the purpose of presentation, described this as happening in two stages: (a) there is some common ground, (b) the identification takes place. But the process as we watch it in our analytic work is not so divided. For the individual to feel that he has a good deal in common with another person is concurrent with projecting himself into that person (and the same applies to introjecting him). These processes vary in intensity and duration and on these variations depend the strength and importance of such identifications and their vicissitudes. In this connection I wish to draw attention to the fact that while the processes I described often appear to operate simultaneously, we have to consider carefully in each state or situation whether, for instance, projective identification has the upper hand over introjective processes or vice versa.[1]

I have suggested in my "Notes on Some Schizoid Mechanisms" that the process of reintrojecting a projected part of the self includes internalizing a part of the object into whom the projection has taken place, a part which the patient may feel to be hostile, dangerous, and most undesirable to reintroject. In addition, since the projection of a part of the self includes the projection of internal objects, these too are re-introjected. All this has a bearing on how far in the individual's mind the projected parts of the self are able to retain their strength within the object into which they have intruded. I shall now make a few suggestions about this aspect of the problem, which takes me to my third point.

(iii) In the story, as I have pointed out earlier, Fabian succumbs to the Devil and becomes identified with him. Although Fabian seemed deficient in the capacity for love and concern even before that, as

---

[1] This is of great importance in technique. For we have always to choose for interpretation the material which is the most urgent at the moment; and in this context I would say that there are stretches of analysis during which some patients seem completely ruled by projection or by introjection. On the other hand, it is essential to remember that the opposite process remains always to some extent operative and therefore enters sooner or later again into the picture as the predominant factor.

soon as he follows the Devil's lead he is completely ruled by ruth-lessness. This implies that, in identifying himself with the Devil, Fabian fully succumbs to the greedy, omnipotent, and destructive part of his self. When Fabian has turned himself into Poujars, he retains some of his own attitudes, and particularly a critical opinion of the person whom he has entered. He dreads losing himself com-pletely inside Poujars, and it is only because he has retained some of Fabian's initiative that he is able to bring about the next transforma-tion. However, he comes near to losing his former self entirely when he turns himself into the murderer Esménard. Yet since the Devil, whom we assume to be also part of Fabian—here his super-ego—warns him and helps him to escape from the murderer, we should conclude that Fabian has not been entirely submerged in Esménard.[1]

The situation with Fruges is different: in this transformation the original Fabian remains much more active. Fabian is very critical of Fruges, and it is this greater capacity to keep something of his original self alive inside Fruges that makes it possible for him gradually to rejoin his depleted ego and become himself again. Generally speaking, I hold that the extent to which the individual feels his ego to be submerged in the objects with whom it is identi-fied by introjection or projection is of greatest importance for the development of object relations and also determines the strength or weakness of the ego.

Fabian regains parts of his personality after his transformation into Fruges and at the same time something very important happens. Fabian-Fruges notices that his experiences have given him a better understanding of Poujars, Esménard, and even Fruges, and that he is now able to feel sympathy with his victims. Also through Fruges, who is fond of children, Fabian's affection for little George awakens. George, as the author describes him, is an innocent child, fond of his mother and longing to return to her. He awakens in Fabian-Fruges the memory of Fruges' childhood, and the impetuous desire arises to turn himself into George. I believe he is longing to recover the capacity for love, in other words an ideal childhood self.

This resurgence of feelings of love shows itself in various ways: he experiences passionate feelings for the baker-woman which,

[1] I would say that however strongly splitting and projection operate, the disintegration of the ego is never complete as long as life exists. For I believe that the urge towards integration, however disturbed—even at the root—is in some degree inherent in the ego. This is in keep-ing with my view that no infant could survive without possessing in some degree a good object. It is these facts which make it possible for the analysis to bring about some measure of integration sometimes even in very severe cases.

in my view, meant a revival of his early love life. Another step in this direction is his transforming himself into a married man and thereby entering into a family circle. But the one person whom Fabian finds likeable and of whom he becomes fond is Elise. I have already described the various meanings Elise has for him. In particular he has discovered in her that part of himself which is capable of love, and he is deeply attracted towards this side of his own personality; that is to say, he has also discovered some love for himself. Physically and mentally, by retracing the steps he has taken in his transformations, he is driven back with increasing urgency closer and closer to his home and to the ill Fabian whom he had forsaken and who by now has come to represent the good part of his personality. We have seen that the sympathy with his victims, the tenderness towards George, the concern for Elise, and the identification with her unhappy passion for Camille, as well as the wish for a sister—all these steps are an unfolding of his capacity to love. I suggest that this development was a precondition for Fabian's passionate need to find his old self again, that is to say for integration. Even before his transformations occurred, the longing to recover the best part of his personality—which because it had been lost, appeared to be ideal—had, as I suggested, contributed to his loneliness and restlessness; had given impetus to his projective identifications[1] and was complementary to his self-hatred, another factor impelling him to force himself into other people. The search for the lost ideal self,[2] which is an important feature of mental life, inevitably includes the search for lost ideal objects; for the good self is that part of the personality which is felt to be in a loving relation to its good objects. The prototype of such a relation is the bond between the baby and his mother. In fact, when Fabian rejoins his lost self, he also recovers his love for his mother.

With Fabian we note that he seemed incapable of an identification with a good or admired object. A variety of reasons would have to be discussed in this connection, but I wish to single out one as a possible explanation. I have already pointed out that in order to identify strongly with another person, it is essential to feel that there is within the self enough common ground with that object. Since

[1] The feeling of having dispersed goodness and good parts of the self into the external world adds to the sense of grievance and envy of others who are felt to contain the lost goodness.

[2] Freud's concept of the ego ideal was, as we know, the precursor of his super-ego concept. But there are some features of the ego ideal which have not been fully taken over into his super-ego concept. My description of the ideal self which Fabian is trying to regain comes, I think, much closer to Freud's original views about the ego ideal than to his views about the super-ego.

Fabian had lost—so it seemed—his good self, he did not feel that there was enough goodness within him for identification with a very good object. There might also have been the anxiety, characteristic of such states of mind, lest an admired object should be taken into an inner world which is too much deprived of goodness. The good object is then kept outside (with Fabian, I think, the distant stars). But when he rediscovered his good self, then he found his good objects as well and could identify with them.

In the story, as we have seen, the depleted part of Fabian also longs to be re-united with the projected parts of his self. The nearer Fabian-Camille comes to the house, the more restless Fabian grows on his sickbed. He regains consciousness and walks to the door through which his other half, Fabian-Camille, utters the magic formula. According to the author's description, the two halves of Fabian are longing to be re-united. This means that Fabian was longing to integrate his self. As we have seen, this urge was bound up with a growing capacity to love. This corresponds to Freud's theory of synthesis as a function of the libido—ultimately of the Life Instinct.

I have suggested earlier that although Fabian was searching for a good father, he was unable to find him because envy and greed, increased by grievance and hatred, determined his choice of father-figures. When he becomes less resentful and more tolerant, his objects appear to him in a better light; but then he is also less demanding than he was in the past. It appears that he no longer claims that his parents should be ideal and therefore he can forgive them for their short-comings. To his greater capacity for love corresponds a diminution of hatred, and this in turn results in a lessening of feelings of persecution—all of which has a bearing on the lessening of greed and envy. Self-hatred was one of the outstanding features in his character; together with the greater capacity for love and for tolerance towards others arose the greater tolerance and love towards his own self.

In the end Fabian recovers his love for his mother and makes his peace with her. It is significant that he recognizes her lack of tenderness but feels that she might have been better had *he* been a better son. He obeys his mother's injunction to pray and seems to have recovered after all his struggles his belief and trust in God. Fabian's last words are "Our Father", and it would appear that at that moment, when he is filled with love for humanity, the love for his father returns. Those persecutory and depressive anxieties

On Identification

which were bound to be stirred up by the approach of death would
to some extent be counteracted by idealization and elation.

As we have seen, Fabian-Camille is driven home by an irresistible
impulse. It seems probable that his sense of impending death gives
impetus to his urge to rejoin the deserted part of his self. For I believe
that the fear of death which he has denied, although he knew of his
severe illness, has come out in full force. Maybe he had denied this
fear because its nature was so intensely persecutory. We know how
full of grievance he was against fate and against his parents; how persecuted he felt by his own unsatisfactory personality. In my experience, the fear of death is very much intensified if death is felt as an
attack by hostile internal and external objects or if it arouses depressive anxiety lest the good objects be destroyed by those hostile figures. (These persecutory and depressive phantasies may of course co-
exist.) Anxieties of a psychotic nature are the cause for this excessive fear of death from which many individuals suffer throughout
their lives; and the intense mental sufferings which, as a few observations have shown me, some people experience on their deathbed
are due in my view to the revival of infantile psychotic anxieties.

Considering that the author describes Fabian as a restless and
unhappy person, full of grievances, one would expect that his
death should be painful and give rise to the persecutory anxieties
which I have just mentioned. However, this is not what happens
in the story, for Fabian dies happily and at peace. Any explanation
for this sudden ending can only be tentative. From the artistic
point of view it was probably the author's best solution. But,
in keeping with my conception of Fabian's experiences which I
have put forward in this paper, I am inclined to explain the unexpected ending by the story presenting to us two sides of Fabian.
Up to the point where the transformations begin, it is the adult
Fabian whom we meet. In the course of his transformations we
encounter the emotions, the persecutory and depressive anxieties
which characterized, as I believe, his early development. But whereas in childhood he had not been able to overcome these anxieties and
to achieve integration, in the three days covered by the novel, he
successfully traverses a world of emotional experiences which in my
view entails a working through of the paranoid-schizoid and the
depressive positions. As a result of overcoming the fundamental
psychotic anxieties of infancy, the intrinsic need for integration comes
out in full force. He achieves integration concurrently with good
object relations and thereby repairs what had gone wrong in his life.

345

14

THE UNCONSCIOUS PHANTASY OF AN INNER WORLD REFLECTED IN EXAMPLES FROM LITERATURE

JOAN RIVIERE

THE inner world which in our unconscious phantasy each of us contains inside ourselves is one of those psycho-analytical concepts that most people find especially difficult to accept or understand. It is a world of figures formed on the pattern of the persons we first loved and hated in life, who also represent aspects of ourselves. The existence even in unconscious phantasy of these inner figures and of their apparently independent activities within us (which can be as real, or more real and actual, to us in unconscious feeling than external events) may seem incredible and incomprehensible; it might therefore perhaps be useful to approach the problem from the opposite end, as it were, that is from the conscious level. My aim in this contribution is essentially to forge a link between certain conscious experiences, which will be familiar to most people, and the proposition that phantasies of our containing other persons inside ourselves, though deeply unconscious, do exist. For this purpose I have selected some relevant passages from literature. Before discussing these, however, I will consider shortly the question why this proposition of internal objects seems so difficult to accept.

It was of course Freud who first recognized the existence of the "introjected object" as a regular phenomenon, a normal part of the personality, namely, in his formulation of the mental institution he called the super-ego, mainly based on the person of the father and represented consciously in our minds by what we call the conscience in each of us. Melanie Klein, however, in her explorations of unconscious phantasy through her work with very young children, has pursued this theme and brought to light much more concerning the persons in the inner world whom each of us individually has felt or feels to be part of himself. There is a difference between

Freud's super-ego, a single differentiated function of our mental make-up, modelled though it may be on the personalities of parents, and the "personal relations", however primitive and fantastic, we have had with the figures who people our inner worlds. When Freud published his *The Ego and The Id* his concept of the internalized parent as the super-ego did not rouse much resistance; it is true that it had already been introduced in a more acceptable form under the title of ego-ideal. Nevertheless, before very long an emotional reaction to the concept of the super-ego was manifested in a new view of analytic therapy; a move for the "dissolution of the super-ego" was even initiated by Alexander at the Salzburg Congress, 1924, and found considerable support at the time. (This view is to be distinguished from the general recognition that the curative effects of analysis are in part attributable to a reduction of the severity of the super-ego.) The point I wish to recall here is the emotional enthusiasm greeting Alexander's idea which virtually stigmatized the independent internal object in the self as something morbid. In the enthusiasm for this view, which Freud himself did what he could to discourage, we had, I think, the first flicker of the suspicion and intolerance often enough manifested against the concept of internal objects.

The "inner world", like other psycho-analytical concepts, meets with a twofold resistance; on the one hand, the incapacity to understand it, and on the other a direct emotional rejection of it as an unwelcome suggestion which is hardly rationalized by serious discussion. Emotional rejection is an acute reaction which arises, as experience teaches, from an acute anxiety; arguments and explanation have little influence on it. When anxiety is not too overmastering, however, one means of allaying it consists in obtaining control of the alarming phenomenon by knowledge and understanding. The urge to master the terrors of superstition and so to find and to make life and the world safer for ourselves was undoubtedly one main source from which scientific curiosity sprang.

The debatable point in question here is that we all had originally and still have in some form an emotional relation with persons felt to exist inside ourselves. When this proposition meets with an intense emotional rejection there is clearly a direct association in the hearer's mind of this idea with danger, as though anything inside one which is not "oneself" pure and simple is and must be dangerous—or pathological; in fact the association of such an idea with madness is often conscious. Less acute reactions can yet be seen to have a similar quality even when the objects inside are not directly imagined as dangerous, but are felt to be *unknown* and therefore alarming. This condition is similar to the common experience of looking into a medical book with drawings of internal organs and feeling extremely repelled—and in effect alarmed—at the sight of things which we "did not know" were inside us. This tendency to fear the unknown[1] plays its part in our difficulties in forming a conscious idea of the internal objects which unconsciously have so much reality to us; on this line of feeling any such unknown relation to objects inside one must be morbid and dangerous. There is, nevertheless, another quality of feeling in us towards such figures, one entirely distinct from this apprehensiveness or suspicion about them. From this other angle these internal figures represent what we most love, admire and crave to possess—they constitute the good properties and aspects in our lives and personalities.[2] The value and beneficence of these figures in us is usually even less in evidence consciously than their bad aspects, since in their good aspects they do not give rise to fear reactions which then become noticeable.

Freud formulated the pleasure-pain principle, but the degree to which it rules our lives often seems overlooked. Melanie Klein's work has emphasized a fact that sounds like a platitude in its obviousness, yet seems not fully recognized in all its simplicity. The life of the emotions which is continuously active in us from birth to death is based on a simple pattern: fundamentally everything in it is either "bad" or "good", nothing is neutral. Events, circumstances, things, people, everything we have to deal with in life and, above all, our own feelings and experiences are felt in the depths as essentially bad, i.e. disappointing, alarming, sad or painful; or good, i.e. satisfying, reassuring, hopeful, happy. Less fundamentally we may be aware of experiences and of our own feelings as mixed good and bad; but offhand and spontaneously, as it were, things in us and about us seem to split naturally into "good" or "bad". One day "all's right with the world", another day "all's wrong"; instinctively there are often no half-measures. I am not to be misunderstood to mean that apparently normal adults are consciously in a mental state approximating to a manic-depressive condition—though that may be less uncommon than is generally supposed. I am saying that there is always a general undertone of feeling even consciously in normal adults,

[1] The tendency discussed by Freud in "The Uncanny", *Collected Papers*, Vol. IV (London, 1925).

[2] Cf. Freud on the good, protective, tender aspects of the super-ego in "Humour", *Collected Papers*, Vol. V (London, 1950).

which can be defined as predominantly good or bad, although the condition will be by no means entirely related to external causes, or even appropriate to the external situation of the person at the moment. There is, however, less conscious awareness of feelings of contentment and satisfaction (unless they arise suddenly from changes for the better) than of unpleasant feelings, because satisfying feelings are taken for granted as our right, whereas an unpleasant state tends to rouse a reaction of protest immediately.

This brings me back to the inner world: good inner objects are to some extent taken for granted. Unless their presence has to be emphasized unconsciously and demonstrably insisted on (e.g. as in peoply who are continually needing praise and recognition—unconsciously *about* their internal goodness), the good things within us do not excite attention and they remain unconscious. This state of things again has its corollary in our relation to our physical bodies; so long as our digestive or other organs are functioning well and are in a "good" condition, we take them for granted and either remain unconscious of them, or it may be that in so far as we are aware of pleasurable bodily sensations they are frequently felt consciously to be self-ordained and self-induced and thus suggest no connection with any other agency internally. It is especially when such sensations are "bad" in some way or may become so that we pay them much attention and recognize their existence; thus it happens that when we are required to recognize the existence of anything inside us, we may almost automatically expect it to be bad and think of it as bad. Along with this expectation there goes as a corollary a constant claim by us that all should be perpetually well and giving no trouble within us, namely, that everything in us should be "good".[1]

At first sight there appears to be no connection between the proposition that we imagine ourselves to contain within us other persons and the sharp differentiation in feeling just described between good or bad states of mind or body which colour all our emotional experiences. But in fact the connection is simple: the people we unconsciously feel to be within us, parts of ourselves or alien to

[1] The words "good" and "bad" are obviously used here in the simplest possible sense—in fact, much as a small child would use them—as expressing the quality of feeling concerned and unrelated to any other standard. Moral judgments, for instance, as to what is good or bad do not necessarily coincide with what is spontaneously felt by the person in himself to be so—often quite the contrary. The same applies to matters of health, of pleasure, of taste; the sole criterion is the pleasure-principle. In the cradle we were all originally in the condition of the despised person who "knows nothing about" any external criteria but "simply knows what he likes", namely, what gives him pleasure or unpleasure; and however much the forms taken by our pleasures may alter as life proceeds, it is fundamentally always on that same principle that our good and bad experiences arise.

ourselves are not neutral, they also are felt as either good or bad. They are essential parts of ourselves and as such we require them to be "good"—perfect, in fact; all our vanity and self-esteem is disturbed if they are not. Melanie Klein's work has clearly shown that the phenomenon of narcissism—one's relation to oneself—is unconsciously bound up with the inner world, the relation one has to the figures inside one and their relation to oneself. But if we feel wrong, guilty, and bad, then one of the purposes for which we need or use our internal objects is that of attributing our own badness to them inside us. Thus our narcissism is relieved and enabled to escape blemish in some degree. This demand that we should have everything in perfection and without pain or effort of course extends beyond our own persons and internal economy to what is outside us, to our external needs, circumstances and belongings; obviously, our narcissism requires that we should have the best of everything outside us as well as inside, e.g. our possessions, reputations, or, say, our children particularly, should have no flaws. The demands of external reality, however, the pressure of Necessity, to quote Freud's phrase, train us to inhibit or modify these egoistic claims in the external world to some degree and at least superficially; whereas in our inner worlds we tend to maintain our infantile assumption of autocratic intolerance of all interference with our self-satisfaction and well-being.

It is not my aim here to give a description of the inner world of unconscious phantasy, still less to give a theoretical exposition of how or why this phenomenon occurs. The work of Melanie Klein and Paula Heimann contains such accounts. But it seems that the following illustrations, which may help to bridge the gap between a difficult concept and conscious understanding, should be prefaced with a few provisos to obviate misunderstandings.

Although in psycho-analysis we speak of the inner world, it must be remarked that this phrase does not denote anything like a replica of the external world contained within us. The inner world is exclusively one of *personal* relations, in which nothing is external, in the sense that everything happening in it refers to the self, to the individual in whom it is a part. It is formed solely on the basis of the individual's own urges and desires towards other persons and of his reactions to them as the objects of his desires. This inner life originates at least at birth and our relation to our inner world has its own development from birth onwards, just as that to the external world has. Our relation to both worlds is at first of an extremely primitive character, based on bodily needs such as sucking at the breast; this relation comprises also the emotional elements, the love and hate, springing from our two main instincts—desire and aggression—at first felt only in relation to such limited objects as the nipple or breast. (But to the baby this one and only object is to begin with the be-all and end-all of existence.) The bodily sensations of taking in and containing are accompanied by the emotional corollary of pleasure, or of pain when frustration occurs, in varying degrees.

These early experiences of taking in, with their accompaniment of emotional pleasure, constitute the foundation and prototype of the phantasy-process of internalization, which persists throughout life in more developed forms as a main feature of our mental functioning. The inner world of our instinctual objects in its primitive form is thus first peopled with our mother and father or the parts of them internalized at this time, e.g. by the sucking act or by looking, perceiving and registering within; and those two persons remain as the prototypes of all our later developed reactions with other persons. In later life, moreover, these objects, external or internal, no longer need be exclusively persons, but may be represented by non-human, inanimate, or abstract interests. To the infant in particular, in whom life is governed by pleasure and pain, both his own feelings and the objects to whom they refer are never neutral; both his feelings and his objects are either pleasurable or painful, good or bad. For the infant, moreover, it is especially characteristic that his own bad painful sensations and impulses may be projected internally and attributed to his inner people or parts of them, which to some extent he feels are not himself, thus helping to relieve his fears about inherent or uncontrollable evil or danger in himself. The sway of pleasure or pain diminishes with growth and the course of later development progresses beyond the stage at which the internalized figures are so much needed in their original primitive forms; we can become less dependent on our objects, both external and internal, less subject to the crudely violent forces felt both in our own spontaneous impulses and in the good and bad objects whom we love and hate. As we gradually assimilate and work over into components of ourselves the good and bad properties we recognized in our loved and hated parents, or with which we endowed them, their nature as distinct and separate entities in ourselves alters, recedes and diminishes. The residue of these primitive figures in us, formed so largely on our own primitive characteristics,

Joan Riviere

will ultimately consist mainly of qualities or characters in our personality which still retain and crystallize the strong charges of emotional feeling once attaching to the original persons from whom they are derived.

Nevertheless, in the depths our loving or hating relationships to the good or bad mother and father remain—an experience in our past life which is unconsciously indestructible and which on occasions becomes reactivated and relived, its reality re-established. At moments such as these in adult life, poets and writers have become aware of this reality in the depths and have sometimes been able to transmute it into convincing expression.

In my first example a poet describes his inward possession of his beloved who in the outside world is far away, while he nevertheless has her clasped within himself.

> Absence, hear thou my protestation
> Against thy strength,
> Distance and length;
>
> . . . .
> . . . .
>
> To hearts that cannot vary
> Absence is presence;
> Time doth tarry.
>
> My senses want their outward motion,
> Which now within
> Reason doth win,
> Redoubled by her secret notion;
> Like rich men that take pleasure
> In hiding more than handling treasure.
>
> By absence this good means I gain,
> That I can catch her
> Where none can watch her,
> In some close corner of my brain:
> There I embrace and kiss her,
> And so enjoy her, and none miss her.[1]

These lovely lines express with matchless simplicity a happening that no one who has ever loved can have failed to experience—undisclosed and unconsidered though it may ordinarily be. It constitutes a feature of human experience, part of the human heritage. We should find allusions to it in most of the famous love-letters of history; but a poet alone can bring such an experience out into full daylight.

[1] John Donne, 1573–1631.

352

Yet the description given in this poem of a relation to another person inside oneself confirms the proposition of the existence of an emotional inner world only to a special and limited extent. It relates to only one person contained within the speaker—his beloved—and she and his relation to her are in the highest degree "good"—in fact, they are idealized, as is typical in a highly developed love-relation. This idealization of the loved one is achieved, as we know, by the process of divesting him or her of all unwelcome or evil associations and locating them elsewhere; a splitting into two, good and bad aspects, of the original single object of both love and hate has taken place. A strong denial is then set up that the pair, the good and bad figures, can have anything in common; they are kept at opposite poles. The denial or banishment of all "badness"—pain, deprivation or danger—in the relation to the loved one is very explicitly represented in the poem quoted. Its message consists in a denial, a "protestation" against the plain emotional fact that the absence of the loved one is painful, and this denial it is which produces the idealization of the situation and also results in its fantastic quality.

The driving force behind the poetic creation reveals itself, though in the setting of an adult love-relation, as one of the simplest, if not the most primordial of all human reactions—namely, fear of the loss and the craving for possession of something outside oneself, here another person, on which one's life seems to depend. The inevitable reaction to this need must be the drive to obtain possession of such an object, to acquire it, absorb it and make it one's own. Food would be the evident prototype of such a desire and need; and the earliest experience in life of such a longing, and of the joy expressed in the poem, must be the infant's craving for his or her mother along with the life-giving breast she represents, and the phantasy of taking her into the self in order nevermore to be without her. This primordial human phantasy belongs of course to the order of instinctual impulses classed as cannibalistic, although the overmastering intensity of the love-longing and the terror of loss which are inherent elements in it were not originally appreciated by those psycho-analysts who first recognized the existence of such impulses in all human beings.[1] It is through Melanie Klein's work that we are now able to understand the common meaning and origin of what appear to be two such totally unrelated human experiences of incorporation as that of the poem and those cannibalistic acts which take place in

[1] Cf. Freud, "Mourning and Melancholia", for the relation between loss and incorporation of the object.

Joan Riviere

dreams or in savage rites. Yet there is again an undeniable link between the two in the physical impulse that often becomes conscious in the intensity of sexual passion to incorporate the loved one by biting and absorbing, as well as by clasping and embracing. Devouring with the eyes, too, is perhaps the commonest, because the least prohibited, of all activities between lovers.

In all these forms the wish to incorporate a desired object is manifest and conscious; as such it cannot be denied. What is denied, however, to conscious recognition is that all these and many similar manifestations are but varied expressions of a major human tendency. Each of such examples can be treated as an isolated phenomenon, belittled as unimportant or without significance; the associations between them which build them into a whole are kept unconscious, so that the inevitable inferences are ignored. In referring above to the infant's earliest experience of this desire to incorporate whatever is intensely craved and needed, I quoted the fear of its loss as one great incentive. This fear is in fact an indissoluble element of the wish; desire on the one hand, and fear of frustration, still more of total deprivation of desire's fulfilment on the other, are but two aspects of *one* emotion. Now the superficial disregard of the intensity and significance of human impulses to possess and incorporate operate largely by admitting the wish to some extent, it is true; though denying it any "meaning". But it operates still more by total denial and exclusion of the great factor of *fear of loss* from which so largely springs the dynamic process of this wish to possess. The fundamental connection between the two is plainly manifest in one universal human response, namely, in the reflex action of hugging and embracing, clasping and clinging to a person (or a thing) which one has regained after a parting or loss. Because it is regarded as so natural, the significance of this quite unequivocal expression of a desire to incorporate what has been (and therefore may be again) lost remains unrecognized.[1] In my view it is our rejection of and blindness to our dread of total loss and deprivation of good objects which results in the lack of understanding of these manifestations and the failure to recognize that in the vast field of human life this dynamic causation is a constant force.

In the poem I have quoted this fear is actually expressed, though the main content of ecstatic joy in it almost entirely outweighs the allusions in it to fear. "To *hearts that cannot vary*, absence is presence;

[1] The relation between the symptom of kleptomania and experiences of deprivation in early life has been to some extent recognized.

354

time doth tarry": it is clear that the pain which is being extinguished by the thought of the beloved's secret presence inside himself, her "secret notion", is not that merely of her absence, but of the fear that her heart may vary; if she is not with him she is loving and giving herself to another, *she has left him*, not merely in the flesh but with her love, and he has *lost her finally*. It is hinted at too in the last verse, where he insists on the secrecy of his possession, as if he would have lost her if she were known to be his. Those who are familiar with Donne's love-poems will know how constant and repetitive in them, despite their wealth of unique imagery and the varied forms of love-relation described, these two themes are: the rapturous union of the lovers is yet invariably shot through with the dread of loss of her and her love. A few of the poems consist simply of the certain expectation of this loss, or of his absolute conviction of it and his own intense despair.

I will digress here from my main point for a moment to refer to the middle verse of the poem in question:

> "My senses want their outward motion
> Which now within
> Reason doth win,
> Redoubled by her secret notion"

.   .   .   .   .

In the poem's plainspoken description of the incorporation of an object it is interesting to find direct illustrations of the following themes: a withdrawal of cathexis from external objects leading to the reinforcement of narcissistic pleasure (Freud); compensation for disappointment by an external object by turning to the internal counterpart object (Klein); the suggestion contained in it that narcissistic well-being depends on or is greatly augmented by the existence of good internal objects (Klein); and the "manic" quality (Klein) of the idea that the phantasy of inward possession of the loved one "redoubles reason". Even if "Reason" in the seventeenth century did not mean exactly what it connotes to us to-day, the prevalent split between reason and feeling was already well established; no doubt it was born or reborn in the Renaissance. Was Donne's peculiar melancholy and tendency to despair, which epitomizes one aspect of the Renaissance spirit, perhaps an expression of grief and mourning for the coming degradation in Western life of the status of feeling and for the foreseen victory of intellect and objectivity over feeling and subjective experiences? And is his use of the word "reason" here a flat repudiation of the truth that he does *not* possess the objective person of the beloved, and a direct assertion that the omnipotence of his subjective thought can override and arrogate to itself the omnipotence of external reality? "Time doth tarry!"

To revert to my theme: that the fear of loss is a dynamic factor in the need to possess and incorporate. There is much to be understood about this fear of loss, and the more so by reason of our blindness to it and refusal to take it into account. Why should we unconsciously have such an "unreasoning" expectation and terror of loss? To begin with, all terrors are to be regarded as fears of some kind of loss. Freud regarded castration as the greatest fear in man (and woman) and that consists of the loss of the penis. This view did not satisfy everyone. Ernest Jones found a deeper and broader explanation of anxiety in his suggestion that it is rooted in the fear of "aphanisis", the loss of the capacity for experiencing pleasure in life, ultimately sexual pleasure. Finally, the work of Melanie Klein has shown that whereas both these roots of anxiety are true and valid, there is a yet deeper source of fear—fear of the loss of life itself.[1] All fears are intrinsically related to the deepest fear of all: that in the last resort any "loss" may mean "total loss"; in other words, if it persists or increases, loss may mean loss of life itself and unconsciously any loss brings that fear nearer. All fears come back to the fear of death: to the destructive tendency that might be called the capacity for death in oneself, which must be turned outward in aggression if it is not to work out in and on oneself. Yet in turning this destructive force outward the loved and needed objects become its target and so the danger of their loss arises. Faced with the loss of them and their death, as a result of one's own destructiveness and hate, one's own death appears imminent; thus the fear of "total loss" takes shape. It is ultimately the fear of death which is behind our cravings to acquire, possess, and incorporate, behind our greed and sadism and the predatory aspects of our modes of life.

And why should this fear be so acute in human beings and lead to so many differences between us and the rest of animal life? Here I think Freud gave us an answer, though he did not explicitly link it with the craving to possess and acquire: Freud was always impressed with the lengthy period of immaturity which human beings alone are subject to, with the long condition of dependence and helplessness of our early years. He clearly felt that it had fateful conse-

[1] See her papers, especially "Anxiety and Guilt", Ch. VIII, also "Notes on the Life and Death Instincts", Ch. X, by Paula Heimann, in *Developments in Psycho-Analysis*, London, 1952.

quences on our psychical development, even if he did not altogether succeed in formulating them.[1] Thus, as I see it, the helplessness and dependence of human children must, in conjunction with their phantasy-life, presuppose that the fear of death is even part of their experience. They cannot maintain themselves; absence of the parents, the means of life, entails loss of life. Even to-day in this country children die of neglect by the parents; older children see it happening. Many people have conscious memories of their terror as small children of being turned out by their parents to starve, as it might be. The small child's ego is quite sufficiently rational to appreciate its dependence on adults, and in addition in its phantasies the angry and revengeful parents threaten it with starvation, exposure, and all the terrors of death at their hands, which the child has willed that the parents shall undergo. It may well be that the id, which represents the mental expression of life and death instincts in fusion, cannot experience their total defusion and the extinction of life until bodily death ensues. But the ego, of which there is some nascent core from the very beginning of life, must have some capacity in that direction, since self-preservation is its primary function. To the unconscious of the child the worst terror, as Freud recognized, is that of the loss of the parents' love, and that loss means loss of all their needed goodness and in its place incurring their hate and revenge, so being alone and destitute with death as the consequence. This frightful thought is plainly dealt with by many and various methods of defence, among which denial of any such possibility or any such fear will be one of the first. Such an idea thus becomes inaccessible and taboo.[2]

We cannot escape the conclusion that an intense fear of dying by active aggression or passive neglect is a fundamental element in our emotional life, is as deeply-rooted in our unconscious minds as life itself and is barricaded off from conscious experience by every known mechanism of defence.[3] My thesis is that this fear is one fundamental source of the danger and terror giving rise to the drive to *incorporate* whatever is longed for and needed and the loss of

[1] Freud's decisive rejection of the possibility of an unconscious fear of death evidently played its part in this. Even if this view represents an aspect of truth, it appears to be only a partial one.

[2] I mention these objective factors in their bearing on a child's feelings and phantasies, not because I believe them to be a first cause of the fears in question, the root of which lies in a child's own instinctual endowment, but because such factors and their influence are denied and ignored by adults.

[3] I cannot here discuss the point further, but would refer the reader to recent papers on the topic by Melanie Klein and Paula Heimann, notably Chapters VIII and X in *Developments in Psycho-Analysis* (London, 1952).

Joan Riviere

which is dreaded. But in what sense does life depend on security in the love and possession of loved and needed persons, so that they must be internalized and kept alive within? It is true that people as well as animals are known to pine away and die when their loved ones vanish. We are not concerned here with material realities only; death is not only a matter of whether the breath leaves the body and the heart ceases to beat. That is one item of the experience of death, it is true; but is that all that death means to us? It is probably the most important factor in death because it is irrevocable, and thus all else that death means becomes irrevocable: namely, the cessation, the disappearance, so comparatively sudden, of a living existence, an entity, a person, a personality, a most complex and composite structure of attributes, tendencies, experiences, memories, idiosyncrasies good and bad, as well as the body they belong to. It is all this which disappears; from one moment to the next it was here and it is gone. So when one fears one's own death, it is all that which one will lose, one's "life"—in both senses—one's present breath of life, and one's "past life" out of which one's identity is constituted. And evidently it is to the loss of the latter, bound up with the death of the body, that the fear of death largely relates; the belief in the immortality of the soul even points to the wish that the death of the body might be negligible if only the personality could survive.

This complex personality of ours, unique in every individual, then, is what we cling to in life.[1] And now I must consider what this personality consists of, how it is composed. We tend to think of any one individual in isolation; it is a convenient fiction. We may isolate him physically, as in the analytic room; in two minutes we find he has brought his world in with him, and that, even before he set eyes on the analyst, he had developed inside himself an elaborate relation with him. There is no such thing as a single human being, pure and simple, unmixed with other human beings. Each personality is a world in himself, a company of many. That self, that life of one's own, which is in fact so precious though so casually taken for granted, is a composite structure which has been and is being formed and built up since the day of our birth out of countless never-ending influences and exchanges between ourselves and others. They begin with heredity and are succeeded by every emotional experience undergone as the days of life pass; and every one of these emotional experiences is

---

[1] The fear of the *loss of one's own identity*, by the disintegration and splitting of the ego, can be seen to be one of the most acute and painful anxieties accompanying or underlying schizophrenic disorders.

358

bound up in feeling with one or more other persons in our lives, with "loved and hated objects". From the earliest and simplest infantile situations of receiving or giving pleasure, of receiving or giving frustration and pain, of love of power, of hatred of authority or necessity, of fear of losses—from life itself to loss of the imperatively claimed, needed and desired persons on whom and on whose life our life depends—from these ultimates have expanded all our experiences, memories, qualities and idiosyncrasies which form our own identity —our loves and hates, our likes and dislikes, our habit of mind, our tendencies and reactions—every one of which is ultimately founded on experiences with other persons in our lives and every one of which is an integral part of our personality. These other persons are in fact therefore parts of ourselves, not indeed the whole of them but such parts or aspects of them as we had our relation with, and as have thus become parts of us. And we ourselves similarly have and have had effects and influences, intended or not, on all others who have an emotional relation to us, have loved or hated us.[1] We are members one of another.

All this, which must be theoretically well known and obvious to any analyst, still seems to be insufficiently appreciated by us emotionally. We cling to the fiction of our absolute individuality, our independence, as if we owed nothing to anyone and nothing in us had been begged, borrowed or stolen. I will not go into the motives which create and maintain this fiction—the deep-rooted egoisms omnipotent self-importance, the denial of debts which demand to be repaid; I will only point in passing to this attitude as another facet of the lack of comprehension of—resistance against— the notion of other individuals being within us and yet parts of ourselves. Nevertheless, there are moods and there are moments when we can be and are deeply conscious of the extent to which our lives and our being are interwoven with those of others. Everyone realizes at times, and normally with strong feeling, how much his life and his experience, if not his character and personality, is or has been enriched by a relation with other men and women (whether or not consciously he includes his parents among them). One thinks of the phrase "To have loved her is a liberal education".

Now it is not without significance that such moments most commonly occur in two particular situations: on the one hand, it is

[1]As will be seen, what I have here attempted to describe in non-technical terms is something of the operation of introjection and projection in the formation of the personality, though excluding arbitrarily for the moment the dynamic instinctual forces behind their functioning.

characteristic that the awareness of boons and benefits derived through
the relation with another is part of the state of being in love, and
especially when the love is returned; the other situation in which
such emotions are typical is that of mourning the death or loss of
someone whose value to one has been very great.[1] When, however,
the awareness of all that one has gained in experience and personality
from other people is connected with their loss this recognition of
what such a person has meant to one is manifestly bound up with
conscious *memories*. It can be said perhaps that the nearest a normal
person, at any rate in the Western culture, comes to conscious realization of his own inner world is through the processes of memory.
When we think such a thought as "I shall always have him or her
with me wherever I go", what we consciously mean is that our
memory of the person is so vivid and established so firmly in us that
it is part of ourselves and cannot be lost. We can see them with
"that *inward eye* which is the bliss of solitude", as Wordsworth says.

The experience and functions of "memories" in the life of the
emotions is a large subject, not yet adequately explored. Memories
have perhaps been awarded a somewhat back-handed evaluation in
psycho-analysis. To begin with, Freud credited them with being the
origin of neurotic symptoms, after which we all expected to unearth
traumatic incidents in the childhood of our patients. Since those days
other factors in ætiology have come into the foreground, and we
hear far less of "memories". But this is too superficial a description of
what has happened. Analysis is not now seen so much as the process
of recovering the memory of certain specific early events, but as a
process in which every significant *relation* to others throughout life,
whether permanent, constant, temporary, or incidental, has to be recalled and realized; all the important emotional experiences of one's
life comprise the "memories" which the analysis of to-day finds it
necessary to recover, and these important experiences consist, as we
know well, as much or more of feeling and phantasy in reference to
other persons as of real occurrences in which they figured. What
matters is what we "did with them inside ourselves" (a phrase used
by a patient) "in our own minds", usually much more than what
happened with them outside in "real life". The memories to be recovered in analysis consist so much of these inner happenings, to
which external events such as we consciously call memories are often

[1] It would seem to be worth remarking that they are both situations in which a measure of
defusion of instincts has taken place; for the time being either Eros or Thanatos has gained
some victory and the equilibrium which balances on so many compensatory denials has given
way.

not much more than labels or signposts—in a sense but "screen-memories". As such nevertheless they have their great emotional importance to us; just as a person's name, which is but a label, can represent his whole being to us.

I will now illustrate this significance of past memories in our lives with another verse—a more familiar and, because it expresses such a universal experience, even a hackneyed one.

> . . . "At moments which he calls his own,
> Then, never less alone than when alone,
> Those whom he loved so long and sees no more,
> Loved and still loves—not dead, but gone before—
> He gathers round him."[1]

The meaning which is conveyed to us consciously by these lines is that the poet, when alone, becomes so deeply immersed in his thoughts and memories of those whom he has loved and lost by death that they seem to him to be still alive as they were in the past and their death and absence is thus for the time annulled. We recognize this to be a natural and familiar experience and so we attribute this meaning to the poem. In fact, however, the poet does not say that at all; he says nothing whatever about memory or the past. He simply says that when he is alone loved ones whom he no longer sees can be called to him, and he is then not alone, for he has them round him. His words are based on the assumption that they are *still present* and available to him; his words contradict the supposition that his relation with them lies in the past and can be enjoyed no longer. Yet it is incontestable that what this poetic phantasy relates to in external reality is his acts of absorption when alone in thoughts and memories of his *past*. The contradiction which is so remarkable here between past and present is to be resolved only in one way, namely, by the realization that the two opposites, past and present experience, are one and the same thing—two aspects of *one phenomenon*. It represents very much more than the banal fact that memories are always present with us to be called up when required. The appeal of these lines to so many thousands rests on their forthright statement that all those who have been emotionally important to us are still with us and inseparable from us—the unconscious truth behind the words being that they are *in us* and part of us and therefore inseparable and available to us. Memory, relating to external events and to the corporeal reality of loved figures as beings distinct from ourselves, is one facet of our relation to them; the other facet is

[1] Samuel Rogers, *Human Life*.

361

the life they lead within us indivisible from ourselves, their existence in our inner worlds.[1]

I will digress here to give a significant instance of these two facets of a relation to another, past and present, coming to expression in one and the same breath, as it were. R. L. Stevenson was a writer whose mind was unusually open to the idea that other persons can be contained in oneself, whether for good or ill; such stories as *Dr. Jekyll and Mr. Hyde* and *The Bottle Imp*, for instance, are evidence enough. In his essay, "The Manse", he gives a picture of his grandfather's house and the grandfather himself, as he saw him and remembered him from his own childhood—silver hair, pale face, aloofness, the solemn light in which he was beheld in the pulpit, a somewhat awful figure. He wonders what of himself derives from this old minister, and would like to have inherited his noble presence.

"I cannot join myself on with the reverend doctor; yet all the while, no doubt, and even as I write the phrase, *he moves in my blood and whispers words to me*, and sits efficient in the very knot and centre of my being."[2] The whimsical R.L.S. then goes on most sensibly and plausibly to describe the converse: not only is the grandfather alive in him now, but he, R.L.S., was alive (part of him) in the grandfather when *he* was young, and went to school in him and was thrashed perhaps by Dr. Adam, and fell in love and married a daughter of Burns's Dr. Smith, and heard stories of Burns at first hand. "I have forgotten it but I was there all the same." So his past memories of the actual grandfather he knew in his childhood slide imperceptibly into his present phantasies of containing his grandfather alive in him now and of being alive in him before he himself was born. Time doth tarry in this inner world, indeed.

The two poems I quoted represent first and foremost the psychological truth that other persons can exist within us; besides

[1] It will be seen that in the lines from *Human Life* the poet does not actually state in words that these men and women are alive *in him*. The phrase he uses is that they can be gathered "round him". The content of the poem, however, states that they are not dead but are *still present to him*, and it is of interest to find that he chooses the idea that they are "round him" to express this thought since it is one of the most frequent symbols for internal objects. As Melanie Klein has mentioned in *Contributions to Psycho-Analysis*, p. 303, also p. 333 note, a house, a car, a train or whatever contains people commonly represents the inner world; and conversely, whatever is closely round a person or on top of him (close but invisible) may represent his internal objects. Another aspect of the inner world, its mysterious, inaccessible quality, is also commonly represented symbolically by *far away*, by *looking into space*, both not tangible, incapable of exploration; again, by *farthest away*, equivalent to nearest, one's own inside; by *looking into a mirror*, into one's own inside; or by *the sky, heaven high above*, inaccessible, unknowable and again *above*.

In the lines quoted the explicitly omnipotent character of the poetic phantasy, together with the speaker's *solitude*, are further indications of inner world phantasy-manipulation.

[2] (My italics) *Memories and Portraits*.

expressing this thought more or less unequivocally, however, both these poems at the same time refer manifestly to situations of the loss of loved objects in external reality by death or absence. I tried to show in these two cases the special compensatory connection between external loss and internal acquisition or possession. This particular causative connection does not, however, exhaust the functions or significance of internal objects in our minds; and though I am not inclined to suppose that this dynamic element can ever be entirely inoperative during life, there are other and equally important factors at work which create and maintain our inner worlds.

It is an essential element in these poems that the persons inside, or spoken of as "round", the speaker are exclusively those he feels great love for. Not only is there no question in these instances of any alarm or revulsion at the idea of alien entities existing within the self; on the contrary, it is precisely the assurance that "good", loved and loving, ones are present that serves to ward off alarm in the speaker's mind and recoil from thoughts of loneliness, sadness and despair. In the case of Donne's poem about *Absence* I pointed to the extreme idealization in it as an inherent feature of the phantasy-situation: the implied idealization and perfection of the beloved herself has radiated and extended into the ecstasy of possessing her which the poet actually describes. In the lines from *Human Life*, too, there is a strong idealization of the man's relation with the dead men and women from his past: there is in it the asseveration that nothing but love is felt for them or by them. What is assumed in the first poem is explicit in the second, that it is the presence of the *love*-feelings between the speaker and those he can recall and possess that gives rise to the happiness, the fulfilment, reassurance, and peace they express and constitutes the effective barrier against the depression, loneliness, and alarm more natural in such a situation.

It appears therefore that these two poems would have had no meaning and served no purpose without their content of strong predominating love-feelings: anything indifferent or antagonistic in the speaker's relation with those within him must be totally excluded. And it is equally clear that just as it is the strong accentuation on possessing love which successfully excludes the thoughts of loss, so the emphasis on the loving relation between those concerned just as effectively averts the thought of any hostility, hurtfulness, or pain between them. What is explicitly denied in the poems is the experience and the fear of loss, as I commented to begin with; what is implicit in the poems is that the loss feared and denied is specifically of the *love* in the relation with another human being. Thus we see, what as analysts we already know, that the loss and absence of loved ones can be equivalent in our unconscious to *lack of love*, hostility, hate, even malevolence, in them to us and in us to them. Donne's poems betray the failure of love, the tendency to cynicism and despair, behind which lies the dread of hate, in his jealous expectations of losing the beloved. The second poem, about those who have died, cannot fail to remind us that the dread, guilt, and hate felt towards the dead in the unconscious, and the projected hate they feel for us, which psycho-analysis recognized so early, inevitably play their part here, and that the essential impulse prompting the verse is to dispel this fear. If love is not present there will be hate, there must be hate. Deep in the dynamic reservoir of instinctual forces, in the id, Eros the life and Thanatos the death force are in never-ending strife, one always aiming at ascendancy over the other. Whether in absence, or in death, or in other situations of estrangement, the intolerable fear rises that it is our own deadly hate which brings about the loss; and the greater is the love, the more hate is feared.

This brings me back to the split between love and hate, and between loved and hated, good and bad, objects, which I discussed to begin with; the simple "good or bad" pattern of our emotional life. I referred to the prevailing expectation we have that anything unknown, "not oneself" and alien inside us must be bad and dangerous, and to the corresponding claim and assumption that everything belonging to and part of us *must* be good—in itself a denial of the fear that it is not. I have further tried to show that our loving and hating of others relate as much (and more crudely) to their aspects inside us as to those outside us. In our earliest days, but later in life too, when the self within feels full of ruthless egoism or hate, destructive and painful, intense anxiety arises, both for ourselves and for the endangered objects; the violence of the fierce greed and hate raging within, and felt to be uncontrollable, is unutterably terrifying. It is then omnipotently denied and dissociated from the self, but is attributed instead to the persons inside who are the objects of the hate or greed, and are then felt to have provoked hate by their hate. It is they who are felt as bad: envious, robbing, ruthless, murderous. Thus it happens that a good helping person or part of a person, who was needed and craved, changes shape and turns into a terrifying and dangerous enemy inside one; one is felt to be "possessed of a devil" inside.

The bad objects within thus take their origin from our own dangerous and evil tendencies, disowned by us; characteristically therefore they are felt as "foreign objects", as an incubus, a nightmare, an appalling, gratuitous and inescapable persecution.[1] This phantasy-situation takes particular symptomatic form in hypochondriasis, in which the feelings about the evil persons who are parts of oneself are replaced consciously by feelings about various organs or parts of the body supposed to be diseased and dangerous.[2] Thus the persons outside us whom we once needed and depended on as life-giving come to be taken into us in phantasy; as they then become attacked and hated for further satisfactions they come to represent our own evil, until they are at the opposite pole and personify death-dealing influences. Then a defence against this danger will be sought by externalizing them again, projecting and finding them outside in the external world, in the effort to rid the self of them again.

The projection of persecutory phantasies concerning the inner world has manifestly found its most widespread expression in the myths of frightful and horrible forms of existence, e.g. as in nether worlds, notably in the Hell of medieval times. Such regions are explicitly of an "inner" description, circumscribed and contained, and the inmates are immured *within* them; their underground siting links, among other things, with the inner depths of the unconscious and the "bad" inner world.[3] Hell is a mythological projection of a personal region within the individual in which all one's own "bad", cruel, torturing and destructive impulses are raging against the "badness" of others and vice versa; the fires of Hell too symbolize the guilt and shame, not felt by the persecuted as part of them and arising spontaneously, but as attacking them aggressively. Dante's *Inferno* is the classic portrayal of this inner life.

Apart from descriptions of such terrible regions, there are in literature of course innumerable instances of less generalized representations of the bad inner world, transposed into the external world. Modern poetry abounds in them; such, for instance, as in

[1] The classical and emotionally most significant example of these unconscious phantasies of inner activities with and by inner objects is that of the primal scene, the parents in intercourse, typically of a monstrous and unutterably terrifying character, inside one. By the child originally they are felt as enacting what one set of urges in him is aiming at with each of them, but these aims are denied as his own and transferred on to them.

[2] For a study of hypochondriasis, see Paula Heimann, *Developments in Psycho-Analysis*, (London, 1952), Ch. IV.

[3] The symbolic association of the *lower* parts of the body and the "lower" aspects of human nature with the deep internal regions of Hell and the sadistic-anal and genital allusions in this context have long been recognized by psycho-analysis.

Joan Riviere

T. S. Eliot's *Waste Land* and also in his *Murder in the Cathedral*, where the action takes place in the innermost sanctuary *inside* a sacred building. The cathedral represents both the person of the thinker in his most precious and valued aspects, his highest aspirations and capacities—love, truth, nobility and so on—as well as the inside of the idealized mother's body. In the depths, nevertheless, the bloody outrage happens with its accompaniments of desecration, ruin, and corruption. The idealization of creative love and goodwill breaks down and the persecution by evil, in the murder of the father by the son, resurges within it.

The fears of malevolent and dangerous beings inside us unconsciously representing those we love, desire, hate, misuse, and treat despitefully, and thus by our own persecution of them transform into persecutors of us, are, moreover, bound up in a particularly complex and specific way with the detailed phantasies relating to the act of their incorporation. I have already attempted to give some general idea of the way our lives and personalities are interwoven with those of others and how we become integral parts of them and they of us. I shall now quote a passage from a love-story which puts into words something of the emotion belonging to the act of incorporating another and even expresses some details in the process which are part of the underlying unconscious phantasy itself.

In this story, a man who believes his beloved to be far away comes back unexpectedly at night to a house where he and she had once spent much time, but actually he discovers her there. They talk; and then after a silence:

"What are you thinking of?" she said.
"Can I think of anything but you?" I murmured, taking a seat near the foot of the couch. "Or rather, it isn't thinking; it is more like a consciousness of you always being present in me, complete to the last hair, the faintest shade of expression, and that not only when we are apart but when we are together, alone, as close as this. I see you now lying on this couch, but it is only the insensible phantom of the real you: the real you is in me. How am I to know that the image is anything else but an enchanting mist?
"I will tell you how it is. When I have you before my eyes there is such a projection of my whole being towards you that I fail to see you distinctly. I never saw you distinctly till after we had parted and I thought you had gone from my sight for ever. Then you took body in my imagination and my mind seized on a definite form of you for all its adorations—for its profanations too."[1]

Not only does the writer give us here an absolutely explicit description of one human being's act of incorporation of another,

[1] Joseph Conrad, *The Arrow of Gold*, p. 283.

366

but he tells us of several accompaniments of the process. There is again the association of it with parting and loss which I have dwelt on already. There is the statement that the other whom he has within him is *more real* than the woman outside him, thus bringing into the foreground the connection between the directness and immediacy of the experience and the unconscious instinctual sources of our being, the *reality* of sensation, emotion, and the surges of instinct in us being so much more actual and vivid than any perceptions of the external world. It is here that lies the origin of the mystical tendencies in human nature, bound up as they are with immediate experience of body and mind; their explanation is found in phantasies of bodily incorporation, union, fusion, and inner possession.[1] In the quotation above there is, further, a direct statement of the phantasy of self-*projection* into the object which appears to be bound up and simultaneous with the process of *introjection* of the object; this is a most remarkable direct intuitive emergence into the author's conscious thought of the deepest unconscious processes which only through the work of Melanie Klein have now been uncovered and recognized in a scientific sense. Finally and most important is the last sentence in the passage: "you took body" in me and my mind "seized" you, "for its adorations *and its profanations too*".

This final utterance it is which completes the picture; with this nothing is left out. In spite of the intensity of the love which infuses the speaker and his words, the phantasy of incorporating another person is not here bound up, as it is in the other cases quoted, with an idealization of the lover's feelings. Ruthless and egoistic impulses towards the woman are scarcely veiled in his speech and purely antagonistic hate and revenge are almost manifest in it. The egoism of the lover and his hate of the frustrating object are here felt by him *as part of his love of her* and are recognized by him as such. There is a differentiation of his motives indeed into "adorations and profanations", but here it does not develop fully into the split between love and hate, good and bad, the split of idealization *versus* persecution, with the persecutory aspects denied and obliterated; in this passage the fundamental truth of their co-existence is laid bare. The open admission of intense love, longing, craving for possession, hand in hand with the impulse to profane

[1] These phantasies of "projective identification" are the kernel of the "cannibalistic" stage of development, already mentioned; they accompany the earliest oral phase of breast-feeding, the former being in any case an offshoot of impulses and phantasies belonging to the latter.

367

Joan Riviere

—to maltreat, abuse, and degrade—is almost unique and it yields the solution to all our problems about the inner world. Those whom we love and crave for—first the mother, and later the long procession of all who come after her—who "take body" in us, whom we seize, devour, and immure, we have not only loved, not only yearned to be fed by and to feed, not only longed to satisfy and delight, but have craved to engulf and possess for ourselves and to use for our own ruthless purposes, in total disregard of their needs, and have wreaked on them the greed and savage impulses that are inherent in us along with our capacity for love. These savage impulses gain ground when love and desire are frustrated; they spring from the forces of death in us which are reinforced when love fails, and the fear of such danger to the self within impels us to direct them outward on to the other. In its primitive form perhaps the impulse to possess and incorporate the desired object can be regarded as a sort of half-way process, a manifest fusion of Eros and Thanatos, a compromise between loving and killing, in which both have a share but neither prevail and by means of which the life of both subject and object is felt to be secured. Nevertheless, in one of its aspects it entails the imprisonment, subjection, and torture of the loved, desired, and hated objects, and from that circumstance spring the torments and agonies suffered by them and by us in our inner worlds. Thus it is that one and the same figure in our inner worlds can bear two different aspects, can be felt as ideally perfect, without a flaw, or as vile and monstrous, as bounteously loving and protecting, or as terrifying and persecuting.

Now to conclude I will come back from the theme that good and bad cannot be isolated from each other, that all life and therefore ourselves contain them both in varying degrees, to the corollary of this that none of us can be isolated, that each of us is a company of many, and that our being is contained in all those others we have been and are occupied with as we live, just as they are contained in us. The following translation of verses by a French poet expresses this aspect of life with the peculiar concrete realism of such phantasies.

> The stream of life went past me and I looked for my body there
> All those who followed on and on and who were not myself
> Were bringing one by one the pieces of myself
> There I was built up piece by piece as one erects a tower
> The men and women piled up high and I appeared —myself
> Who had been made of all the bodies all the stuff of man

368

The Unconscious Phantasy of an Inner World reflected in literature

Times past—passed out—ye gods who made me
As you lived so I in passing only live
My eyes averted from the empty future
Within myself I see the past all gaining growth

Nothing is dead but what is yet to come
Beside the luminous past to-morrow is colourless
And shapeless too beside what perfectly
Presents at once both effort and effect[1]

My attempt has been to convey some introductory idea, as it were, of the phantasies we all unconsciously create of harbouring others inside ourselves. I have scarcely touched on what they are, what we feel they do with us or we do with them.[2] I have wished to show that even the *conscious* phantasy of other beings existing within us is not in the least uncommon in the imagination of man, and is far from being an outrage on human nature or a sign of derangement. The understanding of the part played in our lives by the *unconscious* phantasy can only come through the widening knowledge of psycho-analysis.

[1] Le cortège passait et j'y cherchais mon corps
Tous ceux qui survenaient et n'étaient pas moi-même
Amenaient un à un les morceaux de moi-même
On me bâtit peu à peu comme on élève une tour
Les peuples s'entassaient et je parus moi-même
Qu'ont formé tous les corps et les choses humaines
Temps passés Trépassés Les dieux qui me formâtes
Je ne vis que passant ainsi qui vous passâtes
Et détournant mes yeux de ce vide avenir
En moi-même je vois tout le passé grandir

Rien n'est mort que ce qui n'existe pas encore
Près du passé luisant demain est incolore
Il est informe aussi près de ce qui parfait
Présente tout ensemble et l'effort et l'effet

Guillaume Apollinaire: *Alcools*, p. 57, 1920.
[2] In my paper (p. 370) on "The Inner World in Ibsen's *Master-Builder*" some pathological aspects of the activities of internal objects are illustrated.

15

THE INNER WORLD IN IBSEN'S MASTER-BUILDER

JOAN RIVIERE

IN my paper "The Unconscious Phantasy of an Inner World reflected in Examples from Literature"[1] I brought together a few instances from poetry and prose in which a conscious awareness of containing other persons inside them, and of themselves existing in others, is more or less directly acknowledged by the writers. Here I have chosen a different kind of illustration of this theme, one in which conscious awareness of having beings inside one is not quite directly expressed, although it does appear in a special guise; nevertheless the whole meaning and content of the work has this and can have no other significance. It is a play; and the allusions in it to what is happening in the inner world are not occasional and transitory, nor are they elaborately overlaid by a realistic pattern of everyday life. The whole action and even the characters belong so predominantly to the inner world that the entire drama is a representation of that world; and moreover, to such a degree is this so that from the standpoint of external life the story seems to have no apparent motivation, and to some has even appeared ridiculous. The play is Ibsen's *Master-Builder*, whose meaning and message remains as mysterious to-day as it was when first performed more than fifty years ago, when nearly all the critics reacted to it with contempt.[2] In spite of its insoluble and fantastic story, however, the play has

---

[1] See p. 346.

[2] This play was written by Ibsen in 1892; the English translation by E. Gosse and W. Archer was published by Heinemann in February, 1893. The play was put on in London in the same month by E. Robins and H. Waring. In a preface to the translation dated May, 1893, E. Gosse refers to the "delightful want of proportion between the scorn of the British critics on the first appearance of the book and the excessive and sustained curiosity of the public itself". The critics, with few exceptions, "explained to us at once that the *Master-Builder* would fall still-born from the press and would not be tolerated an hour upon the stage". It was pronounced "fantastic balderdash devoid of the slightest interest"; "a bewildering farrago of tiresome rubbish". Admittedly, Gosse says, *what it all means* is of course the crux; he also admits that "the faith of the two translators in the play's acceptability for the stage was at times far from robust", until the enthusiasm of E. Robins relieved their minds.

from the beginning had a profound appeal, drawing audiences and moving them by powerful emotional forces in it which yet defy precise definition.

A full psycho-analysis of Ibsen's *Master-Builder* would be of great interest; here I shall give only a sketch of it and deal chiefly with the references in it to the inner world. The story is that of a builder, Solness, who has reached the pinnacle of success in his profession and has apparently attained everything or almost everything that life has to offer. In spite of being supreme, however, with his whole environment at his service, he is revealed as moody and unreasonable, overtly or tacitly harsh to all and preyed upon by anxiety. In particular he has intense feelings of insecurity in regard to the future, dread of being superseded by "the younger generation", and he is haunted by the past. Alongside the story of his fears and his final fate, there is woven into the play the theme of dæmonic forces influencing and impelling him both for and against his will. More than once Solness recounts solemnly, with awe and some uncertainty, that something he had "wished and willed—silently and inwardly—" had come to pass; for instance, when he first met the young woman who was betrothed to his assistant he silently wished very ardently to attract her to him, to make a "helper and server" of her—a phrase which is constantly on his lips—in order to keep the young man under him by her means; and then the next day she appeared, assuming she was to work for him as his book-keeper! In these connections casual references are made in the play to hypnotism or thought-transference, but no weight attaches to them. The weight of feeling lies in Solness's personal experience that some power in him which is not fully himself, but which he is responsible for, is at work on people round him. Conversely, he himself is restrained or impelled by an inner force, "held back as by a hand" from some actions without understanding or strength to resist, and driven or lured on to others.

The major action of the play takes place between the Master-Builder and a young girl, Hilda, a remarkable character; with her appearance the dæmonic forces advance into the foreground and are treated between him and her almost as real, at first playfully, later in all seriousness. They are named and defined; the major power is the "troll" or dæmon; there is also another category of minor beings, less magical and great than the dæmon, who work for his ends, to carry out good tasks or evil acts for him. They are "his good or bad spirits", "black or white devils", and they are aligned with the helpers and servers in the real world, such as the book-keeper, whom he puts his spell upon and uses to do his will. Although this feature of the drama no doubt contributed to the scorn originally cast on the play by the English critics, the gravity and depth of feeling which invests these mysterious forces in the minds of his characters is in fact conveyed to the reader or spectator with inescapable conviction by the masterly power of Ibsen's art.

The play opens by introducing us to the Builder's past, the effects of which are persecuting and troubling him now. Solness began as a poor boy from a country village, worked his way up as a builder and has had astounding luck. When an old firm of architects became bankrupt he took the owner and his son into his office and exploits their experience and abilities to offset his own lack of training on the technical side of building. Now this old architect is worn out with illness, hate, and despair, and is very near death, though still working in an effort to prevail on Solness to allow the son some recognition and some work on his own account, so that he may attain the independence and success he deserves before the father dies. Solness's persecutory dread of being ousted by the young makes it impossible for him to agree; he refuses brutally and insists on the young man remaining as his assistant. To achieve this end we see how he has been impelled even to exert his powers of fascinating women over the book-keeper in his office who is betrothed to the young architect, so that she becomes enslaved by him and is in this way secretly used to keep his hold on the young man and maintain his supremacy.

This situation contains the play's most realistic aspect; there is nothing incomprehensible in it. And unconsciously it is virtually an Œdipus situation; the builder is the son who unconsciously forced himself into the father's place, ruined and enslaved him; now the young couple represent the parents who would ruin him in retribution if they could be united and defy him. But he still decoys the woman, prevents their marriage, makes her no return, and by his secret use of her love and her misery keeps the man in his power. As the play develops, this aspect of the story which deals mainly with external reality, and predominantly with the man's relation to his father, recedes into the background, and the matter becomes more and more fantastic. We regress, as it were, from the genital Œdipus position to the man's primary relation to his mother, and with that the forces of the inner world begin to emerge into the picture.

The Master-Builder's success had also been greatly assisted in the past by another piece of "luck". Twelve years before, soon after his marriage, the gloomy old family mansion inherited by his wife from her parents, in which he and she lived, was burnt to the ground and the insurance compensation obtained from it enabled him to extend his business very substantially. But this advantage was accompanied by a tragedy; his young wife had given birth to twin sons just before the fire, and the shock and effects of the catastrophic destruction of her home and of her removal with the babies during the fire had disastrous consequences for her and them. She lost her milk; the babies died and she was thrown into a depression from which she will never recover. We see her now as a withdrawn and depressed figure, almost without contacts, either sunk in melancholy, self-reproaches and regrets or mechanically occupied with her "duty" in small household tasks; alongside these aspects, moreover, she manifests penetrating suspicion and jealousy of Solness's relations with younger women, such as at the beginning with the book-keeper. The unconscious significance of this past trauma in the hero's relation to his wife and her possessions is clear; it represents the child's pregenital sadistic relation to his mother. The fire—it transpires that he had imagined and wished for a fire to abolish the dreary old mansion of her family and to supply him with funds for his own building—the fire represents his attack on the mother's body; it destroys her breasts, the children in her, as well as her parents inside her, represented by their house. He is left with the ashes, the sterile lifeless wife and pile of fæces, the gold—and with his terrors, of the "younger generation", those murdered children breaking in as avengers in place of the parents.

The Master-Builder's own emotions and morbid fears and phantasies are soon expressed, when he tells the family doctor that his wife's suspicions of his affairs with young women have no basis in fact, but that still he does not relieve her mind about them. Her suspicions are a "salutary self-torture" to him; to endure them "is like paying off a little bit of a huge immeasurable debt; he can breathe more freely for a while"; it relieves *his* mind that she should *doubt* him. He goes on with an access of paranoid feeling: the doctor has been "set on by his wife to draw him out; the wife believes he is crazy—mad—and the doctor is to detect it". Then his "fear of his luck turning" bursts out in panic: "It terrifies me—terrifies me every hour of the day. Sooner or later my luck must turn. I know it—I feel the day approaching. One of the younger generation will come knocking at the door, saying 'Give *me* a chance' and all the rest will come clamouring after him and shouting 'make room for us, make room, make room'. . . . Then there's an end of Halvard Solness! It means retribution." Since his guilt is rooted in his unconscious relation to his father and mother, Solness never defines the crime for which he expects this retribution. In external life there are no sufficient grounds for it; the doctor laughs at his fears, expostulates at his talk of madness, reminds him of his success. He is guiltless in fact of the actual fire that destroyed his wife's happiness and health and the children. Even his hidden tyrannical and dishonourable exploitation of the old architect and his son and the son's bride would not give grounds for anticipating such a calamity. It is evident that such anxieties derive from his inner world; clearest among its characters is his "sick conscience", the super-ego, which in him is not an integrated ego-ideal guiding and controlling him, but a horde of pursuers terrifying and persecuting him, spectres of his own id, the inner unconscious greed and ruthless egoism of his own youth.

The action of the play now moves suddenly from past to present. There is a knock at the door and a young girl walks in, and with her Solness's inner world and his relation with those in it comes to the fore. Hilda is a completely fantastic and unique creation; she exerts a magnetic attraction on some and in some she produces a revulsion. Solness yields to her spell; although she is not a "good figure" in the ordinary sense of the word, she is the best, the only "good" that Solness can entertain. His first reaction to her is his invariable one; she is another piece of "luck" which he will use for his own ends. But we see that she is not, like the hapless real human beings, his to exploit and enslave; she is a dæmonic force herself and becomes at last the antithesis of his luck. She proves to be his doom; in her dæmonic struggle to enslave and exploit *him*, she forces him to a virtual suicide and he is killed before her eyes. So the younger generation in the person of one young girl, instead of the many young men he feared, carries out the retribution Solness had so mortally dreaded.

None of this is apparent on the surface. As I said, the meaning of Hilda and Solness's relation to her is the enigma of the play. We see dimly that her influence over him is finally disastrous; we feel a catastrophe impending, but we do not know how or why. Hilda's other-world origin, her personification of Solness's inner self and inner objects is not hinted at directly; although she herself and the nature of her acquaintance with him are, if not incredible, exceedingly unusual.

Ten years before Solness had built a church with a high tower on it in Hilda's native town and she as a child of eleven had watched the celebrations at its completion, when he had climbed to its pinnacle by the scaffolding and had hung a wreath there. The little girl was intoxicated by the excitement of the incident, cheered and sang among the loudest, afterwards waylaid him in her father's house, evoked such a response in him that he kissed her ardently, promised her to come back "like a troll" for her in ten years' time, make her a Princess and give her a kingdom. It is ten years to the day when she walks upon the stage and says she has come for her kingdom!

She is life, youth, vitality personified, blooming health, above all, independence, self-assurance, and fearless daring. She comes alone, walking with a pack from her home miles away, indifferent to ordinary feminine concerns; there is more than a hint of masculinity in her. What she lives for is dangerous excitement; she will defy everything for that. The episode ten years before when she saw Solness court danger and overcome it, even with the added danger of her wild shouting, intoxicated her, filled her with an infatuation for him which was sealed that evening by the excitement of his sensual responses and his glittering promises to the little girl. The craving for dangerous excitement in her so fully roused that day has possessed her all the ten years since then; she has waited in the assured belief that this hero-father of her dreams will fulfil her hopes and raise her beside him to the dizzy pinnacle of her "kingdom".

With her entry, two poles of an emotional state become personified in her and the Master-Builder; where life offers him only a decline into gloom and danger she incarnates sunshine, youth, and promise; he is uncertain, irascible, full of torment, while she is gay assurance and determination that she can gain her ends. She is thrilling with daring and defiance against any opposition, in contrast with the shuddering dread of madness, the torturing terror of retribution that we catch clear sight of in him. She can be gentle and understanding to his unhappy wife, while he alternates between agonies of remorse and harsh intolerance towards her. In the heart of his house the cold empty rooms of the dead children still remain; in the heart of Hilda is the vision of her castle in the air, the Princess enthroned over all.[1]

[1] There could not be a plainer representation of the manic defence personified in Hilda, as against the depressive and persecutory anxieties which are overwhelming the Builder.

When Hilda arrives, Solness is first amused with her, regarding her as of no importance, and then he attempts to make use of her—in the office. Her contempt for this suggestion has its effect and he is gradually impressed by the totally forgotten incident of his promise to her years before and by the insistence of her demands on him to fulfil it. When she proudly declares that "no one but he should be allowed to build at all", she is "not such a child as he thought". He cannot do without her; she shall be his ally; with her he will triumph over his fears. She too is the "younger generation", as he has yearned for it, however, and not as he feared it. He will pit her against the generation he dreads; it shall be "youth marching against youth". "He needs her"; he even feels he "called her to him"; he has been "torturing himself trying to remember something he had forgotten" and he "never had the slightest inkling what it could be!" His inner dæmon has stood between; the "hand has held him back". He will no longer be the "half-mad, crazy man" he is, ground down by the dæmon of his super-ego, with his "terrible burden of debt" to his wife. He tells Hilda the story of the fire and the dead children: "And now I am chained alive to a dead woman—I who *cannot* live without the joy of life!" But to look at Hilda is "like looking at the sunrise", "like the dawn of day".

The meaning, unconscious or not, of Hilda's phantasy of the Princess and the kingdom is plainly to capture for herself the hero-father who had so entranced her in her identification of him with the high tower he had built up and climbed up. But in her too, as in Solness, the genital relation to the love-object cannot develop fully. She shows womanliness and goodness at moments, but they struggle with the aggressive greed in her and are lost. The woman's oral greed towards the man and his penis, the urge to seize and absorb them sadistically, to become fused with them in masculine identification and to triumph in possession of them "on top of the world", is insuperable; Hilda cannot surrender fully to love for a man. To the audience the tension of the drama consists largely in the question whether the need of Solness and Hilda for each other will or can develop normally, at any moment whether they will or will not fall into each other's arms. Though they know and refer to the possibility of that, they avoid it. It does not happen. Instead we see repeatedly how "the hand holds them back"—one of the forces of the other world, the internal dæmon in one of his shapes, always interposes. There can be no happy ending to their story.

They avoid thinking of the future; they talk of the past, for the inner forces which inhibit their relation are figures from the past, from their *pre*-genital existence. Hilda diagnoses the "sick conscience" in Solness; she yearns for a "strong, radiant, robust conscience, for then one *could dare* to do what one would". She talks of Vikings, who captured and carried off the women they desired; Solness says there is something of the bird of prey in her and she bursts out "Why not? Why shouldn't *I* carry off the prey I want, get my claws into it and do what I want with it! There are dæmons in women as well as in men."

They talk about the dæmon, and the black and white spirits. The dæmon shows one the vision, the illusion, "the *impossible*"! which yet beckons and calls, attracts and allures irresistibly. One has a faculty, says Solness, for desiring, craving, *willing* a thing so inexorably that it *has* to happen; and the good and bad spirits and devils, the helpers and servers, must play their part too if it is to come out right; but they must be *called*, they never come of themselves. The fire happened because he never stopped thinking of a fire and never mended a chimney which might have caused a fire.[1] So those who *did* cause the fire were merely his helpers and servers, his black or white spirits; and so it *is* his fault that the children died and his wife's life is ruined. "That's what people call having all the luck; but what does this kind of luck make you feel! It's like a great raw place here on my breast, and the helpers and servers keep flaying off pieces of flesh from *other* people in order to heal my wound— but still it never heals—never, never!" He created homes, happy homes, with the money from the fire; but the terrible price he had to pay for it; he had to forgo for ever the home *he* might have had, "with a troop of children, and a father and mother too!" The ruin of his wife's home and her illness have destroyed it. "The dæmon within me has drawn all the life-blood out of her; and the spirits too do it for *my happiness!*" "All I have done and succeeded in has to be made up and paid for with *other* people's happiness—over and over and over again—for ever!" "The fight I am fighting has cost heart's blood enough. And I'm afraid the helpers and servers won't obey me any longer. Retribution is inexorable."

Hilda cries out at this: "Do you want to take from me what is more than my life?" (What is that?) "The longing to see you great,

[1] The devil who held his hand back was his own greed which meant to have a fire and profit by it, and also his father or mother whom *he* had thought so greedy.

to see you again with a wreath in your hand, high, high up upon a church-tower." For her, life consists in her illusions, her phantasies. Where Solness tried to escape from necessity and frustration by imposing his will on reality and forcing it to his pattern, she tries to escape them, and guilt and persecution too, by denying reality and living in idealized dreams, as she did for ten years in dreaming of her Master-Builder's return. The factor of illusion, the snares and the trickery of the dæmon, along with his compulsions and denials, in a sense constitutes the major theme of the play. Indeed, such is the capacity of both Solness and Hilda for illusion that in this analysis it might seem that their grandiosity merits nothing but ridicule. But in the play itself, under the hands of Ibsen, we are moved to much compassion by their pitiful struggles. Solness describes how he had first built his churches out of a pure and heart-felt devotion to God and his glory; but he "found he was tricked"; God wanted more and more for Himself. *God* put the dæmon into Solness and made him able to lord it over everyone, gave him the devils to burn his home down, but all so that Solness should build more and more for *His* glory. So the Builder swore he would be even with God, he achieved the impossible, in spite of his terror of heights; one day, when Hilda saw him, he climbed the tower he had built and defied God. Thenceforth he would build no more churches, only happy homes. But that was all delusion too—God's turn came again. "Happy homes are not worth a straw, Hilda. Now I *see* it. People don't want their homes—not to be *happy* in! I shouldn't have been able to enjoy it if I'd had one." It is all a de-lusion: "Children and parents cannot be and don't want to be happy together" is what he means. So, he says, nothing, nothing comes of it all. "Castles in the air is all one *can* build." Everything is trickery. At one moment of miserable indecision he says "Oh, there are innumerable devils that you *never see*. If only you could always tell if it's the white or the black ones that have got hold of you!"

A new tower on a new house he is building is to be finished that evening; Hilda has been insisting that he must climb it and again set a wreath on the height; he must grant her that pleasure "to see him great again". His wife, who knows his dizziness and mortal dread of heights, is in terror at the thought. But as Hilda sees her kingdom on earth with Solness fade farther and farther off, with the figure of the broken and helpless wife coming ever more and more between them, she takes her last refuge in this desperate throw. Castles in the air are what they *shall* build; the Master-Builder *shall* place the wreath on the tower to-night, and silently he accepts her will. He climbs to the top, but as he waves to her and she to him, he falls. The beginning of his story was tragedy and the end must be so, for them both: disillusionment and dispossession for her, retribution and death for him.

★   ★   ★

And who and what then precisely are the people of the inner world who appear, as I claim, so plainly in this play? The inner world starts to be formed in us along with our perceptions of the outer world; the prototypes of its inhabitants consist therefore in our earliest instinctual objects: mother, father, and the family, and the figures who are their successors in later life. It is these figures in the guises they wear in the inner world whom we find dramatized and effecting the action in the play. Superficially, the dæmon and the white spirits or black devils are not to be taken seriously; that is so, but though they are imaginary personifications and names, they are names given by Solness to something that is serious and is real, that has actual power and directs the lives of the real bodily persons with far stronger influence than any rational motives do.

The dæmon, who is the king of this underworld, is not difficult to identify. He is a figuration of that part-object, the great penis, the essential source of life and death, of magic power for good or evil. Though this magic penis is a separate entity, it originates as the father's penis and is always related to him. The father-figure himself in the Builder's inner world is clearly represented by two figures: one the old architect whom he forces into his service, whose ability and whose young son (both representing the father's potency) Solness grinds down and keeps in slavery for himself. The other father-figure is represented by God, in the story of Solness's first delusional belief that he was building for God's glory and not his own; in that way cheating God and himself and secretly robbing Him; and then in finding projectively that the father-figure had turned deceptive and grasping against *him*, so that he, Solness, was being defrauded of glory. Then the fight between himself and God came out into the open. Solness *did the impossible*, climbed the tower, and arrogated the magic penis, the power over life and death, to himself, stole it from God. *He* would be the Creator God, creating happy homes, happy families, and cut out churches and

Joan Riviere

God. But God triumphed; Solness's home and his family were
ruined and came to nothing—dead ashes.[1]

The mother-figure of the Builder's inner world is, one could say,
almost conspicuous by her absence. True, she it is whom he is for
ever creating and recreating anew in his churches and homes; but
that relation is far from the simple direct one to a mother. It is
largely a reversal of the original relation to his mother, and it is
much complicated by his relation to the father. There is no woman
in the play who is actually a mother, or any reference to one. The
relation to his mother in Solness's inner world is plainly outlined
in broad strokes, however, in the figure of his wife, who seems all
but dead, who is *not* a mother, and who had suffered, at his hands
as he feels, the loss of all her love-objects and treasured possessions,
all that should have made life worth living to her as a woman and
mother. She is there, but as little more than a negation of a woman;
she cannot live or enjoy anything in life, at best she can only do her
duty. She has, however, one aspect which is not a negation, one in
which she seems to the Builder alive, namely, her persecuting side.
Her jealousy of the younger women and her suspicions of Solness
torment him and reproach him frequently; but (as Melanie Klein
has shown us is typical) he maintains these suspicions in her because
they relieve his guilt. He is not in fact sexually unfaithful to her;
and, further, the torment she causes him expiates the guilt he does
feel. Externally Mrs. Solness is the dead, ruined, "depressed" love-
object, and with some persecutory features, as always. Yet there is a
moment in the play when she speaks as a person in her own right,
and is not merely the Builder's mother-figure. There is a wonderful
conversation between her and Hilda about the dead children she
had had, in which her role as mother is seen from the inside, from
the side of *her* inner world. The "dead", mute, self-effacing woman
then talks freely, with terrible emotion and tears; but it is not her
actual babies she is grieving for! They are better in heaven, she says,
where they belong; her suffocating grief is for her home that was
burnt and all her beloved things that had belonged to the family for
generations, the portraits, the old dresses, the lace and jewels—
but above all, *her dolls.* The nine dolls she had kept hidden away and
cherished, had gone on "always living with" even after her marriage
—all were burnt. "You see," she says to Hilda, "there was life in

[1] The Builder has no confidence in a good father-figure in himself; for he had denied,
attacked, and stolen the goodness of his father, as shown in his relation to God; lacking a good
inner father as part of himself, therefore, he cannot himself live the life of such a person in
reality. And because there is no such good human figure, the dæmon rules in his inner world.

them too. They were always with me; I carried them under my heart, like little unborn children!" The children of the inner world it was whom she loved, her phantasy-children and phantasy-parents, and it was the dæmon of this love and grief that wrecked her relation to her real children and caused their death.[1]

I will continue this theme of the children in the inner world before taking up the other aspect of the Builder's inner relation with his mother in the character of Hilda. I do not know if Ibsen was an eldest son, but I would swear that Solness was. His whole setting in the story shows him like a big boy dominating, bullying, and coaxing the group of weaker mortals, most of whom are his willing helpers and servers, though one or two younger brothers only sullenly obey. The old architect-father's son who is kept in subjection by the Builder is one of these "younger ones"; his fiancée the bookkeeper is a sister-figure who has had a close relation with the younger brother but has been seduced away from him secretly by Solness, the elder. The black and white devils or spirits, too, little gnomes, are clearly the younger children, devoted servers of the gangleader at one moment, but invisible mischievous rebels against him at the next, and always liable to betray him to the dæmon father.

The Builder's feelings about real children of his own are highly ambivalent; he appears indifferent to the death of his sons in reality and to feel their loss only as his wife's. When we remember that the babies died because their mother's breasts dried up, we understand why Solness is indifferent![2] There is a curious detail in the play which adds not a little to its obscurity for the lay reader, but which has much meaning psycho-analytically. There are *three* children's rooms still in his house, although only twin boys were born, and there are again to be three children's rooms in the new house he is building for himself and his wife, although they can never have children again. When Hilda arrives, however, she is given one of the children's empty rooms—"the *middle* one", says Solness. So we see that the twin younger brothers (or two parents) are to be dead, but in his inner world the Builder means to create a fair daughter and install her in the centre of the house, in place of the

---

[1] The actress who plays the part of Mrs. Solness needs a fine intuition and deep feeling. If, as does happen, this comparatively small part is portrayed as nothing more than a suspicious, jealous wife, the play loses greatly in emotional impact on us. Her grief for the dolls should touch a note "of such helpless sadness that it beggars all pity", as one of our finest critics said.

[2] His greed towards his mother, and his hate of her for having other children beside himself, caused him in phantasy to attack her breasts, so that they wither and her children starve.

rest of the family—father, brothers, ruined mother—and so possess a virgin mother at last for himself alone.[1]

Hilda's own relation to children is very inhibited. The hints that she desires children by the Builder are extremely slight, hardly to be detected. Her penis-envy of the man is intensified as a defence against her own anxieties about her capacity for maternal love and devotion. In the inner world this anxiety proceeds from her own attacks on her parents' intercourse and then from the embargo laid by the persecuting parents on her wishes to become the mother. These inner persecutory figures do not appear in the play, i.e. this conflict is not faced by her; it is only seen in projection externally, e.g. in her response to the story of the fire and the dead children when told by Solness. "Was anyone burnt?" she says excitedly. When Mrs. Solness tells her about the fire, Hilda grieves for her about the dead babies, again too about the dolls when that grief comes into the open. Hilda understands that there can be *no* living children for them. Her hate and jealousy of brothers and sisters, however, is manifest; she can hardly endure the book-keeper and the young assistant whom Solness exploits. Since the hate is largely conscious, however, she is able to overcome it enough to help them and tries to help the Builder to do them justice.

The other aspect, besides that to his wife, of the Master-Builder's inner relation to women, ultimately to his mother, is of course portrayed in Hilda and his responses to her. Whereas his wife is the mother he destroys, Hilda is the longed-for radiant and young woman, unhurt, full of life, hope, and promise. She corresponds to the churches or the houses he created, just as he "created" the vision of the future and the assurance of her happiness in her by his promise to return. Can he be assured that he can recreate the destroyed mother, all will be well; he can live again. But the old greed is behind this hope; almost as soon as he sees her, he wants her, but in order to *use her for himself*, to obtain a new lease of life from her, not to give her life. He will make her a helper and server; he will turn her against his foes and his fears and she shall fight for him, shelter and protect him; while his wife and others accuse him, she shall defend and support him. He alone shall possess the mother in the home. In this he cannot succeed. Hilda's own dæmon interferes

[1] This detail is highly over-determined. Hilda here also represents the feminine side of Solness, his wishes to rob his wife and mother of children by coming between the parents (twins) in intercourse. His envy and rivalry of the mother and frustrated wish to "build" babies himself impels him to force himself as Hilda into his wife's nursery (mother's body)—where the wife in fact is no mother.

too in various ways. The greed in Hilda which could respond to this aim is not sufficiently unmixed and direct to enable her at any price to take what she can get. But Solness is aware of it in her and also afraid of it; he calls her a bird of prey. Nevertheless, her greed is infused with very great love, and it is idealized to the point where the greed seems almost outweighed. Much as she hates "the other children" who have claims on the Builder, the young assistant and the book-keeper, and the old man, she cannot take her prize at the cost of their destruction. She must attempt, instead of supporting him against "the younger generation", to make Solness restore them their due. Neither can she face a final and utter death-blow to Mrs. Solness by taking him, who is all she has left in life, from her. But Hilda's love and her greed on the oral pattern are almost indistinguishable, largely moreover because they are highly idealized. The aggression and hate in the greed are too much denied and split off and the illusory idealization enables them to break through and to overthrow the love. We see Solness unable to resist her; half of him surrendering to the magic of his recreated mother's belief in his power to achieve the "impossible", half of him surrendering the power of life and death again to the father God, though his life is lost in the act. To Hilda it seems that it is solely in love for him that she must "see him great and free once more", not bound by the shackles of earthly obligations. From behind this mask her devouring love for her father, her abiding envy of his magic powers, and her buried hatred of the father who disappointed her in infancy, well up and annihilate him utterly. After he falls, she is left alone on the stage, still gazing upward, but suddenly she cries out "*My —my* Master-Builder!" She has lost the man himself, but in her inner world of illusion she seems to have gained him at last.

16

A PSYCHO-ANALYTICAL APPROACH TO AESTHETICS

HANNA SEGAL

"Denn das Schöne ist nichts
als des Schrecklichen Anfang, den wir noch gerade ertragen,
und wir bewundern es so, weil es gelassen verschmäht,
uns zu zerstören."[1]

IN 1908 Freud wrote: "We laymen have always wondered greatly
—like the cardinal who put the question to Ariosto—how that
strange being, the poet, comes by his material. What makes him
able to carry us with him in such a way and to arouse emotions in
us of which we thought ourselves perhaps not even capable?"[2] And
as the science of psycho-analysis developed, repeated attempts were
made to answer that question. Freud's discovery of unconscious
phantasy life and of symbolism made it possible to attempt a psychological interpretation of works of art. Many papers have been
written since, dealing with the problem of the individual artist and
reconstructing his early history from an analysis of his work. The
foremost of these is Freud's book on Leonardo da Vinci. Other
papers have dealt with general psychological problems expressed
in works of art, showing, for instance, how the latent content of
universal infantile anxieties is symbolically expressed in them.
Such was Freud's paper "The Theme of the Three Caskets",[3]
Ernest Jones's "The Conception of the Madonna through the Ear",[4]
or Melanie Klein's "Infantile Anxiety Situations Reflected in a
Work of Art and the Creative Impulse."[5]
  Until recently such papers were not mainly concerned with

[1] ... For Beauty is nothing but beginning of Terror we're still just able to bear and why
we admire it so is because it serenely disdains to destroy us.... Rilke, *Duineser Elegien* (trans.
Leishman and Spender).

[2] "The Relation of the Poet to Day-dreaming", *Collected Papers*, Vol. IV (London, 1925).

[3] (1913). *Ibid.*

[4] (1914). *Essays in Applied Psycho-Analysis*, Vol. II (London, 1951).

[5] (1925). *Contributions to Psycho-Analysis, 1921–45* (London, 1948).

A Psycho-Analytical approach to Aesthetics

æsthetics. They dealt with points of psychological interest but not with the central problem of æsthetics, which is: what constitutes good art, in what essential respect is it different from other human works, more particularly from bad art? Psychological writers attempted to answer questions like: "How does the poet work?" "What is he like?" "What does he express?" In the paper "The Relation of the Poet to Day-dreaming",[1] Freud has shown how the work of the artist is a product of phantasy and has its roots, like the children's play and dreams, in unconscious phantasy life. But he did not attempt to explain "why we should derive such pleasure from listening to the day-dreams of a poet". How he achieves his effects is, to Freud, the poet's "innermost secret". Indeed, Freud was not especially interested in æsthetic problems. In "The Moses of Michelangelo"[2] he says: "I have often observed that the subject-matter of works of art has a stronger attraction for me than their formal and technical qualities, though to the artist their value lies first and foremost in this latter. I am unable rightly to appreciate many of the methods used and the effects obtained in art." He was also aware of the limitations of analytical theory in approaching æsthetics. In the preface to the book on Leonardo da Vinci[3] he says that he has no intention of discussing why Leonardo was a great painter, since to do that, he would have to know more about the ultimate sources of the creative impulse and of sublimation. This was written in 1910. Since that time the work of Melanie Klein has thrown more light on the problem of the creative impulse and sublimation, and has provided a new stimulus to analytical writers on art. In the last fifteen years a number of papers have appeared dealing with problems of creation, beauty, and ugliness. I would mention, in particular, those by Ella Sharpe, Paula Heimann, John Rickman, and Fairbairn in Britain, and H. B. Lee in the U.S.A.

Maybe it is possible now, in the light of new analytical discoveries, to ask new questions. Can we isolate in the psychology of the artist the specific factors which enable him to produce a satisfactory work of art? And if we can, will that further our understanding of the æsthetic value of the work of art, and of the æsthetic experience of the audience?

It seems to me that Melanie Klein's concept of the depressive

[1] (1908). *Collected Papers*, Vol. IV (London, 1935).
[2] (1914). *Ibid.*
[3] (1920). *Leonardo da Vinci* (London, 1922).

385

position makes it possible at least to attempt an answer to these questions.

The "depressive position", as described by Melanie Klein, is reached by the infant when he recognizes his mother and other people, and amongst them his father, as real persons. His object relations then undergo a fundamental change.[1] Where earlier he was aware of "part objects" he now perceives complete persons; instead of "split" objects—ideally good or overwhelmingly persecuting—he sees a whole object both good and bad. The whole object is loved and introjected and forms the core of an integrated ego. But this new constellation ushers in a new anxiety situation: where earlier the infant feared an attack on the ego by persecutory objects, now the predominant fear is that of the loss of the loved object in the external world and in his own inside. The infant at that stage is still under the sway of uncontrollable greedy and sadistic impulses. In phantasy his loved object is continually attacked in greed and hatred, is destroyed, torn into pieces and fragments; and not only is the external object so attacked but also the internal one, and then the whole internal world feels destroyed and shattered as well. Bits of the destroyed object may turn into persecutors, and there is a fear of internal persecution as well as a pining for the lost loved object and guilt for the attack. The memory of the good situation, where the infant's ego contained the whole loved object, and the realization that it has been lost through his own attacks, gives rise to an intense feeling of loss and guilt, and to the wish to restore and re-create the lost loved object outside and within the ego. This wish to restore and re-create is the basis of later sublimation and creativity.

It is also at this point that a sense of inner reality is developed. If the object is remembered as a whole object, then the ego is faced with the recognition of its own ambivalence towards the object; it holds itself responsible for its impulses and for the damage done to the external and to the internal object. Where, earlier, impulses and parts of the infant's self were projected into the object with the result that a false picture of it was formed, that his own impulses were denied, and that there was often a lack of differentiation between the self and the external object; in the depressive phase, a sense of inner reality is developed and in its wake a sense of outer reality as well.

[1] For the description of the preceding phase of development see Melanie Klein's *Contributions to Psycho-Analysis, 1921–45*, and Herbert Rosenfeld's paper in this volume.

Depressive phantasies give rise to the wish to repair and restore, and become a stimulus to further development, only in so far as the depressive anxiety can be tolerated by the ego and the sense of psychic reality retained. If there is little belief in the capacity to restore, the good object outside and inside is felt to be irretrievably lost and destroyed, the destroyed fragments turn into persecutors, and the internal situation is felt to be hopeless. The infant's ego is at the mercy of intolerable feelings of guilt, loss, and internal persecution. To protect itself from total despair the ego must have recourse to violent defence mechanisms. Those defence mechanisms which protect it from the feelings arising out of the loss of the good object form a system of manic defences. The essential features of manic defences are denial of psychic reality, omnipotent control, and a partial regression to the paranoid position and its defences: splitting, idealization, denial, projective identification, etc. This regression strengthens the fear of persecution and that in turn leads to the strengthening of omnipotent control.

But in successful development the experience of love from the environment slowly reassures the infant about his objects. His growing love, strength, and skill give him increasing confidence in his own capacities to restore. And as his confidence increases he can gradually relinquish the manic defences and experience more and more fully the underlying feelings of loss, guilt, and love, and he can make renewed and increasingly successful attempts at reparation.

By repeated experiences of loss and restoration of the internal objects they become more firmly established and more fully assimilated in the ego.

A successful working through of the depressive anxieties has far-reaching consequences; the ego becomes integrated and enriched through the assimilation of loved objects; the dependence on the external objects is lessened and deprivation can be better dealt with. Aggression and love can be tolerated and guilt gives rise to the need to restore and re-create.

Feelings of guilt probably play a role before the depressive position is fully established; they already exist in relation to the part object, and they contribute to later sublimation; but they are then simpler impulses acting in a predominantly paranoid setting, isolated and unintegrated. With the establishment of the depressive position the object becomes more personal and unique and the ego more integrated, and an awareness of an integrated, internal world is gradually achieved. Only when this happens does the attack on the object lead to real despair at the destruction of an existing complex and organized internal world, and with it, to the wish to recover such a complete world again.

*   *   *

The task of the artist lies in the creation of a world of his own.

In his introduction to the second Post-Impressionist Exhibition, Roger Fry writes: "Now these artists do not seek to give what can, after all, be but a pale reflex of actual appearance, but to arouse a conviction of a new and different reality. They do not seek to imitate life but to find an equivalent for life." What Roger Fry says of post-impressionists undoubtedly applies to all genuine art. One of the great differences between art and imitation or a super-ficial "pretty" achievement is that neither the imitation nor the "pretty" production ever achieves this creation of an entirely new reality.

Every creative artist produces a world of his own. Even when he believes himself to be a complete realist and sets himself the task of faithfully reproducing the external world, he, in fact, only uses elements of the existing external world to create with them a reality of his own. When, for instance, two realistic writers like Zola and Flaubert try to portray life in the same country, and very nearly at the same time, the two worlds they show us differ from each other as widely as if they were the most phantastic creations of surrealist poets. If two great painters paint the same landscape we have two different worlds.

> ".... and dream
> Of waves, flowers, clouds, woods,
> Rocks, and all that we
> Read in their smiles
> And call reality."
>
> (Shelley).

How does this creation come about? Of all artists the one who gives us the fullest description of the creative process is Marcel Proust: a description based on years of self-observation and the fruit of an amazing insight. According to Proust, an artist is compelled to create by his need to recover his lost past. But a purely intellectual memory of the past, even when it is available, is emotionally value-less and dead. A real remembrance sometimes comes about unex-pectedly by chance association. The flavour of a cake brings back to

388

his mind a fragment of his childhood with full emotional vividness. Stumbling over a stone revives a recollection of a holiday in Venice which before he had vainly tried to recapture. For years he tries in vain to remember and re-create in his mind a living picture of his beloved grandmother. But only a chance association revives her picture and at last enables him to remember her, and to experience his loss and mourn her. He calls these fleeting associations: "inter-mittences du cœur", but he says that such memories come and then disappear again, so that the past remains elusive. To capture them, to give them permanent life, to integrate them with the rest of his life, he must create a work of art. "Il fallait . . . faire sortir de la pénombre ce que j'avais senti, de le reconvertir en un équivalent spirituel. Or ce moyen qui me paraissait le seul, qu'était-ce autre chose que de créer une œuvre d'art?" ("I had to recapture from the shade that which I had felt, to reconvert it into its psychic equivalent. But the way to do it, the only one I could see, what was it—but to create a work of art?")

Through the many volumes of his work the past is being recap-tured; all his lost, destroyed, and loved objects are being brought back to life: his parents, his grandmother, his beloved Albertine. "Et certes il n'y aurait pas qu'Albertine, que ma grandmère, mais bien d'autres encore dont j'aurais pu assimiler une parole, un regard, mais en tant que créatures individuelles je ne m'en rappellais plus; un livre est un grand cimetière où sur la plupart des tombes on ne peut plus lire les noms effacés." ("And indeed it was not only Albertine, not only my grandmother, but many others still from whom I might well have assimilated a gesture or a word, but whom I could not even remember as distinct persons. A book is a vast graveyard where on most of the tombstones one can read no more the faded names.")

And, according to Proust, it is only the lost past and the lost or dead object that can be made into a work of art. He makes the pain-ter, Elstir, say: "On ne peut récréer ce qu'on aime qu'en le renon-çant." ("It is only by renouncing that one can re-create what one loves.") It is only when the loss has been acknowledged and the mourning experienced that re-creation can take place.

In the last volume of his work Proust describes how at last he de-cided to sacrifice the rest of his life to writing. He came back after a long absence to seek his old friends at a party, and all of them ap-peared to him as ruins of the real people he knew—useless, ridiculous, ill, on the threshold of death. Others, he found, had died long ago. And on realizing the destruction of a whole world that had been his he decides to write, to sacrifice himself to the re-creation of the dying and the dead. By virtue of his art he can give his objects an eternal life in his work. And since they represent his internal world too, if he can do that, he himself will no longer be afraid of death.

What Proust describes corresponds to a situation of mourning: he sees that his loved objects are dying or dead. Writing a book is for him like the work of mourning in that gradually the external objects are given up, they are reinstated in the ego, and re-created in the book. In her paper "Mourning and its Relation to Manic-Depressive States",[1] Melanie Klein has shown how mourning in grown-up life is a re-living of the early depressive anxieties; not only is the present object in the external world felt to be lost, but also the early objects, the parents; and they are lost as internal objects as well as in the external world. In the process of mourning it is these earliest objects which are lost again, and then re-created. Proust describes how this mourning leads to a wish to re-create the lost world.

I have quoted Proust at length because he reveals such an acute awareness of what I believe is present in the unconscious of all artists: namely, that all creation is really a re-creation of a once loved and once whole, but now lost and ruined object, a ruined internal world and self. It is when the world within us is destroyed, when it is dead and loveless, when our loved ones are in fragments, and we ourselves in helpless despair—it is then that we must re-create our world anew, reassemble the pieces, infuse life into dead fragments, re-create life.

If the wish to create is rooted in the depressive position and the capacity to create depends on a successful working through it, it would follow that the inability to acknowledge and overcome depressive anxiety must lead to inhibitions in artistic expression.

I should now like to give a few clinical examples from artists who have been inhibited in their creative activities by neurosis, and I shall try to show that in them it was the inability to work through their depressive anxieties which led to inhibitions of artistic activity, or to the production of an unsuccessful artistic product.

Case A is a young girl with a definite gift for painting. An acute rivalry with her mother made her give up painting in her early teens. After some analysis she started to paint again and was working as a decorative artist. She did decorative handicraft work in preference to what she sometimes called "real painting", and this was because she knew that, though correct, neat, and pretty, her work failed to be

[1] (1940). *Op. cit.*

moving and æsthetically significant. In her manic way she usually denied that this caused her any concern. At the time when I was trying to interpret her unconscious sadistic attacks on her father, the internalization of her mutilated and destroyed father and the resulting depression, she told me the following dream: "She saw a picture in a shop which represented a wounded man lying alone and desolate in a dark forest. She felt quite overwhelmed with emotion and admiration for this picture; she thought it represented the actual essence of life; if she could only paint like that she would be a really great painter."

It soon appeared that the meaning of the dream was that if she could only acknowledge her depression about the wounding and destruction of her father, she would then be able to express it in her painting and would achieve real art. In fact, however, it was impossible for her to do this, since the unusual strength of her sadism and her resulting despair, and her small capacity to tolerate depression, led to its manic denial and to a constant make-believe that all was well with the world. In her dream she confirmed my interpretation about the attack on her father, but she did more than this. Her dream showed something that had not been in any way interpreted or indicated by me: namely, the effect on her painting of her persistent denial of depression. In relation to her painting the denial of the depth and seriousness of her depressive feelings produced the effect of superficiality and prettiness in whatever she chose to do—the dead father is completely denied and no ugliness or conflict is ever allowed to disturb the neat and correct form of her work.

Case B is that of a journalist aged a little over thirty, whose ambition was to be a writer, and who suffered, among other symptoms, from an ever-increasing inhibition in creative writing. An important feature of his character was a tendency to regress from the depressive to the paranoid position. The following dream illustrates his problem: "He found himself in a room with Goebbels, Goering, and some other Nazis. He was aware that these men were completely amoral. He knew that they were going to poison him and therefore he tried to make a bargain with them; he suggested that it would be a good thing for them to let him live, since he was a journalist and could write about them and make them live for a time after their death. But this stratagem failed and he knew that he would finally be poisoned."

An important factor in this patient's psychology was his introjection of an extremely bad father-figure who was then blamed for all that the patient did. And one of the results was an unbearable feeling of being internally persecuted by this bad internal father-figure, which was sometimes expressed in hypochondriacal symptoms. He tried to defend himself against it by placating and serving this bad internal figure. He was often driven to do things that he disapproved of and disliked. In the dream he showed how it interfered with his writing: to avoid death at the hands of internal persecutors he has to write for them to keep them immortal; but there is, of course, no real wish to keep such bad figures alive, and consequently he was inhibited in his capacity for writing. He often complained, too, that he had no style of his own; in his associations to the dream it became clear that he had to write not only for the benefit of the poisoners, and to serve their purposes, but also at their command. Thus the style of his writing belonged to the internal parental figure. The case, I think, resembles one described by Paula Heimann.[1] A patient of hers drew a sketch with which she was very displeased; the style was not her own, it was Victorian. It appeared clearly during the session that it was the result of a quarrel with another woman who stood for her mother. After the quarrel the painter had introjected her as a bad and revengeful mother, and, through guilt and fear, she had to submit to this bad internal figure; it was really the Victorian mother who had dictated the painting.

Paula Heimann described this example of an acute impairment of an already established sublimation. In my patient his submission to a very bad internal figure was a chronic situation preventing him from achieving any internal freedom to create. Moreover, although he was trying to appease his persecutors, as a secondary defence against them, he was basically fixed in the paranoid position and returned to it whenever depressive feelings were aroused, so that his love and reparative impulses could not become fully active.

*   *   *

All the patients mentioned suffered from sexual maladjustments as well as creative inhibitions. There is clearly a genital aspect of artistic creation which is of paramount importance. Creating a work of art is a psychic equivalent of procreation. It is a genital bisexual activity necessitating a good identification with the father who gives, and the mother who receives and bears, the child. The ability to deal with the depressive position, however, is the precondition of both genital and artistic maturity. If the parents are felt to be so

[1] "A Contribution to the Problem of Sublimation and its Relation to Processes of Internalization", *Int. J. Psycho-Anal.*, Vol. XXIII, Part I, 1942.

completely destroyed that there is no hope of ever re-creating them, a successful identification is not possible, and neither can the genital position be maintained nor the sublimation in art develop.

This relation between feelings of depression and genital and artistic problems is clearly shown by another patient of mine. C, a man of thirty-five, was a really gifted artist, but at the same time a very ill person. Since the age of eighteen he had suffered from depression, from a variety of conversion symptoms of great intensity, and from what he described as "a complete lack of freedom and spontaneity". This lack of spontaneity interfered considerably with his work, and, though he was physically potent, it also deprived him of all the enjoyment of sexual intercourse. A feeling of impending failure, worthlessness and hopelessness, marred all his efforts. He came to analysis at the age of thirty-five because of a conversion symptom: he suffered from a constant pain in the small of his back and the lower abdomen, which was aggravated by frequent spasms. He described it as "a constant state of childbirth". It appeared in his analysis that the pain started soon after he learned that the wife of his twin brother was pregnant, and he actually came to me for treatment a week before her confinement. He felt that if I could only liberate him from the spasm he would do marvellous things. In his case identification with the pregnant woman, representing the mother, was very obvious, but it was not a happy identification. He felt his mother and the babies inside her had been so completely destroyed by his sadism, and his hope of re-creating them was so slight, that the identification with the pregnant mother meant to him a state of anguish, ruin, and abortive pregnancy. Instead of producing the baby, he, like the mother, was destroyed. Feeling destroyed inside and unable to restore the mother, he felt persecuted by her; the internal attacked mother attacked him in turn and robbed him of his babies. Unlike the other three patients described, this one recognized his depression and his reparative drive was therefore very much stronger. The inhibition both in his sexual and artistic achievements was due mainly to a feeling of the inadequacy of his reparative capacity in comparison with the devastation that he felt he had brought about. This feeling of inadequacy made him regress to a paranoid position whenever his anxiety was aroused.

*   *   *

Patient E, a woman writer, was the most disturbed of the patients described here. She was a severe chronic hypochondriac, she suffered from frequent depersonalization and endless phobias, amongst them food phobias leading at times to almost complete anorexia.

She had been a writer, but had not been able to write for a number of years. I want to describe here how her inability to experience depression led to an inhibition of symbolic expression.

One day she told me the following dream: "She was in a Nursing Home, and the Matron of this Home, dressed in black, was going to kill a man and a woman. She herself was going to a fancy dress ball. She kept running out of the Nursing Home in various fancy disguises, but somehow something always went wrong, and she had to come back to the Nursing Home, and to meet the Matron. At some point of the dream she was with her friend Joan."

Her friend, Joan, was for my patient the embodiment of mental health and stability. After telling me the dream she said: "Joan was not in a fancy dress, she was undisguised, and I felt her to be so much more vulnerable than me." Then she immediately corrected herself: "Oh, of course I meant she was so much less vulnerable than me." This slip of the patient gave us the key to the dream. The mentally healthy person is more vulnerable than my patient, she wears no disguises and she is vulnerable to illness and death. My patient herself escapes death, represented by the Matron, by using various disguises. Her associations to this dream led us to a review of some of her leading symptoms in terms of her fear of, and attempted escape from, death. The disguises in the dream represented personifications, projective and introjective identifications, all three used by her as means of not living her own life and—in the light of the dream—not dying her own death. She also connected other symptoms of hers with the fear of death. For instance her spending almost half her lifetime lying in bed, "half-dead", was a shamming of death, a way of cheating death. Her phobia of bread, her fear of sex, appeared to her now as ways of escaping full living, which would mean that one day she would have "spent her life" and would have to face death. So far, she had almost lived on "borrowed" life. For instance, she felt extremely well and alive when she was pregnant, she then felt she lived on the baby's life; but immediately after the baby's birth she felt depersonalized and half-dead.

I mention here only some of her more striking symptoms which all pointed in the same direction; to a constant preoccupation with the fear of death. The analyst, represented by the Matron, tears off her disguises one after another, and forces her to lead her own life and so eventually to die.

After some three sessions completely taken up with the elaboration of this theme, she started the next one with what appeared to be a completely new trend of thought. She started complaining of her inability to write. Her associations led her to remember her early dislike of using words. She felt that her dislike was still present and she did not really want to use words at all. Using words, she said, made her break "an endless unity into bits". It was like "chopping up", like "cutting things". It was obviously felt by her as an aggressive act. Besides, using words was "making things finite and separate". To use words meant acknowledging the separateness of the world from herself, and gave her a feeling of loss. She felt that using words made her lose the illusion of possessing and being at one with an endless, undivided world: "When you name a thing you really lose it."[1] It became clear to her that using a symbol (language) meant an acceptance of the separateness of her object from herself, the acknowledgment of her own aggressiveness, "chopping up", "cutting", and finally losing the object.

In this patient the loss of the object was always felt as an imminent threat to her own survival. So we could eventually connect her difficulties in using language with the material of the earlier sessions. Refusing to face this threat of death to her object and to herself, she had to form the various symptoms devised magically to control and avoid death. She also had to give up her creative writing. In order to write again, she would have to be stripped of her disguises, admit reality, and become vulnerable to loss and death.

I shall now describe shortly a session with the same patient two years later.

She had known for some time that she would have to give up her analysis at the end of the term, through external circumstances. She came to this session very sad, for the first time since it became clear that she would end her analysis. In preceding sessions she felt nausea, felt internally persecuted and "all in bits and pieces". She said at the beginning of the session that she could hardly wait to see me for fear that her sadness would turn into a "sickness and badness". She thought of the end of her analysis, wondered if she would be able to go on liking me and how much would she be able to remember me. She also wondered if she in any way resembled me. There were two things she would wish to resemble me in: the truthfulness and the capacity to care for people which she attributed to me. She hoped she

---

[1] This theme became later linked with the "Rumpelstiltskin" theme of stealing the baby and the penis, but I cannot follow it up here.

may have learned these from me. She also felt I was an ordinary kind of person, and she liked that thought. I interpreted her material as a wish to take me in and identify herself with me as a real "ordinary" feeding breast, in contrast to an earlier situation when an idealized breast was internalized, which subsequently turned into a persecuting one.

She then told me the following dream: "A baby has died—or grown up—she didn't know which; and as a result her breasts were full of milk. She was feeding a baby of another woman whose breasts were dry."

The transference meaning of that dream was that I weaned her— my breast was dry—but she had acquired a breast and could be a mother herself. The baby who "died or grew up" is herself. The baby dies and the grown woman takes its place. The losing of the analyst is here an experience involving sadness, guilt (about the rivalry with me in relation to the baby), and anxiety (will she be able to go on remembering me?). But it is also an experience leading to the enrichment of her ego—she now has the breasts full of milk and therefore need no longer depend on me.

Towards the end of the hour, she said: "Words seem to have a meaning again, they are rich", and she added that she was quite sure she could now write "provided I can go on being sad for a while, without being sick and hating food"—i.e. provided she could mourn me instead of feeling me as an internal persecutor.

Words acquired a meaning and the wish to write returned again when she could give up my breast as an external object and internalize it. This giving up was experienced by her as the death of the breast, which is dried up in the dream and the death of a part of herself—the baby part—which in growing up also dies. In so far as she could mourn me words became rich in meaning.[1]

This patient's material confirmed an impression derived from many other patients, that successful symbol formation is rooted in the depressive position.

One of Freud's greatest contributions to psychology was the discovery that sublimation is the outcome of a successful renunciation of an instinctual aim; I would like to suggest here that such a successful renunciation can only happen through a process of mourning. The giving up of an instinctual aim, or object, is a repetition and at

---

[1] I have given here only the transference meaning of the dream in order not to detract from my main theme. This transference situation was linked with past experiences of weaning, birth of the new baby, and the patient's failure in the past to be a "good" mother to the new baby.

the same time a re-living of the giving up of the breast. It can be successful, like this first situation, if the object to be given up can be assimilated in the ego, by the process of loss and internal restoration. I suggest that such an assimilated object becomes a symbol within the ego. Every aspect of the object, every situation that has to be given up in the process of growing, gives rise to symbol formation.

In this view symbol formation is the outcome of a loss, it is a creative act involving the pain and the whole work of mourning. If psychic reality is experienced and differentiated from external reality, the symbol is differentiated from the object; it is felt to be created by the self and can be freely used by the self.

I cannot deal here extensively with the problem of symbols; I have brought it up only in so far as it is relevant to my main theme. And it is relevant in that the creation of symbols, the symbolic elaboration of a theme, are the very essence of art.

*   *   *

I should now like to attempt to formulate an answer to the question whether there is a specific factor in the psychology of the successful artist which would differentiate him from the unsuccessful one. In Freud's words: "What distinguishes the poet, the artist, from the neurotic day-dreamer?" In his paper "Formulations Regarding the Two Principles in Mental Functioning", Freud says: "The artist finds a way of returning from the world of phantasy back to reality, with his special gifts he moulds his phantasies into a new kind of reality." Indeed, one could say that the artist has an acute reality sense. He is often neurotic and in many situations may show a complete lack of objectivity, but in two respects, at least, he shows an extremely high reality sense. One is in relation to his own internal reality, and the other in relation to the material of his art. However neurotic Proust was in his attachment to his mother, his homosexuality, his asthma, etc., he had a real insight into the phantastic world of the people inside him, and he knew it was internal, and he knew it was phantasy. He showed an awareness that does not exist in a neurotic who splits off, represses, denies, or acts out his phantasy. The second, the reality sense of the artist in relation to his material, is a highly specialized reality assessment of the nature, needs, possibilities, and limitations of his material, be it words, sounds, paints, or clay. The neurotic uses his material in a magic way, and so does the bad artist. The real artist, being aware of his internal world which he must express, and of the external materials with which he works, can

397

in all consciousness use the material to express the phantasy. He shares with the neurotic all the difficulties of unresolved depression, the constant threat of the collapse of his internal world; but he differs from the neurotic in that he has a greater capacity for tolerating anxiety and depression. The patients I described could not tolerate depressive phantasies and anxieties; they all made use of manic defences leading to a denial of psychic reality. Patient A denied both the loss of her father and his importance to her: Patient B projected his impulses on to an internal bad object, with the result that his ego was split and that he was internally persecuted: Patient C did the same, though to a lesser extent: Patient E regressed to the schizoid mechanisms of splitting and projective identification which led to depersonalization and inhibition in the use of symbols.

In contrast to that, Proust could fully experience depressive mourning. This gave him the possibility of insight into himself, and with it a sense of internal and external reality. Further, this reality sense enabled him to have and to maintain a relationship with other people through the medium of his art. The neurotic's phantasy interferes with his relationships in which he acts it out. The artist withdraws into a world of phantasy, but he can communicate his phantasies and share them. In that way he makes reparation, not only to his own internal objects, but to the external world as well.

*   *   *

I have tried, so far, to show how Melanie Klein's work, especially her concept of the depressive position and the reparative drives that are set in motion by it, and her description of the world of inner objects, throws new light on the psychology of the artist, on the conditions necessary for him to be successful, and on those which can inhibit or vitiate his artistic activities. Can this new light on the psychology of the artist help us to understand the æsthetic pleasure experienced by the artist's public? If, for the artist, the work of art is his most complete and satisfactory way of allaying the guilt and despair arising out of the depressive position and of restoring his destroyed objects, it is but one of the many human ways of achieving this end. What is it that makes a work of art such a satisfactory experience for the artist's public? Freud says that he "bribes us with the formal and æsthetic pleasures".

To begin with, we should distinguish between the æsthetic pleasure and other incidental pleasures to be found in works of art. For instance, the satisfaction derived from identification with particular scenes or characters can also arise in other ways, and it can be derived from bad as well as from good art. The same would apply to the sentimental interests originating in memories and associations. The æsthetic pleasure proper, that is, the pleasure derived from a work of art and unique in that it can only be obtained through a work of art, is due to an identification of ourselves with the work of art as a whole and with the whole internal world of the artist as represented by his work. In my view all æsthetic pleasure includes an unconscious re-living of the artist's experience of creation. In his paper on "The Moses of Michelangelo", Freud says "What the artist aims at is to awaken in us the same mental constellation as that which in him produced the impetus to create."

We find in Dilthey's philosophy a concept called by him "nach-erleben".[1] This means to him that we can understand other people from their behaviour and expression, we intuitively reconstruct their mental and emotional state, we live after them, we re-live them. This process he calls "nach-erleben". It is, he says, often deeper than introspection can discover. His concept, I think, is equivalent to unconscious identification. I assume that this kind of unconscious re-living of the creator's state of mind is the foundation of all æsthetic pleasure.

To illustrate what I mean I will take as an example the case of "classical" tragedy. In a tragedy the hero commits a crime: the crime is fated, it is an "innocent" crime, he is driven to it. Whatever the nature of the crime the result is always complete destruction— the parental figures and child figures alike are engulfed by it. That is, at whatever level the conflict starts—*Œdipus Rex*, for instance, states a genital conflict—in the end we arrive at a picture of the phantasies belonging to the earliest depressive position where all the objects are destroyed. What is the psychological mechanism of the listener's "nach-erleben"? As I see it, he makes two identifications. He identifies himself with the author, and he identifies the whole tragedy with the author's internal world. He identifies himself with the author while the latter is facing and expressing his depression. In a simplified way one can summarize the listener's reaction as follows: "The author has, in his hatred, destroyed all his loved objects just as I have done, and like me he felt death and desolation inside him. Yet he can face it and he can make me face it, and despite the ruin and devastation we and the world around us survive. What

---

[1] Hodges, H. A., *Wilhelm Dilthey: Selected Readings from his Works and an introduction to his Sociological and Philosophical Work*, London.

is more, his objects, which have become evil and were destroyed, have been made alive again and have become immortal by his art. Out of all the chaos and destruction he has created a world which is whole, complete and unified."

It would appear then that two factors are essential to the excellence of a tragedy: the unshrinking expression of the full horror of the depressive phantasy and the achieving of an impression of wholeness and harmony. The external form of "classical" tragedy is in complete contrast with its content. The formal modes of speech, the unities of time, place and action, the strictness and rigidity of the rules are all, I believe, an unconscious demonstration of the fact that order can emerge out of chaos. Without this formal harmony the depression of the audience would be aroused but not resolved. There can be no æsthetic pleasure without perfect form.[1]

In creating a tragedy I suggest the success of the artist depends on his being able fully to acknowledge and express his depressive phantasies and anxieties. In expressing them he does work similar to the work of mourning in that he internally re-creates a harmonious world which is projected into his work of art.

The reader identifies with the author through the medium of his work of art. In that way he re-experiences his own early depressive anxieties, and through identifying with the artist he experiences a successful mourning, re-establishes his own internal objects and his own internal world, and feels, therefore, re-integrated and enriched.

*   *   *

But is this experience specific to a work of art that is tragic, or is it an essential part of any æsthetic experience? I think I could generalize my argument. To do so I shall have to introduce the more usual terminology of æsthetics and re-state my problems in new terms. The terms I need are "ugly" and "beautiful". For Rickman, in his paper "The Nature of Ugliness and the Creative

---

[1] Roger Fry says, "All the essential æsthetic quality has to do with pure form", and I agree, but he adds later: "The odd thing is that it is, apparently, dangerous for the artist to know about this." Fry feels that it is odd, I think, because of an inherent weakness of the formalist school he represents. The formalists discount the importance of emotional factors in art. According to Fry, art must be completely detached from emotions, all emotion is impurity, and the more the form gets freed from the emotional content the nearer it is to the ideal. What the formalists ignore is that form as much as content is in itself an expression of unconscious emotion. What Fry, following Clive Bell, calls "significant form", a term he confesses himself incapable of defining, is form expressing and embodying an unconscious emotional experience. The artist is not trying to produce pretty or even beautiful form, he is engaged on the most important task of re-creating his ruined internal world and the resulting form will depend on how well he succeeds in his task.

Impulse",[1] the "ugly" is the destroyed, the incomplete object. For Ella Sharpe[2] "ugly" is destroyed, arhythmic, and connected with painful tension. I think both these views would be included if we say that "ugliness" is what expresses the state of the internal world in depression. It includes tension, hatred and its results—the destruction of good and whole objects and their change into persecutory fragments. Rickman, however, when he contrasts ugly and beautiful, seems to equate "beautiful" with what is æsthetically satisfying. With that I cannot agree. Ugly and beautiful are two categories of æsthetic experience and, in certain ways, they can be contrasted; but if beautiful is used as synonymous with æsthetically satisfying, then its contradictory is not "ugly", but unæsthetic, or indifferent, or dull. Rickman says that we recoil from the ugly; my contention is that "ugly" is a most important and necessary component of a satisfying æsthetic experience. The concept of ugliness as one element in æsthetic satisfaction is not uncommon in the tradition of philosophical æsthetics; it has been most strikingly expressed, however, by the artists themselves. Rodin writes: "We call ugly that which is formless, unhealthy, which suggests illness, suffering, destruction, which is contrary to regularity—the sign of health. We also call ugly the immoral, the vicious, the criminal and all abnormality which brings evil—the soul of the parricide, the traitor, the self-seeker. But let a great artist get hold of this ugliness; immediately he transfigures it—with a touch of his magic wand he makes it into beauty."

What is "beautiful"? Taking again the beautiful as but one of the categories of the æsthetically satisfying, most writers agree that the main elements of the beautiful—the whole, the complete, and the rhythmical—are in contrast with the ugly. Amongst analytical writers—Rickman equates the beautiful with the whole object; Ella Sharpe considers beauty essentially as rhythm and equates it with the experience of goodness in rhythmical sucking, satisfactory defæcation and sexual intercourse. I should add to this rhythmical breathing and the rhythm of our heart-beats. An undisturbed rhythm in a composed whole seems to correspond to the state in which our inner world is at peace. Of non-analytical writers, Herbert Read comes to a similar conclusion when he says that we find rhythmical, simple arithmetical proportions which correspond

[1] *Int. J. Psycho-Anal.*, Vol. XXI, Part III (1940).
[2] "Certain Aspects of Sublimation and Delusion" (1930). "Similar and Divergent Unconscious Determinants underlying the Sublimations of Pure Art and Pure Science" (1935).

to the way we are built and our bodies work. But these elements of "beauty" are in themselves insufficient. If they were enough then we would find it most satisfactory to contemplate a circle or listen to a regular tattoo on a drum. I suggest that both beauty, in the narrow sense of the word, and ugliness must be present for a full æsthetic experience.

I would re-word my attempt at analysing the tragic in terms of ugliness and beauty. Broadly speaking, in tragedy "ugly" is the content—the complete ruin and destruction—and "beautiful" is the form. "Ugly" is also an essential part of the comic. The comic here is ugly in that, as in caricature, the overstressing of one or two characteristics ruins the wholeness—the balance—of the character. Ugly and tragic is also the defeat of the comic hero by the same world. How near the comic hero is to the tragic can be seen from the fact that outstanding comic heroes of past ages are felt, at a later date, to be mainly tragic figures; few people to-day take Shylock or Falstaff as figures of fun only; we are aware of the tragedy implied. The difference between tragedy and comedy lies then in the comic writer's attempt to dissociate himself from the tragedy of his hero, to feel superior to it in a kind of successful manic defence. But the manic defence is never complete; the original depression is still expressed and it must therefore have been to a large extent acknowledged and lived by the author. The audience re-lives depression, the fear of it, and the aggression against it which are expressed in a comedy and its final successful outcome.

It is easier to discover this pattern of overcoming depression in literature, with its explicit verbal content, than in other forms of art. The further away from literature the more difficult is the task. In music, for instance, we would have to study the introduction of discords, disharmonies, new disorders which are so invariably considered to be ugly before they are universally accepted. New art is considered "difficult", it is resisted, misunderstood, treated with bitter hatred, contempt; or, on the other hand, it may be idealized to such an extent that the apparent admiration defeats its aim and makes its object a butt of ridicule. These prevalent reactions of the public are, I think, manifestations of a manic defence against the depressive anxieties stirred by art. The artists find ever new ways of revealing a repressed and denied depression. The public use against it all their powers of defence until they find the courage to follow the new artist into the depths of his depression, and eventually to share his triumphs.

The idea that ugliness is an essential component of a complete experience seems to be true of the tragic, the comic, the realistic, in fact of all the commonly accepted categories of the æsthetic except one—and this single exception is of great importance.

There is, undoubtedly, a category of art which shows to the greatest extent all the elements of beauty in the narrow sense of the word, and no apparent sign of ugliness; it is often called "classical" beauty. The beauty of the Parthenon, of the Discobolos, is whole, rhythmical, undisturbed.   But soulless imitations of beauty, "pretty" creations are also whole and rhythmical; yet they fail to stir and rouse nothing but boredom. Thus classical beauty must have some other not immediately obvious element.

Returning to the concept of *nach-erleben*, of experiencing along with another, we may say that in order to move us deeply the artist must have embodied in his work some deep experience of his own. And all our analytical experience as well as the knowledge derived from other forms of art suggest that the deep experience must have been what we call, clinically, a depression, and that the stimulus to create such a perfect whole must have lain in the drive to overcome an unusually strong depression. If we consider what is commonly said about beauty by laymen, we find a confirmation of this conclusion. They say that complete beauty makes one both sad and happy at the same time, and that it is a purge for the soul—that it is awe-inspiring. Great artists themselves have been very much aware of the depression and terror embodied in works of classical beauty which are apparently so peaceful. When Faust goes in search of Helen, the perfect classical beauty, he has to face unnamed terrors; to go where there is no road:

> "Kein Weg! Ins Unbetretene
> Nicht zu Betretende; ein Weg ins Unerbetene,
> Nicht zu Erbittende."

He must face endless emptiness:

> "—Nichts wirst du sehn in ewig leerer Ferne,
> Den Schritt nicht hören den du tust,
> Nichts Festes finden, wo du ruhst."

Rilke writes: "Beauty is nothing but the beginning of terror that we are still just able to bear."

Thus to the sensitive onlooker, every work of beauty still

embodies the terrifying experience of depression and death. Hanns Sachs, in his book, *Beauty, Life and Death*, pays particular attention to the awesome aspect of beauty; he says the difficulty is not to understand beauty but to bear it, and he connects this terror with the very peacefulness of the perfect work of art. He calls it the static element; it is peaceful because it seems unchangeable, eternal. And it is terrifying because this eternal unchangeability is the expression of the death instinct—the static element opposed to life and change.

Following quite a different trend of thought I come to similar conclusions about the role of the death instinct in a work of art. Thus far my contention has been that a satisfactory work of art is achieved by a realization and sublimation of the depressive position, and that the effect on the audience is that they unconsciously re-live the artist's experience and share his triumph of achievement and his final detachment. But to realize and symbolically to express depression the artist must acknowledge the death instinct, both in its aggressive and self-destructive aspects, and accept the reality of death for the object and the self. One of the patients I described could not use symbols because of her failure to work through the depressive position; her failure clearly lay in her inability to accept and use her death instinct and to acknowledge death.

Re-stated in terms of instincts, ugliness—destruction—is the expression of the death instinct; beauty—the desire to unite into rhythms and wholes—is that of the life instinct. The achievement of the artist is in giving the fullest expression to the conflict and the union between those two.

This is a conclusion which Freud has brought out in two of his essays, though he did not generalize it as applicable to all art. One of these essays is that on Michelangelo's Moses, where he clearly shows that the latent meaning of this work is the overcoming of wrath. The other essay is his analysis of the theme of the Three Caskets. He shows there that in the choice between the three caskets, or three women, the final choice is always symbolical of death. He interprets Cordelia in *King Lear* as a symbol of death, and for him the solution of the play is Lear's final overcoming of the fear of death and his reconciliation to it. He says: "Thus man overcomes death, which in thought he has acknowledged. No greater triumph of wish-fulfilment is conceivable."

All artists aim at immortality; their objects must not only be brought back to life, but also the life has to be eternal. And of all human activities art comes nearest to achieving immortality; a great work of art is likely to escape destruction and oblivion.

It is tempting to suggest that this is so because in a great work of art the degree of denial of the death instinct is less than in any other human activity, that the death instinct is acknowledged, as fully as can be borne. It is expressed and curbed to the needs of the life instinct and creation.

BIBLIOGRAPHY

BELL, CLIVE, *Art*, 1914.

EHRENZWEIG, A., "Unconscious Form Creation in Art", *Brit. J. med. Psychol.*, Vol. XXI, Parts II and III (1948).

FAIRBAIRN, W. R. D., "The Ultimate Basis of Æsthetic Experience", *Brit. J. Psychol.*, Vol. 29, Part II.

FREUD, S., "The Relation of the Poet to Day-Dreaming" (1908); "Formulations Regarding the Two Principles of Mental Functioning" (1911); "The Theme of the Three Caskets" (1913); "The Moses of Michelangelo" (1914), *Collected Papers*, Vol. IV. London, Hogarth Press, 1925.

FRY, R., *Vision and Design*, 1920.

—— *Transformations*, 1926.

JONES, E., *The Conception of the Madonna Through the Ear*, 1914.

—— *The Theory of Symbolism*, 1916.

HEIMANN, PAULA, "A Contribution to the Problem of Sublimation and its Relation to Processes of Internalization", *Int. J. Psycho-Anal.*, Vol. XXIII, Part I.

KLEIN, MELANIE, "Infantile Anxiety Situations Reflected in a Work of Art and the Creative Impulse" (1929); "A Contribution to the Psychogenesis of Manic-Depressive States", (1935); "Mourning and its Relation to Manic-Depressive States" (1940); *Contributions to Psycho-Analysis, 1921-45*. London, Hogarth Press, 1948.

LEE, H. B., "A Critique of the Theory of Sublimation", *Psychiatry*, Vol. 2, May, 1939.

—— "A Theory Concerning Free Creation in the Inventive Arts", *Psychiatry*, Vol. 3, May, 1940.

LISTOWELL, *A Critical History of Modern Æsthetics*. London, Allen and Unwin, 1933.

READ, H., *The Meaning of Art*. London, Faber & Faber, 1931.

—— *Art and Society*. London, Faber & Faber, 1934.

RICKMAN, J., "The Nature of Ugliness and the Creative Impulse", *Int. J. Psycho-Anal.*, Vol. XXI, Part III.

SHARPE, ELLA, "Certain Aspects of Sublimation and Delusion" (1930); "Similar and Divergent Determinants Underlying the Sublimation of Pure Art and Pure Science" (1935). *Collected Papers on Psycho-Analysis*. London, Hogarth Press, 1950.

SACHS, H., "Beauty, Life and Death".

17

FORM IN ART

ADRIAN STOKES

I[1]

I FIND in the clouds to-day the splendid shapes of T'ang figures.
I turn my back to the fabulous scene, except to the invariable
quality of all æsthetic sensation.

Art re-creates experience, projects emotional stress. Much conversation does likewise. Art cannot be distinguished from some
other "useless" activities except by what in modern jargon is called
Form. If that quality is much in evidence, it may please us to call
conversation an art, and we may find that it is practised, consciously
or unconsciously, with the predominant aim of achieving Form.
Then every part should have a felicitous note as if pervaded with a
certain music: conversation becomes an entity, one might feel, an
epitome of much that goes beyond it, of much that happens psychic-
ally and physically, transformed into "a world of its own". This
metaphor is pertinent so far as the greater physical actuality causes
visual art to become representative of all art. (The artist *par excellence* of popular idiom is the painter.) If this word "entity" is felt to
be gross and inappropriate to the nebulosity, perhaps airiness, equi-
vocation, that some works of art are deemed to convey, in that case
we can be sure that full æsthetic experience has not been transmitted.

The work of art, then, because it is expressively self-subsistent,
should invoke in us some such idea as the one of "entity". It is as if
the various emotions had been rounded like a stone. We compare
occasionally a many-sided yet harmonious personality to a work of
art: the comparison suggests the notion of a psyche for once so
integrated, that in contemplating it we experience the kind of pleasure we have in a well-proportioned object and the uniformity of its

---

[1] Since I am not a psycho-analyst I shall put second what must therefore be tentative
arguing, together with some elaboration of the speculative statements in Part I.

surrounding space. But together with the sense of a clear totality, of an individual yet varied object (one among many), the notion, it must be remarked, contains a reference to a non-differential medium (space) which embraces the whole visible world. Now, an impression occupies real salience for an artist when it suggests an entire and separate unity, though, at the same time, it seems to be joined to the heart of other, diverse, experiences, to possess with them a pulse in common: that is the feeling the artist strives to re-create. Thus, a good poem has the closed air of an entity, of something compact that makes a dent, but its poetry is a contagion that spreads and spreads. We can always discover from æsthetic experience that sense of homogeneity or fusion combined, in differing proportions, with the sense of object-otherness.

As well as the vivid impress of self-contained totalities, we renew, at the instance of æsthetic sensation, the "oceanic" feeling, upheld by some of the qualities of id "language", such as interchangeability, from which poetic identifications flow.

Because it combines the sense of fusion with the sense of object-otherness, we might say that art is an emblem of the state of being in love: this seems true if we emphasize the infantile introjections and reparative attitudes that are strengthened by that state. These attitudes are the fount of Form. When the artist joins them in the creative process, infantile psychic tensions concerning sense-data renew in him some freshness of vision, some ability to meet, as if for the first time, the phenomenal world and the emotion it carries.

The sublimation is highly wrought. Art, is, of course, a cultural activity: the "good" imagos at the back of Form are identified with the actualities or potentialities of a particular culture: indeed, the artist, "child of his age", is limited by the parent culture he serves, whose immediate yet deeper moods he portrays, as well as his own, however isolated he may be. He labours also with artistic tradition and convention, whether to swell their fruit or whether, upon desiccation, to re-combine the stock.

The face is another indispensable metaphor for the work of art. We all construe faces every day, interpreting the physical showing of lifelong experience. Art divagates upon this coalescence of inner and outer, particularly upon the instantaneous impact of its apprehension (sometimes, perhaps, with the intention of unifying the "good" and the "bad" into one physical unity). For this reason alone it is inevitable that visual art should be much taken up with human, animal, and vegetable form whether by a treatment that is generalized, or whether of the kind from which portraiture has evolved. But this matter goes further. We look first to building for style or period. By changes of surface and texture, by proportion, by void and solid, the architect, for long ages supported by his craftsmen, made walls "speak", imputed a radiant flowering. That is one reason why this extreme or abstract yet ubiquitous art was often the mother of the rest. No other art could show as well how strongly the material itself, the medium can be cathected.

Now the artist or would-be artist may be distinguished by the extent to which he cathects a medium. Specific forms are derived from that intense engrossment with a material through which a "face", a physical epitome of experience can be envisaged. For the poet, words, for the sculptor, stone, are pregnant materials with which they are in communion, through which they crystallize particular phantasies. In a sense the work of art is not new enactment but re-affirmation of a pre-existent entity.[1] This entity is allowed once more a full and separate life: it is restored. The dancer's body, whether or no in relation with music, is not the sole æsthetic hub of the dance. She ornaments an all-embracing space on which she weaves a pattern, whose directions she will have shown to be harmonious at the conclusion of the dance. An old contact will have sustained her attack upon these vistas now left in new repose. The stage or space which the dancer's movement, in a kind of plastic interplay with music, has particularized, is the æsthetic object also. Music itself, perhaps, first cooed and crowed, was pinned as an enhancement to blissful silence. "Music creates her own disorder like doves sent circling from the cote to which they readily return." In art an all-embracing element, the stage, silence, the blank canvas, can serve as the sleep of which dreams, though wakeful and rapid, are the guardians. I shall identify the interchange, between an all-embracing and particularized element (thus antithetical but blended), with "good" imagos that are the basis of Form.

Form bestows not only pattern but completeness, not only the sense of separate life, but the sense of fusion. In art, repose will in some manner encompass energy. This point is crucial. Whatever the rhythm, the force, the fierceness, the furore, there is yet calm, for

---

[1] Cf. the opening lines of Michelangelo's famous sonnet (trans. J. A. Symonds)
> "The best of artists hath no thought to show
> Which the rough stone in its superfluous shell
> Doth not include: to break the marble spell
> Is all the hand that serves the brain can do."

As is well known, Michelangelo tended to preserve in parts of his sculpture, the original surfaces of the marble.

there is also completeness. An identity has been established amid the manifold to whose differences full value is given: just as a mirror's surface makes more comprehensive the turbulent scene reflected there.

Let us now visit the new Rembrandt room at the National Gallery. Here, on the walls, faces come softly but vividly from dark backgrounds, faces and hands that "realize" the sitters. Drawing, texture, disposition, echoing toppling shape, seem to be a rich fructi- fication of character rather than the physical representatives. Such an effect depends on eliciting from us muscular response to the draw- ing and an increase of the usual correlating activities of vision. We feel this apprehension of inner and outer actuality in prior terms of our muscular responses, let us say, to be benign. I would stress the benignity of the synthesis effected by art, whatever the subject matter. Thomas Mann has pointed out that artists themselves tend to speak more of the goodness or badness of a work of art than of its beauty or ugliness. I think that particularly two shades of meaning in the word "good" are taken up here, the excellent or loved and the beneficent. These meanings in their depth are of course uncon- scious: they spur the artist to the creation of Form, a benign or uni- fying experience, however dire his subject matter. Pre-Columbian Mexican stone masks often express a powerful sadism or blood- thirstiness: it comes through to us as we look at the masks. It comes through to us, as it was meant to do, in terms of the calm, suave yet austere curves that it feeds. No other form of communication is likely to be more expressive of this blood-curdling content, yet the mask does not horrify the æsthete. He is aware, of course, of the blood-thirsty intensity and he perhaps values all the more—but it is obvious that taste will oscillate here a good deal—the powerful serenity, the spare enclosure, the beauty of the form. Mexican artists discovered an enduring pattern for strong emotions without belittling them, without (manic) protestation. There comes to us the perception of a fructifying object, inanimate though it be.

By the side of what I have called the benignity of art I put the non- anxious character or guiltlessness of æsthetic experience. It is not that the artist is without guilt or anxiety—far from it—nor that his sub- ject matter, the content of his work, must be divorced from these emotions. Such inhibition would entail a falsifying that would rule out art. Better than most, the artist remembers an actual taste, how- ever bitter. In this respect like the scientist, though himself *engagé*, he is also the observer and recorder. No, it is simply that in æsthetic experience we have something inexhaustible on which we feed, a pabulum without surfeit or waste product: something—and, remember, all experience comes within these terms—something nourishing, beneficent, that denotes at the same time an independent object, excellent or loved. These "good" objects, then, are out of harm's way and they preside over a world more unexpurgated than is usual. A cohesive load of experience—it must be as broad as possible if there is to be weight in so wide a reparative homage—is put by Form at the service of their universal dominion.

The psycho-analytic approach, then, to the æsthetic experience must be primarily in terms of the depressive position and of the ensuing drive to reparation, as conceived by Melanie Klein. I have attempted this approach in a discursive manner, in connection with architecture (1951); but the reference can only be to Dr. Segal's paper (1952). In contemplating the character of art as I have outlined it, I find it necessary to posit the prevalence, the universal prevalence, in this act of reparation, of two unconscious "good" imagos (to be specified a little later) in virtue of which Form embraces the artist's subject matter: whatever other introjected objects are supporting them, the two imagos, identified with a cultural background, are the main, invariable filter, often most narrow, through which content must pass. This filter, if it can be contemplated apart from the cultural identification, the cultural refinement —the metaphor here breaks down—has a primitive content of its own that tends to influence the general content: that is, Form has a content of its own. But if I say that the content of Form sometimes imposes an idealizing as well as a connective touch on manifest content, let it not be thought that I am unaware of ferocious treatments, sometimes well within the bounds of Form in modern art especially, or of undisguised obsessional and paranoiac traits; or of the protest not only that idealization is not essential but that art is in contact with the whole man and with the actualities of the cultural chaos which she must take to her heart.

But these negative expressions may figure successfully in art only if there is present as well a reparative nucleus: one sign of it, we have said, is a richness or excellence attributed to the medium: perhaps not to medium but at any rate to art in general. Indeed, it is because there is excellence in art's succinctness and pattern that some trends which are usually inhibited can so freely be displayed: this is part of the bringing together, of a coalescence that provides an emblem to the difficult organization of the ego. Art is a powerful means for the harmless expression of aggressive trends.

It may be thought that my least equivocal statements have been those concerned with the portraits of Rembrandt, namely, that our apprehension of the sitters' characters in terms of our visual and muscular responses to pictorial textures or realizations of shape, is a benign or unifying experience. I would recall to the reader that my first words were of clouds and of images they embody. We cannot look out upon the external world without any trace of such projection. Its nature will normally be somewhat circumscribed by the character, as it appears to the reality principle, of the object present to the senses. There are a thousand and one gradations between the power, as we feel it, of the object to suggest associations to us and the imputation, as we feel it, of our mood to this object. Anyone who, looking at clouds, with or without conscious phantasy, is increasingly arrested by their shape, tone, disposition, or the spaces between them, by every detail and its inter-relation, experiences an æsthetic sensation. In asserting this I am presuming that conscious phantasy, if it makes an appearance, does not merely use the condition of the clouds as a point of departure but that, on the contrary, the movements of phantasy or of judgment have been transposed into, and therefore restricted by, the very particular visual and tactile terms of these cloudy forms: only an animating content that exalts or sharpens the shape and detail of the clouds is felicitous or æsthetic; only what is continuously apprehended in terms of the eye's correlations and of the muscular sense. Then only is it an æsthetic projection, worthy of the epithet "benign". It seems to me that this is so because in such kind of apprehension we are as one with the *virtu* of the object while at the same time we, in turn, are giving to its intrinsic structure in bodily terms, to its actuality or distinctiveness, to its separateness from ourselves, full value. Such experiences are at the back of art: the artist re-creates them, and in so doing he is re-creating, preserving also, enlivening, older experiences, among them the basic experiences in object relationship, those which, when successfully fused, could have been the benign key to psychical integration (now declared, instead, in a form of art); namely, the sensation of one-ness with the satisfying breast no less than an acceptance of the whole mother as a separate person, as the sum of conflicting attributes. And so, we come to this definition: Form in art *is* content conceived in terms of a medium and of a culture that have been profoundly associated by the artist with the imagos described above (or with their prime surrogates).

I have said nothing about creativeness in general except to refer to the reparative aspect. Art epitomizes creativeness. This vague term, *tout court*, is permissible for a metapsychological context only, as a synonym for Eros in cultural dress.

But the homage to Eros would be formless were the heavier gifts from Thanatos excluded. I have insisted on certain metaphors and an abstraction: for emotion, a rounded stone; for the work of art, an entity; on something final, comprehensive and at rest. As *basso continuo* such intonations accompanying the melody of the integrative imagos with which they are used in harmony to make the music of Form.

At the service of life and health, the fusion into sleep may elongate bliss at the satisfying breast: not entirely removed from so single a world is utter ceasing. . . . The more constant entities are those inanimate. . . . Agent for resurrection and for death, the artist furnishes enshrinement.

II

In order to restore, and to communicate what he repairs, the artist must elaborate that part of the psyche, his ego, directly in touch with the external world. He busies himself arranging substances or sounds; and whereas all communications are received through the senses, his are distinguished, as we have seen, by unexampled sensuousness. Art descants in this way upon object-relationships and their introjection-projection, from the start of their history to their climax in the genital position, in relation with the breast and in relation with the whole, self-subsisting person. While communicating an intellectual content, art revivifies the impact of sensuous impressions under the ægis as well of the all-embracing sensations of early infanthood, particularly those connected with the mother's breast and with the hallucinations it evoked. Dr. Heimann writes in *Developments in Psycho-Analysis* (1952): "The most primitive psychic processes are bound up with sensation. The original experience, of which we can render the content only by using words, is certainly in the form of sensation, and it might be said that (to begin with) the infant has only his body with which to express his mental processes. Analytic work uncovers the unconscious contents as basic formations in the psyche, and within the analytic situation words seem a sufficient means for understanding. When, however, these phantasies are spontaneously expressed outside the analytic situation in language, that is, by the insane or by the poet, it is clear that words are handled as a material with sensual qualities."

To turn to the other end of the matter. Psycho-analysis has failed to emphasize the trait in æsthetic experience of full object-relationship. I know of only two passages in the literature[1]—there may well be a few others—which forge a link between artistic sublimation and the genital position. I think the gap occurs because the manifest quality I have discussed, the otherness or "entity" character that figures massively in æsthetic appreciation, has not been recognized. On the other hand, foundational or pre-genital full object-relationship, the first encounter with whole objects in the depressive position, as conceived by Melanie Klein (1934), is the subject of Dr. Segal's paper, *A Psycho-analytical Approach to Aesthetics* (1952), elsewhere in this book. She emphasizes two points especially, first, that the loss and the mourning in the depressive position is for a whole object: second, that since he has full capacity to experience loss, the artist retains a strong grip upon psychic reality. Indeed, since æsthetic pleasure lies in the perception of a reconstructed whole, it must be one built upon the recognition of the object's previous loss or ruin (whether or not this ruin also is shown), in contrast with manic denial. Art, if only by implication, bears witness to the world of depression or chaos overcome. It would otherwise possess no perennial attraction. Calm beauty is nothing without the collapse from which it arose: or, rather, it is mere prettiness.

This is a profound and a poetic conclusion. We all feel that though consumed with phantasy construction and idealization, art communicates in this way the broader actualities; it is often overt conflict that inspires an artist's imaginative flights. But this is not to endorse Rilke's sentence which Dr. Segal quotes: "Beauty is nothing but the beginning of terror which we are just able to bear." Certainly, the element of depression implicit in true creativeness brings a whiff of death: yet, to the æsthete at any rate, not only is ugliness a great deal more "depressing"—the occasion for re-depression, however momentary—but so is the manic, protesting, character of the vulgar and of the "merely pretty" which Dr. Segal has so well separated with a few words from beauty.

[1] Thus, Ella Sharpe, in her unfinished paper on *Hamlet* (1947). "It seems to me that the conception of a work of art in its total harmonious unity, is only possible when a unification of component trends under genital primacy has occurred, even though this may have been maintained only for a very brief period. It may indeed be that the artist himself fails to re-attain full sexual development in maturity but his work will continue to bear witness to the strongest drive in nature, the impulse to create. This impulse may be foreshadowed in the pre-genital impulses and is often expressed in their terms, but is nevertheless dynamized by genital libido." This is in accord with a passage from Melanie Klein (1923), where it is inferred that one of the determinants for artistic creation is the degree of genital activity deflected into sublimation.

In defining æsthetic Form I have indicated that subject-matter is organized under the dominion of two imagos or prototypical experiences that have been introjected: first, the feeling of one-ness with the breast and so, with the world; secondly, the keen recognition of a separate object, originally the mother's whole person whose loss was mourned in the infantile depressive position. The second postulate is in accord with Dr. Segal's analysis of the æsthetic approach to the solution of depressive phantasies. But is my first postulate (merging with the breast) at variance?

At first sight it would seem so. Dr. Segal is rightly at pains to demarcate the æsthetic from the manic solution, beauty from the denial of depressive actuality. What, then, is to be made of oceanic feeling or merging with the breast as a constant initiator of the Form in art? It testifies, surely, to a manic element?

Referring to Freud's statement that in mania the ego is merged into the super-ego, Rado says (1928) in a sentence that has often been quoted: "This process is the faithful intra-psychic repetition of the experience of that fusing with the mother that takes place during drinking at the breast." And so, conversely, if merging with the breast is an experience that underlies the creation of Form, then it might seem likely that an element of manic denial governs artistic creation. I have insisted on identifying the two ill-assorted imagos with the ethics, as it were, of a medium: and moreover, these early super-ego introjects are said to have become associated with the ample extensions of a cultural heritage. So far as he can be called "pure" artist, the artist's ego, with all his elaboration of the senses, has been closely confined by those introjects: it is the same, I think, for the observer, in the act of æsthetic appreciation.

We have reached entire genetic confusion: an emphasis upon the ego and object-relationship, at the same time upon a merging of ego with super-ego: yet an emphasis also upon a non-manic grip of psychic reality, upon unblushing display of conflict.

The muddle hardly matters if it helps to indicate the central problem of art from a psycho-analytic point of view. That problem may be put as follows: How can it be that the homogeneity associated with idealization (the inexhaustible breast), is harnessed by the work of art to an acute sense of otherness and of actuality? (Thus, space is a homogeneous "state" into which we are drawn and freely plunged by the representations of visual art; concurrently it figures there as the mode of order and distinctiveness for "pre-existent" objects.) It is my conviction not only that these are contrary elements fused in art but that there is a just proportion, founded upon a once simple link between them, which make their harmony poignant and health-giving.

I think we may often discern in the views of artists especially, in matters outside art, more than a trace of this amalgam. There is no all-embracing, non-differentiating doctrine to which, rather more, perhaps, than their fellows, they are not prone to subscribe. Their facile idealism is often in harness with an otherwise cynical attitude to generalization. Artists are the first debunkers, satire their prime offensive weapon. We have the stubborn Bohemianism of the studios, a refusal of the uneasy disguises of conventional living (except where it possesses æsthetic value), in combination, very often, with political, philosophical, religious panaceas, not to mention romantic attachment to Bohemia itself. But this last, the most typical, is in no way hostile to truth: and investigators tend to agree that the hypothetical "pure" artist cares only for an æsthetic solution of conflict: were it so, dogmas would at best have an æsthetic value for him. The man in the street sometimes appears to display a similar attitude. But what does this mean: what does this tendency—it cannot be put higher, even in the case of Michelangelo and his stern, deeply founded religion tempered with neo-Platonism—amount to, in the face of religious belief, for instance? An optimistic answer might point to the not uncommon use of the word "æsthetic" as a *judgment*, in effect, upon world-embracing systems of thought that are by no means scientific. For instance, we may feel that universal religions and philosophical systems, huge constructions of passion and intellect, solid, rounded as hill towns, are fine enough *in themselves*, that is to to say if viewed æsthetically, as works of art, as polished reflectors of human endeavour rather than as vehicles of truth. (The reader may be reminded of the fused ingredients that go to make up Form.) The word "æsthetic" in this context, then, covers the amalgam we are examining in a matter outside art: and if acknowledged art shall extend wider, the better it will be for truth.

But it would be absurd to equate the artist with the normal man. For one thing, the artist's depression is far more acute. And again, some artists undoubtedly have strong hypomanic tendencies, to say the least. Nevertheless, since art is compact, articulated, æsthetic activity cannot be identified with ecstatic states, though it may be impossible to assert a clean-cut distinction between poets, for instance, the saga makers, and prophets or others who speak of current affairs from a state of trance. The artist, however, seeks inspiration

415

no less for his *mode* of utterance, for poem as well as for poetry: the mode makes utterance a "thing", an object like a person with a viewpoint of his own: such individuality may be recognized even by those who least identify themselves with the "message". The second basic imago of Form, the emphasis it brings upon full object-relationship, possesses a temperate power over the first unity, the blissful merging with the breast: it provides æsthetic experience with a definition that would be disturbing to mere ecstacy, brings to art a second principle of unification; so that the one is wide, the other crisp.

It seems to me then, that in relation to depressive states, the æsthetic position perhaps deserves a category of its own, between the predominant manic defence and a normal outcome; a position, however, not without relevance to an analysis of integration, since it uncover a more creative role than usual for the manic defence mechanism: one that is potentially non-stultifying. Were this so, it would appear that the germ of the æsthetic attitude would be discoverable in infancy. Ella Sharpe wrote (1935): "Seeing, hearing, bodily sensations are the instruments by which we first learn to know external reality and first introject what we see and hear and feel." . . . "The artist's moral code, his range of values, is in terms of good and bad form, line, colour, sound, and movement. His ethics are in these things because of the intensity of his feelings, good and bad, associated with sight, sound, intake and output, during infancy." But this must be true of every infant, and we are used to hearing now that all children are artists. The question is whether children's drawings, and sometimes, too, their play, can be said to be projected under the dominion of the elements I have associated with æsthetic Form.

My answer, such as it is, cannot be made firmly since I have not alluded to the vast kingdom of symbolization except with regard to the symbolism of Form that in art incites and rules this populace from which it has sprung.

For vitality and rhythm, above all as pregnant symbol-formation, children's drawings, so similar under favourable circumstances throughout the world (and, one suspects, throughout the ages), win admiration from modern artists; the more so since the chaotic nature of our culture to-day precludes an easily communicable "world on its own": the identifications that produce inevitable symbols are not easily made between ourselves and our cultural environment. On the other hand, the contrast in æsthetic value between

416

children's drawings and primitive art which is, of course, the mature expression of a culture, tends to justify the introduction of this word in my definition of Form. Apart from the ego's growth, art needs for its powerful syntheses the ramifying of the super-ego formations I have singled out.

We know that many kinds of anxiety, most psychical situations, are "acted out" in children's play and in their drawings. It must be very doubtful whether this compulsiveness has a discoverable reparative nucleus in general, such as I have attributed to æsthetic Form. All the same, even the scrappiest of children's drawings tend to be vivid, self-contained "things": whatever is predominantly symbolized—parents in sadistic intercourse, let us say—the primary content proceeds by way of manifest content to the terms of a static configuration: although the child is entirely implicated, he disguises his own role, too, as the palpable fruit of the medium he employs. There is, maybe, to be found in this situation, not only the defence of projective identification or of other distortions, but also a picking up through the medium of a calmer aspect in the outside world of objects, since the primary content is now *composed* by means of rhythm and design and the reciprocities of vivid colour. Such integration in a new setting of divergent symbols allows to each a more marked significance. Melanie Klein has said (1930) that both dread of an original object and the loss of an object tend to entail their substitution by symbols. It is not surprising that symbols of a dreaded object and of a lost, loved object often coalesce to make a work of art: that is to say, when the first contributes to the particular content and the other contributes to Form whereby the particular content achieves an absolute, a final air.

In regard to the other aspect of Form, the element of one-ness and fusion, I will quote some sentences from Marion Milner's paper, *Aspects of Symbolism in Comprehension of Not-Self* (1952), elsewhere in this book, which is concerned, in the analysis of a boy of ten, not only with just this element, but also with the link between the sense of one-ness and the sense of other-ness. She suggests that the first is necessary to the second: that "states (of one-ness) are a necessary phase in the development of object-relationships and that the understanding of their function gives a meaning to the phrase 'Art creates Nature'". . . . "The idea that these states of illusion of oneness are perhaps a recurrently necessary phase in the continued growth of the sense of two-ness leads to a further question: What happens when they are prevented from occurring with sufficient

417

frequency or at the right moment? I think this boy was trying to tell me that what may happen is that the world becomes grey, lacking in affective colouring, prosaic." It is because "the basic identifications which make it possible to find new objects, to find the familiar in the unfamiliar, requires an ability to tolerate a temporary loss of sense of self, a temporary giving up of the discriminating ego".[1]

Any further connection to be found in the literature between one-ness, or fusion with the breast, and the sense of otherness, may help to resolve the problem I have stated and to explain the genesis of æsthetic Form. I can offer only two examples.

Dr. Rycroft writes (1951) of a so-called dream-screen dream (merging with the breast). "It represented the successful fulfilment in sleep of the wish for oral union with the analyst, who was taking the role of the mother's breast and the father's penis conceived of as a breast. This oral union was an external object-relationship, and the real importance of the dream was that it marked the shift from a narcissistic attitude of identification with an internal object to one of turning towards an external object, even though the external object still bore the projected image of the phantasied breast."

Melanie Klein has averred a basic connection between relationship with the breast and object-relationship. "I have often expressed my view", she wrote (1946), "that object relations exist from the beginning of life, the first object being the mother's breast." . . . "The introjection of the good object, first of all the mother's breast, is a precondition of normal development." (A successful assimilation of introjects prepares the way for sublimatory processes. P. Heimann (1942).) "This first internal good object", continues Melanie Klein, "acts as a focal point in the ego. It counteracts the processes of splitting and dispersal, makes for cohesiveness and integration, and is instrumental in building up the ego. The infant's feeling of having inside a good and complete breast may, however, be shaken by frustration and anxiety. As a result, the division between the good and bad breast may be difficult to maintain, and the infant may feel that the good breast too is in bits. . . . With the splitting of the object, idealization is bound up, for the good aspects of the breast are exaggerated as a safeguard against the fear of the

[1] One of Mrs. Milner's remarks about symbolism has much bearing on the present subject. She writes: "Earlier psycho-analytic discussion of symbol formation most often emphasized the child's attempts to find substitution for those original objects of interest that are the parents' organs. But some also emphasized the aspect of the child's attempts to find his own organs and their functioning in every object. In more recent work these two views tend to be combined and the idea develops that the primary 'object' that the infant seeks to find again is a fusion of self and object, it is breast and mouth felt as fused into one."

persecuting breast. Idealization is thus the corollary of persecuting fear, but it also springs from the power of the instinctual desires which aim at unlimited gratification and therefore create the picture of an inexhaustible and always bountiful breast—an ideal breast."[1] Melanie Klein is chiefly concerned in the paper I have quoted with the dangers inseparable from the early splitting processes. Excessive projective identification is one of these, whereby even good parts of the self may be lost. "It is not only an object about whom guilt is experienced but also parts of the self which the subject is driven to repair or restore."

One of the ways by which he can do so once more, I feel, is in the creating of art. There is a close connection between definition of the ego and of the whole and separate object first encountered in the depressive position (Klein, 1935). Similarly, if, in a work of art, one of the objects re-defined, renewed, and found by the artist is, at root, himself, nevertheless the model for self-subsistence has been the other person or thing: or, at least, the one cannot be distinguished without its reflections from the other. We may suspect that the work of art constantly symbolizes such percipience, just as it symbolizes the restoration of truly self-sufficient objects to which have accrued, all the same, propensities of the inexhaustible breast.

When he is viewed from a related ego angle, it is sometimes obvious that the artist appropriates objects in terms of his subject-matter, controls them, reduces them, without much ado, to the needs of his own idiosyncrasy, that is to say, to aspects of dominant ego trends. Needless to say the exhibitionism and omnipotence remarked by Freud is then much to the fore. But again, if the product is æsthetic, the artist will have made of himself an "entity"; and he will have accommodated omnipotence with the oceanic feeling. Then, however summary and masterful his treatment, the affirmation of enduring other-ness survives. I have previously called this affirmation the carving, as opposed to the more summary, or modelling, aspect of art with which it is welded (1934 and 1937).

A powerful sublimation of aggression contributes to the "attack", as it is called, in the use of the medium of an art, irrespective of what content is communicated. This sublimation combines with the one

---

[1] In *A Contribution to the Theory of Anxiety and Guilt* (1948), Melanie Klein has stated that "depressive anxiety or guilt already play some part in the infant's earliest object-relation, i.e. in relation to his mother's breast". Here is a link that may be deemed invaluable to the present argument. The connecting of the earliest object-relationships (bodily sensations) with idealization and omnipotence as well as persecution, provides one of the many rich themes within the projection-introjection key, worked out by Joan Riviere, Paula Heimann and Melanie Klein herself in *Developments in Psycho-Analysis*, Hogarth Press (1952).

of the depressive position in its positive or reparative aspect. For many an unsuccessful or would-be artist, "attack" will have been impeded, or exaggerated, by anxiety; but of course, such inhibition is not usually as stultifying as an inhibition of the depressive viewpoint itself by a major regression to the earlier schizoid or paranoid phases (Klein, 1946), a state of affairs that rules out any question of æsthetic paramountcy owing to the inability to undergo depressive suffering.

A consideration of "attack" is not immediately relevant to Form in art as I have defined it. I make this mention of "attack" in order to assure the reader that though I think my main argument brushes, however lightly, the centre of æsthetic value, I know that a hundred and one further psycho-analytic questions are involved.

18

PSYCHO-ANALYSIS AND ETHICS

R. E. MONEY-KYRLE

I. THE TRANSFER OF AN ETHICAL PROBLEM FROM PHILOSOPHY TO SCIENCE

Philosophers are now divided into two main schools of thought: those who try to ask and answer metaphysical questions, and those who try to show that all metaphysical questions are meaningless.[1] But if logic is on the side of the second school, we still need not dismiss all speculative philosophy as a sterile pursuit. The questions it formulated may often have been grammatically meaningless, but those who formulated them were clearly wrestling with some problem which they felt to be important. What was wrong was not that there was no problem, but that there was a failure to formulate it in such a way that an answer would be possible. So the essential difference between science and philosophy would seem to be, not that science deals with significant and philosophy with meaningless problems, but that science deals with those that are clear cut and philosophy with those which have not got beyond the stage of being only dimly felt.[2] Many centuries of philosophical endeavour may be required before such questions get beyond this stage, and when they do they cease to be philosophical and are immediately transferred to science. In other words, the task of philosophy is perhaps always a preliminary one: that of formulating new problems for science.

Among the oldest questions of philosophy are: What is a good individual? And what is a good society or state? It is not difficult to see what the philosopher who asks, and tries to answer, these

---

[1] According to Wittgenstein, the right method of teaching philosophy would be to confine oneself to propositions of the sciences, leaving philosophical assertions to the learner, and proving to him, whenever he made them, that they are meaningless. *Tractatus Logico-Philosophicus*, 1922.

[2] Professor Jerusalem of Vienna expressed this well by saying that philosophy begins with an "intellectual discomfort".

questions is trying to do. He is trying to defend his moral and political preferences—both from doubts within himself and from the hostility of others—and he is trying to do this in a particular way, by argument rather than by force.

It is clear that success in these tasks would be a very notable achievement. It would—at least in theory, though not necessarily in practice—transfer the ultimate arbitrament of moral and political disputes from the arena of force to the court of rational discussion. But is it even theoretically possible?

If what is being sought is a "proof" of a "preference",[1] this is certainly a futile quest, which would never have been attempted but for a confusion between two senses of the word "belief". We may say, for instance, that we "believe in" democracy when what we really mean is that we desire it and may thus mislead ourselves linguistically into treating our desire as if it were a belief which could be "true" or "false". But strictly speaking, a desire or preference is not an object of belief, can be neither true nor false, and is therefore not susceptible to "proof".

The discovery that preferences cannot be proved may be an important negative achievement of "positivist" philosophy. But I no longer think that this disposes of ethics. It would do so if beliefs and preferences were entirely independent of each other. But they are not. We know that our preferences affect our beliefs; and it is equally true that our beliefs affect our preferences. As we acquire knowledge—and this consists in the substitution of true beliefs for false ones—our moral and political preferences undergo a change. Now consider the way in which such changes could occur in different individuals, whom we may suppose to start with very different preferences. There are three possibilities: the preferences may remain divergent, or they may converge, or they may converge in some respects and remain divergent in others. There is no *a priori* means of knowing which of these three alternatives is correct. If the first, then such preferences are relative, and all attempts to find a rational argument to justify some one against the rest must necessarily fail. If, however, either of the two alternatives should prove to be the case, if preferences converge, either wholly or in part, with increasing knowledge, then such preferences, or at least some aspect of them, could be justified as being held by all wise men. Moreover,

---

[1] Many ethical arguments can be shown to have been circular. For instance, a preference for a particular moral code or political system is first expressed in a definition. Then the definition is treated as a proposition and an attempt is made to prove it "true".

since knowledge, that is, true beliefs, can be proved and communicated, it would be logically possible, though not perhaps feasible in practice, for the wise to convert others to their preferences.

Some such possibility as this must have been in Plato's mind when he formulated the basic problems of ethics. His question, in effect, was not "What is a good man or a good society?" but "What are the morals and politics of the wise?" We may try to reconstruct from a trivial example some of the background of his thought. If a man prefers pork pie to caviare, this may be either because, while acquainted with both, he really prefers pork pie, or because he is unacquainted with caviare. Plato seems to have taken the second alternative for granted, and proceeds to inquire about the taste of the truly wise who are acquainted with everything.

Now this question could have a unique answer only if Plato's assumption is correct, that is to say, if differences of æsthetic or moral and political taste result solely from the limitations of our knowledge or experience. But whether it has a unique or a multiple answer, it is a significant question of a kind which could transfer ethics from philosophy to science.

Unfortunately he does not seem to have tried to find an empirical answer. Instead, he became enmeshed in the coils of a concealed tautology. For his answer—that the wise prefer the good—results solely from his definitions: that the good is what is most desirable, and that what is most desirable is what we should desire if we were acquainted with everything.

Moreover, for Plato, wisdom did not consist in any empirical knowledge, but in acquaintance with the ideal prototypes of things.

Nevertheless, there can be no doubt, I think, that Plato's formulation of the problem as one about the morals and politics of the wise is the only formulation that can lead to significant and important results. Unlike the question "What is a good man or a good society?" which can only be answered by a definition, the question "What are the morals and politics of the wise?" is, at least in theory, capable of an empirical answer, which may or may not prove to be unique.

To make it also a practical question, we must modify it a little further. In the first place, we must specify the type of wisdom we refer to. Obviously some kinds of knowledge are more relevant than others. Neither our moral nor our political preferences are much influenced by our knowledge of motor-cars or aircraft. But both are modified, often profoundly, by our knowledge of what is

broadly called the humanities—or, more specifically, by our understanding of ourselves and so of other people, that is, by our knowledge of psychology. Our politics, if not our morals, must also be
influenced by other forms of knowledge, for example, of economics
and the technique of production and of general sociology. But
since these influence our choice of means to a pre-determined social
end, rather than of the end itself, we may ignore them for the
moment, and begin by considering only the influence of our knowledge of ourselves.

In the second place, wisdom—which for our immediate purpose
we have now equated with psychological insight—although increasing, is always incomplete. No one can claim to be all wise,
or even very wise, though if he studies he may hope to be becoming
wiser. If therefore the ethical question is not to be purely academic,
we must stop asking about the ethics of the wise, and ask instead
about the changing ethics of those whose wisdom is increasing. Taking account of these modifications, our question now becomes:
How do our moral and political preferences change with increasing
psychological insight? Do the preferences of different people remain
divergent? Do they tend to converge? Or do they converge in
some respects and remain divergent in others? If so, what is the type
of morality and ideology towards which they converge?

These questions, or so it seems, to me, have always been latent
in ethics. The task of philosophy is to make them manifest by so
formulating them that an empirical answer is possible. From then
on the task of answering them belongs to science—in this case, to
psychology.

2. PSYCHO-ANALYSIS AS A METHOD OF PSYCHOLOGICAL RESEARCH

Plato put his question nearly two and a half millennia ago; and even
had he put it clearly, that is, in a form admitting an empirical answer, we might have had to wait until now before a correct answer
could have been given. The relevant science might not have been
sufficiently developed.

Suppose this question to have been asked in this form at some previous time. We should have seen that the moral and political preferences of any individual usually changed, at least to some extent,
as his knowledge of the sciences of man increased. But I do not
think we should have been able to observe any certain convergence

between the preferences of different individuals as they each advanced in learning. Indeed, it would have seemed clear enough that an equally profound knowledge of history, of economics, and of every other branch of the humanities was compatible with the widest moral and political divergencies. We should therefore have been forced to the conclusion that there was no rational means by which one set of values could be defended against others. The essential relativity of values would have seemed well established—each being right only for those who held them and wrong for others.

Almost within the last half century, however, a new branch of learning has developed which is particularly relevant to our inquiry; for more than any other it profoundly affects all our feelings and desires. This science investigates a field the very existence of which was only recently discovered—namely the field of our own unconscious minds. We may therefore reopen the old question in a new form and ask: How are our morals and politics affected as we become more conscious of ourselves?

The technique that enables us to widen the boundaries of our consciousness is psycho-analysis. That the effect it has on our emotions and desires is solely the result of the knowledge it conveys, and not of some other influence, is a point vital to the argument to be developed. To prove that we meet our obligations to the patient we need only show that these changes diminish his distress by helping to restore his capacity for both work and pleasure. To justify them to any society that sets itself above the individual, we might also have to show that they make him a more efficient functioning unit. But these are both arbitrary courts. To justify them to science, which is not arbitrary, we have to show that they are the result of having helped him to see the truth about himself. To increase in him this kind of wisdom is the analyst's overriding aim.

Everyone knows that analysis is a form of therapy for mental illness. But there is some uncertainty—perhaps even among analysts —about its aims and the way in which they are achieved. If the analyst has a sense of responsibility towards his patients—and it is impossible to imagine a competent analyst who has not—he certainly desires to lighten their distress. If he has a sense of responsibility towards society—and this is a less important asset—he may wish to improve their adaptation to it. But if either of these were his primary aim he might sometimes have to use a different method. He might have to prevent his patients becoming conscious of some troubles which they had hitherto successfully evaded. Or he might

425

R. E. Money-Kyrle

have to prevent them from becoming wiser than the society they lived in, lest their adaptation to it should be worsened rather than improved.

In general, however—and in the long run perhaps always—the hedonic interests of the patient, and the utilitarian interest of society, are best served by the pursuit of truth. That this should be so is very far from obvious. The content of the unconscious consists of insatiable libidinal desires, passionate destructive hatreds, terrible anxieties and all the abysses of depression and despair. What hedonic, what utilitarian, purpose can possibly be served by bringing these to light? That it does serve such purposes has been proved by every analysis that has succeeded in its primary purpose of raising the iron curtain of repression. But how are we to explain so unexpected a result? One part of the explanation is that opposite impulses, which have been dissociated from each other, are necessarily modified when brought together in the light. But I think a more important part is that some of these impulses are diminished in intensity by the discovery that they are reactions to imaginary situations, which they themselves created, rather than to real ones.[1] The patient, in fact, learns two sorts of truth about himself: first, that he has many impulses and emotions which he had previously denied. And secondly, that these impulses (which seemed omnipotent at a time when there was no distinction between sensation and idea) have first created, and are now maintained by, an unconscious phantasy world which is a gross distortion of the conscious world of sensory perception. It is, I think, this last discovery that most changes his emotional behaviour.

Of course the emotional and the intellectual aspects of the process react reciprocally upon each other. An interpretation that lessens a patient's anxiety improves his emotional relation to his analyst and this in turn removes an impediment to further insight. But if the emotional change is achieved by a "reassurance" rather than an interpretation, there is no durable advance. So it is always the increase in insight—the successive flashes of self-knowledge awakened by interpretation—that initiates and maintains the therapeutic process.

A grossly over-simplified example may best serve to illustrate this single point. A young man complains of exaggerated nervousness

[1] The therapeutic process has been examined in detail by James Strachey in two papers: "The Nature of the Therapeutic Action of Psycho-Analysis" (1934), and "Symposium on the Theory of the Therapeutic Results of Psycho-Analysis" (1937), *Int. J. Psycho-Anal.* Vols. XV and XVII.

in the presence of authority. This soon shows itself in his relation to his analyst. Consciously, he regards him as helpful and sympathetic, and indeed over-estimates the extent of his skill and benevolence. But he begins to behave as if he believed him to have the exact opposite of these qualities—as if he believed him to be a sinister, almost a diabolic, figure who had both the power and the wish to injure him. This, in fact, is what he does unconsciously believe. If true, such a belief would amply justify his symptoms, which are neurotic only in so far as it is contrary to all the evidence. His analyst's task is to help him free himself from it by showing him how it was developed. They begin by discovering that all authoritative figures in his life, from his present analyst to his father, of whom he was once extremely jealous, have been consciously admired and loved, but unconsciously hated. This goes some way to explain his fear, because he naturally expects to be hated in return. What reduces the fear, however, is not, I think, the mere discovery of the hatred, but the discovery that the hatred has distorted its object. A vicious spiral had been in operation: his unconscious hatred had painted his father blacker than he was, and this increased blackness had in turn increased his hatred, until he had built up, in unconscious phantasy, a truly diabolic figure of which he lived in mortal dread.[1] Meanwhile, at the conscious level, all this was not only denied but actually reversed; for he had tried to defend himself against his dread by over-idealizing its object. Consciously, he had painted every authority, from his father to his analyst, much whiter than they really were, and so had sought to turn them into wholly benevolent guardians of himself—into gods to protect him from his devils. With these discoveries, the two opposite pictures begin to converge to a reality which is somewhere in between the two, and the fear, together with the exaggerated admiration, is appreciably diminished.

Even in an over-simplified example, I cannot pretend that this is the end of the story. Hatred based on jealousy does not fully account for the sadistic malevolence of that phantom of his unconscious imagination of which he stood so much in awe. The sadism was originally his own. Its first object was his mother. He had later projected it upon his father whom he had thus made its agent in his early quarrels with her; and he had then become terrified of the Frankenstein monster which his omnipotent phantasy seemed to have created. So what we ultimately arrive at is the fear of a

---

[1] As is well known, such figures are unconsciously felt to be internal persecutors, which are projected into the analyst and other figures in the external world.

destructive impulse within himself—and here perhaps remains a nucleus of ineradicable conflict and anxiety.

All this and more has to be laid bare by slow and painful steps before his fear of authority can be reduced to that rational minimum which is justified by the extent to which any given authority has the power and will to do him harm. But perhaps I have said enough to show how analysis achieves its results. The patient's emotional behaviour is irrational. It is not justified by the situation he is really in. He behaves as if he were in different situations. He unconsciously believes he is in them; he is in them in unconscious phantasy; he is unconsciously deluded. Analysis seeks to show him what are these beliefs, these phantasies, or these delusions, and how they are produced. So far as it succeeds in this, it frees him from them; he may still have conflicts, and he may still have some fear of his own aggressiveness, but he no longer has delusions, and no longer fears the phantoms his aggressiveness created. So far as he ceases to believe in his phantasy world, he behaves rationally in the world of his perceptions. Thus analysis is a rational process which operates solely by exposing error and replacing it by truth.

We know from the records of many past analyses a good deal about the various types of unconscious belief or phantasy we are likely to meet, and experience is continually adding to the list. As several usually operate at once, the art consists, not only in seeing which are there, and one's own role in them, but also in choosing which to interpret first. Different analysts, even when they belong to the same school and have the same degree of technical ability, may perhaps take them in rather different orders; but, if these analysts are relatively free from individual blind spots, no important theme is likely to be missed, and the end result will be very much the same. For what has been pieced together is the truth of which there can be no two versions.[1]

III. TWO TYPES OF CONSCIENCE

Among the various changes of feeling and desire that occur in analysis, as the patient gradually learns the truth about himself, are changes in his moral attitude. A moral impulse may be defined as an impulse to do, or to refrain from doing, something because to

---

[1] As to the wider differences between different schools, it is not always easy to distinguish between those which are real and those which are apparent. The real differences, which are considerable, are between the different contents attributed to the unconscious. The apparent ones are between different conceptual systems used to represent the same content.

refrain from doing, or to do, it would arouse a sense of guilt. Obviously such impulses can change their object, or increase or diminish in intensity. But what is less obvious, and was for a long time overlooked, is that there can also be a qualitative change in the guilt which is their motive.

We are accustomed to think of guilt as an elementary feeling. We now know that it is a compound of at least two elements. In a deep analysis, there is a fundamental change in the relative intensity of these components, or, to be more exact, in the patient's relative capacity to feel them; he becomes less sensitive to one and, on the whole, more sensitive to the other. But this distinction, which we owe to Melanie Klein, is comparatively recent. In earlier analyses, which did not penetrate into the deeper levels of infantile experience, only the diminishing component in guilt attracted much attention. We will consider separately the moral changes brought about by these earlier analyses and compare them with the changes occurring in the more recent and fuller analyses which those influenced by Melanie Klein's work on the very early levels of infantile experience endeavour to conduct.[1]

Unlike psychopathic delinquents and some psychotics, who often give the (incorrect) impression of having no capacity for guilt at all, most neurotics and especially obsessionals are extremely conscientious. And it was with neurotics that analysis was at first concerned. Their guilt seemed to have been first aroused in early childhood by certain primitive sexual wishes and to have subsequently become attached to, and so interfered with, many non-sexual sublimations. The result was a crippling, and often progressive, inhibition of whatever activities they tried. They seemed to be suffering from an excess of guilt, so that the diminution of this guilt appeared as the ultimate aim of their analyses.

A prolonged study of such over-conscientiousness in neurotics led Freud to the discovery of the super-ego—one of the major achievements of analysis. The first step, and by no means a small one, was to recognise the guilt motive at all in what to the patient seemed a meaningless symptom which gratuitously condemned him to impotence in whatever he strove to undertake—indeed often in whatever his conscious morality bade him undertake. And when this was done, the way in which such a crippling, and often self-defeating, morality could have been developed remained

---

[1] Of course the terms "deep" and "shallow" are relative. What seems deep to-day may seem shallow enough to our successors.

to be unearthed. Freud's well-known explanation is certainly true, but is no longer generally believed to be the whole truth. It may be briefly stated thus: the child's Œdipean jealousy brings him into conflict with the parent of the same sex as himself, whom he may have loved and admired but now also, though less consciously hates, and wishes to mutilate and to destroy. His sense of guilt is originally his fear of a talion punishment from this parent, and in particular his fear of being castrated by him. After a period of conflict, of varying intensity and duration, he succeeds in repressing his jealousy, and good relations with this parent are once more restored. But the change is brought about in a very special way. The image of the loved, hated, and feared parent is split into two. The more realistic aspect continues to be identified with the external parent of perception. But the less realistic and more terrifying aspect is incorporated in phantasy as an unconscious part of the self. To this "introjected" parent Freud gave the name of super-ego. In his view, it is the necessary guardian of morality; but when over-developed, it condemns its possessor to mental illness, and by so doing defeats part of its own purpose which is to transmit the positive as well as the negative demands of the society we live in.

Freud by no means ignored, indeed he stressed, the fact that the same parent who is feared and hated is also admired and loved.[1] Nevertheless the super-ego morality described by him is predominately a morality of fear.

Moreover, it is an essentially relative morality. Its primary taboos —those on incest and parricide—are of course common to all mankind; but since its basic aim is to appease, by obedience, a feared authority, it is as varied in its superstructure as the will of the authority to be obeyed. Its immediate sanction is the introjected parents whose moral code was in turn derived from their parents and so from the traditional mores of the society in which they lived. And since the super-ego is readily identified with the sanctions of this society, it is further strengthened by them, and becomes both indirectly and directly the precipitate of these mores. Thus the super-ego morality of a "good" German Nazi is very different from that of a "good" British Socialist, and still further removed from that of a "good" Trobriander or Dobuan. There is indeed only one common element in the super-ego moralities of different societies or sub-groups; they all alike demand the same unquestioning obedience, but to codes of very different kinds.

[1] "Humour", *Int. J. Psycho-Anal.*, Vol. IX, 1928.

If we next inquire about the changes effected in super-ego morality by the self-knowledge which analysis endeavours to extend, there can be little doubt about the answer. So far as this morality is based on irrational fears, for example, on a castration anxiety which is no longer, as it may have been in primal times, justified by the actual situation, the effect of analysis is to weaken the fear and the morality based upon it. Of course the process is never complete; a varying amount of "persecutory guilt" remains. But the direction of the change is always and inevitably the same—towards the liquidation of a morality based on an irrational anxiety.

No special analytic knowledge is required to convince us that there must be another aspect of morality based not on fear but love. Yet its unconscious ramifications have proved even harder to unravel. What we have now learnt about them we owe to Melanie Klein's discovery of early persecutory and depressive states in the development of children, which we must now examine.[1]

Those analysts who accept her results are quite as concerned as those who have not yet done so with the exposure of the phantasies underlying the persecutory element in guilt. Indeed, they seek to carry this process much further; for in their view the super-ego, which Freud discovered, does not begin, as he believed, about the age of five, but is already at that age approaching its final form after five years of previous development. In its earlier stages, however, it consists of unintegrated phantasy objects, by which the infant believes himself to be persecuted from within, and has not yet acquired its final character of an integrated internal mentor. The phase in which these persecutory anxieties reach a maximum intensity has been called by Melanie Klein the "paranoid position". Its discovery has of course greatly increased the chances of successful treatment of adult paranoics. It has also enabled us better to analyse the paranoid elements in all patients—including "normal" people— and so further to diminish the persecutory elements in their conscious and unconscious sense of guilt.

Now sooner or later, in any deep analysis, as the sense of persecution is diminished, depressive feelings begin to appear. As these are analysed in turn they are always found to express grief and remorse for injuries to a loved object for which the patient feels himself to be responsible. This grief and remorse constitute the other element in guilt which we may describe as depressive as distinct from persecutory.

---

[1] Melanie Klein, *The Psycho-Analysis of Children* (London, 1932), and *Contributions to Psycho-Analysis*, 1921-45 (London, 1948).

In order to understand its origin, and its relation to the persecutory element, we must try to reconstruct the first stage in the intellectual and emotional development of a newborn baby. This is the association of percepts with memory images to form concepts of enduring objects. Since to him the most noticeable attribute of any percept or memory image is the pain or pleasure it provides, he begins by linking all similar percepts and memory images that are pain-giving or frustrating to form one object and all similar pleasurable or gratifying ones to form another. Thus, for example, his first concept of the breast is not of one object but of two, which are as wholly incompatible with each other as night and day. Moreover, since he attributes to, or "projects" upon, the frustrating breast all his own rage at the frustration, it is felt as persecutory as well as disappointing. And, similarly, by the projection of his love, the gratifying breast is also felt to be actively benevolent.

That these ideally "good" and ideally "bad" objects are different aspects of the same one (and the same child both loves and hates them)[1] is a discovery which is delayed because it is so intensely painful. But sooner or later this discovery is made, and with it comes the first onset of depression, which later forms the depressive element in guilt.

Since the good object which is injured, either in phantasy or fact tends to turn into a persecutor, the two elements are, perhaps from the beginning of the depressive phase, almost inseparably combined. But they can be combined in very different proportions, and the proportions in which they are combined in any given individual will determine the type of his conscience, the kind of situation that arouses it and the nature of the action it impels.

All true guilt, as Freud long ago discovered, is aroused by what is basically the same situation, namely conflict with the inner representative of an integrated parental figure. But the two elements in it will be combined in proportions determined by the extent to which this figure is felt to be bad and persecutory or good and beneficent. And from this it follows that the external situations that arouse guilt can be very different for different individuals. Those whose superegos are predominantly persecutory will experience guilt, and of a predominantly persecutory kind, in situations where they are tempted to defy this figure or some external power which represents it. But the situations that will arouse guilt in those whose inner

---

[1] See W. Clifford M. Scott, "A Psycho-Analytic Concept of the Origin of Depression", *Brit. med. J.*, 1949.

figures are predominantly good, will be such as imply an injury to, a betrayal of, or a failure to protect, the people or values that symbolize their good internal objects.

There will also be a fundamental difference, not only in the quality of the guilt and in the type of situation that arouses it, but in the reaction to the guilt aroused. Those with predominantly persecutory consciences react by propitiation. Those in whom the persecutory element is slight and are in consequence relatively more sensitive to the depressive element react by reparation.

It is obvious that these two types of conscience, which are characteristic of different individuals, can coexist in the same one. To some extent they always do so. Every child, especially in the Œdipean phase of his development, is faced with situations that evoke a direct conflict between them. In the boy, for instance, to disobey an autocratic father is felt as wrong because it arouses great quantities of guilt in which persecutory feelings predominate. But to obey this father may involve the desertion, not only in phantasy but also to some extent in fact, of a defenceless mother. Then obedience too is felt as wrong because it arouses the other type of guilt in which the predominant feeling is depressive. In some people this kind of conflict persists throughout life. But in the majority, it is settled one way or the other fairly early, and with it the subsequent pattern of their consciences.

We have next to inquire about the way in which the depressive element in guilt is affected by a deep analysis. In the case of the persecutory element, as we have seen, the effect is to diminish it. And the theoretical limit of this process—never of course achieved in practice—would be a state in which the patient feared only real dangers in the external world and had ceased to fear, because he had ceased to believe in, those existing only in unconscious phantasy. He might still fear the disapproval of his fellows, or the long arm of the law, but he would have ceased to be afraid of being castrated or eaten by his super-ego. In the case of depressive guilt, however, the effect is somewhat different. Since much of this guilt arises from acts performed in unconscious phantasy, the exposure of the phantasy as distinct from fact certainty relieves it. But phantasied acts imply a desire to commit them. That the patient has wished to destroy, to injure, to desert or to betray his loved objects is itself a fact, which analysis cannot disprove but rather exposes to the light of day. Thus a substantial reduction in this kind of guilt cannot be achieved merely by showing that the destructive impulses have not in reality

R. E. Money-Kyrle

achieved their aim—unless these impulses themselves are also reduced. What analysis does do is to weaken these impulses indirectly; for aggression toward loved objects, while partly primary and irreducible, is greatly increased by the persecutory anxieties the phantastic basis of which analysis does undermine. It also helps to free the reparative response to the irreducible destructiveness that still remains.

Thus analysis, while diminishing the conflicts that lead to depression, increases rather than diminishes the capacity to feel guilt of a depressive kind whenever a "good" object is in any way injured or betrayed.

IV. HUMANISM AS AN ATTRIBUTE OF INSIGHT

We can now see what must be the end of at least the first part of our inquiry—that concerned with morals. We have discovered that there is a causal link between the possession of a certain kind of conscience and the possession of a certain kind of wisdom. This gives us, in broad outline, the answer to our question. All that remains is to fill in some of the more salient details.

We may begin by classifying people into four main groups according to their attitude to morals. Of course some people will belong to more than one group, and indeed everyone will do so to some extent; but this is a complication which for simplicity we may here disregard. In the first group are those who do not appear to have any morality at all. They do not consciously experience either form of guilt themselves, and regard those who claim to be influenced by moral obligations or scruples as hypocrites or weaklings. But this is because they deny their unconscious guilt, not because they do not have any to deny. They pride themselves on being super-normal; but in reality they are hypomanic, for their freedom from anxiety and depression is achieved at the cost of their capacity to understand themselves. The second group contains those who are at once self-righteous and censorious. Their guilt is for export only. They deny it in themselves, but see it most clearly in others on to whom they project their own share as well. So they live in a state of moral indignation with the scapegoats for their own offences. They too believe themselves to be normal people, who indeed excel others in virtue; but they are really hypo-paranoid and live in terror of discovering the truth about themselves.

The two remaining groups are composed of people who are conscious of a conscience. The distinction between them is not so clear

434

cut, for it is formed, as it were, by the middle point on a scale stretching between two theoretical extremes. At one end of the scale are those in whom the persecutory element in guilt predominates. They are concerned mainly with obedience to an exacting super-ego or its external representatives. They tend to be self-disciplined but hard. Their consciences may be described as authoritarian. The other end of the scale contains those who have little sense of persecution and in whom the capacity for the depressive element in guilt is relatively unimpaired. Such people are less afraid of disobedience; but they are more consciously distressed by any disloyalty to the values or persons who symbolize their good internal objects. In practice they may be less law-abiding citizens, but they are more kindly and more ready to take up arms in the defence of other people's wrongs. In short, they have more freedom within themselves and more responsibility towards their neighbours.

These distinctions may be illustrated by different attitudes to the morality of war. The hypomanics have no guilt about attacking neighbours they despise, and may do so with elation. The hypoparanoids are over-anxious to start crusades against neighbours on whom they have projected their own unadmitted crimes. Unlike either of these, the attitude of those with an authoritarian conscience will depend on the nature of the inner authority they serve. If it tells them to fight, they will do so with obedient zeal irrespective of the real issues involved. If it tells them not to, they will remain obstinately pacific, and will not even defend the people or values they love. In this they are in sharp contrast with the humanists who are prepared to fight whatever threatens what they care for, but who do not initiate aggression.

Similar differences characterize the attitude of these last two groups to sexual morality. The authoritarians conform with the conventions of society; the humanists are influenced more by positive loyalties than by restrictive codes.

Passing from descriptive to causal differences, we have already seen that the humanist conscience is possessed by, and only by, those who are relatively free from blind spots and capable of feeling what is in themselves. They surpass all other groups in the insight which, on the one hand, diminishes their irrational persecutory anxieties, and, on the other, enables them to feel grief if they injure or abandon what they love. Thus a movement away from the authoritarian and towards the humanist type of conscience is the moral effect of any increase in that kind of wisdom which consists in insight or

435

self-knowledge. And this is true however the increase in insight is brought about—whether by a formal analysis or by some other means.

But the humanist consciences of different individuals are by no means necessarily identical. Being based on love rather than fear, they do not display the almost limitless variability of the authoritarian conscience, which springs from a pliable subservience to whatever code has been imposed. But they do differ from each other in so far as the current symbols of good objects to be cherished and defended are different. This gives the answer to the first half of the question we began with; as people become wiser in self-knowledge, their morality converges in some respects and remains divergent in others. Their consciences become more humanist in form, but this common form is compatible with a certain variety of content.

V. THE INFLUENCE OF INSIGHT ON POLITICAL OPINION

There still remains the second half of our question—that concerned with politics. Can we also say that increased insight would bring about some convergence in the form or content of our political preferences?

That it would do so at least so far as insight influences morals and morals influence politics must be already clear. I do not think, for example, that a humanist politician could tolerate the guilt of attacking a comparatively harmless neighbour, as Germany did in 1939, or of abandoning a friendly one, as Britain did in 1938. So both active and passive forms of non-humanist political behaviour would tend to be reduced. And, in general, a predominance of the humanist type of conscience would modify the political behaviour of any group, whether nation, class, or party, to other groups in much the same way as it would modify the private behaviour of individuals to each other. Since each group would be likely to be the priority "good object" to its own members, they would still be likely to put its interests first, which, if threatened, they might indeed defend more stoutly than at present. But they would not be able to ride rough shod over the interests of another group, or to desert those of a friendly one, without a sense of guilt; nor would they be so prone, in resisting an aggressive group, to project their own guilt feelings upon it and so to paint it blacker than it is. In other words, our political behaviour would not only be more consistently loyal to our own values, but also less callous towards its rivals and less vindictive towards its enemies. In short, there would be a measure of convergence towards a humanist standard of political behaviour.

There would also be some convergence in our political beliefs, by which I mean our beliefs about political affairs. Such beliefs—for example, those expressed in our idea of other nations, parties or classes, or in our sociological, including economic, theories—are by no means solely determined by our contacts and our studies. They are often very greatly influenced by unconscious phantasies surviving from early childhood which distort our conscious inferences and deductions. So insight by reducing these impediments to social science would help to bring us nearer to a common truth.

But can we go still further and say that increasing insight would bring about some convergence in political ideology, that is, in the different "ideal" states or societies which different individuals would like to live in?

Anthropology has taught us that any fairly homogeneous people tends to create a society congenial to itself, and that many different kinds of society exist each of which is "good" to its own members, but "bad" to members of the others. The anthropologist, who himself has a specific character, will naturally prefer some kinds of people and some kinds of society above the rest. But, in the absence of any independent standard against which to measure his own subjective one, he will usually dismiss such judgments as relative and therefore outside the bounds of science. This attitude may be in itself a healthy reaction against a too naïve assumption of superiority by earlier travellers. But it seems to me to be carried much too far in the relativist denial that any independent standard can be found.

The relativist position culminates in the relativist definition of normality, according to which a normal person is one well adapted to the society he lives in. Definitions cannot be false; but they can be ill chosen, or they can fail to fit the pre-existing concept they are endeavouring to express in words. Now the clinical concept of normality may be vague. But it certainly does not depend on adaptation to society; for, if it did, some people whom every clinician would class as ill would have to be classed as normal in some societies. A verbal definition of normality that both fits the clinical concept and is absolute in the sense of being independent of the standards of any arbitrarily chosen culture may be difficult to find. But it seems to me to emerge, at least in outline, from the following considerations. What we call illness, whether this is a specific symptom or a

437

"character defect" is something we try to cure, or at least to lessen, by analysis, that is, by helping the patient to achieve a higher degree of insight or self-understanding than he had before. Sometimes the task is beyond our present technical ability. But this does not lessen our belief that insight, if we could only awaken it, would still effect the cure. In other words, we believe that what we call health is something that can be achieved by insight. Now, if this causal connection between health and insight exists, we can use it to give a verbal definition of normality that does fit the clinical concept and is independent of any arbitrarily chosen cultural standards. We can define a normal—that is, a healthy—mind, as one that knows itself.[1]

Since in reality self-knowledge is always incomplete, it follows from our definition that there can be no completely normal person. But this conclusion, with which no analyst will quarrel, does not lessen the value of a term to denote a limit to which real people approximate in various degrees.

Having reached a definition of a normal mind as one that knows itself, we have next to inquire about its other attributes. These are not included in the definition and can only be discovered empirically. Some of the moral attributes we have already found: they comprise what we called a "humanistic" as opposed to other forms of conscience. Two qualities which Freud used to define normality in a wider sense are certainly attributes of anyone who is approximately normal in the narrow one. These are a well-developed capacity for both work and enjoyment. But, for our present purpose, the most comprehensive and significant attribute is perhaps maturity.

We can now re-word our question about the ideological effects of insight in rather different terms and ask what kind of state would be most congenial to people who, as a result of insight, are humanist in conscience and have also attained a fairly high level of psychological maturity in other respects too. There can be no doubt that such people would be most unhappy (and maladjusted) in any state that sought to dominate their consciences or to control their labours. They would therefore be opposed to totalitarianism in all of its many different forms. But neither would they be content to thrive in a *laissez faire* society which accepted no obligations towards those who were less fortunate or less efficient in the economic struggle for existence. So their political aim would be a state that accepted

[1] The two expressions: "A mind that knows itself" and "an integrated mind" are I think equivalent. Integration as a criterion of mental health has been stressed by Marjorie Brierley (1947) in her paper "Notes on Psycho-Analysis and Integrative Living", *Int. J. Psycho-Anal.*, Vol. XXVIII. Chapter VI in *Trends in Psycho-Analysis*, (London, 1951).

responsibility for welfare without curtailing independence.[1] This also gives us the answer to our question in its original form. The effect of increasing insight would be to bring about some convergence in political ideology towards what may still be called, in spite of totalitarian attempts to misappropriate the term, the democratic aim.

VI. CONCLUSION

How little, or how much, have we achieved by this inquiry? Certainly there is nothing new in the conclusion that wise men are humanist in morals and democratic in their politics. Most people in democratic countries believe it already. But to prove it empirically has, I think, only been made possible by the more recent discoveries of analysis—in particular by those we owe to Melanie Klein's pioneering work which she began with children. These discoveries, as I have tried to show, enable us for the first time to construct an argument capable both of confirming this belief in those who already have it, and perhaps, in the long run, also of convincing those who at present hold a contrary opinion.[2]

[1] The political cleavage in this country since the war has been roughly between those who stress the first to the partial neglect of the second, and those who stress the second to the partial neglect of the first, of these two desiderata. But in the last few years each party seems to have borrowed—if without acknowledgment—from the other a good deal of what it had previously neglected.
[2] The argument briefly outlined in this paper is developed further in my book *Psycho-Analysis and Politics*, (London, 1951).

19

GROUP DYNAMICS: A RE-VIEW

W. R. BION

USING his psycho-analytic experience Freud[1] attempted to illuminate some of the obscurities revealed by Le Bon, McDougall, and others in their studies of the human group. I propose to discuss the bearing of modern developments of psycho-analysis, in particular those associated with the work of Melanie Klein, on the same problems. Her work shows that at the start of life itself the individual is in contact with the breast and, by rapid extension of primitive awareness, with the family group; further-more she has shown that the nature of this contact displays qualities peculiar to itself, which are of profound significance both in the development of the individual and for a fuller understanding of the mechanisms already demonstrated by the intuitive genius of Freud.

I hope to show that in his contact with the complexities of life in a group the adult resorts, in what may be a massive regression, to mechanisms described by Melanie Klein[2] as typical of the earliest phases of mental life. The adult must establish contact with the emotional life of the group in which he lives; this task would appear to be as formidable to the adult as the relation-ship with the breast appears to be to the infant, and the failure to meet the demands of this task is revealed in his regression. The belief that a group exists, as distinct from an aggregate of indiv-iduals, is an essential part of this regression, as are also the charac-teristics with which the supposed group is endowed by the individual. Substance is given to the phantasy that the group exists by the fact that the regression involves the individual in a loss of his

---

[1] Notably in *Totem and Taboo*, London, 1919, and *Group Psychology and the Analysis of the Ego*, (London, 1922).

[2] Melanie Klein, "Notes on some Schizoid Mechanisms", in *Developments in Psycho-Analysis* (London, 1952), and "A Contribution to the Psychogenesis of Manic-Depressive States" in *Contributions to Psycho-Analysis*, (London, 1948).

"individual distinctiveness",[1] indistinguishable from depersonalization, and therefore obscures observation that the aggregation is of individuals. It follows that if the observer judges a group to be in existence, the individuals composing it must have experienced this regression. Conversely, should the individuals composing a "group" (using that word to mean an aggregation of individuals all in the same state of regression) for some reason or other become threatened by awareness of their individual distinctiveness, then the group is in the emotional state known as panic. This does not mean that the group is disintegrating, and it will be seen later that I do not agree that in panic the group has lost its cohesiveness.

In this paper I shall summarize certain theories at which I have arrived by applying in groups the intuitions developed by present-day psycho-analytic training. These theories differ from many others, in merits and defects alike, in being educed in the situations of emotional stress which they are intended to describe. I introduce some concepts new to psycho-analysis, partly because I deal with different subject matter, partly because I wanted to see if a start disencumbered by previous theories might lead to a point at which my views of the group and psycho-analytic views of the individual could be compared, and thereby judged to be either complementary or divergent.

There are times when I think that the group has an attitude to me, and that I can state in words what the attitude is; there are times when another individual acts as if he also thought the group had an attitude to him, and I believe I can deduce what his belief is; there are times when I think that the group has an attitude to an individual, and that I can say what it is. These occasions provide the raw material on which interpretations are based, but the interpretation itself is an attempt to translate into precise speech what I suppose to be the attitude of the group to me or to some other individual, and of the individual to the group. Only some of these occasions are used by me; I judge the occasion to be ripe for an interpretation when the interpretation would seem to be both obvious and unobserved.

The groups in which I have attempted to fill this role pass through a series of complex emotional episodes which permit the deduction of theories of group dynamics which I have found useful both in the illumination of what is taking place and in the exposure of nuclei of further developments. What follows is a summary of these theories.

[1] Freud, S., *Group Psychology and the Analysis of the Ego*, (London, 1922) (p. 9).

W. R. Bion

THE WORK GROUP

In any group there may be discerned trends of mental activity. Every group, however casual, meets to "do" something; in this activity, according to the capacities of the individuals, they co-operate. This co-operation is voluntary and depends on some degree of sophisticated skill in the individual. Participation in this activity is only possible to individuals with years of training and a capacity for experience which has permitted them to develop mentally. Since this activity is geared to a task, it is related to reality, its methods are rational, and, therefore, in however embryonic a form, scientific. Its characteristics are similar to those attributed by Freud to the Ego.[1] This facet of mental activity in a group I have called the Work Group. The term embraces only mental activity of a particular kind, not the people who indulge it.

When patients meet for a group therapy session it can always be seen that some mental activity is directed to the solution of the problems for which the individuals seek help. Here is an example of a passing phase in such a group:

Six patients and I are seated round a small room. Miss A suggests that it would be a good idea if members agreed to call each other by their Christian names.[2] There is some relief that a topic has been broached, glances are exchanged, and a flicker of synthetic animation is momentarily visible. Mr. B ventures that it is a good idea, and Mr. C says it would "make things more friendly". Miss A is encouraged to divulge her name but is forestalled by Miss D who says she does not like her Christian name and would rather it were not known. Mr. E suggests pseudonyms; Miss F examines her fingernails. Within a few minutes of Miss A's suggestion, the discussion has languished, and its place has been taken by furtive glances, an increasing number of which are directed towards me. Mr. B rouses himself to say that we must call each other something. The mood is now a compound of anxiety and increasing frustration. Long before I am mentioned it is clear that my name has become a preoccupation of the group. Left to its own devices the group promises to pass into apathy and silence.

For my present purposes I shall display such aspects of the episode as illustrate my use of the term work group. In the group itself I

---

[1] (1911) "Formulations Regarding the Two Principles in Mental Functioning", in *Collected Papers*, IV, London, 1925.
[2] See also the discussion of taboo on names in *Totem and Taboo*, p. 54.

might well do the same, but that would depend on my assessment of the significance of the episode in the context of the group mental life, as far as it had then emerged. First, it is clear that if seven people are to talk together it would help the discussion if names were available. In so far as the discussion has arisen through awareness of that fact it is a product of work group activity. But the group has gone further than to propose a step that would be helpful in any group no matter what its task might be. The proposal has been made that Christian names should be used because that would make for friendliness. In the group of which I am speaking it would have been accurate to say that the production of friendliness was regarded as strictly relevant to therapeutic need. At the point in its history from which the example is taken, it would also be true to say that both Miss D's objection and Mr. E's proposed solution would be regarded as dictated by therapeutic need; and in fact I pointed out that the suggestions fitted in with a theory, not yet explicitly stated, that our diseases would be cured if the group could be conducted in such a way that only pleasant emotions were experienced. It will be seen that the demonstration of work group function must include: the development of thought designed for translation into action; the theory, in this instance the need for friendliness, on which it is based; the belief in environmental change as in itself sufficient for cure without any corresponding change in the individual; and finally a demonstration of the kind of fact that is believed to be "real".

It so happened, in the instance I have given, that I was subsequently able to demonstrate that work group function, though I did not call it that, based on the idea that cure could be obtained from a group in which pleasant feelings only were experienced, did not appear to have produced the hoped-for cure; and indeed was being obstructed by some sort of difficulty in achieving a limited translation into the apparently simple act of assigning names. Before passing to the discussion of the nature of the obstructions to work group activity I would mention here a difficulty, which must already be evident, in the exposition of my theories. For me to describe a group episode, such as the one I have been discussing, and then to attempt the deduction of theories from it, is only to say that I have a theory that such-and-such took place and that I can say it again only in different language. The only way in which the reader can deliver himself from the dilemma is to recall to himself the memory of some committee or other gathering in which he has participated and consider to what extent he can recall evidence that could point to the existence of what I call work group function, not forgetting the actual administrative structure, chairman and so forth, as material to be included in his review.

THE BASIC ASSUMPTIONS[1]

The interpretations in terms of work group activity leave much unsaid; is the suggested use of pseudonyms motivated only with a view to meeting the demands of reality? The furtive glances, the preoccupation with the correct mode for addressing the analyst, which became quite overt subsequently, cannot profitably be interpreted as related to work group function.

Work group activity is obstructed, diverted, and on occasion assisted, by certain other mental activities which have in common the attribute of powerful emotional drives. These activities, at first sight chaotic, are given a certain cohesion if it is assumed that they spring from basic assumptions common to all the group. In the example I have given it was easy to recognize that one assumption common to all the group was that they were met together to receive some form of treatment from me. But exploration of this idea as part of work group function showed that ideas existed, invested with reality by force of the emotion attached to them, that were not in conformity even with the somewhat naïve expectation consciously entertained by the less sophisticated members. Furthermore, even sophisticated individuals, one member for example being a graduate in science, showed by their behaviour that they shared these ideas.

The first assumption is that the group is met in order to be sustained by a leader on whom it depends for nourishment, material and spiritual, and protection. Stated thus, my first basic assumption might be regarded as a repetition of my remark, above, that the group assumed that "they were met together to receive some form of treatment from me", only differing from it in being couched in metaphorical terms. But the essential point is that the basic assumption can only be understood if the words in which I have stated it are taken as literal and not metaphorical.

Here is a description of a therapeutic group in which the dependent assumption, as I shall call it, is active.

Three women and two men were present. The group had on a

[1] See also R. W. Bion, "Experiences in Groups", *Human Relations*, Vol. I, 3 and 4; Vol. II, 1 and 4; Vol. III, 1 and 4.

previous occasion shown signs of work group function directed towards curing the disability of its members; on this occasion they might be supposed to have reacted from this with despair, placing all their reliance on me to sort out their difficulties while they contented themselves with individually posing questions to which I was to provide the answers. One woman had brought some chocolate, which she diffidently invited her right-hand neighbour, another woman, to share. One man was eating a sandwich. A graduate in philosophy, who had in earlier sessions told the group he had no belief in God, and no religion, sat silent, as indeed he often did, until one of the women with a touch of acerbity in her tone, remarked that he had asked no questions. He replied, "I do not need to talk because I know that I only have to come here long enough and all my questions will be answered without my having to do anything."

I then said that I had become a kind of group deity; that the questions were directed to me as one who knew the answers without need to resort to work, that the eating was part of a manipulation of the group to give substance to a belief they wished to preserve about me, and that the philosopher's reply indicated a disbelief in the efficacy of prayer but seemed otherwise to belie earlier statements he had made about his disbelief in God. When I began my interpretation I was not only convinced of its truth but felt no doubt that I could convince the others by confrontation with the mass of material—only some of which I can convey in this printed account. By the time I had finished speaking I felt I had committed some kind of gaffe; I was surrounded by blank looks; the evidence had disappeared. After a time, the man, who had finished his sandwich and placed the carefully folded paper in his pocket, looked round the room, eyebrows slightly raised, interrogation in his glance. A woman looked tensely at me, another with hands folded gazed meditatively at the floor. In me a conviction began to harden that I had been guilty of blasphemy in a group of true believers. The second man, with elbow draped over the back of his chair, played with his fingers. The woman who was eating, hurriedly swallowed the last of her chocolate. I now interpreted that I had become a very bad person, casting doubts on the group deity, but that this had been followed by an increase of anxiety and guilt as the group had failed to dissociate itself from the impiety.

In this account I have dwelt on my own reactions in the group for a reason which I hope may become more apparent later. It can be justly argued that interpretations for which the strongest evidence lies, not in the observed facts in the group but in the subjective reactions of the analyst, are more likely to find their explanation in the psychopathology of the analyst than in the dynamics of the group. It is a just criticism, and one which will have to be met by years of careful work by more than one analyst, but for that very reason I shall leave it on one side and pass on to state now a contention which I shall support throughout this paper. It is that in group treatment many interpretations, and amongst them the most important, have to be made on the strength of the analyst's own emotional reactions. It is my belief that these reactions are dependent on the fact that the analyst in the group is at the receiving end of what Melanie Klein has called projective identification,[1] and that this mechanism plays a very important role in groups. Now the experience of counter-transference appears to me to have quite a distinct quality which should enable the analyst to differentiate the occasion when he is the object of a projective identification from the occasion when he is not. The analyst feels he is being manipulated so as to be playing a part, no matter how difficult to recognize, in somebody's else's phantasy—or he would do if it were not for what in recollection I can only call a temporary loss of insight, a sense of experiencing strong feelings and at the same time a belief that their existence is quite adequately justified by the objective situation without recourse to recondite explanation of their causation. Speaking as an analyst, the experience consists of two closely related phases: in the first there is a feeling that whatever else one has done, one has certainly not given a correct interpretation; in the second there is a sense of being a particular kind of person in a particular emotional situation. I believe ability to shake one's self out of the numbing feeling of reality that is a concomitant of this state is the prime requisite of the analyst in the group: if he can do this he is in a position to give what I believe is the correct interpretation, and thereby to see its connection with the previous interpretation, the validity of which he has been caused to doubt.

I must return to consider the second basic assumption. Like the first, this also concerns the purpose for which the group has met. My attention was first aroused by a session in which the conversation was monopolized by a man and woman who appeared more or less to ignore the rest of the group. The occasional exchange of glances amongst the others seemed to suggest the view, not very

[1] "Notes on some Schizoid Mechanisms".

446

seriously entertained, that the relationship was amatory, although one would hardly say that the overt content of the conversation was very different from other interchanges in the group. I was, however, impressed with the fact that individuals, who were usually sensitive to any exclusion from supposedly therapeutic activity, which at that time had come to mean talking and obtaining an "interpretation" from me or some other member of the group, seemed not to mind leaving the stage entirely to this pair. Later it became clear that the sex of the pair was of no particular consequence to the assumption that pairing was taking place. There was a peculiar air of hopefulness and expectation about these sessions which made them rather different from the usual run of hours of boredom and frustration. It must not be supposed that the elements to which I would draw attention, under the title of pairing group, are exclusively or even predominantly in evidence. In fact there is plenty of evidence of states of mind of the kind we are familiar with in psycho-analysis; it would indeed be extraordinary, to take one example, if one did not see in individuals evidence of reaction to a group situation that could approximate to an acting out of the primal scene. But, in my opinion, to allow one's attention to be absorbed by these reactions is to make difficult any observation of what is peculiar to the group; furthermore I think such concentration at worst can lead to a debased psycho-analysis rather than an exploration of the therapeutic possibilities of the group. The reader must then, assume, that in this, as in other situations, there will always be a plethora of material familiar in a psycho-analysis, but still awaiting its evaluation in the situation of the group; this material I propose for the present to ignore and to turn to a consideration of the air of hopeful expectation that I have mentioned as a characteristic of the pairing group. It usually finds expression verbally in ideas that marriage would put an end to neurotic disabilities; that group therapy would revolutionize society when it had spread sufficiently; that the coming season, spring, summer, autumn, or winter, as the case may be, will be more agreeable; that some new kind of community—an improved group —should be developed, and so on. These expressions tend to divert attention to some supposedly future event, but for the analyst the crux is not a future event but the immediate present—the feeling of hope itself. This feeling is characteristic of the pairing group and must be taken by itself as evidence that the pairing group is in existence, even when other evidence appears to be lacking. It is

447

itself both a precursor of sexuality and a part of it. The optimistic ideas that are verbally expressed are rationalizations intended to effect a displacement in time and a compromise with feelings of guilt—the enjoyment of the feeling is justified by appeal to an outcome supposedly morally unexceptionable. The feelings thus associated in the pairing group are at the opposite pole to feelings of hatred, destructiveness, and despair. For the feelings of hope to be sustained it is essential that the "leader" of the group, unlike the leader of the dependent group, and the fight-flight group (which I shall later explain), should be unborn. It is a person or idea that will save the group—in fact from feelings of hatred, destructiveness and despair, of its own or of another group, but in order to do this, obviously the Messianic hope must never be fulfilled. Only by remaining a hope does hope persist. The difficulty is that, thanks to the rationalization of the dawning sexuality of the group, the premonition of sex which obtrudes as hope, there is a tendency for the work group to be influenced in the direction of producing a Messiah, be it person, idea, or Utopia. In so far as it succeeds, hope is weakened; for obviously nothing is then to hope for, and, since destructiveness, hatred, and despair have in no way been radically influenced their existence again makes itself felt. This in turn accelerates a further weakening of hope. If, for purposes of discussion, we accept the idea that the group should be manipulated in order to compass hopefulness in the group, then it is necessary that those who concern themselves with such a task, either in their capacity as members of a specialized work group such as I shall describe shortly, or as individuals, should see to it that Messianic hopes do not materialize. The danger, of course, is that such specialized work groups will either suffer through excess of zeal and thereby interfere with innocent, creative work group function or alternatively allow themselves to be forestalled and so put to the troublesome necessity of liquidating the Messiah and then recreating the Messianic hope. In the therapeutic group the problem is to enable the group to be consciously aware of the feelings of hope, and its affiliations, and at the same time tolerant of them. That it is tolerant of them in the pairing group is a function of the basic assumption and cannot be regarded as a sign of individual development.

The third basic assumption is that the group has met to fight something or to run away from it. It is prepared to do either indifferently. I shall call this state of mind the fight-flight group;

the accepted leader of a group in this state is one whose demands on the group are felt to afford opportunity for flight or aggression and if he makes demands that do not do so, he is ignored. In a therapeutic group the analyst is the work group leader. The emotional backing that he can command is subject to fluctuation according to the active basic assumption and the extent to which his activities are felt to fit in with what is required of a leader in these differing states of mind. In the fight-flight group the analyst finds that attempts to illuminate what is taking place are obstructed by the ease with which emotional support is obtained for such proposals as express either hatred of all psychological difficulty or alternatively the means by which it can be evaded. In this context I would remark that the proposal to use Christian names, in the first example I gave, might well have been interpreted as an expression of the desire for flight in a fight-flight group though, in fact, for reasons connected with the stage of development that the group had reached, I interpreted it in terms of work group function.

CHARACTERISTICS COMMON TO ALL BASIC ASSUMPTION GROUPS

Participation in basic assumption activity requires no training, experience, or mental development. It is instantaneous, inevitable, and instinctive: I have not felt the need to postulate the existence of a herd instinct to account for such phenomena as I have witnessed in the group.[1] In contrast with work group function basic assumption activity makes no demands on the individual for a capacity to co-operate but depends on the individual's possession of what I call valency—a term I borrow from the physicists to express a capacity for instantaneous involuntary combination of one individual with another for sharing and acting on a basic assumption. Work group function is always in evidence with one, and only one, basic assumption. Though the work group function may remain unaltered the contemporary basic assumption that pervades its activities can be changing frequently; there may be two or three changes in an hour or the same basic assumption may be dominant for months on end. To account for the fate of the inactive basic assumptions I have postulated the existence of a proto-mental system in which physical and mental activity is undifferentiated, and which lies

[1] In contrast with W. Trotter, *Instincts of the Herd in Peace and War*, but in agreement with Freud, *Group Psychology and the Analysis of the Ego*, p. 3.

449

outside the field ordinarily considered profitable for psychological investigations. It must be borne in mind that the question whether a field is suitable for psychological investigation depends on other factors besides the nature of the field to be investigated, one being the potency of the investigating psychological technique. The recognition of a field of psycho-somatic medicine illustrates the difficulty that attends any attempt at determination of the line that separates psychological from physical phenomena. I propose therefore to leave indeterminate the limits that separate the active basic assumption from those I have relegated to the hypothetical proto-mental system.

Many techniques are in daily use for the investigation of work group function. For the investigation of basic assumption phenomena, I consider psycho-analysis, or some extension of technique derived directly from it, to be essential. But since work group functions are always pervaded by basic assumption phenomena it is clear that techniques that ignore the latter will give misleading impressions of the former.

Emotions associated with basic assumptions may be described by the usual terms, anxiety, fear, hate, love, and the like. But the emotions common to any basic assumption are subtly affected by each other as if they were held in a combination peculiar to the active basic assumption. That is to say, anxiety in the dependent group has a different quality from anxiety evident in the pairing group, and so on with other feelings.

All basic assumptions include the existence of a leader, although in the pairing group, as I have said, the leader is "non-existent", i.e. unborn. This leader need not be identified with any individual in the group; it need not be a person at all but may be identified with an idea or an inanimate object. In the dependent group the place of leader may be filled by the history of the group. A group, complaining of an inability to remember what took place on a previous occasion, sets about making a record of its meetings. This record then becomes a "bible" to which appeal is made, if, for example, the individual whom the group has invested with leadership proves to be refractory material for moulding into the likeness proper to the dependent leader. The group resorts to bible-making when threatened with an idea, the acceptance of which would entail development on the part of the individuals comprising the group. Such ideas derive emotional force, and excite emotional opposition from their association with characteristics appropriate to the pairing group leader. When the dependent group or the fight-flight group are active a struggle takes place to suppress the new idea because it is felt that the emergence of the new idea threatens the *status quo*. In war, the new idea—be it a tank or a new method for selecting officers—is felt to be "new-fangled", i.e. opposed to the military bible. In the dependent group it is felt to threaten the dependent leader, be that leader "bible" or person. But the same is true of the pairing group, for here the new idea or person, being equated with the unborn genius or Messiah, must, as I have said before, remain unborn if it, or he, is to fulfil the pairing group function.

ABERRANT FORMS OF CHANGE FROM ONE BASIC ASSUMPTION TO ANOTHER

Change in the mentality of the group need not be due to the displacement of one basic assumption by another and can take certain aberrant forms which depend on what basic assumption is active when tension increases. These aberrant forms always involve an extraneous group. If the dependent group is active, and is threatened by pressure of the pairing group leader, particularly perhaps in the form of an idea which is suffused with Messianic hope, then if methods such as a resort to bible-making prove inadequate, the threat is countered by provoking the influx of another group. If the fight-flight group is active, the tendency is to absorb another group. If the pairing group is active, the tendency is to schism. This last reaction may appear anomalous unless it is remembered that in the pairing group the Messianic hope, be it person or idea, must remain unrealized. The crux of the matter lies in the threat of the new idea to demand development and the inability of the basic assumption groups to tolerate development. The reasons for this I shall educe later.

THE SPECIALIZED WORK GROUP

There are certain specialized work groups, to which Freud[1] has drawn attention though not under this name, whose task is peculiarly prone to stimulate the activity of a particular basic assumption. Typical groups of this nature are provided by a Church or an Army. A Church is liable to interference from dependent group phenomena,

[1] *Group Psychology and the Analysis of the Ego*, p. 41 ff.

and the Army suffers a similar liability from fight-flight group phenomena. But another possibility has to be considered, namely that these groups are budded off by the main group of which they form a part, for the specific purpose of neutralizing dependent group and fight-flight group respectively and thus preventing their obstruction of the work group function of the main group. If we adopt the latter hypothesis, it must be regarded as a failure in the specialized work group if dependent or fight-flight group activity either ceases to manifest itself within the specialized work groups or else grow to overwhelming strength. In either case the result is the same—the main group has to take over the functions proper to the specialized work group, and yet fulfil its work group functions. If the specialized work group cannot, or does not, cope with the basic assumption phenomena which are its province, then the work group functions of the main group are vitiated by the pressure of these basic assumptions. As work group function consists essentially of the translation of thoughts and feelings into behaviour which is adapted to reality, it is ill-adapted to give expression to basic assumptions. For basic assumptions become dangerous in proportion as the attempt is made to translate them into action. Indeed, the specialized work group has tended to recognize this and shows it by the attempt to carry out the reverse process, namely to translate action into terms of basic assumption mentality—a much safer proceeding. Thus, a Church, when presented with some notable achievement of work group function, will adjure the group to give thanks to its deity and not to its capacity for realistic hard work, "*non nobis, Domine*". The prosperous and successful Church, from the point of view of easing work group function, must combine fortification of religious belief with the insistence that it must never be acted on; the successful fighting service must encourage the belief that anything can be done by force provided always it is never used. In both cases it comes to this—basic assumption mentality does not lend itself to translation into action, since action requires work group function to maintain contact with reality.

In the small therapeutic group, the tendency, when the dependent group is active, is to produce a sub-group which then takes on the function of interpreting the dependent group leader—usually located in the analyst—to the group. In the fight-flight group a similar sub-group fulfils a similar function. If the analyst proves obdurate material, he is liable to evoke reactions which I have already described as associated with the threat of the new idea.

I have not mentioned any specialized work group which fulfils for the pairing group functions similar to those which Church or army fulfil for the dependent and fight-flight groups respectively, but an aristocracy may be such a group. The function of this sub-group is to provide an outlet for feelings which centre on ideas of breeding and birth, that is to say for Messianic hope which I have already suggested is a precursor to sexual desire, without ever arousing the fear that such feelings will give rise to an event which will demand development. The aristocracy must inspire Messianic hope but at the same time confidence that the pairing group leader, if he materializes, will be born in a palace but be just like ourselves—"democratic" is probably the modern cant term for the desired quality. In the therapeutic group the "aristocratic" sub-group usually helps the group to understand that the new idea is one with which they are already quite familiar.

BASIC ASSUMPTIONS, TIME, AND DEVELOPMENT

There are two characteristics of basic assumption mentality to which I would draw attention. Time plays no part in it; it is a dimension of mental function which is not recognized; consequently all activities that require an awareness of time are imperfectly comprehended and tend to arouse feelings of persecution. Interpretations of activity on the level of the basic assumptions lay bare a disturbed relationship to time. The second characteristic, which I mentioned earlier, is the absence of any process of development as a part of basic assumption mentality; stimuli to development meet with a hostile response. It will be appreciated that this is a matter of importance in any group which purports, by the study of the group, to promote a therapeutic development of insight. Hostility thus engendered tends to determine that the reaction to the emergence of the Messianic person or idea will take an aberrant form rather than spend itself in the cyclic change from one basic assumption to another. For, if a group wishes to prevent development, the simplest way to do so is to allow itself to be overwhelmed by basic assumption mentality and thus become approximated to the one kind of mental life in which a capacity for development is not required. The main compensation for such a shift appears to be an increase in a pleasurable feeling of vitality.

The defence that schism affords against the development-threatening idea can be seen in the operation of the schismatic groups, ostensibly opposed but in fact promoting the same end. One group adheres to the dependent group, often in the form of the group "bible". This group popularizes the established ideas by denuding them of any quality that might demand painful effort and thereby secures a numerous adherence of those who oppose the pains of development. Thought thus becomes stabilized on a level which is platitudinous and dogmatic. The reciprocal group, supposedly supporting the new idea, becomes so exacting in its demands that it ceases to recruit itself. Thus both groups avoid the painful bringing together of the primitive and the sophisticated which is the essence of the developmental conflict. The superficial but numerous schismatics are thus opposed by the profound but numerically negligible schismatics. The result reminds one of the fear expressed sometimes that a society breeds copiously from its least cultured members while the "best" people remain obdurately sterile.

RELATION OF ONE BASIC ASSUMPTION TO ANOTHER

We may now reconsider the three basic assumption groups and the work group to see if they are not capable of resolution into something more fundamental. Granting that the postulate of basic assumptions helps to give form and meaning to the complex and chaotic emotional state that the group unfolds to the investigating participant, there is yet no reasonable explanation of why such assumptions should exist. It is clear that no one of the three basic assumptions about the group satisfactorily allays fear of the group and its emotions, otherwise there would be none of the shifts and changes from one to another and no need for the formation, which I have sketched out, of the corresponding specialized work groups. All three basic assumptions contain the idea of a leader. The fight-flight group shows a total absence of recognition of understanding as a technique. All are opposed to development which is itself dependent on understanding. The work group, on the other hand, recognizes a need both to understand and to develop. If we consider the specialized work groups, all three are concerned with matters which appear to lie outside the province of the basic assumption, with which they appear primarily to be concerned. Thus the specialized work group of the dependent basic assumption is not free from preoccupation with Messianic ideas that appear to be more in the sphere of pairing-group activity than of the dependent group.

Effort here seems to be devoted to a Messiah born, out of wedlock, in a bed of bulrushes, or a manger, with one exalted parent, Pharaoh's daughter or the Deity, and one less exalted. In the pairing group the aristocratic sub-group allows exalted parents, wedlock, and a palatial crib, but the child is notable only in being one with the rest of us. A scrutiny of the facts seems to lead to a central difficulty in bringing together sexual love, equal parents, an infant like ourselves, the Messianic hope which I consider to be an essential component of the sexual love, and a compulsion to develop which in itself necessitates a capacity for understanding. The fight-flight group expresses a sense of incapacity for understanding and the love without which understanding cannot exist. But the leader of the fight-flight group brings back into view one of the feared components, an approximation either to the dreaded father or the infant.

Furthermore, the three basic assumption groups seem each in turn to be aggregates of individuals sharing out between them the characteristics of one character in the Œdipal situation, which one depending on whichever basic assumption is active. The parallel with the characters in the Œdipal situation is however marked by important divergences. The relationship appears to be between the individual and the group. But the group is felt as one fragmented individual with another, hidden, in attendance. The hidden individual is the leader, and although this appears to contradict the constantly reiterated statement that the analyst is the leader, the contradiction is resolved if it is remembered that in the therapeutic group the analyst is the work group leader, and if attention is paid to the many indications that he is suspected of leading, but apparently only rarely perceived to be leading. It is quite common, in my experience, to be told I am not taking any part in the group or ever giving the group a chance to know what my views are, although the probability is I am doing more talking than anyone else. The essential point here, as always in a group, is the feeling with which the idea expressed is accompanied, and the point I would emphasize again is that I am suspected of, but not perceived to be, leading the group.

On the emotional plane, where basic assumptions are dominant, Œdipal figures, as I have indicated, can be discerned in the material just as they are in a psycho-analysis. But they include one component of the Œdipus myth of which little has been said, and that is the sphinx. In so far as I am felt to be leader of work group function, and recognition of that fact is seldom absent, I, and the work group function with which I am identified, am invested with feelings that would be quite appropriate to the enigmatic, brooding, and questioning sphinx from whom disaster emanates. In fact terms are sometimes employed, on occasions when my intervention has provoked more than usual anxiety, which hardly require interpretation to enable the group to grasp the similarity. I know of no experience that demonstrates more clearly than the group experience the dread with which a questioning attitude is regarded. This anxiety is not directed only towards the questioner but also to the object of the inquiry and is, I suspect, secondary to the latter. For the group, as being the object of inquiry, itself arouses fears of an extremely primitive kind. My impression is that the group approximates too closely, in the minds of the individuals composing it, to very primitive phantasies about the contents of the mother's body.[1] The attempt to make a rational investigation of the dynamics of the group is therefore perturbed by fears, and mechanisms for dealing with them, which are characteristic of the paranoid-schizoid position. The investigation cannot be carried out without the stimulation and activation of these levels.

We are now in a better position to consider if the basic assumptions are capable of resolution into something more fundamental. I have drawn attention already to the fact that these three states of mind have resemblances to each other which would lead me to suppose that they may not be fundamental phenomena, but rather expressions of, or reactions against, some state more worthy of being regarded as primary. In fact, although I have found the hypothesis of basic assumptions a valuable aid in producing order out of the chaos of material in a group session, it is soon clear that further investigation demands fresh hypotheses. The need, and the way to the hypothesis that might satisfy it, became apparent to me in considering what could precipitate the change from one basic assumption to another. I include in this discussion the aberrant forms I have already described.

In brief, no matter what basic assumption is active, investigation discloses that the elements in the emotional situation are so closely allied to phantasies of the earliest anxieties that the group is compelled, whenever the pressure of anxiety becomes too great, to take defensive action. Approached from this primitive level, the basic assumptions take on a different aspect from that which they present

[1] Melanie Klein.

in the descriptions I have already given. The impulse to pair may now be seen to possess a component derived from psychotic anxiety associated with primitive Œdipal conflicts working on a foundation of part object relationships. This anxiety compels individuals to seek allies. This derivation of the impulse to pair is cloaked by the apparently rational explanation in the pairing group that the motive is sexual and the object reproduction.

But if the pairing group is active, again we find that many of its components are too close to primitive part objects to escape identification with them so that it is only a matter of time before psychotic anxiety is aroused with such force that new defence must be found. Let us suppose that it takes the form of the fight-flight group, that is to say the release of hate which finds an outlet either in destructive attacks on a supposed enemy or flight from the hated object. The indifference of the group to the individual, and still more the inability of the group to escape by this means from the primitive primal scene, again leads to release of anxiety and the need for another change of basic assumption.

It will be seen from this description that the basic assumptions now emerge as formations secondary to an extremely early primal scene worked out on a level of part objects, and associated with psychotic anxiety and mechanisms of splitting and projective identification such as Melanie Klein has described as characteristic of the paranoid-schizoid and depressive positions. Introjection and projection of the group,[1] which is now the feared investigator, now the feared object of investigation, form an essential part of the picture and help to add confusion to the scene unless recognized as being very active.

The classical view of the primal scene does not go far enough to deal with the dynamics of the group. I must stress the point that I consider it essential to work out very thoroughly the primitive primal scene as it discloses itself in the group. This differs markedly from the primal scene in its classical description in that it is much more bizarre and seems to assume that a part of one parent, the breast or the mother's body, contains amongst other objects a part of the father. In her paper on early stages of the Œdipus conflict[2] Melanie Klein gives a description of these phantasies as she discovered

---

[1] How this appears in psycho-analysis is described by Paula Heimann in her paper "Certain Functions of Introjection and Projection in Early Infancy", *Developments in Psycho-Analysis*, p. 155.
[2] *Contributions to Psycho-Analysis*, p. 204 ff. Also: "The Œdipus Complex in the Light of Early Anxieties," p. 339 ff.

W. R. Bion

them in the process of individual analysis.[1] The group experience seems to me to give ample material to support the view that these phantasies are of paramount importance for the group.[2] The more disturbed the group, the more easily discernible are these primitive phantasies and mechanisms; the more stable the group, the more it corresponds with Freud's description of the group as a repetition of family group patterns and neurotic mechanisms. But even in the "stable" group the deep psychotic levels should be demonstrated though it may involve temporarily an apparent increase in the "illness" of the group.

SUMMARY

Before turning to discuss psycho-analytic views of the group I think it is necessary to sum up the theories I have described so far. It will be remembered that I attempted deliberately, in so far as it is possible to a psycho-analyst admittedly proposing to investigate the group through psycho-analytically developed intuitions, to divest myself of any earlier psycho-analytic theories of the group in order to achieve an unprejudiced view. In the result I have arrived at a theory of the group as giving evidence of work group functions together with behaviour, often strongly emotionally coloured, which suggested that groups were reacting emotionally to one of three basic assumptions. The idea that such basic assumptions are made involuntarily, automatically, inevitably has seemed useful in illuminating the behaviour of the group. Nevertheless, there is much to suggest that these supposed "basic assumptions" cannot be regarded as distinct states of mind. By that I do not mean to claim that they are "basic" explanations which between them explain all conduct in the group—that would indeed be extravagant nonsense—but that each state, even when it is possible to differentiate it with reasonable certainty from the other two, has about it a quality that suggests it may in some way be the dual, or reciprocal of one of the other two, or perhaps simply another view of what one had thought to be a different basic assumption. For example, the Messianic hope of the pairing group has some similarity to the group deity of the

---

[1] See also Paula Heimann, "A Contribution to the Re-evaluation of the Œdipus Complex—The early Stages", *Int. J. Psycho-Anal.*, Vol. XXXIII, Part II (1952), and p. 23 in this book.
[2] It is worth noting that Melanie Klein's description of the psychotic reaction to external objects in her paper on "Early Stages of the Œdipus Conflict", p. 204 in *The Psycho-Analysis of Children*, is markedly similar to the group's reaction to ideas. Bible-making is one form of defence against them.

dependent group. It may be difficult to see because the presenting emotional tone is so different. Anxiety, fear, hate, love, all, as I have said, exist in each basic assumption group. The modification that feelings suffer in combination in the respective basic assumption group may arise because the "cement", so to speak, that joined them to each other, is guilt and depression in the dependent group, Messianic hope in the pairing group, anger and hate in the fight-flight group. Be that as it may, the result is that the thought content of the discussion may appear as a result to be deceptively different in the three groups. It is possible at times to feel that the unborn genius of the pairing group is very similar to the god of the dependent group; certainly on those occasions when the dependent group appeals to the authority of a "past" leader it comes very close to the pairing group which appeals to a "future" leader. In both the leader does not exist; there is a difference of tense and a difference in emotion.

I reiterate these points to show that the hypothesis of the basic assumptions which I have put forward cannot be regarded as rigid formulations.

THE PSYCHO-ANALYTIC VIEW

Freud's theories of the group derive from his study of the transference. Since the pair relationship of psycho-analysis can be regarded as a part of the larger group situation the transference relationship could be expected, for the reasons I have already given, to be coloured by the characteristics associated with the pairing group. If analysis is regarded as part of the total group situation, we should expect to find sexual elements prominent in the material there presented and the suspicions and hostilities of psycho-analysis as a sexual activity active in that part of the group which is in fact excluded from the analysis.

From his experience of analysis Freud was able to deduce the significance of two of what I have called specialized work groups, army and Church, but did not discuss the specialized work group which attaches most importance to breeding, and is therefore most likely to have to deal with pairing group phenomena, namely the aristocracy. If the aristocracy were concerned simply with the external reality, its activity would far more closely resemble the work of a genetics department in a university than it does. But the interest shown in breeding has not the scientific aura we should associate

459

with mental activity directed to external reality: it is a specialized work group split off to deal with pairing group phenomena in much the same way as the army has to deal with fight-flight phenomena and the Church with dependent group phenomena. Therefore, the relationship of this sub-group with the main group will not be determined by the degree of fidelity to the strict genetic principles with which it conducts its affairs but rather by the efficiency with which it satisfies the main group demand that pairing group phenomena are dealt with so that work group functions of the total group are not obstructed by emotional drives from that source. Although he expressly disavowed any but a superficial study of the group problem,[1] and made his observations in the course of a discussion of the views of Le Bon, McDougall, and Wilfred Trotter,[2] Freud in fact had ample experience of the group and what it means to be an individual caught up in its emotional stresses—as I have indicated by my picture of the position psycho-analysis is likely to occupy in a group in which it stimulates pairing group.

Freud says individual and group psychology cannot be absolutely differentiated because the psychology of the individual is itself a function of the relationship between one person and another.[3] He objects that it is difficult to attribute to number a significance so great as to make it capable by itself of arousing in our mental life a new instinct that is otherwise not brought into play. In this view I think Freud right; I have not at any time met with any phenomena that require explanation by a postulation of a herd instinct. The individual is, and always has been, a member of a group, even if his membership of it consists of behaving in such a way that reality is given to an idea that he does not belong to a group at all. The individual is a group animal at war, both with the group and with those aspects of his personality that constitute his "groupishness". Freud limits this war to a struggle with "culture"[4] but I hope to show that this requires further expansion.

McDougall and Le Bon seem to speak as if group psychology comes into being only when a number of people are collected together in one place at one time, and Freud does not disavow this. For my part this is not necessary except to make study possible: the aggregation of individuals is only necessary in the way that it is

[1] *Totem and Taboo*, p. 75 ff.
[2] *Group Psychology and the Analysis of the Ego*, passim.
[3] *Civilization and Its Discontents*, p. 44 ff.
[4] Freud, S., *Group Psychology and the Analysis of the Ego*, p. 29.

necessary for analyst and analysed to come together for the transfer-ence relationship to be demonstrable. Only by coming together are adequate conditions provided for the demonstration of the char--acteristics of the group; only if individuals come sufficiently close to each other is it possible to give an interpretation without shouting it; equally, it is necessary for all members of the group to be able to witness the evidence on which interpretations are based. For these reasons the numbers of the group, and the degree of dispersion, must be limited. The congregation of the group in a particular place at a particular time is, for these mechanical reasons, important, but it has no significance for the production of group phenomena; the idea that it has springs from the impression that a thing must commence at the moment when its existence becomes demonstrable. In fact no individual, however isolated in time and space, should be regarded as outside a group or lacking in active manifestations of group psychology. Nevertheless, the existence of group behaviour is, as I say, clearly more easy to demonstrate, and even to observe, if the group is brought together; and I think it is this increased ease of ob-servation and demonstration that is responsible for the idea of a herd instinct, such as Trotter postulates, or of the various other theories I have already mentioned which amount in the end to the idea that a group is more than the sum of its members. My experience con-vinces me that Freud was right to reject any such concept as, on present evidence, unnecessary. The apparent difference between group psychology and individual psychology is an illusion produced by the fact that the group brings into prominence phenomena which appear alien to an observer unaccustomed to using the group.[1]

I attribute great force and influence to the work group which, through its concern with reality, is compelled to employ the methods of science in no matter how rudimentary a form; despite the in-fluence of the basic assumptions, and sometimes in harmony with them, it is the work group which triumphs in the long run. Le Bon said that the group never thirsts after the truth. I agree with Freud's opinion—given particularly in discussing the part played by the group in the production of language,[2] folk-song, folk-lore, etc.—that in saying this Le Bon is unfair to the group. When McDougall says that conditions in the highly organized group remove "the psychological disadvantages of group formation" he approximates

---

[1] It is also a matter of historical development; there are aspects of group behaviour which appear strange unless there is some understanding of M. Klein's work on the psychoses. See particularly papers on symbol formation and schizoid mechanisms. I develop this point later.
[2] Later in this paper I discuss one aspect of the development of language.

to my view that the function of the specialized work group is to manipulate the basic assumption so as to prevent obstruction of the work group. Freud describes the problem as one of procuring for the group "precisely those features that were characteristic of the individual and are extinguished in him by the formation of the group". He postulates an individual outside the primitive group who possessed his own continuity, his self-consciousness, his traditions and customs, his own particular functions and position. He says that owing to his entry into an "unorganized" group, the individual had lost his distinctiveness for a time. I think the struggle of the individual to preserve his distinctiveness assumes different characteristics according to the state of mind of the group at any given moment. Group organization gives stability and permanence to the work group, which is felt to be more easily submerged by the basic assumptions if the group is unorganized. Individual distinctiveness is no part of life in a group which is acting on the basic assumptions. Organization and structure are weapons of the work group. They are the product of co-operation between members of the group and their effect, once established in the group, is to demand still further co-operation from the individuals in the group. In this respect McDougall's organized group is always a work group and never a basic assumption group. A group acting on basic assumption would need neither organization nor a capacity for co-operation. The counterpart of co-operation in the basic assumption group is valency—a spontaneous, unconscious function of the gregarious quality in the personality of man. It is only when a group begins to act on a basic assumption that difficulties arise. Action inevitably means contact with reality and contact with reality compels regard for truth; scientific method is imposed and the evocation of the work group follows. Le Bon described the leader as one under whom a collection of human beings instinctively place themselves, accepting his authority as their chief; the leader must fit in with the group in his personal qualities and must himself be held by a strong faith in order to awaken the group's faith. His view of the leader as one who must fit in with the group in his personal qualities is compatible with my view that any leader is ignored by the group when his behaviour or characteristics fall outside the limits set by the prevalent basic assumption. Further, the leader must be held by the same "faith" that holds the group—not in order to awaken the group's faith but because the attitude of group and leader alike are functions of the active basic assumption.

462

McDougall's distinction between the simple "unorganized" group and the "organized" group seems to me to apply, not to two different groups but to two states of mind which can be observed to co-exist in the same group. The "organized" group, for reasons I have already given, is likely to display the characteristic features of the work group, the "unorganized" of the basic assumption group. Freud discusses McDougall's views, quoting his description of the "unorganized" group.[1] With regard to the suggestibility of the group, I think it depends what the suggestion is. If it falls within the terms of the active basic assumption, the group will follow it, if it does not, the group will ignore it. This characteristic seems to me to come out very clearly in panic to which I refer later.

McDougall, discussed by Freud in the above-mentioned passage, draws up certain conditions for raising the level of collective mental life.[2] "The first of these conditions", he says, "which is the basis of all the rest, is some degree of continuity of existence of the group." This convinces me that in the organized group McDougall is describing what I call the work group. Meyer Fortes,[3] discussing Radcliffe Brown's views on social structure, particularly the distinction between "structure as an actually existing concrete reality" and "structural form", says that the distinction is associated with the continuity of social structure through time. In my view the continuity of social structure through time is a function of the work group. Meyer Fortes states that the time factor in social structure is by no means uniform in its incidence and adds that all corporate groups, by definition, must have continuity. As with McDougall's distinction between organized and unorganized groups, so with the incidence of the time factor, I do not believe that we are dealing with two different kinds of group, in the sense of two different aggregates of individuals, but rather with two different categories of mental activity co-existing in the same group of individuals. In work group activity time is intrinsic: in basic assumption activity it has no place. Basic assumption group functions are active before ever a group comes together in a room, and continue after the group has dispersed. There is neither development nor decay in basic assumption functions, and in this respect they differ totally from work group. It is therefore to be expected that observation of the group's continuity in time will produce anomalous and contradictory results

[1] McDougall, W., *The Group Mind* (Cambridge, 1927), p. 45.
[2] *The Group Mind*, p. 49.
[3] Meyer Fortes, *Time and Social Structure: an Ashanti Case Study*.

if it has not been recognized that two different kinds of mental functioning operate within the group at the same time. The man who asks, "When does the group meet again?" is referring, in so far as he is talking about mental phenomena, to work group. The basic assumption group does not disperse or meet and references to time have no meaning in the basic assumption group. I have known a group of intelligent men, to whom the hours of the sessions were perfectly well known, express anger because the session had ended, and to be quite unable for an appreciable time to grasp a fact which could not be a matter of doubt in work group mentality. What is ordinarily called impatience must therefore, in the basic assumption group, be considered as an expression of the anxiety which is aroused by phenomenal intrinsically co-mingled with a dimension of which basic assumption mentality knows nothing. It is as if a blind man were made aware of phenomena that could only be understood by one to whom the properties of light were familiar.

I would describe McDougall's principles for raising collective mental life to a higher level as an expression of the attempt to prevent obstruction of work group by basic assumption group. His second condition stresses the need for the individual to have a clear view of the aims of the work group. His fourth point desiderates the existence of a body of traditions and customs and habits in the minds of the members of the group, that will determine their relations to one another and to the group as a whole; this approximates to Plato's view that group harmony must be based on individual function and the firmness with which the individual is restricted to it. But it also has affinities with St. Augustine's view, in the 19th Book of *The City of God*, that a right relation with his fellows can only be achieved by a man who has first regulated his relationship with God. This may seem to contradict my statement that McDougall is concerned in his description of the organized group primarily with work group phenomena. The difference between the two writers would seem to be this: McDougall is concerned to cope with basic assumptions by strengthening the work group's capacity to retain contact with external reality, while St. Augustine is elaborating a technique by which a specialized work group is formed with the specific function of maintaining contact with the basic assumption—in particular with the dependent basic assumption. It is worth remembering that he was concerned to defend Christianity against the charge of having so undermined morale that Rome had been unable to resist the onslaught of Alaric. Put in other terms, a body or group had arisen which was under suspicion of having dealt with basic assumptions in a manner less efficient than that of their pagan predecessors. St. Augustine is uneasily concerned to refute this. It is a predicament with which those who purport to lead both public and group are not unfamiliar: the stimulation, and manipulation, of basic assumption, especially when done, as in some sort it must always be done, without anything like adequate knowledge, or even awareness, must lead to untoward results and sometimes even to the dock.

I shall now consider that part of Freud's discussion which turns on the statement that in a group an individual's emotions become extraordinarily intensified, while his intellectual ability becomes markedly reduced. About this I shall have something to say later when considering the group from the point of view of the individual, but I wish for the present to approach the matter, as Freud does, as a group phenomenon.[1] In the groups I have studied it has been natural for the group to expect me to take the lead in organizing its activities. As I take advantage of the position thus accorded me to lead the group in the direction of demonstrating group dynamics, the "organization" of the group does not do what McDougall says the organization of the group is intended to do. The desire for an "organized" group, in McDougall's sense, is frustrated. Fear of the basic assumptions, which cannot be satisfactorily dealt with by structure and organization, therefore expresses itself in the suppression of emotion, emotion being an essential part of the basic assumptions. The tension thus produced appears to the individual as an intensification of emotion; the lack of structure promotes the obtrusion of the basic assumption group, and since in such a group the intellectual activity is, as I have already said, of an extremely limited kind, the individual, conforming with the behaviour imposed by participation in the basic assumption group, feels as if his intellectual capacity were being reduced. The belief that this really is so is reinforced because the individual tends to ignore all intellectual activity that does not fit in with the basic assumption. In fact I do not in the least believe that there is a reduction of intellectual ability in the group, nor yet that "great decisions in the realm of thought and momentous discoveries and solutions of problems are only possible to an individual working in solitude"[2]; although the belief that this is so is commonly expressed in the group discussion, and all sorts of plans are elaborated

[1] *Group Psychology and the Analysis of the Ego*, p. 33.
[2] *Ibid.*

for circumventing the supposedly pernicious influence of the emotions of the group. Indeed I give interpretations because I believe that intellectual activity of a high order is possible in a group together with an awareness (and not an evasion) of the emotions of the basic assumption groups. If group therapy is found to have a value, I believe it will be in the conscious experiencing of group activity of this kind.

Freud turns to discussion of something that crops up under a variety of names, such as "suggestion", "imitation", "prestige of leaders", "contagion". I have used "valency" partly because I would avoid the meanings which already adhere to the terms I have listed, partly because the term "valency", as used in physics to denote the power of combination of atoms, carries with it the greatest penumbra of suggestiveness useful for my purpose. By it I mean the capacity of the individual for instantaneous combination with other individuals in an established pattern of behaviour—the basic assumptions. Later I shall consider in greater detail what meaning we should attribute to this term when I am dealing with the psycho-analytic view of the individual's contribution.

I shall not follow Freud's discussion in detail, but will pass on to his use of the term "libido", which he takes from his study of the psycho-neuroses.[1] He thus approaches the group by way of psycho-analysis, and psycho-analysis, in the light of my experience of groups, can be regarded as a work group likely to stimulate the basic assumption of pairing; that being so, psycho-analytic investigation, as itself a part of pairing group, is likely to reveal sexuality in a central position. Further, it is likely to be attacked as itself a sexual activity since, according to my view of the pairing group, the group must assume that if two people come together, they can only do so for sexual purposes. It is therefore natural that Freud should see the nature of the bond between individuals in a group as libidinous. In the group, the libidinous component in the bond is characteristic of the pairing group, but I think it has a different complexion in the dependent group and the fight-flight group. Freud describes the commander-in-chief of the Church as Christ, but I would say that it is the Deity. Christ, or the Messiah, is the leader, not of the dependent group but of the pairing group. In psycho-analysis, regarded as a part of the pairing group, the Messiah, or Messianic idea, occupies a central position, and the bond between individuals is libidinous. The Messianic idea betrays itself in the supposition that

[1] *Ibid.*

466

the individual patient is worth the analyst's very considerable devotion; as also in the view, sometimes openly expressed, that as a result of psycho-analytic work a technique will be perfected that will, ultimately, save mankind. In short, I regard Freud's use of the term libido as correct only for one phase, though an important one, and feel the need for some more neutral term that will describe the tie on all basic assumption levels. The tie in the work group, which I regard as being of a sophisticated nature, is more aptly described by the word co-operation.

Freud's notion of the leader as one on whom the group depends, and from whose personality it derives its qualities, seems to me to derive from his view of identification as almost entirely a process of introjection by the ego; to me the leader is as much the creature of the basic assumption as any other member of the group, and this, I think, is to be expected if we envisage identification of the individual with the leader as depending not on introjection alone but on a simultaneous process of projective identification[1] as well. The leader, on the basic assumption level, does not create the group by virtue of his fanatical adherence to an idea, but is rather an individual whose personality renders him peculiarly susceptible to the obliteration of individuality by the basic assumption groups' leadership requirements. The "loss of individual distinctiveness" applies to the leader of the group as much as to anyone else—a fact which probably accounts for some of the posturing to which leading figures are prone. Thus the leader in the fight-flight group, for example, appears to have a distinctive personality because his personality is of a kind that lends itself to exploitation by the group demand for a leader who requires of it only a capacity for fighting or for flight; the leader has no greater freedom to be himself than any other member of the group. It will be appreciated that this differs from Le Bon's idea that the leader must possess a strong and imposing will, and with Freud's idea that he corresponds to a hypnotist. Such power as he has derives from the fact that he has become, in common with every other member of the group, what Le Bon describes as "an automaton who has ceased to be guided by his will". In short, he is leader by virtue of his capacity for instantaneous, involuntary (maybe voluntary too) combination with every other member of his group, and only differs from them in that, whatever his function in the work group, he is the incarnation of the basic assumption group leader.

[1] Klein, Melanie, "Notes on some Schizoid Mechanisms."

Freud's view seems not to make explicit the dangerous possibilities that exist in the phenomenon of leadership. His view of the leader, and indeed all other views of which I am aware, is not easily reconciled with my experience of leadership as it emerges in practice. The leader of the work group at least has the merit of possessing contact with external reality, but no such qualification is required of the leader of the basic assumption group. The usual description of the leader seems to be a mixture embodying various group phenomena, the characteristics of the work group leader predominating. For reasons I have given, the work group leader is either harmless through lack of influence with the group, or else a man whose grasp of reality is such that it carries authority. It is likely therefore that discussions of leadership coloured mostly by views of work group leader qualities will be optimistically tinged. My view of the basic assumption group leader does not rule out the possibility of identity with the work group leader, but it allows for the existence of a leader apparently evoking the enthusiastic allegiance of the group, but devoid of contact with any reality other than the reality of the basic assumption group demands. When it is realized that this can mean that the group is being led by an individual whose qualification for the job is that his personality has been obliterated', an automaton, "an individual who has lost his distinctiveness", but who yet is so suffused by the emotions of the basic assumption group that he carries all the prestige one would like to believe was the especial perquisite of the work group leader, it becomes possible to explain some of the disasters into which groups have been led by leaders whose qualifications for the post seem, when the emotions prevalent at their prime have died down, to be devoid of substance.

Freud says that panic is best studied in military groups.[1] I have experienced panic with troops in action on two occasions, and have on several other occasions in small civilian groups had reason to think that the emotional experience bore a sufficiently close resemblance to my military experience to deserve the name panic. I think Freud is discussing the same phenomenon, though these experiences do not appear in all respects to bear out Freud's theories. McDougall's description of panic refers to an experience which I think is similar, in essentials, to my own and I am confirmed in this when he says, "Other of the cruder, primary emotions may spread through a crowd in very similar fashion though the process

[1] *Group Psychology and the Analysis of the Ego*, p. 45.

is rarely so rapid and intense as in the case of fear",[1] and then describes in a footnote an instance he witnessed in Borneo of the almost instantaneous spread of anger through a crowd.[2] McDougall has thus brought very close together, though without making the connection, anger and fear, and thus supports my view that panic is an aspect of the fight-flight group. It is my contention that panic flight and uncontrolled attack are really the same. I am not acquainted with Nestroy's parody, quoted by Freud,[3] but taking the story as he gives it, I would agree that it could be taken as typifying panic, but I would say this: there can be no more absolute a way of leaving a battle than by dying. There is nothing in the story of panic flight following the death of the general, that we may regard as incompatible with fidelity to the fight-flight leader; he is followed even when dead, for his death is an act of leadership.

Panic does not arise in any situation unless it is one that might as easily have given rise to rage. The rage or fear are offered no readily available outlet: frustration, which is thus inescapable, cannot be tolerated because frustration requires awareness of the passage of time, and time is not a dimension of basic assumption phenomena. Flight offers an immediately available opportunity for expression of the emotion in the fight-flight group and therefore meets the demand for instantaneous satisfaction—therefore the group will fly. Alternatively, attack offers a similarly immediate outlet—then the group will fight. The fight-flight group will follow any leader (and, contrary to views hitherto expressed, retains its coherence in doing so) who will give such orders as license instantaneous flight or instantaneous attack. Provided that an individual in the group conforms to the limitations of the fight-flight leader he will have no difficulty in turning a group from headlong flight to attack or from headlong attack to panic.

The stimulus for panic, or the rage which I consider to be interchangeable, must always be an event that falls outside the work group functions of the group involved. That is to say, the degree of organization of the group is not a factor in panic unless the organization (which is, as I have said, a part of work group function) has been evolved for coping with the specific external event responsible for the panic. In Freud's example of a fire in a theatre or place of amusement,[4] the work group is devoted to the watching of

[1] *The Group Mind*, p. 24.
[2] *Ibid.*, p. 26.
[3] *Group Psychology and the Analysis of the Ego*, p. 49.
[4] *Ibid.*, p. 47.

play but not to the witnessing of a conflagration, still less to the extinguishing of it. The essential point about organization is that it should be suitable both to the external aim of the group and to the manipulation of the basic assumption that such a pursuit is most calculated to evoke. Panic in an army is not produced by a military danger, though military danger is, in the nature of things, very likely to be present. It is not likely to be produced by any situation in which attack or flight are appropriate expressions of work group. If it appears to arise in such a situation it is because the actual cause is not observed.

It is clear that between the theories advanced by Freud and those I have sketched out here there is a gap. It may appear to be more considerable than it is because of my deliberate use of a new terminology with which to clothe the apparatus of mechanisms that I think I have detected. It will be necessary to test this by looking at the group more from the standpoint of the individual. But, before I do this, I shall sum up by saying that Freud sees the group as a repetition of part object relationships. It follows from this that groups would, in Freud's view, approximate to neurotic patterns of behaviour while in my view they would approximate to the patterns of psychotic behaviour.

The society or group that is healthy shows its resemblance to the family group as Freud describes it. The more disturbed the group, the less it is likely to be understood on the basis of family patterns or neurotic behaviour as we know it in the individual.

This does not mean that I consider my descriptions apply only to sick groups. On the contrary, I very much doubt if any real therapy could result unless these psychotic patterns were laid bare with no matter what group. In some groups their existence is early discernible; in others, work has to be done before they become manifest. These groups resemble the analytic patient who appears much more ill after many months of analysis than he did before he had had any analysis at all.

The individual who attends a group for treatment is entitled to believe that he is going to experience something which will lead to his cure. Almost without exception—and the exceptions have themselves to be demonstrated as more apparent than real—patients are convinced that the group is no good and cannot cure them. It is something of a shock to them to find, at any rate when I am a member of the group, that what takes place is not something which allays these anxieties, but appears rather to be a detailed and painstaking demonstration that their vague and ill-formulated suspicions and resentments about the group are based, as often as not, on only too substantial group attitudes towards them and their troubles. Their suspicions are well grounded; they are anchored, at one end at any rate, in what seems to be a perfectly genuine indifference to them, or worse still, hatred of them. For example: A woman is talking in a group consisting, on this occasion, of six people and myself. She complains of a difficulty about food, her fear of choking if she eats at a restaurant, and of her embarrassment at the presence, during a recent meal, of an attractive woman at her table. "I don't feel like that", says Mr. A, and his remark is met by a murmur of sound from one or two others which could indicate that they were at one with him; could indicate it and does indicate it, but at the same time leaves them free to say, for this group had now become wily, if need arose, that they "hadn't said anything". The remainder looked as if the matter were of no interest or concern to them. If a patient spoke in analysis as the woman had spoken, it is clear that according to the state of her analysis the analyst would not expect to have any great difficulty in seeing that a number of interpretations were possible. I cannot see how any of these interpretations, which are based on years of psycho-analytic study of the pair, can possibly be regarded as appropriate to the group; either that, or we have to revise our ideas of what constitutes the analytic situation. In fact the interpretations I gave were concerned almost entirely with pointing out that the material that followed the woman's confidence to the group indicated the group's anxiety to repudiate that the woman's difficulty, whatever it was, was theirs, and furthermore that they were, in that respect, superior to the woman. I was then able to show that the reception the group had given to the woman's candour had now made it very difficult for any of the remainder of the group to speak, individually, of those other respects in which, in a burst of frankness, they were prepared to admit that they were "inferior". In short, it was not difficult to show that if a patient did go so far as to come to the group for help with a difficulty, what she got was an increase of feelings of inferiority, and a reinforcement of feelings of loneliness and lack of worth.

Now this situation is not similar to that which obtains in an analysis when the analyst has succeeded in making overt unconscious fears and anxieties. In the instance that I have given, no interpretation was made which would elucidate for the woman the significance of her anxieties when eating in the presence of "an attractive woman". The

471

series of interpretations that I gave could, in so far as they were successful, have made clear to her the disagreeable emotions associated
with being the receptor in a group which is resorting freely to projective identification. I could have made clear to her that her "meal"
in the session was causing her embarrassment, and to some extent
this was implicit in the interpretations I was giving to the group as a
whole. But it seems fair to say that, from an analytic point of view,
the woman is not getting a satisfactory interpretation, and is suffering
an experience the discomfort of which is not intrinsic to her disability, but inheres in the fact that group treatment is the wrong
treatment. There is, however, another possibility, and it is this: when
this woman was speaking, although I had no reason to suppose and
still do not suppose that she was anything but a case of psychoneurosis, the whole manner in which she expressed herself reminded
me strongly of the candour and coherence of unconscious expression
which so often contrasts, in the psychotic, with the confusion that
attends his attempts at rational communication. I can make my point
clearer by saying that I believe that if this patient had spoken when
in analysis with me as she did in the group, her intonation and
manner would never have led me to doubt that the correct interpretation would be one appropriate to a neurotic disability; in the
group I felt that manner and intonation alike indicated that her
behaviour would be more accurately assessed if it were regarded as
akin to the formulations of the psychotic. Regarded in this light I
would say that she felt that there was a single object, called the
group, that had been split up into pieces (the individual members of
the group) by her eating, and that the belief that this was so reinforced guilty feelings that the emotions associated with being the
receptor of projective identifications were the fault of her behaviour.
These feelings of guilt again make it difficult for her to understand
the part played in her emotions by the actions of the other members
of the group.

So far I have considered the "badness of the group" as it touches the
patient trying to get treatment; we may now turn to consider this
from the point of view of the members of the group who have been
trying to achieve "cure" by the splitting and projective mechanisms
described by Melanie Klein.[1] Not only have they divested themselves of any of the troubles of the woman patient, but, if this
mechanism is to be effective, they have laid themselves open to the
necessity for getting rid of any sense of responsibility towards the

[1] "Notes on some Schizoid Mechanisms".

woman. This they do by splitting off good parts of their personality and placing them in the analyst. In this way the "treatment" that these individuals receive from the group is the achievement of a state of mind recognizably akin to the "loss of individual distinctiveness", spoken of by Freud, on the one hand, and the depersonalization which we meet with in psychotics, on the other. At this point the group is in the state I have described as having the basic assumption of dependence dominant.

I shall not go further with the description of subsequent development in this group except to mention one peculiarity of its subsequent behaviour which is very common to all kinds of group situations; subsequent communications were in terms of short interjections, long silences, sighs of boredom, movements of discomfort. This state of affairs in a group deserves close attention. The group appears to be capable of enduring almost endless periods of such conversation, or none at all. There are protests, but endurance of this monotony appears to be a lesser evil than action to end it. It is impossible to give all my reasons for thinking this phase of group behaviour to be significant. I shall content myself with saying that it is closely linked with the splitting and depersonalization mentioned above. I also believe it to be linked with feelings of depression probably in much the same way as maintenance of the schizoid position serves to suppress the depressive position.[1]

VERBAL COMMUNICATION

In this state, when interpretations are made, they are disregarded. This disregard may be, as in psycho-analysis, more apparent than real; it may be that the interpretations are faulty and on that account inefficacious; or it may be that the basic assumptions are so dominant that any lead is ignored that does not fall within the limitations of those states. But even allowing for these possibilities, there is an unexplained residue. I have been forced to the conclusion that verbal exchange is a function of the work group. The more the group corresponds with the basic assumption group the less it makes any rational use of verbal communication. Words serve as a vehicle for the communication of sound. Melanie Klein has stressed the importance of symbol formation in the development of the individual, and her discussion of the breakdown of a capacity for symbol

[1] Klein, Melanie, "Notes on some Schizoid Mechanisms".

formation appears to me to be relevant to the group state I am describing.[1] The work group understands that particular use of symbols which is involved in communication; the basic assumption group does not. I have heard it suggested that the "language" of the basic assumption group is primitive. I do not believe this to be true. It seems to me to be debased rather than primitive. Instead of developing language as a method of thought, the group uses an existing language as a mode of action. This "simplified" method of communication has none of the vitality of primitive or early language. Its simplicity is degenerate and debased. Contrast to this state of affairs is provided by the occasions when a group, aware of the inadequacies of its vocabulary, tries to discuss and agree upon terms which they want to use in the group. In this instance, one might say one sees the evolution of a "primitive" scientific method as a part of work group function, but there is nothing debased about it. The "language" of the basic assumption group lacks the precision and scope that is conferred by a capacity for the formation and use of symbols: this aid to development is therefore missing, and stimuli that would ordinarily promote development have no effect. But one might well claim for the methods of communication that the group employs the title of Universal Linguistic, which Croce conferred on æsthetic. Every human group instantaneously understands every other human group, no matter how diverse its culture, language, and tradition, on the level of the basic assumptions.

As an exercise in the application of some of the theories I have been putting forward, I will instance the biblical account of the building of the Tower of Babel.[2] The myth brings together—rather in the way that a psycho-analytic patient's associations bring together—the following components: a universal language, the building by the group of a tower which is felt by the Deity to be a menace to his position; a confounding of the universal language and a scattering abroad of the people on the face of the earth. What kind of event is embedded in this myth? I shall use my theories to interpret the myth as embodying an account of the development of language in a group with the dependent basic assumption dominant. The new development—it is worth remembering that Freud chose the development of language as an instance of group activity of high mental order—

---

[1] "The Importance of Symbol Formation in the Development of the Ego", in *Contributions to Psycho-Analysis*.

[2] Genesis xi, 1–9. This account is a part of the so-called Jahvistic code and could therefore be regarded as an example of recording by a group with dependent basic assumption dominant when threatened by the emergence of the basic assumption of pairing.

in itself demands further development in the group; this I take to be implicit in the symbolism of the tower, the building of which menaces the supremacy of the Deity. The idea that the tower would reach to Heaven introduces the element of Messianic hope which I regard as intrinsic to the pairing group. But a Messianic hope that is fulfilled violates the canon of the pairing basic assumption, and the group dissolves in schisms.

Melanie Klein has shown that the inability to form symbols is characteristic of certain individuals[1]; I would extend this to include all individuals in their functions as members of the basic assumption group.

SUMMARY

Freud's view of the dynamics of the group seem to me to require supplementation rather than correction. There are many occasions when the apposite interpretation is one which draws attention to behaviour in the group which would be appropriate if it were a reaction to a family situation. In other words there is ample evidence for Freud's idea that the family group provides the basic pattern for all groups. If I have not stressed the evidence for this, it is because that view does not seem to me to go far enough. I doubt whether any attempt to establish a group therapeutic procedure can be successful if it is limited to an investigation of mechanisms deriving from this source. I would go further; I think that the central position in group dynamics is occupied by the more primitive mechanisms which Melanie Klein has described as peculiar to the paranoid-schizoid and depressive positions. In other words I feel, but would not like to be challenged with my limited experience to prove, that it is not simply a matter of the incompleteness of the illumination provided by Freud's discovery of the family group as the prototype of all groups, but the fact that this incompleteness leaves out the source of the main emotional drives in the group.

It may be, of course, that this is an artefact produced by the frustration of the individual's desire to be alone with me in the group. I do not wish to minimize the importance of this, but in fact I do not believe that the phenomena I have witnessed are peculiar to a therapeutic group. All groups stimulate and at the same time frustrate the individuals composing them; for the individual is impelled to seek the satisfaction of his needs in his group and is at the same time

---

[1] "The Importance of Symbol Formation in the Development of the Ego."

inhibited in this aim by the primitive fears which the group arouses.

To recapitulate: any group of individuals met together for work shows work group activity, that is mental functioning designed to further the task in hand. Investigation shows that these aims are sometimes hindered, occasionally furthered, by emotional drives of obscure origin. A certain cohesion is given to these anomalous mental activities if it is assumed that emotionally the group acts as if it had certain basic assumptions about its aims. These basic assumptions, which appear to be fairly adequately adumbrated by three formulations, dependence, pairing, and fighting or flight, are, on further investigation, seen to displace each other, as if in response to some unexplained impulse. They appear, furthermore, to have some common link, or, perhaps, even to be different aspects of each other. Further investigation shows that each basic assumption contains features that correspond so closely with extremely primitive part objects that sooner or later psychotic anxiety, appertaining to these primitive relationships, is released. These anxieties, and the mechanisms peculiar to them, have been already displayed in psychoanalysis by Melanie Klein, and her descriptions tally well with the emotional states which find an outlet in mass action of the group in behaviour that seems to have coherence if it is considered to be the outcome of a basic assumption. Approached from the angle of sophisticated work group activity the basic assumptions appear to be the source of emotional drives to aims far different either from the overt task of the group or even from the tasks that would appear to be appropriate to Freud's view of the group as based on the family group. But approached from the angle of psychotic anxiety associated with phantasies of primitive part object relationships, described by Melanie Klein and her co-workers, the basic assumption phenomena appear far more to have the characteristics of defensive reactions to psychotic anxiety, and to be not so much at variance with Freud's views as supplementary to them. In my view, it is necessary to work through both the stresses that appertain to family patterns and the still more primitive anxieties of part object relationships. In fact I consider the latter to contain the ultimate sources of all group behaviour.

If it is felt that the attempt to establish a group therapeutic procedure as a method for treating the individual is worth while, psychoanalysts would be well advised to find a new name for it. I cannot see that there is any scientific justification for describing work of the kind I have attempted as psycho-analysis—I have already given my reasons for this (pages 470–2). In addition to this there is the fact, of which we are all aware, that "bitter experience has taught us that resistance against the unconscious can be so subtle that it may distort the analytical findings and reinterpret them in support of some personal defence"[1] and therefore the term psycho-analysis should continue to be applied, in so far as we can control the situation, to the fundamental principles of psycho-analysis. There remains the question of what therapeutic value is to be attached to the procedure I have tried to describe. I do not think that the time has come to give a definite opinion, and I believe that there may be room for fully qualified psycho-analysts to carry on research into its value, possibly with groups composed of individuals who themselves are having or have had a psycho-analysis.

As a description of group dynamics, each individual is in a position to decide for himself whether the theories I have adumbrated give meaning to the phenomena which he, in the course of his daily life as a member of a group, can witness.

[1] Jones, E., in Preface to Developments in Psycho-Analysis.

20

SOCIAL SYSTEMS AS DEFENCE AGAINST PERSECUTORY AND DEPRESSIVE ANXIETY

A Contribution to the Psycho-Analytical Study of Social Processes

ELLIOTT JAQUES

IT has often been noted that many social phenomena show a strikingly close correspondence with psychotic processes in individuals. Melitta Schmideberg[1] for instance, has pointed to the psychotic content of many primitive ceremonies and rites. And Bion[2] has suggested that the emotional life of the group is only understandable in terms of psychotic mechanisms. My own recent experience[3] has impressed upon me how much institutions are used by their individual members to reinforce individual mechanisms of defence against anxiety, and in particular against recurrence of the early paranoid and depressive anxieties first described by Melanie Klein.[4] In connecting social behaviour with defence against psychotic anxiety, I do not wish in any way to suggest that social relationships serve none other than a defensive function of this kind. Instances of other functions include the equally important expression and gratification of libidinal impulses in constructive social activities, as well as social co-operation in·institutions providing creative, sublimatory opportunities. In the present paper, however, I propose to limit myself to a consideration of certain defensive functions; and in so doing I hope to illustrate and define how the mechanisms of projective and introjective identification operate in linking individual and social behaviour.

[1] "The role of psychotic mechanisms in cultural development", *Int. J. Psycho-Anal.*, Vol. XII.
[2] "Group Dynamics: A re-view", in this book.
[3] *The Changing Culture of a Factory* (London, 1951).
[4] The views of Mrs. Klein drawn upon in this paper are described in her two books, *The Psycho-Analysis of Children* (London, 1932), and *Contributions to Psycho-Analysis* (London, 1948), and in papers recently published in *Developments in Psycho-Analysis* (London, 1952).

Social Systems as defence against Persecutory and Depressive Anxiety

The specific hypothesis I shall consider is that *one* of the primary cohesive elements binding individuals into institutionalized human association is that of defence against psychotic anxiety. In this sense individuals may be thought of as externalizing those impulses and internal objects that would otherwise give rise to psychotic anxiety, and pooling them in the life of the social institutions in which they associate. This is not to say that the institutions so used thereby become "psychotic". But it does imply that we would expect to find in group relationships manifestations of unreality, splitting, hostility, suspicion, and other forms of maladaptive behaviour. These would be the social counterpart of—although not identical with—what would appear as psychotic symptoms in individuals who have not developed the ability to use the mechanism of association in social groups to avoid psychotic anxiety.

If the above hypothesis holds true, then observation of social process is likely to provide a magnified view of the psychotic mechanisms observable in individuals, while also providing a setting in which more than one observer can share. Moreover, many social problems—economic and political—which are often laid at the door of human ignorance, stupidity, wrong attitudes, selfishness, or power seeking, may become more understandable if seen as containing unconsciously motivated attempts by human beings to defend themselves in the best way available at the moment against the experience of anxieties whose sources could not be consciously controlled. And the reasons for the intractability to change of many social stresses and group tensions may be more clearly appreciated if seen as the "resistances" of groups of people unconsciously clinging to the institutions that they have, because changes in social relationships threaten to disturb existing social defences against psychotic anxiety.

Social institutions, as I shall here use the term, are social structures with the cultural mechanisms governing relationships within them. Social structures are systems of roles, or positions, which may be taken up and occupied by persons. Cultural mechanisms are conventions, customs, taboos, rules, etc., which are used in regulating the relations among members of a society. For purposes of analysis, institutions can be defined independently of the particular individuals occupying roles and operating a culture. But the actual working of institutions takes place through real people using cultural mechanisms within a social structure; and the unconscious or implicit functions of an institution are specifically determined by the particular individuals associated in the institution, occupying

479

Elliott Jaques

roles within a structure and operating the culture. Changes may occur in the unconscious functions of an institution through change in personnel, without there necessarily being any apparent change in manifest structure or functions. And conversely, as is so often noted, the imposition of a change in manifest structure or culture for the purpose of resolving a problem, may often leave the problem unsolved because the unconscious relationships remain unchanged.

PROJECTION, INTROJECTION, AND IDENTIFICATION IN SOCIAL
RELATIONSHIPS

In *Group Psychology and the Analysis of the Ego*, Freud takes as his starting point in group psychology the relationship between the group and its leader. The essence of this relationship he sees in the mechanisms of identification: of the members of the group with the leader and with each other.[1] Group processes in this sense can be linked to earlier forms of behaviour, since "identification is known to psycho-analysis as the earliest expression of an emotional tie with another person".[2] But Freud did not explicitly develop the concept of identification beyond that of identification by introjection, a conception deriving from his work on the retention of lost objects through introjection.[3] In his analysis of group life, he does, however, differentiate between identification of the ego with an object (or identification by introjection) and what he terms replacement of the ego ideal by an external object.[4] Thus, in the two cases he describes, the Army and the Church, he points out that the soldier replaces his ego ideal by the leader who becomes his ideal, whereas the Christian takes Christ into himself as his ideal and identifies himself with Him.

Like Freud, Melanie Klein sees introjection as one of the primary processes whereby the infant makes emotional relationships with its objects. But she considers that introjection interacts with the process of projection in the making of these relationships.[5] Such a formula-

[1] *Op. cit.*, p. 80: he states, "A primary group... is a number of individuals who have substituted one and the same object for their ego ideal and have consequently identified themselves with one another in their ego".
[2] *Op. cit.*, p. 60.
[3] "Mourning and Melancholia", *Collected Papers*, Vol. IV (London, 1925).
[4] *Op. cit.*, p. 110.
[5] Cf. "Notes on some Schizoid Mechanisms", p. 293: "I have often expressed my view that object relations exist from the beginning of life.... I have further suggested that the relation to the first object implies its introjection and projection, and that from the beginning object relations are moulded by an interaction between introjection and projection, between internal and external objects and situations." In *Developments in Psycho-Analysis*.

tion seems to me to be consistent with, although not explicit in, the views of Freud expressed above. That is to say, identification of the ego with an object is identification by introjection; this is explicit in Freud. But replacement of the ego ideal by an external object seems to me implicitly to contain the conception of identification by projection. Thus, the soldiers who take their leader for their ego ideal are in effect projectively identifying with him, or putting part of themselves into him. It is this common or shared projective identification which enables the soldiers to identify with each other. In the extreme form of projective identification of this kind, the followers become totally dependent on the leader, because each has given up a part of himself to the leader.[1] Indeed, it is just such an extreme of projective identification which might explain the case of panic described by Freud,[2] where the Assyrians take to flight on learning that Holofernes, their leader, has had his head cut off by Judith. For not only has the commonly shared external object (the figure-head) binding them all together been lost, but the leader having lost his head, every soldier has lost his head through being inside the leader by projective identification.

I shall take as the basis of my analysis of group processes, the conception of identification in group formation, as described by Freud, but with particular reference to the processes of introjective and projective identification, as elaborated by Melanie Klein. Such a form of analysis has been suggested in another context by Paula Heimann[3] who puts forward the notion that introjection and projection may be at the bottom of even the most complex social processes. I shall try to show how individuals make unconscious use of institutions by associating in these institutions and unconsciously co-operating to reinforce internal defences against anxiety and guilt. These social defences bear a reciprocal relationship with the internal defence

---

[1] Cf. "Notes on some Schizoid Mechanisms", p. 301: "The projection of good feelings and good parts of the self into the mother is essential for the infant's ability to develop good object relations and to integrate his ego. However, if this projective process is carried out excessively, good parts of the personality are felt to be lost, and in this way the mother becomes the ego ideal; this process too results in weakening and impoverishing the ego. Very soon such processes extend to other people, and the result may be an over strong dependence on these external representatives of one's own good parts." In *Developments in Psycho-Analysis*.

[2] *Op. cit.*, p. 49.

[3] Cf. "Functions of Introjection and Projection", p. 129: "Such taking in and expelling consists of an active interplay between the organism and the outer world; on this primordial pattern rests all intercourse between subject and object, no matter how complex and sophisticated such intercourse appears. (I believe that in the last analysis we may find it at the bottom of all our complicated dealings with one another.) The patterns Nature uses seem to be few, but she is inexhaustible in their variation." In *Developments in Psycho-Analysis*.

Elliott Jaques

mechanisms. For instance, the schizoid and manic defences against anxiety and guilt both involve splitting and projection mechanisms, and, through projection, a link with the outside world. When external objects are shared with others and used in common for purposes of projection, phantasy social relationships may be established through projective identification with the common object. These phantasy relationships are further elaborated by introjection; and the two-way character of social relationships is mediated by virtue of the two-way play of projective and introjective identification.

I shall speak of the "phantasy social form and content of an institution" to refer to the form and content of social relationships at the level of the common individual phantasies which the members of an institution share by projective and introjective identification. Phantasy is used in the sense of completely unconscious intra-psychic activity, as defined by Susan Isaacs.[1] From this point of view the character of institutions is determined and coloured not only by their explicit or consciously agreed and accepted functions, but also by their manifold unrecognized functions at the phantasy level.

ILLUSTRATIONS OF SOCIALLY STRUCTURED DEFENCE MECHANISMS

It is not my intention in this article to explore either systematically or comprehensively the manner in which social defence mechanisms operate. I shall first examine certain paranoid anxieties and defences, and then depressive anxieties and defences, keeping them to some extent separate for purposes of explication, and giving illustrations from everyday experience. Then I shall present case material from a social study in industry which may make clearer some of the theoretical considerations by showing the interaction of paranoid and depressive phenomena.

Defences against paranoid anxiety

One example of social mechanisms of defence against paranoid anxieties is that of putting bad internal objects[2] and impulses into particular members of an institution who, whatever their explicit

---

[1] "The Nature and Function of Phantasy". In *Developments in Psycho-Analysis*.

[2] The nature of the objects projected and introjected (e.g. fæces, penis, breast), the medium of introjection and projection (e.g. anal, urethral, oral) and the sensory mechanism of introjection and projection (kinæsthetic, visual, auditory, etc.), are variables of fundamental importance in the analysis of group relationships. I shall not, however, consider these variables to any extent here, but I hope to show in subsequent publications that their introduction makes possible a systematic explanation of differences between many types of institution.

function in a society, are unconsciously selected, or themselves choose to introject these projected objects and impulses and either to *absorb* them or *deflect* them. By absorption is meant the process of introjecting the objects and impulses and containing them; whereas in deflection they are again projected but not into the same members from whom they were introjected.

The phantasy social structuring of the process of absorption may be seen, for example, in the case of a first officer in a ship, who, in addition to his normal duty, is held responsible for many things that go wrong, but for which he was not actually responsible. Everyone's bad objects and impulses may unconsciously be put into the first officer, who is consciously regarded by common consent as the source of the trouble. By this mechanism the members of the crew can unconsciously find relief from their own internal persecutors. And the ship's captain can thereby be more readily idealized and identified with as a good protective figure. The anal content of the phantasy attack on the first officer is indicated in the colloquialism that "the first officer must take all the shit; and he must be prepared to be a shit". Naval officers in the normal course of promotion are expected to accept this masochistic role; and the norm is to accept it without demur.

The process of deflection may be seen in certain aspects of the complex situation of nations at war. The manifest social structure is that of two opposing armies, each backed and supported by its community. At the phantasy level, however, we may consider the following possibility. The members of each community put their bad objects and sadistic impulses into the commonly shared and accepted external enemy. They rid themselves of their hostile, destructive impulses by projecting them into their armies for deflection against the enemy. Paranoid anxiety in the total community, Army and civilian alike, may be alleviated, or at least transmuted into fear of known and identifiable enemies, since the bad impulses and objects projected into the enemy return, not in the form of introjected phantastic persecutors, but of actual physical attack, which can be experienced in reality. Under appropriate conditions, objective fear may be more readily coped with than phantasy persecution. The bad sadistic enemy is fought against, not in the solitary isolation of the unconscious inner world, but in co-operation with comrades-in-arms in real life. Individuals not only rid themselves of phantastic persecution in this way; but further, the members of the Army are temporarily freed from depressive anxiety because their own sadistic impulses can be denied by attributing their aggressiveness to doing their duty, that is expressing the aggressive impulses collected and introjected from all the community. And members of the community may also avoid guilt by introjecting the socially sanctioned hatred of the enemy. Such introjected sanction reinforces the denial of unconscious hatred and destructive impulses against good objects by allowing for conscious expression of these impulses against a commonly shared and publicly hated real external enemy.

Social co-operation at the reality level may thus allow for a redistribution of the bad objects and impulses in the phantasy relations obtaining among the members of a society.[1] In conjunction with such a redistribution, introjective identification makes it possible for individuals to take in social sanction and support. The primitive aim of the absorption and deflection mechanisms is to achieve a non-return at the phantasy level of the projected phantasy bad objects and impulses.

But even where absorption and deflection are not entirely successful (and mechanisms at the phantasy level can never be completely controlled), the social defence mechanisms provide some gain. Paula Heimann[2] has described the introjection of projected bad objects, and their related impulses, into the ego, where they are maintained in a split-off state, subjected to intra-psychic projection, and kept under attack. In the cases described above, the ego receives support from the social sanctions which are introjected, and which legitimize the intra-psychic projection and aggression. The first officer, for example, may be introjected, and the impulses projected into him introjected as well. But in the phantasy social situation other members of the crew who also attack the first officer are identified with by introjection, partly into the ego, and partly into the super-ego. Hence the ego is reinforced by possession of the internalized members of the crew, all of whom take part in the attack on the segregated bad objects within the ego. And there is an alleviation of the harshness of the super-ego by adding to it objects that socially sanction and legitimize the attack.

These illustrations are obviously not completely elaborated; nor are they intended to be so. They are abstractions from real life situations in which a fuller analysis would show defences against perse-

---

[1] Cf. Freud's description of the re-distribution of libido in the group, *op. cit.*, p. 43.
[2] "Preliminary notes on some defence mechanisms in paranoid states", *Int. J. Psycho-Anal.* (1952).

cutory and depressive anxiety interacting with each other, and with other more explicit functions of the group. But perhaps they suffice to indicate how the use of the concepts of introjective and projective identifications, regarded as interacting mechanisms, may serve to add further dimensions to Freud's analysis of the Army and the Church. We may also note that the social mechanisms described contain in their most primitive aspects features which may be related to the earliest attempts of the infant, described by Melanie Klein,[1] to deal with persecutory anxiety in relation to part objects by means of splitting and projection and introjection of both the good and bad objects and impulses. If we now turn to the question of social defences against depressive anxieties, we shall be able to illustrate further some of the general points.

Defences against depressive anxiety

Let us consider first certain aspects of the problems of the scape-goating of a minority group. As seen from the viewpoint of the community at large, the community is split into a good majority and a bad minority—a split consistent with the splitting of internal objects into good and bad, and the creation of a good and bad internal world. The persecuting group's belief in its own good is preserved by heaping contempt upon and attacking the scape-goated group. The internal splitting mechanisms and preservation of the internal good objects of individuals, and the attack upon, and contempt for, internal, bad persecutory objects, are reinforced by introjective identification of individuals with other members taking part in the group-sanctioned attack upon the scapegoat.[2]

If we now turn to the minority groups, we may ask why only some minorities are selected for persecution while others are not. Here a feature often overlooked in consideration of minority prob-lems may be of help. The members of the persecuted minority com-monly entertain a precise and defined hatred and contempt for their persecutors matching in intensity the contempt and aggression to which they are themselves subjected. That this should be so is per-haps not surprising. But in view of the selective factor in choice of persecuted minorities, we must consider the possibility that one of the operative factors in this selection is the consensus in the minority

[1] Cf. (1945) "The Œdipus Complex in the light of early anxieties", in *Contributions to Psycho-Analysis*, and (1946) "Notes on some schizoid mechanisms". in *Developments in Psycho-Analysis*.

[2] Cf. Melanie Klein's description of the operation of splitting mechanisms in the depressive position (1934) "A contribution to the psychogenesis of manic-depressive states", in *Contri-butions to Psycho-Analysis*.

group, at the phantasy level, to seek contempt and suffering in order to alleviate unconscious guilt. That is to say, there is an unconscious co-operation (or collusion) at the phantasy level between persecutor and persecuted. For the members of the minority group, such a collusion reinforces their own defences against depressive anxiety—by such mechanisms as social justification for feelings of contempt and hatred for an external persecutor, with consequent alleviation of guilt and reinforcement of denial in the protection of internal good objects.

Another way in which depressive anxiety may be alleviated by social mechanisms is through manic denial of destructive impulses, and destroyed good objects, and the reinforcement of good impulses and good objects, by participation in group idealization. These social mechanisms are the reflection in the group of mechanisms of denial and idealization shown by Melanie Klein to be important mechanisms of defence against depressive anxiety.[1]

The operation of these social mechanisms may be seen in mourning ceremonies. The bereaved are joined by others in common display of grief and public reiteration of the good qualities of the deceased. There is a common sharing of guilt, through comparison of the shortcomings of the survivors with the good qualities of the deceased. Bad objects and impulses are got rid of by unconscious projection into the corpse, disguised by the decoration of the corpse, and safely put out of the way through projective identification with the dead during the burial ceremony; such mechanisms are unconsciously aimed at the avoidance of persecution by dæmonic figures. At the same time good objects and impulses are also projected into the dead person. Public and socially sanctioned idealization of the deceased then reinforces the sense that the good object has after all not been destroyed, for "his good works" are held to live on in the memory of the community as well as the surviving family, a memory which is reified in the tombstone. These mechanisms are unconsciously aimed at the avoidance of haunting by guilt-provoking ghosts. Hence, through mourning ceremonies, the community and the bereaved are provided with the opportunity of unconsciously co-operating in splitting the destroyed bad part of the loved object from the loved part, of burying the destroyed bad objects and impulses, and of protecting the good loved part as an eternal memory.

One general feature of each of the instances cited is that the phantasy social systems established have survival value for the group

[1] "Mourning and its relation to manic-depressive states" in *Contributions to Psycho-Analysis*.

as well as affording protection against anxiety in the individual. Thus, for example, in the case of the mourning ceremony the social idealizing and manic denial make it possible for a bereaved person to reduce the internal chaos, to weather the immediate and intense impact of death, and to undertake the process of mature internal mourning at his own time and his own pace.[1] But there is a general social gain as well, in that all those associated in the mourning ceremony can further their internal mourning and continue the lifelong process of working through the unresolved conflicts of the infantile depressive position. As Melanie Klein has described the process "It seems that every advance in the process of mourning results in a deepening in the individual's relation to his inner objects, in the happiness of regaining them after they were felt to be lost ('Paradise Lost and Regained'), in an increased trust in them and love for them because they proved to be good and helpful after all".[2] Hence, through the mourning ceremony, the toleration of ambivalence is increased and friendship in the community can be strengthened. Or again, in the case of the first officer, the ship's crew, in a situation made difficult by close confinement and isolation from other groups, is enabled to co-operate with the captain in carrying out the required and consciously planned tasks by isolating and concentrating their bad objects and impulses within an available human receptacle.

CASE STUDY

I shall now turn to a more detailed and precise examination of phantasy social systems as defence mechanisms for the individual and as mechanisms allowing the group to proceed with its sophisticated or survival tasks, by examining a case study from industry. It may be noted that the conception of sophisticated tasks derives from Bion's conception of the sophisticated task of the work or W group.[3] I am refraining from using Bion's more elaborate conceptual scheme defining what he terms the "basic assumptions" of groups, since the relationship between the operation of basic assumptions and of depressive and persecutory phenomena remains to be worked out.

[1] Cf. Melanie Klein, "Many mourners can only make slow steps in re-establishing the bonds with the external world because they are struggling against the chaos inside," *Contributions to Psycho-Analysis*, p. 329.

[2] *Op cit.*, p. 328.

[3] "Group Dynamics: A re-view".

Elliott Jaques

The case to be presented is one part of a larger study carried out in a light engineering factory, the Glacier Metal Company, between June, 1948, and the present time. The relationship with the firm is a therapeutic one; work is done only on request, from groups or individuals within the firm, for assistance in working through intra-group stresses or in dealing with organizational problems. The relationship between the social consultant (or therapist) and the people with whom he works is a confidential one; and the only reports published are those which have been worked through with the people concerned and agreed by them for publication. Within these terms of reference, I have published a detailed report on the first three years of the project.[1]

The illustration I shall use is taken from work done with one department in the factory.[2] The department employs roughly sixty people. It was organized with a departmental manager as head. Under him was a superintendent, who was in turn responsible for four foremen, each of whom had a working group of ten to sixteen operatives. The operatives had elected five representatives, two of whom were shop stewards, to negotiate with the departmental manager on matters affecting the department. One such matter had to do with a change in methods of wages payment. The shop had been on piece rates (i.e. the operatives were paid a basic wage, plus a bonus dependent on their output). This method of payment had, for a number of years, been felt to be unsatisfactory. From the workers' point of view it meant uncertainty about the amount of their weekly wage, and for the management it meant complicated rate-fixing, and administrative arrangements. For all concerned, the not infrequent wrangling about rates that took place was felt to be unnecessarily disturbing. The possibility of changing over to a flat rate method of payment had been discussed for over a year before the project began. In spite of the fact that the change was commonly desired they had not been able to come to a decision.

A period of negotiation

Work with the department began in January, 1949, by attendance at discussions of a sub-committee composed of the departmental

---

[1] *The Changing Culture of a Factory.*

[2] This case material is a condensation of material which is given in much greater detail in two published articles: Jaques, E., "Collaborative group methods in a wage negotiation situation", *Human Relations*, Vol. III (1950); and Jaques, Rice and Hill, "The social and psychological impact of a change in method of wage payment", *Human Relations*, Vol. IV (1951).

manager, the superintendent, and three workers' representatives. The general tone of the discussions was friendly. The committee members laid stress upon the fact that good relationships existed in the department and that they all wanted to strive for further improvement. From time to time, however, there was sharp disagreement over specific points, and these disagreements led the workers' representatives to state that there were many matters on which they felt they could not trust the management. This statement of suspicion was answered by the management members, who emphasized that they for their part had great trust in the workers' sense of responsibility.

The workers' suspicion of management also revealed itself in discussions held at shop floor level between the elected representatives and their worker constituents. The purpose of these discussions was to elicit in a detailed and concrete manner the views of the workers about the proposed change-over. The workers were on the whole in favour of the change-over, but they had some doubt as to whether they could trust the management to implement and to administer the change-over in a fair manner. What guarantees did they have, they asked, that management had nothing up its sleeve? At the same time, the workers showed an ambivalent attitude towards their own representatives. They urged and trusted them to carry on negotiations with management, but at the same time suspected that the representatives were management "stooges" and did not take the workers' views sufficiently into account. This negative attitude towards their representatives came out more clearly in interviews with the workers alone, in which opinions were expressed that although the elected representatives were known as militant trade unionists, nevertheless they were seen as liable to be outwitted by the management and as not carrying their representative role as effectively as they might.

The day-to-day working relationships between supervisors and workers were quite different from what would be expected as the consequence of these views. Work in the shop was carried out with good morale, and the supervisors were felt to do their best for the workers. A high proportion of the shop had been employed in the company for five years or more, and genuinely good personal relationships had been established.

The discussions in the committee composed of the managers and elected representatives went on for seven months, between January and July, 1949. They had a great deal of difficulty in working

Elliott Jaques

towards a decision, becoming embroiled in arguments that were
sometimes quite heated and had no obvious cause—other than the
workers' suspicion of the management, counterbalanced by the
management's idealization of the workers. Much of the suspicion
and idealization, however, was autistic, in the sense that although
consciously experienced, it was not expressed openly as between
managers and workers. These attitudes came out much more
sharply when the elected representatives and the managers were
meeting separately. The workers expressed deep suspicion and mis-
trust, while the managers expressed some of their anxieties about
how responsible the workers could be—anxieties which existed
alongside their strong sense of the workers' responsibility and of
their faith in them.

Analysis of the negotiation phase

I now wish to apply certain of our theoretical formulations to
the above data. This is in no sense intended to be a complete analysis
of the material. Many important factors, such as changes in the
executive organization of the shop, personal attitudes, changes in
personnel, and variations in the economic and production situation
all played a part in determining the changes which occurred. I do
wish, however, to demonstrate how, if we assume the operation
of defences against paranoid and depressive anxiety at the phantasy
social level, we may be able to explain some of the very great difficulties encountered by the members of the department. And I would
emphasize here that these difficulties were encountered in spite of the
high morale implied in the willingness of those concerned to face,
and to work through in a serious manner, the group stresses they
experienced in trying to arrive at a commonly desired goal.

The degree of inhibition of the autistic suspicion and idealization
becomes understandable, I think, if we make the following assumptions about unconscious attitudes at the phantasy level. The workers
in the shop had split the managers into good and bad—the good
managers being the ones with whom they worked, and the bad being
the same managers but in the negotiation situation. They had unconsciously projected their hostile destructive impulses into their
elected representatives so that the representatives could deflect, or
redirect, these impulses against the bad "management" with whom
negotiations were carried on, while the good objects and impulses
could be put into individual real managers in the day-to-day work
situation. This splitting of the management into good and bad, and

the projective identification with the elected representatives against the bad management served two purposes. At the reality level it allowed the good relations necessary to the work task of the department to be maintained; at the phantasy level it provided a system of social relationships reinforcing individual defences against paranoid and depressive anxiety.

Putting their good impulses into managers in the work situation allowed the workers to reintroject the good relations with management, and hence to preserve an undamaged good object and alleviate depressive anxiety. This depressive anxiety was further avoided by reversion to the paranoid position in the negotiating situation.[1] During the negotiations paranoid anxiety was partially avoided by the workers by putting their bad impulses into their elected representatives. The representatives, while consciously the negotiating representatives of the workers, became unconsciously the representatives of their bad impulses. These split-off bad impulses were partially dealt with and avoided because they were directed against the bad objects put into management in the negotiation situation by the workers and their representatives.

Another mechanism for dealing with the workers' own projected bad objects and impulses was to attack their representatives, with an accompanying despair that not much good would come of the negotiations. These feelings tended to be expressed privately by individuals. The workers who felt like this had introjected their representatives as bad objects and maintained them as a segregated part of the ego. Intra-psychic projection and aggression against these internal bad objects were supported by introjective identification with other workers, who held that the representatives were not doing their job properly. That is to say, other members of the department were introjected to reinforce the intra-psychic projection, and as protection against the internal bad representatives attacking back. In addition to defence against internal persecution, the introjection of the other workers provided social sanction for considering the internalized representatives as bad, offsetting the harshness of super-ego recrimination for attacking objects containing a good as well as a persecuting component.

From the point of view of the elected representatives, anxiety about bad impulses was diminished by unconsciously accepting

---

[1] Melanie Klein has described how paranoid fears and suspicions are often used as a defence against the depressive position. Cf., for instance (1934) "The Psychogenesis of Manic-Depressive States", in *Contributions to Psycho-Analysis*, p. 295.

Elliott Jaques

the bad impulses and objects of all the workers they represented. They could feel that their own hostile and aggressive impulses did not belong to them but belonged to the people on whose behalf they were acting. They were thus able to derive external social sanction for their aggression and hostile suspicion. But the mechanism did not operate with complete success, for there still remained their own unconscious suspicion and hostility to be dealt with, and the reality of what they considered to be the good external management. Hence, there was some anxiety and guilt about damaging the good managers. The primary defence mechanism against the onset of depressive anxiety was that of retreat to the paranoid position. This came out as a rigid clinging to attitudes of suspicion and hostility even in circumstances where they consciously felt that some of this suspicion was not justified by the situation they were actually experiencing.

From the management side, the paranoid attitude of the elected representatives was countered by the reiteration of the view that the workers could be trusted to do their part. This positive attitude unconsciously contained both idealization of the workers and placation of the hostile representatives. The idealization can be understood as an unconscious mechanism for diminishing guilt, stimulated by fears of injuring or destroying workers in the day-to-day work situation through the exercise of managerial authority—an authority which there is good reason to believe is, at least to some extent, felt unconsciously to be uncontrolled and omnipotent. To the extent that managers unconsciously felt their authority to be bad, they feared retaliation by the operatives. This in turn led to a reinforcement of the idealization of the elected representatives as a defence against paranoid anxiety; that is to say, as a means of placating the hostility of the workers, and hence of placating internal persecutors. These idealizing and placatory mechanisms were employed in the meetings with the elected representatives, so that reality mechanisms could operate in the relationships with workers in the work situation, less encumbered with the content of uncontrolled phantasy.

It can thus be seen that the unconscious use of paranoid attitudes by the workers and idealizing and placatory attitudes by the management were complementary, and reinforced each other. A circular process was set in motion. The more the workers' representatives attacked the managers, the more the managers idealized them in order to placate them. The greater the concessions given by management to the workers, the greater was the guilt and fear of

492

depressive anxiety in the workers, and hence the greater the retreat to paranoid attitudes as a means of avoiding depressive anxiety.

Description and analysis of the post-negotiation phase

In June, six months after the discussions began, these attitudes, rather than the wages problem, were for a time taken as the main focus of consideration. A partial resolution occurred,[1] and the workers decided, after a ballot in the whole department, to try out a flat-rate method of payment. The condition for the change-over, however, was the setting up of a council, composed of managers and elected representatives, which would have the authority to determine departmental policy—a procedure for which the principles had already been established in the company. The prime principle was that of unanimous agreement on all decisions, and the agreement to work through all obstacles to unanimous decision by discovering sources of disagreement so that they could be resolved.

It appeared as though the open discussion of autistic attitudes facilitated a restructuring of the phantasy social relations in the department—a restructuring which brought with it a greater degree of conscious or ego control over their relationships. The fact, however, that there was only a partial restructuring of social relations at the phantasy level showed itself in the subsequent history of the shop council. For, following the change-over to a flat-rate method of payment, the council came up against the major question of reassessing the times in which given jobs ought to be done.

Under piece rates such assessment of times was necessary, both for calculation of the bonus to operatives and for giving estimated prices to customers. On flat rates, it was required only for estimating to customers; but the times thus set inevitably constituted targets for the workers. Under piece rates, if a worker did not achieve the target, it meant that he lost his bonus; in other words, he himself paid for any drop in effort. Under flat rates, however, a drop below the target meant that the worker was getting paid for work that he was not doing. A detailed exploration of workers' attitudes[2] showed that the change-over from piece rates to flat rates had in no way altered their personal targets and personal rate of work. They felt guilty

---

[1] The work-through process is in part described in the articles referred to above, and includes an account of the manner in which transference phenomena were handled in the face-to-face group situation. An analysis of the work-through process is outside the scope of the present paper, and hence there is only passing reference to it in the text.
[2] Cf. "The social and psychological impact of a change in method of wage payment", *Human Relations* (1951).

Elliott Jaques

whenever they fell below their estimated targets, because they were no longer paying for the difference. In order to avoid this guilt, the workers applied strong pressure to keep the estimated times on jobs as high as possible, as well as pressure to get the so-called tight times (times on jobs that were difficult to achieve), re-assessed. There were strong resistances to any changes in job assessment methods which the workers suspected might set difficult targets for them.

On the management side, the change-over to flat rates inevitably stirred whatever unconscious anxieties they might have about authority. For under piece rates, the bonus payment itself acted as an impersonal and independent disciplinarian, ensuring that workers put in the necessary effort. Under flat rates it was up to managers to see that a reasonable rate of work was carried on. This forced upon them more direct responsibility for the supervision of their subordinates, and brought them more directly into contact with the authority that they held.

The newly-constituted council, with its managers and elected representatives, had great difficulty in coping with the more manifest depressive anxiety both in the managers and in the workers. This showed in managers' views that the council might possibly turn out to be a bad thing because it slowed down administrative developments in the department. Similar opinions that the council would not work and might not prove worth while played some part in the decision of five out of six of the elected representatives not to stand for re-election in the shop elections which occurred sixteen months after the setting up of the council. These five were replaced by five newly-elected representatives, who in turn brought with them a considerable amount of suspicion. That is, there was again a retreat to the paranoid position while the managers' depressive anxiety continued to show to some extent in the form of depressive feelings that the council would not work. It has only been slowly, over a period of two years, that the council has been able to operate in the new situation as a constitutional mechanism for getting agreement on policy and at the same time intuitively to be used for the containment of the phantasy social relationships. An exploration of the re-rating problem has been agreed and is being carried on with the assistance of an outside industrial consultant.

This case study, then, illustrates the development of an explicit social institution, that of meetings between management and elected representatives, which allowed for the establishment of unconscious mechanisms at the phantasy level for dealing with paranoid and

494

depressive anxieties. The main mechanisms were those of management idealizing the hostile workers, and the workers maintaining an attitude of suspicion towards the idealizing management. To the extent that splitting and projective identification operated successfully, these unconscious mechanisms helped individuals to deal with anxiety, by getting their anxieties into the phantasy social relations structured in the management elected-representative group. In this way the anxieties were eliminated from the day-to-day work situation, and allowed for the efficient operation of the sophisticated work task and the achievement of good working relationships.

However, it will be noted that the elected representative-management group was also charged with a sophisticated work task—that of negotiating new methods of wages payment. They found it difficult to get on with the sophisticated task itself. In terms of the theory here propounded, these difficulties have been explained as arising from the manner in which the predominant unconscious phantasy relations in the negotiating group ran counter to the requirements of the sophisticated task. In other words, an essentially constitutional procedure, that of elected representatives meeting with an executive body, was difficult to operate because it was being used in an unrecognized fashion at the phantasy level to help deal with the depressive and paranoid anxieties of the members of the department as a whole.

SOME OBSERVATIONS ON SOCIAL CHANGE

In the above case study, it might be said that social change was sought when the structure and culture no longer met the requirements of the individual members of the department, and in particular of the managers and the elected representatives. Manifest changes were brought about, and in turn appeared to lead to a considerable restructuring of the phantasy social form and content of the institution. Change having taken place, however, the individual members found themselves in the grip of new relationships, to which they had to conform because they were self made. But they had brought about more than they had bargained for, in the sense that the new relationships under flat rates and the policy-making council had to be experienced before their implications could be fully appreciated.

The effects of the change on individuals were different according to the roles they occupied. The elected representatives were able to change roles by the simple expedient of not standing for re-election. And this expedient, it will be noted, was resorted to by five of the six representatives. The managers, however, were in a very different position. They could not relinquish or change their roles without in a major sense changing their positions, and possibly status, in the organization as a whole. They had, therefore, individually to bear considerable personal stress in adjusting themselves to the new situation.

It is unlikely that members of an institution can ever bring about social changes that suit perfectly the needs of each individual. Once change is undertaken, it is more than likely that individuals will have to adjust and change personally in order to catch up with the changes they have produced. And until some readjustment is made at the phantasy level, the individual's social defences against psychotic anxiety are likely to be weakened. It may well be because of the effects on the unconscious defence systems of individuals against psychotic anxiety, that social change is resisted—and in particular, imposed social change. For it is one thing to readjust to changes that the individual has himself helped to bring about. It is quite another to be required to adjust one's internal defence systems in order to conform to changes brought about by some outside agency.

SUMMARY AND CONCLUSIONS

Freud has argued that two main processes operate in the formation of what he calls artificial groups, like the Army and the Church; one is identification by introjection, and the other is replacement of the ego-ideal by an object. I have suggested that this latter process implicitly contains the concept, formulated by Melanie Klein, of identification by projection. Further, Melanie Klein states explicitly that in the interaction between introjective and projective identification lies the basis of the infant's earliest relations with its objects. The character of these early relations is determined by the way in which the infant attempts to deal with its paranoid and depressive anxieties, and by the intensity of these anxieties.

Taking these conceptions of Freud and Melanie Klein, the view has here been advanced that one of the primary dynamic forces pulling individuals into institutionalized human association is that of defence against paranoid and depressive anxiety; and, conversely, that all institutions are unconsciously used by their members as mechanisms of defence against these psychotic anxieties. Individuals may put their internal conflicts into persons in the external world, unconsciously follow the course of the conflict by means of projective identification, and re-internalize the course and outcome of the externally perceived conflict by means of introjective identification. Societies provide institutionalized roles whose occupants are sanctioned, or required, to take into themselves the projected objects or impulses of other members. The occupants of such roles may absorb the objects and impulses—take them into themselves and become either the good or bad object with corresponding impulses; or, they may deflect the objects and impulses—put them into an externally perceived ally, or enemy, who is then loved, or attacked. The gain for the individual in projecting objects and impulses and introjecting their careers in the external world, lies in the unconscious co-operation with other members of the institution or group who are using similar projection mechanisms. Introjective identification then allows more than the return of the projected objects and impulses. The other members are also taken inside, and legitimize and reinforce attacks upon internal persecutors, or support manic idealization of loved objects, thereby reinforcing the denial of destructive impulses against them.

The unconscious co-operation at the phantasy level among members of an institution is structured in terms of what is here called the phantasy social form and content of institutions. The form and content of institutions may thus be considered from two distinct levels: that of the manifest and consciously agreed form and content (including structure and function, which, although possibly unrecognized, are nevertheless in the preconscious of members of the institution, and hence are relatively accessible to identification by means of conscious study); and that of the phantasy form and content, which are unconsciously avoided and denied, and, because they are totally unconscious, remain unidentified by members of the institution.

A case study is presented to illustrate how within one department in a factory a sub-institution, a committee of managers and elected workers' representatives, was used at the phantasy level for segregating hostile relations from good relations, which were maintained in the day-to-day production work of the department. When, however, the committee was charged with a serious and conscious negotiating task, its members encountered great difficulties because of the socially sanctioned phantasy content of their relationships with each other.

Some observations are made on the dynamics of social change. Change occurs where the phantasy social relations within an institution no longer serve to reinforce individual defences against psychotic anxiety. The institution may be restructured at the manifest and phantasy level; or the manifest structure may be maintained, but the phantasy structure modified. Individuals may change roles or leave the institution altogether. Or, apparent change at the manifest level may often conceal the fact that no real change has taken place, the phantasy social form and content of the institution being left untouched. Imposed social change which does not take account of the use of institutions by individuals, to cope with unconscious psychotic anxieties, is likely to be resisted.

Finally, if the mechanisms herein described have any validity, then at least two consequences may follow. First, observation of social processes may provide one means of studying, as through a magnifying glass, the operation of paranoid and depressive anxieties and the defences built up against them. Unlike the psycho-analytical situation, such observations can be made by more than one person at the same time. And second, it may become more clear why social change is so difficult to achieve, and why many social problems are so intractable. For from the point of view here elaborated, changes in social relationships and procedures call for a restructuring of relationships at the phantasy level, with a consequent demand upon individuals to accept and tolerate changes in their existing pattern of defences against psychotic anxiety. Effective social change is likely to require analysis of the common anxieties and unconscious collusions underlying the social defences determining phantasy social relationships.

21

AN INCONCLUSIVE CONTRIBUTION TO THE THEORY OF THE DEATH INSTINCT

R. E. MONEY-KYRLE

BEFORE coming to my main theme of the death instinct, a few words on the concept of instinct in general may not be out of place.

If, as external observers, we study any animal, we note that it has certain dispositions to behave in certain ways in certain situations.[1] We say these dispositions are partly innate and partly acquired, but a difficulty arises when we try to say which part is which. At least in the higher species, and especially in man, every behaviour pattern is the joint product of heredity and environment. We know that the two contributions are not separate entities like the foundation and superstructure of a building, but we often speak of them as if they were, and so become involved in such misleading dichotomies as that between what is there at birth and what develops subsequently, or between what develops in a "normal" environment and what deviates from it in an abnormal one. We should come nearer the implied distinction if we regarded what is innate as a range of potentialities, and what is acquired as an actuality selected from them under the influence of a particular environment. Thus we have an instinct to eat and acquire specific eating habits.

The range of potentialities comprised by instincts has widened in the course of evolution. The instincts of lower forms of life are relatively stereotyped; those of the higher animals are much more plastic, and include mechanisms for modifying themselves in accordance with the experience encountered. Both the stereotyped and the plastic dispositions could be described by conditional statements of the form, "if a then A, then if b then B, etc.", where a and b are patterns of stimuli—both internal and external—and A and B are

---

[1] The term "situation" here includes an internal stimulus to appetitive behaviour as well as an external pattern eliciting consummatory behaviour.

R. E. *Money-Kyrle*

patterns of response. But in the case of the higher plastic instincts, propositions giving the precise way in which such patterns are progressively modified by their own outcome would have to be included. In other words, a complete description of a higher plastic instinct would take the form of a pyramid of conditional statements giving the widening alternative developments in every conceivable environment. Then the actual development in the actual environment would be represented by one line from the apex to the base. In man the instincts are particularly plastic, and the "width" of the pyramid needed to describe them, correspondingly great. Biology has not got beyond a rough and uncertain classification of some of the main forms common to our species. Future work may also list the racial and individual differences—for it may be presumed that we differ innately from each other as much in our instinctive potentialities of function, which express the minutiae of cerebral structure, as in our more easily recorded, overt structure.

So far we have considered instincts from the external, biological, point of view—that is, behaviouristically. But as psychologists we are not only concerned with behaviour. Indeed, strictly speaking, we are concerned with behaviour only because we depend on it to infer states of mind, which it is our business to study and describe. By a process of controlled identification we imagine we have these before us. We can then again abstract what I have called the dispositions. But we seek to go beyond the behavioural factors to the underlying tendencies to think and feel, either consciously or unconsciously, in certain ways in certain "perceptual situations".[1] In other words, we are concerned with the phantasy responses which may precede and initiate behaviour.[2] In this field, the analytic technique invented by Freud has reaped a steady harvest. He and those who have followed him have listed a number of innate phantasy patterns and can describe how they are likely to develop under the influence of different environments. The psycho-analytic study of these phantasy patterns is the study of instinct in man.

One unforeseen result of this study was that old classifications of a number of distinguishable instincts tended to break down. Not only did apparently homogeneous instincts turn out to be the ex-

[1] The term "perceptual situation" is taken to include the conscious or unconscious perception of an inner need, such as hunger, as well as the perception of a pattern of external objects. It denotes the psychological equivalent of the biological definition of "situation" in the footnote to page 499.
[2] To be precise, what the psychologist studies are the psychic correlates of those cerebral processes which the biologist assumes, though cannot observe, to be the "effects" of stimuli patterns and the "cause" of behaviour.

500

pression of a number of component phantasies, but the same primary phantasies, divided and recombined in an extremely complex way in the course of their development, were found expressed in a number of apparently unconnected instincts. But from the beginning, Freud saw conflict to be a basic character of the inner world of phantasy, and was therefore led to believe that all instincts must at least be divisible into two main groups. The classification he at length evolved into life and death instincts is still highly controversial. But it is not a mere metapsychology divorced from practice;[1] for the view we take of it profoundly affects our working theories and our clinical technique. This is because we are basically concerned with anxiety, the origin of which the theory of the death instinct may possibly explain.

While many analysts are unable to follow Freud and accept this theory, Melanie Klein goes further than he did. She not only accepts the death instinct, but believes the fear of death to be at the root of persecutory, and so indirectly of all, anxiety. Against this, both Freud and Ernest Jones had already argued that one cannot fear what one cannot conceive of, and that it is psychologically impossible to form a positive idea of anything so negative as being nothing. I used to be much impressed by this argument, which corresponded with my own epistemological approach, but I have since come to feel it to be something of a quibble; for if we cannot form an idea of being dead, we can certainly form an idea of, and fear, the experience of dying.

Now Freud's theory of a death instinct and Melanie Klein's view that there is also a basic fear of death are conceptually distinct. The first postulates a primary impulse to seek death; the second a primary impulse to fear and to avoid death. There is no *a priori* reason why we should not have both; for though they conflict, they do not logically exclude each other—indeed the first may be supposed to stimulate the second. But neither do they necessarily imply each other. Let us therefore consider them in turn, beginning with the second.

The old analytic argument against the existence of a basic fear of death rests, implicitly if not explicitly, on the discovery that what is consciously thought to be a fear of death often turns out to cover other unconscious fears, such as the fear of castration. But it is now

[1] Or perhaps it would be more correct to say that the metapsychological and the empirical aspects of the theory are so interwoven, in analytic thought, that it has become difficult to distinguish between them.

R. E. Money-Kyrle

fairly generally agreed that there are fears more basic than the fear of castration or loss of love (Freud), or even the loss of all capacity for pleasure (aphanisis, Ernest Jones). There is, for instance, the terror of disintegration.[1] It may not be easy to be sure—still less to convince the doubters—that such anxiety attacks express the fear of dying. But there are other pointers, of a more general kind, which are perhaps easier to follow. Why, if there is no fear of death, are nearly all religions so concerned with immortality? Why, in our ambitions, are we so passionately anxious for something of ourselves, a work of art, a scientific contribution, a business, or just our good name, to be accepted and to survive? Why, not only for our pleasure but for our peace of mind, do we need children who should create grandchildren, and so on? Why, in short, do we so strive for immortality—or at least for immortality by proxy? Or how better can we describe those moments of deep despondency, which no one altogether escapes, than as a feeling that there is no joy in fighting an enemy who must ultimately defeat us—no joy in living if death or destruction must surely overtake us and all our works, those offshoots of ourselves we try to save?[2] And why, if there is nothing in it, have the biologists so much stressed an instinct of self-preservation? We may not be able to form an idea of our own annihilation, but in common with other animals we are certainly predisposed to anxiety at threats of it.[3] If we were not, our line would have died out long ago and we should not have existed. Indeed, it is a mere tautology to assert that the only instincts that can be developed by selection are such as tend to promote the survival of offspring to inherit them. So the instinct to preserve ourselves to produce offspring must be basic; and the instinct to protect them, if necessary before ourselves, must be a derivative of it to improve the survival prospects of the species. In other words, all the striving that fills life is the expression of a ceaseless battle against death.

But it is still a long way from the acceptance of the fear of death—

[1] The terror of disintegration may perhaps be equated with Freud's concept of traumatic anxiety.

[2] We feel these moments to be cowardly, to be the antithesis of that courage which can find joy even in fighting for lost causes. This is the theme of Russell's *A Free Man's Worship*, that people should enjoy striving for what they value without the consolation of myths that deny the ultimate destruction of the world.

[3] Perhaps the nearest we can get to the idea of our own annihilation is the idea of the annihilation of all our good objects, both internal and external, and of being left with nothing but the bad ones—the containers of our own destructiveness. But then this is terrifying because these bad impulses threaten to destroy us. So the ultimate object of fear, if it is not the idea of being nothing, is at least the idea of the painful process of being reduced to this condition—if not of death, of dying.

or at least of situations likely to cause death—as a basic instinct, to the acceptance of Freud's theory of a death instinct. Indeed, the very arguments in favour of the one seem, at first sight, to militate against the other. Since instincts, in the Darwinian sense, are developed by the selection of such mutations as favour the survival of offspring, and so of parents to produce them, how can we imagine the development by selection of an instinct of self-destruction? Of course this argument, by starting with the Darwinian conception of instinct, really begs the question. But the Darwinian conception, which certainly holds for all of what Freud called the life instincts, has been immeasurably fertile in biology, and is not something to be lightly thrown away as a general explanatory principle. So before accepting the death instinct, that is, the existence of an instinct with a self-destructive aim which cannot have been evolved by selection to promote survival, we must do our best to see how far the analytic facts can be explained without it.

The following theory seems to me to go some way to explain most of these facts on Darwinian lines without the assumption of a death instinct. But I shall also argue that it does not go quite far enough.

To every organism another organism has three basic potential meanings. It is something to eat (or reject),[1] something to be eaten by, or something to unite (or reunite) with. And it is tempting to suppose that the corresponding impulses aggressively to desire and consume the first, to fear and avoid the second, and to love and preserve while combining with the third, may have been developed, both phylogenetically and ontogenetically, from each other in this order. According to the theory of the death instinct, the aggression in the first of these impulses has been, as it were, diverted from an originally self-destructive aim, and used in the service of the life instincts. But let us, for a moment, consider the contrary (Darwinian) hypothesis, that it was originally evolved as an appropriate response to the threat of death by hunger. Assume further that aggressive greed towards the outer world when under the influence of hunger is the primary impulse, and let us try to imagine how the next impulse, that to fear and avoid other organisms when they are dangerous, can have been evolved from it. In evolving something new, Nature tends to make use of

---

[1] The impulse to reject or discard what is unpleasant or disgusting provides, as it were, another thread to be woven into a complete account of the development of object relations. But for simplicity I have ignored it here.

what is already there. So it is not unlikely that an organism's capacity to "recognize" the danger from its potential enemies results from the evolution of a tendency to project into them the aggression felt within itself. We know from analysis and especially from Melanie Klein's work with children, that this is the way in which persecutory anxiety either originates or is at least augmented in human beings. And such facts of analytic observation suggest the hypothesis that the paranoid mechanism, which is so fundamental in our lives and which we see so clearly in its exaggerated forms, may be the innate mechanism through which self-preservative behaviour in the face of external danger is achieved, at least in the higher, and perhaps in every species. If so, the fear of death in this specific form would be not the fear of a death instinct originally directed against the organism itself, but the fear of a projected aggression originally evolved in the interests of self-preservation.

Coming to the third stage, the evolution of the sex impulse to unite and reproduce: as we experience it, we can detect, in addition to identification and protective love, a not altogether stable fusion between a sadistic impulse to mastery and a masochistic impulse to surrender.[1] Each partner is, as it were, at once the eater and the eaten, yet both are preserved from actual damage. And we may reasonably suppose that the safety of each partner is somehow achieved by a partial turning of aggression against the aggressive self—for this, too, is in accordance with analytic findings. And we may again conclude that a tendency to such inversion has been evolved to protect the partner—and later the offspring and whatever we identify ourselves with—against an original predatoriness which, if unchecked by such a mechanism, would endeavour to consume the world. This seems plausible enough. If we accept it, we have a hypothesis which may seem at least to lessen the need for a theory of a death instinct. For the assumption of an aggression, originally evolved to secure our own survival,[2] and now partially turned inwards to secure the survival of those we identify ourselves with and love, is sufficient to account for at least some of the self-destructive impulses we find.

Such a mechanism would seem necessary to the survival of any

---

[1] The common view that sadism is masculine and masochism feminine may be qualified by the consideration that this applies only to the phallic component. The allocation of the active and passive aspects of the oral component tends to be reversed: the active oral component being more conspicuous in female genitality.

[2] Both directly by the active pursuit of prey, and indirectly by warning us of danger by other predators.

species that reproduces sexually; and could have been further evolved to protect the offspring. It could even—though this is a digression from my main theme—have been used to produce in each species some acquiescence in its optimum longevity. In bacteria and insects, and in all those forms of life which, when faced with a changing environment, rely for their survival more on improvements through mutations in germ plasm in successive generations than on adaptation in soma, the life span of individuals is relatively short. In those which rely more on learning, and the transfer of acquired knowledge to other younger members of the species, the life span is relatively long. We must suppose this to be because, in each species, an optimum longevity has been selected. We can go further and suppose that in our own species our life span is determined by a neurological limit to our capacity to acquire and store knowledge, and that we are predisposed to die when, this capacity having been exhausted, we begin to become more a liability than an asset to our fellows. An innate tendency for the progressive transfer of concern for survival from ourselves to those of our products with which we identify ourselves could promote the survival of our species in two ways: positively, by making the old protect the young; and negatively, by helping the old to acquiesce in their extinction instead of harmfully competing.

There is therefore much to be said for a phylogenetic hypothesis which derives the fear of objects from the projection of aggressive greed, and self-destructiveness from the need to divert this greed from loved objects, that is, from objects at once desired by, and projectively identified with "good" parts of, the self. And ontogenetically, we are familiar with an inverted aggressiveness of this kind. But we believe we can also detect a primary threat to the self from within the self which is not derived from anything. It is indeed this apparent fact of observation that is the analytic basis of the theory of the death instinct, and that must be capable of being explained in some other way before that theory can be discarded as empirically redundant. To do so, it might be thought sufficient to remember that, ontogenetically, the distinction between self and object is only gradually achieved. It is a philosophic truism that we can never be aware, in the sense of being directly acquainted with, anything beyond our own sensations and ideas. So in fact the dualistic conception of self and outer world expresses a rather arbitrary, and by no means constant, distinction between those sensations and ideas which we define as constituting ourselves and those we define as constituting the outer world. In the new-born infant the distinction is rudimentary, or still non-existent; so fear of death by hunger, aggressive greed, and fear of aggressive greed in a projected form, are played out between entities not yet separated into self and outer world. This, so it seems to me, might well give rise to that primary sense of being threatened from within which we assume in infants and which perhaps recurs whenever the boundaries between self and outer world are again disturbed.

At first sight, the conclusion to be drawn from such considerations is that the theory of the death instinct is not necessary to account for the facts observed. But before discarding it other more general arguments in its support have still to be assessed. Freud himself, as we know, based it not only on analytic studies of masochism and the compulsion to repeat the past but also on a wide philosophical survey embracing, if not the universe, at least the whole of life. And although we are accustomed to think of his philosophy as a super-structure designed to explain his discoveries, it perhaps deserves to be taken more seriously on its own account.

In this philosophy or "metapsychology", he derived the destructiveness he found in man from a conservatism in organisms which reacts against the forces that brought them into being. If it is not too fanciful to link this concept of conservatism with that of catabolism in biology and entropy[1] in physics, Freud's metapsychology of the death instinct could perhaps be restated in the following terms.

If we revert to the behaviouristic standpoint and use the word behaviour in its widest sense, we observe a basic conflict of forces. The organism is threatened both from within and from without by the forces of destruction—that is, by catabolic processes as well as by external enemies. It reacts against them in such a way as to maintain its integrity as a system. And we may add that, as an additional precaution, the system also tends to multiply itself. From the point of view of physics, no new laws have to be introduced to explain why this should be so. If chance once produced a boundary maintaining system of molecules which reproduced itself in a limited environment, competition and selection would automatically ensure the evolution of ever more adaptable systems capable of maintaining themselves in an ever wider range of possible environments. Thus, given the existence of reproductive organisms in a limited environment, logic alone should have led us to expect the bio-

[1] Entropy can perhaps be personified as a kind of "levelling" principle in nature.

logical part of the universe to run counter to the entropy of the whole.[1]

From the point of view of psychology we attribute at least to the higher systems in this small part something we deny to the inorganic part of nature, namely awareness and the will to live; and this would seem to be the psychic correlate of the forces which maintain them as organic systems. We are directly acquainted with the will to live in ourselves and have no hesitation in projecting it into our picture of our fellows, as well as into other animals so far as they behave as we do. But at what level in the organic hierarchy are we to draw the line? And are we to attribute psychic equivalents only to the system maintaining processes, and not to the disruptive processes they counteract?

Where we are acquainted with a psyche in ourselves we believe it to be conditional on the integrity of the particular and highly complex system of our brains. And as brains, like other organs, are presumably evolved to preserve and multiply their owners' lives, it is not easy to associate a primary self-destructive impulse with neural processes in evolved cerebral structure.[2] For these reasons, the body-mind correlations we assume in scientific thought tend to be restricted, on the one hand to such organisms as are possessed of brains, and on the other to such psychic processes as are correlated with self and species preservation. But the limits we thus impose on the spontaneous animism of prescientific thought begin to seem arbitrary as soon as we remember that imperceptible links of evolution connect the complex neural system of a brain to ever simpler patterns of reactive tissue. We can find no obvious place to draw a line below which mind should disappear and only matter remain. So after all the old animistic conception of the world, which scientific people pride themselves on having outgrown, may have erred only in attributing complex mental processes to simple systems; and perhaps we should be prepared to follow Leibnitz in attributing some *petits perceptions* even to the simplest systems of all. And our hesitation in doing so may be diminished when we remember that

[1] Perhaps Darwin's main contribution to science was not the empirical discovery of evolution, but a piece of pure deductive reasoning: that, given the well-known facts of inheritance with variation in a limited world, evolution must logically occur. Whether these facts alone are sufficient to explain the pace of the evolution that has actually occurred, or whether the inheritance of acquired characters must also be assumed is, on the other hand, an empirical question which was left by him, and still remains, without a certain answer.

[2] N. Tinbergen, *The Study of Instinct* (Oxford, 1951), defines an instinct as a hierarchically organized nervous mechanism which is susceptible to certain priming, releasing, and directing impulses of internal as well as external origin, and which responds to these impulses by co-ordinated movements *that contribute to the maintenance of the individual and the species* (my italics).

there is a sense in which the mental world with which we are alone acquainted, and which includes what we call our perceptions of the external world, is more "real" than this external world of physics which physicists themselves now regard as only a mathematical construction.[1]

The argument we have embarked on may lead to conclusions repugnant to our current thought, which is still predominantly materialistic. But we cannot escape these conclusions without abandoning our belief in continuous development.[2] We can observe that our own behaviour "expresses" psychic impulses, and we attribute such impulses to other organisms so far as they are like ourselves in structure and behaviour. Then, having made this initial step, the principle of continuity forces us to attribute some psychic correlate, of however indefinite a kind, to all observed behaviour.

But can we, at the risk of becoming altogether lost in the fogs of mysticism, venture to be more precise in such a revised animistic conception of the universe? If behaviour in the widest sense is any guide, we see the two opposite tendencies which so impressed General Smuts and led him to write Holism and Evolution: on the one hand entropy, on the other the organic development of ever more complex and adaptable systems. The principle of continuity suggests that we may have to attribute psychic correlates to both.[3]

At least there seem good biological as well as analytic reasons for regarding the fear of death[4]—either our own or that of those with whom we are identified—as the basic motive in life. And when, in analysis, we meet this fear in its more primitive forms, it seems to be linked with the awareness of a self-destructive force. Whether our awareness of this force can be explained as the awareness of aggression at a time when the distinction between self and outer world has not been achieved or has broken down; or whether it can in some way be conceived of as a psychic representative of entropy—of the catabolic process in our brains and bodies—seems to me an open question. But as a major cause, and an effect, of anxiety in man it is a force that certainly exists.

[1] Clifford Scott's concept of the "body scheme" (which is in part derived from Schilder's concept of the "body image") includes the external world.

[2] The alternative to the principle of continuity would seem to be some form of "emergent vitalism"—a doctrine which I find much harder to accept.

[3] It can be argued that in conceiving a model of the universe in which events are the resultant of these opposing forces, we are merely "projecting" the forces we experience within ourselves. But this argument, while attacking animism, implies the admission that both forces are in fact within us.

[4] To avoid logical difficulties, we can always substitute the "fear of dying" for the "fear of death".

In conclusion, I should like again to stress my point that the fear of death, or of dying, and the death instinct are logically distinct. Empirically we know that the fear of death is either derived from, or at least greatly increased by, our own aggression. But an aggression felt to threaten the self because it has been projected or inverted, or, still more fundamentally, because the distinction between self and outer world has not yet developed, or has disappeared, is not the same as the death instinct conceived by Freud. If no such instinct exists, we must assume that the fear of death (e.g. by hunger) is primary and that aggression (e.g. aggressive greed) is an instinctive response to it which, if not clearly directed against an external object, serves only to increase the sense of danger. If, however, there is a death instinct we can hardly doubt that the fear of death is a response to it. As Paula Heimann says: "Danger arising primarily within the organism provides the stimulus for the human being's innate capacity for fear."[1] The difficulty consists, not in how the death "instinct" works if it exists, but in seeing how it can exist at all. It cannot be an instinct in the ordinary sense—something evolved in the interests of self- and species-preservation.[2] It can therefore hardly be conceived except as a kind of psychic correlate of entropy—something prior to the instincts proper which were presumably evolved to counteract it.[3]

[1] "Notes on the Theory of the Life and Death Instincts" in *Developments of Psycho-Analysis* (London, 1952).
[2] An instinct to secure no more than an optimum longevity (p. 504) might conceivably have been evolved. But, if so, it would be something far more specific and limited in scope than the general death instinct envisaged by Freud.
[3] If we do accept the death instinct in some such terms as these, there still remains the possibility of a further open question: that of the relation of the death instinct to aggression. With Freud, we can imagine the one as the outward expression of the other. Or we can imagine a secondary aggression as evolved, in the interests of self- and species-preservation, to counteract a primary self-destructive force, and then becoming inverted and so confused with this "death instinct" when in fact it was only the death instinct's temporary ally. But if there is no difference between the observable effects of these two hypotheses, the distinction is perhaps unreal.

INDEX

Abraham, Karl, xii, 4, 17
  on coprophagic phantasies, 211
  and death instinct, 34
  and delusions of persecution, 262
  and depression, 39
  and fixation-points of psychosis, 241
  and infantile sexuality, 34
  on melancholia, 309n.
Absorption, of introjected objects, 483
  see also Concentration
Acting-out,
  of aggressive phantasies in child, 9
  in psychotics, 225
Action,
  and basic assumption mentality, 452
  preference for, in schizophrenics, 225–6
Adaptation (Adjustment) to reality, 221
  and schizophrenics, 239
  and symbolism, 84
Adolescence, re-emergence of infantile sexuality in, 27
Adult role, of child in play analysis, 8
"Aesthetic moment", 97
Aesthetics,
  central problem of, 385
  Freud and, 385
  psycho-analysis and, 410
  see also Pleasure
Aggression, xi-xii, 92, 103
  art and, 410
  and death instinct, 503, 509
  denial of, in autistic children, 176
  expressed as envy, 208
  expression in play analysis, 50
  fear of, and transfer of interest, 82
  and feeling of inner bad object, 289
  incapacity to display in act, 149
  inhibition of, 150
  inversion of, 504
  mother's unconscious, 129
  and persecution, 171

  projected, death-fear as fear of, 504
  projection of, 289
  in schizophrenic, 195
  turning against self, in schizophrenia, 195
  uncontrolled, fear of, 71
Aggressive
  action, incapacity for, 149
  instinct, and hypochondria, 302
  phantasies, against breast, 310
    in child patients, 9
    prime movers of, 324
Aggressiveness,
  expression in play analysis, 8–9, 10
  and fear of retaliation, 18
Agoraphobia, 266
Alexander, F., 347
  denies super-ego in schizophrenics, 183
Aloofness, 294
Ambivalence,
  beginning of, 25
  conflict of, in paranoia, 263
  towards family, 11, 21
  towards father, 12, 333
  in infants, 25
  towards mother, 5, 15
  mother's, towards analyst, 6
  towards siblings, 48
  see also Love and Hate
Anal
  element, in phantasy attack on leader, 483
  evacuation into analyst, 246–7
  impulses, in children, 16
  interests, heightened as defences, 36
  trends, in paranoid position, 36
  stage, first, 35–6
    second, 36
    and oral stage, 36
    polymorphous stage and, 36

Index

Freud, Sigmund (*contd.*),
  on groups and leaders, 480
  on heavenly and earthly love, 333
  and hypochondria, 301
  and identification by projection, 313n.
  and introjected object, 346–7
  on introjection, 249–50
  on memories, 360
  on narcissistic women, 178–9
  and origin of super-ego, 15, 32
  on polymorphous-perverse sexuality, 34
  on primitive group behaviour, 252
  on prolonged immaturity in man, 356
  on psycho-analysis and psychosis, 220–22
  and schizophrenia, 185
  on Schreber case, 293n.
  on sublimation, 396
  on super-ego, 429–30
  theories of group, 459–60, 466ff., 475
Frigidity, 283
"Fritz", case of, 4
Fromm Reichmann, F., 181, 191n.
Frustration,
  in children, 29, 101
  expression in play analysis, 10
  fear of, 354
  inability to tolerate, 5
  of infant, and anger, 40
  of mother by father, 328
  need for, 270
  reinforces greed, 329
Fry, Roger, 388, 400n.
Fusion,
  feeling of, with ideal breast, 161
  and illusion, 85ff.
  prelogical, 105
  of self and object, 87

Games, in play-analysis, 8
Garma, A., 205n.
Gate (symbol), 155
Generalization, 83
Genital
  urges, in second half of first year, 27
  woman's, child's views of, 29

Giggling, 190
Glacier Metal Co., 488ff.
Gnomes, as symbols, 54–5
"Good" and "bad",
  use of terms, 349
  division of objects into, 122, 187
Goodness, independent, toleration of, 104
Gosse, Edmund, 370n.
Gracefulness, in autistic children, 178
Grandeur, delusions of, 262
Gratification, sadistic, from feeling or suffering, 246
Greed,
  and aggressive phantasies, 324
  and depressive position, 385
  excessive, and curiosity, 150
  as origin of fear, 505
  as primary impulse, 503
  and projective identification, 323n., 329
  projection of, 289, 290
  reinforced by frustration, 329
  and relation to father, 332
  splitting mechanisms as ministering to, 223
  in *The Master-Builder*, 377, 382
Green, Julian, 314ff.
Grief, 431;
  see also Depression; Mourning
Group,
  artificial, Freud on, 496
  attitude to individuals, 441
  "badness" of the, 472–3
  behaviour, maladaptive, in, 479
    primitive, 252, 264
  contacts, and early mental life, 440
  desire for organization in, 465
  dynamics, 440ff.
  and individual, 460–2
  introjection and projection of, 457
  neurotic and psychotic behaviour in, 470
  organized and unorganized, 463
  psycho-analytic view, 459ff.
  psychology, Freud on, 480
  therapy sessions, 442
  treatment, and analyst's reactions, 446

Index

Guilt,
absence of, in æsthetic experience, 409
and castration fears, 430
and depressive position, 312, 387
effect of analysis on, 433
and ego/super-ego tensions, 32
and father's death, 331, 332
feelings, 259
  absence in paranoia, 256
  emotional basis of, 186
  in play analysis, 9–10, 15
institutions as defences against, 181
and lack of affection for father, 66
and mourning ceremonies, 486
need of punishment to relieve, 201
over neglect of part of personality, 337
in oral stage, 186
reactions to, 433
in *The Master-Builder*, 374
situations arousing, 432
two elements of, 429
varying attitudes to, 434
in work group, 445

Hallucinations,
analysis of, 233
?n autistic children, 174n.
blissful, 156–7
change into phobias, 173
frightening, 157–8, 159
localized, 160
negative, 159, 175
in case of "Raul", 155ff.
in schizophrenic, 191, 197
wish-fulfilling, 325
Hand(s),
gestures of, as symbols of cathexes, 209
objects held in, as symbols of internalized object, 70
Handkerchief, search for, meaning, 206
Hate (hatred), 427
and aggressive phantasies, 324
of father, 29
and loss, 364
in paranoids, 257
projected, of the dead, 364
see also Love and Hate

Hayward, M. L., 184
Health and insight, connection, 438
Heater, car, as symbol of genital, 66
Hebephrenia, 190
Heimann, Paula, 113, 297–8, 336n., 385, 412, 418
on assimilation, 154n.
and counter-transference, 95, 141, 193n.
and death instinct, 509
impairment of sublimation, 392
on introjection and projection, 481, 484
Hell, 365
Herd instinct, 449, 460–1
Heredity, *see* Environment
Heterosexuality, establishment of, 29
Home, unsuitable for child analysis, 6
Homosexual
identification, 76
impulses, defence against, and paranoia, 257
phantasy, 58
situation, anxiety in, 74
trends, in girl, 31
  guilt and, 62
Homosexuality, 334–5, 339
ego-ideal and, 185
male, roots of, 28
and need for protection, 134
repressed, 335
stimulus to, 332
Hope, feeling of, in group, 447–8
see also Messianic Hope
Horse, symbolizing mother, 76
Hug-Hellmuth, Dr., 3
Humanism, *see* Conscience
Humpty-dumpty Christmas-tree game 114ff.
Hunger, effects of, 41
Hypersensibility, 173
Hypnotism, x
Hypochondria(sis), 80, 289, 291, 301ff. 365
Hysteria, 287ff., 302
Hysterical conversion, 301ff.

'I', pronoun, first use of, 125, 128
Ibsen, Henrik, 370ff.

Index

Normality,
absolute, non-existent, 241
definition, 437–8
Nose, as penis symbol, 75
Nose-picking, compulsive, 67
Notation, 221, 222
Nunberg, H., 186

Obedience, automatic, 142, 144n.
Object,
bad, fear of intrusion of, 322
concern for, 162
external, intrusion of, 322
psychotic reaction to, 458
fear of loss of, 353
forces forbidding interest in, 82
good, feeling of destruction of, 327
good internalized, condition for stable ego, 312
ideal, failure to assimilate, 154
ideal internal, in autistic children, 178
internal, in adults, 252n.
loss of, and transfer of interest, 82
loved, desire to possess, 163
meaning of, 41
primary, meaning of, 87
Object-relationship, and æsthetic experience, 413, 416
Object relations,
defences against, 93
and depressive positive, 385
early, 21, 24–5
establishment of, 97
influenced by splitting, 311
and integration, 312
intra-psychic, 250ff.
in schizophrenics, 222, 226
Object stage, 25–6
Objectivity, achievement of, and anxiety, 102
Objectless condition, original, 100
Observation, in paranoids, 261
Obsession,
anxiety underlying, 6
rituals of, 110–11, 267
Obsessional,
case of, needing to be "kept", 266ff.

neurosis, 5
"undoing" in, 15
rituals, see Rituals
"Oceanic"
feeling, and art, 100, 407, 414
states, 95
Œdipal
situation, in basic assumption groups, 455
inverted, 334, 339
in *The Master-Builder*, 372
wishes, expression in play, 116
Œdipus complex, xi, 17, 23ff., 329, 332
beginning of, 26
in boys, 28ff.
and depressive position, 241, 258
direct and inverted, 28, 32
early stages, 26ff., 326
final stage of process, 33
in girls, 30ff.
introjection and, 32–3
is nuclear complex, 33
roots of, 241
ubiquity of, 241
Offspring, instinct to protect, 502
Omnipotence,
in autistic children, 176
of evil, belief in, 25
illusion of, 275
infantile, 104–5, 300
lessening of, 163
relief from abandonment of illusory, 104
see also Control
Omnipotent possession of object, 24
Oneness, illusion of, 100, 101–2, 417
Ontogenesis, 503, 505
Opposition, need for, 270
Oral
aims, 37
anxieties, connection with sadistic phantasies, 18
desires, consequences of failure to modify, 335
desires and anxieties, role of, 17
greed, in schizophrenic, 205
impulses, 37
leaders in polymorphous urges, 27
inhibition, 127

526

Projection *(contd.)*,
  develops from phantasy of object
    expulsion, 24
  Fenichel on, 100
  of "good" parts of self, 310
  internalized breast and, 310
  and introjection, 309, 321
    in Conrad, 367
    in schizophrenia, 198-9
  role in personality formation, 359
  and unconscious phantasies, 24
  see also Introjection
Projective Identification, 37, 117, 151,
    176, 177, 178, 188, 297, 300,
    311ff.
  as defence mechanism, 189
  Freud and, 313n.
  in groups, 445, 467
  inordinate use of, 177
  and primitive thinking, 298ff.
  processes underlying, 336
  rise of, 323n.
  in schizophrenia, 194, 222, 225, 226
  in story of "Fabian", 321ff.
Projective mechanisms, importance for
    identification, 311
Pronominal inversal, 51, 174, 177
Propitiation, 433
Prostitute, equation of mother and, 330
Proto-mental system, 449-50
Proust, Marcel, 388-90, 397, 398
Psychiatry, diagnoses in, and psycho-
    analysis, 242
Psycho-analysis,
  aims of, 425
  isolation of, through terminology,
    106
  and psychiatry, 242
  and schizophrenia, 180ff., 216ff.
  and widening of consciousness, 425
Psychology, influence on knowledge,
    424
Psycho-somatic medicine, 450
Psycho-surgery, 285
Psychosis (-es),
  adult, and infant emotional life, 22
  analysis of, and child analysis, 181
  difference from neurosis, 220
  early super-ego and, 17

  Freud on, 185, 220
  as id-ego conflict, 185
  psycho-analysis and, 181, 220
  transference, 182
Psychotic
  anxieties, in some measure normal, 19
  behaviour, 138
  nature of infantile anxieties, 19n.
Puberty rites, and examinations, 283
Punishment,
  desire for, 205
  need of, 15, 201
Puppy, as penis symbol, 70, 71
Puritanism, in analytic writing, 83

Rabbit, toy, as symbol, 93
Racker, Mrs. G., 177
Rado, Sandor, 414
  and depression, 39
Rage,
  in groups, 469
  outbursts of, 52, 55
  see also Anger; Panic
Rank, Otto, 83-4, 283
  on art and play, 98
Rapoport, J., 175n.
"Raul", case of, 140ff.
Reaction-formation, and reparation, 15
Read, [Sir] Herbert, 83, 85, 401
Reading, as retreat from masculine
    activity, 76
Reality,
  denial of, in *The Master-Builder*, 378
  inner, development of sense of, 385
  principle, institution of, 221
  relation to, and identification, 83
  sense, in artist, 397
Reason and feeling, split between, 355
Reassurance, 63, 426
  temptation to, with paranoid patients,
    243
  in treatment of schizophrenia, 218
  use is psychosis, 181, 184
Re-creation, and art, 388-90
Redistribution, of bad objects, in
    phantasy relations, 484
Re-entry, of object into ego, 198
Regression,
  as defence, 75

Index

Social structures, 479
Sounds,
first, in mute schizophrenic, 167
overheard, and guilt, 330
and symbol formation, 99n.
Space, and art, 407, 414
Speech,
appearance of, in mute schizophrenic,
170
features in autistic children, 174
and symbolism, 99
Sphinx, in work groups, 455–6
Spiders, as symbols, 56–7
red, dream of, 285–6
Splitting,
in case of "Colin", 117
counteracted by good breast, 312
defence against fear or annihilation,
312
persecutory anxiety, 311, 312
in different planes, 296
earliest ego defence, 25
establishment of ego–ideal by, 253
importance of, 21
and incorporation, 368
of object, and idealization, 353
use of language for, 226
and paranoid–schizoid position, 323n.
phantasies underlying, 336
and projective identification, 311
symbolization of, 55–6
varieties of, 313
of verbal thought, 223
Spontaneity, lack of, 393
Stamp attachment label, as penis
symbol, 79
Stamps, as symbols of internalized
parents, 78–9
Starcke, A., 284
Stealing, 60–1, 73
Stengel, E., 283
Stevenson, R. L., 362
Strachey, James, 113, 245n., 426n.
on introjection, 250
Sublimation,
and assimilation, 154n.
basis of, 385
contribution of reparation to, 15
impairment of, 392

as renunciation of instinctual aim, 396
Substitutes, and symbols, 299n.
Suggestibility, in groups, 463
Suicide, 42
impulses to, 51, 57, 190
Sullivan, H. S., 181
Super-ego, 50, 322
analyst as, 184
archaic, 183–4
in child, 15, 431
control, exercised by analyst, 184
depressive, 188
depressive states and, 44
difficulty of dealing with, in analysis,
183
discovery of, xi, 309, 429
dissolution of, 347
early, underlies psychosis, 17
early origins of, 15, 217–18
and ego-splitting, 205
harsh, 15, 16, 17
helpful, 206–7
inner object and, 346
internalization of breast the core of,
18
and internalization of parents, 32
as introjected object, 252
parent, 430
and introjection, 251, 309
introjection into, 484
persecutory quality of, 187
primitive, in schizophrenics, 189
projection of, 205
into analyst, 201
relation to ego–ideal, 343n.
relative morality of, 430
in schizophrenia, 180ff.
symbolized by gnome, 54–5
in The Master-Builder, 374, 376
Surrender, altruistic, 313n.
Survival, desire for, 502
Symbol, different uses of word, 83, 84–5
Symbol formation, 20
anxiety and, 86
conditions of capacity for, 228
and depressive position, 172, 396–7
and groups, 473–4
illusion and, 82ff.
inhibition of, 20

533

Index